NIʻIHAU

Niʻihau

PELE'S HAWAIIAN LANDFALL

– A HISTORY –

STEVEN GENTRY

STEELE ROBERTS
AOTEAROA

DISTRIBUTION BY UNIVERSITY OF HAWAIʻI PRESS

© Steven Gentry 2023

IMAGES

FRONT COVER: TOP Niʻihau at sunset from the Kōkeʻe Road (photo by Christine Faye). LOWER, left to right: Eliza Sinclair (Robinson family); Whales in Kaulakahi Channel (Nancy Shaw); Keiki at Puʻuwai with Governor Cayetano (*Honolulu Advertiser*); Laysan albatross over Niʻihau (Nancy Shaw); Coastal hibiscus or hau (*Indigenous Flowers of the Hawaiian Islands* by Isabella Sinclair).

BACK COVER The Niʻihau poetic saying is quoted verbatim from *Niihau: The Traditions of an Hawaiian Island* by Rerioterai Tava & Moses K Keale Sr, Mutual Publishing, 1984. The lower quote is from the *Honolulu Advertiser* of 30 September 1961 in an article by Jack Teehan after he visited the island.
IMAGES (from top to bottom and left to right): Niʻihau east coast pali (Marcia Braden); Sailing canoes off Niʻihau (John Webber, Hawaiian Historical Society); Niʻihau shell lei (*Honolulu Star Bulletin*); Paniolo on Niʻihau in the 1920s (private collection); Monk seal (Wikimedia Commons); Niihauan carved gourd (Robinson family); Eland (Michael Anderson, Kauaʻi Historical Society); Governor Ariyoshi speaking in front of the church at Puʻuwai (Greg Vaughn); Cattle loading at Nonopapa (Robinson family).

ENDPAPERS: FRONT Niihauan fishermen, 1870s; see page 202.
BACK: left, Sinclair/Gay/Robinson family tree; right, United States Geological Survey map of Niʻihau, 1929.

PRELIMINARY PAGES Part of a moena pāwehe, a decorated makaloa mat from Niʻihau (Robinson family/Nancy Shaw). A photo of the full mat is on page 44.

Abbreviations: ATL Alexander Turnbull Library, Wellington, New Zealand
DLNR (United States) Department of Land and Natural Resources
RAC Russian-American Company
USGS United States Geological Survey

ISBN 978-1-99-115384-5

STEELE ROBERTS AOTEAROA PUBLISHERS
299 Manly Street, Paraparaumu Beach 5032, Aotearoa New Zealand
info@SteeleRoberts.co.nz • www.SteeleRoberts.co.nz

Distribution: University of Hawaiʻi Press

CONTENTS

	Introduction	7
ONE	A volcanic ark	11
TWO	Polynesian footfall	31
THREE	A fateful European encounter	57
FOUR	Early Western voyagers	75
FIVE	Rebellion on Kauaʻi	105
SIX	Sinclairs, Gays and Robinsons in New Zealand	127
SEVEN	The Pacific journey and purchase of Niʻihau	163
EIGHT	A fledgling ranch	187
NINE	Aubrey Robinson takes the reins	219
TEN	Aylmer's stewardship	247
ELEVEN	An enduring culture	281
	The lei images on chapter heading pages	311
	Acknowledgements	313

Appendices

A	Timeline	316
B	The Niihauan dialect: past and present	320
C	The Battle of Niʻihau	327
D	Niʻihau population numbers	333
E	Botanical exploration on Niʻihau	335
	Bibliography	342
	Endnotes	347
	Hawaiian words in the text	367
	Index	368

Ni'ihau, from the northeast, in 2007.
Christopher Becket / Wikimedia Commons

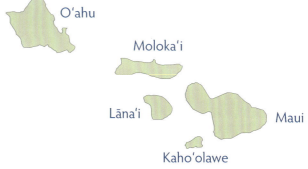

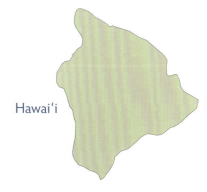

The Hawaiian Islands

50 miles

INTRODUCTION

Islands fascinate me. Is it because they are bounded on all sides by water and have a sense of integrity for plants, animals and people? Or is it something intangible, their suggestion of adventure and romance? Having published *Raoul and the Kermadecs: New Zealand's Northernmost Islands* in 2013, the idea for this present book came about fortuitously via an encounter in Honolulu with a member of the Robinson family, long-time owners of Niʻihau. When I learned that the family spent twenty years in New Zealand before purchasing Niʻihau in 1864 and that their descendants still maintained New Zealand links, I became intrigued. The general advice in Hawaiʻi was, however, that writing about Niʻihau would be a challenge — 'Try writing about any other island, but not Niʻihau' was the comment. That only quickened my interest.

Writing this book has been a journey of discovery. It has proved a larger task than originally envisaged because of the amount of material available, but the research has been easier because so much original source material is now online and can be accessed from anywhere.

Much has been written about individuals marooned, or choosing a solitary life on islands, from Daniel Defoe in the 18th century to Adam Nicolson and Gavin Francis in recent times. Francis has suggested that islands *simplify*. This they may do for individuals, but not so much apparently for small societies that find themselves on isolated islands. These have not fared so well — the Bounty mutineers on Pitcairn Island are a good example, and this situation was the subject of a novel in William Golding's *Lord of the Flies*. Fortunately this has not been the case on Niʻihau — whether because of the island's closeness to Kauaʻi, which has been a bolthole in times of trouble, or the missionary philosophy taking hold in the community very early in historical times.

The story of the island has two interwoven realities: the ever-present need for water, and the vital synergy with the much larger and more productive neighbor of Kauaʻi.

The first chapter concerns the natural world of Niʻihau, placing the island in its context geographically, geologically and as an element in the Hawaiian chain. It then describes how the island's biota has evolved over time and adapted to Polynesian and European arrivals.

The second chapter has two parts. The first covers what science tells us about the origins and the movements of the proto-Polynesian people over time, their arrival in Polynesia and finally to the Hawaiian islands. This is complemented by the Niihauan people's own creation myths, their voyaging traditions, and the development of a distinctive Niihauan culture.

In 1778 Captain James Cook came upon the islands on his third voyage. Ni'ihau's pivotal role in this encounter is the topic of the third chapter. Bad weather prevented Cook's ships from returning to Waimea on Kaua'i, and a number of his crew had to spend two nights on Ni'ihau — with dire consequences for the islanders.

The return of Cook's ships to England caused a flurry of interest in the sea otter trade from the West Coast of America, and Ni'ihau briefly profited as a supplier of yams, a valuable food for seafarers. The succession of ships visiting the island in the immediate aftermath of Cook's visit is the substance of the fourth chapter.

The focus of the next chapter shifts briefly to Kaua'i, with Ni'ihau in the shadow of the power struggles there, exacerbated by the introduction of European firearms. The chapter covers the period to 1824 when political stability was finally achieved on the two islands.

Chapter Six relates the background to the story of the Sinclairs as the future purchasers of Ni'ihau. It follows the family's journey from Scotland to New Zealand in the 1840s and their twenty-year stay in Pigeon Bay on Banks Peninsula, before their decision to move on.

The Sinclair family's journey from New Zealand, across the Pacific to Vancouver Island, and finally to their purchase of Ni'ihau from King Kamehameha V in 1864 is the focus of Chapter Seven.

The Protestant missionary church was established on Ni'ihau almost a generation before the Sinclairs arrived. Chapter Eight covers this and the early years of ranching by the family, the integration of the Niihauan way of life into the farming operation, and the cultural strictures the new owners placed upon the Niihauans.

Chapter Nine outlines the development of ranching under Aubrey Robinson's leadership and the way of life of the family, which relied heavily on the synergy between the ranching on Ni'ihau and their Kaua'i landholdings, centered on Makaweli. The chapter covers the 1880s to the 1920s.

Aylmer Robinson's stewardship of the island and its inhabitants features in Chapter Ten. Aylmer dedicated his life to making the island stand on its own feet economically while ensuring the needs of the Niihauans were always addressed. He was involved in the island's affairs from the First World War until his death in 1967.

The territory — and later the state — of Hawai'i became ever more involved in Ni'ihau, beginning in Aylmer's time, but more extensively towards the present. The final chapter centers on the state's attempts to erode the private ownership of the island, and the wish of the Niihauans to live their lives as they choose. The retention of the Niihauan language is crucial to their distinctive lifestyle, and the chapter outlines current efforts to maintain this as the core of their culture.

Then follows a series of appendices on aspects of island life, and incidents better outlined away from the main narrative to maintain its flow and integrity.

Introduction

This 'island biography' tells the story of the Sinclair/Robinson family, so intimately connected to the island that they provide a useful touchstone for this story. I hope the combination of natural history and the accounts of Polynesian settlement and more recent European involvement provide points of interest for readers at many levels.

There has been much discussion as to whether the 'okina (') and the kahakō (macron) should be used in the narrative. Traditionally Niihauans do not use these conventions, whereas contemporary Hawaiian does. Since the book aims for a readership across Hawaiian society, I have opted to use 'okina and kahakō throughout. The exception is that all quotations appear exactly as per the source, and generally do not include them.

Steven Gentry
Wellington, Aotearoa New Zealand
June 2023

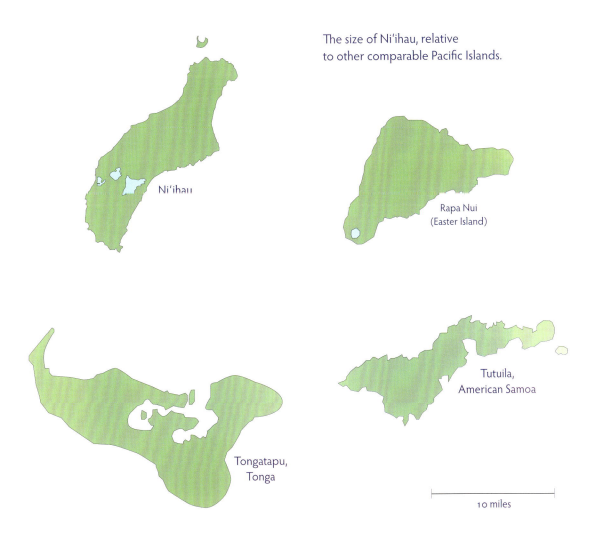

The size of Ni'ihau, relative to other comparable Pacific Islands.

▲ 'A living amethyst' — Niʻihau seen from the Kōkeʻe Road on Kauaʻi as the sun sinks over the island, evocative of Isabella Bird's remarks quoted opposite.
Christine Faye

CHAPTER ONE

A VOLCANIC ARK

Brooding off the western coast of Kaua'i, the hazy outline of Ni'ihau looms across the unruly Kaulakahi Channel. The Victorian traveler, Isabella Bird, was enraptured with the view from the uplands of Makaweli on Kaua'i in 1874:

> Behind rise the forest covered mountains and in front a beautiful wooded ravine very precipitous widens to the rolling grassy hills and the blue sea 5 miles off on which at a distance of about 18 miles floats the island of Niihau which the sun turns every night to a living amethyst.[1]

A precious jewel indeed, and a vision particularly treasured by the émigré Niihauans living on the western side of Kaua'i in Kekaha and Waimea. The island is presently home to considerably fewer than a hundred Hawaiians proudly calling themselves Niihauan, but is the spiritual home to many more Niihauans living on western Kaua'i and elsewhere in Hawai'i.

Another image used to describe the island when seen from western Kaua'i is that of a gently basking whale. It is easy to imagine the island as a giant whale, and indeed humpbacks are often seen in the Kaulakahi Channel.

The prevailing northeast trade winds blow unkindly across Ni'ihau, having deposited the bulk of their moisture on the high mountains of Kaua'i to the east. Infrequent westerly kona winds bring the relief of rain to the low-lying landscape.

An irregular lozenge-shaped island, 18 miles long and 6.2 miles wide at most, Ni'ihau is 69.5 square miles (180 km²), reaching an altitude of 1280 feet (390 m) at Pani'au (for comparison, another extreme of the Polynesian diaspora, Easter Island/Rapa Nui is comparable in area at 67 square miles and rises to 1600 feet).

▼ Whales cruise through the Kaulakahi Channel between Ni'ihau and Kaua'i.
Nancy Shaw

▶ A watercolor from Kaua'i by Maud Knudsen Garstin, which she named 'Niihau May be Seen in the Distance.' The painting has been loaned to the Kaua'i Museum by the Blackwell family, in honor of Mrs Cynthia Blackwell.
Kaua'i Museum

Ni'ihau is an island like no other in the Hawaiian chain — no lofty snow-clad peaks, no lush, craggy pinnacles, no fertile plains — but nevertheless with a mysterious, earthy fascination all its own.

The tiny sickle-shaped volcanic island of Lehua lies a mile away, off Ni'ihau's northern tip, while Ka'ula Island's rugged outline may be seen 17 miles away to the southwest.

The oldest and the most westerly island in the main Hawaiian archipelago, Ni'ihau rose from the depths of the ocean five to six million years ago — little more than a blink of the eye in geologic time, but still earlier than the other islands. Slowly the island's vegetation and fauna arrived by wind, wave and wandering seabird, followed eons later by humans, first Polynesians and then Europeans. Each colonization has had its effect upon the landscape.

Lying on the fringe of the tropics in latitude 22° north, the sun beats down incessantly on Ni'ihau, leavened intermittently, and particularly in the winter months, by the kona winds. The land is generally dry and dusty, except when these conditions prevail. While the higher tableland may once have been covered by forest, this has long since gone.

A depiction of the island's terrain by Charles Forbes in 1913 reveals the island as:

> About one-third consists of volcanic table land, this being surrounded on all but the eastern side by a low rolling plain composed of both volcanic and coral rock.
>
> The northern end is a low plain of volcanic material, fringed in the proximity of the sea with dunes of coral sand …

▼ A 1924 aerial photo of the southern end of the island, showing the eroded volcanic cone of Kawaihoa Point and Kawanahaki Bay.
Kaua'i Historical Society

◀ This ethereal painting of Ni'ihau by Howard Hitchcock was commissioned by Eliza Gay Welcker, Jane Gay's daughter. Family tradition has it that when Eliza saw the painting she asked that clouds be painted above Ni'ihau, as she had never seen the island without clouds. Hitchcock duly complied. The painting is undoubtedly the island as seen from Polihale Beach, as he painted there and it fits with the landscape. It is still in family hands. D. Howard Hitchcock (1861–1943) was the foremost Hawaiian painter of his generation and is regarded as the first homegrown artist to achieve international recognition.
Robinson family

The plateau is also of volcanic material. The highest points are on the northern and northeastern boundaries, where the vertical cliffs reach 1304 feet at Paniau. From here the ground slopes downward to the south and west on a somewhat even grade, interrupted by several deep gorges, and by the high and prominent cone of Ka'eo …

Between the west coast and the plateau there is a low cliff of lime sandstone. The plain south of the plateau is composed of coral sand and sandstone, with an undulating volcanic belt near and parallel to the west coast. It has a low elevation and is frequently under water. Sand dunes and coral sandstone follow around the east and west coasts of this part. The southern point of the island [Kawaihoa Point] consists of an eroded volcanic cone, reaching a height of 600 feet.[2]

Forbes was a botanist and his portrait lays the landscape bare. In broad landform terms the predominant feature is the weathered remnant of a deeply furrowed dome-shaped volcano that drops precipitously into the sea on its eastern side, with the remaining two-thirds of the island coastal plain. It is well vegetated, having the aspect of an African savannah in the lowlands, with the covering of kiawe trees giving the rolling grassland some substance. Eland (antelope) add a further exotic touch to the sheep and pigs roaming the island. On the empty white-sand beaches the rare monk seals lounge and seabirds whirl overhead.

Geology

All the Hawaiian islands are geologically dynamic and exciting, and Ni'ihau is no exception. James Dana, the geologist on the United States Exploring Expedition led by Charles Wilkes to the Pacific Ocean and surrounding lands, wrote in 1849:

Among the [island] groups of Polynesia, the Hawaiian exceeds all others in geological interest. The agency of both fire and water in the formation of rocks, is exemplified not only by results, but also by processes now in action; and the student of nature may watch the steps through the successive changes.[3]

Niʻihau is now nearly 390 miles from the Hawaiian hotspot on the eastern edge of the Big Island, where volcanic activity is rife. The hotspot's location has remained constant relative to the earth's axis over time, while the whole archipelago has rumbled its way northwest at a rate of over four inches per year.

Almost six million years ago, what is now the island of Niʻihau emerged slowly over the hotspot. What caused the pause in volcanic activity since the formation of Nihoa Island — 138 miles to the northwest, and 1.5 million years earlier — is still uncertain, but a new volcanic vent sprang to life at this time on the seabed about 15,000 feet below the surface, beginning the formation of a new shield volcano. Shield volcanoes are formed by flows of extremely fluid lava and typically have slopes of only 2–3°. Their shape has been likened to a shield lying flat on the ground, hence the name.

Although no definite proof has yet been found, it is considered that because of Niʻihau's location to the west of Kauaʻi, it is likely it emerged before the Kauaian shield volcano, although there may have been some overlap.

The earliest geologist to write about Niʻihau was James Dana, the doyen of American geologists of the time, who suggested in 1890 that in earlier times Niʻihau had been a part of Kauaʻi.[4] When Dana was the geologist on the Wilkes Exploring Expedition of 1838–42 he visited Kauaʻi but did not set foot on Niʻihau, and did not include this assertion in his expedition report of 1849. Later writers generally agree that Dana was incorrect and that the geological structure of Niʻihau indicates it was an independent volcano.

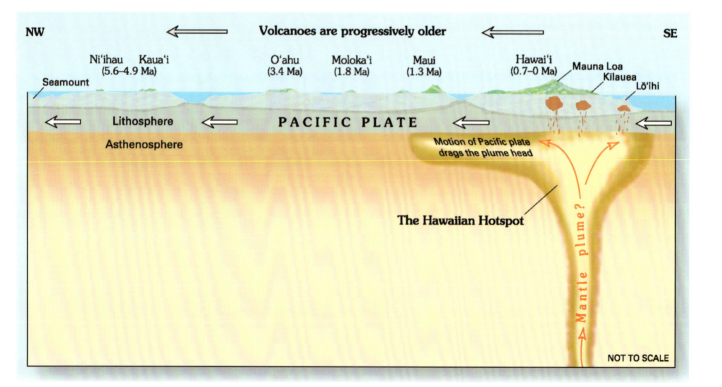

▼ A cross-section along the Hawaiian chain, showing the assumed mantle plume of magma that has fed the Hawaiian hotspot as the Pacific Plate moves northwest. The plume is a large volume of hot rock rising through the earth's mantle which causes rocks in the lower lithosphere (crust) to melt. The ages of the oldest rocks on each island are shown, with Niʻihau and Kauaʻi being the oldest.

Diagram derived from *This Dynamic Planet* by Simkin et al (2006) / Wikimedia Commons

◀ The east coast cliffs of Niʻihau, from the north.
Marcia Braden

The first geologist to land on Niʻihau was Sidney Powers, who spent a few hours there in 1915 and collected rock samples to examine. Many of his observations about the island's geology have not stood the test of time.[35]

In 1921 Norman Hinds, a Bishop Museum geologist, spent eight days on Niʻihau and visited most of the island. His studies confirmed that the lava exposed in the eastern cliffs had no relation to those of northwestern Kauaʻi, and therefore Niʻihau was not a fragment of Kauaʻi.[6]

In the 1940s, geologist Harold Stearns set down a model of the evolutionary stages through which all the Hawaiian volcanoes progressed. His report on Niʻihau was published in 1947,[5] and proposed four stages for the evolution of the single shield volcano that formed Niʻihau. The dates are drawn from Clague and Dalrymple's 1989 paper on the Hawaiian-Emperor Volcanic Chain.

1. Submarine and emergent stage (5.7–4.8 million years ago)[7]

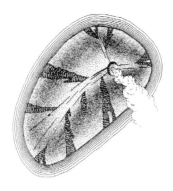

A dome-shaped volcanic island emerged by the outpouring of basalt flows. It extended 2500 feet above the present sea level and 13,000 feet above the ocean floor. Its eruptive center was about two miles east of Niʻihau, and a large crater probably indented the summit. The eastern rim of the crater may have been lower than the western, as the eastern side was destroyed by subsequent erosion more rapidly than the western side.

2. Weathering and erosion (4.8–2.5 million years ago)[8]

The cessation of volcanism was followed by a long period of weathering, during which high marine cliffs were formed on the eastern and south-eastern coasts of the dome, and lower ones on the other coasts. Streams cut canyons in the dome. This was followed, in common with other islands of the Hawaiian archipelago, by a gradual submergence of the island by a large but unknown amount. The island probably finally reached stability around 2.5 million years ago.

From 2.5 million to 12 thousand years ago many shifts in sea level occurred — from about 250 feet above the present level to 300 feet below. A shelf 0.5 to 1.5 miles wide was cut 300 feet below the current sea level, indicating long periods at that level. Reefs grew during rising seas.

3. Volcanism renews (2.5–0.5 million years ago)

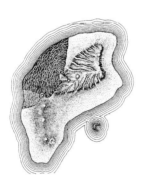

Concurrent with the shifting sea levels, volcanism was renewed and lava and tuff cones (light porous rock formed by consolidation of volcanic ash) built the submarine shelf to above sea level. Buried cones lie below sea level.

During a 60-foot lower sea level period a lava dome formed the northern part of the coastal plain to above sea level and Lehua Island was created by a submarine explosion. Ash from Lehua fell over most of Niʻihau and was blown into dunes on the northern plain.

4. Volcanism ceases and sea levels change again (0.5 million years ago to the present)

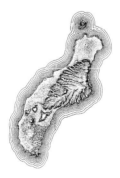

In this final stage, the sea level rose about 85 feet from the minus 60-foot level, drowning the seaward parts of the dunes. Later the sea fell twenty feet and formed benches and beaches five feet above the present sea level. The sea then fell a further five feet and formed today's beaches and dunes.

A large portion of the Niʻihau shield dome, together with its postulated summit caldera two miles east of the present coastline, apparently collapsed into the sea in a massive landslide eons ago, leaving a huge amount of debris scattered on the ocean floor.

Stearns also recognized Kawaihoa at the south end of the island as a tuff cone, as well as a series of tuff cones around Kiʻekiʻe, and several others formed during the resurgence of volcanic activity in the relatively recent past. This appears to have been much more extensive on Niʻihau and Kauaʻi than on the other islands in the group.

The coastal plain to the west of the dome remnant was formed during this resurgence, by lava and tuff which emerged from offshore vents. This volcanic formation has now been partially overlain by wind-blown sand, which has been cemented during sea-level changes to form the current landscape.

▲ Stearns' diagrams of the four stages in the evolution of the volcano that formed Niʻihau.

5 miles

◀ Towards the southern end of Niʻihau lie two lakes — Halulu & Halāliʻi. While Halāliʻi is by far the larger at over 800 acres when full after winter rains, it can shrink almost completely to a salty pan in the summer and is regarded as a 'playa' or intermittent lake. Halulu (pictured, almost full), on the other hand, is regarded as the largest true lake in all of Hawaiʻi. It also shrinks in the summer, but has been used over many years by the locals as a mullet fishery, as mullet are able to enter the lake through a lava tube.
Marcia Braden

While beaches are extensive, coral reefs are not, because of extreme wave energy from all directions. A powerful northwest swell frequently impacts the northern and western coasts during the winter, and Kauaʻi is too distant to provide shelter from the northeast trade winds impinging on the eastern coast. Hurricanes can cause extensive reef damage. Where coral communities exist, they grow as thin veneers on limestone and basalt outcrops.

Kaʻula Island, 20 miles southwest of Niʻihau, Stearns identified as a tuff cone based upon a submerged independent shield volcano.[9]

Volcano Watch, the US Geological Survey's Hawaiian Volcano Observatory's newsletter, confirmed in 2016 that Stearns' model is still accepted:

> The stages of Hawaiian volcanism are defined by the vigor of eruptive activity, as well as the chemical composition of the erupted lava, which changes over time as the volcano is rafted away from the hotspot. New data and insights continually refine this model, but the overall tenets remain largely unchanged since first proposed by Stearns over 70 years ago.[10]

In his 1947 paper Stearns also discussed Niʻihau's water resources. There are no permanent streams, and only a few perennial springs. All are brackish due to salt spray, but most can be used for stock. There are a number of lakes fed almost exclusively from run-off, most of which hold water only intermittently, as they soon evaporate and are reduced to salt pans. The biggest is Halāliʻi, which is the largest lake in the Hawaiian islands, although even it can almost become a complete salt pan if there is no rain.

▼ A typical sandy beach on the west coast of Niʻihau — looking northeast, with Lehua Island in the distance.
Greg Vaughn

Stearns noted that groundwater 'occurs in all formations that extend below sea level and is the chief supply of water on the island.' He listed 57 wells and waterholes, with depths, salinity, aquifer type and comments on each, concluding:

> ... the total quantity of recoverable ground water is small and amounts to thousands of gallons per day. This results from low rainfall, adverse geologic structures, large quantities of salt carried inland by spray, and deposits of ... salts in some of the earthy formations. There is no possibility of developing supplies of millions of gallons of water per day, such as are common in the larger Hawaiian islands.[11]

This must have confirmed the worst fears of the people of Niʻihau.

Flora — now a kiawe savannah

Flying over the island today, it's hard not to be struck at how different it must have looked when the early Hawaiians first saw it, and how different again it must have been when Europeans came upon it after several hundred years of Polynesian occupation. Today the dominant vegetation is the kiawe first planted by Aubrey Robinson in the early 1900s. While some savannah areas remain, much of the island is now a dense forest of kiawe trees. Early European botanical explorers, though, saw a somewhat barren island without much vegetation, while Harold St John, after his 1940s fieldwork, describes it as 'dominated by *Prosopis pallida* [kiawe] which forms a dry, open, sparse stand over the lowlands ... and is also found on the upland except near the crest and on the cliffs' (see Appendix E for the island's botanical exploration history). St John fears for the endangered species:

> The original vegetation of Niihau has been decimated by the grazing of goats, sheep and cattle. Native plants of the sandy or salty shores of the island still occur, and perhaps only one (*Scaevola coriacea*) of this group has been exterminated. Native plants of the lowlands, and uplands, have been so much depleted that most of the surviving ones can only be found in crevices, or rock faces, or other places, that cannot be reached by grazing animals.[12]

▶ A dense forest of kiawe now covers large areas of the island. The contrast between the aerial photograph on page 6, taken in 2007, and the one shown here, taken in 2018, is quite marked in this respect. Although large areas of relatively sparse kiawe still exist, the kiawe canopy appears to be becoming more extensive over time.
Steven Gentry

The most complete compilation of the Niʻihau flora is to be found in the 1990 book *A Chronicle and Flora of Niihau*, which lists 243 species of flowering plants. Written by local historian Juliet Rice Wichman and Harold St John, this book is based upon the fieldwork St John undertook in 1947 and 1949, but incorporates all the earlier botanical collections (see Appendix E) and the later botanical studies of 1976 and 1977 carried out by John Fay and Charles Christensen.

As Table 1 (page 20) indicates, of the 243 species and varieties of flowering plants listed in the book 100 can be considered indigenous, and eight of these are endemic (i.e. found only on Niʻihau). By 'indigenous' is meant any species believed to have arrived naturally as a result of animal, wind or ocean transport, rather than through human activities. With plants of worldwide tropical distribution it is sometimes impossible to ascertain whether a species arrived on Niʻihau naturally or was introduced by humans, and an educated guess has been made in some instances.

It seems 143 species were introduced, with 19 of them likely early introductions by Hawaiians, and the remaining 124 introduced since the arrival of Europeans, either accidentally or deliberately. The causes of the European introductions are basically twofold: the demand for improved grasses for the ranching operation, and inhabitants importing exotic plants, both ornamental and useful, for their gardens.

Of the 19 species thought to have been brought by the early Hawaiians, 15 are considered essential to their culture and four arrived as stowaways and are regarded as weeds. The 15 species likely to have been brought by the early Hawaiians and essential to the Hawaiian culture are shown in Table 2 (page 20).

A surprising omission in Harold St John's list is the bottle gourd, ipu (*Lagenaria siceraria*) which he did not find. It had earlier been grown, but apparently never listed by any of the earlier botanists. Ipu pāwehe (carved gourds) provided an item of trade with Kauaʻi in pre-European times (see also Chapter Two).

Because of a lack of suitable habitat taro was unlikely to have been grown successfully on Niʻihau for food in the Hawaiian era, although a few plants were found when Cook visited and when later botanical collections were made.

In a 1978 paper St John concludes that the Polynesians also inadvertently brought weeds to the islands on their migration voyages. He names seven, four of which are growing on Niʻihau.[13] Two of those not present on Niʻihau are those associated with irrigated taro fields, lending credence to the view that taro has never been grown on the island. The third missing weed also grows in wet situations.

Table 3 (page 21) shows the eight endemic species mentioned in Table 1 — two grasses, a palm, a vine, a shrub and three daisies.

The most recently discovered of these endemic species on Niʻihau was found in the wild by St John in 1947. He saw several palms growing in cliff-bound areas in the center of the island and named the new species *Pritchardia aylmer-robinsonii* after the island's owner, Aylmer Robinson.[14] The palm is widely cultivated as an ornamental by the residents of Niʻihau and is found in many botanical collections internationally, as well as in private gardens, so its survival is assured.

The endemic *Delissea undulata* subsp. *niihauensis* (also known as *Delissea niihauensis* subsp. *niihauensis*), a shrub of the lobelia family, was collected on Niʻihau by James

▲ Harold St John (1892–1991) was a professor of botany at the University of Hawaiʻi, Mānoa, from 1929 to 1958. In the course of his field research over the years he visited Niʻihau twice. As a result he wrote, with Juliet Rice Wichman, *A Chronicle and Flora of Niihau*, which was published in 1990 by the National Tropical Botanical Garden, the most complete flora of the island to date.
University of Hawaiʻi, Mānoa

▲ Wāhane was found growing wild on Niʻihau in 1947 by Harold St John, who named it after rancher Aylmer Robinson.
National Tropical Botanical Garden, Kauaʻi

Table 1: Origins of the Niihauan plant species listed by St John

Origin	No. of species
Indigenous but not endemic to Niʻihau	92
Endemic to Niʻihau	8
Polynesian introductions	19
European introductions	124
Total	243

▲ *Sesbania tomentosa* (ʻohai): probably extinct on Niʻihau and endangered elsewhere in the islands.
National Tropical Botanical Garden

▲ The delicate flower of the ʻōlulu or 'cabbage on a stick' belies the plant's rugged appearance (photo on page 22).
Wikimedia Commons

Table 2: Plants listed by St John likely to have been brought to Niʻihau by early Hawaiians and essential to their culture

Common name	Hawaiian name	Botanical name	Comment
pandanus	hala	*Pandanus tectorius* (originally considered to be *P. odoratissimus*)	Now thought to have arrived naturally.
sugar cane	kō	*Saccharum officinarum*	The species now grown on the island is not an early Hawaiian introduction, but many early reports exist of cane growing on Niʻihau.
bamboo	ʻohe	*Schizostachyum glaucifolium*	
ti	lāʻī (plant) ki (root)	*Cordyline terminalis* (now *C. fruticosa*)	
yam	uhi	*Dioscorea alata*	
banana	maiʻa	*Musa paradisiaca*	
breadfruit	ʻulu	*Artocarpus altilis*	
kapa	wauke	*Broussonetia papyrifera*	Possibly too slow-growing on Niʻihau for clothing production.
candlenut	kukui	*Aleurites moluccanus*	
beach hibiscus	hao	*Hibiscus tiliaceus*	
sweet potato	ʻuala	*Ipomoea batatas*	
beach mulberry	noni	*Morinda citrifolia*	
hola	hola	*Tephrosia purpurea*	Used for catching fish by poison. Extinct by 1947.
coconut	niu	*Cocos nucifera*	May have floated rather than been introduced by humans.
taro	kalo	*Colocasia esculenta*	

Table 3: Species endemic to Ni'ihau, as listed by St John

Eragrostis niihauensis		grass
Panicum heupeuo		grass
Pritchardii aylmer-robinsonii	wāhane	palm
Canavalia pubescens		vine
Delissea niihauensis (now D. undulata subsp. niihauensis)		shrub
Lipochaeta kawaihoaensis		daisy
Lipochaeta lobata var. incisior (now L. connata)	nehe	daisy
Lipochaeta niihauensis	shrubland nehe	daisy

Table 4: Species collected by earlier botanists on Ni'ihau but regarded as extinct in St John's listing

Cenchrus agriminoides		grass
Panicum ramosius		grass
Schiedea amplexicaulis		shrub
Gynandropsis gynandra		weed
Lepidium o-waihiense		shrub
Tephrosia purpurea	hola	pea family flowering shrub
Isodendrum remyi		shrub
Cheirodendron trigynum	'olapa	medium-sized tree
Reynoldsia sandwicensis (now Polyscias sandwicensis)	'ohe'ohe	medium-sized tree
Lysimachia mauritiana		small shrub
Delissea undulata subsp. niihauensis		shrub/tree
Scaevola coriacea	dwarf naupaka	low seaside shrub

Table 5: Ni'ihau species listed as endangered or threatened by the US Fish and Wildlife Service in 2003

Brighamia insignis	'ōlulu	'cabbage on a stick'
Cyperus trachysanthos	pu'uka'a	sedge
† Delissea undulata subsp. niihauensis	no Hawaiian name	shrub
Isodendrion pyrifolium	wahine noho kula	shrub
* Lobelia niihauensis	no Hawaiian name	woody, grasslike shrub
Panicum niihauensis	lau ehu	grass
Pritchardia aylmer-robinsonii	wāhane	palm
* Sesbania tomentosa	'ōhai	pea family shrub
Vigna o-wahuensis	no Hawaiian name	legume family shrub

† likely extinct   * now likely extinct on Ni'ihau

▲ One of four specimens of the now extinct *Delissea niihauensis* in the Bishop Museum herbarium, collected by James Sinclair.
David Eickhoff / Flickr

▲ Although Harold St John found a few straggly bushes of *Lobelia niihauensis* (above) on Ni'ihau it is now probably extinct on the island; elsewhere it is endangered.
National Tropical Botanical Garden

Sinclair after he arrived in 1864, and four specimens pressed by Ann Knudsen are in the Bishop Museum. The species has not been seen since, although it was collected earlier by Rémy and Brigham. A close relative on Kauaʻi is endangered.

Of the 243 species listed by St John, he records twelve as extinct or probably extinct on Niʻihau (see Table 4, page 21). To these extinctions must be added the cactus or pāpipi (*Opuntia ficus-indica*), the makaloa sedge (*Cyperus laevigatus*), *Sesbania tomentosa* and *Lobelia undulata* subsp. *niihauensis*, remnant populations of which were still existing when St John did his 1947 and 1949 fieldwork, but are now extinct on Niʻihau. The effect of the catastrophic loss of the introduced cactus on the ranching operation is discussed in Chapter Ten.

In 2003 the US Fish and Wildlife Service listed nine Niʻihau plant species as endangered or threatened.[15] Endangered species are considered to be on the brink of extinction now, while threatened species are likely to be extinct in the near future. 'Probably extinct' means the species has not been seen on the island for over 30 years. The nine species listed as endangered or threatened are shown in Table 5, page 21.

The ʻōlulu is also found on Kauaʻi (it could now be extinct on Niʻihau).[16]

The wāhane is unique to Niʻihau and exists nowhere else in the wild. *Delissea undulata* subsp. *niihauensis* has not been seen since 1864 and must be regarded as extinct. The remaining endangered or threatened species on Niʻihau are found on other islands of the group.

If the makaloa sedge, and the lobelia and sesbania in Table 5 are added to the twelve species of Table 4 which St John considered extinct on Niʻihau, the total is fifteen probable indigenous species extinctions since the first European botanical explorations in the early 1800s. With one hundred indigenous species identified by St John as present on Niʻihau, this gives a probable extinction rate of 15%. Fortunately, apart from the Delissea, all of the indigenous species apparently extinct on Niʻihau are growing elsewhere in the archipelago.

After lengthy consultation the US Fish and Wildlife Service designated 347 acres on Niʻihau as a 'critical habitat' for the protection of the ʻōlulu. This is the only plant on Niʻihau afforded such protection, compared to 82 species and 52,549 acres of critical habitat on Kauaʻi. No designation was made to protect the Niʻihau palm or wāhane, nor the two palm species on Kauaʻi, as publication of their locations could invite theft. The third endangered species not considered probably extinct, the sedge puʻukaʻa, is also found on Kauaʻi and no critical habitat for it has been designated on Niʻihau.[17]

Critical habitat designation as defined by the US Fish and Wildlife Service does not affect normal activities on state or private land unless federal funding or permits are involved. Ranching, hunting and other recreational uses are not therefore affected by such designation. If federal agencies are funding projects in critical habitat areas they must ensure that their activities do not endanger the survival of a listed species.[18]

In its 2003 document setting out the final designation for the critical habitat area on Niʻihau the US Fish and Wildlife Service comments on how the island's relative isolation and harsh environmental conditions have produced few endemic species and that unfortunately human disturbance, mainly ranching, has left few of the native vegetation communities extant.[19]

▲ Makaloa sedge is extinct on Niʻihau due to the effect of browsing animals. It is, however, growing on other islands in the chain. This photo shows the sedge in a pond on Maui.
Kim & Forest Starr / Wikimedia Commons

▲ ʻŌlulu (*Brighamia insignis*) — 'cabbage on a stick' (or baseball bat), one of the stranger plants growing on Kauaʻi and previously on Niʻihau. Extremely rare in the wild, it is now widely cultivated.
David Eickhoff / Wikimedia Commons

The report regrets the lack of recent botanical work on the island and hence the paucity of reliable data on the flora. While botanists have spent time on Niʻihau from the earliest European visits (see Appendix E), the later history of botanical work has been patchy at best.

While the Hawaiians brought their own particular plant and animal imports, they essentially lived lightly on the land, as the aridity of the island limited the population. With the introduction of European grazing animals — and goats in particular — the character of the vegetation started to change, and this accelerated manyfold once ranching proper began in 1864. With the end of ranching in 1999 the character is slowly changing yet again.

Fauna — food sources and stowaways

As with the flora, the effects on the fauna caused by human interventions have been enormous. The Polynesian voyagers brought with them to Niʻihau their rats, chickens, pigs and dogs. As stowaways they also unwittingly brought with them on their canoes skinks, geckoes, some land snail species, and doubtless also insects and other arthropods. Over a millennium ago, they then modified the landscape to suit their needs.

Patrick Kirch concluded his paper on the impact of the Polynesians on the Hawaiian archipelago forthrightly:

> [T]here can no longer be any doubt that the island chain as first viewed through European eyes was a land already transformed by centuries of intensive exploitation, modification, manipulation and, frequently, degradation. The vast tracts of grassland that covered the lowlands … were products of human action. Recent studies have suggested that the endemic biota was drastically affected by this habitat destruction…[20]

▲ Pāpipi or prickly pear cactus (*Opuntia ficus-indica*) dying from a fungal blight on Niʻihau during St John's visit in 1947. It was extinct on the island not long after, much to the displeasure of rancher Aylmer Robinson as the leaves provided a valuable water source for his cattle.

Harold St John, in *A Chronicle and Flora of Niihau*, National Tropical Botanical Garden, 1990

Just how much the early Hawaiians may have changed the Niihauan ecology as population pressure mounted and more resources were required is unknown. Evidence shows that the Hawaiian population peaked in the 16th or 17th century and then declined, well before Europeans arrived, presumably because food was hard to come by. There are hints from the land-snail fossil record in particular that Niʻihau must have been more densely wooded in prehistoric times. Everywhere else on the islands the early Hawaiians cleared much of the lowland forest, and the same would have happened on Niʻihau, if there was forest there.

Then came the Europeans bringing goats, sheep, cattle, horses and cats, as well as the ubiquitous black rat (*Rattus rattus*), and another assorted contingent of lizards, insects, spiders and land snails. Deliberate introductions to Niʻihau in later years established further exotic grazing animals and wildfowl. Fortunately the mongoose, so prevalent on the Hawaiian windward islands, is not present on Niʻihau and the feral rabbit has yet to find its way here.

The biota of volcanic islands, totally reliant on chance arrivals and the successful establishment of breeding colonies, has inevitable gaps in the spectrum of life. On the Hawaiian islands there are no native lizards, amphibians or ants, for instance. All are common now and all were introduced by humans. The islands can boast only two native mammals: the Hawaiian hoary bat, now restricted to just Kauaʻi and the Big Island, and the Hawaiian monk seal.

As Niʻihau and Kauaʻi are the oldest islands in the main Hawaiian group, the time span for plants and animals to arrive and evolve since the islands emerged from the ocean has been the longest. While this 'age' effect may be true for Kauaʻi, the ecological niches available for colonizing plants and animals on Niʻihau are limited due to the island's relatively low altitude and the rain-shadow effect of Kauaʻi to the east, capturing the available moisture.

To achieve greater understanding of the fauna on Niʻihau, and the changes to it over historic time, considerably more research is needed.

Monk seals

In 2008 the monk seal was named state mammal for Hawaiʻi in recognition of its place in the hearts and minds of the people. To see a monk seal 'hauled out' on a beach and quietly resting after a morning's fishing is a memorable experience.

The seal's Hawaiian name is ʻĪlio-holo-i-ka-uaua, meaning 'the dog that runs in rough water,' while its scientific name comes from the German scientist Hugo Schauinsland, who found a skull on Laysan Island in 1899.

Niʻihau is home to the largest population of the endangered Hawaiian monk seal in the main Hawaiian islands and as such it deserves a special place in this island biography. Worldwide this seal is found only on the Hawaiian archipelago and Johnston Atoll, around 860 miles southwest of Hawaiʻi. With a total population of about 1400, the bulk of which is in the northwestern Hawaiian islands, around 100 inhabit Niʻihau.[21]

Numbers on Niʻihau and the other main islands have been increasing since the 1970s, while numbers in the northwestern islands have been decreasing over an even longer period. Despite efforts by parties under the leadership of the National Oceanic and Atmospheric Administration (NOAA), the population continues to decline, but the rate has slowed considerably or even plateaued over the last few years.[22]

A low seal-pup survival rate has been the chief cause of the decline in the northwestern islands, caused mainly by lack of food, and by predation by Galapagos sharks

▲ The Polynesian rat (*Rattus exulans*) is found throughout Polynesia and is believed to have been brought with the Polynesians on their colonizing canoe voyages as a source of food, and to have also arrived as stowaways.
Kim & Forest Starr / Wikimedia Commons

◂ A Hawaiian monk seal (*Neomonachus schauinslandi*) lolls on a Niʻihau beach, scratching against a log from time to time.
Nancy Shaw

and other shark species. Adults have suffered from entanglement in abandoned fishing nets and there has been some loss of beach habitat. The situation is different in the main islands. Pup survival rates have been much higher, but threats to adult seals include interference by humans, by-catch from commercial fishing, and disease transmission from dogs, cats, humans and other pathogen carriers.

It is thought that the progenitor of the monk seal evolved twelve million years ago and arrived in the Hawaiian archipelago between twelve and four million years ago, when North and South America were still separated. When the Central American Seaway closed about three million years ago the Hawaiian monk seal became cut off from its Caribbean cousins (now extinct) and developed into the distinct species we have today.[23] Whether the main Hawaiian islands had been thrust from the ocean when the seals first arrived is a matter for conjecture, but given their predilection for sandy beaches for 'hauling out' and pupping, the northwestern islands were a natural home.

If monk seals were present on the main Hawaiian islands when the Polynesians arrived, it appears they were eaten to the point of extinction there within a few generations.[24] In the early 19th century Europeans discovered their northwestern habitats and the seals were hunted almost to extinction for their skins.

Monk seals are generally solitary animals, and while they do move from island to island to some extent, they have an affinity for their home island. Their diet is variable, consisting of crustacea, squid and fish. They are not particularly selective, and hunt and eat whatever is most easily accessible, generally in relatively shallow waters.

Adult seals can weigh as much as 400 pounds, with females larger than males. Pups weigh 30–40 pounds at birth and are much darker in color than their parents. The pups put on weight rapidly and become half the adult size at weaning in just a few months. Their lifespan is around 30 years.

Extensive efforts have been made since the 1950s to stem the decline in numbers. In 1976 the seal was declared endangered and critical habitat areas in the northwestern Hawaiian islands were designated. In 2015 these were revised and critical habitat areas were designated in the main islands as well.[25]

Generally these designations run from the 200-meter depth contour to five meters above the wash of the waves (debris or vegetation line). For Niʻihau, having regard to the contract Niihau Ranch has with the navy's Pacific Missile Range Facility (see Chapter Eleven), the critical habitat designation runs from the 200-meter depth contour to the 10-meter depth contour right around the island. To protect the monk seals' habitat in the coastal and marine area out to the 10-meter depth there are requirements on the navy for Niʻihau. They include a coastal monitoring program for monk seals, periodic removal of feral pigs, a ban on all-terrain vehicles and on dogs, and limited access for visitors.[26]

On Niʻihau, pup survival rates have been good, and interactions with humans will continue to be minimal with the above regime, so there is every hope that this subpopulation will continue to increase. NOAA's monk seal recovery program targets 500 seals in the main Hawaiian islands, which on present distributions would mean around 250 seals on Niʻihau.

▲ While monk seals are awkward on land and never stray inland as a consequence, once in the water their agility is astonishing. They are inquisitive and have no fear of humans underwater, just curiosity.
Wikimedia Commons

Any major rise in monk seal numbers concerns the Niihauans living there who depend on fishing for their way of life. They raised the issue (along with the increase in recreational fishing around the island) with Governor Linda Lingle when she visited the island in June 2003.[27] The governor discussed the possibility of regulating fishing in the waters around the island, which could benefit both the Niihauans and the monk seals (see also Chapter Eleven). The critical habitat designation does not in any way impinge on fishing rights.

Actions by which NOAA hopes to achieve the target of 500 seals are set out in the agency's 2016 *Main Hawaiian Islands Monk Seal Management Plan*[28] with strategies to reduce disease-related seal deaths, reduce the impact of fishing, engage with communities, increase public education, and manage interactions between monk seals and humans.

All of these relate to the special situation on Niʻihau, where there are essentially three communities: the navy, the island's owners (Niihau Ranch), and the Niihauans (residents and their ʻohana), each of whom has different interests in the island.

The Robinson brothers, who own the island, have been fully cooperating with NOAA on the seal management plan.[29]

Interactions between monk seals and feral animals or livestock on Niʻihau, as on the other islands, raises the possibility of disease transmission, and interactions will increase as seal numbers rise. The same is true for monk seal–fisheries interactions, whether it be from the fishing activities of those living on Niʻihau or from out of island (principally Kauaʻi) commercial and recreational fishing.

The Niihauan community living on the island is likely to be better informed on monk seal behavior than any other Hawaiians, but will still need to continually be made aware of the monk seal management plan objectives and strategies.

Further research will be necessary to achieve the 500 seal number outcome in the main Hawaiian islands. As seal numbers rise, funding will also have to rise, and this is especially true if a catastrophic disease outbreak is to be avoided.

Despite the monk seal's apparently indolent nature when on land, the creature appeals to the public imagination in some indefinable way — perhaps due to its large brown eyes and doleful expression. The island of Niʻihau is playing its part in the slow restoration in numbers that can bring this charismatic seal back from the brink of extinction.

Birdlife

Three scientists from the University of Hawaiʻi visited Niʻihau in 1947 and produced a comprehensive body of work. The team consisted of ornithologist Harvey Fisher; entomologist Leonard Tuthill and botanist Harold St John.

Polynesian transformation of the lowland landscape led to the extinction of at least half the known bird species of the Hawaiian archipelago, according to Patrick Kirch in *Pacific Science*.[30] How true this is of the island of Niʻihau we just don't know, but after the Polynesians came the Europeans, and to quote Harvey Fisher's work regarding the birdlife he found on Niʻihau in 1947:

▼ A visitor to Niʻihau when the lakes have water, the black-necked Hawaiian stilt — aeʻo — has proportionately the longest legs of any stilt.
Wikimedia Commons

The avifauna of Niihau has particular interest to the ornithologist because all native birds have been eliminated and their places taken by successful exotic birds. Since the introduction by humans of exotic species has been under the control and supervision of one family [the Robinsons, the island's owners], it is possible to note dates of introduction of many species. It is even feasible to judge the probable dates of entry of birds which have moved without human aid to Niihau from Kauai Island some 25 miles upwind. These latter dates are fairly accurate because the Robinson family has long been interested and informed on the birds of both Kauai and Niihau.[31]

Thus, to borrow a phrase, 'the birds had already flown' when Fisher was on the island, and we have little knowledge of the pre-human avian inhabitants. Fisher draws upon the findings of the few previous ornithologists to have visited and lists 45 current bird species in his paper, but only 17 of these might be considered fully terrestrial and all of the latter except one indigenous bird (the short-eared owl or pueo, *Asio flammeus sandwichensis*) have been either intentionally introduced or are adventive exotics from Kauaʻi. The remaining 28 bird species described are migratory or other seabirds, or birds of the seashore and lakes, and none can be considered exotic introductions. Fisher's paper, therefore, rather overstates the situation. Fisher feels that the natural establishment of further adventive species of exotic and even native birds from Kauaʻi is likely, if and when feed conditions permit.

▲▲ A Laysan albatross (*Phoebastria immutabilis*) flies over a beach on northern Niʻihau in December 2018. They are occasional visitors from the northwestern islands and may be breeding on Lehua Island, now mammalian pests there have been removed.
Nancy Shaw

▲ At the moment of take-off from Niʻihau — a Laysan albatross.
Mike Anderson, 2018, Kauaʻi Historical Society

Since Fisher's time on Niʻihau few, if any, local bird studies specific to the island have been done. Avibase, the world bird database, lists only eight established introduced species on Niʻihau and only four that are on Fisher's list (two dove species, the house finch and the northern cardinal). The four exotic species now established there that are not in Fisher's list are the common barn owl, the African silverbill, the scaly-breasted munia and the house sparrow. The overall species count is given as 31, down from 45 in Fisher's paper.[32] Has there been a substantial decrease in species over the last 70 years, or is the database incomplete? It is probably a mixture of the two, and a visit by an ornithologist is well overdue.

The US Fish and Wildlife Service lists 35 endangered or threatened Hawaiian birds, only one of which, the Hawaiian stilt, aeʻo (*Himantopus mexicanus knudseni*) is present on Niʻihau. It also inhabits the other Hawaiian islands.[33]

Insects

Leonard Tuthill's 1947 visit to the island enabled him to build on the work of David Fullaway, which in turn relied upon the collecting of two of his assistants, who made the first entomological survey in October 1945.[34] Fullaway acknowledged that the list was small, consisting of 70 species from eleven orders, adding, 'It may never be extended greatly, as it is well known that continued grazing by cattle and sheep has long since denuded whatever forest cover was on this low island, and under the circumstances a great variety of insects cannot be expected.' Fullaway's prediction has not come to pass, however, as Beardsley and Tuthill's paper, based upon the collection from Tuthill's 1947 visit shows.[35] They list 127 species in all, from eleven orders, with 106 of these not having been found on Niʻihau before.

The latest published number of insect species on Niʻihau is 153:

Native to the Hawaiian islands (endemic and indigenous)	16
Accidental immigrants arriving with humans (adventive)	112
Purposefully introduced by humans	25
Total insect species	153

As the table shows, almost 90% of these are imports — a very high figure, partly due to the effects of long-term ranching. The number of species overall is low when compared with the figure for Hawaiʻi as a whole, with 8706 insect species of which only 30% are exotics.[36]

In 1948 Elwood Zimmerman looked at the ten orders of insects known on the archipelago at that time, and more particularly the orders that were missing, and concluded that most had arrived on the wind. The likely number of ancestral native species was around 250; probably fewer. With Niʻihau arguably the oldest of the main Hawaiian islands, and no interisland arrivals possible as the other islands had yet to emerge, a reasonable number of the ancestral arrivals may well have been on Niʻihau, and may have later colonized other islands. This is pure speculation and many populations will have met their fate on Niʻihau.

The limited ecological niches available on Niʻihau have favored introduced species, and a number of the native species on David Fullaway's initial list will have succumbed, as many original inhabitants did before his work was published.

Knowledge of the insect life on Niʻihau is fragmentary at best, but none of the sixteen native species remaining are unique to Niʻihau, and none are on the US Fish and Wildlife's endangered species list.

Spiders, scorpions, centipedes

Nishida's 2002 Terrestrial Arthropod Checklist[37] identifies 235 spider species on the Hawaiian islands, but none are shown as inhabiting Niʻihau alone. This is a result of the complete lack of knowledge of spiders on the island, as apparently no entomologist interested in spiders has ever visited.

The same is true of scorpions and their close relatives. Twenty species are recorded for the islands as a whole, but none particularly for Niʻihau. The only circumstantial evidence for the presence of scorpions is in a newspaper report from 1978 that speaks of the homestead at Kiʻekiʻe as infested with scorpions.[38]

With centipedes and their relatives the story is the same. One hundred and six centipede and millipede species are listed for all the islands, but none given as

▲ Of the 20 species of scorpion recorded in the islands, the Lesser Brown is the most common.
Wikimedia Commons

specifically found on Ni'ihau. The island has been forgotten in the scholarly work done on this class of animals.

While some academic papers have been written on the arthropods in Hawai'i's main islands and in its northwestern islands, none have included Ni'ihau, perhaps because of a perceived difficulty in getting there or in obtaining funding. The papers that have been written are therefore not complete, but this has not been overtly recognized by their authors.[39] Perhaps this book will serve as a wake-up call to entomological institutions. Science just does not know what is there.

Land snails (terrestrial molluscs)

Hawai'i's snails are an exemplar of the evolutionary process of adaptive radiation, whereby organisms diversify rapidly from an ancestral species into a multitude of new forms when new environmental niches become available. In 1948 Elwood Zimmerman estimated that just 22–24 accidental arrivals on the islands gave rise to the 1064 native species and subspecies of land snails known at that date.[40] The numbers would be different now, but these figures serve to show the explosion in species that has occurred from only a few ancestral accidental immigrants.*

Using slightly different criteria in 1995, Robert Cowie listed 898 species of native land snails on the islands, with six of these on Ni'ihau. Two are endemic to Ni'ihau and four are also found on other islands.[41] Only ten out of the worldwide total of about 90 families of molluscs found their way to the Hawaiian islands, and species from four of these families have been collected on Ni'ihau.

Perhaps the best known of these snails is elegant, sculptured *Carelia sinclairi*, which is also found on Kaua'i and is 35mm long and 15mm at its widest. It was formally described by a well-known French conchologist César Marie Félix Ancey in 1892 from specimens found on Ni'ihau. It is likely they were sent to him by a member of the Sinclair family, the owners of Ni'ihau as the species name of *sinclairi* is of some significance. Eliza Sinclair, the family matriarch, died that same year, and it seems the naming of *sinclairi* was done as a mark of respect for Eliza, who features heavily in later chapters of this book.

Charles Montague Cooke Jnr, undoubtedly the father of Hawaiian land snail studies, visited Ni'ihau in 1908 and collected them at Halehaa on the west coast near Ki'eki'e.[42] He found abundant *sinclairi* shells in fossil deposits near the seashore, in calcareous beach sand and disintegrated lava mixed with sand. The shells were in perfect condition, indicating that they had lived nearby. He was in little doubt that the species was extinct.[43]

Cooke noted that the Bishop Museum collection had about 1000 specimens, so the shells were not rare finds. The *Carelia* land snails were ground dwellers, living off leaf litter, so vegetation of lowland Ni'ihau may have been much denser in prehuman times. No work appears to have been done on dating the shells.

Marie Neal has described two of the other species discovered on Ni'ihau, *Pleuropoma laciniosa kiekieensis* and *Pleuropoma niihauensis*.[44] Shells of both of these small (2.5 mm) species were found on the western side of the island near Ki'eki'e by John Stokes in 1912 (along with those of *Carelia sinclairi*).

▲ The extinct endemic Hawaiian land snail *Carelia sinclairi*, a species of small air-breathing snail first found on Ni'ihau in 1892 and named after Eliza Sinclair.
Wikimedia Commons

* *In his 1990 paper, 'How many Hawaiian land snail species are left? and what we can do for them,' Alan Solem notes: 'Evidence exists for a minimum of 1461 recognisable endemic taxonomic units of Hawaiian land snails, comprising 931 species, 332 subspecies, and 198 unjudged "varieties".'*
(Bishop Museum Occasional Papers Vol. 30)

The three other species of shells found relate to two land snail families. One of these families is of small snails (0.75–2.5 mm) while the other, of which two species have been identified on Niʻihau, has snails of around 10–25 mm and the family is, perhaps surprisingly, tree-dwelling.⁴⁵

There is little doubt that all six species of snails once found on Niʻihau have long been extinct there. Elwood Zimmerman said that the fossils of land snails were good indicators of the pre-existing forest cover in a given region, and whether it was dry or wet. He thought that many species had become extinct since with the impact of humans on native life in the lowlands.⁴⁶

Lizards, snakes and frogs

Nothing is known of the reptiles and amphibians on Niʻihau. There are at least 17 species of introduced lizards on the islands as a whole, and a single native species clinging to existence in a remote corner of Hawaiʻi Island. Six species of introduced frogs and toads are known to exist in the state and a single established exotic Blind Snake. No work has been done to ascertain how many of these species (and maybe others) inhabit Niʻihau.

▲ César Ancey (1860–1906) was a French colonial administrator and avid collector of shells from around the world. He wrote 140 papers on molluscs and achieved an enduring reputation for his work in the field.
Wikimedia Commons; colorised

Note that because this book is about the island, the surrounding reefs with their myriad life forms have not been explored. Nevertheless, as the next chapter indicates, the marine environment has been essential to the Hawaiian culture that developed on Niʻihau.

The changes humans have wrought to the ecology of the island have been hinted at and more will be written of these in succeeding chapters. There is no question that the effect has been massive.

This chapter began with a European view of Niʻihau from high on the hills of western Kauaʻi. It is appropriate to end with a Hawaiian word-picture of the island from the same general area: 'Inu mai ana Niihau ma i ke kai-e.'⁴⁷ Literally, 'Niʻihau and the others are drinking the sea' — the 'others' are Nihoa and Kaʻula.

CHAPTER TWO

POLYNESIAN FOOTFALL

With exultant shouts and cries of relief from all aboard, the goddess Pele's canoe crunched on the sand of a golden Niihauan beach. Land had been sighted many days before, with a strange white-capped peak emerging from the mists, but a strong northeast wind had kept them offshore. There was much jubilation when they finally made landfall and the goddess was able to dig for fire. It was to no avail, however. The island had long since given up its ability to provide fire from the depths.

The Polynesian dawn — the science

As Chapter One indicated, Niʻihau arose from the ocean steaming and hissing some six million years ago and in time hosted a panoply of plant and animal life. There were extinctions as the more recent lava cones emerged and massive island erosion took place. Niʻihau, together with its Kauaʻi cousin, and their ever-changing biota, evolved over the next several millennia in the absence of all human life.

▼ The diagram indicates the migratory flows of people, deduced from the spread of the Austronesian group of languages. Similar diagrams have been developed for the 'Austronesian Diaspora' based upon genetics (both human and coexisting organisms), cultural patterns, and archeology, all of which lead to generally the same conclusions, as discussed in the text.
Based on Chambers & Edinur (see Endnote 1)

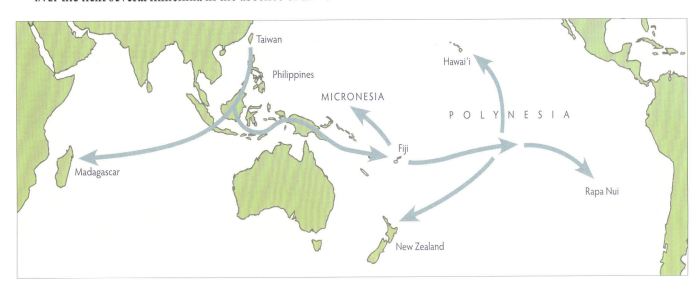

Only in the last few hundreds of thousands of years did humans evolve in Central Africa and then *Homo sapiens* began to slowly extend its domain, reaching Southeast Asia and the islands to the south (including Australia) 50,000 or more years ago.

According to the latest broadly based scientific evidence, the progenitors of the Polynesian peoples emerged from this region and began the Austronesian Diaspora 5000 years ago, with one branch eventually becoming the Polynesian people. DNA sampling shows that the maternal ancestors of the Polynesians can be traced back to Taiwan, while the fraternal side shows a limited inclusion of genes from the Papuan region. This indicates a southerly movement of some of the proto-Polynesians along the north coast of Papua about 3000 years ago. They then all moved eastwards to settle the widely separated islands of the Pacific, finally reaching the Samoan/Tongan area 2800–2900 years ago.[1]

There was then a long hiatus before further migrations took place, during which time it is theorized that the true Polynesian culture developed. It was 1700 years before settlement voyages again took place, when the Society Islands and the Marquesas were inhabited for the first time, between AD 1025–1121. The latest radiocarbon evidence shows that the Hawaiian islands had to wait until AD 1200–1290 before Polynesian

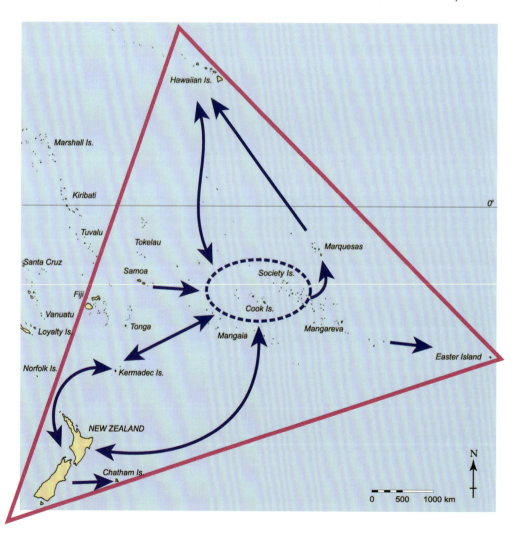

▶ Canoe voyaging patterns and human dispersal within the 'Polynesian Triangle', as determined by mitochondrial DNA from the Polynesian rat ('iore) and other studies.
Lisa Matisoo-Smith

colonization took place, and when it did it was rapid. This is a much later initial settlement date than previous work indicated, but has been accepted by the scientific community.²

The linguistic, archeological and cultural evidence for this pattern of settlement is reinforced by DNA studies, such as compelling results from a study of mitochondrial DNA (mtDNA) in the Polynesian rat, 'iore (*Rattus exulans*) by Lisa Matisoo-Smith in the late 1990s. mtDNA is inherited almost exclusively through the maternal side, and was used as the basis for tracing the female lineage of the Polynesians back to Taiwan. Lisa Matisoo-Smith's research investigated whether the pattern of Polynesian settlement in the Pacific could be elucidated by focusing on genetic variations in the 'iore, an animal that appears to have traveled with Polynesians on all their voyages. The rat was a culturally significant animal and valued source of food throughout most of Polynesia. 'Iore are poor swimmers and staying on flotsam for the length of time necessary to drift between islands seemed impossible. It is unlikely they could have become so widespread throughout Polynesia without human agency.

▲ The bark of the paper mulberry was used for kapa cloth-making throughout the Austronesian Diaspora and has been used as one marker for the movement of peoples throughout the region. It is a mid-sized deciduous tree with distinctive fruit, and cuttings were taken by the canoe voyagers on all their travels. Ni'ihau was, however, too arid for the paper mulberry to grow economically for kapa making, and this, combined with the difficulty of growing pandanus (hala) on the island, may have led to the development of the distinctive makaloa mats.
Wikimedia Commons

For Lisa's study 'iore were trapped throughout Polynesia, from Hawai'i to New Zealand to Rapa Nui (Easter Island). 132 rats were collected and mtDNA analysis performed on samples from them. The evolutionary history of the samples in regard to Hawai'i suggested:

(i) Colonization of the islands of east Polynesia [i.e. within the 'Polynesian Triangle'] and subsequent contact occurred from a broad central region that included at least the Southern Cook and Society Islands, but the Marquesas Islands probably should not be considered a part of this central region to the same degree.

(ii) A minimum of two introductions of the rat into Hawaii supports suggestions of postsettlement human contact with central east Polynesia.³

The conclusions substantiate the legends that there were return voyages to central Polynesia, but perhaps only one-way from the Marquesas.

Analysis of DNA data cannot construct the chronology, but the 'iore results do reinforce the settlement pattern derived from radiocarbon analysis.

Further evidence for this pattern of settlement comes from the dispersal of the paper mulberry or wauke (*Broussonetia papyrifera*) introduced and vegetatively propagated (i.e. using cuttings) from prehistoric times across the Pacific. The paper mulberry is used to make barkcloth or kapa. 604 samples from East Asia, Southeast Asia and Pacific islands were DNA tested for the presence of certain defining features, and on analysing the results the researchers concluded: 'our data concur with expectations of Taiwan as the Austronesian homeland, providing circumstantial support for the "out of Taiwan" hypothesis.'⁴

One of the most important plants in the Polynesian culture was the tī (*Cordyline fruticosa*), the tubers of which were used as food, and the leaves for medicinal, cultural and religious purposes. Anya Hinkle's research on the sterile form of the tī plant throughout Polynesia lends further credence to the 'long pause' before further migrations took place out of the Polynesian heartland of Sāmoa/Tonga. She found that while in the heartland tī was composed of both fertile and sterile forms, on all the later settlement islands within the Polynesian Triangle only the sterile form was growing, perhaps indicating that it was developed in the heartland because of its larger tuber size, and was carried on all later settlement voyages throughout Polynesia.[5]

Other studies attempting to track the movement of the Austronesian people from their Taiwanese homeland to their settlement of the Polynesian Triangle have used as human proxies the breadfruit tree, and Polynesian pigs and chickens. Although results from these studies have not been as definitive as the examples outlined here, none have been found contrary to the thrust of the general pattern described. Even the pre-historical spread of unwelcome stowaways such as the stomach ulcer-forming bacterium, *Helicobacter pylori*, the tapeworm and the Hepatitis B virus have been investigated.

It is a fast-moving field of research, but the evidence for the 'Out of Taiwan' hypothesis with the slow movement of the Austronesian people southward and one branch reaching the Polynesian heartland 2800–2900 years ago seems solid. The 'long pause' of 1700 years which then took place before the voyaging and colonization throughout the Polynesian Triangle is baffling.

▲ Tī (*Cordyline fruticosa*) was of great importance in Polynesian cultures and tubers were carried on all the major canoe voyages.
Wikimedia Commons

To put this in context, this is roughly the same length of time as that between the reign of the Roman emperor Constantine (AD 306–337) and the present. Time enough for massive cultural development, and given the right incentives (such as population pressure), for the evolution of canoe design, sailing technologies, the refinement of navigation skills and the development of the living requirements for long ocean voyages. When these voyages did take place it is contended they were, initially at least, most likely to have been purposeful voyages of exploration. Inevitably many canoes would have been lost, but with the Polynesians' ability to navigate successfully, as exemplified by the travels of the *Hokule'a* and other replica double canoes, many would have returned. These exploratory voyages would have been followed by organized settlement of the lands discovered. The evidence points towards rapid colonization — for the Hawaiian islands, a period of only 90 years — before the long-distance voyages apparently ceased. We can only speculate on the reasons for the collapse of ocean voyaging both to and from the homeland, but as far as Hawaiians are concerned all lines of descent stem from this relatively brief period of migration.

This then is the story of the Polynesian peopling of the Hawaii from the perspective of the scientific community. On the assumption that all the islands were settled at approximately the same time, this is as much as can be said about the timing of the initial human settlement of Ni'ihau. Some compelling evidence from a future Ni'ihau radiocarbon dated sample is still a possibility.

> *this is roughly the same length of time as that between the reign of the Roman emperor Constantine and the present*

The Hawaiian dawn — the creation myths

People and nature are inseparable in the world of the Hawaiians, and the presence of the gods may be seen everywhere. The origin of humankind was intimately linked to the origin of the islands. The life force was expressed in everything around them — landforms, plants, animals and human beings themselves. It was an animist belief system.

The social importance of genealogical descent was paramount — particularly if it could be shown to be from the gods, which then had reverberations back into the creation stories.

Hawaiian cultural traditions were remembered and told in chant or story form until the arrival of the missionaries in 1820. The written language was then developed and widely taught — one of the missionaries' lasting legacies. Before that time the spoken word allowed changes to be made at will, but despite severe sanctions arising from verbal alterations apparent during chanting, there are many versions of the creation myths.

Martha Beckwith, one of the earliest European collectors of Hawaiian myths, characterizes the Hawaiians' view of creation in this way:

> Hawaiian mythology recognises a prehuman period before mankind was born when spirits alone peopled first the sea and then the land, which was born of the gods and thrust up out of the sea. In Hawaii, myths about this prehuman period are rare. No story is told of the long incubation of thought which finally becomes active and generates the material universe and mankind; the creation story in Hawaii begins at the active stage and conforms as closely as possible to the biblical account. No story is told of the rending apart of earth and heaven, after the birth of the gods.[6]

▲ Martha Beckwith (1871–1959), folklorist and ethnographer, was brought up on Maui before graduating from Mt Holyoke in Massachusetts. She eventually became founding Professor of Folklore at Vassar, the first such school in the United States. Her work in Jamaica and among indigenous Americans won her recognition, and her collection of Hawaiian folklore was regarded as outstanding. Her translation of the Kumulipo is seen as her most important work.

Vassar Foundation/Wikimedia Commons; colorised

The best known of the creation myths is the Kumulipo ('Beginning in Deep Darkness'), originally transcribed by King Kalākaua in Hawaiian from the chant, and published in 1889. It consists of 2102 lines, the last half giving the genealogy of the royal family. Chanting it took several hours and was a prodigious feat of memory. Queen Liliʻuokalani (1838–1917)

▶ 'The Birth of the Hawaiian Islands', a depiction by Joseph Feher showing Haumea, the mother of Pele, successively giving birth to the islands. In another mythological version, the various wives of Wākea, including Papahānaumoku, give birth to them.

Sanna Deutsch

translated her brother's transcription into English while under house arrest in the 'Iolani Palace and this was published in Boston in 1897.[7] Several scholarly partial translations followed, but it wasn't until 1951 that a second full translation was published, a task that took Martha Beckwith many years.[8]

The Kumulipo has 16 wā or ages, in each of which a different life form is born. The first seven wā are set in the period of darkness (pō), in the realm of spirit rather than the physical universe, and during this time all plants and animals, both male and female are created). The first seven ages of the Kumulipo are:

- Wā 1: Sea urchins and seaweed are born. Ferns, upland taro and other plants connected by name to these are born to protect their sea cousins.
- Wā 2: 73 types of fish are born and certain plants with similar names are born as protectors. Slivers of the dawn light appear in the darkness.
- Wā 3: 52 types of flying creatures are born, both birds and insects. The darkness barely breaks.
- Wā 4: Turtles, lobsters, lizards and jellyfish are born, together with the maile vine and bamboo in the earliest dawn.
- Wā 5: Taro is born.
- Wā 6: Rats and fleas are born.
- Wā 7: Dogs and bats are born. The dawn light comes across the land.

The following nine wā are set in the period of daylight (ao), the divinities are born (wā eight to eleven), and finally the first humans are born in wā twelve when Wākea (Sky Father) and Papahānaumoku (Earth Mother) have a son, Haloa, who is regarded as the ancestor of all people. The Hawaiian islands are regarded as having been created by Wākea and Papa. Then follows the complex genealogy of the chiefly family through to the 18th century, interspersed with Māui's adventures and genealogy.

There are many variations of the Kumulipo, but all tend to follow the almost biblical pattern of the creation. Beckwith, who saw missionary influence in some of the other Hawaiian legends, came to the conclusion that the Kumulipo predated the missionaries and stood on its own free from their influence. This has been confirmed by later scholars. The two key translations by Queen Lili'uokalani and Martha Beckwith differ in some respects. The queen maintained that the chant stemmed from the early 1700s, a date not accepted by Martha Beckwith, who regarded it as a composite piece from various times and sources, and many times revised. Beckwith's view, as expressed by Katharine Luomala in the foreword to the 1971 edition of Beckwith's Kumulipo:

> Basically, the chant represents a series of name chants linked into a unity by over a thousand lines consisting of genealogical pairs of names. These name chants were composed by Masters of Song who incorporated into them legendary and timely allusions to enhance the glorious name of the family or individual they were celebrating. The Kumulipo enhanced the prestige and fortified the political bid for power of the family to which it belonged by using ancient cosmogonic beliefs, common elsewhere in Polynesia as in Hawaii, in such a way as to trace the family back to the 'beginning in deep darkness.'[9]

▲ King David Kalākaua and his sister and successor, Queen Lili'uokalani, the Hawaiian kingdom's last monarch. While under house arrest she translated the Kumulipo chant of her brother King Kalākaua, wrote her life story, composed songs and worked on traditional quilts.

Wikimedia Commons; Queen Lili'uokalani Trust

Queen Liliʻuokalani:	**Martha Beckwith:**
At the time that turned the heat of the earth,	At the time when the earth became hot
At the time when the heavens turned and changed,	At the time when the heavens turned about
At the time when the light of the sun was subdued	At the time when the sun was darkened
To cause light to break forth,	To cause the moon to shine
At the time of the night of Makalii (winter)	The time of the rise of the Pleaides
Then began the slime which established the earth,	The slime, this was the source of the earth
The source of deepest darkness,	The source of the darkness that made darkness
Of the depth of darkness, of the depth of darkness,	The source of the night that made night
Of the darkness of the sun, in the depth of night	The intense darkness, the deep darkness
It is night,	Darkness of the sun, darkness of the night
So was night born.	Nothing but night.

The queen's translation undoubtedly shows more overt evidence of the realpolitik of the day, but not in the first eleven lines of the two translations (above).

The ideas and emotions conjured up here in the two translations are very similar, but to native English speakers the Beckwith version seems more poetic, particularly when thought of as the spoken chant from which it is derived.

Five other alternate versions of the creation are given in Beckwith's *Hawaiian Mythology*, with all attributing the creation of the world to the triumvirate of gods Kāne, Kū and Lono in varied ways,[10] and different again to the Kumulipo version given in wā eight.

Encyclopedia Mythica, along with several other allied variations, has perhaps the most colorful version:

> In the midst of Chaos there was a great void. It was a time of deep darkness, before the memory of mankind.
>
> Into this void came Kāne, the god of creation. He picked up a giant calabash, threw it high into the air where it broke into two enormous pieces. The top piece was curved like a bowl, and became the Sky. The seeds scattered and became the stars. The remainder of the calabash fell downward, and became the Earth.[11]

Hawaiian voyaging traditions

Unexpectedly, the Kumulipo makes negligible mention of the migrations from the Polynesian homeland. While it is largely a genealogical chant, other legends are enfolded within it, but little reference is made to the great chiefs and navigators who led the exploratory and settlement voyages. In Hawaiian culture much greater importance was attached to descent from the gods, rather than descent from a particular canoe and its leader. Unlike some other Polynesian cultures, descent from a particular canoe was not important and canoe names have generally been forgotten.

▼ 'Early Hawaiians,' a painting by Arman Manookian (1904–31) — with his colorful depiction of the seafaring Hawaiians of old on a voyage of discovery. Of Armenian descent, Manookian came to the United States in 1920. He studied at art school in Rhode Island and New York before joining the Marine Corps in 1923 and serving in Hawaiʻi where he was honorably discharged in 1927. He stayed in the islands until his death in 1931. His body of work is small, but he is regarded as one of Hawaiʻi's most significant artists. Much of his work is held in the Honolulu Museum of Art.
Wikimedia Commons

> The traditional site on Niʻihau where Pele used her divine digging stick to look for fire is called Kaluakawila and is quite close to Kiʻekiʻe.

▼ Pele finally found her resting place at Kilauea, Hawaiʻi. 'Pele Over Kilauea,' a 1953 painting by Paul Rockwood (1895–1972).
US National Parks Service, Hawaiʻi Volcanoes National Park HAVO 799

The Kumulipo aside, there are many engaging voyaging stories, mostly involving return visits to the legendary Kahiki, which may well have been Tahiti, but which was also seen as the dwelling place of the gods. Although it is not universally agreed, Hawaiʻi-loa is regarded by many as the founding father of Polynesian settlement on the islands. Te Rangi Hiroa (Sir Peter Buck) in *Vikings of the Sunrise* gives one account:

> Legend states that Hawaiʻi was first settled by Hawaiʻi-loa, who dwelt on the eastern shores of the land of Kapakapa-ua-a-Kāne ... Hawaiʻi-loa and his navigator Makaliʻi (Pleiades) made many fishing trips to a sea on the east named the Sea-where-the-fish-do-run. On one of his long trips his navigator urged him to sail farther on. They sailed in the direction of the Pleiades and the planet Jupiter (Iao) as a morning star. They sailed into another sea named Many-colored-ocean-of-Kāne. They passed on to the Deep-colored-sea, where they came to an island. The discoverer named the island after himself, Hawaiʻi. Pleased with his discovery, Hawaiʻi-loa returned to his home, picked up his wife, family, and retinue, and sailed back to Hawaiʻi, where he remained to become the first settler.[12]

Other versions state that he named Oʻahu, Molokaʻi and Kauaʻi after his three sons and that the smaller islands of Niʻihau, Lānaʻi and Kahoʻolawe were fished from the ocean by them.

Not the least of the many other travelers' tales are those of Mōʻīkeha, Laʻa and Pāʻao, but the first voyage in which Niʻihau is a specific destination, and perhaps the best known of all the legendary journeys, is that of Pele, goddess of volcanoes. The account of how Pele came to Hawaiʻi comes in many forms. One is elegantly described by William Westervelt in his *Hawaiian Legends of Volcanoes: How Pele Came to Hawaii*:

> Pele's story is that of wander-lust. She was living in a happy home in the presence of her parents, and yet for a long time she was 'stirred by thoughts of far-away lands.' At last she asked her father to send her away. This meant that he must provide a sea-going canoe with mat sails, sufficiently large to carry a number of persons and food for many days.

Other versions describe a conflict within the family as the reason for her journey.

> "What will you do with your little egg sister?" asked her father.
> Pele caught the egg, wrapped it in her skirt to keep it warm near her body, and said that it should always be with her. Evidently in a very short time the egg was changed into a beautiful little girl who bore the name Hii-aka-i-ka-poli-o-Pele (Hiiaka-in-the-bosom-of-Pele), the youngest one of the Pele family.

All versions feature Pele carrying and nurturing the egg of her little sister Hiʻiaka. Pele's subsequent relationship with Hiʻiaka is the subject of several other stories.

After the care of the helpless one had been provided for, Pele was sent to her oldest brother, Ka-moho-alii, the king of dragons, or, as he was later known in Hawaiian mythology, 'the god of sharks.' He was a sea-god and would provide the great canoe for the journey. While he was getting all things ready, he asked Pele where she was going. She replied, 'I am going to Bola-bola; to Kuai-he-lani; to Kāne-huna-moku; then to Moku-mana-mana; then to see a queen, Kaoahi her name and Niihau her island.' Apparently her journey would be first to Bola-bola in the Society Islands, then among the mysterious ancestral islands, and then to the northwest until she found Niihau, the most northerly of the Hawaiian group.

Although Pele's homeland is not mentioned in Westervelt's account, Niʻihau is clearly her final target.

> The god of sharks prepared his large canoe and put it in the care of some of their relatives, Kāne-pu-a-hio-hio (Kāne-the-whirlwind), Ke-au-miki (The-strong-current), and Ke-au-ka (Moving-seas).
>
> Pele was carried from land to land by these wise boatmen until at last she landed on the island Niihau. Then she sent back the boat to her brother, the shark-god. It is said that after a time he brought all the brothers and sisters to Hawaiʻi.
>
> Pele was welcomed and entertained. Soon she went over to Kauai, the large, beautiful garden island of the Hawaiian group. There is a story of her appearance as a dream maiden before the king of Kauai, whose name was Lohiau, whom she married, but with whom she could not stay until she had found a place where she could build a permanent home for herself and all who belonged to her.
>
> She had a magic digging tool, Pa-oa. When she struck this down into the earth it made a fire-pit. It was with this Pa-oa that she was to build a home for herself and Lohiau. She dug along the lowlands of Kauai, but water drowned the fires she kindled, so she went from island to island but could only dig along the beach near the sea. All her fire-pits were so near the water that they burst out in great explosions of steam and sand, and quickly died, until at last she found Kilauea on the large island of Hawaii. There she built a mighty enduring palace of fire, but her dream marriage was at an end. The little sister Hiiaka, after many adventures, married Lohiau and lived on Kauai.¹³

The many accounts of Pele's voyage were analyzed by Harry Arlo Nimmo and his work was published in 1987 in *Pacific Studies*. He concludes:

▲ William Westervelt (1849–1939) was born in Ohio and came to Hawai'i in 1899. A theologian, he published several books popularizing Hawaiian legends and history. He became an authority on island folklore and his writings are considered some of the best on the subject in the English language.
Wikimedia Commons, colorised

▲ An impression by Dietrich Varez (1939–2018) of the great mythological voyaging canoe *Honuaiakea* (great spread-out world) in which Pele and Hiʻiaka set off from their homeland on their journey across the vast Pacific to make landfall at Niʻihau, finally settling in the crater of Halemaʻumaʻu on the island of Hawaiʻi.
Dietrich Varez Estate / Volcano Art Center

> An analysis of the forty-eight versions of Pele's journey to Hawaiʻi reveals a basic structure of seven motifs. All motifs are not found in each version, but an examination of all versions reveals a recurring structure.
>
> Motif 1: Pele is born of divine parents in a mythical homeland. The myths do not always agree as to which gods are Pele's parents, but virtually all are in agreement that she has divine parentage.
>
> Motif 2: Upon reaching adulthood, a conflict develops between Pele and someone else, often her oldest sister Nā-maka-o-Kahaʻi.

▲ 'The Birth of Hiʻiaka', Pele's little sister, a woodcut by Dietrich Varez. His inspiration came from the Hawaiʻi of old when spirits walked the earth and inhabited every tree and stone. His approach to life and business was unconventional, living simply and iconoclastically on his land outside Volcano Village on Hawaiʻi Island.

Dietrich Varez Estate / Volcano Art Center

Motif 3: The conflict ultimately results in Pele leaving her birthplace, usually with an entourage of brothers, sisters, and other relatives.

Motif 4: After leaving her birthplace, Pele and her entourage voyage to Hawaiʻi, sometimes stopping at mythical lands en route.

Motif 5: Pele reaches the Hawaiian islands and searches for a suitable home, traveling in a northwest to southeast direction, from Niʻihau to Hawaiʻi.

Motif 6: As she digs in the islands seeking a home, Pele encounters the sea and must look elsewhere. Frequently, it is her encounters with Nā-maka-o-Kahaʻi (sometimes described as a sea goddess) that necessitate her seeking another home.

Motif 7: Eventually, after trying many places throughout the Hawaiian archipelago, Pele settles into Kī-lau-ea volcano on the island of Hawaiʻi which becomes her permanent home.[14]

The traditional site on Niʻihau where Pele used her divine digging stick to look for fire is called Kaluakawila and is quite close to Kiʻekiʻe.[15] The legendary pit she created is elongated and extends for some distance. Presumably it is close to where she grounded her canoe — named as *Honua-i-a-kea* in some versions of the legend, and given her by her shark-god brother Ka-moho-aliʻi.

As the myth makes clear, she found an island already inhabited, so her voyage was not a founding one.

It is most likely that Niʻihau was first peopled by emigrants from Kauaʻi although, as the Pele legend shows, long-distance voyagers from the south may well have arrived there directly and settled. They would have been aided by the prevailing northeasterly trade winds, which may have sometimes made landings on the more easterly islands impossible.

If the latest science is correct, the islands — including Niʻihau —were settled in the 12th century by Polynesians. They brought the plants and animals necessary for their survival with them, and their culture developed over millennia. From initial settlement to the arrival of the first Europeans in the late 18th century is a mere 600 years, but over this time a distinctive Niihauan culture developed, despite what must have always been a symbiotic relationship with Kauaʻi. An element in this cultural development is the distinctive Niihauan language, which is discussed in Appendix B.

Hanohano Niihau i kau ike, aka Naulu ae hooipo nei.
Majestic is the Niʻihau I see, caressed and loved by the Naulu wind.

— Old Niihauan saying [16]

Niʻihau rulers — between myth and history

While there is no surviving genealogical record of the ruling chiefs (aliʻi ʻai moku) of Niʻihau, nor of the early relationships between the people of Niʻihau and Kauaʻi, there is a genealogical record of the ruling chiefs of Kauaʻi going back, in some versions, to the four key Hawaiian gods — Kāne, Kū, Lono and Kanaloa — or to Wākea and Papa.

Mōʻīkeha, one of the first voyagers from Kahiki in the 12th century, is regarded as the first aliʻi ʻai moku of Kauaʻi, fourteen generations removed from Wākea and Papa.[17] The names of some of the early Niʻihau ruling aliʻi are remembered — Puwalu, Queen Manoʻopupaipai, Makaliʻi, Kaneoneo, Kaʻeo, Queen Kaoahi, Halāliʻi, Halulu, Kupoloula, Kahelelani — but not exactly when they reigned.[18]

Kahelelani, born in the late 17th century, is the first roughly dateable aliʻi of Niʻihau and it seems that at about this time Niʻihau formally became part of the kingdom of Kauaʻi. Peleʻioholani, the 21st Kauaian aliʻi ʻai moku, reigned from 1730 to 1770 and amassed an empire stretching from Niʻihau in the west to Oʻahu and Molokaʻi in the east. During this period, for governance purposes, Kauaʻi was divided into six districts, one of which was Niʻihau. Given the disparity in size and population, it is likely that Niʻihau had before this time come under the control of the Kauaian ruler.

Niʻihau itself was not always a united island, and the great aliʻi Kaʻeo, the much-loved ruler of the northern half of the island, is credited with bringing about unification. His rival and the ruler of the southern portion, the warlike Kawaihoa, was continually causing strife and there was much bad feeling between the two. To demarcate their landholdings a stone wall was built across the southern quarter of the island with Kaʻeo's identifying stones being black, and Kawaihoa's white. The wall was not effective, however, in preventing further arguments. Finally, with the help of his two brothers from Maui, Kawaihoa was defeated in battle and Kaʻeo was successful in unifying the island. Kawaihoa was banished to the southern tip, with the volcanic cone there now bearing his name. Kaʻeo himself is remembered by Mount Kaʻeo, the second highest hill on the island.[19]

A distinctive Niihauan culture develops — subsistence and crafts

Ever since human settlement, lack of water has been the critical factor in the development of the Niihauan economic system. Many of the plants they brought with them on their ocean voyages would not grow on Niʻihau, or only marginally so, e.g. paper mulberry, taro, breadfruit and pandanus. They had to adapt, and adapt they did. They had always lived close to nature, and were master agriculturalists. On Niʻihau they grew a limited amount of taro (kalo) in selected locations close to springs with water fed to the plants using bamboo conduits. The supply of poi from home-grown taro was never enough, and trade with Kauaʻi must have been established almost immediately.

The ʻuala or sweet potato was grown as a staple, but needed careful nurturing. Slips were planted out at the start of the rainy season, but in the months prior the mounds of earth to receive them were carefully prepared. The largest potatoes were always picked first to allow the smaller ones to mature, and the mounds were loosened periodically during the growing season. It is said that in times of old there could be up to 100 acres of ʻuala growing in the Kamalino area.[20]

Something of a mystery surrounds the yam or uhi. At the time of first European contact they were grown in large quantities on Niʻihau and were a favorite of the early European ships' captains as a substitute for bread, because of their keeping qualities — particularly when compared to taro or sweet potato. Large quantities were traded. Growing them cannot have been easy as they favor moist, damp situations, which makes the quantities traded even more surprising.

▲ Sweet potatoes or ʻuala (*Ipomoea batatas*) have long been cultivated on Niʻihau as a staple item of diet.
A Chronicle and Flora of Niihau, National Tropical Botanical Garden

▲ The tuber of a yam or uhi (*Dioscorea alata*). Yams were grown extensively on the island at the time of first European contact and were much prized by the early ships' captains as they lasted well at sea. The trade dwindled due to lack of supply and within a generation had practically disappeared. There are many species of yam, but the only one that reached Polynesia was *Dioscorea alata*. All are vines. The tubers can be purple or white and can grow to an enormous size, with the world record standing at 180 pounds. The Niihauan yams were apparently unique, of a large size, hairy and white-fleshed.
eattheweeds.com

It was not many years, though, before supplies of yams at Niʻihau by visiting ships became unobtainable. Why was this? There may have been a drought year or two, but this wouldn't have discouraged the Niihauans from trying again, given their adaptability and resourcefulness. Unlike sweet potatoes, which produce after a few months it takes a full year to produce a crop. This may have been part of the reason, but in any event the trade completely dried up and yams have not been grown on the island for many years.

The yams from Niʻihau appear to have been quite distinctive — large and particularly hairy. In *Niihau: The Traditions of an Hawaiian Island*, the authors speak of some of them being so heavy that a horse could only carry two at a time.[21] They were apparently regarded as a famine food by the Niihauans, and were only eaten hot, directly out of an imu (underground oven). Cold leftovers were regarded as inedible and fed to pigs.

Bananas and sugar cane were also grown, and at the time of European arrival a few breadfruit trees were in evidence, deftly planted in deep holes in the coral to maximize water availability for the trees.

Fish was the main source of protein, although pigs, dogs, chicken and rats, all of which had come with them on their voyaging, were also eaten. Fish drying racks were a feature of island life. Seaweed was also a staple. For self-sufficiency the sea was essential and the harvest was strictly controlled to maintain sustainability. But fish were more than just food:

> Certain sea creatures, most commonly sharks, sometimes became ʻaumakua (personal gods) and were fed with regularity and recognized as individuals. Legends and chants contain some characters that change at will to sea creatures, and there are numerous incidents in Hawaiian oral literature that reflect intimate knowledge of fish, their characteristics, habits and domain.[22]

Fish were also central in the exchange of items and services between households within the ʻohana, particularly for those on Niʻihau who lacked some basic necessities. What was largely missing from their diet was the staple item, poi, made from taro. Supplies were available from Kauaʻi, but items of trade to barter were required. While dried fish was one component, it may have been this economic necessity which drove the Niihauans to develop their distinctive crafts — decorated gourds, makaloa mats and shell lei.

Gourds or ipu were planted among the sweet potatoes and were used as dippers, pots and utensils such as dishes, bowls and mugs. They were also used to store and carry water and other goods, and even as burial receptacles for bones. Niʻihau was renowned for the quality of its gourds and for their unique ornamentation. Abraham Fornander, researching at the end of the 19th century wrote: 'The best calabashes and water-gourds, with spotted marks, are found on Niihau. That is the untiring land in work of ornamentation.' But as a footnote he added: 'The ornamented gourds of olden times are so seldom seen now that it may be said to be a lost art. The markings having the appearance of tatuing [sic], were done while the gourd was fresh and green, before the removal of its outer skin, at times even while it was still on the vine.'[23]

▲ Two examples of the unique Niihauan decorated gourds (ipu pāwehe). The typically geometric pattern (pāwehe) was incised in the outer skin of the gourd. After soaking in a bark infusion the gourd (ipu) was immersed in black mud in a swamp, with the result that the incised areas were dyed a darker brown. The upper ipu pāwehe is from the Kauaʻi Museum and the lower one is part of the Robinson family collection.
Steven Gentry

▶ A watercolor of a complete makaloa sedge plant (*Cyperus laevigatus*) in the Kauaʻi Museum. See also page 22 for the plant growing in its normal habitat.
Kauaʻi Museum

Polynesian footfall

◀ A makaloa mat owned by Princess Likelike hung up for display. The contrasting colors in the original design are obvious.
Hawaiian Historical Society, HH Arning Collection

▲ Abraham Fornander (1812–87), author of *An Account of the Polynesian Race: Its Origins and Migrations and the Ancient History of the Hawaiian People to the Times of Kamehameha I*, was a man of many talents. Born a clergyman's son and university-educated in Sweden, he left the country in disgrace after a torrid affair with his mother's sister. He roamed the world as a whaler for over a decade before deserting his ship in Honolulu in 1844 and becoming a Hawaiian citizen. He was a journalist for the next 15 years, owning and writing for several local newspapers. In 1865 King Kamehameha V appointed him to his privy council and he became the inspector-general of schools for the kingdom. This role let him develop his great interest in the Hawaiian people, leading to his monumental work referred to above. He was also a judge for 12 years.
Wikipedia

The decorated gourd was developed over many centuries and would have been an article of trade between the islands. Evidently the art died out with the advent of the Europeans, when metal containers and utensils became available. Fortunately there are several fine examples of this craftsmanship in the Bishop and Kauaʻi Museums.

The makaloa mats (moena makaloa) of Niʻihau were famous throughout the islands in prehistoric times. While some makaloa mats were made on other islands, it was the mats from Niʻihau that were particularly prized for their fineness and softness. The normal material used for plaiting mats was the prepared leaves of the pandanus tree or hala, but this did not grow well on Niʻihau and this fact probably initiated a search for alternatives. Several sedges grew around the margins of the intermittent lakes on the island, and *Cyperus laevigatus* — makaloa — was found to be ideal as a substitute — if considerably more labor-intensive to plait because of its narrow width in comparison to hala. Strands in the plaited mat could be from 10 to 25 to the inch, compared to hala with generally four at most — hence the makaloa mats' softness. Although the literature is inconclusive it appears the makaloa, because of its growing pattern, could only be harvested for plaiting for two or three months of the year. Useful strands could be up to five feet long. The tubular stems were flattened as the sedge was dried, giving a shiny surface on both sides. Plaiting was generally done in the common crosscheck manner.

A detailed description of the making of the mats is given in *Arts and Crafts of Hawaii* by Te Rangi Hiroa (Sir Peter Buck), published by the Bishop Museum from his notes as a posthumous tribute to him in 1957.

The art of decorating the mats (moena pāwehe) developed using different colored sedges — kohekohe (*Eleocharis calva*) which has a bright red basal sheath, and neki (*Scirpus spp*) which was green. It was thought originally that the colored strands were only obtained from the sheath at the base of the *Cyperus* sedge stems, but from the remaining examples of mats Harold St John considers that other species of sedge were

▲ This fine example of a moena pāwehe (patterned makaloa mat) measuring 9 × 6 feet was given to the Robinson family in the late 19th century by an unknown Niihauan. Family tradition has it that it was made as a sampler for one of the nine customary pāwehe designs.
Robinson family

▼ A 16-inch (40 cm) multi-strand shell lei (necklace) collected by Captain Cook during his voyage to the Hawaiian islands in 1778–79. The lei is almost certainly from Ni'ihau and consists mainly of reddish-brown kahelelani shells (*Leptothyra verruca*) interspersed with white ones of different species.
British Museum

used for this purpose.[24] Tava and Keale have confirmed this.[25]

Beatrice Krauss, in her book *Plants in Hawaiian Culture,* describes the technique used and the patterns formed:

Makaloa mats were not only famous for their fine plait but because of their beautiful decoration. This consisted of the introduction of colored geometrical motifs on the upper surface by overlaying colored wefts [crosswise strands] on the foundation wefts and plaiting them as double wefts for the area covered by the design. The colored wefts were laid on both the left and right crossing wefts to obtain a solid motif in one color; they were cut off at the far edge of the last crossing weft. The colored motifs are visible only on the upper surface of the mat since the colored wefts were applied on the upper surface of the foundation wefts.

The generic term for the colored motifs in makaloa mats was *pāwehe*, thus the name moena pāwehe as an alternate name for these mats. The geometrical designs consisted of lines, usually zigzag (*ke'eke'e* pattern); triangles, such as one with opposing triangles with their apexes touching to give the appearance of hourglasses (*papa'ula* pattern); a horizontal row of triangles each with its base vertical and its apex touching the base of the next triangle in the row (*puahala* pattern); and two vertical rows of triangles with the bases below and the apices touching the bases above (*nene* pattern). Another motif was produced with lozenges, such as red bands that were internally enhanced with a continuous row of white lozenges (*humuniki* pattern); and continuous rows of lozenges with all angles touching (*papakonane* pattern).[26]

The mats, particularly the decorated ones, were prized possessions and commanded high prices in trade or in payment of tributes to the ali'i. As such they were never used as floor coverings, but rather as blankets, wall coverings, wall dividers and, on Ni'ihau especially, as an item of clothing. The art was flourishing at the time of European exploration, and the earliest remaining mats date from Cook's voyage. As with gourd decoration, the art has died out and one of the last mats to be plaited is the 'protest mat' described in Chapter Eight.[27]

The one and only distinctive Niihauan craft that has survived from pre-European days is shell lei making. More will be said on this in later chapters, but while those on the other islands were decorating themselves with lei of flowers, the Hawaiians on Ni'ihau were making decorative use of the tiny shells found on their beaches at certain times of the year. While many of the shells used were found on other islands, they were prolific on Ni'ihau and it was there that the art of shell lei threading developed and reached its zenith.

The earliest known use of the tiny shells for decorative purposes is the fragment of a child's armband found during a Bishop Museum archeological dig at Nu'alolo Kai on Kaua'i. This was found in a layer which has been dated to between 1700 and 1850. The unpublished paper on the armlet find reads:

A small armlet, probably for a child, was found 20 inches (50.8 cm.) below the surface (level III) of site K5 (K5/117-4; plate 1-21) Although the ends are damaged and incomplete, its overall length must have been about 160 mm., exclusive of ties. It consists of four parallel strands of *Columbella varians* Sowerby (*pupu Niʻihau*) shells, each about 8 mm. long. …

Each shell is perforated by punching through the slightly flared lip, then strung on a cord and secured by half-hitches with lateral cords on each side. The resulting strands of shells are joined by whipping, the cord passing back and forth between the adjacent lateral cords of the strands of shells … The cord is two-ply S twist throughout and is probably of *olona* (*Touchardia latifolia*) fiber.[28]

The Bishop Museum's 1978 exhibition *Artificial Curiosities*, which brought together artifacts and ornaments collected on Cook's three voyages did not feature any shell lei as the term is understood today, but did include one shorter multi-strand shell necklace from Niʻihau. Several feather necklaces of about the same length were also in the exhibition.[29]

The use of the tiny shells in making ornaments for personal adornment was well developed by the time of European contact and Niihauans continue the tradition today, as we shall see in later chapters.

Religion and ritual

Throughout the 500 years from Polynesian settlement to the time of European contact, and even to this day, Niʻihau has been associated politically, economically and spiritually with its much larger neighbor, Kauaʻi. The island did not have the resources to compete with 'the Garden Island', and above all else was the problem of water supply. Some authorities say that in times of severe drought the whole population of Niʻihau had to move to Kauaʻi, settling on the Na Pali coast, Mana and points further south.[30] Certainly the ebb and flow of the population has been well documented in historic times.

Aside from water, the absence of forest trees and olonā vines (*Touchardia latifolia*)* meant that canoes, fishing nets and lines and even suitable poles for building had to be obtained in exchange for trade items. These goods may have included dried fish as well as craft items. The Niihauan economy must have been extremely heavily dependent on trade with Kauaʻi — probably largely between families living on both islands. Nevertheless it worked.

The founding settlers on Niʻihau, whether from faraway Kahiki or nearby Kauaʻi, brought with them not only their useful plants and animals, but also their existing culture — their worship of nature, their tribal customs, their skills and their language, all of which had evolved over millennia.

Society was stratified and became more rigid over time. At the apex were the ruling chiefs or aliʻi and their closely associated priests or kahuna. The majority of people were commoners or makaʻāinana (those who lived on the land). Beneath them again were the slaves (kauwa).

This caste system was maintained by a matrix of rules known as kapu (taboos), mostly permanent, but some of a periodic or seasonal nature. The penalties for

▲ Te Rangi Hiroa (Sir Peter Buck). Born in New Zealand in 1877 of a Māori mother and an Anglo-Irish father, he attended Te Aute College, alma mater to many Māori leaders. He graduated from Otago University as a doctor in 1904 and was appointed medical officer to Māori in 1905 before being elected to parliament. During World War I he served as a medical officer at Gallipoli and in France where his heroism was recognized with a Distinguished Service Order. After the war he took up several appointments within the New Zealand Health Department before gaining a five-year research fellowship at the Bishop Museum in 1927. He became director in 1936, a position he held until his death in 1951. He was knighted in 1946.
ATL 1/1-019099-F

* *The endemic olonā vine was one of the few crops the Hawaiians planted and grew for anything other than food. The cordage derived from its fibers was highly valued and often used as an item of trade. It was an exceedingly strong natural fiber, as evinced by its use by European mariners.*

breaking a kapu, intentionally or not, were severe, and often fatal. The kapu system was interwoven with nature worship and the sacredness of their many gods to explain the natural world all around them. It placed some severe restrictions on daily life, and with its cruel punishments ensured subordination of the commoners. Only the aliʻi could institute or lift kapu, and over time they used the system to consolidate ever more power into their hands.

In a societal sense it seems Niʻihau was always regarded by the Kauaʻi rulers as a vassal state, so politically as well as economically, the island's fortunes were tied to those of Kauaʻi.

For some considerable time after Polynesian settlement Kauaʻi prospered, as more settlers arrived and more land was developed and irrigated for growing taro. The island, with Niʻihau was ruled from Waimea, where the first Polynesians had landed many generations prior. Then, according to Fornander and Wichman,[31] in the time of King Kaikipaʻanānea some voyagers from the Marquesas arrived, led by their chief Punanuikaiaʻāina. Kaikipaʻanānea allowed them to settle on the Wailua river, where plenty of land was available. The lands were subsequently named Puna. The Marquesan arrivals also prospered, to the extent that they rivalled the original Waimea kingdom, known as Kona.

The stage was set for civil war, which reputedly raged for over a century. Niihauan warriors would undoubtedly have become involved to supplement the forces of successive Kona kings. It was a difficult time for the islands, but many are the heroic tales told of this era. The tides of war ebbed and flowed between the two kingdoms with Puna under King Kūkona finally being victorious, and the center of power shifting from Waimea to Wailua. The date for the unification of Kauaʻi is generally thought to be late-17th century. The overlord was now a little more distant from Niʻihau.

Kūkona (the aliʻi nui) now concentrated on consolidating his power by setting up a more formal political arrangement based on moku (land districts). Kauaʻi was divided into five moku (Kona, Puna, Koʻolau, Haleleʻa, Nā Pali), while Niʻihau was a sixth, each governed by an aliʻi ʻai moku (one who leads the land). Within the districts were a number of ahupuaʻa led by a konohiki appointed by the aliʻi ʻai moku.

The aliʻi nui (king or paramount chief), as the descendant and personal representative of the gods, owned all the land and all the life thereon. He had the responsibility,

▲ Bruce Wichman (1928–2014), teacher and author. From an early age he became fascinated with the old Kauaian legends and determined to preserve them. His collecting and writings complemented his teaching activities, and in his later years he was regarded as one of Kauaʻi's greatest historians. He wrote seven books of legends and the scholarly *Ruling Chiefs of Kauaʻi*, as well as many historical articles.
Kauaʻi Historical Society

▶ A view of Kaunuapua puʻuhonua from the early 1900s.
Robinson family

Heiau — sacred sites on Niʻihau

In *Niihau: The Traditions of an Hawaiian Island,* Tava and Keale identified eight heiau on Niʻihau. Clockwise from Pueo Point, they describe the heiau thus:

Pueo	'where several other temples are located' (see also caption on pueo — owls — on page 65).
Pahau	'in addition to the temple, there are remnants of an old village found at this site'.
Puhihula	'reported in 1912 by John Stokes to be at Puli Ula although the remains cannot be seen.' (Actually called Puhiola, at Kamalino in Stokes' field notes. Noted, but not seen by Stokes.)
Kauwaha	'hidden by nature and buried under the sands at Kaununui. The temple exposes itself only in certain circumstances. This unveiling takes place when there is a tidal wave or extremely rough waters. Kauwaha is a very large *heiau*. Its upright walls are made of black rock … There is a special name for Kaununui which also includes the name of the *heiau*: "*Kaununui heiau kapu noho ana i ka poli o Kauwaha*" meaning "the sacred temple Kauwaha is cradled in the bosom of Kaununui".' (Not mentioned by Stokes in his field notes.)
Kaunuapua	'is a *puuhonua* or place of refuge located next to Puu Koae at Kihawahine. It is an oblong enclosure built of limestone slabs with a low bench encircling the exterior walls. The bench on the outside and the entrance facing inland (east) are unusual features. In many places, the bases of the walls are faced with large slabs placed on edge. There were interior enclosures at each end for altars.' Stokes described and photographed Kaunuapua, which he called Kihawahine. A person who had broken a kapu would be safe if he could elude his accusers in getting there. Provided he remained there for several days and performed certain rituals prescribed by the kahuna, his crime was regarded as having been propitiated and he could leave a free man. It was also a place of safety in times of war.
Kahalekuamano	'at Nanina, which is about 1000 feet east of Kalanihale Point. The temple is a low embankment, thirty-five feet long and five feet wide.' (Seen by Stokes, who called it Halekuamano.)
Kaunuokaha	(or Kaunuohiki) 'south of Lehua landing on shore about one mile northeast of Kaunuapua. This *heiau* is a small, low platform.' (Stokes thought it was probably a koʻa or fishing shrine.)
Kaunuopou	Another koʻa or fishing shrine Stokes saw and photographed.

Based on *Niihau: The Traditions of an Hawaiian Island,* by Rerioterai Tava & Moses K Keale Snr, 1984. Tava and Keale do not use ʻokina (ʻ) and kahakō (macrons).

with advice from his kahuna nui (chief priest), of ensuring the proper prayers and propitiations were made to the gods. In the worldly sphere he was supported by his kālaimoku (prime minister), who among many other duties, made sure the commoners paid their annual tribute to the ali'i nui in the form of crops, food items, fine mats, etc.

The only visible evidence remaining of the old religion and its rituals are the stone heiau (temples) and pōhaku (sacred stones) scattered over all the islands. The single archeologist to visit Ni'ihau has been John Stokes of the Bishop Museum, who in 1912 identified four heiau on the island while gathering information for William Brigham's book *Ancient Hawaiian Worship* (which he never completed). Brigham comments on Stokes' visit:

> Mr. Stokes had expected to gather much heiau lore from the natives of the island on account of its seclusion, but on landing it was found that the original inhabitants had gradually become scattered over the other islands of the group since the establishment, between 1860 and 1870, of the present ranch, and that the natives now living there know nothing of the history of the island.[32]

▲ Eric Knudsen (1872–1957) was the son of Ann (née Sinclair) and Valdemar Knudsen, pioneer rancher and sugar plantation owner on Kaua'i. He graduated from Harvard Law School in 1898 and returned to the islands to manage the family ranch on Kaua'i. He served as a representative and later as a senator in the Hawai'i legislature, but ranching and the great outdoors of Kaua'i were his passion. After retiring from politics in 1932 he began a writing and broadcasting career which, during World War II, led him to entertain troops, becoming known as 'The Teller of Hawaiian Tales.' He published these stories under this title and wrote other similar books as well as a biography of his father, *Kanuka of Kauai*.
Wikimedia Commons

Stokes, in his field notes comments:

> A brief visit was paid to Niihau in January 1912, where I was the guest of the owner of the island, Mr. Aubrey Robinson. I am also indebted to this gentleman for the information obtained, as the last of the original native inhabitants migrated from the island about the year 1865. The natives living in Niihau at present were born in other islands of the group.[33]

It is not surprising that no information was available as the kapu and the old religion had been done away with in 1819, almost a century before Stokes' visit, so any memories of the old religion would have been secondhand at best.

It is clear that Stokes only visited the north end of the island. For the heiau he did see, the descriptions above from Tava and Keale are summaries drawn from his field notes.

On this same 1912 visit to Ni'ihau John Stokes also investigated the possible existence of petroglyphs at Ki'i, and William Brigham, director of the Bishop Museum, reported bad news:

> Of the field work Mr. Stokes reports: 'In January I went to Niihau, through the kindness of Mr. Aubrey Robinson, with the intention of investigating the report of the existence of petroglyphs at the boat landing at Kii, and collecting plants and shells for the other departments. One heiau was measured and photographed and the sites of two other heiau (?) noted. The results in the case of the petroglyphs were negative.'[34]

Apart from some archeological work done by the navy for a possible runway at the south end of the island (see Chapter Eleven) no further archeological work has been done on Ni'ihau since Stokes' visit more than 100 years ago. With all the advances in techniques and understanding of the past that have been achieved since then, further work would be timely and would enhance our knowledge of the island's history. (Stokes' plant collection is discussed in Appendix E.)

Legends and sayings

Polynesians have always been skilled at storytelling, an artform that communicates a shared heritage and spirituality. Each island has its own store of legends and stories, and Niʻihau is no exception. One that has been told in many different ways is entitled *The Three Old Ogres of Niihau* in Eric Knudsen's book *Teller of Hawaiian Tales*. In other publications, ogres have been replaced by man-eating spirits, evil spirits or even akua (gods). Eric Knudsen's version goes like this:

The three old ogres of Niʻihau

Once upon a time, long, long ago, three old ogres lived on Niihau near the landing called Kii. They were cannibals, and everyone who landed on Niihau was promptly killed and eaten.

One day a young chief named Ola decided he would rid the island of these ogres. He carved four little men [kiʻi] out of lehua wood and put mother-of-pearl eyes in each one.

Loading them into his canoe, and taking some fish and poi and his magic war club, he paddled boldly across the stormy channel towards Kii. One of the old ogres was on the lookout, and when he spied something moving on the ocean, he called out, 'I see a boat!'

'It's only a log!' came back the answer.

He watched for a long time, and again cried, 'I see a boat and there are men paddling in it. They are headed straight for Kii.'

When the ogres were certain it was really a canoe and was coming in to land, they hid behind the sand dunes and watched. Young Ola meantime drove his canoe safely through the breakers and ran it up on the sand.

On the beach was an old boathouse. He carried one of the passengers up and set him down against the wall facing the door. 'Two go up, and one goes back,' counted the old ogres. Then as Ola carried his three companions up beside the first one, the ogres could see there were five in the party. After Ola had set his four little men in a row, he hid behind the door and soon fell fast asleep.

The old ogres waited for some time and then one crawled up to the door and peeped in. When he returned to his companions he said, 'They are still awake. I can see the whites of their eyes.'

They waited a long time, then one crept up to the door again. There stood the four little men as before.

After Ola had slept for two or three hours, he awoke, ate some fish and poi, and soon felt his strength and vigor return. He then laid his four little men on their sides with their backs to the door, and again hid behind the door with his magic war club in his hand.

By and by one old ogre crept up and, seeing the men asleep, signaled the other two; whereupon all three crawled in.

The first ogre stooped over the nearest sleeper and bit him behind the ear to kill him; but instead he broke his long tooth!

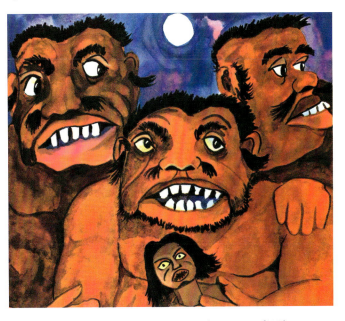

▲ The three ogres of Niʻihau, on the cover of the 1974 children's book *Spooky Stuffs: Hawaiian Ghost Stories* written by Eric Knudsen and illustrated by Guy Buffet.

Island Heritage

◂ The rock-throwing giants of Niʻihau and Kauaʻi, seen here hurling immense rocks at one another across the broad Kaulakahi Channel in the heat of the summer sun. An original pen and ink drawing by talented Niihauan, Kuramatsu Kuuwaimalamalamaokalani Kahokuloa. ('Matsu'), a 2021 graduate of Ke Kula Niihau O Kekaha. Matsu is the great-great-grandson of Ishimatsu Shintani, the Niʻihau beekeeper at the time of the 'Battle of Niʻihau' in the week following the Pearl Harbor attack on 7 December 1941 (see Appendix C and Chapter Ten).

Kuramatsu Kahokuloa

'Auwe!' he cried. 'Paakiki na kanaka o Kauai.' (The men of Kauai are tough.)

'Paakiki we are, indeed!' cried the young chief, as he stepped out from behind the door. He swung his magic war club; and before the ogres knew what was happening, they had been killed!

Ola dragged their bodies to the beach and cast them into the ocean for the sharks and eels to devour. Then he loaded his canoe and paddled back to Kauai.

Great was the rejoicing among the people of Kauai. Niihau was free at last, and many families moved over and settled there.[35]

The landing place was reputedly named Kiʻi after the four little wooden statues.

Another favorite legend, which may have grown out of the friendly rivalry and interdependence between Niʻihau and Kauaʻi, is retold here:

The rock-throwing giants

In the middle of the northern plains of Niʻihau rises a small, seemingly out-of-place, conical hill called Pakehoʻolua. This is the story of how it got here …

Eons ago both Niʻihau and Kauaʻi were inhabited by a race of powerful giants. The chiefs on both islands were enormous and prided themselves on their physical prowess. They continually raised their voices and thundered taunts at one another across the Kaulakahi Channel. The land shook as their tempers rose and their jeers became more scornful.

One day the teasing became too much. From Niʻihau a giant shouted, 'I eat sweet potato for my strength while you only eat poi.' This incensed the Kauaʻi giant and he began throwing rocks, to which the Niʻihau giant responded in kind. But try as he might, the Niʻihau giant could not reach the Kauaʻi shore and all his boulders landed just offshore on rocks at Mana. The white cross where they fell may still be seen today.

The Kauaʻi giant was having more success, and finally, in his rage, he tore a piece off the pali behind him, and with one enormous heave, flung it across the Kaulakahi Channel where it landed directly on the other giant, killing him instantly. The poi thus proved better nourishment than sweet potatoes and yams.

The distinctive hill of Kauaʻi soil is today called Pakehoʻolua and the Niihauan giant's bones lie buried underneath.[36]

In days of old, with their strong animist beliefs, all families had a benevolent guardian spirit or ʻaumakua and often this was a shark (manō). Sharks have a special place in Hawaiian mythology, and none more so than the exploits of Pele's brother, the supreme shark-god Kuhaimoana and his son Kukaiʻaiki. Part of their legend follows:

The shark-god Kuhaimoana and his three sons

Kuhaimoana lived on Kaʻula Island and was born a god, with the ability to assume both shark and human forms. From his union with Kaluaikaikona, who lived on Lehua Island, were born three sons, the youngest of whom was Kukaiʻaiki.

The supreme shark-god Kuhaimoana was extremely keen to ascertain whether any of his three sons had inherited his supernatural powers and he lengthened his body so that his head rested on Kaʻula while his tail was on Niʻihau. He instructed his eldest son to swim the length of his body from Kaʻula to Niʻihau and then return down his other side. His eldest son attempted the swim first, but given the size of the task, only got as far as the shark-god's first dorsal fin (kualā).

It was now the turn of his second son. He got as far as Kuhaimoana's second kualā, but could go no further. He too was exhausted. Neither had evidently inherited their father's magical powers; a disappointment to Kuhaimoana.

His third son, Kukaiʻaiki, now stepped up, and sensing his father's chagrin, was determined to do better. He reached Kuhaimoana's third kualā, but realizing he could go no further in that bodily form he changed to that of a trevally (papio). He was then able to swim as far as Kuhaimoana's tail and he nibbled it to make sure his father knew he had reached it. For the return swim he changed form yet again, this time to a dorado or mahimahi, and finally to his natural body form, the rare, tiny, bright-red maʻuluʻula, just a few inches long, found in deep waters off Niʻihau. He was instantly recognizable to Kuhaimoana, who was elated to find at last he had a son who had inherited his supernatural powers.

After many adventures Kukaiʻaiki made his home in a cave on Lehua Island, while his father remained at Kaʻula.[37]

▼ A pen and ink drawing of the shark-god Kuhaimoana by Niihauan Matsu Kahokuloa.
Kuramatsu Kahokuloa

Niihauans have always prided themselves on their physical prowess, and fleetness of foot was regarded as an admirable attribute. The following legend exemplifies this:

Keliʻimalolo and the fleet-footed runners of Niʻihau

Two sons of the bird-god Halulu (after whom the Niihauan lake is named) were the fastest runners on Niʻihau and were reputed to be able to make ten circuits of Kauaʻi in a single day. They were so swift they could run on land or sea and even from the earth to the sky.

Keliʻimalolo, one of the fastest runners on Oʻahu had an unfortunate experience on Molokaʻi when he was on a fishing trip there. As he landed on Molokaʻi the locals called out to him to leave his canoe and fishing gear in the canoe shed to prevent it being stolen by young Maniniholokaukau, known as Mani, who had a reputation for such thefts.

Keliʻimalolo's retort was to ask if Mani was a fast runner, to which there was no reply, so he ignored the advice and undressed to wash in a freshwater pool. As soon as he was in the pool Mani arrived and approached the canoe, and from the pool Keliʻimalolo warned him to stay away. With that Mani hoisted the canoe with all the fishing gear inside on his back and ran off at tremendous speed.

Keliʻimalolo scrambled out of the water and ran off after him as fast as he could, but could not catch him. Mani ran to the bottom of what appeared to be an impenetrable pali (cliff) and cried out, 'Open up, O cave!' The pali wall parted revealing a cave, and Mani disappeared inside with the canoe before an exhausted Keliʻimalolo arrived — just as Mani called, 'Close up, O cave!' and he was faced with the solid pali wall. He hunted for an opening, but all was in vain and he left Molokaʻi in disgust.

On his return to Oʻahu, Keliʻimalolo determined to find someone to help him retrieve his canoe and he searched for the fastest runner in the islands. His search led him to Kauaʻi and he landed at Mana, carried his canoe ashore, and following his habit, went for a swim in a nearby pool. Just as he did so the two sons of Halulu arrived from Niʻihau. Espying Keliʻimalolo's loincloth (malo) on the beach, they picked it up and ran away with it. He immediately leapt out of the pool and gave chase, but couldn't catch them. The two brothers ran out to sea on the surface and stood looking at him. Realizing their speed and supernatural powers Keliʻimalolo called out to them, 'Come ashore and let's be friends. You two may be the means of returning to me my rightful belongings.' They came ashore and he told them how his canoe and fishing gear had been stolen by Mani on Molokaʻi. The brothers agreed to help and said to Keliʻimalolo, 'Return to Oʻahu and when you see the two narrow pointed clouds on the horizon we will come, but in the meantime let us all make a circuit of Kauaʻi in one day.'

Keliʻimalolo agreed and the next morning they set out on their run around the island. The two brothers quickly completed a circuit and found Keliʻimalolo still struggling to finish the first land district (ahupuaʻa). The brothers ran around again, overtaking Keliʻimalolo as he was completing the second ahupuaʻa. In all they completed ten circuits in the day, while Keliʻimalolo couldn't complete one. The Niihauan brothers were shown to be great runners, having no equal in all the islands.

The following morning Keliʻimalolo embarked for Oʻahu and awaited the arrival of his two new friends. Some days later he saw the two pointed clouds on the horizon and shortly the two brothers appeared. They then all boarded a double canoe for Moloka'i, landing at the place where Keli'imalolo's canoe had been stolen. As before, they all then undressed and swam in the freshwater pool.

Mani had seen the canoe in the distance and set off for the landing place. He was impressed with the double canoe, patting its sides and exclaiming 'My canoe, my canoe!' Keli'imalolo saw him and whispered to the brothers, 'That's the thief,' calling out to Mani, 'Leave that canoe alone!'

Taking no notice, Mani picked up the canoe and ran off with it as fast as he could. The brothers took off after him, telling Keli'imalolo that if he saw a fire burning it was a sign that they had caught up with Mani and killed him.

When Mani was almost up to the cave he called out 'Open up, O cave!,' but the brothers were upon him and immediately called out 'Close up, O cave!' The cave opened and as suddenly shut again, crushing Mani and the canoe in its mighty jaws and killing him.

With another cry of 'Open up, O cave!,' this time from the brothers, they entered and saw it was filled with canoes of every description, as well as many other valuables. They thereupon lit a fire and soon the people of the village arrived to reclaim their stolen goods.

The fame of the two sons of Halulu from Ni'ihau spread far and wide throughout the islands.[38]

▲ An 11-inch tall hula ki'i puppet from the late 18th century. Carved from soft wood and wearing a crested helmet, the face is covered with kapa cloth except for the nose, which is of animal skin. The eyes are made of pearl shell. The helmet, upper lip and neck are wrapped with twisted coir cordage. The open mouth is irregularly set with shark's teeth.
British Museum Oc.HAW.77

Niihauans pride themselves on their island being the ancestral home of the hula ki'i, or 'dance of the images,' in which dancers move stiffly like the wooden puppets or ki'i they are portraying. The story of the birth of hula ki'i is retold here:

Kewelani and the Birth of Hula Ki'i

As part of the Pele legend it is recorded that in the time of chief Halāli'i, Pele and her two sisters Kapoulakinau (Kapo) and Kewelani, daughters of goddess Haumea, visited Ni'ihau. At that time the chief was holding a series of nightly entertainments, to which all were invited. The sisters entered the chief's hale nui and he motioned them to sit by him. Kapo, in her wind form, perched on the great man's shoulder and using her spiritual powers of possession, chanted through him.

When Halāli'i had finished chanting, Kapo turned to her sister Kewelani and asked her to dance for the chief. Kewelani was always full of fun and chose a dance that fully reflected her personality.

As the audience became quiet, five people rose holding up between them a large makaloa mat as a screen. While Kapo chanted, the mischievous Kewelani remained hidden behind the mat, waiting for the right moment to reveal herself. As the chant ended Kewelani appeared and began to dance. It was a dance like no other, and one that had never been seen before on Ni'ihau or elsewhere.

It is said that her voice rose and fell like the song of the gentle-eyed Iale (a legendary sweet-singing bird) and with her hands uplifted and moving in time to her singing she danced to the rapturous delight of chief Halāli'i.

As the dance was ending she strutted like a bird onto the makaloa mat and rolled back her eyes till only the whites were visible, as bright and shiny as mother-of-pearl, which caused everyone to shout in amazement and stamp their feet. Halāliʻi and all the people watching applauded her comical act and kept laughing and shouting for more.

This was the ancestral hula kiʻi, danced for the first time on Niʻihau, and which became popular throughout the islands.[39]

Sayings

The above stories or legends are but a few of those pertaining to Niʻihau, and there are also many sayings, some of which are derived from the legends. Niihauans, like all Hawaiians, do not always speak in a straightforward fashion. They delight in riddles, jokes, epithets, allusion and proverbs. A large number of such sayings, nearly 3000 in all, were collected over many years by Mary Kawena Pukui and published in her canonical work *ʻOlelo Noʻeau: Hawaiian Proverbs and Poetical Sayings*. Several relate specifically to Niʻihau and its adjacent islets of Lehua and Kaʻula. In the preface to her work the book's editors explain the uniqueness of these sayings, which

> … present a variety of literary techniques such as metaphor, analogy, allegory, personification, irony, pun, and repetition. It is worth noting, however, that the sayings were spoken, and that their meanings and purposes should not be assessed by the Western concepts of literary types and techniques.[40]

The editors found it impossible to categorize them thematically and instead presented them alphabetically. Each saying is given in Hawaiian, followed by a literal English translation, and where necessary, a commentary or clarification. Those relevant to Niʻihau are given below as they appear in the book:

Aia i ka mole o Lehua.

At the taproot of Lehua, said of one who is out of sight for a long time, neither seen or heard of. Lehua is an island off the northern tip of Niʻihau.

ʻEna aku la manu o Kaʻula.

Untamed is the bird of Kaʻula, said of a shy person. Kaʻula is a small island southwest of Niʻihau inhabited by many birds.

Hāiki Kaʻula i ka hoʻokē a na manu.

There isn't room enough on Kaʻula, for the birds are crowding. A reference to overcrowding.

Ke kō ʻeli lima o Halāliʻi.

The sugar cane of Halāliʻi, dug out by hand. Winds blowing over this place on Niʻihau buried the sugar cane. Here and there the leaves were seen and the people dug them out by hand.

Moena pāwehe o Niʻihau.

Patterned mat of Niʻihau, a poetic expression often used in reference to Niʻihau. Its makaloa mats, beautifully patterned, were famed far and wide.

▲ Mary Kawena Pukui (1895–1986), renowned Hawaiian scholar and educator, was born on the Big Island to a Hawaiian mother and an American father, and reared by her maternal grandparents who steeped her in native Hawaiian culture. She attended Seventh Day Adventist schools before teaching Hawaiiana at Punahou School. At the age of 15 she began collecting and translating Hawaiian folk tales, an interest that fitted her well for her ethnological role at the Bishop Museum, where she worked from 1938 to 1961. She published over 50 scholarly works, as well as coauthoring the still definitive Hawaiian-English Dictionary. In 2017 *Hawaiʻi Magazine* included her in their list of the most influential women in Hawaiian history.
Wikimedia Commons

Na ʻulu hua i ka hāpapa.

The breadfruit that bears on the ground. Breadfruit trees were grown in sinkholes. The trunks were not visible and the branches seemed to spread along the ground. These trees are famed in the chants of Niʻihau.

Niʻihau a Kahelelani.

Niʻihau, land of Kahelelani. Kahelelani was an ancient ruler of Niʻihau. The tiny seashell that is made into the finest lei now bears his name.

Niʻihau i ka uhi paheʻe.

Niʻihau of the slippery yam. Niʻihau was known for its fine yams, which when grated raw for medicine are slippery.

Niʻihau i ke kīkū.

Niʻihau leans back firmly. Niʻihau people are independent.

Puaēa ka manu o Kaʻula i ke kai.

The bird of Kaʻula expires over the sea, said of utter destruction, as of birds that drop dead while flying over the sea.

Kūʻonoʻono ka lua o Kuhaimoana.

Deep indeed is the cave of Kuhaimoana, said of a prosperous person. Kūʻonoʻono (deep) also means 'well supplied.' The cave of Kuhaimoana, a shark god, is at the islet of Kaʻula.

Wawā na manu o Kaʻula.

Noisy are the birds o Kaʻula. A lot of gossip is going around.

The above sayings are a mixture of types, from practical reality to metaphor. Another rich source of wisdom is Tava and Keale's book, *Niihau: The Traditions of an Hawaiian Island*.[41] The authors chose not to include ʻokina (ʻ) and kahakō (macrons) in their book on the grounds that most of the sources used did not contain them (see preface). This has been followed in these sayings selected from the book:

Aina nui o Niihau piliwale mai o Lehua.

Great is the land of Nʻiihau and Lehua is nearby.

Aina o Kaula ike komohana hoa paio no ke Konahea.

The island of Kaula lies to the west, an opponent of the Konahea winds.

Hanau Niihau he aina, he motu, he aina i ke aa i ka mole o ta aina.

Born the island of Niʻihau, the land that is the stem of all the islands. Niʻihau is the oldest of all the islands.

Kauai kaili la, o Niihau ka la kau.

Kauaʻi steals the sun; Niʻihau is the sun.

O kanaka o ka wai.

The people of the water, used in reference to Kauaʻi.

> **Niʻihau i ke kīkū.**
> *Niʻihau people are independent.*

Rerioterai Tava (1930–2010), Tahitian-born, became an author, teacher, nurse and professional entertainer. Adopted by Methodist missionaries, she was educated in the United States, but by 1950 Rerioterai felt the need to revitalise her Polynesian roots. She studied at the Bishop Museum with anthropologist Dr Kenneth Emory and was a board member of the Hawaiian Music Foundation. An accomplished Pacific arts performer and teacher, her art has been exhibited at the Honolulu Museum of Art and the Kauaʻi Museum. She coauthored *Niihau: The Traditions of an Hawaiian Island* with Moses Keale.

Moses Kapalekilahao Keale Snr (1938–2000) was born at Puʻuwai on Niʻihau and attended school on Kauaʻi, later entering the Officer Training School on Oʻahu, and graduating as a lieutenant. He became an accomplished Hawaiian language instructor, translator and pastor, working for the Hawaiʻi State Department of Social Services before being appointed Niʻihau/Kauaʻi representative on the board of the Office of Hawaiian Affairs (OHA) in 1980, where he served until his retirement in 1999.

I ka lani no ka ua wai e no ke pulu.

The rain is still in the clouds. It's time to prepare the mulch. Months in advance Niihauans prepared the land for planting, usually for uwala (sweet potato). Don't wait for the rain to come; you may find yourself with little or no crop.

He ku pu maia ike ala.

The banana stalk that stands by the road, a sexually impotent person. The stalk was pithy and no good.

Note how often the islets of Ka'ula and Lehua enter into these legends and aphorisms. The ancestral Niihauans regarded them as integral elements of their intellectual and spiritual domain.

The stories in this chapter have relied almost entirely on oral traditions, supplemented by artifacts and early European travelers' accounts. When we see what was found on Nihoa and Necker (Mokumanamana) Islands in the 1920s by the *Tanager* expedition, and similarly at the dig in the 1950s at Nu'alolo Kai on Kaua'i, we have to wonder if there are archeological discoveries still to be made on Ni'ihau, despite the ranching that has occurred over the last 150 years.

> 'Aina nui ō Ni'ihau, piliwale mai ō Lehua.
> *Great is the land of Ni'ihau, and Lehua is close by.*

▲ Aerial view of Ni'ihau and Lehua.
James L. Amos/Getty images 523662554

CHAPTER THREE

A FATEFUL EUROPEAN ENCOUNTER

The way of life described in the previous chapter, which had been developing on Niʻihau for over 500 years, was about to irrevocably change with an extraordinary apparition off the southwestern coast on 29 January 1778.

> Some were terrified and shrieked with fear … they saw the boat with its masts and its sails shaped like a gigantic sting ray. One asked another, "What are those branching things?" and the other answered, "They are trees moving about on the sea." Still another thought, "A double canoe of the hairless ones of Mana!" A certain kahuna named Ku-ʻohu declared, "That can be nothing else than the heiau of Lono, the tower of Ke-o-lewa, and the place of sacrifice at the altar.' … The excitement became more intense and louder grew the shouting.[1]

Although the above quotation was written by Samuel Kamakau about the appearance of Captain James Cook's ships, the *Resolution* and the *Discovery,* off Kauaʻi ten days earlier, it applied equally well to the situation at Niʻihau. For many of those on shore, seeing the ships for the first time, they appeared to be a single unfathomable entity — hence the author's use of the singular for what they saw.

▼ James Cook arrived off the south side of Kauaʻi on 19 January 1778. 'The next morning we stood in for the land and were met by several Canoes filled with people, some of them took courage and ventured on board. I never saw Indians so much astonished at entering a ship before, their eyes were continually flying from object to object.' This sketch, by William Ellis, surgeon's mate on the *Resolution*, is the first known image of the Hawaiian islands drawn by a Westerner.
Wikimedia Commons

▲ US Postal Service stamp issued to commemorate the bicentenary of Cook's landing at Waimea on 21 January 1778; he landed on Ni'ihau nine days later. He and his crew became the first Westerners to set foot on the Hawaiian Islands.
US Postal Service

▼ 'An Inland View in Atooi' [Kaua'i] by John Webber. In the center a cask of water is being rolled and bartering is proceeding to the left center while other interactions and activities are taking place in the village. An engraving by Samuel Middiman from the drawing done by Webber on Cook's first visit to Waimea in 1778.
Hawaiian Historical Society

The two vessels had left Bora Bora northwest of Tahiti on 8 December 1777, and after coming upon and naming Christmas Island, sailed on northwards towards Bering Strait in their quest for a northwest passage, the major object of their voyage. Cook' eyes were wide-open:

We continued to see birds every day … All these are looked upon as signs of the vecinity of land; we however saw none till day break on the morning of the 18th [January] when an island was descovered bearing N E B E and soon after we saw more land bearing North and intirely ditatched from the first; both had the appearance of being high land. …

On the 19th at Sun rise the island first seen bore East [blank] leagues distant at least; this being directly to windward there was no getting nearer it so that I stood for the other, and not long after discovered a third island in the direction of W N W and as far distant as an island could be seen.[2]

The first island seen was O'ahu, then Kaua'i and the third, Ni'ihau; the first known sightings by any Europeans. But were the islands inhabited? This was answered for them when the ships were still six or seven miles off Kaua'i. Several canoes were observed heading towards them and the vessels stopped and waited for them to arrive. To their surprise they found the islanders spoke a language similar to that spoken in Tahiti, so that communication was relatively effortless (see Appendix B).

Captain James Cook had left Plymouth on his third voyage on 12 July 1776 in command of HMS *Resolution*, with Charles Clerke in command of HMS *Discovery*. When he left England, Cook had three officers with him on the *Resolution*: James King, John Gore and John Williamson. The surgeon was William Anderson, assisted by David Samwell, and William Bligh, later of *Bounty* fame, was sailing master.

Charles Clerke had two officers with him on the *Discovery*: John Rickman and James Burney. The surgeon was John Law, assisted by William Ellis, and the sailing master was Thomas Edgar. This was still the disposition of the senior personnel when they came upon the Hawaiian islands. They cruised slowly westwards along the south coast of Kaua'i, looking for an anchorage and suitable watering place. All along the coast

every vantage point was thronged with people watching this strange apparition as it glided past them. No suitable watering spot was found by nightfall, but the following afternoon, 20 January, after a reconnaissance, the ships anchored a mile off the Waimea river mouth, thronged by canoes. Cook immediately went ashore and the next two days were spent watering, bartering and exploring the immediate hinterland.

On the following morning, the 23rd, an onshore breeze having sprung up, Cook felt it prudent to move the *Resolution* further offshore, but having weighed anchor, was prevented from so doing by a windshift. For the next five frustrating days he cruised back and forth in the Kaulakahi Channel before giving up hope of returning to Waimea. The *Discovery* followed suit, but as she was moored further from the shore, weighed anchor three days later after completing provisioning. Thus thwarted, on the morning of 29 January Cook decided to investigate the leeward (western) side of Ni'ihau to see if the rest of the water and food supplies needed for his venture to the Arctic might be obtained there:

> Weary with plying so unsuccessfully, Captain Cook laid aside all thoughts of returning to Atooi [Kaua'i], and resumed his intention of paying a visit to Oneeheow [Ni'ihau]. With this view, he dispatched the master [Bligh] in a boat to sound along the coast, and search for a landing-place, and afterwards for fresh water. In the mean time the ships followed under an easy sail. The master, at his return, reported, that there was tolerable anchorage all along the coast; and that he had landed in one place, but could not find any fresh water.

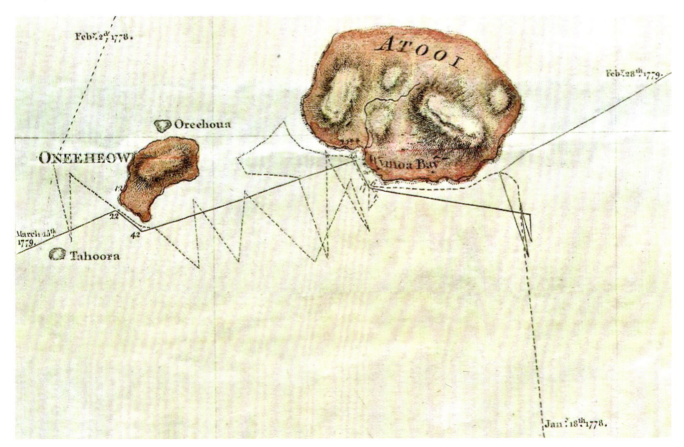

▼ A detail from the map of the expedition's tracks through the Hawaiian islands, drawn by the *Resolution*'s master, William Bligh. The dotted line shows Cook's course and particularly his difficulties in the Kaulakahi Channel from 17 January 1778 to departure from Ni'ihau on 2 February 1778. The solid line shows the vessel's return track from 28 February to 25 March 1779.
Wikimedia Commons

▲ Cook's vessels approaching Ni'ihau on 29 January 1778. The first depiction of the island of Ni'ihau by a European.
Watercolor by William Ellis, Bishop Museum

Captain Cook being informed by some of the natives, who had come off to the ships, that fresh water might be obtained at a village which they saw at a little distance, ran down, and cast anchor before it, about six furlongs [three-quarters of a mile] from the shore, the depth of water being twenty-six fathoms. The Discovery anchored at a greater distance from the shore, in twenty-three fathoms.

The south-eastern point of Oneeheow bore south, 65 deg. east, about one league [three miles] distant; and another island which they had discovered the preceding night, named Tahoora, [Ka'ula] bore south, 61 deg. west, at the distance of seven leagues.[3]

The anchorage location has never been pinpointed. Cook scholar J.C. (John) Beaglehole speculates in his edit of Cook's journals:

> Neither Chart LV nor its engraved copy marks the anchorage, but from these bearings and other indications it seems to have been not far from Leahi Point, towards the now disused village of Kamalino — or rather perhaps off a village a mile or two south of that.[4]

Whether any of the inhabitants of Ni'ihau had foreknowledge of the mysterious 'apparition' when it appeared offshore at Ni'ihau is not known. Most likely they did, as it was now ten days since it had first been seen off Kaua'i.

Lieutenant John Rickman, second officer on the *Discovery*, gives a brief view of their arrival and the attractions of Ni'ihau:

> On the 29th we bore away to another lee island [Ni'ihau], which abounded with hogs and fruit, and where the natives were equally hospitable with those we had just left; but, there being no water to be procured at a moderate distance, and the reefs being

▲ Cook's chart of the west side of Ni'ihau, as seen from the *Resolution* at anchor, drawn by William Bligh as a guide for future navigators. The cinder cone of Kawaihoa is prominent on the right.
Journal of Cook's Third Voyage, Hawaiian Historical Society

dangerous, and the surf running high, Capt. Cook, after surveying the island, and taking possession of it, in the name of his Royal master, (calling the whole cluster Sandwich's Isles) was preparing to depart, when a storm came on from the eastward, and again obliged the Resolution to put to sea.[5]

Cook on the *Resolution* was not as fortunate as the *Discovery*. Having been unable to totally replenish his supplies at Kaua'i due to the weather, he was more reliant than the *Discovery* on obtaining produce from Ni'ihau. His comments on their arrival are considerably more extensive than Rickman's:

> Before we anchored, several canoes had come off to us, bringing potatoes, yams, and small pigs, besides mats. The people who were in them resembled in their persons the inhabitants of Atooi; and, like them, were acquainted with the use of iron [from flotsam, likely from Japanese vessel wreckage given the prevailing currents], which they asked for by the names of *toe* and *hamaite*, readily parting with all their commodities for pieces of this metal. Some more canoes soon reached our ships, after they had come to anchor; but the islanders who were in these had apparently no other object, than to make us a formal visit. Many of them came on board, and crouched down upon the deck; nor did they quit that humble posture, till they were requested to rise.[6]

It would appear that the Niihauans were still entertaining the notion that the apparition indicated the return of the god Lono. Cook had much to attract his attention:

> Several women, whom they had brought with them, remained along-side in the canoes, behaving with much less modesty than the females of Atooi; and, at intervals, they all joined in a song, which, though not very melodious, was performed in the exactest concert, by beating time upon their breasts with their hands. The men who had come on board did not continue long with us; and before their departure, some of them desired permission to lay down locks of their hair on the deck.[7]

Captain Clerke of the *Discovery* came aboard the *Resolution* at this time and Lt King, his first officer, added detail of the encounter and also noted the locks of hair being left, a custom evidently done to memorialize such a formal meeting:

> On C Clerke's coming on board & perceiving by some bustle in getting the Canoes out of his way, that he was a Chief, those on board crouch'd down & did not rise till they were told to do so. After staying on board some time many desir'd permission to leave a lock of their hair on the deck after which they all left us.[8]

The Britishers were intrigued to learn whether or not the locals were cannibals like the Māori of New Zealand:

> The curious enquiry, whether these islanders were cannibals, was this day renewed; and the subject did not arise from any questions put by us, but from a circumstance that seemed to remove all doubt. One of the natives, who wished to get in at the gun-room port, was refused, and he then asked, whether we should kill and eat him, if he should come in? accompanying this question with signs so expressive, that we did not entertain a doubt with

▲ James King (1750–84), Cook's second officer on the *Resolution*, who commanded the ship after the deaths of Cook and Clerke, and later steered publication of the journals of the voyage.
Portrait by John Webber / National Library Australia

▼ The first known image of hale pili (grass houses) on Ni'ihau. Pili grass was favored for thatching. It grows in clumps and when used for thatching the whole clump was removed, the ends trimmed and the bundle attached to the frame, root-end upward. The drawing is by William Ellis and appears in his journal.
Courtesy Mary Ann McCrea

respect to his meaning. We had now an opportunity of retorting the question as to this practice; and a man behind the other, in the canoe, instantly replied, that, if we were killed on shore, they would not scruple to eat us: not that he meant they would destroy us for that purpose, but that their devouring us would be the consequence of our being at enmity with them.[9]

In the afternoon Cook sent Lieutenant Gore with three armed boats to look for water and a suitable landing place. He returned in the evening having been to a village, presumably Kamalino, where he was taken to a water source about half a mile inland. This proved to be only a trickle and difficult of access. The following morning Gore went ashore again with a complement of marines, this time to trade for food supplies. Cook himself had intended to follow, but judged that the sea was rising and he may not get back to the *Resolution*, so he didn't go.

This is exactly what happened to the first officer and his party of 'about twenty men,' who could not get back to the *Resolution* and had to spend the night in the village. This was a major blow to Cook in his stated aim of preventing venereal disease reaching the islands. In the evening Gore had signalled for boats to be sent, but as King relates:

▲ Lieutenant (later Captain) John Gore (c.1730–90), Cook's first officer on the *Resolution* who led the search for water on Ni'ihau. A portrait by John Webber, painted later when Gore had assumed command of the expedition after the deaths of Cook and Clerke.

National Library of Australia

> ... the Surf broke so violently on the shore, that Mr Gore & the Marines did not venture to come off in the boats that were sent for them, & for what they had purchas'd, most of which was lost & spoilt in getting into the boats; the Captain was very uneasy at their staying on shore, being apprehinsive, that his endeavours in hindring any connexions with the women woud be now frustrat'd ...[10]

The allure of the women was described by Lt Rickman of the *Discovery*:

> The women in general have shock hair, which they were at great pains to ornament. They had large holes in their ears, that, filled as they were with most beautifully coloured shells made up in clusters, served for jewels, and had no bad effect. Their head-dress consisted of wreaths of flowers, decorated with feathers chiefly red; and having, in general, lively piercing black eyes, white teeth, small features, and round faces, were not a little inviting, had not Capt. Cook's severe prohibition put a check to the predominant passion of our men.[11]

Lt Williamson, one of Cook's officers on the *Resolution*, was even more pointed as to the temptations facing the men with the actions of the women villagers:

> ... & ye extreme reservedness of the party excited so great a curiosity in the women, that they were determined to see wether our people were men or not, & us'd every means in their power to provoke them to do that, which ye dread of punishment would have kept them from.[12]

Cook reconciled himself to the inevitable and rued: '... thus the very thing happened that I had above all others wished to prevent.'

Most of the stores secured during the day were brought out by the islanders, as Gore's purchases were mostly lost, as King relates above. Cook describes the traders:

> The violence of the surf did not deter the natives from coming off in canoes to our ships. They brought with them some refreshments for which we gave them, in exchange, some nails and pieces of iron hoops; and we distributed among the women in the canoes, many pieces of ribbon, and some buttons, as bracelets. Some of the men had representations of human figures punctured upon their breasts, and one of them had a lizard represented.[13]

The Niihauans, who had visited Cook and Clerke when the vessels were at Waimea, confirmed that 'there was no chief of this island, but that it was subject to one of the chiefs of Atooi, whose name was Teneooneoo [Kaneoneo].'[14]

Later in the evening it started to blow and Cook thought it prudent to move the *Resolution* further offshore, where he anchored in 42 fathoms.

The next day, 31 January, the northeast trades continued so strongly that there was no possibility of communicating with Gore and his men, and they had to spend a second night ashore, much to Cook's annoyance. Later in the day Cook was, however, able to send Bligh on a reconnaissance to the southeast point from where the ship lay (presumably Lēʻahi Point) to see if a boat might be able to land in its lee. He reported favorably, but it was too late in the day by then to embark the shore party.

In the morning (1 February) Cook sent an order to Gore to march his men to the point, but as the boat could still not land by the village, a doughty sailor had to swim ashore with the message. Cook was in a generous frame of mind:

> ... on the return of the boat I went my self with the Pinnace and Launch up to the point to bring the party on board, taking with me a Ram goat and two Ewes, a Boar and Sow pig of the English breed, the seeds of Millons [melons], Pumpkins and onions. I landed with great ease under the west side of the point, and found the party already there, with a few of the Natives among them. There was one man whom Mr Gore had observed to have some command over the others, to him I gave the Goats, Pigs and seeds. I should have left these things at the other island [Kauaʻi], had we not been so unexpectedly driven from it.[15]

▲ 'Man of Atooi [Kauaʻi],' a pencil sketch by William Ellis, 1778. The sketch has the subject in a Windsor chair, which can only have come from Cook's cabin on the *Resolution*.
ATL A-264-045

Having presented the animals and seeds, the first given by a European to a Hawaiian, Captain Cook explored the hinterland, a warm proposition in full dress uniform:

> While the people were filling four water casks from a small stream occasioned by the late rain, I took a little walk into the island attended by the man above mentioned, and followed by two others carrying the two pigs. As soon as we got upon a rising ground I stoped to look round me, a woman on the other side of the vally where I landed, called to the men with me, on which the Chief began to mutter something like a prayer and the two men with the pigs continued to walk round me all the time, not less than ten or dozen times before the other had finished. This ceremony being ended, we proceeded and presently met people coming from all parts, who, on the men with me calling to them laid down till I was out of sight.[16]

Was Cook seen as the embodiment of Lono on the latter's legendary predicted return to the island, or as Beaglehole suggests at least an aliʻi ʻai moku — a chief of the highest rank? Cook then gives a brief impression of the countryside he walked through:

> The ground over which I walked was in a state of nature, very stony and the soil seemed poor; it was however covered with shrubs and plants, some of which sent forth the most fragrant smell I had met with in this sea.[17]

▲ Flowers of the coastal sandalwood, ʻiliahe aloʻe, which perfumed the air during Cook's walk on Niʻihau. It is a sprawling shrub or small tree, extremely variable in size and shape, inhabiting low shrublands and lava plains. The species is endemic to the Hawaiian islands.
Kim and Forrest Starr / Wikimedia Commons

The fragrance might have come from the coastal sandalwood, *Santalum ellipticum*, known as ʻiliahe aloʻe to the Hawaiians. It was still found to be in the vicinity by Harold St John in 1947, despite the ravages of stock since Cook's time. Another source of the aroma could have been the flowers of the native caper, *Capparis sandwichiana*, pilo to the Niihauans, which was found at Lēʻahi Point by St John.

When the water casks were filled and a few further stores of roots, dried fish and salt purchased from the islanders, Cook returned to the *Resolution*, intending to visit the island again the next day, but it wasn't to be. That evening the *Resolution*'s anchor started dragging and Cook felt it judicious to set sail. This took some time as they had so much chain out and by the time it was completed they were nine miles leeward of their previous location off Niʻihau. His journal records his change of plan: 'And foreseeing that it would take some time to recover it [i.e. the distance], more at least than I chused to spend I made signal to the *Discovery* to weigh and join us which was done about Noon when we stood away to the Northward.'[18]

With this, on 2 February, he left the islands, but not before naming them the Sandwich Islands after the expedition's sponsor, the Earl of Sandwich. Rickman, in his journal, states that Cook took possession of the islands in the name of his master, King George, but Cook doesn't mention this in his own journal. Nor is it covered in any other account.

It had not been a very satisfactory time for the *Resolution*, but the *Discovery* had fared better:

> Thus after spending more time about these islands than was necessary to have answered all our purposes, we were obliged to leave them before we had compleated our Water, and got from them such a quantity of refreshments as the inhabitants were able and willing to supply us with. But as it was we procured from them full three weeks provisions and Captain Clerke got roots sufficient for two months or upwards.[19]

▲ Captain Charles Clerke (1741–79) served on all three of Cook's voyages — as master's mate on the first, as second lieutenant on the second voyage, and in command of the *Discovery* on the third. Upon Cook's death in February 1779 he assumed command of the expedition, but succumbed to tuberculosis in August while searching for a northwest passage. From the portrait by Nathaniel Dance-Holland.
Wikimedia Commons

Rickman is pleased with the haul:

> Our boats [the *Discovery*'s], while the shore was accessible, were employed in bringing on board the product of the island, and, on the evening of the 1st of February we had more than 250 hogs, besides three months allowance of sweet potatoes, bananoes [sic], plantains, sugar-cane and vegetables in abundance.[20]

Rickman doesn't allude to yams, which Cook says are Niʻihau's main vegetable produce. This is probably a simple omission as the *Discovery* certainly stocked up with yams. Yams were a premium substitute for bread as they lasted two to three months at sea, whereas sweet potatoes lasted only ten days or so.

Cook was impatient to proceed with his main mission, the discovery of a northwest passage. As he left the islands he reflected on the experiences of Lt Gore's party while marooned on Niʻihau, the only crew members who had the opportunity to see something of the island and the islanders' way of life:

> Our party who had been detained so long on shore, found, in those parts of the island which they had traversed, several salt ponds, some of which had a small quantity of water remaining, but others had none. They saw no appearance of a running stream; and though, in some small wells which they met with, the fresh water was pretty good, it seemed to be scarce.
>
> The houses of the natives were thinly scattered about; and it was supposed, that there were not more than five hundred persons in the whole island. The method of living among these people was decent and cleanly. No instance was observed of the men and women eating together; and the latter seemed in general to be associated in companies by themselves.

> The oily nuts of the *dooe dooe* [kukui] are burned by these islanders for lights during the night; and they dress their hogs by baking them in ovens, splitting the carcases through the whole length. Our people met with a sufficient proof of the existence of the *taboo* among them; for one woman was employed in feeding another who was under that interdiction. Several other mysterious ceremonies were also observed; one of which was performed by a woman, who threw a pig into the surf, and drowned it, and then tied up a bundle of wood, which she disposed of in the like manner. The same female, at another time, beat a man's shoulders with a stick, after he had seated himself for that purpose.
>
> An extraordinary veneration seemed to be paid here to owls, which they keep very tame. It appeared to be pretty general practice among them, to pull out one of their teeth; and when they were asked the reason of this remarkable custom, the only answer they gave was, that it was *teeha*; which was also the reason assigned by them for giving a lock of their hair.[21]

With that brief description Cook and his crews turned their attention to the task at hand — the journey to a possible northwest passage. From the Niihauans' point of view the apparition disappeared from view as quickly as it had appeared, but their way of life had already begun to change, with the iron and other goods the strangers brought. The goats Cook left were to become an instant source of friction. There was no turning back.

Oneeheeou revisited

Leaving Oneeheeou (as Cook spelled Niʻihau in his journal), the ships sailed almost due north until they were able to pick up the prevailing westerly winds in the higher latitudes. Cook had previously arranged to rendezvous with Clerke off the coast of North America in latitude 45° should the vessels become separated, but this was not necessary. The ships made landfall together on 7 March off the coast of what is now Oregon in latitude 44° 20'. They proceeded northwards up the coast looking for a harbor, charting as they went, until they came to Nootka Sound on the western coast of Vancouver Island. Here they spent a month refitting their vessels before pushing northwards along the Alaskan coast and into the approaches to the Bering Strait.

The summer months saw the ships probing the Bering Strait area. Their highest latitude of 70° 44' was reached on 18 August, when they were confronted with advancing ice from horizon to horizon. Realizing there was no possibility of progress, the vessels retreated to Unalaska in the Aleutian Islands, where they spent three weeks repairing sails and rigging before sailing south for Hawaiʻi on 24 October.

Maui was sighted a month later, on 26 November. Cook cruised east along the coast and then clockwise around Hawaiʻi looking for a suitable harbor. Winds were light, progress was slow, crews were disgruntled, and it wasn't until 17 January 1779 that he sailed into Kealakekua Bay and the vessels came to anchor. The tragic events that took place there are fairly well known: Cook was attacked and killed while attempting to kidnap the ruling chief of the island of Hawaiʻi, Kalaniʻōpuʻu, in order to reclaim a cutter taken from one of his ships after his crew took wood from a burial ground.

After Cook's recovered remains were consigned to the deep with all due ceremony, they departed Kealakekua Bay on 22 February. The ships were now under the command of Captain Clerke, who was determined to complete the expedition as Cook would

▲ The Hawaiian owl, pueo (*Asio flammeus sandwichensis*). Cook wrote after his initial visit to Niʻihau: 'A particular veneration seems to be paid here to owls, which they have very tame.' The pueo was revered in Hawaiian culture as a protector and guide, and even as an interlocutor for the gods. Their great eyes were seen to watch over the peace of families, guiding them when called upon as their ʻaumakua or family god. There is debate as to whether the pueo arrived in the islands shortly before or shortly after the Polynesians. In view of Cook's comment that they tamed them, could it be that they brought them with them on their sea voyages? Pueo are unusual for owls in that they hunt during the day, and lay their eggs in nests on the ground.
mauinui.com

have wished. Cook's plan had been to make a second attempt at finding a northwest passage, and hence his decision to return to Hawai'i to winter over.

With the loss of Cook and the death at sea of William Anderson, the *Resolution*'s surgeon, on their return to Ni'ihau fourteen months later Charles Clerke was at the helm of the *Resolution* and John Gore of the *Discovery*. William Harvey, a midshipman, was made an officer on the *Resolution*. David Samwell transferred to the *Discovery* as surgeon, while William Ellis and John Law went to the *Resolution* in that role.

While they had largely revictualled at Kealakekua Bay, the water they had obtained was brackish and they were short on yams. Clerke therefore sailed west along the north side of Maui and Moloka'i looking for a haven, and then on to O'ahu where he stopped briefly in Waimea Bay on 28 February in the hope of watering there. The two captains, Clerke and Gore, went ashore with Lt King, and all were quite taken with the roadstead. King comments: 'the banks of this river, and indeed the whole we saw of the North West part of Woahoo, are well cultivated, and full of villages; and the face of the country is uncommonly beautiful and picturesque …'[22] Of the search for water Clerke writes:

> On landing I was receiv'd with every token of respect and friendship by a great number of the Natives who were collected upon the occasion; they every one of them prostrated themselves around me which is the first mark of respect at these Isles, indeed I dont know how any People can devise a more expressive one; however I immediately made motions for them to rise; when one who seem'd the most consequential of this assembly arose and came forward … I beg'd to be shewn some good Water in which they readily undertook to oblige me and brought me to a run of water which empties itself into the sea, but unfortunately for near a quarter of a Mile up the Country the course of this Water is along a flat over which the Tide constantly flows; now tho' it was quite low Water when I was onshore the stream was rather brackish merely with the drainings of the Tide, at any other periods it must be much worse. As this was the only Water to be found I thought it best immediately to repair to A'tou'i [Kaua'i] …[23]

This landing was the first by Europeans on O'ahu, and Clerke was touched by his welcome. The news of the tragic events at Kealakekua Bay had apparently not reached Waimea Bay. Clerke's narrative explains the significance of yams:

> At A'tou'i I can get good Water and much more Fruit & Hogs than I shall want, but a stock of Yams is now my principal Aim; they are the only roots that will keep, the Eastern Isles produce very few of them, nor did we see many at A'tou'i during our last visit, but O'nee'how [Ni'ihau] a small Isle to the Westward of A'tou'i we found to produce great abundance. These are to me the most essential acquisition now I must proceed to N°ward, as they are a substitute for the Bread which is the most exhausted Article.[24]

It is intriguing that only at Ni'ihau were they able to obtain yams in quantity, and we may wonder why. It may have been for the same reason that Clerke wanted them — their keeping qualities. With Ni'ihau's aridity and intermittent droughts, yams may well have been grown there as a form of insurance that was unnecessary on the other islands. But with its small population and unreliable climate the supply of yams was limited.

The two ships sailed on to Kaua'i, anchoring at their old watering hole at Waimea on the morning of 2 March 1779. They were not met with the cordiality of their previous visit, and initially suspected that news had arrived about what had happened

a stock of Yams is now my principal Aim … O'nee'how [Ni'ihau] a small Isle to the Westward of A'tou'i we found to produce great abundance.

at Kealakekua Bay, but this was not so. There had been a battle the day before in which several were killed and Kaneoneo, whom they had met last year, was driven into the mountains. The new chief was Kaʻeo. Feelings were still running high. The goats which had been given by Cook to Kaneoneo had also become casualties of the conflict.

Adding to their distress was the legacy of venereal disease left behind from their last visit, which the Hawaiians were quick to point out, and sheeted home the blame to last year's apparition.

That afternoon Lt King took a watering party ashore and the islanders became quite menacing in their attempts to steal anything of iron, including the marines' muskets, to the point where King shot a man to protect his party. The following day Clerke sent his men ashore well prepared, with good result:

> In the Morning I sent Mr King again upon the Watering business with all the Boats of both Ships and 50 Men under arms to protect those who were employ'd about the Casks &c, with orders not by any means to suffer a Native to come near them — they now went on very well, the Natives assembled to the amount of some thousands but were merely distant Spectators, they gave our Party no kind of interruption.[25]

▲ Carved gourd water container obtained on Cook's third voyage. Decorated gourds, achieved by incising the skin and rubbing in mud or vegetable dye, were a Niihauan speciality.
Weltmuseum, Vienna

The watering continued for a further four days without incident, and was completed on 7 March. The carpenters from both ships were meanwhile recaulking the *Resolution*'s planking and decks — a task which seemed never-ending, as the vessel had evidently been poorly constructed.

Captain Clerke received several visits from the new queen of the island, Kamakahelei, and her retinue, including her third husband, the chief Kaʻeo. The first visit was on 4 March, and presents were exchanged, and a second took place two days later, with more presents given. The queen arrived again on 7 March, and surprised Clerke:

> This Fore Noon I had a visit from the old Queen with her retinue, and for the first time from Ta'ma'ha'no [Kaneoneo]. They met upon deck when poor Ta'ma'ha'no's looks bespoke his broken fortunes. The Queen order'd him peremptorily not to come into the Cabin during her stay there, which hurt the poor fellow so much he took his Canoe and return'd to the shore. There is something in the Police* of these people wholly unintelligible to us …[26]

* *In this context, 'police' is an archaic term for the system of regulation for the preservation of law and order.*

Clerke was astounded that two antagonists at open war with each other could meet in such a relatively civil fashion after a battle in which he says Kaneoneo lost 26 men and Kaʻeo one. The following morning the two ships set sail for Niʻihau and in the afternoon of 9 March anchored in their previous place on the western side of Niʻihau, close by Lēʻahi Point. Clerke was of a mind to trade:

> The Weather so boisterous that few Canoes will venture to us; these however bring off what Yams they can conveniently stow. I sent the Launch into a small sandy Bay abreast of us … with Orders to the Officer to come to a Grapling in the Bay and try if the Natives would then bring off their Yams (which is now the only trade I shall give any great attention too) for I could plainly percieve from the Ship that the Surfe was far too heavy, even in this Bay for our boats to keep up any kind of connection with the Shore. At Noon the Launch return'd with a Cargo of these roots but they were a very bad sample of what I fear we have now to expect, being very deficient both in respect to size and firmness.[27]

The 'Grapling' was an anchor and attached buoy at which the trading and transfer of cargo from canoes to ships' boats could take place, as the ships themselves were anchored two miles offshore. Trading for yams went on in this fashion for the following three days. On 12 March a canoe arrived at the *Resolution* from Kaua'i, a not inconsiderable distance, and in inclement weather, bringing presents of hogs and fruit for Clerke from the Queen. This gives an indication of the extent of travel between the islands that was routinely undertaken.

On 13 March Clerke sent Bligh with two boats to search for a more sheltered anchorage anywhere along the western side of Ni'ihau. Bligh returned on the evening of the following day, having been far enough north to establish that Lehua was definitely a separate island. He had encouraging news:

> … he had found a Bay well shelter'd from the prevailing Winds here, just to the N°ward of the Western point of this road, which is also the Western point of the Island. The soundings from 10 to 18 fathom with a good clear sandy bottom, and that there was Water in small wells, about a ¼ of a mile from the shore, which might with a little trouble be got into Casks and convey'd to the Boats, the land being tolerably level between these Wells and the shore; to which place I wou'd recommend any ships that may hereafter have occasion to Anchor at this Isle.[28]

▲ The young William Bligh (1754–1817), painted by John Webber shortly before they both left on the *Resolution* on Cook's third voyage, Bligh as sailing master and Webber as official artist. Bligh had training as a cartographer and produced the charts of the voyage. Note the dividers he is holding in the portrait. Bligh's later career was mired in controversy, but he was twice exonerated in courts-martial and completed his career as a vice-admiral and governor of New South Wales.
Wikimedia Commons

Bligh had found the anchorage now known as Nonopapa, but which was called Yam Bay by the next few explorers and visitors to the islands. That morning, 14 March, Clerke received 'another Cargo of Hogs, Roots &c from my Royal friend at A'tou'i who is indeed a most social old Lady, and I am much obliged to her for her attention at this distance.' Clerke had made a hit with Queen Kamakahelei — or were there more subtle political overtones in her gestures of friendship? We will never know.

The following morning, 15 March, Clerke judged that while plenty of hogs were still available, the supply of yams was almost exhausted:

> I am sorry to have occasion to observe they have fallen exceedingly short of my expectations both in respect to quality and quantity, they are now almost all small and Watery, infinitely inferior to those we were supply'd with from this Island in the beginning of Feb[ry] last Year, nor are they by any means so abundant, but vastly more costly.[29]

As his only objective in visiting Ni'ihau was to secure yams, he judged that there would be few more forthcoming and he therefore made arrangements to sail at seven the following morning on a second attempt to force a northwest passage. The vessels never returned to Hawai'i.

Clerke sailed directly north to the Kamchatka Peninsula, where the Russians assisted with ship repairs and the expedition picked up further supplies. By then Clerke was suffering with tuberculosis, but the expedition made a second attempt to sail beyond Bering Strait, albeit without success. Clerke died in Petropavlosk on 22 August, and command of the expedition fell upon John Gore, with James King captaining the *Discovery*. The ships returned home via the east coast of Japan, Macao and the East India Company trade route around the Cape of Good Hope, arriving at Sheerness, England, on 4 October 1780. It was to a subdued welcome, news of Cook's and Clerke's deaths having reached England some months before.

A fateful European encounter

> Wednesday's *and* Thursday's Posts.
> *From the* LONDON GAZETTE.
> *Admiralty-Office, January* 11, 1780.
> CAPT. Clerke, of his Majesty's Sloop the Resolution, in a Letter to Mr. Stephens, dated the 8th of June, 1779, in the Harbour of St. Peter and St. Paul, Kampfchatka, which was received Yesterday, gives the melancholy Account of the celebrated Capt. Cook, late Commander of that Sloop, with four of his private Mariners, having been killed on the 14th of February last at the Island of O'why'he, one of a Group of new-discovered Islands, in the 22d Degree of North Latitude, in an Affray with a numerous and tumultuous Body of the Natives. Capt. Clerke adds, that he had received every friendly Supply from the Russian Government; and that as the Companies of the Resolution and her Consort the Discovery were in perfect Health, and the two Sloops had twelve Months Stores and Provisions on board, he was preparing to make another Attempt to explore a Northern Passage to Europe. *Gaz.*

◀ Headlined 'Melancholy Account of the Celebrated Capt. Cook', the first report the British public had of Cook's death was in a letter written by Captain Charles Clerke from Kamchatka in Russia to Philip Stevens, Secretary to the Admiralty and Member of Parliament.
Wikimedia Commons

Other voices

The previous accounts of the Cook expedition's two visits to Niʻihau are drawn almost exclusively from the journals of the expedition's leaders. There are several other accounts of these visits, which in some instances shine a little more light on events. Perhaps the most insightful is that of David Samwell, assistant surgeon on the *Resolution* on the ships' first visit to Niʻihau, and surgeon on the *Discovery* on their second. Samwell was the son of a Welsh vicar and received a grammar school education before being apprenticed to a naval surgeon. He obtained his certificate as second mate from the Royal College of Surgeons in 1775, and was subsequently appointed surgeon's mate on the *Resolution*.

Although according to his writings, the prohibition of any contact with the women on Niʻihau by the crews was paramount in Cook's mind, Samwell's journal indicates that Lieutenant Gore and his men were deliberately left ashore overnight for procurement of supplies, rather than being marooned ashore by the weather. This is at odds with Cook's own account. On 29 January 1778 Samwell writes: 'The first Lieut. with some more people staid on shore to attend the market & purchase Hogs and other Provisions from the Natives & took up Residence in one of their Houses.'[30]

And on 31 January, Samwell gives, in rather poetic language, a more extensive picture of the priestess Cook saw across the valley while on his stroll through the Niihauan countryside.

▲ David Samwell (1751–98), a Welshman, was surgeon's mate on the *Resolution* during the greater part of Cook's third voyage. After Cook's death he became surgeon on the *Discovery*. His journal of the voyage adds useful sidelights to the official account. He was described as 'tall, stout, blackhaired, pockmarked, fierce looking, wondrous friendly in company'.
Wikimedia Commons

> An old woman named Waratoi whom we supposed to be mad lived with our people all the time they were on shore; she performed daily some religious Ceremonies as we supposed them to be, & offered Up some small pigs as Sacrifices for some purpose, and used many Extravagant Gestures like the Thracian Priestesses of old as if possessed with some fury; this woman had much Influence over the Indians & was of some use to us in causing them to bring Provisions to Market &c. However her Function which we

◆ Sailing canoes off Ni'ihau: John Webber's sketch from the *Resolution*'s anchorage. The formidable peak of Kawaihoa is at right.
Hawaiian Historical Society

supposed to be that of a Priestess was no bar to the Performance of her Devotions at the Temple of Venus, for like the rest of her Countrywomen she scrupled not to grant every favour to our people, tho' with no mercenary View as she would take nothing from them in return. Indeed we found all the Women of these Islands but little influenced by interested motives in their intercourse with us, as they would almost use violence to force you into their Embrace regardless whether we gave them any thing or not, and in general they were as fine Girls as any we had seen in the south Sea Islands.[31]

When Cook was finally able to bring his men off Ni'ihau, Samwell reports:

> … on their coming away the old Priestess performed various Ceremonies & killed several small Pigs by striking their Heads against a Stone, which were intended as Tokens of Friendship towards us & the Indians seemed to regret much our leaving the Island so soon. They behaved all the time in a very peaceable & friendly manner.[32]

That same evening the *Resolution* departed her Ni'ihau anchorage. From the tone of his journal, we can assume that Samwell himself did not stay ashore and experience these scenes at first hand. He must, however, have talked at length to those who had been involved to have written such a detailed account of Waratoi's unusual behavior.

On their return to the islands 14 months later the ships anchored again off Waimea, Kaua'i, to get water and, as mentioned earlier, a menacing incident occurred on 1 March 1779, which Samwell records:

> In the Afternoon the Resolution's Launch & Pinnace were sent ashore for water under the Command of the 1st Lieutenant. A great number of Indians were collected together at the Town of Owaimea and our people had hardly landed before the Natives stole a Bucket, and presently after attempted to snatch away the Cooper's Bag of Tools; they grew very troublesome & many of them were armed with Clubs and Spears, so that our people were obliged to be strictly on their guard to prevent a general attack from them; they made several attempts to seize their Arms from the Marines, one of them snatched the Serjeant's Hat off his head & got clear off with it, for it would have been rash to fire at any of them while our people were ashore … As they were getting into the Boats they

snatched the Lieut's Hanger [small sword] from him, when our people had all embarked they fired three Muskets at them & killed one Man but not the Thief.³³

This rendering of the incident accords with that of Lt King, the officer in charge, but contrasts wildly with John Rickman's in his 1781 book on the voyage:

> … but when our casks were landed, in order to exchange our water (that of O-why-he being both bitter and brackish, and the water here excellent) the coopers were no sooner set to work, than one Indian snatched up his adze, another his bucket, a third his bag of nails, and so on; and this among a croud of natives of 4 or 500 in number. To put a stop to these depredations, orders were given to fire over their heads; but this not having the desired effect, a gun from the ships threw them all into confusion. Two were seen to drop, and by the shrieks and cries of the women, more were supposed to have been killed or wounded. For a while the multitude retreated; but being rallied by some of their chiefs, who doubtless had heard that we were not invulnerable, they returned in greater numbers than before, when it was thought prudent to lay aside watering, and to provide for our own safety. All hands were now ordered to their posts, and an engagement commenced in earnest, when the Indians instantly gave way, after a few being killed and wounded by our fire, and they never again offered the least violence during our stay.³⁴

Rickman's book, published anonymously, was the first to be sold, in a market which was itching for an authoritative account. J.C. Beaglehole, in his magisterial publication on the third voyage, was dismissive of Rickman's effort: 'The book can be taken as a source, where it is verifiable, or even likely … but on the whole it is a fanciful and ridiculously exaggerated production, done exclusively for the market. The romantic strain is strong …'³⁵

The above extract would appear to bear this out. Although the incident took place on Kauaʻi just before the expedition's second visit to Niʻihau, it is included as an example of the differences between accounts, for political, marketing or other reasons.

Surgeon William Ellis gives a further, apparently unadorned, version of the event, more akin to Lieutenant King's:

> At one in the afternoon, the Resolution's launch was sent on shore for a load of water, attended by the large cutter, to traffick with the natives. Upon the first landing of our people, they were very civil, but soon began their old trade of thieving, which they were the more encouraged to do, as our party was but small. The first attempt was upon one of the water buckets; which one of them made off with: a musket was fired at him, but without effect. The next thing was the cooper's bag, in which there luckily was nothing but a few bungs; the third was Mr. King's hanger, which they snatched out of his hand. Having with much difficulty filled all the casks, they were got off, and our people were preparing to embark: some of them were already in the boats, when the Indians pressed close upon them, and attempted to wrench the muskets out of their hands; and one of them threw a stone at the serjeant of marines, which knocked off his hat, upon which orders were given to fire, which three of the marines did, and killed or mortally wounded one of them. This threw them into some confusion, which our people took the advantage of, and put off.³⁶

Ellis was reputed to have been educated at Cambridge University and St Bartholomew's Hospital. Samwell says of Ellis's two-volume account of the expedition, '… the Language is good but there is no Spirit in the Narrative … he tells no Lies 'tis true

▲ John Webber (1751–93) was the official artist on Cook's final voyage. His output of sketches and finished paintings during the voyage was prodigious. He was born in London, educated in Bern, and studied painting in Paris before being selected for the voyage on the recommendation of Daniel Solander, botanist on Cook's first voyage. Back in England after the voyage in 1780 he exhibited works at the Royal Academy, of which he was made a member in 1791.

Painting by Johann Daniel Mottet. Bernisches Historiches Museum, Bern / Wikimedia Commons

▲ After the ships' first visit to Kaua'i and Ni'ihau, William Ellis reflected on the lives of the Hawaiians: 'Besides these [canoes] they have another means of conveying themselves in the water upon very light flat pieces of board …' Lieutenant James King also marvels at their surfing skills in his journal. This image, the first known depiction of a surfer by a European artist, is an enlargement from an etching of John Webber's watercolor of Kealakekua Bay with the ships at anchor.
'A view of Karakakooa, in Owyhee', John Webber

but then he does not tell you half the odd adventures we met with; it is an unentertaining outline of the voyage …'[37] From this short extract we can perhaps identify with Samwell's comments, even if they were made by an interested party.

Another quite different view of these happenings is given by John Ledyard, an American recruited as a marine on the *Resolution*, whose account was published in Connecticut in 1783. He writes that from the canoes that approached the ships on their arrival at Waimea this second time they understood that the Hawaiians were justifiably angry on account of the sickness and deaths venereal disease had caused, which they rightly attributed to the ships' first visit. He says they were also aware of what had taken place at Kealakekua Bay, which had shown the Europeans to be mere mortals:

The only hopes then that we had of being able to land and water here, were either those that originated from bestowing great presents on all the chiefs at least: and those of mere force, or perhaps a little of each, which indeed was the case. We were on shore three successive days with all the force we could spare from the ships, but had not the chiefs exerted themselves in the most strenuous manner in our favor, they certainly would have attacked us, though they still stood awed when they saw our little intrepid handfull; and so far our force was of service to us: and it was best not put to a further proof, for there were more than 15000 of the natives round us every day, and above half that number fighting men.[38]

He makes no mention of the affray that took place on the first day, but from the way he writes he cannot have been a participant, despite being a marine on the *Resolution*. Certainly on the following days, when all the marines from both ships were ashore to protect the watering party, he writes as if he were involved, but his interest is in the causes of the unrest rather than the actions taken. He makes no attempt to describe his involvement, but wildly overestimates the number of locals.

Although these matters took place on Kaua'i rather than Ni'ihau, the various accounts show how the different writers dealt with the same subject, and in general how each contributed to a more colorful and rounded picture of what took place, even if requiring some reflection on the part of the reader. The affair also serves to indicate the trepidation with which the expedition approached Ni'ihau in search of yams to complete their victualling for the journey to Bering Strait.

The accounts by Ledyard and Rickman of their visits to Ni'ihau add little to what has already been said, but all the writers, upon leaving the archipelago for the second and last time, made observations on the islands and their inhabitants. Later commentators have been amazed at the knowledge obtained during these brief stays, although the writers had the advantage of a considerable sojourn in Polynesia with the time spent in both New Zealand and the Society Islands, and thus had a basis for cultural comparisons.

A fateful European encounter

The most relevant account from the point of view of Ni'ihau is that of William Ellis, whose comments were made at the conclusion of his first visit, before their time at Kealakekua Bay on their second visit. About their houses, canoes and surfing he writes:

> The houses of the natives are in general situated near the shore, and placed in clusters, so as to form small towns or villages. Their external appearance greatly resembles the top of a barn placed upon the ground, with a small entrance in the middle. Some of them were elevated upon posts about three feet high, particularly those nearest the sea; from which we may conclude, that they are during some parts of the year subject to inundations. They are well thatched on the outside with dry grass, so as totally to prevent the entrance of rain. The floor is also well strewed with dry grass, upon which mats of various sizes and dimensions are placed. These mats are of a very close, compact texture, and made of different patterns, some of which are really elegant. They vary greatly in their degree of fineness. Their canoes or boats are the neatest we ever saw, and composed of two different coloured woods, the bottom being dark, the upper part light, and furnished with an out-rigger. Besides these, they have another means of conveying themselves in the water, upon very light flat pieces of board, which we called shark-boards, from the similitude the anterior part bore to the head of that fish. Upon these they will venture into the heaviest surfs, and paddling with their hands and feet, get on at a great rate. Indeed, we never saw people so active in the water, which almost seems their natural element.
>
> O'neehow [Ni'ihau], which is the westernmost island, is very small, and rather low. It produces sugar-cane, plantains, sweet potatoes, yams, and salt; in the two latter articles it exceeds A'towi [Kaua'i]. The inhabitants are not numerous; their houses, &c. are exactly like those of the above mentioned isle.[39]

▲ John Ledyard (1751–89) was a marine on the *Resolution* on Cook's third voyage. Born in Connecticut, he briefly attended Dartmouth College before signing on as a seaman on trading voyages to Europe. He eventually jumped ship in England, where he was pressganged into the Royal Navy and joined Cook's expedition. As a marine he later fought briefly for the British in the American Revolution, before deserting and retiring to Dartmouth where he completed writing a colorful account of the voyage with Cook. His later life was one of travel and adventure, before accidentally poisoning himself with sulphuric acid in Egypt at the age of 38.
Wikimedia Commons

◀ After the traumatic events at Kealakekua Bay on 14 February 1779 and revictualling in the islands, the *Resolution* and *Discovery* depart Ni'ihau and the Sandwich Islands for the second and last time on 15 March 1779. Whilst there is controversy over Cook's role as 'an enabler of colonialism' and the violence associated with his contacts with indigenous peoples, he left a legacy of scientific and geographical knowledge that influenced his successors well into the 20th century. Numerous memorials worldwide have been dedicated to him.
Wikimedia Commons

As well as describing the Niihauan houses and canoes, this is the first portrayal for European readers of the sport of surfing, in which Niihauans excelled.

The news of the first documented contact with the Hawaiian archipelago and its inhabitants by Europeans, along with the death of Captain James Cook at the hands of the Hawaiians, reached Europe overland many months before the two ships arrived back at Sheerness at the mouth of the River Medway in Kent, downstream from Chatham Naval Dockyard, in October 1780. The news set in motion a wave of explorers, traders, adventurers and scientists who visited and interacted with the people of the land, and Niʻihau in particular, which is the subject of the following chapter.

▶ Makaloa mat presented by Charles Clerke to the governor of Kamchatka.

From the collection of the Peter the Great Museum of Anthropology and Ethnography (Kunstkamera), Russian Academy of Sciences

CHAPTER FOUR

EARLY WESTERN VOYAGERS

It was over seven years before the next European ships appeared on the horizon. On 8 June 1786 Captains Nathaniel Portlock and George Dixon arrived in their British vessels *King George* and *Queen Charlotte* and anchored off the spot William Bligh had discovered on the west side of Niʻihau, known as Yam Bay. Both Portlock and Dixon had been with Cook on his third voyage — Portlock as master's mate on the *Discovery* (and after Clerke's death in August 1779, on the *Resolution*) and Dixon as armorer on the *Discovery*.

Yams and the sea otter fur trade

From their experiences on the Cook voyage they saw opportunities for sea otter skin trading on the northwest coast of America and lobbied influential people in London who were aware of the burgeoning market for furs in China. In 1785 a partnership was formed, which included Portlock and Dixon, and was commonly known as the King George's Sound Company, to develop the fur trade in the region. King George's Sound (now known as Nootka Sound) is a series of inlets on the rugged west coast of Vancouver Island, and was intended as a base. Portlock and Dixon knew the area, having visited it with Cook seven years earlier.

◀ The sea otter (*Enhydra lutris*). In April 1778 Captain Cook wrote: 'The fur of these animals … is certainly softer and finer than that of any others we know of; and, therefore, the discovery of this part of the continent of North America, where so valuable an article of commerce may be met with, cannot be a matter of indifference.'

Engraving by Peter Mazell based on a drawing by John Webber/Wikimedia Commons

The two ships left England on 2 September 1785 and rounded Cape Horn in January 1786, before reaching Hawai'i on 24 May 1786. They anchored in Kealakekua Bay on the Big Island, but the crush of canoes and people around the ships and on the beach was such that they didn't venture ashore, and instead set sail. They ranged along the south side of O'ahu, replenishing their water from calabashes brought out by the Hawaiians, before making for Ni'ihau. Portlock wanted yams:

> Having completed our water, and procured such refreshments as Woahoo [O'ahu] afforded, I determined to proceed to Oneehow [Ni'ihau] without loss of time, in order to get a supply of yams, which I knew that island produced in great plenty and perfection.[1]

Some days later, having reached Yam Bay:

> No sooner were we moored, than several canoes visited us, bringing yams, sweet potatoes, and a few small pigs; for which we gave in exchange nails and beads. Amongst the people in these canoes were several whose faces I remembered to have seen when at this island before; particularly an old priest, in whose house a party of us took up our abode, when detained all night on shore by a heavy surf, and who treated us in a very friendly manner.[2]

So Portlock had been one of the party which Cook had to leave on shore overnight in 1778, and the stay is credited with introducing venereal disease to the islands. The following morning …

> A chief, named Abbenooe, whom I knew when at this island before, also paid me a visit, and recognized his old acquaintance the moment he came on board. Having appointed six persons to trade with the natives for yams, and given orders to have them dried and stowed away, I went on shore in search of the wells mentioned by Mr. Bligh, accompanied by Abbenooe as a guide.[3]

Abbenooe — 'Ōpūnui — is also named in Dixon's parallel account of the voyage as the principal chief of Ni'ihau and is described as 'a very active, intelligent person.' The travelers understood that Ni'ihau 'belonged to Ta'aao [Ka'eo], king of Atou'i [Kaua'i]' and that 'Ōpūnui governed the island in the king's absence. 'Ōpūnui is not named in the journals of Cook's voyage seven years earlier. Portlock ventured further:

> After examining these wells, I made an excursion into the country, accompanied by Abbenooe, and a few of the natives. The island appears well cultivated; its principal produce is yams. There are besides, sweet potatoes, sugar-cane, and the sweet root which is called *tee* by the natives. A few trees are scattered here and there, but in little order or variety. Some that grew near the well just mentioned were about fifteen feet high, and proportionably thick; with spreading branches, and a smooth bark; the leaves were round, and they bore a kind of nut somewhat resembling our walnut. Another kind were nine feet high, and had blossoms of a beautiful pink colour. I also noticed another variety, with nuts growing on them like our horse chestnut. These nuts, I understand, the inhabitants use as a substitute for candles, and they give a most excellent light.[4]

Nathaniel Portlock thus became the next European person after Cook himself to walk through the Niihauan countryside. The ships spent the next four days trading for yams and pigs. Although Ka'eo was not present, Portlock sent some gifts for him and two days later the king reciprocated, his messenger returning from Kaua'i 'accompanied by

▲ Nathaniel Portlock (c.1748–1817), a British naval officer who sailed as master's mate on Cook's third voyage. After the voyage he formed a consortium, the King George's Sound Company, to exploit the sea otter fur trade on the northwest coast of America and sailed in command of the company's two ships in 1785. Later he returned to the Royal Navy, retiring as a commander in 1807.
Wikimedia Commons

▲ The leaves, flowers and nuts of the kukui or candlenut tree. The trees were one of those commented upon as growing on Ni'ihau as Portlock walked about the island.
Kim and Forest Starr / Wikimedia Commons

Early Western voyagers

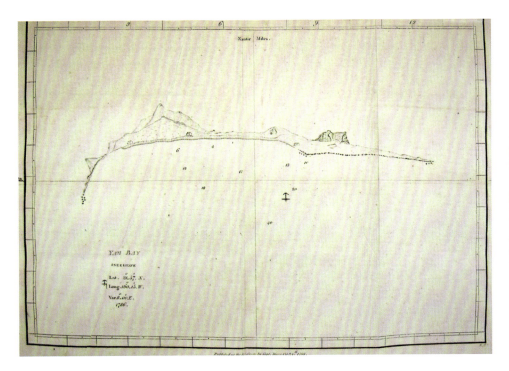

◀ A perspective of Yam Bay — Nonopapa — on the west coast of Ni'ihau. It was drawn from the ship in 1786 and included in George Dixon's journal of the voyage of the *Queen Charlotte*. The map has north to the left, and land features are shown in elevation. Depths are in fathoms and the *Queen Charlotte*'s anchorage location is shown.
Hawaiian Historical Society

◀◀ The 305-ton *King George*, Nathaniel Portlock's flagship on his trading voyage to the northwest coast of America. Bought 'off the stocks' in 1785 by the King George's Sound Company, she carried a crew of 59 for her three-year journey.
Part of an engraving by Peter Mazell based on a sketch by I Woodcock / Wikimedia Commons

◀ The *Queen Charlotte* was ordered by the King George's Sound Company, and launched in 1785. Under George Dixon she sailed with the *King George* on their voyage which began the sea otter fur trade from the northwest coast of America to China. The 220-ton vessel carried a complement of 33.
Part of an engraving by Peter Mazell from a drawing by I Woodcock / Wikimedia Commons

two double canoes which brought a number of fine hogs to be disposed of, together with taro and sugar-cane.' Portlock's mission was successful:

> Since our arrival at the Sandwich Islands, we had salted on board the King George seven tierces [casks holding 42 US gallons] and two hogsheads [63 US gallons] of pork, besides two tierces of bones …
>
> … we had procured near ten tons of fine yams, and captain Dixon had got about eight tons on the Queen Charlotte. The health of both ships crews was well re-established …
>
> At five o'clock in the morning of the 13th [June 1786] we unmoored, and at eight o'clock we weighed and got under sail, standing out of the bay (which obtained the name of Yam Bay, from the great quantity of yams we procured in it) with a fresh breeze at North East…⁵

A little over a month later they made landfall off Alaska at Cook's River. The vessels stayed on the coast for almost three months purchasing sea otter and other furs before retracing their steps to Hawai'i, with a snow-clad Mauna Kea joyfully sighted on 14 November. Two weeks later, having been resupplied by the islanders as they sailed

77

west along the north coast of Hawai'i and Maui, the ships anchored in Wai'alae Bay for repairs. Almost three weeks were spent in the bay, and a ready supply of pigs, vegetables, water and firewood was brought to the ships as the weather allowed. They sailed for Kaua'i on 20 December and anchored off Waimea two days later. Having walked the coast from Waimea to the Nā Pali cliffs in an unsuccessful search for a safer haven for his vessels, Portlock concluded:

> Being now well assured that Atoui afforded no place for the ships to ride in equal to Wymoa Bay, I determined to keep our situation a short time, for the purpose of salting pork for sea-store, and afterwards to proceed to Oneehow [Ni'ihau] for a supply of yams, and to remain there till the proper season for the prosecution of our voyage to the coast of America.[6]

This was not quite to be. After reprovisioning in Waimea, it was 16 January 1787 before they anchored at their old location in Yam Bay at Ni'ihau. 'Ōpūnui ('Abbenooe') had come from Waimea with them, and after lunch, when the surf had moderated, he and Portlock took the whaleboat and found a place to anchor it safely while they transferred to a canoe. The canoe overturned in the violent waves, however, and they swam for shore. As at Waimea, they searched along the coast for a more sheltered anchorage, to no avail:

> The country seemed very poorly cultivated, and Abbenooe told me, that since we took our stock of yams in [six months earlier], the people have in a great measure neglected the island, barely planting enough for their own use; and that some had entirely left the island, and taken up their future residence in Atoui.[7]

And later Portlock reflects in a similarly downcast vein:

> … probably the iron which they procured from us formerly, enabled them to purchase possessions in Atoui; as Oneehow is but a poor spot, abounding in scarce anything but yams, potatoes, sugar-cane, and the sweet root, with a very trifling quantity of wood: whereas Atoui is amply provided with many articles of provisions, particularly the taro, which the natives prefer to yams or potatoes; and I am sensible that none of them will live at Oneehow that can procure a sufficiency to reside at Atoui.[8]

This is very different from his comments on the cultivations seen during his visit six months earlier. There is no mention of drought. Knowing that the vessels were coming back, they might have planted yams for further trading. If Portlock is correct in his musings, there seems to be no element of greed in their nature. The situation is difficult at this distance to fathom, but the explanation may be as simple as that yams took a year or more to grow and their seed stock may have been depleted.

The surf ran high for the next few days and there were further boat overturnings. On 20 January, in a rising gale, Portlock had to run out of Yam Bay, leaving three invalids ashore. It was almost a week before he could regain his anchorage and pick up his crew members. Valuable anchors were lost in the process. Two days later he abandoned Yam Bay again because of the weather and sailed back to Waimea, where conditions were easier. The ships stayed almost a month for reprovisioning and maintenance, but Portlock was determined to recover the anchors he had lost. This he achieved on 17 February, and also secured a small store of yams before returning to Waimea. Both ships sailed on 3 March 1787 for their second visit to North America. Niʻihau had been a disappointment in terms of the weather and the supply of yams.

Their passage to the northwest coast took six weeks and they arrived at the entrance to Prince William Sound on 24 April in latitude 60°. On 10 May they met the trading vessel *Nootka*, captained by John Meares. He had wintered over in Prince William Sound and had lost half of his crew to the cold and scurvy. Portlock gave him supplies and even two seamen to assist his voyage back to China. As trading was slack Portlock and Dixon separated, with the *Queen Charlotte* under Dixon going direct to King George's Sound to forestall other possible traders. The *King George* under Portlock traded along the coast, finally leaving for a third wintering visit to Hawaiʻi on 22 August 1787.

Having stocked up with hogs and vegetables as the *King George* sailed along the coast of Hawaiʻi, Portlock made directly for Kauaʻi in the hope of making contact with the *Queen Charlotte* at Waimea. Two days later, off the southern point of Kauaʻi, he learned that the *Nootka* and the *Queen Charlotte* had visited the island. The *Nootka* sailed straight to Niʻihau without anchoring and stayed there for a few days, presumably purchasing yams. Portlock also learned that Dixon had left a letter for him with ʻŌpūnui.[9]

The letter was kapu and could only be released under ʻŌpūnui's direction, and as he was on Niʻihau with the king, Portlock headed immediately to Niʻihau. He would seek yams and send a messenger to Kauaʻi for the letter.[10] On his arrival at Yam Bay:

> My old friend [ʻŌpūnui] acquainted me of the Nootka having sailed from this place about a month ago, and captain Dixon having sailed from Atooi about eighteen or twenty days ago. He gave me to understand that the Nootka and them parted on bad terms, but that captain Dixon and they parted on terms perfectly friendly. He told me that they had been fired on by the Nootka, but that no person had been hurt … [11]

ʻŌpūnui sent to Waimea for Dixon's letter and it arrived on 7 October:

> … at eight in the morning the messenger returned from Atoui with captain Dixon's letter, which I found dated the 18th of September; and that he had left the [American] coast on the 9th of August, all well, and with fifteen hundred skins. He likewise informed me, that off King George's Sound he fell in with a ship and sloop under Company's colours; I should suppose our Company's [The King George's Sound Company], the ship called the Prince of Wales, commanded by a captain Colnett … Captain Colnett informed him that he had just come out of King George's Sound; at which place he had found lying a ship under Imperial colours, commanded by captain Barclay, and manned by Englishmen.[12]

As far as the supply of yams was concerned, Portlock's visit to Niʻihau was more successful than the last. On the same day (7 October) he wrote:

> In the evening busily employed in purchasing yams and water; and by six o'clock had completed that business; having procured about twelve tons of yams, a quantity of potatoes, and filled seven butts and two puncheons of water … [13]

Having written a letter for Captain Colnett that he left with ʻŌpūnui, he sailed later in the evening for Macao, and on to England.

So ended the second set of visits to Niʻihau by a pair of European ships. The visit of the *Nootka* under Captain Meares was clearly not a success and marks the first time Europeans used violence against the Niihauans. No other records of the incident appear

▲ John Meares (c.1756–1809), an entrepreneurial and controversial trader of sea otter skins in the late 1780s. He visited Niʻihau at least three times for yams. Meares began his career in the Royal Navy before becoming attracted by the otter fur possibilities on the northwest coast. He later returned to the navy, retiring with the rank of commander.
Wikimedia Commons

◤ *The Launch of the North West America at Nootka Sound*, an engraving in John Meares' journal of the voyage. The sloop *North West America* was the first European vessel constructed on the northwest coast and the launch took place in September 1788. The engraving is regarded as a fanciful representation of the occasion. In the background may be seen Meares' two vessels, the *Felice Adventurero* and the *Iphigenia Nubiana*, the latter captained by William Douglas.

Engraving by R Pollard based on a drawing by C. Metz / Wikimedia Commons

to exist other than those quoted, and what provoked the hostilities is not recorded. Meares' own published journal does not mention the incident, nor the *Nootka*'s stay at Ni'ihau, speaking only of the vessel's visit to Hawai'i in general terms.[14]

John Meares' backers for the *Nootka* voyage were a consortium of British expatriates centered on Calcutta. The voyage was a financial failure, but Meares had considerable powers of persuasion and it wasn't long before he found financiers to back a second voyage, and the Bengal Fur Company was founded. The company secured and fitted out two vessels, the *Felice Adventurero*, captained by Meares, and the *Iphigenia Nubiana*.

Thus in October 1788 John Meares paid a second visit to Ni'ihau, this time on the *Felice Adventurero*, sailing under the Portuguese flag, but in reality a British vessel. The East India Company had a statutory monopoly on British trade in the Pacific, and the King George's Sound Company had obtained the necessary licenses from them to trade. The Bengal Fur Company had not, and traded out of Macao under the Portuguese flag.

The two ships left for the American seaboard in January 1788 and spent the summer on the Alaskan coast. The *Felice* was carrying Chinese construction workers and building materials for a Nootka Sound trading post and a coastal trading vessel. The *North West America*, a 40-ton schooner, was launched in September 1788. After his experience on his first voyage, Meares left Nootka Sound for Hawai'i, reaching Maui on 18 October, and Ni'ihau on 25 October for yams, before returning to Macao. Meares' journal does not allude to what had occurred on his first visit:

> On arriving off this island [Ni'ihau] we did not experience the operations of any prohibition against us; on the contrary, we were surrounded by a crowd of natives, among whom were many of our old friends, whom we perfectly recollected, so that the ship was very shortly filled with visitors of all ages and both sexes ...

> We had at this time neither bread or flour on board, and depended on procuring a quantity of yams sufficient to supply our wants during the remainder of the voyage. But as this was not the season for them, and they were too young to be dug up, we should have found it a matter of great difficulty to have obtained a sufficient quantity, if our friend Friday [a Niihauan who had befriended them on their first visit] had not undertaken the important negotiation. ... we at length obtained several tons of these most necessary provisions by the morning of the 27th; and at noon prepared to put to sea.
>
> I am really at a loss how to describe the very marked concern, both in words and looks, that the inhabitants of this island expressed, when they were informed of our approaching departure.[15]

'Friday' was well paid for his negotiating skills and there is perhaps a lesson here for other seafaring captains. 'Friday' was doubtless from the aliʻi, but he was not ʻŌpūnui, who is mentioned earlier in John Meares' account. ʻŌpūnui was on Kauaʻi at this time.

Meares' account is at odds with his private view of the Niihauans and their leaders. As he left the American coast he wrote to Captain Douglas of the *Iphigenia Nubiana*:

> The savage fierceness of the people of Wahoo [Oʻahu], will, I should suppose, render your stay at that island very short. The populousness of Atooi [Kauaʻi] may deter you from making any long stay in Wymeo Bay [Waimea Bay]. You will therefore finally close your route at Onehow [Niʻihau] where I trust you will guard carefully against the art and cunning of Taheo [Kaʻeo] and Abinui [ʻŌpūnui] for I think them dreadful, mercenary, artful villians.[16]

Was he referring obliquely here to whatever had happened on his first visit to Niʻihau?

Meanwhile the *Iphigenia* and the *North West America* were making ready to winter over in Hawaiʻi, which they reached on 6 December 1788. They spent over three months around the coasts of the islands, but only the last couple of days at Niʻihau to pick up yams for the return journey.

Cruising around tropical islands for three months playing a waiting game for the northern spring to return cannot have been easy for Captain Douglas and his crew on the *Iphigenia*. Idleness tends to breed dissatisfaction, particularly when living conditions are necessarily cramped. This boiled over at Niʻihau when a plot was discovered, led by the quartermaster, to steal the jolly boat (see illustration) and burn the ship — to what purpose is not entirely clear. Despite a strict watch being kept to foil any action, the ringleader and two sailors escaped ashore in canoes. The two sailors were caught and promptly returned to the ship by 'Friday,' Douglas's local ally. But when the quartermaster was found he could not be taken off in the rising surf and was left behind, thus becoming the first European inhabitant of Niʻihau.[17]

The *Iphigenia* visited the islands again for a month in July/August 1789, but Meares' journal (written on William Douglas's behalf) gives no detail. In all probability the ship visited Niʻihau to barter for yams again for the journey back to China.

While Meares and Douglas had been trading on the American coast, the King George's Sound Company had not been idle. Captain Dixon of the *Queen Charlotte* had met another company vessel, the *Prince of Wales*, commanded by James Colnett, in Nootka Sound. The latter sailed from England in September 1786, a year after Portlock and Dixon, together with another company vessel, the *Princess Royal*, under James

▲ In the 18th century the jolly boat was the smallest boat carried on sailing ships, used to take people and goods from ship to shore and to enable maintenance on the exterior of the ship. The jolly boat was between 16 and 18 feet long, clinker built, and rowed by four or six oarsmen. When not in use it was normally slung across the stern of the ship on davits. Some, such as the one illustrated, could also be sailed.
Wikipedia Commons, colorised

Duncan. The two ships rounded Cape Horn together and traded for furs in the late summer of 1787.

Colnett and Dixon then wintered over together in Hawai'i, arriving on 2 January 1788 for a ten-week stay. Their main objective was to obtain food, water, wood — and women, while awaiting the opening of the 1788 fur trading season on the northwest coast. The crews had not eaten fresh food for 15 months. They arrived off the north coast of Hawai'i purchasing supplies from canoes, and slowly worked their way west, with their first anchorage off the western end of Moloka'i on 15 January where they stayed five days. Stealing of iron of any sort, particularly boat fittings, was a major problem with ever more devious stratagems being used. The two ships moved on to anchor off Waikīkī:, which they found to be a much more bounteous area, but the pilfering was even more of a problem with over 1000 canoes surrounding the ships at times. Trading for supplies was no problem, but security was, and they sailed for Kaua'i a few days later.

In reading Colnett's account, wintering over in the islands between fur trading seasons was a time for rest and recreation for all concerned, and Colnett's liberal leadership style does not seem to have engendered any discontent among the crew. There was no urgency to their travels around the islands as the American northwest coast could not sensibly be approached until April.

The two vessels anchored off Waimea, Kaua'i, on 30 January 1788, still wary of the locals after Dixon's warnings and the incessant attempts at thieving. 'Ōpūnui again proved helpful in assisting in trading, but the relationship was uneasy. Captain Duncan was less tolerant than Colnett and on 14 February fired on two swimmers, which caused 'Ōpūnui to place a kapu on the *Princess Royal* and not a single canoe came near until the kapu was lifted a day later. Several other kapu followed and relations deteriorated until on 23 February 'Ōpūnui banned all women from the ships on pain of death to their fathers. This was too much for two of the girls, who confessed to some crew members that it was the intention of the priests to poison the two crews on the following day, using the food to be supplied as the vehicle. Thus forewarned, the plan could not be enacted, but the bower anchor cable of the *Prince of Wales* was found slack and on hauling in the cable it was revealed the cable had been cut just above the anchor — the loss of an anchor was a most serious matter. The anchor was swept for using a grapnel, but without success. All Hawaiians were kept away from the ships by firing warning shots to prevent the loss of a further anchor. Duncan was more ruthless and fired a cannon full of musket balls at an approaching canoe, killing all aboard.

This event triggered a rapid exit by both vessels to Ni'ihau before news of the massacre arrived, as yams were still required for the onward journey. Colnett's journal:

> I told Capt. Duncan we would beat up to windward for a day or two but he advis'd me to go to Oneehow [Ni'ihau] before the news, & get our stock of Yams which advice I follow'd.[18]

The ships anchored in Yam Bay (Nonopapa), and the following morning:

> Wednesday Morning February 27th many Canoes from all parts of the Isle loaded with Yams, wood, water, salt, salt fish, & fresh fish, which they readily bartered for small nails, beads, & fish Hooks ...[19]

Colnett, however, had seen one of the anchors Portlock had lost the previous year on the beach at Waimea:

> I had determin'd with myself to get under weigh beat over to Atooi [Kauaʻi] & by some Strategem get the Anchor We saw near Tyo's [Kaʻeo's] house which was nearly the weight of our bower [anchor] …[20]

This he proceeded to do and having first negotiated a truce, Colnett persevered, and after over two weeks of discussions the anchor was brought aboard in exchange for two muskets, two pistols, ammunition, five iron bars and sundry tools. He then sailed back to Niʻihau where he was able to barter for yams and other articles.[21]

On 18 March the two ships returned to the northwest coast for another summer's fur trading. It had certainly been an eventful winter at the islands. This second season they operated separately, but agreed to rendezvous in Hawaiʻi in September 1788, before sailing to Canton where they arrived late November. Colnett's journal finishes when the *Prince of Wales* left the coast but a second journal of the voyage, written by the third mate, Andrew Taylor, still exists. The *Prince of Wales* 'stood in for the land' on 10 September at Hawaiʻi where the *Princess Royal* joined her two days later. The ships worked their way west, anchoring off Molokaʻi and Oʻahu for supplies, before reaching Kauaʻi on 18 September. Their time here was uneasy with many kapu proclaimed and provisions not easily obtained. As a consequence on 25 September the vessels sailed for Niʻihau after a most frustrating visit to Waimea.

Having first anchored in Cook's old spot, they moved to Yam Bay where trading 'in great abundance' took place. 'Abanuez [ʻŌpūnui] received a good quantity of Powder by Barter.' Colnett had few scruples when it came to supplying guns and ammunition and 'ʻŌpūnui couldn't get enough. By the time they left Taylor comments 'they Will shortly have a tolerable stock of Guns.' Their friendship with 'ʻŌpūnui, sparked by his interest in muskets and powder, and their interest in securing supplies and women, brought lavish results in terms of provisions. Taylor again: 'by being in friendship with Abanuez we received Bananas Plantains Cocoa nuts Bread fruit sweet potatoes'[22] in addition to the usual yams. Were these all being grown on Niʻihau at this time or were they being brought from Kauaʻi? The latter would have been a massive logistical exercise.

After four days at Yam Bay, on 29 September they sailed away with heavy hearts. As Taylor says, 'I declare for myself it was some hours ere I rallied my spirits … but the females particularly made one feel rather uncomfortable at parting.' The vessels had spent just two weeks at the islands, ostensibly for supplies for the long journey to Macao.

The voyage has been described as one of the most profitable to that date. John Meares had remained in China and successful discussions took place over the winter on merging the Bengal Fur Company with the King George's Sound Company to form a combined enterprise — known by several names, but called here the South Seas Company of London. The venture funded a further voyage to the northwest coast, retaining James Colnett as overall commander, this time on the newly purchased *Argonaut*. He was accompanied by the *Princess Royal* sailing under Thomas Hudson.

The *Argonaut* and the *Prince of Wales* arrived at Nootka Sound within hours of one another on 2 July 1789, to find a Spanish warship in the sound and a fort under construction. They learned that on 14 May the Spanish had seized the *Iphigenia* and

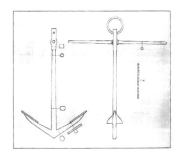

▲ An anchor is one of the most critical functional elements in any seagoing vessel and in 18th-century sailing ships, far from home, the loss of an anchor was serious. A typical anchor of the time is shown here — one recovered in the 1990s in Tahiti from HMS *Adventure*, lost in 1773 during Cook's second voyage. The shank is over ten feet (3.1m) long and the anchor weighs more than 1000 pounds (480kg).
Heritage Office, New South Wales, Australia

* San Blas is on the Pacific coast of the Mexican mainland in latitude 21° 32.' It lies about 100 miles south and 300 miles east of the southern tip of Baja California. It was founded as a Spanish naval base in 1768.

arrested her captain, William Douglas. This began what came to be called the Nootka Incident, an affair that brought Britain and Spain to the brink of war. Spain was determined to assert sovereignty over Nootka Sound and intended to establish a colonial outpost there. British activity in the region was increasing, and Spain had sent an armed naval expedition under Esteban José Martinez consisting of the warship *Princessa* and an armed supply ship, the *San Carlos*, to the sound from their Pacific naval base at San Blas* in Mexico for this purpose. After two weeks' imprisonment William Douglas and his crew were released and the *Iphigenia* was allowed to leave — with only minimal supplies of food and trade goods. Douglas sailed directly to Hawai'i for food, water and wood, where he arrived on 20 July. Although Ni'ihau is not specifically mentioned in the written record, yams were on his 'shopping list' so he must have presumably called there before departing for Macao on 10 August.[23]

On the arrival of the *Princess Royal* at Nootka Sound on 2 July the Spanish authorities arrested Captain Hudson and the vessel, with a Spanish crew commanded by Manuel Quimper, was sailed to San Blas. Later the same day the *Argonaut* sailed into the Sound and Martinez similarly seized the ship and arrested James Colnett and his crew. On 14 July, under a Spanish crew, the *Argonaut* also set sail for San Blas. Colnett and his crew were aboard as prisoners. The news of these actions and other Spanish provocations in the area reached London in January 1790.

The *Argonaut* and her crew were eventually released (on 9 July 1790) in San Blas after twelve months' incarceration and Colnett sailed north again to resume fur trading. The *Princess Royal*, now in the service of Spain, was not able to be immediately recalled when the Spanish Viceroy had a change of heart and decided the vessel should be returned to the British authorities in Manila.

The following year (1791) Colnett and Quimper, who become acquainted in Las Blas, met by chance in the Hawaiian islands as Quimper was sailing to Manila to return

▶ The capture of the *Argonaut* at Nootka Sound by the Spanish. Captain Colnett is shown being taken prisoner by Esteban José Martinez of the Spanish navy in this 1791 aquatinted etching by Robert Dodd, 'The Spanish Insult to the British Flag at Nootka Sound.'
By courtesy of the trustees of the British Museum

Early Western voyagers

◀ The *Argonaut*, in a rough sketch from Colnett's journal, as she sailed along the coast of Japan on her way from Hawai'i to Macao in July 1791.
Champlain Society, Toronto

the *Princess Royal* and Colnett was returning from the northwest coast to Macao with his cargo of furs. When Colnett arrived off Hawai'i on 1 April 1791 and heard that the *Princess Royal* was in the vicinity he determined to attack her in retribution for the stores the Spanish had taken from the *Argonaut* in San Blas. The attack never eventuated, but the force of arms shown by Colnett cowed Quimper into the realization that he should placate him, which he did, and they concluded their discussions with a friendly exchange of charts. Colnett felt he had won the day and spent effort in denigrating the Spanish in the eyes of the islanders, on the suspicion that Quimper was looking for a site for a Spanish settlement.

Both vessels sailed direct from Kailua on Hawai'i to Waimea on Kaua'i, with Colnett deliberately arriving first so he could sow seeds of discontent regarding the impending Spanish visit. The weather was bad and Colnett's journal reveals:

> I overtook the Princess Royal next day and whether his intentions were what I thought I cannot say, but I miss'd him in the night and stood on for Atooi [Kaua'i] where I let go my Anchor in 17 fathoms, but Blowing a gale of wind the Ship blew off the Bank, and attempting to work up sprang my main mast, which obliged me to bear up for Oneehow [Ni'ihau] where I anchor'd the same Evening in Poor-or-re [Puhiula] Bay Latitude 21° 56'. I fish'd [strengthened] my main mast and Completed with wood and water, Yams, and Hogs. All the Chiefs of Atooi and Oneehow were gone to windward to war with the Owhyheeans [Hawaiians].[24]

Colnett had no cause to return to Waimea, but in case the Spanish attempted to settle there he sent to Waimea by canoe 'Powder, Shot, arms and ammunition and a number of other presents for the Chiefs, their wives, Daughters, and Children, our old and worthy ^friends.' He also left at Ni'ihau his remaining livestock, consisting of 'a Ram and two Ewes, a Cock and two Hen Turkeys, with Beans, peas, Indian Corn and Callavances [a variety of bean].' As a Royal Navy officer on half pay while on this trading voyage, Colnett had

▲ Esteban José Martinez (1742–98) a central figure in the Nootka Incident which left the British and Spanish on the brink of hostilities in 1789. A career naval officer, he was tasked by the viceroy of New Spain (Mexico) with establishing a fort in Nootka Sound on Vancouver Island. This led to conflict with the British fur traders and the arrest of British ships, including the *Argonaut*.
Museo Naval, Madrid

▲ A bust of Manuel Quimper at Sooke, British Columbia. Quimper (c.1757–1844), a Peruvian-born career Spanish naval officer and later colonial official, played a part in the Nootka Incident. Quimper's later career was long and distinguished, encompassing naval cartography and colonial administration in Peru before retiring in Spain.
Wikimedia Commons

no qualms about supplying arms where Britain's interests could be threatened. He left Niʻihau for Macao on 18 April 1791; this was his last visit to the islands.

John Meares arrived in London in April 1790 to press the case for action against Spain, the Royal Navy made preparations for war and an ultimatum was delivered to Spain. Spain called upon France for assistance, but when that wasn't forthcoming due to the French Revolution, the Spanish decided to negotiate (while simultaneously reinforcing their naval presence in Nootka Sound). The negotiator sent by the British government to Nootka Sound was George Vancouver, who reached there in August 1792 and his travels figure further in this story of Niʻihau. The outcome of the negotiations became known as the Nootka Conventions.*

The difficulties over Nootka Sound, coupled with the East India Company's monopoly, largely brought an end to the British sea otter fur trade in which Niʻihau had figured so prominently. The ventures had not been the success hoped for, but a pattern of fur-trading ships wintering over in Hawaiʻi to acquire food, wood and water from the four main islands had developed. A visit to Niʻihau for yams became the last call for British vessels before returning to the northwest coast or to the Chinese market.

American fur trading vessels also visited the Hawaiian islands during this period, with the *Eleanora* and the *Fair American* arriving in 1790.[25] Both ships were involved in the Nootka Sound crisis, but did not visit Niʻihau. Neither did the *Hope,* which paid two visits to the islands in 1791.[26]

The first American vessel to circumnavigate the globe, the *Columbia*, made two voyages out of Boston to the northwest coast and visited the Hawaiian archipelago each time. On the first voyage the vessel arrived on 24 August 1789 and spent 24 days in the islands buying supplies. The ship's log has been lost so it is not known whether it called at Niʻihau, but the following extract from John Boit's log of the second voyage shows that the *Columbia* called there in early November 1792:

> *November* 1. This day, having on board 93 Hogs and great quantities of Fruits and Vegetables, we bore away from this enchanting Island [Hawaiʻi, where the ship arrived on 30 October] bound to *Onehow*, after more Yams and to put a Native on shore, which the Capt had taken from that Isle on his former voyage.
>
> [November] 2 … Pass'd Atooi [Kauaʻi], and steer'd for Yam bay in Onehow. In the morning was well into the bay. Vast many canoes off, in one of which was the Father and other relations of our Sandwich Islands Lad. [T]hey came on board and the meeting was very affectionate, but still our Lad refused to go on shore and Capt. Gray did not think proper for to force him. However made his freinds many presents.
>
> [November] 3. Bore off and made all sail for the Coast of China …[27]

* Of the Nootka Conventions the first was of the most immediate importance, with agreement being reached that the northwest coast should be open to trading ships from both Britain and Spain, that all captured British ships were to be released, and that compensation was to be paid. Land held by the British was to be restored, but this proved difficult with the opposing parties having different views on the land purchased. There were also widely divergent opinions on where the Spanish/British boundary should lie. Agreement could not be reached on these matters by Vancouver and his Spanish counterpart (Bodega y Quadra) and these issues were referred back to their respective governments, to form the substance of the later conventions. Both nations finally agreed to abandon Nootka Sound, and the substance of the agreements reached in these conventions laid the groundwork for the much later border agreement between the United States and Canada at the 49th parallel.

◀ The *Columbia*, in 1790, was the first American vessel to circumnavigate the globe. As an American ship she played a neutral role while in Nootka Sound during the Nootka Incident in 1789, the Spanish allowing her to continue to trade for furs along with her accompanying ship, the *Lady Washington*. In November 1792 she paid a short visit to Niʻihau for yams. The *Columbia* was not large for her time, at 213 tons. This 1793 drawing is by George Davidson, the ship's artist.
Wikimedia Commons

The fate of 'our Lad' is unknown, as this is the only mention of him. The *Columbia*'s companion vessel on her first voyage, the sloop *Lady Washington*, sailed independently to China via Hawai'i, and was at the islands in October/November 1791, but it is not known if she visited Ni'ihau. She probably did. Under various captains the vessel also called at the islands in October/November 1793, December 1794 and in February 1796, but again her interisland itinerary is unknown.[28] She was at Waimea in February 1796 under Captain Roger Simpson at the same time as the *Ruby* under Charles Bishop, but there is no mention in Bishop's journal of the *Lady Washington*'s intention to visit Ni'ihau.[29]

—

The next section outlines Captain George Vancouver's visits between 1791 and 1794, and the rise of Honolulu as the major trading port after Kamehameha's conquest of the windward islands in 1795. Gradually the availability of imported supplies, and flour in particular, supplanted the need for yams as a staple.

The final two sections in this chapter detail two major incidents involving Ni'ihau that occurred during the height of the yam trade, and a table summarises the ship visits made to Ni'ihau for yams.

Vancouver's visits and the demise of the Ni'ihau yam trade

The first few years of the Niihauan yam trade — allied as it was to the North American coast fur trade, and so reliant on the buoyant market for furs in China — was inspired by the writings from James Cook's third voyage.[30] The master navigator and his successor commanders kindled a commercial pattern that existed for a generation despite the changing mix of nationalities involved as the trade waxed and finally waned. Despite several British stratagems, the strictures of the East India Company (essentially demanding a percentage of the sale of pelts in return for a license to operate) and the demoralizing effect of the Nootka Incident meant that by 1797 only a single British vessel (the *Dragon*) was working on the American coast. The slack was rapidly picked up by American ships, mostly financed by wealthy Bostonians with their home ports in New England. By 1801 their numbers had increased to over 20 from six in 1792.[31]

George Vancouver, although not a fur trader, was one of the last of the British ship captains of the early era to visit Ni'ihau. In 1791 he was sent by the British government to negotiate with the Spanish at Nootka Sound, and while there to chart the Hawaiian islands and the northwest coast. Vancouver had accompanied Cook on his second and third voyages. He sailed via the Cape of Good Hope to Australia and thence to Hawai'i in his ship HMS *Discovery* (a new vessel, not Cook's *Discovery*) together with an associated tender, HMS *Chatham* under Lieutenant William Broughton.

He made Ni'ihau his last stop, to secure yams which were not available at all on Kaua'i at the time, before leaving the islands in March 1792.

> About three in the morning of the 14th, we sailed [from Waimea] with a fine northerly breeze for Onehow [Ni'ihau], in order, whilst the decks of the Chatham were caulking, to take on board such yams and other vegetables as we might be able to procure …

▲ John Boit (1774–1829), who sailed in 1790 at the age of 16 as fifth officer on the second voyage of the *Columbia*. One of his duties was to keep a journal of the voyage, which he did admirably, and his visit to Ni'ihau is quoted in the text. He did well on the voyage and on his return he sailed as captain on a sloop, the *Union*, on a trading voyage to the northwest coast which involved a circumnavigation of the globe in a small vessel. Subsequent trading voyages followed for Boit, and a time ashore as a merchant. His final voyage was in 1826.
Oregon Historical Society

87

> [Two days later] by friday in the afternoon, we had purchased a very ample supply: and the Chatham's deck being now finished, about six in the evening we proceeded together towards the coast of America.[32]

Thomas Manby, master's mate on the *Discovery* during this Niʻihau visit, kept a journal and made some perceptive comments on Niʻihau and its inhabitants. They had a rough crossing from Kauaʻi:

> At 9 a.m. tranquility was again restored by the ship's coming to anchor in a small bay under the south point of the island, about three quarters of a mile from the shore.
>
> The reason of our touching here was to procure yams, Onehow being famous for the growth of this most excellent root.
>
> Some canoes came off immediately on our anchoring and our traffic commenced for this nutritious branch of commerce.
>
> By the 16th [March 1792] we had purchased five hundred weight of yams for nails and pieces of iron, besides a great plenty of sweet potatoes. They have but few hogs and trust to the produce of the sea for animal food. Being expert and diligent fishermen, they salt a great deal and barter it with the people of Atooi for cloth and mats. The fish they take are principally bonettas and dolphin, albacores and cavallies of a very large size. An ample supply of these were laid in for our sea stock, making a pleasing variety in our diet.
>
> I made an excursion with the botanist [Archibald Menzies] nearly round the island. It is very inferior in point of beauty to all other of the Sandwich group. It produces very few trees of any kind, and is only remarkable for the fineness of its yams and sweet potatoes. I killed a few ducks in my walk, some curlews and some other birds of a smaller kind.
>
> Onehow is considered as under the government of Atooi. It is but thinly inhabited and had no chief of any consequence residing on it … [33]

As he departed the islands, Vancouver took the opportunity to note the changing behavior of the locals since his last visit in 1779 (and indeed since Colnett's visit in 1788):

▲ Captain George Vancouver (1757–98). Vancouver was a career naval officer, entering the service as a thirteen-year-old. He served as a midshipman on the *Resolution* during Cook's second voyage, and on the *Discovery* on Cook's fateful voyage to the Hawaiian islands. He was commissioned as a lieutenant on his return. When the Nootka Crisis arose in 1789 he led an expedition of two ships which left England in 1791 to enforce the Nootka Conventions, and survey the Hawaiian islands and the northwest coast of America. He returned in 1795 and began publishing his findings, a task completed by his brother as he died in 1798. The National Portrait Gallery holds this painting, by an unknown artist, labeling it 'probably' George Vancouver.

National Portrait Gallery, UK

▲ The ships of the Vancouver Expedition. An undignified image of HMS *Discovery* on the rocks on the northwest coast in 1792. In the background is HMS *Chatham*, which pulled *Discovery* off the rocks with little damage. The sloop *Discovery* was launched in 1789 as a 330-ton, ten-gun survey ship, almost 100 feet long overall, with 100 personnel. The brig *Chatham* was launched in 1788 as a 133-ton, four-gun survey ship, 80 feet long with a crew of 45. The original sketch by Zachary Mudge was colored by William Alexander for inclusion in Vancouver's published journal of 1801.

University of Illinois

Early Western voyagers

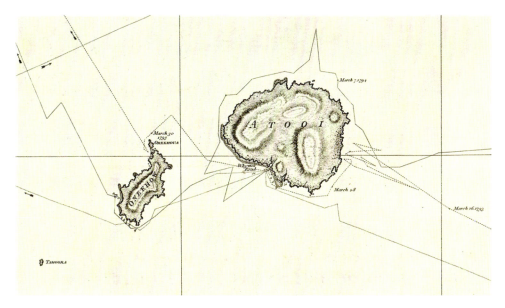

◀ Vancouver's chart, showing his tracks around Niʻihau and Kauaʻi. Part of his sailing instructions from the Lords of the Admiralty was to chart the Sandwich Islands, as Hawaiʻi was then known. This he did meticulously, and this is part of the chart produced, focusing on his visits to Niʻihau and Kauaʻi.
Smithsonian Institution, Washington DC

▼ *View on the South Side of Onehow SE point bear[in]g EbN offshore a mile*, a watercolor and pencil drawing by Midshipman John Sykes on the Vancouver expedition. No official artist was on board, but Sykes and three others of the crew left an artistic record of sorts. Sykes was a career naval officer, retiring in 1855 as a full admiral.
Bancroft Library, Honeyman Collection, University of California, Berkeley

The supply of refreshments which the Sandwich islands on this occasion had afforded us, was undeniably a very scanty one. This, however, I did not solely attribute to scarcity, as I had frequently great reason to believe an abundant stock might have been procured, had we been inclined to have purchased them with arms and ammunition; with which, through the unpardonable conduct of the various traders who have visited these islands, the inhabitants have become very familiar, and use these weapons with an adroitness that would not disgrace the generality of European soldiers.[34]

The days of trading for supplies using only nails and beads disappeared, with arms and ammunition now taking precedence.

Vancouver paid two further visits to the islands (in March 1793 and March 1794) during the course of his extensive voyage. Only on his final visit did he return to Niʻihau for yams, but his expectations were not met in the promised supply.[35] Was this because he refused to trade in muskets or ammunition, using as a pretext, so he says, that they all belonged not to him, but to his chief, King George?

One of the later visits to Niʻihau during this period was that of Captain Charles Bishop in the 101-ton vessel *Ruby*, owned by Sydenham Teast of Bristol (who also owned the *Jenny* which figures in this chapter). With a license to trade from the East India Company, the *Ruby* left England in late 1794, rounded Cape Horn and traded up the northwest coast in the summer of 1795. Bishop then wintered over in Hawaiʻi, with his last port of call being Niʻihau to stock up on yams for his voyage to Canton. From Bishop's journal:

> At daylight [27 February 1796] we made sail and Passing the South East Point [of Niʻihau] hauled up to the Northward for Yam Bay. In a short time the Cannoes came off and a brisk trade was Carried on for vegetables. At Noon it being nearly Calm we anchored in 26 fathems over a Sandy Bottom about 2 miles South from Yam Bay and about that distance from the Shore.
>
> [On the following day] we continued trading 'till noon, when having Procured a Sufficiency of yams, which are by no means Plentiful at this time, to last us to China, we weighed and made all sail for Canton.[36]

Fortunately he needed considerably fewer yams than Vancouver two years earlier, who had well over 200 personnel to feed on his two vessels.

Bishop comments on a minor incident that occurred on their departure from the island, which perhaps presages the tragic events that occurred a few months later, in July 1796, when Lt William Broughton on HMS *Providence* visited for yams:

> Many Islanders wanted to go with us to 'Pretannee' [Britain]. A youth who had rendered himself familiar by his great good humour was after much Solicitation received on board. His Sister (by no means an unhansome young Woman) pressed much to accompany her Brother, and had actually got on board, and it was not without a Present and some harsh words we could Perswade her to return to her cannoe. Their Parting was like Brother and Sister. It was affectionate nor could they refrain from Tears. She continued to follow us 'till the Breeze Freshening they found the Ship haistily leaving them, when with seeming reluctance they paddled slowly back towards their Native Isle [37]

New opportunities

The trading landscape was changing. Kamehameha had conquered Oʻahu in 1795 and then had all the windward islands under his control. But all the while he had designs on Kauaʻi and its satellite Niʻihau. He moved his court from Hawaiʻi to Oʻahu and took up residence in the Waikīkī: area. Realizing the opportunities for trade with passing vessels he shrewdly began growing crops, and charging plenty for them. Apart from a foray to quell a rebellion in Hawaiʻi in 1796, Kamehameha continued living on Oʻahu, initially at Waikīkī:, and later in Honolulu until 1810 when he returned to Hawaiʻi. In that same year he finally came to an agreement with the king of Kauaʻi and Niʻihau, Kaumualiʻi, in which the latter recognized Kamehameha as the supreme ruler of all the islands (see Chapter Five).

Given its natural harbor and the adjacent royal court, in the early 1800s Honolulu became the center of trading activity in the islands. The days of ships moving from island to island in search of water, food and wood were waning. As well as growing crops at Waikīkī: and Mānoa, food supplies for sale were being brought to Honolulu from the other islands.[38]

One typical comment from this period (from John Turnbull, second officer on the British brig *Margaret*) was that in Honolulu, compared with Niʻihau: 'Every article we wanted was at least three times, and many of them six times the price.' Thus there was still a market for Niʻihau yams.

The *Margaret* arrived at Oʻahu on 17 December 1802, where the crew traded, particularly for salt. There, to avoid the ship being overrun, 'we resolved as much as

◀ Honolulu's port in 1816, depicted by Louis Choris.
Wikimedia Commons

possible to assume the appearance of a ship of war: and therefore dressed six seamen in soldier's uniforms, and made them walk the deck under arms, and kept our colours and pendant always flying.' Supplies were so expensive they resolved to sail to Kaua'i, where they arrived in foul weather on 26 December, but being unable to anchor

> … we bore up for Onehow [Ni'ihau], the other small island still remaining faithful to the rightful king of Attowaie [Kaua'i]' …³⁹
>
> … on our making the island, the natives flocked about us, furnishing abundance of yams at a very moderate rate: we there also laid in a small addition to our stock of salt. Here, as at the other islands, all were eager to be admitted on board; but the notion of our ship being a man of war, and the formidable appearance of our marines, kept them in awe.⁴⁰
>
> Having in the course of four days collected about three tons of yams, an invaluable treasure to us in such circumstances, we set sail to the eastward for Owyhee [Hawai'i] …⁴¹

So yams were still available at Ni'ihau, 23 years after Captain Cook's visit.

After buying further supplies at Hawai'i, the *Margaret* sailed south to the Tuamotu islands looking for trading opportunities.

Archibald Campbell,* who was on O'ahu in 1809–10, describes Honolulu at that time: 'The village of Hanaroora … consisted of several hundred houses' and the countryside was 'in the highest state of cultivation.' He notes that 'At one time during my stay, there were nearly sixty white people upon Wahoo [O'ahu] alone, but the number was constantly varying …' and that 'many inducements are held out to sailors to remain here.' Kamehameha was keen to learn all he could from Europeans and 'had a considerable number in his service, chiefly carpenters, joiners, masons, blacksmiths and bricklayers.'⁴² At least twelve vessels called there during Campbell's thirteen months on the island.⁴³

This gives a snapshot of the patterns of trade as Honolulu began to be the center of commerce and the Ni'ihau yam trade faded. For ten years the sandalwood trade with

---

* Campbell arrived on O'ahu in 1809 on the Russian ship Neva (Captain Hargomeister) having had both feet amputated due to frostbite in the Aleutian Islands. He spent three months in Kamehameha's household, then lived with Isaac Davis, and then on his own land in the Pearl Harbor area gifted him by the king. He was a weaver by trade and spent his time in Kamehameha's household repairing sails and rigging. His journal was edited by James Smith, to whom he told his story.

China, using the resources on the islands, flourished, and supplemented the fur traders' activities as prices for skins declined, but Niʻihau as a destination was being overtaken by the rise of commercial activity in Honolulu, and it had no sandalwood trees.

In 1816 Peter Corney, mate of the British schooner *Columbia*, was looking after two shiploads of sandalwood which were stored in Honolulu. This was not the same vessel as the American ship *Columbia* mentioned earlier. She was much smaller, at 185 tons, with a crew of 25. Corney reported that by then:

> The Island of Woahoo [Oʻahu] is by far the most important of the group of the Sandwich Islands, chiefly on account of its excellent harbours and good water. It is in a high state of cultivation: and abounds with cattle, hogs, sheep, goats, horses, etc., as well as vegetables and fruit of every description.[44]

The days of relying on Niʻihau yams for sustenance on the perilous journey to the northwest coast of America or to China were finished. Ship visits to Niʻihau became few and far between.

Even the enormous growth in the American whaling fleet in the Pacific after 1820 did nothing to resurrect the Niihauan yam trade. Figures from over 2500 whalers' logbooks show that while there were more than 1500 whaling ship visits to Oʻahu (Honolulu) between 1820 and 1869, and over 1000 to Maui (Lahaina), only eight whaling vessels visited Niʻihau in the same period.[45]

The Niʻihau yam trading era was well and truly over.

Two hijacked teenagers

Having spent the northern summer surveying the northwest coast of America, when Captain George Vancouver arrived at Nootka Sound on the *Discovery* at the end of August 1792 to implement the Nootka Conventions with the Spanish authorities, he was surprised at the shipping activity there, with upwards of ten ships from four nations at anchor. Relations with the Spanish were friendly, but discussions had become deadlocked. Both parties referred matters back to their governments for further direction, a process that was bound to be slow.

On 6 October 1792 the British schooner *Jenny*, out of Bristol, arrived in Nootka Sound. Captain James Baker and his crew had spent the summer fur trading and intended continuing doing so down the coast on their way home to England via Cape Horn. On their outward voyage they had sojourned in Hawaiʻi and had taken with them to 'the coast' two Niihauan girls, in somewhat dubious circumstances. Archibald Menzies, the surgeon and naturalist on Vancouver's *Discovery*, describes matters thus:

> These two girls were about ten months absent from their friends and constantly declared to us that they were taken away in the 'Jenny' from Niihau, without either their own consent or that of their parents or relations, as they were kept below confined in the cabin while the vessel was getting under way and leaving the island.[46]

The girls stated that they went on board the *Jenny* with several others, but when the others left they were forcibly shut in the cabin. Captain Baker, of course, denied all knowledge of their being aboard until they were well at sea. The actual truth will never be known.*

---

* A non-judgemental view of the girls' voyage on the *Discovery* is given by Edward Bell, clerk on the *Chatham*: 'There these poor Girls found themselves happy & satisfied not only with the pleasing idea of getting soon home to their friends & Country, but having a Companion on board the Discovery (one of their Countrymen that Capt. Vancouver brought with him from Owyhee [Hawaiʻi] …) to whom they cou'd converse, and who from his knowledge of our Language wou'd contribute much to their wants & desires.' (See Bell, Journal on the Chatham for 6 & 7 October 1792, Alexander Turnbull Library Wellington, manuscript qMs-2071, Journal pp 242–243.)

According to Menzies, 'one of them was about 14 years of age named *Teheeopea* & the other was a few years older named *Tahemeeraoo*.' (Teheeopea shortly decided to call herself Raheina, and was so known for the rest of the voyage.) According to Vancouver, they were related to one another and both were of some consequence on Ni'ihau. Menzies comes to Captain Baker's defense: 'But they spoke of no further ill-treatment during their stay on board.' Vancouver himself echoes this, saying that they had been treated 'with every kindness and attention' while on Baker's ship. How they were accommodated for four months alongside perhaps twenty crew on such a small vessel without major disruptions can only be imagined.

The *Jenny* was wrecked in the Bristol Channel in 1794, shortly after her return to England. James Baker, his crew, and the logbook survived, but the logbook was subsequently destroyed in a fire in 1832.[47]

Captain Baker became aware on his arrival at Nootka Sound that Captain Vancouver and his vessels were shortly to leave for California and Hawai'i, so he asked if Vancouver would take the girls home to Ni'ihau. Despite what was apparently a kidnapping, Vancouver liked the cut of Baker's jib and agreed. Rumors that Baker was proposing to sell the girls into slavery were rife in Nootka at the time, but Vancouver gave him the benefit of the doubt:

> Although I had not any personal knowledge of Mr. Baker previous to his entering Nootka, yet I should conceive him totally incapable of such an act of barbarity and injustice; and if there were the least sincerity in the solicitude he expressed to me for the future happiness and welfare of these young women, it is impossible he could ever have meditated such a design. I do not, however, mean to vindicate the propriety of Mr. Baker's conduct, in bringing these girls from their native country; for I am decidedly of opinion it was highly improper; and if the young women are to be credited, their seduction and detention on board Mr. Baker's vessel were inexcusable.[48]

Vancouver left Nootka Sound on 13 October and worked his way down the coast as far as Monterey Bay. According to Menzies:

> During the time [the two girls] were on the Discovery, they lived at Captain Vancouver's table in the cabin, and conducted themselves with such propriety and decorum that they gained the friendship and esteem of everyone on board.[49]

They spent over five months on the *Discovery* and were obviously quite remarkable young women. Vancouver was very taken with them, and with Raheina in particular. His normally matter-of-fact journal is most expansive:

> The elegance of Raheina's figure, the regularity and softness of her features, and the delicacy which she naturally possessed, gave her a superiority in point of personal accomplishments over the generality of her sex amongst the Sandwich islanders; in addition to which, her sensibility and turn of mind, her sweetness of temper and complacency of manners, were beyond any thing that could have been expected from her birth, or native education; so that if it were fair to judge of the dispositions of a whole nation from the qualities of these two young women, it would seem that they are endued with much affection and tenderness. At least, such was their deportment towards us; by which they gained the regard and good wishes of, I believe, every one on board, whilst I became in no small degree solicitous for their future happiness and prosperity.[50]

▲ Archibald Menzies (1754–1842), a Scottish naval surgeon and naturalist who spent a long time at sea, first in the Royal Navy on the American station, then as surgeon with James Colnett on the Prince of Wales from 1786–89. Then followed his selection as naturalist to accompany George Vancouver on his voyage around the world in HMS *Discovery* from 1791–95. On both these latter voyages he visited Ni'ihau several times. He was an avid plant collector and has several species named after him. He was also the first Westerner to climb Mauna Loa, on Hawai'i. He later served with the navy in the West Indies and upon his retirement from the sea practiced medicine in London.
Wikimedia Commons

> *I became in no small degree solicitous for their future happiness and prosperity*

The Lords of the Admiralty must have been surprised at this unexpected description of pulchritude and sophistication. Vancouver continues:

> They seemed much pleased with the European fashions, and in conforming to this new system of manners, they conducted themselves in company with a degree of propriety beyond all expectation. Their European dress contributed most probably to this effect, and produced, particularly in Raheina, a degree of personal delicacy that was conspicuous on many occasions.[51]

The 'European fashions' were made from sailcloth or cheap cotton by the *Discovery*'s sailmakers, at least one of whom must have had an eye for such clothes. Archibald Menzies remarks that 'They constantly wore shoes and stockings and a sort of English habit that was made for them on board …'

The vessels anchored at the infant San Francisco to replenish supplies of wood and water, spending time at the Presidio (35 soldiers and their families) and the Franciscan mission (three priests). The girls were not fazed by new sights and experiences. Vancouver continued to be impressed:

> The sight of horses, cattle, and other animals, with a variety of objects to which [the girls] were intire strangers, produced in them the highest entertainment; and without the least hesitation or alarm, they were placed on horseback on their first landing, and, with a man to lead the animal, they rode without fear, and were by that means enabled to partake of all the civilities and diversions which our Spanish friends so obligingly offered and provided.[52]

After ten days in the San Francisco Bay area, Vancouver sailed down to Monterey, the residence of the governor-general of the Spanish province of California. Advance warning of their visit had been sent on horseback by the San Francisco Commandant so the Monterey governor was most welcoming and arranged entertainments for them. This included a dance at the governor's house which Menzies describes in detail, and included a hula by the two Hawaiian girls, preceded by 'some country dances, but even in this remote region they seem'd most attach'd to the Spanish exhilerating dance the *Fandango*, a performance which requires no little elasticity of limbs as well as nimbleness of capers & gestures.' Menzies reports a culture clash:

▶ The Presidio of San Francisco in an 1817 watercolor by Louis Choris, over 20 years after Vancouver called with the two young Niihauan women. John Sykes on the Vancouver Expedition does not appear to have had the opportunity to paint this presidio as he did in Monterey (see page 99). The San Francisco presidio was built by the Spanish in 1776 to protect their interests in the Bay area.
Wikimedia Commons

Early Western voyagers

◀ Lahaina on Maui, where Vancouver's two vessels spent three weeks refitting in 1793 before the *Discovery* and the *Chatham* went their separate ways. On the hill can be seen Lahainaluna Seminary, built in 1831, long after Vancouver's stay.
Engraving by Jean-Pierre Moynet/Mary Ann McCrea

> The two Sandwish Island Women at the request of Captain Vancouver exhibited their manner of singing & dancing, which did not appear to afford much entertainment to the Spanish Ladies, indeed I believe they thought this crude performance was introduced by way of ridiculing their favourite dance the Fandango, as they soon after departed.[53]

It appears that Menzies himself was also not a hula aficionado. In return Vancouver hosted a dinner party on the *Discovery* that did not turn out well, as the motion of the vessel proved too much for his Spanish guests who retired early, a little the worse for wear.

Vancouver was visiting in pursuance of his Nootka Conventions mission with the Spaniards. He sailed from Monterey for the Hawaiian islands on 14 January 1793 after a stay of over two weeks, arriving off the northeast coast of Hawaiʻi on 12 February 1793, after a month-long passage. He spent over three weeks at the island, sending the *Chatham* to survey the east and south coasts while the *Discovery* visited Kawaihae and Kealakekua Bay where Kamehameha was in residence. The two vessels then sailed on to Maui and anchored off Lahaina for some days before the *Discovery* proceeded along the south side of Oʻahu to spend a few days at anchor off Waikīkī:. The *Chatham* left from Lahaina to sail back to Nootka.

One incident, related by Menzies, which occurred at Lahaina serves to indicate Vancouver's volatile nature, and his feelings for the girls. Maui was then under the control of King Kahekili, and both he and his half-brother Kaʻeo were spending the night on the *Discovery*, when:

> Next morning one of the Niihau women missed a piece of ribbon which it is supposed some of those who slept in the cabin stole from her. Captain Vancouver in endeavoring to recover this trifle put himself into such a passion and threatened the chiefs with such menacing threats that he terrified some of them out of the ship with great precipitation. The king [Kahekili] in particular came running into my cabin before I knew anything of the business and instantly jumping into his canoe through the port hole, paddled hastily to the shore and we saw no more of him.[54]

Kaʻeo was evidently not so easily frightened and it was he who explained to Menzies what had happened. History does not relate whether the ribbon was ever found.

▶ 'View down Whymea River, Atooi' — a sketch by John Sykes, probably drawn when Vancouver dropped the two Niihauan girls off at Waimea in 1793.

Bancroft Library Honeyman Collection, University of California, Berkeley

On 24 March 1793 the *Discovery* left Oʻahu for Kauaʻi. Vancouver had learned that in the year since he had last visited the islands Niʻihau had been stricken with drought. No yams were available and most of the population had left to live on Kauaʻi. Menzies records that the two Niihauan women, on hearing this and meeting with a number of their relations on Kauaʻi, wanted to land there instead of Niʻihau. This was relayed to the regent, acting for the young king, Kaumualiʻi, and

> … they were strongly recommended to his care and protection, when we had that chief aboard off the east end. He then readily gave his consent, and particular directions that they should be left under the chief of Waimea in whose district a house and a portion of land should be given to each of them, and where all of their effects should be protected in safety.[55]

Vancouver was particularly concerned that the pair should suffer no harm on their return because they had broken the prohibition on eating with men. In the presence of the two girls he entreated the regent, Inamoʻo, to give him his word that this would be so, 'and had the satisfaction of receiving from him … assurances of his protection; not only of their persons, but their property.'

The offer of land and houses seemed so generous to both Vancouver and Menzies that they entertained some suspicions. Vancouver emphasized that they would be returning in a year's time, and to reinforce the women's position he 'desired that the houses and land should be given to me, that the property should be considered as vested in me, and that no person whatever should have any right in it but by my permission; and that I would allow Raheina and Tymarow [Tahemeeraoo] to live on the estate.' This was agreed to by the chiefs. He came to terms with his doubts:

> We found the situation proposed … to be a very large portion of the fertile valley, noticed on our former visit on the western side of the river, commencing at the sea beach, and extending along the banks of the river to a certain established landmark, including a very considerable extent of the inland mountainous country. … [This] was in value so far above our most sanguine expectations, I was led to suspect the sincerity of the intended donation. But to this we became reconciled, from the protestations of the chief himself, as also from the universal declaration of many of the natives who had accompanied us …[56]

We can only sympathize with Menzies and Vancouver's suspicions, as it was a generous gift of some of the most valuable land in Waimea. But Vancouver says that the declarations 'seemed perfectly to satisfy the young women, that they would be put into possession of these estates; and that their persons and property would be protected according to the assurances we had now received.'

The young women were landed on the beach that afternoon (29 March) with all their effects, which by now 'were pretty considerable', in the words of Menzies. These effects 'were instantly carried to a house a little way back from the beach' and the house was placed under kapu. Menzies again:

> After this we walked a little distance through the plantations, where we were shown the houses that were to be put in repair for these women, and the extent of ground that was to be allotted to each of them …[57]

Vancouver's care and attention to ensure the young women's ongoing welfare was admirable and a measure of the respect which the whole crew had for them both. Then it was time for farewells:

> They followed us back to the beach, where they took leave of Captain Vancouver and other officers with tears trickling down their cheeks … and did not quit the beach until the last of our people had left the shore and the vessel getting under weigh in the evening got out of their sight.[58]

After a brief look to confirm that Lehua was indeed separated from Ni'ihau, the *Discovery* departed for the northwest coast and another summer of surveying, first in the north and then down as far as Baja California. From there the vessel returned to Hawai'i, and sailing westwards through the islands, ultimately to Kaua'i. At Waimea Vancouver found:

> Our arrival was soon known, and we were early visited by many of our former friends and acquaintances. Amongst the number were the two young women I had brought from Nootka and settled here; during our late absence they had been treated with great kindness and civility, yet they were both very apprehensive that, on our finally quitting these seas, the attentive behaviour they had hitherto experienced would be discontinued. I however embraced the first opportunity of obtaining from all the principal chiefs the most solemn assurances of the contrary.[59]

Both girls were keen to visit their old home of Ni'ihau, even though they were aware that the *Discovery* would not be returning to Waimea. Vancouver was happy to take them as he thought they might assist in securing the supply of yams he needed. The island, however, had not yet recovered from the drought and yams were certainly not plentiful so the *Discovery* accompanied by the *Chatham* left Ni'ihau the following day (14 March 1794) to return to the northwest coast of America.

▼ The view of Lehua Island from the northern end of Ni'ihau across the three-quarter-mile-wide strait separating the islands. Lehua is now a Hawai'i State Wildlife Sanctuary and a permit is required to pass beyond the high tide mark. The island is in the process of restoration of the natural habitat for the many seabirds that nest there. Rabbits were removed in 2006 and monitoring is continuing to determine whether the Polynesian rat eradication project has been completely successful. The National Tropical Botanic Gardens is also carrying out a replanting program of indigenous species on the 284-acre island.
Nancy Shaw

There were fond farewells again as the vessels left the young women for the last time. As Archibald Menzies put it: 'A little past 5 we weighed anchor & as we were dropping out of the bay, the two girls & our other friends went on shore, after taking an affectionate leave of us.'[60]

But this is not quite the last we hear of the young women. In July 1796, over two years after Vancouver's departure, events took place on Niʻihau which are related in the next section, and the two women were peripherally involved.

Dale La Tendresse, in his introduction to Thomas Manby's *Journal of the Voyages of HMS Discovery and Chatham* asserts that '[Vancouver] fell in love with one of these lovely young women' and that 'the remaining 3½ years of his voyage and 6 years of his life were profoundly affected by this unresolvable matter of the heart.'[61] From his writings it is obvious that he was captivated by the two Niihauan women, and Raheina in particular, and did all he could to ensure their future happiness, but nothing has been found in any of the journals (Vancouver, Menzies, Manby, Bell) that lends full credence to La Tendresse's statements.[62]

▲ Captain William Broughton (1762–1821), c.1800. Broughton was a successful Royal Navy captain who commanded HMS *Chatham* on Vancouver's voyage, and later HMS *Providence* which called twice at Niʻihau in 1796, with tragic consequences.
Wikimedia Commons

Murder on the island

William Broughton, as captain of HMS *Chatham*, accompanied Vancouver on the earlier portion of his pioneering survey of the northwest coast of America. When negotiations with the Spanish over Nootka Sound reached an impasse, Vancouver determined to send the *Chatham* home to request further instructions. In the event the Spanish offered to help Broughton himself to go to England via Central America to the east coast, and so on to England. Vancouver readily accepted this, and leaving Monterey in January 1793, Broughton finally reached England in July.[63]

In October 1793 Broughton, with the new rank of commander, was appointed to HMS *Providence*. She was a relatively large sloop of 406 tons, with a crew of 115. His mission can only be surmised. Despite an exhaustive search through archival records his admiralty instructions could not be found for inclusion in the 2010 publication *William Robert Broughton's Voyage of Discovery to the North Pacific 1795–1798*.[64]

Fitting out the *Providence* took many months and it wasn't until February 1795, in convoy as France and England were by now at war, that Broughton sailed. His route was around the Cape of Good Hope to Sydney and on to Tahiti and Hawaiʻi. The latter was sighted on 1 January 1796. Broughton visited all the major islands and had considerable contact with his old friends, including Kamehameha. Relations were cordial throughout, although there was pressure to barter for arms, which Broughton refused. He anchored off Niʻihau at Yam Bay in the afternoon of 19 February 1796, where:

> Some canoes came off the next day bartering yams, potatoes, water-melons, and pumpkins: our boat also in the evening arrived laden with roots. The weather from the South occasioned a great swell in the Bay, and prevented us from receiving the supplies we had been promised. … The wind increased, and we had rain with strong squalls that split the main-topsail. After hoisting in the boats and securing the anchor, we stood in shore and bent another main-topsail … but the surf was so great that canoes could not reach us without risque. I therefore gave up the idea of anchoring, as there was no probability of doing so while this wind continued, which seemed likely to be the case.[65]

The following day was breezy, but some supplies were obtained, and a full sufficiency of yams, pumpkins, sweet potatoes and watermelons the next day, so on the morning of 22 February: 'We sailed for Nootka Sound. The ship's crew was generally healthy, excepting those who were infected with the venereal disease, contracted at the Sandwich Islands. The symptoms of this disorder were not very violent.'[66] The weather was not kind at Yam Bay, but there was no talk of drought, let alone the possibility of trouble ashore. The scourge of venereal disease had now gone full circle after their six-week stay, but Broughton doesn't seem to have been too perturbed.

They arrived at Nootka in March 1796 to find the Spanish had fulfilled their obligations under the Nootka Conventions and a tribal village now stood where the Spanish facilities had been. Broughton learned that Vancouver had departed from Monterey for England via Cape Horn in December 1794, some 15 months earlier. Not being entirely certain of Vancouver's intentions, Broughton decided to sail down to Monterey in the hope that Vancouver had left a message for him there. Both Vancouver and Broughton had orders from the admiralty to survey the southern portion of the west coast of South America, and given Vancouver's timings, Broughton became convinced that Vancouver would have been able to fulfil his instructions, and there was no point in following in his wake down the South American coast. What to do next?:

▲ The Presidio of Monterey, as sketched by John Sykes on Vancouver's expedition in 1794. The presidio (fort) was founded by the Spanish in 1770 in the face of a perceived Russian threat.
Wikimedia Commons

> As this was the case, my proceedings in future depended upon my own discretion; and I wished to employ his Majesty's sloop, under my command, in such a manner as might be deemed most eligible for the improvement of geography and navigation. I therefore demanded of the officers their sentiments in writing, respecting the manner in which these discretionary powers allowed to me might most effectually be employed. The result of their opinions, I was happy to find, coincided with my own, which was to survey the coast of Asia, commencing at the island of Sakhalin … and ending at the Nanking river in 30° N lat.[67]

Sakhalin is a Russian island in the Pacific, north of Japan, and Nanking —Nanjing — in China. The decision to proceed to Asia set the stage for a second visit to Hawai'i to restock supplies before the long voyage. Broughton left Monterey on 20 June 1796 and anchored in Kealakekua Bay on 6 July after a fast passage. Having checked his chronometers, a task which took some time, he left for Waikīkī: where he met with Kamehameha before proceeding to Kaua'i. At Waimea obtaining water proved difficult, 'the natives strongly maintained it was private property and that we should not take any away unless we paid for it with powder.' Broughton refused and it was only by sending an armed party ashore they were able to top up their water.

Provisioning likewise proved difficult as 'we understood, orders had been sent over [by the king] to prevent the selling of any article, unless we paid for it either by musquets or powder; of course we made no purchases.' As a consequence 'in the morning [of 28 July] we got under way, and made sail for the island of Onehow [Ni'ihau]' where in the afternoon the sloop anchored in Yam Bay a mile and a half offshore.

As Broughton intended staying at the island for 48 hours it wasn't until the following morning that he sent a boat ashore with three marines and a small tent to protect whatever they purchased, their prime objective being, of course, to buy yams. It was not a simple matter:

> In the evening I landed, and was sorry to find so small a collection: willing, therefore, to make it larger, I walked to some of the plantations, but was told there was a general scarcity over the island. On my return, I met with a party which had just come from Atooi [Kaua'i], and with them Tupararo, the man who was directed to follow us, that he might supply us with provisions.[68]

Tupararo told him there would be plenty of yams and sweet potatoes in the morning and asked Broughton to come on shore then and to bring a present of red cloth. Broughton, slightly suspicious, countered by suggesting Tupararo come aboard to receive his presents when the boat returned to the ship with their purchases later in the evening. At this stage he was unworried:

> ... I walked along shore to the South, where the pinnace waited for me about one mile distant. Only one of the natives accompanied me; and I walked unmolested, meeting several of the inhabitants, till I reached the boat, which was further off than I had imagined. As I had visited this island twice before, and many of the officers had made shooting parties in the interior without any interruption, I had not the least fear for my own safety; but the unhappy event which took place the next day will shew my fortunate escape.[69]

The next morning some provisions were received on board from Tupararo 'who left the ship with a design, as he said, of sending me more.' Broughton sent the cutter to receive whatever he had. The master's mate (John Cawley) was ordered to go ashore with two armed marines and Alexander Bishop (the cook/botanist) to barter, while the cutter and its crew anchored offshore under a midshipman so that they could assist if anything untoward occurred.

The boat had been gone an hour when Broughton was told by the deck officer that all the canoes around the sloop had left for the shore, a sign that something was perhaps amiss. Broughton immediately signalled the cutter to return to the ship with those on shore:

> We saw them strike the tent, and immediately after heard a firing from the boat. As no signal was made, I thought this firing was intended to recall those who were absent; but soon after, the signal was hoisted for the pinnace, when I sent an officer with marines to their assistance.[70]

As Cawley and Bishop later told Broughton, the tragic events unfolded as follows:

> The mate, on seeing the signal, ordered the boat in, and struck the tent. The marines unfixed their bayonets; and one of them gave his firelock to the botanist, while he put the tent in the bag. At this instant, when they suspected no danger, the botanist was knocked down from behind; and Tupararo run away with the musket, which the botanist had dropped. The marines were served in the same manner. After they recovered themselves, there was not time to fire the remaining musket, as the natives pressed upon them with the greatest eagerness on their retreat to the surf.[71]

At this stage the cutter was about 50 yards from the shore and the crew were frantically rowing shorewards while keeping up a constant fire with their two muskets. Cawley and Bishop reached the boat safely, the latter only by stabbing a man who had seized him in the water. The two marines, Jonathan Bird and Daniel Dell, weighed down by their uniforms and equipment, could not escape and were killed in the surf.

As the *Providence* was anchored one and a half miles offshore the pinnace was too late to be able to offer any assistance, but:

> The pinnace remained on shore to protect the dead bodies from the natives, who seemed anxious to get them, though they were sunk below the surf. As this unhappy transaction took place without the smallest provocation on our part, I consulted with the officers on the measures necessary to be pursued.[72]

All agreed the bodies had to be protected until they could be recovered, and that 'it [was] necessary to make some example on the spot.'

> The boats were therefore manned, and directions given that the marines should burn every house, canoe, and plantation, within a mile from the beach where the boats were, and should return before sunset. As they went we heard some firing from the pinnace, which occasioned the boats to land without resistance. The natives took care to keep out of the reach of the shot ... The houses were soon in flames, and sixteen canoes on the beach were burnt or destroyed. All this time the natives assembled in great numbers, armed with spears: two of them had the ill-fated marines' muskets and accoutrements. As our people advanced they fled ...[73]

The marines' bodies were recovered from nine feet of water, naked except for remnants of their trousers. One had multiple stab wounds from his own bayonet, while the other appeared to have drowned after being hit on the head. Broughton was numbed: 'Of all the murders that have been committed in these islands, this seems as unprovoked as any. The cause of it I cannot account for ...'[74]

As to what was learned from the incident, Broughton felt that the tent should have been erected on higher ground, and the boat anchored much closer to the shore to provide better protection.

The cause was likely Broughton's refusal to barter provisions for muskets and powder. The civil war on Kaua'i had recently ended, as the next chapter relates, but arms were still highly sought after. The plot was obviously pre-planned and well executed, aiming to secure the marines' muskets at all costs.

Tupararo was the instigator, and one aside in Broughton's account follows:

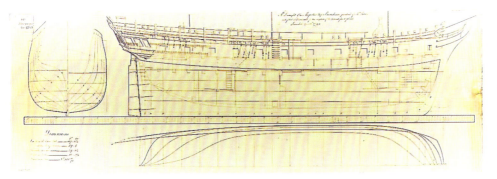

◀ The 'lines' of the sloop HMS *Providence*, launched in 1791, which Broughton commanded on a major voyage, leaving England in February 1795 to join Vancouver's expedition on the west coast of America. Before this journey the vessel under William Bligh, on his second attempt, successfully transported breadfruit trees from Tahiti to the West Indies.
Wikimedia Commons

> It was extraordinary that the two women, Rahina and Timarroe (whom Captain Vancouver brought from the N.W. coast) should have come with us from Atooi, when Tupararo was the husband of the first, and whose child had been sent on board that we might see him. They were much alarmed, and desired to be sent on shore; which request we complied with, giving each a letter, begging they would entrust them to the first vessel that arrived there, but upon no account to let them be seen by the Europeans at Atooi.[75]

Broughton was concerned that one or more of the Europeans may have been involved, or was at least aware of, the plot to secure muskets.

The officers agreed to return to Waimea to endeavor to get the chiefs there to 'deliver up Tupararo, and the other principals in these horrid murders.' The *Providence* thus set sail from Ni'ihau on 31 July, hoping to arrive before the news of the atrocities reached Kaua'i, but as 'the wind being East was directly opposite to our course' Broughton finally abandoned the attempt and after inspecting rocky Nihoa to the northwest, sailed west, intending to track along the 28th parallel in the hope of new discoveries.

It was over two years before another ship touched at Ni'ihau: the *Neptune* out of New Haven on a sealing trip. The supercargo (cargo superintendent) and son of the owner, Ebenezer Townsend Jnr, records an uneventful visit:

▲ A Royal Navy marine private from the 1790s. Their heavy, inflexible uniforms made them highly visible. The musket was the object of desire for the Niihauans in the incident related here.

▲ The Sea Service Pattern 'Brown Bess' musket shown was in service from 1778–1854. It had a smooth bore of 0.75 inches, an overall length of 53.5 inches (plus bayonet), and weighed nine pounds.
Wikipedia Commons

> We arrived [at Ni'ihau] this day, August 30th [1798], and one of our Indians went on shore to forward the getting of some yams, which we found were scarce. I believe a month later we should have found them plenty. We have not anchored and shall not, as we shall square away for Canton in the evening. We find the trade small at this island, but generally a good island for yams. The southern part of the island looks poor but the rest appears pretty well.[76]

There is no mention of being approached by canoes, nor any reference to the murders, which they appear unaware of despite having already called at Hawai'i, O'ahu and Kaua'i before Ni'ihau, and having contact with several other vessels.

After the *Neptune*, the next ship to call for yams was likely the *Margaret*, which has been discussed earlier as the vessel dressed to look like a naval vessel to prevent pilfering. There is no description of the marines' deaths, and masquerading as a naval ship may have brought benefits as they secured three tons of yams.

The only account of Broughton's voyage and the affray is his own, unlike Vancouver's voyage of which there are several descriptions. This may be because, much later in his voyage, on 17 May 1797, the *Providence* was wrecked and abandoned. Fortunately Broughton had earlier bought an English schooner in Macao, the *Prince William Henry*, to help with the surveying. With the *Providence* lying on her beam ends, in Broughton's words: 'the ship's crew were sent into the boats, which was happily effected without any accident; and soon after 11 o'clock they reached the schooner in safety, and with the loss, both officers and men, of everything belonging to them.' Presumably only Broughton's journal and the ship's log were saved. Broughton was cleared of any wrongdoing in

the subsequent court-martial in Macao, and the surveying continued from the *Prince William Henry*.

Could the attack by the Niihauans have been prevented? The visit to Waimea was fraught regarding the provision of supplies and required armed support, which could have alerted the crew to be on their guard on Niʻihau. But once there Broughton was apparently deliberately lulled into a false sense of security sufficient for him to take a stroll along the beach. If he had taken his pistols with him, they would have given him some protection, but also would have been a temptation for the locals. When the attackers seized the moment it was well planned and coordinated, relying heavily on the complacency engendered. Little wonder Broughton and his officers felt duped and thought retaliation was necessary.

Ships known to have called at Niʻihau for yams 1778–96

Vessel(s)	Captain	Dates at Niʻihau
HMS *Resolution*/ HMS *Discovery*	James Cook	29 January – 2 February 1778
HMS *Resolution*/ HMS *Discovery*	James Clerke	9–16 March 1779
King George	Nathaniel Portlock	8–13 June 1786
Queen Charlotte	George Dixon	
Nootka	John Meares	c.10 September 1787
King George	Nathaniel Portlock	?30 September – ?7 October 1787
Prince of Wales	James Colnett	27 February – 18 March 1788 24–29 September 1788
Princess Royal	James Duncan	
Felice Adventurero	John Meares	25–27 October 1788
Iphigenia Nubiana	William Douglas	c. March 1789
North West America	Robert Funter	c. March 1789
Iphigenia Nubiana	William Douglas	Probable visit August 1789
Argonaut	James Colnett	April 1791
Jenny	James Baker	Early 1792
Columbia	Robert Gray	2–3 November 1792
Lady Washington	John Kendrick	Possible visits November 1791, November 1793, December 1794
HMS *Discovery*	George Vancouver	14–16 March 1792
HMS *Chatham*	William Broughton	
Lady Washington	Roger Simpson	Possible visit February/March 1796
HMS *Discovery*	George Vancouver	13–14 March 1794
HMS *Chatham*	William Broughton	
HMS *Providence*	William Broughton	19–21 February, 28–31 July 1796
Ruby	Charles Bishop	27–28 February 1796

This chapter has concentrated on Western visitors to Niʻihau who were searching for supplies for their long journeys to the northwest coast of America, or to China. Other ships visited from other nations in their quest for scientific knowledge, and many of these are covered in Appendix E. The next chapter follows the traumatic political events in Hawaiʻi during this early period of Western contact, and particularly those involving Kauaʻi and, of course, Niʻihau.

▲ This feathered image of Kū (Kūkaʻilimoku), the Hawaiian god of war, was collected by Captain Cook on his third voyage. When the ships returned to England it was given by Lt King to King George III, and he in turn presented it, along with 500 other artifacts, to Göttingen's Institute of Anthropology. It now resides at Göttingen University in Sweden.
Wikimedia Commons

CHAPTER FIVE

REBELLION ON KAUA'I

Over the centuries the political history of Ni'ihau has been dominated by events on Kaua'i, and this pattern intensified after Westerners visited. Likewise the political history of Kaua'i and Ni'ihau has been heavily influenced by the history of the Hawaiian islands as a whole, although the dangerous 72-mile-wide Ka'ie'ie Waho channel between O'ahu and Kaua'i has provided some isolation and protection to the leeward islands of Kaua'i and Ni'ihau. This chapter briefly outlines the political history of these two islands from the time of Captain Cook until their full absorption into the Hawaiian kingdom in 1824.

In the years immediately before Cook's arrival the islands had been in a state of considerable political flux, and war was in the air. At the time Cook landed at Waimea, Kamakahelei, the granddaughter of Pele'ioholani was ali'i 'ai moku (Queen Regent) of the leeward islands, owing allegiance to her grandfather, whose kingly domain stretched at its maximum extent from Ni'ihau to Moloka'i. She was described by surgeon William Ellis of the *Discovery* as 'short and lusty … and very plain with respect to person,' but she came from a most distinguished lineage. Kamakahelei had married high chief Kiha, titular prince of Ni'ihau who paid homage to the Kaua'i ruler. By Kiha she had two daughters and a son, Keawe.[1]

To ensure stability in his realm, Pele'ioholani sent his grandson Kaneoneo from Maui to Kaua'i. Kamakahelei subsequently married Kaneoneo, her first cousin, whereupon Kiha fled with some warriors to Ni'ihau, and from there harassed the south coast of Kaua'i. In one of these skirmishes Kiha was killed and peace was restored. Kaneoneo ruled with Kamakahelei as his consort.[2]

Ka'eo

Pele'ioholani's empire was crumbling, with Kahekili, the new ruler of Maui in the ascendency, having been victorious over Pele'ioholani. Kahekili was planning to invade O'ahu, and also saw an opportunity on Kaua'i, where politics were difficult, and sent his half-brother Ka'eokūlani (known as Ka'eo) to woo Kamakahelei to whom Ka'eo had been betrothed in his early teens. His mission was a success and shortly after Cook's visit in 1779 the newly married couple deposed Kaneoneo in favor of Keawe, Kamakahelei's son by her marriage to Kiha.³ (Other accounts say that Kaneoneo was removed from power in a battle on 29 April 1779.)

A son, Kaumuali'i, was born to Ka'eo and Kamakahelei c.1778.⁴ He was to prove a key figure in subsequent events. The pregnancy was unexpected as Kamakahelei was thought to be past childbearing age, and Keawe had already been named as heir to the kingdom.⁵

By 1786, when Portlock and Dixon visited, Ka'eo was the undisputed king of Kaua'i and Ni'ihau, with 'Ōpūnui ('Abbenooe') his deputy and Ka'eo's man on the ground on Ni'ihau. Kahekili was by this time all-powerful on O'ahu, Maui and the smaller windward islands. Hawai'i was still in a state of political uncertainty, with three warring parties contending for power.⁶

Ka'eo was described by Portlock as 'about forty-five years old, stout and well made, and seemed the best disposed man that we had met with amongst the islands.' He was impressed: 'According to my expectation, I found that Abbenooe was a man highly esteemed by the king, who consulted him on every occasion.'⁷

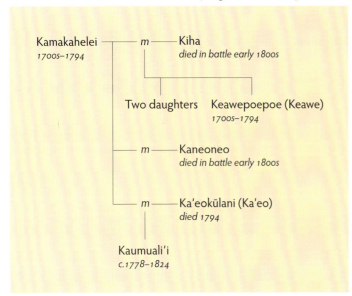

▲ The ancestry of Kaumuali'i.

Western weapons introduced a new dimension to traditional Hawaiian warfare and an arms race ensued, particularly on Hawai'i. The response of visiting ship captains varied, but inevitably muskets and powder were acquired. Ka'eo was one of the first to arm himself with the new weaponry.

When in 1791, Ka'eo was called on to help his half-brother Kahekili fight Kamehameha on Maui, his son Kaumuali'i, still a child, was appointed heir to Kaua'i and Ni'ihau, while the elderly Wailua chief Inamo'o was named regent in his absence. Keawe, Kamakahelei's eldest son was thus passed over, setting the stage for major dispute.⁸

Kamehameha had already consolidated his position on Hawai'i and in 1790 had invaded Maui while Kahekili was absent on O'ahu. Then rebellion broke out on Hawai'i and Kamehameha had to return, leaving the way open for Kahekili to reconquer Maui, Moloka'i and Lāna'i. Kahekili then attempted to invade Hawai'i and his and Kamehameha's fleets clashed off Hawai'i's northeast coast, both deploying western weapons. Kahekili and Ka'eo were defeated and no further attempt was made by either party to join in battle until after Kahekili's death at Waikīkī: in 1794. Ka'eo and one of Kahekili's sons, Kalanikūpule, inherited Kahekili's kingdom.⁹

Ka'eo determined to return to Kaua'i, while Kalanikūpule remained undisputed sovereign of Maui, Moloka'i and Lāna'i. O'ahu became a bone of contention between them and on 12 December 1794 a decisive battle took place on O'ahu at 'Aiea, which was won by Kalanikūpule. Ka'eo was killed in the encounter, leaving Kaua'i and Ni'ihau in the hands of his son, the youthful Kaumuali'i, and his controversial regent Inamo'o.¹⁰

Warring between Keawe and Kaumuali'i

The deaths of Ka'eo and, shortly afterwards, that of Inamo'o, gave Keawe, Kaumuali'i's elder half-brother, the opportunity he had been seeking, and a civil war ensued on Kaua'i. When Charles Bishop visited on the ship *Ruby* in March 1796, he reported:

> This Island [Kaua'i] is the Pleasantest by far we have seen but is now torn to Pieces by the distractions and civil War reigning at this time — Taheo [Ka'eo] the late King dying, left a Son called King George [Kaumuali'i styled himself King George], a youth of about 17 years, whose Mother had bourne several children before she became the wife of Taheo, by a Principal Chief, the Eldest of which is Named Teeavey [Keawe] and also Rerowee — they Both claim the Soveriegnty of the Island and support it by the Sword. Teeavey [Keawe], has got Possession of the West side and by far the best and most Numerous Part of the People in his cause. The other has the East side, and altho' not so strong in Numbers, his Party is Resolute and Firm to his cause. While we were here two Battles or skirmishes had happened in which Teeavey tho' much stronger had no reason to boast a victory.[11]

Bishop describes an aspect of the ritualistic manner in which warfare was conducted:

> A small stream of water in a valley separates the Encampments of the two armys, and I am told it requires the utmost force of the Taboo to Prevent the armies rushing on to Death or Victory and which the contending chiefs Politically exert, for as Soon as the Taboo is Proclaimed in one camp, for one, two, or three days, it immediately takes place in the other for the like time. In this time, these intervals of war, they sit on the opposite banks of the stream conversing with each other as Friends.[12]

Four months later in July 1796, when Robert Broughton arrived on HMS *Providence*, Keawe's forces had been victorious and Kaumuali'i was living with Keawe under house arrest and completely powerless.[13]

Charles Bishop describes Keawe as 'a bold Hawaiian Person and ... renowned Warrior.' His reign as king of Kaua'i and Ni'ihau was, however, short-lived, as he died later that same year. Accounts vary as to whether Keawe's death was from natural causes or assassination but, whatever the circumstances, it gave Kaumuali'i and his supporters the chance to seize power over the Leeward Islands.

Kamehameha's Kaua'i invasion attempts

Meanwhile, in the spring of 1795 Kamehameha invaded O'ahu from Moloka'i, and in the famous battle of Nu'uanu defeated Kalanikūpule. Kamehameha's conquest of the Windward Islands was complete, but his dream was to unite all the islands and he began preparations for an invasion of Kaua'i. He assembled a large military force and naval fleet on O'ahu, which sailed in May 1796 only to encounter a fierce storm in the Ka'ie'ie Waho channel. The attempt was abandoned and the fleet fled in disarray. Soon afterwards, in September, an insurrection occurred on Hawai'i, and Kamehameha had to return there, where he remained for the following six years. Relative peace returned to the islands, but Kamehameha still had a burning desire to unify all the islands.

Six years on and he again gathered his forces for an assault on Kaua'i and Ni'ihau, first assembling in Lahaina and then moving to O'ahu. He continued to send threatening

▲ 19th-century wooden leiomanō, a Hawaiian war club with inset shark teeth and mother-of-pearl inlay. The teeth are fastened with copper pins, showing post-European contact influence. The club is exhibited in the Peabody Essex Museum, doubtless brought back from Hawai'i by an early whaling vessel.
Wikipedia Commons.

messages to Kaumualiʻi. Richard Cleveland was the first Western trader to convey one of these messages, while visiting Kauaʻi on the *Lelia Byrd* in July 1803, and he comments:

> Atoui [Kauaʻi], at this time, was independent of the government of Tamaahmaah [Kamehameha], from whom we were bearers of a message to the King [Kaumualiʻi], purporting, that the ambassador, which had been sent to him, together with one of equal rank, must be sent to Woahoo [Oʻahu], within the space of one month, acknowledging him, Tamaahmaah, as his sovereign, on penalty of a visit with all his forces. As the King did not come on board and we did not land, the message was given to one of the European residents, who promised to convey it, but said it would be disregarded.[14]

▶ Richard Cleveland (1773–60), an American merchant seaman who, in 1800, together with William Shaler, bought the 175-ton Virginia-built brig *Lelia Byrd* to trade for furs along the west coast of America. By the toss of a coin Shaler became the captain and Cleland the supercargo (a representative of the ship's owner, responsible for overseeing the cargo and its sale). Cleveland kept extensive journals of their voyaging and they achieved fame in Hawaiʻi by being the first westerners to take a message from Kamehameha to Kaumualiʻi in his battle for control of Kauaʻi.
Wikimedia Commons

Kamehameha was thwarted in his invasion attempt yet again, however, this time by an outbreak of disease. In 1804 a devastating epidemic (possibly typhoid or bubonic plague, but most likely cholera) broke out among his troops on Oʻahu and he abandoned his plans.

Meanwhile Kaumualiʻi had been consolidating his position on Kauaʻi and Niʻihau. John Turnbull, visiting on the *Margaret* in December 1802, described the population's feelings about Kaumualiʻi: 'He appeared to be loved almost to adoration …'[15] An earlier pen portrait of Kaumualiʻi as a youth was given by Vancouver, who met him in 1792:

> In his countenance was exhibited much affability and cheerfulness; and, on closely observing his features, they had infinitely more the resemblance of an European than of those which generally characterize these islanders; being destitute of that natural ferocity so conspicuous in the persons about him. In these respects, and in the quickness of his comprehension and ideas, he greatly surpassed his young friend and companion *Tipoone* [Kapune]. … if conclusions may be permitted to be drawn from the general deportment and manners of his early years, the riper ones of this young prince must be attended with a very considerable degree of consequence in this part of the world.[16]

▲ The legendary Kamehameha the First (c.1758–1819) in a portrait by Russian artist Mikhail Tikhanov. This stern and mysterious pencil and watercolor rendition dates from 1818, the year before Kamehameha's death, and was painted during the visit to Kailua, Kona by the Russian research vessel *Kamchatka* under Captain Golovnin. It hangs in the Museum of the Russian Academy of the Arts, St Petersburg. The artist was the expedition's draftsman for the global circumnavigation undertaken between 1817 and 1819. Kamehameha's head was shaved in mourning for his sister's death the previous day.
Wikimedia Commons

▲ Kaumualiʻi (c.1737–1824), last king of Kauaʻi and Niʻihau. No portrait exists from life. This painting, which draws upon existing textual records, is in the Kauaʻi Museum.
Kauaʻi Museum

By 1805 he certainly was becoming consequential. In that year William Shaler spent three months in the islands, mostly at Kamehameha's court. Shaler became his next informal ambassador when he sailed to Kauaʻi on the *Atahualpa* in October, and he writes of Kamehameha:

> He has frequently assured me that his ambition would be satisfied with the king of Atooai's [Kauaʻi] acknowledging him as sovereign, and paying him an annual tribute. However this may be, he, like all ambitious men, is determined to have no rival, and is making great preparations for the invasion of that island …[17]

While Shaler didn't agree with Kamehameha's plans for conquest, he firmly believed that all the islands should be under a single government.

◀ A modern depiction of the *Lelia Byrd* being towed by three double canoes into Honolulu Harbor, in a painting by Raymond Massey. The *Lelia Byrd* had a colorful career. During her fur-trading time she was briefly interned in San Diego by the Spanish authorities, but escaped under fire. She paid three visits to Hawai'i and was finally sold there to King Kamehameha in exchange for a smaller vessel. Subsequently she made several voyages to Canton with cargoes of sandalwood.
Raymond Massey

Shaler met with Kaumuali'i off Kaua'i on the *Atahualpa* and 'broached with him the business of my mission, and represented to him the folly of making any resistance to Tamaihamaiha [Kamehameha], and the still greater folly of expecting to amuse him by idle tales of submission …' The upshot was a letter from Kaumuali'i to Kamehameha penned by Shaler which apparently assured Kamehameha 'that he [Kaumuali'i] would comply with whatever terms the king of Owyhee should dictate that were consistent with honour and personal safety.' The fate of the letter is unknown.

Isaac Iselin was in the islands on the *Maryland* in 1807 and left a fascinating account that included a record of conveying 'a chief from Attowai [Kaua'i] with despatches,' from O'ahu to Kaua'i — so the rival parties were still negotiating. Iselin describes Kamehameha at this time:

> The King is a tall stout man of about fifty or sixty. His countenance, rather stern and unpleasant, bespeaks nothing of his remarkable character. His manners are cordial and free — he appears a great observer, viewing every corner and locker of the ship — talks but little, but seems to think much.[18]

Later in his visit Iselin, while off Waimea, makes a brief comment on Kaumuali'i:

> 18th [July 1807] In the afternoon another double canoe hove in sight and soon after we were honored with a visit of King Tamoru [Kaumuali'i] (otherwise called King George) accompanied by a few chiefs and warriors. Tamoru is a fine looking man of about thirty, with an excellent European countenance, and his whole deportment, together with his old French marine uniform coat, makes him more of a Frenchman than a South Sea Islander.[19]

▶ Mahiole (helmet) reputedly given to Kaumualiʻi by Kamehameha for agreeing to a peaceful settlement of their differences. It now resides in the Bishop Museum.
Wikimedia Commons

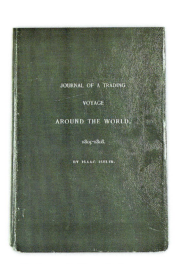

▲ The journal of Isaac Iselin (1783–1841). Isaac emigrated to New York from Switzerland in 1801 and worked in shipping firms before being entrusted as supercargo on the trading vessel *Maryland*. The voyage lasted two and a half years and the ship journeyed around Cape Horn to Canton and back around the Cape of Good Hope. This included the Hawaiian islands, where in 1807 he interacted with both Kamehameha and Kaumualiʻi. Iselin kept a diary throughout the voyage and had it printed as a gift for his son.
Steven Gentry

They must have been testing times for Kaumualiʻi, as Iselin would have been able to tell him of the enormous scale of Kamehameha's weaponry and manpower assembled on Oʻahu.[20]

The meeting and agreement of 1810

Kamehameha had been insisting for some time that a face-to-face meeting was necessary to settle their differences. Kaumualiʻi was naturally wary, and it took the diplomacy of an American captain to make it happen. Many envoys had passed between them since, as the historian Samuel Kamakau says, 'Kamehameha had now given up the thought of going to war with Ka-umu-aliʻi, believing that he could secure annexation by peaceful means.'[21]

Nathan Winship, captain of the trading vessel *Albatross*, arrived in Waimea in March 1810. He had been to the islands in 1806 as mate on the *O'Cain*, captained by his brother Jonathan, and presumably he met Kamehameha and Kaumualiʻi at that time. The last envoy Kaumualiʻi had sent to Oʻahu, his nephew Kamaholelani, had just returned with positive news of the reception he had received, but indicating that Kamehameha was still insisting on a meeting between the two kings to make further progress. Winship offered to take a delegation, including Kaumualiʻi, to treat with Kamehameha at Honolulu, leaving his mate, William Smith, in Waimea as surety for Kaumualiʻi's safe return. After much hesitation, Kaumualiʻi agreed. On arrival off Honolulu, as Kamakau records:

> Kamehameha went out to meet the boat [the *Albatross*] at the sea of Mamala [Bay], accompanied by his chiefs and Ka-lani-moku, his leading counselor. Ka-umu-aliʻi had with him his old kahunas learned in ancient wisdom and his war leaders, Kaheʻe and Puʻu-iki. The fleet of canoes drew near, red with feather cloaks and radiant with the colors of the rainbow. Kamehameha himself was in a single canoe and he drew close to

the boat, thinking to be unrecognised; but Kaumuali'i was ready to receive him, dressed in the costume of the chiefs of old, with Captain Winship and the foreigners of the ship in full dress.[22]

It must have been quite a sight. According to John Papa 'Ī'ī the two absolute rulers 'greeted each other kindly and with true affection.'[23] The parties then went ashore and discussions took place at Pākākā, Kamehameha's compound near the canoe landing place in Honolulu harbor.

The outcome of their discussions, according to historian Ralph Kuykendall, was that 'Kauai should be a tributary kingdom and that Kaumualii should continue to govern [Kaua'i and Ni'ihau], acknowledging Kamehameha as his suzeran.'[24] 'Ī'ī makes it clear that their understanding included a rider that when Kamehameha died, his son Liholiho would be recognized as heir to all the islands.[25]

The agreement essentially put Kaumuali'i's domains in the same camp as the other islands of Kamehameha's realm. Franchere remarks in his 1811 journal that Kamehameha had 40 schooners, 'these vessels served to transport the tributes in kind paid by his vassals in the other islands.'[26] It appears that Kaumuali'i's tribute may have been paid in 1811, but it is doubtful if he made any further payments until 1818.

The first intimation in the written record that the agreement had been breached by Kaumuali'i is in Don Francisco de Paula Marin's journal entry for 19 March 1813, where he notes that Kaumuali'i had declared war on Kamehameha.[27] The log of the American trading vessel *Atahualpa* which is referred to extensively in Peter Mills' book *Hawai'i's Russian Adventure,*[28] corroborates Marin's entry.

Kaumuali'i was feeling more confident in relation to his old foe, due in no small part to his fostering of relationships with American trading captains during the War of 1812 between the British and the Americans. The log of the *Atahualpa* confirms that the American fur traders offered Kaumuali'i support against both Kamehameha and the British.

According to Edwin McClellan's article on John Gamble in the Hawaiian Historical Society's 1927 annual report:

> King Kaumualii of Kauai, at this time, showed a loyalty to principle and a friendly spirit toward Americans that should never be overlooked. On his island was property owned by Captain Whittemore and Jonathan Winship to the value of many thousands of dollars. Captain Tucker 'employed every stratagem to gain possession of it, without effect. He at first began to wheedle Kaumualii, 'using all his efforts to entice him on board the *Cherub*.' But Kaumualii could be neither bought nor persuaded to betray the Americans.[29]

One amusing, but probably apocryphal, story told during the heyday of this relationship with American ship captains is given in John Lydgate's article in the Hawaiian Historical Society's Annual Report for 1915:

> One of these traders (perhaps it was Captain Windship) who was on terms of intimate friendship with Kaumu-alii, was in the habit of filling orders for his Majesty in the Orient. On one particular occasion, as he was preparing to sail, he came to the King for his usual order. Kaumu-alii gave him about the customary list for dry goods, hardware, furniture, weapons, munitions etc., and then in conclusion said: 'I understand that other Kings have jewels of great beauty and value, and I have none at all. What are these jewels?'

▲ John Papa 'Ī'ī (1800–70), a respected adviser to Hawaiian kings for 58 years, beginning at age ten as kahu (guardian) to Kamehameha's son Liholiho, and serving continuously through to the reign of Kamehameha V. His memoirs, *Fragments of Hawaiian History*, were written in the last year of his life as newspaper articles, which were edited and published in 1959 by the Bishop Museum. An excellent biography of 'Ī'ī, *Facing the Spears of Change* by Marie Alohalani Brown, was published in 2016 by the University of Hawai'i Press.
Wikimedia Commons

'Well,' returned the Captain, 'there are various kinds of jewels. I believe diamonds are considered the top-notch thing in the line of jewels.' 'Well, then, I wish you would bring me back a diamond from China.' 'I don't know much about diamonds,' returned the Captain, 'but I will do the best I can for you. How big a diamond would you like?' 'Well,' returned the King, 'say one as big as a cocoanut!'[30]

Kaumuali'i's closeness to the American traders was not to last. Many of his chiefs were not happy with the situation, particularly as it involved collecting sandalwood under contracts that Kaumuali'i had made with the traders. Sandalwood collection was arduous and was becoming increasingly difficult as supplies on Kaua'i diminished. Traders also had problems protecting their property on the island and they were naturally disgruntled.

Despite their agreement, Kaumuali'i believed that Kamehameha was waiting for an opportunity to invade, and felt he could not now rely upon the American vessels for support in that event. By October 1814 the Americans ran out of patience and prepared to take their goods and depart for Canton, at which point Kaumuali'i refused the vessels any further sandalwood. This precipitated a crisis, and as the log of the *Atahualpa* for 1 October 1814 states:

> At 2 PM Capt. Davis [of the fur-trader *Isabella*] ordered his ship to be hauled close in shore at the same time sent a message on shore to know if they intended delivering the Wood. At 3 Received an answer in the Negative. At the same time saw the Natives making evry preparation for action. As Capt. Davis did not think proper to risk the lives of his People in action with the natives, at 8 haul'd ship off to his former berth.[31]

Given these difficulties, some of which were of Kaumuali'i's own making, the fur traders slowly removed their goods from the island and by the spring of 1815 all had departed, leaving Kaumuali'i dependent solely on his own resources again.

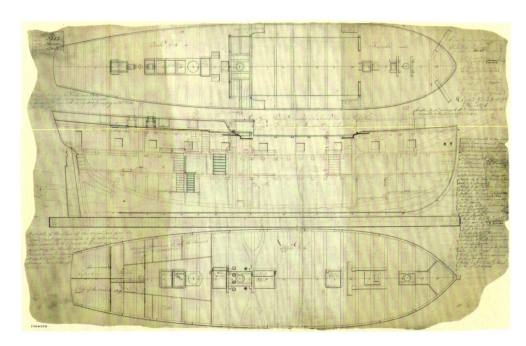

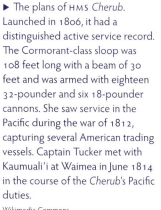

▶ The plans of HMS *Cherub*. Launched in 1806, it had a distinguished active service record. The Cormorant-class sloop was 108 feet long with a beam of 30 feet and was armed with eighteen 32-pounder and six 18-pounder cannons. She saw service in the Pacific during the war of 1812, capturing several American trading vessels. Captain Tucker met with Kaumuali'i at Waimea in June 1814 in the course of the *Cherub*'s Pacific duties.
Wikimedia Commons

Dr Schäffer and the Russians

Into this vacuum, in November 1815, stepped Dr Georg Schäffer. A German by background, he had been sent on behalf of the tsar by the Russian-American Company to negotiate for the return of valuable otter-skin cargo, which had been saved from the wreck of the RAC's vessel *Bering* when she had been driven ashore at Waimea beach on 31 January 1815.

The Russian-American Company (RAC) was Russia's first joint-stock company, and received a charter from the tsar in 1799 to establish settlements in Russian America (i.e. broadly today's Alaska) and trade with the native Americans. It was only dissolved when the United States bought Alaska in 1867.

The *Atahualpa* had, by a quirk of fate, been bought by the RAC in 1814 and renamed the *Bering*, and under an American skipper, James Bennett, was back at Waimea on 30 January 1815. Caught in an on-shore wind she foundered on the beach with a full cargo of furs and ship's stores.

When James Bennett realized the fully laden ship could not be saved, he asked for Kaumuali'i's help to salvage the valuable cargo. This was grudgingly given, and up to 2000 locals were employed on the task for several days in February. Inevitably there was pilfering, and relations between the crew and the workers were not easy. Efforts to salvage the ship itself continued for weeks, but to no avail.

Kaumuali'i saw the loss of the *Bering* and the recovery of its furs as a heaven-sent opportunity. He felt it inevitable that the Russians would attempt to retrieve the cargo now in his storehouses. He had regained foreign leverage to bolster his position with Kamehameha.

On the understanding that the agreement of 1810 was still valid and that Kamehameha was the supreme sovereign, Dr Schäffer was tasked by the RAC with currying Kamehameha's favor to secure release of the cargo and establish mutually profitable trade relations. It was understood by Dr Schäffer that if his negotiations with Kaumuali'i did not appear to be succeeding, the threat of war between the two parties was to be used as a lever.

With the War of 1812 at an end, when Schäffer arrived at Kamehameha's court on Hawai'i, the Americans on the island recognized the threat posed by the Russians to their privileged position and obstructed Schäffer. As a medical doctor, circumstances intervened, and he successfully treated both Kamehameha and Queen Ka'ahumanu for serious illnesses. This won over Kamehameha, and Schäffer reported to his superiors that he had negotiated successfully for the return of the cargo, and had been given land by the Hawaiian king on both Hawai'i and O'ahu to set up trading ventures. Kamehameha was moving slowly, however — so slowly that on 28 May 1816 the impetuous Schäffer sailed from Hawai'i for Kaua'i to meet with Kaumuali'i.

What happened next almost beggars belief. With the arrival of Schäffer, Kaumuali'i saw an opportunity to use the Russians to best Kamehameha.[32] On 2 June, only three days after his arrival, Schäffer and Kaumuali'i signed two formal agreements. As described by Bolkhovitnov in the *Hawaiian Journal of History*:

◀ Georg Schäffer (1779–1836), a German-born surgeon employed in the imperial Russian service and later by the Russian-American Company.
Wikimedia Commons

▼ The statue of Kaumuali'i at Pa'ula'ula.
Nancy Shaw

In a solemn atmosphere, Kaumualii — 'King of the Sandwich Islands of the Pacific Ocean, Atuvai [Kauai] and Nigau [Niihau], and Hereditary Prince of the Islands of Ovagu [Oahu] and Mauvi [Maui]' — humbly requested 'His Majesty the Sovereign Emperor Alexander Pavlovich … to accept the mentioned islands under his protection' and promised eternal allegiance to the 'Russian scepter.' On that same day another agreement was signed, in which Kaumualii promised not only to return the part of the *Bering*'s cargo that had been saved, but also to furnish the RAC with a monopoly in sandalwood trade. The company also received the right to institute its trading stations and plantations on Kaumualii's domains without interference.[33]

Even more extraordinary, five weeks later, on 13 July, a secret treaty was signed between them under which Kaumualiʻi would provide 500 warriors for an expedition to be led by 'the gallant doctor of medicine' to reconquer all of the Windward Islands (except Hawaiʻi), 'belonging to him and taken from him by force.' The treaty continued, 'The King provides Doctor Schäffer carte blanche for this expedition and all assistance in constructing fortresses on all islands.' In addition:

- The RAC was to receive one half of Oʻahu, and the rights to all sandalwood on the island.
- Kaumualiʻi agreed to pay in sandalwood for all that he received under the treaty — vessels, weapons and ammunition.
- He also agreed not to trade with the United States of America.
- For his part Schäffer agreed to the 'setting up of trading stations and a better economy, through which local inhabitants might gain enlightenment and wealth.'[34]

Even with the age-old invasion threat from Kamehameha uppermost in his mind, did Kaumualiʻi really understand what he was signing? While Kaumualiʻi had competent Hawaiian/English speakers around him and both signatories spoke English — of a kind — the treaties were in Russian. The Hawaiian language in written form had to await the arrival of the missionaries. The consensus of the commentators in the literature, however, is that he *did* understand what he was doing.

Schäffer was flushed with success. He sent copies of the agreements by the first available means to his immediate superior, Alexandr Baranov, in New Archangel (today's Sitka), and to the RAC's head office in St Petersburg, with a request for two armed vessels to be sent to the islands. As might have been expected Baranov hedged, requiring main office permission before taking action, and he cautioned Schäffer against any speculative ventures.

Meanwhile on Kauaʻi Schäffer was busy building storehouses for his trading station in Waimea and establishing gardens. With

▲ Tsar Alexander I (1777–1825) reigned from 1801 until his death. The focus throughout his reign was always upon events in Europe and the see-sawing relationship with Napoleon until the latter's final defeat in Russia in 1812. Even after this, the unstable situation to Russia's west continued to consume his energies and he had little interest in expansion of his empire eastwards into Alaska. Nevertheless in 1799 by royal charter he agreed to the formation of the Russian-American Company, but when matters spiralled out of control regarding the Hawaiian islands in 1818 he would not agree to the acquisition by Russia of Niʻihau and Kauaʻi. This 1824 painting is by the English portraitist, George Dawe.
Wikimedia Commons

▶ Alexandr Andreyevich Baranov (1747–1819), the chief manager of the Russian-American Company, and effectively the first Governor of Russian America, who employed Georg Schäffer and set him the task of recovering furs from Kaumualiʻi. This 1818 painting is by Mikhail Tikhanov, who also painted Kamehameha I during the visit of the *Kamchatka* to the Hawaiian islands (see page 108).
Wikimedia Commons

◀ Fort Elizabeth, the Russian fort at Waimea, on Kauai, in a photographic reconstruction indicating how it may have looked when first completed in 1816.
Alexander Molodin and Peter Mills 2015 / Wikimedia Commons

▼ Otto von Kotzebue (1787–1846), an Imperial Russian naval officer who captained the naval brig *Rurik* on an exploration mission to find a passage across the Arctic ocean. In July 1815 he spent three weeks in the Hawaiian islands, mostly at the court of King Kamehameha, making it clear to him that Schäffer was a usurper and that Russia did not have Imperial ambitions for the islands.
Wikimedia Commons

the help of 300 Hawaiians supplied by Kaumuali'i (including three of his wives), construction of the massive Fort Elizabeth, the 'Russian Fort' or Pā'ula'ula o Hipo, commenced in September on the true left bank at the mouth of the Waimea River.

Disillusionment with Schäffer began when Otto von Kotzebue arrived on the Russian naval ship *Rurik* to visit Kamehameha at his court on Hawai'i. Given the rumors abounding about Schäffer's activities, Von Kotzebue emphatically reassured the king that Russia had no interest in taking possession of the islands, and sailed away without even visiting Kaua'i, much to Schäffer's chagrin. This led to rumors that Russian naval vessels would not be arriving to bolster Kaumuali'i's regime — rumors that were true, as Schäffer now knew. American ship captains were also actively working against him and attempted to lower the Russian flag flying in Waimea. Threats of violence were made. At some point Kaumuali'i realized he had been duped and the Russian government was not going to support the treaties, but this did not dawn on Schäffer himself until June 1817.[35]

With much difficulty Schäffer made his way to Honolulu, and finally to Canton in China, where he passes out of the picture as far as Kaua'i and Ni'ihau are concerned. Not so though in Russia, where his reports were carefully considered and passed up through the RAC structure, government departments and finally to Tsar Alexander himself. The tsar's response was unequivocal. As his minister of internal affairs informed the RAC on 8 March 1818:

> His Majesty the Emperor wishes to presume that the acquisition of these islands [Kaua'i and Ni'ihau] and their voluntary acceptance of his protection are not only without any significant benefit to Russia but, on the contrary, in many regards they are burdened with very weighty inconveniences. And therefore it would be pleasing to His Majesty not to accept this act from him [Kaumuali'i] though His Majesty expresses all possible affability and desires to preserve friendly relations with him … [36]

The missive goes on to hope that the friendly relations established will encourage the development of trade between the RAC and the islands. The RAC was instructed that there could be no deviating from the Emperor's 'august will,' but the RAC wished to capitalize on the amicable business dealings already achieved, despite the disastrous ending to Schäffer's time there.

Matters dragged on in Russia between the RAC and various ministries about how best to proceed. Finally, in August 1819, the RAC directors in St Petersburg instructed the company management to send an expedition to Kaua'i 'without delay' to influence Kaumuali'i to gain his consent to the settlement of Russians 'predominantly on Ni'ihau,' or better still, to encourage him to sell the island to the RAC. 'Acquisition of that island is all the more important to the company because it is the nearest to the colonies [i.e. Alaska] and, being sparsely populated, there is less danger of conceit on the part of inhabitants.' Company management was not enthusiastic, to say the least, and moved slowly, resulting in a further instruction to proceed urgently. This resulted in a cogent paper from management on 'the total uselessness of trade relations with the Hawaiian islands.' The matter was finally dropped by the directors, but not until January 1821.[37]

Thus ended the saga of Russian involvement with Kaua'i and Ni'ihau. If the tsar had been looking eastwards rather than towards Europe, the result for the islands and for the world at large may have been very different.

Kaumuali'i's tribute of 1818 to Kamehameha

Meanwhile, back on Kaua'i, with the Russians' fall from grace in 1817, Kaumuali'i felt extremely exposed. He fully anticipated Russian retaliation for what had happened, and Kamehameha's military might was never far from his mind. Kamehameha himself was also concerned there could be Russian reprisals,[38] and this could have worked to Kaumuali'i's advantage. But it didn't stop Kamehameha pressing for his tribute in 1818.

Early in 1818 Kamehameha bought the fully armed brig *Columbia* and then sent it to Waimea to collect sandalwood, two shiploads of which were presumably the current year's tribute required from Kaumuali'i. The sandalwood was duly loaded in Waimea, but then offloaded in Honolulu and stored there by the previous owners of the ship until it could be shipped to Canton. Kaumuali'i and his chiefs at Waimea were evidently most co-operative. As Peter Corney, mate of the *Columbia*, wrote in his journal:

> [Kamehameha's] chiefs landed, and were well received by Tamooree [Kaumuali'i]; and the next morning they commenced sending wood on board. About 500 canoes were employed in bringing it off ... The king behaved extremely well, and sent us off plenty of hogs and vegetables. Our chiefs came on board, as did also some Atooi [Kaua'i] chiefs. We weighed and made sail for Woahoo [O'ahu] ...[39]

Kamehameha's chiefs included his right-hand man Kalanimoku and several lesser chiefs.[40] Kaumuali'i knew he was in a weak position, and a tribute was better than invasion of his islands. This appears to have been the first tribute Kaumuali'i had paid since 1811 or 1812.

By the time all the sandalwood in payment for the ship had been collected and stored in Honolulu it was 1 May 1818 and the vessel was formally handed over the following day in Honolulu to Kalanimoku, Kamehameha's chief minister.

The death of Kamehameha

By 1818 Kamehameha was not a well man, and he died in May 1819. He was to be succeeded by his 21-year-old son Liholiho, but actual administrative power still resided with Ka'ahumanu, Kamehameha's favorite wife. The death of Kamehameha gave Kaumuali'i the opportunity he was looking for. Jacques Arago, visiting Hawai'i, Maui and O'ahu as artist on the Freycinet expedition three months after Kamehameha's death described it this way:

> It had not been without some degree of vexation that the King of Atooi [Kaua'i] saw himself under the necessity of submitting to the yoke that seemed to be imposed on him; he resolved however to shake it off the first favourable opportunity, and that has been furnished him by the death of Tammeamah [Kamehameha]. Perfectly certain of the apathy of Riouriou [Liholiho], he has given the latter to understand 'that he was no longer his tributary, that he considered the engagements which had been forced upon him at an end, and that he would repel force by force. In the event of a contest, it would probably soon be seen which of the two Kings was destined to pay tribute to the other.'[41]

The regime change following the death of Kamehameha required a firm hand, as it also gave an opportunity for rebellion by other chiefs, particularly those disaffected by Kamehameha's monopolization of the sandalwood trade on the Windward Islands. Liholiho was seen as mercurial, but behind his outbursts often lay well thought-out plans. An example was the abolition of the kapu system in early November 1819, an earth-shattering event for the Hawaiian religion and culture. The kapu system — with its rigid rules involving human sacrifice, separation of men and women while eating, prostration in front of ali'i, and ritual prayers for guidance — was the very foundation of Hawaiian society. Even accidentally breaking a kapu could result in death. Contact with Westerners had brought a broader knowledge of the world, and Liholiho, encouraged particularly by Ka'ahumanu, became determined to have the kapu system set aside. He proposed a feast as the symbolic gesture.

As Kuykendall describes the occasion, based on contemporary sources:

> When the young king had finally made his decision and was on the point of putting it into execution — a course requiring no small amount of courage on his part — he caused a feast to be prepared at Kailua, to which all the leading chiefs and several foreigners were invited. Two tables were set in the European fashion, one for men and one for women.
>> "After the guests were seated, and had begun to eat … suddenly, and without any previous warning to any but those in the secret, [the king] seated himself in a vacant chair at the women's table, and began to eat voraciously, but was evidently much perturbed. The guests, astonished at this act, clapped their hands, and cried out '*Ai noa* — the eating tabu is broken.'
>> "When the meal was over, Liholiho issued orders to destroy the heiaus [shrines] and burn the idols, and this was done from one end of the kingdom to the other."[42]

Liholiho unexpectedly visits Kaua'i

While Kuykendall states that the idols were destroyed 'from one end of the kingdom to the other' Liholiho was not so sure if this was so on Kaua'i under Kaumuali'i. A further example of Liholiho's apparently erratic behavior, and one most germane to the subject of this book, is his dramatic visit to Kaua'i in July 1821. By February 1821 Liholiho had moved his principal place of residence from Kailua on Hawai'i to Honolulu. In July he set off from Honolulu on horseback (with his entourage) to Waialua to inspect sandalwood cutting in the Wai'anae Range on O'ahu. (Other accounts say they traveled around the island, some by canoe and some on horseback.) Three days later, at Wai'anae, on his way back to Honolulu, the king suddenly proposed a visit to Kaua'i, and could not be dissuaded despite the obvious dangers of the stormy channel and the reception he might receive from Kaumuali'i.

He set out in a small open sailboat, accompanied by just a few chiefs and 30 retainers. (Other versions of the story say the decision to sail to Kaua'i was made in mid-journey over the remonstrations of those on board.) In retrospect it was not done on impulse, but was a well developed plan which Liholiho had been waiting for a suitable opportunity to execute.

The journey proved fearful, with waves slopping over the gunwales, and twice the vessel was nearly swamped. Bailing was almost continuous, but the outline of Kaua'i finally appeared at dusk on the second day and in the morning they beached on the island.

The visit must have been a huge surprise to Kaumuali'i, who hastened to meet the new king of the Windward Isles. Their greetings were friendly, and hospitality befitting a monarch was arranged. Contemporary records suggest Kaumuali'i was appropriately deferential. The Reverend Hiram Bingham was on Kaua'i at the time. He had been in the islands a little over a year and while he was not yet fluent in Hawaiian, he had an interpreter with him. Writing later, he describes the meeting:

> ... the two kings soon attended to business. Kaumualii, wishing to know the pleasure of Liholiho proposed to give up to him his country, vessels, fort and guns. When the generous proposition was fully made, there was, for a little time, a profound stillness, the parties waiting with deep interest to hear the reply of Liholiho, on which the fortunes of Kaumualii and his family, and of others, seemed to be suspended. At length, his majesty Liholiho replied, 'I did not come to dispossess you. Keep your country and take care of it as before, and do what you please with your vessels.' To this succeeded a shout of cheerful approbation from both parties, and Kaumualii retired from the consultation

▲ Liholiho (Kamehameha II) (c.1797–1824) assumed the kingship on the death of his father in 1819. He had been brought up by his legal guardian Ka'ahumanu, and in the early years of his rule he relied heavily on her advice, to the point that she was in effect the ruler. Only six months after the death of his father the age-old kapu system with its gods, temples and priestly class was forcibly abandoned. This resulted in war with his cousin Kekuaokalani. The decisive battle on the Big Island was won by the king and Ka'ahumanu.
Bishop Museum

▶ Ka'ahumanu (1768–1832), self-proclaimed queen regent after her husband's death, ruled jointly with Liholiho (Kamehameha II) as kuhina nui, a title devised by the council of advisers of the late king. She was hugely influential in the abolition of the kapu and in 1821, to preserve the integrity of the kingdom, married Kaumuali'i after he had been kidnapped off Kaua'i. In 1824 she became a Christian. The original painting was by Louis Choris.
Wikipedia

Rebellion on Kaua'i

with a peaceful smile. In this very singular transaction between the '*emperor and king*' — as Liholiho sometimes styled himself and Kaumualii, it is difficult to say which of them showed the greatest degree of sagacity or magnanimity.[43]

This was a similar interaction to that which had taken place between Liholiho's father, Kamehameha, and Kaumuali'i eleven years earlier, and with the same result. It was a far cry from the warlike rumors expressed by Arago. Following the meeting, at Liholiho's request, the two kings and the principal chiefs set out on a 42-day extended tour around Kaua'i for Liholiho to assure himself that the kapu had been totally removed throughout the island.

While the tour was in progress Kaumuali'i sent word to Ka'ahumanu that Liholiho was on Kaua'i. As soon as she heard, Ka'ahumanu, together with Kalanimoku and the king's five wives, set sail for Kaua'i in Liholiho's recently acquired luxury yacht *Ha'aheo o Hawai'i* (Pride of Hawai'i) formerly named *Cleopatra's Barge*. The vessel arrived off Waimea just as Liholiho and Kaumuali'i's island tour ended.

On 16 September 'the two kings amused themselves with a Sabbath sail on board their respective brigs, coming to anchor at evening' (Kaumuali'i had recently purchased the 130-ton American brig *Becket* which had been built in Massachusetts in 1814). On their return to Waimea, Kaumuali'i went aboard Liholiho's yacht, when abruptly Liholiho gave orders to sail to O'ahu. Kaumuali'i had been deceived and kidnapped. There was much lamenting on Kaua'i when the populace discovered what had happened, with cries of 'Farewell to our king — we shall see him no more.'

Kaumuali'i was landed at Wai'anae, and reached Honolulu on 5 October 1821. Bingham writes: 'There was in his countenance an appearance of dejection, or sadness, which called forth the sympathy of his missionary friends, and others.'[44]

When the party arrived at Liholiho's Honolulu complex Kaumuali'i was given an ultimatum by Ka'ahumanu: marry me and all will be well in your kingdom, refuse and your death will follow, and as a consequence there will be disorder and confusion on Kaua'i and Ni'ihau.[45]

Five days later, on 10 October, with no real choice, Kaumuali'i married Ka'ahumanu and the Leeward and Windward Isles were united, by matrimony at least. Ka'ahumanu was in her early fifties and Kaumuali'i a decade younger. This had undoubtedly been Liholiho's and Ka'ahumanu's plot from the start of the voyage to Kaua'i. To reinforce this bond, Ka'ahumanu later also married Kaumuaili'i's 21-year-old son (and younger half-brother to Humehume), Keali'iahonui, further cementing the relationship between all the islands.

Upon Kaumuaili'i's exile to Honolulu, Maihinenui (Wahinenui), Kaumuali'i's sister, was named by Liholiho as governor of Kaua'i and Ni'ihau, but the real power on the islands still lay with Ka'ahumanu. Kaumuali'i was held a

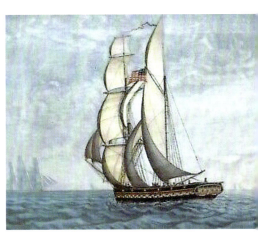

▲ *Cleopatra's Barge* was built as a luxury yacht for the Crowninshield family of Salem, Massachusetts in 1816. In 1817 she crossed the Atlantic and cruised the Mediterranean. Crowds gathered at all ports to tour the vessel. Back in Boston she changed hands within the family and undertook trading voyages, and, after changing hands again, was sailed to Hawai'i via Cape Horn with a view to selling the yacht to the king. Liholiho was entranced and purchased the ship for 8000 piculs (around 500 tons) of sandalwood. In 1821 the vessel played a part in the kidnapping of Kaumuali'i. In 1823 she had a major refit and renamed *Ha 'aheo o Hawai'i* (Pride of Hawai'i). In 1824 she ran aground on a reef in Hanalei Bay, could not be hauled off, and slowly broke up. The 1818 painting by George Ropes is in the Peabody-Essex Museum.
Peabody Essex Museum

◀ Hiram Bingham (1789–1869), the protestant missionary leader, and his wife Sybil (1792–1848) in an 1819 oil painting by Samuel Morse (the renowned American artist who invented Morse code). Bingham was present on Kaua'i when Liholiho visited in 1821 and wrote about the meeting between the two kings.
Wikimedia

▲ Kealiʻiahonui (1800–49), the second son of Kaumualiʻi and half-brother to his eldest son, Humehume.
Wikimedia Commons

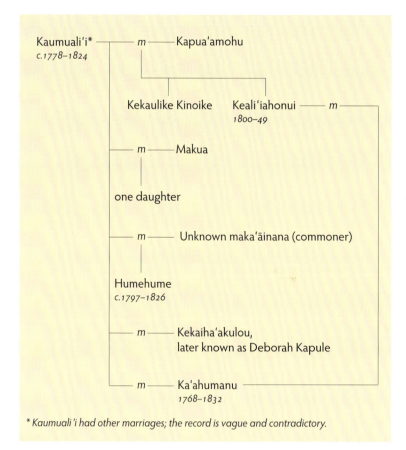

* Kaumualiʻi had other marriages; the record is vague and contradictory.

virtual prisoner on Oʻahu, but together with Kaʻahumanu and many others surprisingly made a trip back to Kauaʻi in August 1822. James Jarves describes the scene when they returned:

> On the 13th, Kaumualii and Kaahumanu, with a retinue of nearly twelve hundred people, sailed for Kauai. Four small vessels conveyed this multitude, which crowded their decks, and even occupied the chains, tops and bowsprits … The object of the voyage was to collect the annual tribute of sandal-wood … In December following they returned.[46]

During this four-month expedition a visit was made to Niʻihau in the *Tartar*, one of the four vessels, and missionary Samuel Whitney was a passenger on what was almost certainly his first visit to the island.[47] Nothing is known about what took place on Niʻihau, but it must be assumed that its overriding purposes were to collect tributes from the people and familiarize the royal party with the extent of the kingdom. They also sailed to Nihoa and formally took possession of the island on behalf of the Hawaiian kingdom.

The return of Humehume

In 1820, Humehume, Kaumualiʻi's son, arrived back on Kauaʻi after 15 years in America, where his father had sent him to be educated. It had not been an easy time for the 22-year-old prince, who sailed back on the *Thaddeus*, which brought the first missionaries to the islands. He was finally reunited with his father on 3 May. His arrival

▲ James Jarves (1818–88), an American art historian and editor who spent 1838 to 1849 in Hawaiʻi. He founded the *Polynesian* newspaper and in the early 1840s wrote and published a major history of the islands.
Wikimedia Commons

also marked the arrival of the first missionaries on Kauaʻi, Samuel Ruggles and Samuel Whitney (see Chapter Eight). The time Humehume had spent with the missionaries certainly influenced his father to accept them into his kingdom with open arms.

In July 1820 Humehume wrote (in his excellent English) to Herman Daggett, his teacher at the Foreign Mission School in Connecticut, saying in part:

> I often take great pleasure in meditating on what you have taught me, in former days; and hope, dear friend, that you will have the pleasure of hearing the virtue of your words to me. You cannot but rejoice to hear that my father has demolished his idols. The event took place before my arrival here. How astonished were all at this information! They seem to think that the Governor of the universe had surely begun to display his mighty power. Now it is peace and harmony; and the female, who was before trodden beneath, is now on the same footing. Now the man and wife, son and daughter, eat and drink in the same social band. It is very pleasing to me …[48]

Kaumualiʻi had 'demolished the idols' and embraced much of Christianity. At about the same time as his son's letter to Daggett he wrote to thank the Board of Commissioners for Foreign Missions for the Bible they had sent him via Humehume:

> Dear Friend, I wish to write a few lines to thank you for the good book you was so kind as to send by my son. I think it is a good book. One that God gave us to read. I hope my people will soon read this and all other good books. I believe that my idols are good for nothing. My gods I have hove away. They are no good. They fool me and they do me no good. I give them coconuts, plantains, hogs and many good things and they fool me at last. Now I throw them all away. I have none now. When your good people learn me I worship your God. I feel glad you good people come here to help us …[49]

On Humehume's return Kaumualiʻi showered him with gifts and titles, but the peace and harmony Humehume speaks of above did not last. It appears all the attention went to his head and he became dissolute, estranged from his father and from his fellow Kauaians. He married the daughter of Isaac Davis, one of Kamehameha's chief advisers, and settled at Wahiawa, some eight miles from Waimea.

It was only a year after his return that his father was kidnapped and taken to live in Honolulu. They doubtless saw one another again in the latter part of 1822 during the royal visit to collect tributes, and there were suggestions made by some that in Kaumualiʻi's absence Humehume should assume royal duties. Then news came in early May of 1824 that Kaumualiʻi was gravely ill in Honolulu, and many chiefly Kauiians left to be with their king in Honolulu. Others returned nervously to their homes to await developments.

News then arrived that Kaumualiʻi had died on 26 May 1824. As Hiram Bingham correctly prophesied, when writing to his fellow missionaries about this news, 'it would be no great departure from the Hawaiian customs if the wildest ebullition of the vilest passions should burst forth around them in the forms of drunkenness, prostitution, revenge, and bloodshed, as on the death of former kings.'

No individual was clearly recognized as Kaumualiʻi's successor. Power still really lay with Kaʻahumanu, rather than 24-year-old Liholiho.

In March 1824 Maihinenui's husband died and she felt she should relinquish the governorship; Kahalaiʻa Luanuʻu, a nephew of the prime minister, Kalanimoku, was

▲ Humehume (c.1798–1826), also known as George Prince Tamoree, the eldest son of Kaumualiʻi and half-brother to Kealiʻiahonui by an unknown mother (in some references she is called Niʻihau but the connection to the island is not recorded). At age of six Kaumualiʻi had his young son shipped off to the east coast of the United States to be educated. After serving in the US Navy and Marines during the war of 1812, he returned home in 1820, and died in 1826.
Samuel Morse, 1820 / Wikimedia Commons, colorised

appointed in her stead. He served until his death in 1826, when chief Kaikioʻewa, a cousin of Kamehameha I, was appointed.

With Kaumualiʻi's death there was much uneasiness on the on Kauaʻi and Niʻihau. Many chiefs were disaffected by the governorship and the terms of Kaumualiʻi's will, which did not make provision for the customary redistribution of land. Kaʻahumanu saw this period as an opportunity to appoint to positions of power on the two islands chiefs amenable to her viewpoint. Prime Minister Kalanimoku was not so hasty.

Prime Minister Kalanimoku's diplomacy

Kalanimoku visited Kauaʻi in an attempt to calm the situation. Bingham happened to be in Waimea at the time:

> [Kalanimoku was conducted] to the cool shade of the large Kou trees, near the bank and mouth of the river, over against the fort, where they strewed the area beneath with grass and rushes, overspread them quickly with mats, and placed for him an armed chair. He pleasantly seated himself in the midst of the multitude, who were gathering from every quarter, to gaze on the old companion of Kamehameha, and prime agent of Kaahumanu. Kahalaia [the governor] crossed the river from the fort, and respectfully welcomed his honored uncle.
>
> It did our hearts good, in our strait, to see the friendly old chieftain. Still, much as we relied on his friendship, experience, and talents, we did not feel even now, that all was safe.⁵⁰

▲ Kalanimoku (c.1768–1827) served as chief minister to Kamehameha I and traveled to Waimea in March 1818 on the *Columbia* to ensure Kamehameha received the full measure of sandalwood from Kaumualiʻi.

Louis Choris / Wikimedia Commons

How right he was to 'not feel that all was safe.' At a second meeting later in the week Kalanimoku confirmed the overlordship, and that there would be no redistribution of land. This left many unhappy and rebellious. Three days after this second meeting, as Hiram Bingham relates:

> Before the dawn of the next morning, August 8th, 1824, the confused noise of the battle of the warrior was heard pealing through the valley, from the fort. The malcontents, surprising the little garrison, had commenced the work of blood.
>
> Roused by the noise of battle so near, and hearing the balls whistle over us, what was our surprise and anguish to hear that George [Humehume] and his coadjutors were attempting to take the fort! We trembled for our friend, Kalanimoku, and his party, and for George too.⁵¹

The shooting lasted over half an hour and soon enough a message was received from across the river that the rebels had fled east in the direction of Hanapēpē. According to historian Edward Joesting, losses in the engagement were ten attackers and six fort defenders, including two Englishmen.⁵² Fearing further violence Kalanimoku summoned his schooner, the *New York*, to evacuate the missionary families to Honolulu and to request assistance as his situation on Kauaʻi appeared so perilous. On the arrival of the schooner in Honolulu, Hiram Bingham reported:

> 'He kaua, he kaua — War, war' — rung through the village and valley of Honolulu; and in a few hours a thousand men were ready to join and defend their chieftain, and bring the Kauaians under the same government with the windward islands … This reinforcement embarked the next day, and quickly reached Waimea, to the relief of Kalanimoku, while the insurgents were rallying at Wahiawa, the estate of George.⁵³

The schooner went directly on to Maui to inform Ka'ahumanu, who was still there attending funerary rites for her husband, Kaumuali'i. The frenzy was similar. Further reinforcements were raised from the island, commanded by Hoapili, the governor and a lifelong friend of Kamehameha. Two schooners set sail for Kaua'i. On arrival they combined with the loyal Kauaian warriors and the reinforcements from O'ahu, and on 18 August Hoapili led this force from Waimea towards Wahiawa where the dissidents, perhaps unwisely, had remained since the attempted storming of the fort. The following day was a Sunday and the loyalists rested.

With the insurgents commanding the east side of the Hanapēpē valley, Bingham records:

> The next day they proceeded, crossed the river, and ascended the heights ... and were drawn up in the order of battle ... Then, in a curved line or semicircle, they advanced, the right and left extremes intending to pass the enemy's lines, and capture the whole force. As they drew near, the insurgents, who had taken a station behind a wall with a small field-piece, discharged it a few times ... Some supposed at the moment that this engine of foreign war was doing the work effectually, though it was neither weakening the strength nor daunting the courage of the government troops, who returned the fire and pressed on. The insurgents, unable to stand, were beaten and routed; some forty or fifty were killed,[54] and the rest fled, chiefly to the woods, and some were pursued and taken.[55]

▲ Sheldon Dibble (1809–45) arrived in Hawai'i in 1831 with the fourth company of missionaries. After five years at Hilo he became a teacher at Lahainaluna School, where he started collecting Hawaiian history and interesting the students in their own past. In 1843 he published a *History of the Sandwich Islands*. Among his students were David Malo and Samuel Kamakau, who both went on to become Hawaiian historians. The painting dates from 1838, when he returned briefly to the East Coast.
Wikimedia Commons

Sheldon Dibble, missionary and historian, writing in the early 1840s, describes the action after the battlefield rout:

> In the pursuit many of the enemy were killed, and, with the exception of a few instances, no quarter was given, no mercy shown to captives, and no regard paid to the weak and defenseless. The unarmed, the aged, women and little children were slain indiscriminately. ... This work of destruction continued for many days. The bodies of the slain were left unburied to be devoured by dogs and swine.[56]

The battle became known as 'Aipua'a — 'the pig eating.' Looting of the island by the victors went on for several weeks, as revenge for past perceived wrongs took hold in the minds of the Windward Islands' chiefs. Property was taken at a whim, and many sheep and cattle were shipped to other islands. Ni'ihau was unlikely to have been exempt from this behavior, but no records exist.

Humehume himself escaped on horseback, but was captured several weeks later, starving and disheveled. In a surprising show of clemency he was not killed, but he and his family were exiled to O'ahu where they lived out their days. He caught influenza and died on 3 May 1826, six years after he returned home.

Jarves again:

> The disaffected chiefs and their tenants were distributed among the other islands, where it would be impossible for them to combine in another conspiracy. Their lands were divided among the loyal favorites and chiefs, who filled the minor offices with their creatures.[57]

The Windward Islands chiefs felt many grievances towards the Leeward Islands, centering perhaps on the failed attempts to subjugate the two islands to the Kamehameha family will, and having to accommodate refugees from the Kamehameha

◤ Liholiho and party at Drury Lane Theatre in London, 4 June 1824. Front row from left: King Liholiho, Queen Kamāmalu and Boki's wife Kuini Liliha. Back row: Two unknown Hawaiians, Boki and Frederick Byng, who was supervising the royal visit on behalf of the British government. After the king and queen died of measles in July that year, Boki became leader of the delegation.

Hand-colored lithograph by J W Gear, held in the National Library of Australia. Wikimedia Commons

domains, and earlier historical issues. The news of the rebellion on Kauaʻi came like music to many of these chiefs' ears and hence the spontaneous outbursts of joy, and willingness in Honolulu and Lahaina to participate in the war.

Most of the land owned by rebellious chiefs was given to relations of Kamehameha, with portions being given for services rendered to court favorites and warrior families. No record was kept of those who lost land, and a reconciliation had to await the Great Māhele, over 20 years later.

Tensions still simmered on Kauaʻi for the rest of the year. Kaʻahumanu, now the undisputed regent while the king was on a state visit England, visited Kauaʻi in August 1824 and remained there until the end of the year. She, as ruler, had a major involvement in the land redistribution process, a task which did not endear her to all of her subjects.

Kahalaiʻa, the governor and Kalanimoku's nephew, was replaced by Kaikioʻewa, a companion of Kamehameha in earlier wars, and in Bingham's words 'a more sober and conciliatory chieftain' who 'rendered important service in restoring quietude.'

One small aside concerning Niʻihau is relevant. The schooner, *New York*, owned by premier Kalanimoku, did sterling service during the rebellion. Records show that she shuttled between Kauaʻi, Honolulu and Lahaina from 9 to 22 August carrying troops, equipment and supplies. Later in the year she went aground on Niʻihau. To use Bingham's words: 'Kalanimoku, who thought he could attend to such things better than others, hurried thither, and had his schooner hauled up and repaired.'[58]

Exactly where this happened, and the extent of Niihauan labor employed in repairs to the schooner, are not recorded. The incident is related by Hiram Bingham because during this time on Niʻihau Kalanimoku wrote two letters to him expressing his belief in Christianity. The letters are notable for Kalanimoku's adeptness in English and for his changed feelings towards the missionaries. The first reads:

'Much love to you, Bingham and Mrs. Bingham, and you all. I salute you all. Great affection for you all who remain. Exceedingly great is my love to you. Here I am, earnestly attending to the Word of God. I pray also, to our Lord Jesus Christ, and to the Holy Spirit, who will enlighten me. Let the perseverance of you all be great. Be ye strong to labor for this land of darkness. Love to the children of you all, and to yourselves also. My salutations to you all are ended.[59]

Whether the rebellion was quashed using Christian principles is a question much debated in the missionary literature. The answer seems to be only to a limited extent. Hoapili, who led the government troops, asked missionary William Richards before he left Maui how he should conduct the war, and Richards gave him appropriate Christian advice. The excesses of his troops after the major engagement showed that at this time, at least, the god Kū was still ascendant.

Political stability is achieved

The distressing news of the deaths of the king and queen in England was received in Honolulu when the whaleships *Almira* and *Peru* arrived in March 1825. Their bodies came home on HMS *Blonde* two months later, on 6 May.

Kaikioʻewa governed Kauaʻi and Niʻihau for 14 years until well into the reign of Kamehameha III. With the stability that Kaikioʻewa brought, an independent monarchy on the islands had well and truly come to an end.

Attention on Kauaʻi now turned more to commerce, and Niʻihau, with its lack of natural resources, became even more of a backwater. Along with the rest of the islands, its population had declined massively due to the impact of western diseases. With the island still owned almost entirely by the king, taxes became a major source of friction between the Niihauans and the crown. By 1854, when Kamehameha IV came to the throne, Niʻihau had become an embarrassment to the monarchy.

▲ William Richards (1793–1847) came to Hawaiʻi in 1823 with the second company of missionaries. With the blessing of Liholiho and Kaʻahumanu he and fellow missionary Charles Stewart sailed from Honolulu to Lahaina on *Cleopatra's Barge* to found the first mission on Maui in May 1823. He was a principled churchman and when the Humehume rebellion took place in 1824 advised the leaders of the participants from Maui how war should be conducted. He later became a diplomat of note for the Hawaiian kingdom.

Wikimedia Commons, colorised

◀ HMS *Blonde*, the British navy frigate which brought back the bodies of King Kamehameha II and Queen Kamāmalu to Honolulu. Commanded by Lord Byron (George Anson Byron, who inherited the title on the poet's death in 1824), the frigate arrived in Honolulu on 6 May 1825. The painting is by Robert Dampier, the artist on the voyage, and hangs in Honolulu at Washington Place.

Wikimedia Commons

With the political turmoil on Kaua'i and Ni'ihau at an end, the following two chapters describe events in the life of the Sinclair family: their journey from Scotland to New Zealand and subsequently on to Hawai'i, culminating in their purchase of the island of Ni'ihau in 1864.

▶ Kaua'i/Ni'ihau basalt pōhaku puka ku'i poi (ring poi pounder), 19th century, maker unknown.
Mount Holyoke College Art Museum, South Hadley, Massachusetts; photo Laura Shea, MH 1.19.V.B(a)

CHAPTER SIX

SINCLAIRS, GAYS AND ROBINSONS IN NEW ZEALAND

Since 1864 the island of Ni'ihau has been closely linked with the Robinson family and their forebears, the Sinclairs. Originally from Scotland, the Sinclairs spent twenty-three years in New Zealand as pioneer Scottish immigrants before finally settling on Ni'ihau. Together with their family, Francis and Eliza Sinclair left Scotland for New Zealand in 1840.

Precise details on the family's life before their emigration are few and far between. One fixed point is the record of Francis and Eliza's marriage on 13 January 1824 at Gorbals, Glasgow.[1] Many sources show that Francis was born in 1797, and this is corroborated by the ship's manifest for the voyage to New Zealand. Given the marriage date was early in the year, he would likely have been 26 at the time of the nuptials. Eliza was born on 26 April 1800 so she would have been 23 on her wedding day.[2]

His achievements in New Zealand show that Francis Sinclair was industrious, ingenious and enterprising. He came to New Zealand with a little capital, was skilled in the art of boat design and building, was a well-respected mariner and had farming experience. These skills he must have acquired before leaving Scotland.

Ship-building was a long-established industry on the Clyde, but as a port it suffered from the shallow water in the river as vessels approached Glasgow. Cargo from all large ships had to be transferred to lighters to reach Glasgow itself, until the river was dredged in the late 1800s. While it is speculation, Francis may well have been employed on the Clyde and thus learned how to design and build schooner-sized vessels.

Ship-building also took place at Leith, only two miles from Edinburgh on the Firth of Forth, so alternatively he may have been employed there. Purportedly Francis was born in Edinburgh, but was married in Glasgow, 46 miles or a day's journey away by 'coach and four' in those times.

George Sinclair, Francis's father, was a master mariner and could have initially encouraged Francis into a life at sea where he would have learned his sailing skills. Although many charming stories concerning Francis's involvement in the Royal Navy have become part of early family tradition, Ruth Knudsen Hanner, Ann Sinclair's granddaughter, said in the appendix to the 1985 edition of *Stories of Long Ago* that there were no records in London to show that Francis or George Sinclair served in the navy.[3]

Ruth Knudsen Hanner thus contradicts the notion that Francis was a Royal Navy captain. She says that George Sinclair was the captain of a merchant vessel on the run from Prestonpans (eight miles from Edinburgh) to London through the formidable North Sea. Francis may well have accompanied him and learned his seamanship this way.

The only clue as to where Francis may have gleaned his knowledge of farming is in the name the family gave to their New Zealand property: Craigforth. The countryside around Stirling is dominated by three crags above the River Forth: the one on which Stirling Castle and the city stand, the Abbey Craig and Craigforth. In the early 1800s the land around Craigforth (only a few miles outside Stirling) was farmland and remains so today. The name Craigforth must have had happy connotations for Francis and Eliza, and Francis may have worked in the area for a time.

Early in their married life the couple lived on the outskirts of Edinburgh. Francis would have sailed out of Leith, Edinburgh's port. Their first child, George, was born there in 1824, but by the time their second child, James, was born a year later the family had moved to Stirling (37 miles from Edinburgh and 27 from Glasgow).[4] This was presumably the time when Francis gave up seafaring to spend more time with his family. Until they left for New Zealand the growing family then remained in Stirling. Four more children were born there: Jane,[5] Helen, Francis (Frank) and Ann.

Francis and Eliza were both English speakers; in the Scotland of the time many people spoke only Gaelic. Francis's only surviving letter is in copperplate script, so he had considerable education somewhere.

Francis worked as an official for the Inland Revenue Office after he married.[6] He had a family to provide for, but such employment seems out of character for him. It may be that this was the only work available at the time, and the job itself, coupled with their financial situation, may have been the major factors leading to Francis and Eliza's decision to emigrate to New Zealand.

Eliza was also an adventurous spirit, as well as being a superb homemaker. She was the rock around which the family life was built and took her husband's absences in her stride. If she wasn't making the family's clothes and shoes she was teaching her daughters how to do so, all the while coping with farm duties. She had been well taught by her family, and was said to have been the daughter of the prominent Glasgow merchant James McHutcheson and his wife, Jean Robertson.[7]

Given their circumstances with the growing family, when these two adventurous souls saw the New Zealand Company's advertisements, they recognized an opportunity for land of their own and for a better life in a new colony.

The New Zealand Company

The 1830s were a time of economic turmoil and despair in Britain. Major changes were under way with the industrial revolution transforming people's lives, and with a expanding population, employment opportunities were severely limited. Emigration

▲ The last house the Sinclair family occupied in Stirling before they left for New Zealand in August 1840. Known as Bruce of Auchenbowie's House or Bothwell House, it is a 16th-century listed heritage house under the former title. The address is 39 & 41 John Street. Next door is the guildhall with an extensive garden. A family story has it that the Sinclair children enjoyed climbing out of the upstairs windows onto the wall separating their garden from the guildhall.

Robinson family

to the United States and the colonies — Canada, South Africa and more recently Australia — was widely discussed. Attempts to organize emigration to New Zealand began in 1825, but it wasn't until 1837 that it became a serious contender with the formation of the New Zealand Company.

The company was the brainchild of the political philosopher Edward Gibbon Wakefield. His scheme for 'systematic colonization' involved buying land cheaply from the indigenous population and selling it much more expensively to emigrant capitalists. Emigrants would be balanced in numbers between capitalists and laborers, with the former employing the latter in working the land. Laboring families would be offered free passage, using the proceeds from the sale of the land to those with capital.

Edward Gibbon Wakefield's mantra was 'possess yourselves of the Soil & you are secure.'[8] Judging by their subsequent actions, Wakefield's philosophy must have instantly appealed to Francis and Eliza.

Wakefield's ideas for systematic colonization were used in the founding of Adelaide in 1836 by the South Australian Association with mixed results, but before the Adelaide colony's success could be properly evaluated, attention turned to New Zealand. For the founding settlement there it was proposed that land be sold to prospective settlers for £1 an acre, with parcels consisting of a one-acre town lot combined with a 100-acre country lot. A draw would be held to decide the priority order of selection. One lot in ten was to be reserved for Māori — for chiefs' families.[9]

Much time was spent by the company in lobbying the British government for preferential or exclusive arrangements. New Zealand at that stage was not a British colony, but British missionaries, who had been in New Zealand since 1814, were urging the government to become involved. There were upwards of 2000 British citizens in the country at that time, largely living with Māori and trading with whalers. The government procrastinated to the point where the company took the situation into its own hands, given concerns that any government intervention was likely to be detrimental to the company's interests rather than concessionary.

The company therefore chartered the ship *Tory* for a voyage to the Cook Strait area with Colonel William Wakefield, Edward Gibbon's younger brother, as the company's agent, on a mission to negotiate with the Māori inhabitants of the best harbor he could find and buy land suitable for a British settlement.[10] The colonel was given two months for this task, a ludicrously short time. The *Tory* left London on 12 May 1839, followed by a second ship, the *Cuba*, on 31 July to survey the land secured into lots, and begin to make roads and other essentials for building a settlement.

It was not the company's intention to wait and see if Colonel Wakefield's mission had been successful, and from 2 May 1839 a full-scale marketing campaign for suitable emigrants began in England and Scotland. This was an area at which Edward Gibbon

▲ The New Zealand Company's advertisement for emigrants.
Public Record Office, London.

◀ The political philosopher Edward Gibbon Wakefield (1796–1862). Despite a tumultuous early career which included three years in jail for abduction, his ideas on 'systematic colonization' bore some fruit in Canada, Australia and more particularly in New Zealand. He was a visionary and an enthusiast for his cause, but realized himself that he was not an able administrator and left the detail of his sometimes grandiose plans to others. It was not for twelve years after its founding that he visited Wellington, where he was not well received by the incumbent authorities.
Wikipedia

Wakefield was particularly adept — 'puffery' as the campaign was called in those times. Today we might say there was an air of spin-doctoring about it. As part of this campaign the company published a brochure in June 1839 entitled *Information Relative to New Zealand — Compiled for the use of Colonists*, the first paragraph of which read:

> There is probably no part of the world which presents a more eligible field for exertion of British enterprize or a more promising career of usefulness, to those who labour in the cause of human improvement, than the islands of New Zealand.[11]

Five 300–400-ton ships were initially chartered: the *Oriental*, *Aurora*, *Adelaide*, *Duke of Roxburgh* and the *Bengal Merchant*, all with target sailing dates of 10 September, only six weeks after the *Cuba*, the vessel carrying the land survey party, had left.[12] Each ship carried between 100 and 200 passengers; overall there were 152 cabin passengers (the capitalists) and 704 in steerage.

Meanwhile Colonel Wakefield had searched the Cook Strait area and concluded that Port Nicholson (Te Whanganui-a-Tara) offered the best hope for settlement. He found there a people unaccustomed to Europeans (Pākehā), and who liked the idea of strangers living among them. For the Māori it was easy to put their cross on a piece of paper in exchange for — in the case of Wellington — 120 muskets and ammunition, 100 red blankets, 1200 fish hooks, tobacco, European clothes, tools and miscellaneous other attractive and useful items. How much of the transaction they really understood is most questionable. In a week Wakefield had bought Port Nicholson and the surrounding ranges, and on 27 September had crosses from the chiefs of four of the seven major pā (stockaded villages) around the harbor. The claims of the three pā located in what is now Wellington city's central business district (Te Aro, Kumutoto, and Pipitea) had not been properly dealt with and Wakefield was aware of this, but he still claimed ownership over the whole region.[13]

As Patricia Burns says in her story of the New Zealand Company 'It would be hard to find a colony that began in a greater muddle than that at Port Nicholson.'[14] The surveyors sailed into the harbor on the *Cuba* only four days before the first immigrant ship, the *Aurora*, appeared on 22 January 1840 and no sections would be available for months. Areas of flat land were limited and the site in the Hutt Valley selected for Britannia, the new town, was soon found to be liable to flood. The settlers demanded the town be shifted to Thorndon, adjacent to Pipitea pā, the only other sizeable area of reasonably flat land around the harbor. They eventually won the day and the town was shifted, but communication with the Hutt Valley, seven or eight miles along the rocky shore, was limited to a foot track or a boat trip on an often windswept harbour.

It was in this milieu that the Sinclair family found themselves after their long journey from Scotland when they arrived at Thorndon (by this time called Wellington), only eleven months after the first settlers.

▲ William Wakefield (1801–48) was Edward Gibbon Wakefield's younger brother. Early in his career he was imprisoned alongside his brother. He subsequently became a soldier of fortune in Portugal and elsewhere before being asked by his brother in 1839 to lead the New Zealand Company's expedition to New Zealand and negotiate land purchases from the Māori. He remained the company's principal agent in New Zealand until his death in 1848, and was a key figure in the Sinclairs' land purchase arrangements in New Zealand. This caricature dates from 1826.
ATL PA1-0-511-7

◂ The New Zealand Company's Coat of Arms.
Wikipedia

The voyage to New Zealand

As later events show, both Francis and Eliza were adventurous people and ardently wished to do the best they could for their children. They were motivated by the same passion for land as Edward Gibbon Wakefield — 'possess yourselves of the Soil & you are secure' and undoubtedly had read some of his writings. Wakefield's advertising campaign for the new New Zealand colony started in Scotland as well as England in May 1839, with one of the Company's 'first fleet,' the *Bengal Merchant,* sailing from Greenock on the Clyde with Scottish emigrants on 31 October 1839.

The second Scottish emigrant ship, the *Blenheim,* sailed from Greenock on 25 August 1840 with the Sinclair family aboard. The passenger list, in beautiful handwritten script, is headed:

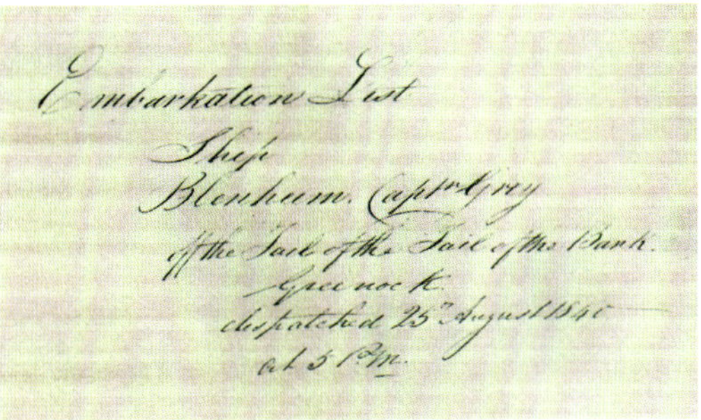

EMBARKATION LIST

Ship
Blenheim Capt. Grey
off the Tail of the Tail of the Bank
Greenock

Despatched 25 August 1840
at 5pm

Embarkation List
Ship
Blenheim. Captn Grey
off the Tail of the Tail of the Bank.
Greenock.
despatched 25th August 1840
at 5 P.M.

▲ The embarkation list for the *Blenheim,* which sailed from 'the tail of the tail of the Bank' at Greenock, near Glasgow in Scotland.

and shows as having aboard:

Francis Sinclair	Age 42, sailor
Eliza Sinclair	Age 40
John Sinclair	Age 20
George Sinclair	Age 15
James Sinclair	Age 14, boy
Jane Sinclair	Age 12, girl
Helen Sinclair	Age 10, girl
Francis Sinclair	Age 6, girl [incorrectly listed]
Ann Sinclair	Age 1, girl

John Sinclair was in fact John McHutcheson, Eliza's brother,[15] so there may have been some cost advantage in including him as their eldest child, although children over the age of 14 were shown as adults on the manifest. John was actually 24.

The New Zealand Company must have felt Francis Senior, at 42, had the skills needed for the new colony as there was generally a cutoff age of 40 for emigrants. Being a sailor may have helped, since he is the only person shown as such on the embarkation list. While the family traveled steerage and probably received free passages, Francis must have been regarded as a 'capitalist,' having sufficient wherewithal to purchase a 100-acre block and a town acre in Wellington, sight unseen, for £101 before they left.[16]

The departure of the *Blenheim* was fully reported in the press of the day:

> On Monday last we had the opportunity of accompanying a select party who paid a farewell visit to the ship 'Blenheim', before her departure with emigrants for the land of promise in the southern seas. The emigrating band numbered nearly 200; they were principally highlanders who are strangers to the language of the Saxon, and as Dr McLeod

*It was normal at this time for a steamer to take passengers to a sailing vessel standing in open waters; in this case to the Tail of the Bank at Greenock.

had consented to address them in Gaelic for the last time before their departure from the shores of old Scotland, the occasion was one calculated to excite both feeling and interest. The 'British Queen' steamer* sailed from the Broomielaw [quay] at 11 o'clock, with the New Zealand flag flying from her mast head, and both there and at Renfrew wharf, passengers for the remote home of Port Nicholson, New Zealand, were received, and placed on board the 'Blenheim' which lay at the Tail of the Bank, shortly after one o'clock … [17]

The *Blenheim*, with 197 steerage passengers and 21 in cabins, was then towed 20 miles down the Firth of Clyde before casting off, and the journey proper began at 11pm on 25 August 1840. It was the New Zealand Company's policy to sail non-stop to New Zealand — the longest emigrant journey in the world — around the Cape of Good Hope and skirting below the Australian continent. Nominal travel time was four months, but with fair winds a three-month journey was possible; in adverse weather, much longer. The average duration of the company's first 17 voyages was five months.[18]

In steerage, family groups were accommodated amidships, with single men and single women separated at either end of the vessel (single men forward, single women aft). Rations and water were supplied daily to the family groups and in communal parcels of six for the single passengers. Water was necessarily limited, but sufficient, given the length of the journey, and the food at least adequate. Lighting was by candles and oil lamps, with sanitation primitive.

With so many people in a confined space, a routine was vital. The company required that all had to be out of bed, washed and dressed by 7.30 each morning. Beds were to be aired, and breakfast was at 8.30. Liquor and gambling were prohibited, and on Sundays a church service was held.

An extensive daily journal was kept by *Blenheim* cabin passenger Jessie Campbell. Ten days into the voyage she describes the fare for different classes of passengers:

> We had for dinner today roast ducks, boiled fowls and curried fowl and pea soup and pickled pork, this is the first day we have been without beautiful cabbage for dinner since leaving Greenock, the potatoes are still very good, our having such a good cook adds much to our comfort; all the steerage passengers got flour, suet and raisins served out to them yesterday to make puddings for their dinners today … they likewise got pickled cabbage, a good many cannot be prevailed on to eat it and were caught throwing it overboard.[19]

Doubtless the Scots got used to their new diet as the journey progressed.

After a damp and drizzly start the *Blenheim* made her way south through the Irish Sea and into the stormy Bay of Biscay, where on 3 September Jessie wrote: 'Passed very uncomfortable night, vessel rolling and pitching so much I could not sleep. Sometimes thought when she went on her side she would not rise again.' This weather proved thankfully short-lived, and pushing out into the Atlantic proper proved much more comfortable, with favorable winds.

On Sunday 6 September the first church service was held on board and Jessie Campbell encounters a member of the Sinclair family: 'Emigrants had prayers and a portion of the bible read to them in Gaelic, we had the same in English by a very respectable steerage passenger of the name of Sinclair from Stirling.'[20]

Francis seems to have performed this role every Sunday throughout the long voyage, evidence of the family's strong Christian faith.

Two days later, north of the Canary Islands, there was a health scare when a passenger was diagnosed with smallpox. He was immediately isolated, but those who had been in contact with him were all fearful of contracting the disease. Fortunately after some time his symptoms disappeared, and after a lengthy quarantine he was released from the ship's hospital.

John Grey, the *Blenheim*'s captain, was a kindly but firm soul who placed great emphasis on ship and passenger hygiene and led by example, having two pails of sea water thrown over him every morning. He insisted on airing the steerage accommodation every single day — determinedly overcoming the reluctance of some steerage passengers to do so.

▲ Emigrants en route to New Zealand in 1840.
ATL A-109-054

Adult deaths were unusual on the company's emigrant ships, but some infants succumbed. Two children died on the *Blenheim*'s voyage and six were born. One of the infants who died was Jessie Campbell's, whose journal I have quoted.

The equator was crossed 39 days out on 2 October with suitable celebrations, and having sighted the island of Trinidad off the Venezuelan coast, the Cape of Good Hope was rounded in 80 days on 12 November. The long eastward haul through the 'Roaring Forties' then began, driven along the 40th latitude by what Captain Grey called 'a glorious breeze,' but which the passengers described as too high a wind for their taste. In the three weeks after the cape had been passed the *Blenheim* averaged 181 miles per day, extremely fast for a sailing ship, so we may sympathise with the passengers.

On 30 November the second great storm of the voyage began, and for 36 hours the ship rolled and pitched in tremendous seas with a frightening noise of wind and water. This wild weather was repeated on 8 December when Jessie Campbell writes:

> Blowing hard, still favourable, was awoke at 4 this morning by the noise on deck in consequence of a violent squall of wind coming on so suddenly that Capt. Gray came on deck almost naked. One sail was torn completely and two very much injured. The emigrants so frightened most of the men ran on deck.[21]

Two days later, on 10 December, the Tasmanian coast was sighted 30 miles to the north — with great relief by some passengers who were sure Captain Grey had overshot, and New Zealand had been missed altogether. It wasn't until 23 December, however, nearly two weeks later, that Jessie Campbell records: 'A cry of land about ½ past 10 o'clock, everyone in such a state of excitement so anxious to get the first peep of the land of our adoption. It was Cape Farewell on the north of the South Island …'[22]

133

The next three days were spent in variable and generally adverse winds. Captain Grey had not been to Cook Strait before, and all were nervous at being in a situation with land visible on both sides and no sheltered anchorage to be found. Nevertheless Christmas Day was suitably celebrated: 'A lovely evening, went up on deck to look at the emigrants dancing, they got some grog to keep their Christmas,' as Jessie says in her journal. The next day, instead of anchoring in Port Nicholson as anticipated, they were blown 30 miles from land. However, 27 December proved to be:

> A beautiful mild morning, just as Capt. Gray expected. The wind went down and changed in our favour about 2 this morning. The Capt. is in rather a dilemma about finding out the harbour; there is not proper chart of it published; he is not sure which of the bays it may be. Very stupid of the Company not to have some signal put up to shew the proper entrance. Went up on deck after breakfast, we were off the bay thought most likely to be the proper entrance. To make sure the Capt. lowered a boat with six hands, they were to make a signal if they found we were in the right place; besides this we had five cannon fired with the hope of bringing a pilot to our assistance. Before the boat had gone any distance from the ship Somes Island and Wards Island were discovered from the mast head which made the Capt. so sure he had at least found the proper place that he made sail into the bay. You may fancy the state of excitement we were all in, the children calling out everything they saw or imagined they saw … [23]

Their first sight of the town and its environs was not what Jessie, at least, was expecting:

> The town consists of a number of small houses some wooden and some thatched, both on the sea beach and a few on an elevated plain behind. We were much disappointed at the wild appearance the country presented. The Bay is so very extensive it would contain the British Navy and more, and surrounded on every side by hills wooded to the top.[24]

After a journey of four months and two days, the Sinclairs and the rest of the emigrants had arrived in their new home.

▼ Charles Heaphy's remarkably accurate 1840 bird's-eye view of Wellington harbor before European settlement, looking north from the harbor entrance. To give an idea of scale, the harbor is roughly five miles across. Thorndon, where the Sinclair family landed, is the far left beach. When he first arrived, Francis Sinclair ferried lumber from the Hutt River in the upper right of the lithograph to the new town being built at Thorndon (Pipitea). The *Richmond* was built on the right hand branch of the Hutt River.

Drawn by Charles Heaphy and lithographed in London by T Allom / ATL C-029-006-b

The Sinclairs' arrival and their beginnings in a new land

As the *Blenheim* nudged her way around Point Jerningham to an anchorage off Kaiwharawhara, passengers were surprised to see as many as twelve vessels of all shapes and sizes in the harbor. More than one trading establishment could also be seen on the shore near the Māori pā at Te Aro, and at the northern end of the harbor at Pito-one (Petone), more buildings were visible. An air of purpose existed in the nascent town; this vision reinforced by the scene that confronted Jessie Campbell:

> The moment our anchor was out a number of boats came off the shore to us. Some of the gentlemen were very superior in appearance and manner to what I expected to see. … Some of the natives came on board dressed in European clothes.[25]

The gentlemen concerned were the New Zealand Company representatives in their best 'meet and greet' clothes for the arrival of the company's eighth emigrant vessel. The settlement was actually in a state of flux with the move from Britannia (in the Hutt Valley) to Wellington still to be completed. Surveying for the land orders paid for in Scotland was far from finished, Māori were unhappy with the large inflow of settlers and what had happened to their land around the harbor. The company's relationship with the colonial government regime centered in the Bay of Islands was also abysmal.

Some temporary accommodation for immigrants may have been built at Kaiwharawhara by this time — earlier, immigrants had been obliged to stay on their ship for a period. This was especially true for the first settlers from Scotland who had arrived on the *Bengal Merchant* eleven months previously, a fact which had not endeared the company to these settlers. Some had already left for greener pastures elsewhere, particularly Sydney.

The Sinclair family seem to have settled in quickly. They were told by the New Zealand Company that their land was to be at Wanganui, 120 miles distant. This didn't necessarily disappoint them, since they understood the land could be more valuable because of the large river which was adjacent. Francis wrote in his first letter to his brother-in-law, William McHutcheson, in Scotland on 3 January 1841, six days after their arrival:

> I have bought a boat and I think that I shall be profitably employed with her till we get our place; the day after we landed I took a cargo of deals [sawn planks] from Petoni to Wellington with her. Geo. Jno. and I started in the evening and landed them the next morning at six o'clock, and we had £2.5.0 for our job. It was the first and I was afraid to load heavyer untill I saw what she would do. I left Jno. and Geo. loading her to start on Monday morning at two o'clock and I shall (weather permitting) make three trips next week at £3- each, perhaps four, so we shall not starve

▼ Pipitea Pā in Wellington, drawn by William Mein Smith in 1842. Smith was surveyor-general for the New Zealand Company until 1843, responsible for laying out the proposed towns. The area now forms part of Wellington city.
ATL PUBL-0011-04-1

Wellington town and harbor in 1842. Engraved by J C Armytage from a drawing by Charles Heaphy, artist and surveyor to the New Zealand Company.
Wikipedia

in the interim. There is, however, a great deal of People idle here in consequence of the surveying being stopt and the Gents not getting to their land.[26]

The letter, the only one we have from Sinclair in his own handwriting, also indicates that the family were in good spirits and that they had already moved from Wellington to Petone. The move was probably to the settlement of Britannia, a short distance up the Hutt River, rather than the beach at Petone. The general move of the settlers in the opposite direction may have left some rudimentary accommodation available.

Francis was certainly a man of action and saw opportunities, both with housing and boat transport. With no road yet between Wellington and Petone (although a daily passenger ferry had begun operating) there was a need for freight capacity and Francis took advantage of the situation. No details exist of the boat he bought, but by March 1841 a twelve-foot-wide road had been punched along the eight miles of coastline to Petone beach. There was, however, still only a track along Petone beach to the mouth of the Hutt River and it would have been from here that he was shipping his cargo, mostly lumber, to Wellington. Freight rates are quoted as £1 per ton, so it would have been a three to four-ton boat.[27]

The family determined to check out the situation in Wanganui, where their land had been allocated, as soon as possible. The township of Wanganui (now Whanganui) was in its formative stage, with the first pioneers leaving Wellington for the new settlement at this time (February 1841). The family myth, which is supported by an unsigned typed paper in the packet with Francis's letter, states that the whole family traveled in a whaleboat, sleeping on the beach each night.

This is corroborated in one of the less fanciful tales of their journey to Wanganui,[28] written as an obituary on the occasion of the death of Eliza's younger brother, John McHutcheson, at the age of 82 in 1899. The writer of the newspaper article is only identified as G J C, but he was obviously a close friend of the family. He talks of the family setting out for Wanganui in:

> ... a fine Deal boat, about 26ft long. In this boat there started for Wanganui Mr and Mrs Sinclair and family of three sons and three daughters, Mr McHutcheson, and another man. Under the lee of Kapiti Island they rode out a gale of wind for two days. During this time they unwittingly took some firewood from a place that was "tapu." A fierce row with some Maoris was the result, and they were glad to make peace and get away. Before leaving Kapiti they took on board a Maori woman who belonged to a Wanganui tribe and had been carried away as a slave. She acted as pilot, and they landed safely at Wanganui on the sixth day.[29]

The boat would have been the one that Francis had bought and used for trading around Port Nicholson. Their return journey is a matter of record. Why they should have chosen to travel to Wanganui in a whaleboat rather than by regular schooner is unknown. The family did, however, voyage back from Wanganui on the schooner *Surprise,* arriving in Wellington on 29 March 1841.[30] How long they spent on the visit is unknown, but they left Wellington some time in February or early March. They returned concerned that the land ownership question had not been settled and Māori were still aggrieved. They came to the conclusion Wanganui was not for them.

Not long after their arrival the Sinclair family met Ebenezer Hay and his family, who had arrived earlier in the *Bengal Merchant*. While the two families were at different stages in their family lives, they became firm friends. Ebenezer was 17 years younger than Francis, having been born in 1814. His family consisted of his wife Agnes, their infant son James, and later in the year included Ebenezer's adult nephew, John Hay, who arrived on the *Mandarin* in December 1841. Ebenezer, a farmer's son with a shrewd eye for promising land, had drawn a high ballot number in the company's land ballot system and was dissatisfied with the land opportunities on offer around the

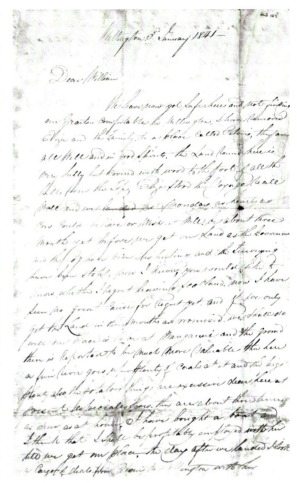

▲ The first page of Francis Sinclair's 3 January 1841 letter to Eliza's brother, William McHutcheson, in Scotland.

ATL fMS-Papers-0460_01

◄ Wanganui, near the mouth of the Whanganui River in September 1841, around the time the Sinclair family made their epic journey up the west coast of the North Island to visit it.

Drawn by William Mein Smith and engraved by Day & Haghe, London. ATL PUBL-0011-05

Wellington region. He had already visited the possibilities around Wellington and in 1842, accompanied by his nephew, walked as far as the Manawatū (90 miles away), but he judged the Māori attitude to European land acquisition there as too threatening.

The two families determined to look further afield in their newly adopted country.

They first sought compensation from Colonel William Wakefield, the New Zealand Company's agent in New Zealand, for their £101 land orders, as they felt it had not been possible to exercise them. They were firmly advised that the company could not compensate them financially, but should they choose to settle in the South Island their land would be protected if and when the New Zealand Company decided to proceed with settlements there.[31]

Whether it was before or after their discussions with Colonel Wakefield that they decided to build a boat is not clear, but given the timings it was probably before, and the vessel may have been initially laid down purely as a trading vessel, which it was for some months. Francis was still presumably trading within the harbor and would have known the Hutt River well. For the Sinclair family to build a schooner they would need to be close to a suitable river and launching spot — which they were at Britannia. The Hays may have joined them there, although Ebenezer took no part in the actual construction.

▶ Ebenezer Hay (1812–63) was Francis Sinclair's partner in building the *Richmond* and in the two families' move to Pigeon Bay. He continued farming in the bay until his life was cut short by an accident in 1863.
ATL PA Coll-7027

◀ Francis Sinclair's land order from the New Zealand Company, dated 30 October 1839, entitling him to 100 country acres in New Zealand, 'with a right of selection in the order of presentation of this Land Order to the Company.'
Archives NZ, Christchurch

The schooner *Richmond*

As the construction would have taken many months, Francis and Ebenezer probably decided to build a vessel in late 1841 or early 1842. It was not a decision to take lightly, as Francis was working mostly from scratch. There was, however, other boat building going on in the Hutt River estuary at the time, so there was some support available. In fact Joseph Robinson had been living there among the Māori since 1823 and making a living constructing and repairing boats.

A daughter-in-law of Ebenezer Hay, Hannah Guthrie Hay, admired Francis Sinclair's skill and inventiveness:

Captain Sinclair was a very clever man, as well as a thorough seaman. He was not long out in New Zealand before he began shipbuilding, his sons [George and James] and brother-in-law [Eliza's brother John] helping him. They set to work to build a schooner on the Hutt River (then called Haeratonga — why the quaint pretty Maori names should be abolished in favour of inelegant English ones remains an unsolved mystery!) They had to cut the timber out of the standing bush, and then let it 'season,' while they manufactured their tools and materials not otherwise procurable. Out of old iron plates and hoops they made nails, screws and bolts, using the butt of an old cannon for their anvil, and making their bellows out of an old musket with a sheep's bladder ingeniously fitted on to it! Fortunately an old sailor appeared on the scene in time to help them with the sails, which they found to be the most puzzling part of the whole undertaking.[32]

There was no shortage of suitable lumber. William Wakefield wrote of his first journey up the Hutt River: 'at about three miles up … commences a grove of fine trees, of the best description for ship and house building, intermixed with large pine trees. One of these called the kaikatea [kahikatea or white pine, *Dacrycarpus dacrydioides*] measured 21 feet in circumference, and was nearly the same size upwards for sixty feet without a branch.'[33] Further up the river grew the mighty tōtara, *Podocarpus totara*, used by the Māori for their waka (canoes). Francis would have used kahikatea for the frames and planking.

While Ebenezer Hay assisted in financing the schooner and became part owner, he did not become involved in her construction. He did, however, accompany Francis on his exploratory voyage to the South Island.

The *Richmond*, as she was named, was launched on 11 August 1842, just 20 months after the family's arrival at Port Nicholson. The launch was noted in the *New Zealand Gazette and Wellington Spectator*:

> Scarcely a week has elapsed since the launching of the *Maori*,* before we have to announce the launch of another fine schooner called the *Richmond*. The Richmond is about 30 tons measurement; she was built on the Okauta,† on the site of the proposed village of Richmond, from which circumstance she has received her name. She has been built under the superintendence, and we believe, we may add, by the manual labour of Mr. Sinclair, the owner and his sons, and we are informed by competent judges, that she is a pretty model and faithfully built. She was launched into her native element on Thursday last, amidst the congratulations of a select party of friends, whom the spirited owner entertained on the occasion. We understand from the agent, Mr. Fitzherbert, that her first trip will be made to Kapiti and Nelson.[34]

The 30-ton cargo capacity of the *Richmond* implies a length of 50 to 55 feet and a beam of about 12 feet, so she was a substantial vessel and building her was no mean feat. Francis must certainly have been involved in the planning and construction of similar vessels in Scotland and knew in detail how to go about it.

She sailed under Captain Sinclair only four days after the launch, bound for Nelson, arriving back with a load of general cargo on 29 August. For the next few months the vessel was engaged in the coastal trade out of Wellington.[35]

Her next voyage was a historic one for the settlement of Canterbury Province. The vessel was chartered for this voyage by William Deans to transport him and, as

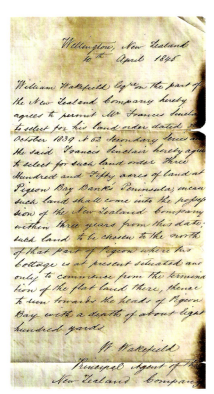

▲ Letter from William Wakefield, as principal agent to the New Zealand Company, to Francis Sinclair, dated 10 April 1845, allowing Francis, in respect of his land order, to select 350 acres at Pigeon Bay 'in case such land shall come into the possession of the New Zealand Company within three years from this date.' It took longer than three years, but via the Canterbury Association, Pigeon Bay did come under the aegis of the New Zealand Company and the company was as good as its word.
Robinson family

* The 'Maori,' a 15-ton schooner, built and owned by local Māori, was launched on 26 July. She was reputed to be the largest vessel built entirely by Māori to that date.

† Okautu, a branch of the Hutt River; now called Black Creek and reduced by earthquakes and river control works to a trickle of its former glory.

September 19, 1842.

▲ Advertisement calling for cargo for the *Richmond* on the schooner's shakedown cruise to Nelson.
NZ Colonist & Port Nicholson Advertiser 22 September 1842

▶ A wholly imaginary 1842 sketch of the lower reaches of the Hutt River (the Okautu Stream branch) by Robert Park. Park was responsible for surveying Richmond, a village that never came to fruition. The church and bridge shown never existed. It is, however, where Francis Sinclair and Ebenezer Hay built their boat, which they named the *Richmond* after the locality.
ATL A-215-004

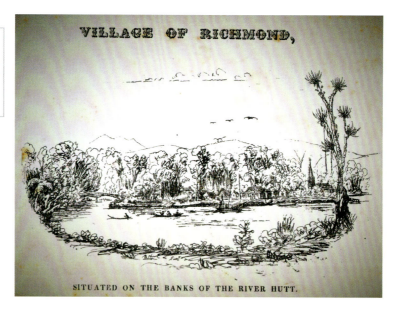

reported in the newspaper, 'ten servants' (actually the Manson and Gebbie families with three children each[36]) to Port Levy on Banks Peninsula. The *Richmond* sailed from Port Nicholson on 10 February 1843 and William Deans, the Mansons and the Gebbies became the first settlers on the Canterbury plains. Having completed the Port Levy charter, Francis, together with Ebenezer Hay, explored the rest of Banks Peninsula and down as far as the Otago Peninsula. The *Richmond* was away more than a month, returning to Wellington from Akaroa on 18 March with a load of potatoes from Moeraki. Having examined all the bays of Banks Peninsula and points south, Francis and Ebenezer decided that Pigeon Bay offered a stunning opportunity for the two families.

With the decision made to settle in Pigeon Bay, the Sinclairs and the Hays began arranging their affairs in Wellington and, with the bulk of their belongings and several months supplies aboard, the *Richmond* sailed for the families' new home on 22 April with the schooner returning in ballast to Port Nicholson on 10 May, the newspaper commenting at the time of their departure:

> The schooner *Richmond*, 30 tons, Sinclair, has sailed for Pigeon Bay, a place on the Middle Island, with one or two families and some stock, for the purpose of forming the nucleus of a settlement there. In this way, Lord Stanley's project* for discountenancing the further colonization of the Middle Island will be thwarted, for numerous individuals are fast peopling that "barren and mountainous" portion of New Zealand.[37]

* Lord Stanley, British Colonial Secretary, was opposed to further expansion of British colonies. In his view, there were too many to manage already.

On his return Francis Sinclair, as quoted in the Wellington newspaper, reported:

> Captain Sinclair of the schooner *Richmond*, from Pigeon Bay, informs us that on his arrival there he heard Mr. Dean[s] had been molested by the Maories, and that they had pulled down his stock-yard. He, in consequence applied to Mr. Robinson,[38] the magistrate of Akaroa, who very promptly, in company with a French gentleman, visited the spot, and told the Natives that if they did not reinstate it forthwith he would send the French man-of-war there. On his return Mr. Robinson told Mr. Dean[s] that he should have applied to him, and not given any consideration for settling on the land in the first instance, as it was an inducement for annoyance; at the same time that he would justify

him in resisting the interruptions of the Natives, and applying force to force, and that he would likewise swear them in as constables, which offer we believe it is their intention to avail themselves of.[39]

This incident did not deter Francis and Ebenezer, and a second sailing to Pigeon Bay took place on 18 May, with the following passengers aboard: 'Messrs. F. Sinclair, G. Sinclair, Hay, Wallace, Cullens, Rhodes, Thorburn, Houree, and three Maories.'[40] The remainder of the two family groups must have been on the first voyage south and remained there. By this time a second son, Thomas, had been born to the Hays. Also aboard were two cows and a calf belonging to Ebenezer. The *Richmond* did not then return to Wellington under Captain Sinclair, but was sold in Akaroa to William Barnard Rhodes, reportedly for either 10 or 18 head of cattle, depending on the reports of the time. Rhodes, a pastoralist and Wellington businessman, had landholdings in Akaroa and reputedly swam the first cattle ashore in the South Island at Akaroa on 12 November 1839.[41] Until then the *Richmond* had been an integral part of the Sinclair family's life in New Zealand.

As an afterword, the schooner returned to Wellington in July 1843 from the Chatham Islands under Captain Finlay, having sailed there from Akaroa to pick up whale oil and bone. A further voyage to the Chathams under Captain Finlay commenced on 8 August, and several subsequent voyages to the Chathams took place under a Captain Brown. Voyages to Kaikōura and Nelson were undertaken too, among others, as part of coastal trading. The vessel was lost with all hands, including Captain Brown, while trying to enter Kāwhia Harbor on 19 July 1845.[42]

Pigeon Bay, the early days

Banks Peninsula was formed over a five-million-year period between eleven and six million years ago from the detritus that spewed forth from two giant volcanoes. Since that time the landscape has been severely eroded. Pigeon Bay, on the northern side, forms one of the four magnificent harbors on the peninsula as a result of these geologic actions.

When the *Richmond* nosed into Pigeon Bay in April 1843, Eliza was afforded her first view of what was to be her home for the next 20 years. After two days uncomfortable sailing down the east coast of the South Island (and Eliza was reputedly not a good sailor), what she saw was a deep, relatively narrow bay six miles long, thrusting into the heart of Banks Peninsula. Although some grassland was apparent at the entrance to the bay, the surrounding hills were clad almost entirely in dark, dense New Zealand rainforest. Smoke could be seen rising from a few Māori encampments, and birdsong filled the air. The hills on both sides were steep, but there was much flattish land at the head of the bay and in an indentation on the western side. Rising up behind the bay loomed what is now called Mount Sinclair at 2759 feet (841m), one of the highest peaks on the peninsula.

The water gently shallowed as the *Richmond* sailed on up the length of the bay and anchored to begin unloading the families' possessions at what Francis and Ebenezer had previously decided was a suitable location for their initial stay. A campsite was prepared and tents erected. These would be their home for the next few months. Leaving

Ebenezer in charge, with the initial establishment complete, Francis, his son George, and Ebenezer's nephew John sailed back to Wellington to collect the remainder of their families and belongings, as well as some extra passengers. Less than three weeks later they returned to Pigeon Bay, but Francis's journeying was not yet over, as the *Richmond* had to be delivered in Akaroa to 'Barney' Rhodes in exchange for some of his cattle. This meant a short journey around the peninsula to the sheltered waters of Akaroa Harbor. Barney had sailed with them from Wellington so the exchange was concluded without difficulty.

Getting the cattle back to Pigeon Bay was not so easy, as Hannah Guthrie Hay relates:

> … they had yet to learn to their cost that there was more to pay, at least indirectly, before they could call the cattle their own. There was then only a Maori track through the otherwise unbroken forest, and a mountain of over 1300 feet interposed its height between them [at Pigeon Bay] and Akaroa, the mountain, as well as the valleys, being covered with dense bush. Over this track in its original state the driving of stock was an

▼ Chart of the north side of Banks Peninsula, 1856, from the survey by Captain Stokes of HMS *Acheron* executed in March/April 1849. (See later sketch of the *Acheron*, page 152.) The relationship of the Sinclair farm in Pigeon Bay (lower right; close-up on opposite page) to the nascent Christchurch and Lyttelton towns can be seen. Neither town was in existence when the area was surveyed, but had been founded before the chart was drawn up in London.
ATL MapColl 834.44aj 1850 10649

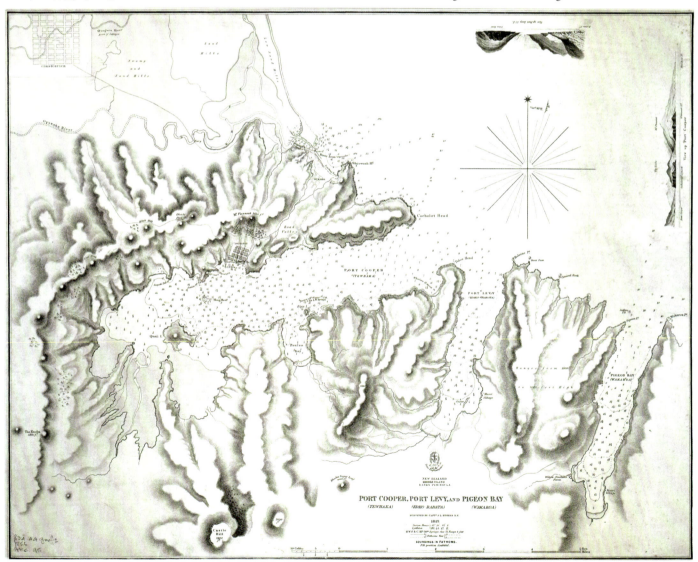

utter impossibility. Nothing daunted, however, our plucky pioneers set to work with a will to widen the track to six feet clear, and completed their task in three weeks, by dint of hard labour. Eight capable men were employed in this undertaking, their numbers having been increased by two, viz.: Alfred Wallace … and a young friend of his named Tom Cullen.[43]

The six family members involved in the task were presumably Francis Sinclair and his sons George and Frank, John McHutcheson, Ebenezer Hay and John Hay. Assuming the cattle were received at the head of the harbor, the distance involved was at least nine miles. Akaroa settlement itself was a further six miles around the eastern side of the harbor. The cattle were all safely driven over the trail in a single day.

On arrival at Pigeon Bay the little community consisted of Francis and Eliza, now 45 and 42, their six children (George 18, James 17, Jane 15, Helen 13, Francis Jnr. 9, Ann 3) and Eliza's brother, John McHutcheson (27). The Hay family was made up of Ebenezer and Agnes, both aged 30, their two small boys James and Thomas, at two and a few months, and Ebenezer's nephew, John Hay. With Alfred Wallace, the Hay family's friend from Wellington, this made a total of fifteen.

One of the first tasks was to provide some more permanent accommodation, and a 'daub and wattle'* house thatched with the long-leaved large tussock, toetoe (*Austroderia richardii*), was erected. The two family groups lived at either end. This arrangement worked well for the two years until each family built their own house in more permanent materials.

One material of which there was no shortage in Pigeon Bay was good durable kahikatea and tōtara lumber and in the fullness of time two charming houses were constructed of kahikatea frames and sidings with tōtara shingle roofs — the Sinclairs,' which they named Craigforth, on the western side of the bay in Sinclairs Bay (now called Holmes Bay) and the Hays,' Annandale, on the eastern side towards the head of the bay, south of the Māori village.

* A wooden frame is first erected and the walls are infilled with woven panels consisting of wooden strips or sticks which are then 'daubed' with wet soil or a clay and straw mixture.

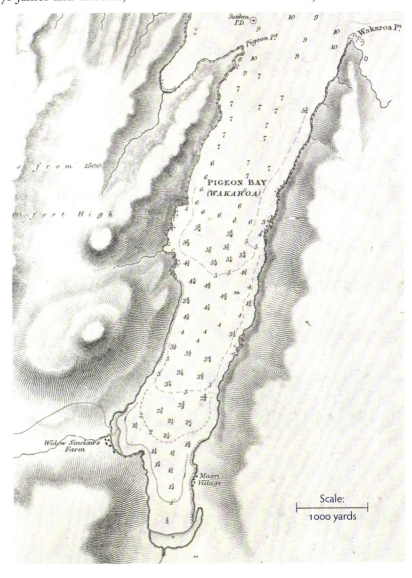

▶ Zoomed image from the chart opposite, showing Pigeon Bay with 'Widow Sinclair's Farm'. The Hays' property, Annandale, has not been identified, but was some distance to the north of the 'Maori Village' shown on the east side of the bay.

► A sketch of the Sinclairs' Pigeon Bay house, drawn on 15 September 1848 by Walter Mantell (1820–95). Mantell had been appointed by the New Zealand government as 'the commissioner for extinguishing native titles in the South Island' so it was only natural that he should call on the Sinclairs. It was an unenviable role for a man of conscience and he remained in the job for only four years. Later in his political career he was, for a time, Native Minister.
ATL E-334-028

A little over a month after the Sinclairs landed, on 17 June, the Wairau Incident occurred in Marlborough when 22 settlers, including the New Zealand Company's Nelson agent, Captain Arthur Wakefield, and four Māori were killed in a clash over the settlers' surveying activities. This disastrous event caused alarm and despondency throughout the New Zealand settler community. Immigration ceased for some months as the killings were seen to be the prelude to a possible general Māori uprising. The dangerous situation had repercussions at Pigeon Bay. Ebenezer wrote to his family in Scotland in January 1844:

> Some natives found their way to the whale fishery (Kaikoura), and told them they would all be killed in a day or two. The whole party fled, some to Port Nicholson, Wellington, and one boat's crew came to Port Cooper (Lyttelton), walked over the hills to our bay, and told us 2000 natives were within two days march of us, killing all the white people as they went along. We could muster about 30 fighting men in the harbour, which included Port Cooper, Port Levy, and Pigeon Bay. We made up our minds to fight to the last, as there was no way of escape; so we cleaned our guns; made bullets, and determined to sell our lives as dearly as we could.[44]

The rumor proved no more than that, but no sooner had this one been quashed than concerns arose about the local Māori who were heard to be plotting to kill all colonists on the peninsula. As the Māori had been friendly, this turn of events was all the more alarming. Their plans were well advanced when, fortunately, they were revealed by the Māori wife of Tom White, an American whaler living in Port Levy, who felt her husband's life was at risk. As the evening of the proposed attack approached, the Māori, knowing their plan had been compromised, thought better of it and abandoned the idea, but for long after this the families kept ready for any contingency.[45]

Despite these events, relations with the Māori inhabitants of the bay remained cordial, but the same couldn't be said regarding their dogs and pigs, which roamed incessantly, and gardens had to be well protected from the pigs in particular. Māori in the bay were already growing potatoes for sale to passing whalers, and the two families employed them clearing the trees in exchange for the first crop off the cleared land.

Dairying was the settlers' first farming priority. Sheep were rare at this early stage in New Zealand. The cows roamed free at first and had to be found and brought in for milking every day. The market for their cheeses was either passing ships or Akaroa village, some 15 rugged miles away. The stronger members of the families made this gruelling journey many times with large loads of butter or cheese on their backs.[46]

Boat building also occupied Francis and his sons. A 20-ton schooner, *Sisters*, was begun almost immediately and launched within a year of their arrival in Pigeon Bay.

In a letter from Francis to his brother William, written in April 1845 and published in the *New Zealand Journal*, the mouthpiece of the New Zealand Company, Francis explains that he built *Sisters* because he knew he was squatting on the land and might have to move on (despite the assurance he had from William Wakefield), and wished a means of transporting his family. In an ironic twist of fate he sold the schooner to the Nanto-Bordelaise Company, who were in final negotiations for the purchase of Banks Peninsula from the Māori, in exchange for the 350 acres the family were occupying in Pigeon Bay. The schooner became part of the company's payment to Māori and as a consequence Francis felt much more secure in the bay.

Between April 1844 and April 1845 *Sisters* made seven trips to Wellington under Francis's command, trading generally between Akaroa, Port Cooper, Pigeon Bay and the growing Wellington town, carrying freight and passengers. The letter referred to above was posted in Wellington on his final trip with George and James as crew and Helen as a passenger.

Having sold *Sisters* for the land he immediately began construction of a 10-ton cutter, the *Jessie Millar*. At the same time Ebenezer was having a 40-ton schooner built in the bay, albeit slowly, by John Hay, Alfred Wallace and Tom Cullen.

Whalers frequented the bay, and potatoes and meat were often traded for flour and sugar from the whaling vessels' supplies. The bay, because of the wood and shelter it afforded, became a popular 'trying out' (boiling oil out of the whale blubber) place for the whalers — a smelly process indeed. As well as the whalers and other welcome visitors, some not-so-welcome also called. In these early days of the New Zealand colony 'Pacific wanderers' of all sorts appeared in Pigeon Bay — and many were the stories told of the hospitality offered and the incidents that occurred. In 1844 a senior government official, Edward Shortland, wrote of his stay with the Sinclairs:

▼ Aotearoa New Zealand, showing places mentioned in the text.

> In the afternoon I returned to Pigeon Bay, where I was invited by Mr. Sinclair to rest at his house. His family was an example for settlers. Everything necessary for their comfort was produced by themselves — two young girls even making their own shoes. Mr. S. told me that he bought very few things; as his family — a wife, three sons, and three daughters — were able to do the work required. They all appeared happy and contented; and as they resided on land which the natives had sold bona fide, they had never been annoyed in any manner by them, although their house stood by the wayside, and numbers passed to and fro daily.[47]

◀ A watercolor of the Sinclair house at Pigeon Bay in 1852, by James Edward Fitzgerald (1818–96), superintendent of the Canterbury Province from 1852–56. Fitzgerald had been involved in planning the new settlement from 1849 and arrived in New Zealand in 1850 with the first group of settlers. He later entered politics in New Zealand at local and national level.
Canterbury Museum

▲ George Selwyn (1809–78) was the first Anglican bishop of New Zealand, from 1841 to 1868. He was an inveterate traveler and by 1847 he had journeyed all over New Zealand by land and sea. His brief visit to Pigeon Bay in 1844 gives an indication of his attention to his flock, be they Anglican or not, despite the fact he was a high churchman who clashed with the low church missionaries of the Church Missionary Society in the North Island.
Author's collection, colorised

In a similar vein New Zealand's first Church of England bishop, George Selwyn, wrote in his journal for 15 February 1844:

> The wind being still contrary, I walked over (from Akaroa) to Pigeon Bay, where I found some Scotch settlers of the right sort, living in great comfort by their own exertions, making every thing for themselves, and, above all, keeping up their religious principles and usages, though far away from any ministerial assistance. The name of this family was Sinclair. I spent the evening with them, and conducted their family prayers.[48]

Francis's April 1845 letter to his brother William, written after two years in Pigeon Bay as he was preparing to depart for Wellington on the *Sisters*, is enthusiastic about the place and their family life:

> I am sure if you saw it you would declare that it is the sweetest spot that you have ever seen. George calls it Craigforth but whether that will be the name or not I cannot yet say; there is nothing wanting to my eyes to make it a perfect paradise but your presence.
>
> As for myself, I say to you honestly, truly and sincerely at no time since I came would I have resumed my former situation in Scotland not for six times the amount of the salary; not that I have made so much money, but that we have been so much happier and every way better.
>
> I left Eliza well and good and beautiful as ever. … I do declare there is not a happier family on the earth than we are.[49]

He did have concerns in the letter at the poor performance of the governor and his officers and how that was contributing to a worsening situation between Māori and settlers. He describes meeting Apie, a Māori friend from the *Richmond* boatbuilding days:

… when he saw me he came running to me, catched my hand in both of his, and looking in my face with perfect delight for a minute or two burst out with the Tangi, or native cry; he found that he could not express his joy at seeing me in any other way; then we sat down and had the Korero [talk]; he inquired for mama, the only name that he knew Eliza by, and then for all the children one by one, and always with a kindly anecdote for each … then we commenced on politics; here Apie was quite at home, as all the natives are. "Ah!" says he "when you stop at Okatu [building the *Richmond*] we all loved one another, every one then were brothers"; now, he says, "all are bad. Typo* (old nick) make the Maori all bad. Typo make all the Pakehas bad, very bad, and every day is very bad for Apie; for both Apie and all the Maoris say Kakeno (no good) this Pakehas; but Apie shall never shall say Kakeno to mama, or the piccaninnies, or you;" and drawing himself up with a grace that you never saw excelled, shook hands, and bade me a most solemn farewell: and his opinion was exactly the same as ours is, with regard to the interference of our rulers.[50]

* *'Typo' is a rendering of the Maori taipo, evil spirit, sometimes referred to as Old Nick, i.e. the Devil.*

One of the earliest letters still in the possession of the family is dated 6 May 1845, and like all the other early letters, must have made the voyage from New Zealand to Niʻihau on the *Bessie*. The letter, written in English by a French settler in Akaroa, would have been carried from Akaroa to Pigeon Bay and refers to an item of work which Francis wished carried out.[51]

The family's industrious efforts continued and three years on from their arrival in Pigeon Bay the toughest of their pioneering days appeared to be over. They were able to slaughter their first cattle beast, having lived largely on wild pig and native pigeons up to that time. The Sinclairs and the Hays were comfortably housed, and their dairying had increased to the extent that a larger market for their produce was required. The obvious choice was Wellington, which by 1846 was a town of a few thousand — many more than the hundred or so in Akaroa. The growing farm produce may have contributed to Ebenezer's decision to have the 40-ton boat built while Francis was completing his 10-ton cutter *Jessie Millar*.

The last voyage

It was May 1846, and over a year since their previous trip to Wellington in *Sisters*, when the *Jessie Millar* was completed and could be readied for her first voyage to Wellington with the dual purpose of selling the families' dairy output on the Wellington market and returning with a cargo of rigging and sails for Ebenezer's schooner. In addition Francis had with him all their combined savings for the purchase of stores and clothing for the two families. The *Jessie Millar* left Pigeon Bay for Wellington on 10 May 1846. Aboard the heavily laden vessel were Francis, his son George, Alfred Wallace (by this time Jane's fiancé), and a shoemaker named McLennan from Akaroa. It was with joyous hearts that the families farewelled the seafarers, looking forward to the prospect of new clothing and supplies.

But as the days passed with no sign of the cutter's return the families became increasingly anxious. At what stage anxiety turned to hopelessness and then certainty of loss no one can say, but it wasn't until 11 July that the following appeared in the Wellington newspaper:

> ... we learn that Mr. Sinclair, of Pigeon Bay, left that place on the 10th of May last in a small cutter of about 10 tons, bound for this port. She has never been heard of since, and there is too much reason to fear that the unfortunate vessel foundered the following day in the heavy south-east gale, which our readers may remember came on very suddenly.[52]

No trace of the vessel was ever found. Four lives had been lost, including their paterfamilias, and the Pigeon Bay families' cash savings and the prospective stores and income from their farming endeavors all vanished at a stroke.

> **the Pigeon Bay families' cash savings and the prospective stores and income from their farming endeavors all vanished**

They were grief-stricken, penurious, and their basic food supplies were dangerously low, but a passing French whaler called wanting fresh beef and gave them supplies in return.[53] The dynamics of the family and their situation had changed forever. Eliza's daughter Helen wrote to a friend:

> Mother's constant activities keep her from brooding too much on our great loss. She supervises so capably all work at Craigforth, up before dawn and never retiring until late at night, cheerful and encouraging, a great source of strength for all of us.[54]

Eliza, in her sorrow, was so overcome that she felt a spell away from her everyday surroundings would be helpful. She therefore arranged with Alexander (Sandy) McIntosh, who had arrived in Wellington with his family on the *London* only two weeks before the Sinclairs, to manage the Pigeon Bay property for two years while she took the family to Wellington, where she had many friends. The family sailed on the cutter *Royal William* in early March of 1847, later returning to Banks Peninsula and living at Akaroa until Sandy McIntosh's lease ran out. Sandy bought the land to the east of Pigeon Bay originally known as McIntosh's Bay[55] (now Menzies Bay), but it is not clear from the record whether this was before or after his two-year stint at Pigeon Bay. Probably it was the latter.

▲ William Fox (1812–93), in his later years. On William Wakefield's death in 1848 Fox was appointed Principal Agent for the New Zealand Company. In the latter stages of Eliza's negotiations over the titles to the Pigeon Bay land, Fox was her main point of contact in Wellington. Oxford-educated, Fox came to New Zealand in 1842 to work as a lawyer, but after a fall-out with the Chief Justice drifted into journalism before taking up appointments with the New Zealand Company. In the 1850s he moved into politics and was four times Premier. Today he is remembered as a gifted watercolorist. The Sinclair family became his lifelong friends, maintaining contact through Frank's many return trips after he moved to Niʻihau.
ATL PA2-2495

Eliza also had reason to visit Wellington, to settle Francis's affairs. The family had essentially been squatting on the land at Pigeon Bay, and while Francis had paid the Nanto-Bordelaise Company for what he thought was their land, the matter of that company's right to Banks Peninsula was still under discussion in Wellington, Paris and London. Eliza's only surety was William Wakefield's word in his discussions with Francis and Ebenezer that the New Zealand Company would honor the Sinclair and Hay land purchases if Canterbury was settled. Although the Canterbury Association, formed to settle Canterbury, was not formally established in London by Edward Gibbon Wakefield until 1848, there would already have been much talk in Wellington of the likely Canterbury settlement. Eliza would have wanted to reinforce her claim to the Pigeon Bay land with William Wakefield, and also with the governor of the colony, George Grey, who was periodically in Wellington.

Wakefield died from a stroke in September 1848, at about the time the family went to Akaroa, and was replaced as the New Zealand Company's agent in New Zealand by William Fox, who later became a firm friend of the family. By the time William left his post in the Nelson colony and was established in Wellington, Eliza was back in Pigeon Bay.

On 6 June 1850, Charles Robinson wrote to Eliza from Wellington, having been asked by Eliza to pursue the family's land claims with William Fox. The letter reads, in part:

I then busied myself about your land and after some difficulty it was agreed between Mr. Fox and myself to leave it to me to arrange if possible, with Carrington [the NZ Company's chief surveyor] that Mr. Fox consents that if Mr. Carrington will change his plan, that he Mr. Fox will not oppose it and that you can thus include any land of not too great an amount to make your land & bay complete and Mr. Fox told me to speak to Carrington about it.[56]

Robinson clearly achieved some success on Eliza's behalf. In any event the claim was subsequently honored and, after much bureaucratic procrastination, Eliza eventually received title to the Pigeon Bay land in 1852.[57]

Thomas Gay

The family returned to Pigeon Bay early in 1849, but during their time at Akaroa, before their return to Pigeon Bay, Jane, aged 21, met 39-year-old Thomas Gay, captain of the 374-ton whaling ship *Offley*. Romance immediately blossomed. According to the journal of the prominent Canterbury land surveyor, Charles Torlesse,[58] the *Offley* was in Pigeon Bay every time Torlesse visited in 1849, and the couple were married on 18 August 1849 in Dunedin by Rev. Charles Creed, a Methodist missionary based at Waikouaiti, north of Dunedin.[59] The wedding took place at the Dunedin courthouse; it was only months after the first immigrants had arrived to settle Otago and churches had yet to be built.

▲ Thomas Gay (1809–65).
Robinson family

Their honeymoon was lengthy, as after the wedding Thomas took Jane on his whaling voyage which arrived back in Hobart on 31 December 1849, before the *Offley* sailed again 'for the South Seas' on 29 January 1850.[60] The record does show though that the *Offley* was in Hobart for two weeks in October 1850 (he had left Hobart originally on 20 February 1849 which appears to have been Thomas's maiden voyage in command of the *Offley*).[61] The marriage took place in Dunedin and a son, George, was born in Pigeon Bay on 26 August 1850.[62]

Thomas arrived back from a second nine-month (unsuccessful) whaling cruise in November 1851 and left Pigeon Bay mid-November, taking Jane and young George with him.[63] There is a record in the Hobart shipping news of Jane returning to New Zealand with George in January 1852, so she had traveled to Hobart for a second time.[64] Thomas and Jane subsequently built a house on the Sinclair property in Pigeon Bay and had five more children.[65]

Thomas Gay was born in Crail, Fifeshire, Scotland in 1809 and went to sea at an early age.[66] His name appears in 1843 as the master of the 97-ton schooner *Adelaide* engaged in the Australian coastal trade. When he met Jane, he was a widower with one son, James, born in 1841. James was living with an aunt in Hobart, as this was Thomas's whaling base. Thomas would undoubtedly have wanted to introduce his new wife to his family in Hobart, hence their honeymoon and subsequent visit. At a later stage James came to live with the Gay family at Pigeon Bay.

From the time of his marriage to Jane Sinclair, Thomas was a crucial figure in the life of the family, as we see in this unfolding tale.

Pigeon Bay, the middle years

The Sinclair family's return to Pigeon Bay in 1849 was back to 'business as usual': dairying, some wheat, oat and potato cropping, forest clearance, fencing, and lumber for passing ships, all with the help of local Māori labor. The children were growing up. Hannah Guthrie Hay commented that the girls could manage a boat as well as their brothers. They were fearless riders when horses became available, were crack shots and capable workers, and the hardships of those first few years did not quell their buoyant spirits.[67]

The family's hospitality to visitors continued unabated. The paddle steamer HMS *Acheron* visited in April 1849 in the course of her survey of the coastline of New Zealand, and crew members came ashore for a picnic and other amusements.[68]

A larger house, Craigforth, was built to cater for the family's expanding needs. Charlotte Godley, the wife of the Chief Agent of the Canterbury settlement, visiting Pigeon Bay in November 1851, describes the new Craigforth and its surroundings in a letter to her mother in England:

> They have just built quite a pretty new house in a most lovely spot; it is in a little bay near the head of the harbour, which they have quite to themselves. There is a beautiful stream under the windows, at one side of the house, with cold clear water, that you would not know how to appreciate, but we from Lyttelton do. It is shaded, too, with trees, quite to the beach. There is a garden in front, with a great many common flowers, and some English grass laid down, and another is being made behind the house, where they are clearing away some trees; but the rest of the valley stretches away into very thick bush, with fern trees, and birds singing so loud that they almost wake you in the morning.[69]

▲ James Walter Gay (1841–93). Jimmy was the son of Thomas Gay by an earlier marriage and came to live with the Sinclairs in Pigeon Bay. At age 22 he traveled with the family on the *Bessie*. He later bought land on Oʻahu in Waialua where he ranched, apparently with money given him by Eliza. The family disapproved and he became estranged from them, except Frank, who took a fatherly interest as the eldest half-uncle. He married Mary Ellen Kaukalilani Richardson and they bought Mokuleia Ranch, and had six children.
Robinson family

▶ Charlotte Godley (1821–1907), wife of the founder of the Canterbury settlement, John Robert Godley. Although they were in New Zealand for less than three years, the Godleys formed a firm friendship with the Sinclairs.
Wikimedia Commons, colorised

The Sinclairs maintained their reputation for unbridled hospitality. Charlotte Godley again, describing the end of a tiring day's walk from Akaroa:

> … and by the time we had pushed across again to Mrs. Sinclair's, it was after eight o'clock and quite dark. We were very glad to get in, and were most kindly received, of course, for they are the kindest people it is possible to conceive …
>
> They are very nice simple people, excessively Scotch, and old-fashioned, and live a regular colonial life, according to one's old ideas of it; plenty of cows, and milk, and butter, and cream, and doing everything for themselves; they have not a servant in the house.[70]

Coastal trading had improved, so marketing produce in Wellington was not the problem it had been earlier. Without Francis, Ebenezer's schooner had no captain and he sold it on the stocks in the boatyard as a consequence.

Ten years after the Sinclairs came to New Zealand, Christchurch was founded in December 1850 with the arrival of the Canterbury Association's 'first four ships' carrying settlers from England. This changed forever the dynamics of the Pigeon Bay settlement. The demand for lumber increased enormously — much of early Christchurch was built from Pigeon Bay frames, planks and shingles. A large market for food had also arrived on their doorstep.

Lyttelton Harbor (known earlier Port Cooper) was decided upon as the port and it grew quickly, becoming important to the Sinclairs. The journey from Pigeon Bay to Lyttelton by whaleboat could take only four hours in favorable winds, but eight was more the norm, and it could take up to twelve. The alternative by foot or horseback meant a trip of 14 miles over two mountains, followed by a whaleboat ride across Lyttelton Harbor.[71]

Having established the Canterbury settlement, John Godley and his wife Charlotte returned to England in December 1852. They had become friendly with the Sinclairs and Godley wrote to Eliza from Lyttelton in August thanking her for all her hospitality and asking her 'if James would be so good as to fill a small case for me with plants out of the bush, for the purpose of taking them home [England was still called home by the colonists until only a generation ago in New Zealand] … the common kinds of trees will be curiosities [there].'[72]

Many more people were appearing in the bay and some were staying permanently. Ebenezer, having young children, was instrumental in building a schoolhouse and recruiting a teacher. The school had 15 pupils in 1852, its founding year.[73]

As settlers continued to arrive in Christchurch, with many checking out prospects on the peninsula, there was a need for more accommodation than these two most hospitable families could provide. John Hay, Ebenezer's nephew, saw the opportunity. In 1852 he leased a portion of Ebenezer's land, built the Pigeon Hotel for travelers, and hired Mrs Elizabeth Brown to manage the establishment. She and her husband had been fellow passengers with the Hays on the *Bengal Merchant*.[74]

The flavor of the settlement in 1852 is given by a *Lyttelton Times* journalist describing the Pigeon Bay section of the overland journey from Port Levy to Akaroa:

> the path leads gently over the hill through thick bush, which extends to the base in Pigeon Bay. On emerging one stumbles rather unexpectedly upon the pretty homestead of Mrs. Sinclair, with its flower garden and lawn in front, and the bush for a background. … a walk of a mile over the macadamised high road to Akaroa, the stony beach, brings you to the head of the bay, and with it to Ebenezer Hay's. Beyond is the Inn, where, if indisposed to proceed, an excellent dinner, made ready in no time, and a comfortable

▲ Craigforth's original title plan, c.1850, giving Eliza Sinclair title to two blocks of land in Pigeon Bay The copy held by Archives NZ is more complete and the note on their copy reads:

No 1 Purchased by the late Mr Francis Sinclair from the Nanto-Bordelaise Company. Contents 157 acres

No 2 Selected by Mrs Sinclair, as per Agreement between her late husband Mr Francis Sinclair and William Wakefield Esq Principal Agent of the New Zealand Company. Contents 370 acres being 20 acres over the quantity which is given as compensation for any PUBLIC WORKS that may be required.
Canterbury Museum/Archives NZ

◀ On the Archives NZ copy a hand-written note has been added:
> The 43 acres to the Southward of the block purchased from the French were added to meet Mrs Sinclair's wishes, and received my assent
>
> Signed William Fox
> PANZ Co [Principal Agent New Zealand Company]
> 27 Dec[ember] 1850
Robinson family

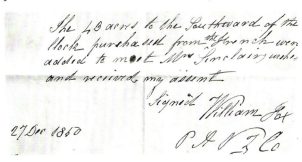

bed-room, can really be obtained as reasonably as in port, under the auspices of the presiding genius, a bustling little Scotchwoman [Elizabeth Brown].

From Pigeon Bay the track again enters the bush — this time, however, on level ground. This fine tract of woodland at the head of Pigeon Bay is about three miles across, and the path is occasionally skirted by large numbers of the tree fern, a very handsome and interesting variation from the pines and totaras.[75]

▲ The 1000-ton paddle steamer HMS *Acheron* was despatched to New Zealand in January 1848 to make a complete survey of the coastline. She had a complement of 100 persons under Captain John Stokes. In the course of the survey she spent 6–9 April 1849 surveying in Pigeon Bay and took full advantage of Eliza's hospitality.
Wikimedia Commons

Thomas Gay disappears from the shipping records from 1852 to 1857 and, while it is only speculation, it is reasonable to suppose that he spent this time in Pigeon Bay among his growing family, becoming a landlubber for a period. There was also always plenty to do helping on the Sinclairs' expanding farm. He was a lucky man; Charlotte Godley comments in her letters: '[Jane] is the nicest of the Sinclairs …'[76]

Charles Barrington Robinson

Although the Sinclair family would not have been aware of it at the time, 2 April 1850 was a significant date for them, when the bark *Monarch*, on her way from Gravesend to Auckland, limped into Akaroa for urgent repairs to her rudder. Aboard was Charles Barrington Robinson, paying his second visit to New Zealand, and Henry Smith, joint charterers of the vessel ostensibly bringing 52 emigrants to Auckland.

Charles Robinson had previously spent 1840 to 1845 in Akaroa as the resident magistrate. In this role he met the Sinclair family shortly after their arrival, probably in connection with the Deans affair on the Canterbury Plains mentioned earlier. Robinson's role in Akaroa was a delicate one — managing the situation between French and British settlers, and between them and the Māori inhabitants. By all accounts he acquitted himself extremely well. He was a fluent French speaker with a good knowledge of French law, having spent several years practising in Paris. During his period in Akaroa he learned Māori and also acquired land in both Akaroa and Pigeon Bay.

Having been recruited in England by Governor Hobson for a police magistrate's position in Wellington, Charles Robinson arrived in the Bay of Islands, then the seat of the colonial government, on the *Chelydra* on 28 June 1840.[77] He was almost immediately shipped down to Akaroa by the governor on the *Britomart* to give an air of British territorial authority to the township after the governor got wind of the imminent arrival there of a group of French settlers. British sovereignty had been declared over the South Island in June, and the arriving French were totally unaware of this development until the French corvette *L'Aube*, sent to protect the settlers, reached the Bay of Islands en route to Akaroa. The *Britomart* sailed into Akaroa Harbor on 10 August 1840, the *L'Aube* on the 15th and the *Comte de Paris*, carrying the French settlers, on the 17th. The pragmatic arrangements arrived at between magistrate Robinson and Captain Lavaud of the *L'Aube* to maintain civil order over the succeeding years were praised by both the French and British governments.

For instance, Captain Lavaud, the French King's Commissioner for Akaroa, writing to Acting Governor Shortland (Governor Hobson having died in office) on the occasion of Captain Lavaud's leaving the Akaroa station in January 1843, says:

◀ William Fox's delicate watercolor 'Mrs. Sinclair's Pigeon Bay' was painted in 1858 during one of his stays with the family.
Hocken Collections, Uare Taoka o Hākena, University of Otago, Acc: 78/22

> After having given you an account of the way in which I have to praise Mr. Robinson, there remains for me a particular request to address to Your Excellency, and that is to call the attention of the Government of the Queen to him, and to help me, at the close of the negotiations pending between France and Britain with regard to the settlement of Akaroa, to cause him to obtain the reward of his conduct since he has represented his Government here.[78]

Likewise Colonel William Wakefield, the agent for the New Zealand Company, writing to the Otago Association in Dunedin in August 1844 after a visit to Akaroa, states:

> We were most cordially welcomed by Mr. Robinson, who, during four years, has fulfilled the duties of his office in a most delicate and difficult position to the entire satisfaction of his Government and in perfect amity with the French authorities and settlers.[79]

Charles Robinson resigned his position as magistrate in 1845 when a transfer to Otago was mooted. After his resignation he seems to have been uncertain about his future plans, writing three letters to Francis Sinclair in the next few months asking him to do several things for him and wishing to discuss the possibility of Francis becoming his agent in New Zealand. The letters are formal by today's standards, and peremptory in tone with a hint of master–servant relationship about them, and an air of fastidiousness here and there. Nevertheless when he finally decided to return to England, and realized he may never see the family again, he wrote to Francis:

> If I should not see you again before I leave I shall not have an opportunity of thanking you for the unvarying kindness I have ever met with from yourself & all your family but I assure you I shall not quickly forget your hospitable conduct so different from that of the great majority of the inhabitants of the Peninsula.[80]

Charles Robinson went back to England in April 1846, returning four years later on the *Monarch* after a horrendous voyage during which only a fortuitous change of wind

▼ The raising of the Union Jack in Akaroa in 1840 was celebrated 100 years later by a commemorative postage stamp.
NZ Post

saved the ship from being driven onto the rocks on Otago Peninsula when the bark's rudder broke for the second time. After such a voyage, it was not surprising that 41 of the prospective Auckland bound settlers (out of 52) opted to remain in Akaroa.

Leaving Henry Smith in Akaroa to manage his property and stock, Charles continued on to Auckland on the *Monarch*, presumably for business reasons. The *Monarch* sailed via Wellington, on 15 May 1850, after six weeks in Akaroa, now sporting a newly made and fitted rudder.

During his times in Akaroa Charles would undoubtedly have visited his property in Pigeon Bay and reacquainted himself with the Sinclair and Hay families. Helen Sinclair was now a pretty woman of 19; her elder sister, Jane, was already married to Thomas Gay and was living at Pigeon Bay with her children; while the youngest daughter, Ann, was a girl of eleven. It may have been then, or even earlier, before he left Akaroa in 1846, that Helen caught his eye. Charles was 19 years her senior and is described by one of his fellow passengers on the *Monarch* as, 'a short, thickset man, with a dark, Jewish-looking face, smart and clever.'[81] Another commentator, writing later, describes him thus: 'He was a clever lawyer, and was always stylishly dressed, wearing a high silk hat, and requiring his boots to be blacked once every day, "even in those times".'[82]

Charles spent the next few months buying livestock in Sydney and selling the animals in New Zealand. The *Lyttelton Times* for 1 February 1851, for instance, advertised for sale in Akaroa ex the *Monarch* twelve merino rams, 550 merino ewes, 50 heifers, one shorthorn bull, twelve brood mares and a pony.

These comings and goings gave him ample time to court Helen Sinclair, and the following notice appeared in the *Lyttelton Times* of 29 January 1853:

> MARRIED,—January 17th, at Akaroa, by the Rev. W. Aylmer, Charles Barrington Robinson, Esq., to Helen, daughter of the late Captain Sinclair, of Craigforth, in Pigeon Bay.[83]

Helen was 22 and Charles 41. The couple set up house in Akaroa and later in the year, on 17 October, a son, Aubrey was born.

The next major event in the family's life is best described in the words of Ida Knudsen von Holt in *Stories of Long Ago*:

> When little Aubrey Robinson was one year old, Helen appeared one forenoon at her mother's house, having walked all the way from Akaroa carrying the child. She announced that she had left her husband and had come home to stay. Mr. Robinson came at once after his wife, and had long interviews with Grandmama [Eliza], but all to no avail. Helen would not even see him, nor let the little boy be taken from her, and no one seemed to know the reason for this absolute estrangement, or what the real trouble was.[84]

It appears the event actually took place in April 1854, when Aubrey was six months old. They had been married for only 16 months.

Charles Robinson was an irascible man, and perhaps in a domestic situation subject to unpredictable outbursts of bad temper. Helen, at the time of her marriage, was seen as 'pretty, but spoilt and inexperienced.'[85] She was also strong-willed and tenacious, as subsequent events show. Her mind was firmly made up and there was to be no going back, despite Charles's pleading via Eliza. When this became obvious to Charles he acceded to Helen's wish that she should henceforth look after Aubrey. In spite of his natural affection for his son, Helen refused to let him see the child, nor would she meet with him herself.

Eliza was usually a shrewd judge of character, but if we are to believe what happened, this time she got it wrong. But whether, given Helen's character, Eliza could have influenced her can only be speculated upon. Like all mothers, but even more so as a widow of seven years standing, Eliza only wanted the best for her children, and any rumors swirling around Akaroa regarding Charles Robinson clearly hadn't reached the Sinclair family during the couple's courting days.

Although Charles Robinson seems to have been well respected in Akaroa (particularly among the French settlers) during his time as a magistrate, the same was certainly not true four years later on his return. Henry Sewell, a senior administrator for the Canterbury Association, visiting Akaroa in June 1853, a few months after the Robinsons' marriage, writes in his journal that he: '…made acquaintance with Mr. Robinson who seems a clever educated man, but every body speaks of him as dangerous and mischievous.'[86] He was regarded as somewhat unscrupulous in his land dealings, which may have set the community against him, and this was followed by his marital troubles, for which the best clue comes from Johannes Andersen's unpublished *Old Identities* journal:

> Mrs Sinclair had three daughters, and they all married old men. The second married Mr. C.B. Robinson, the magistrate. Mr. Hay says he was a scamp: he ill-treated his wife, kicking and beating her, and using her so badly that she was taken away from him. He then threatened to take away the child — 'not because he was fond of it, but in order to cause his wife yet more misery. It appears that old Mr. Hay, Ebenezer, was against the marriage, cautioning Mrs. Sinclair against it — but she answered, "Oh Mr. Hay, I would do anything to please Mr. Robinson." When Robinson threatened to take the child, his wife came to Mr. Hay in her distress, but he reassured her, saying "He doesn't love you, and he loves the child less: we will see to it that he does not get it."[87]

This was told to Johannes Andersen well after the event, by James Hay, Ebenezer's son, who was a boy of 14 when these matters took place. How much of it all he was aware of at the time is not known, but it does appear there was some neighborly assistance given to Helen, both in Akaroa and in Pigeon Bay. James Hay never cared for Charles, only acknowledging in his published book of reminiscences that 'Mr Robinson was specially fitted for his [magistrate's] position in Akaroa, being a remarkably clever lawyer and a good linguist'[88] — without further comment.

Charles Robinson's relationship with the Akaroa community seems to have deteriorated well before his wife's sudden departure. The *Lyttelton Times* in January 1854, in discussing what were obviously Robinson's land dealings, refers to him as 'a person notorious at Akaroa.'[89]

One other incident which gives a window on his character is a famous duel which took place between Charles Robinson and Captain Douglas Muter of the 49th Regiment, ostensibly over a land dispute, but rumors at the time suggested it was a question of Helen Sinclair's honor. As duelling has always been illegal in New Zealand, facts are hard to come by. It appears to have taken place somewhere in Pigeon Bay, some

▲ Johannes Andersen (1873–1962) was born in Denmark, but his parents moved to New Zealand when he was only a few months old. He is best remembered as the first librarian of the Alexander Turnbull Library, a position he held from 1915 until 1937. He was a prolific, and sometimes controversial, writer and speaker on many aspects of Maoridom and New Zealand natural history. His *Place Names of Banks Peninsula* was published in 1927, and it was doubtless through the gathering of these names that he also collected information for his unpublished *Old Identities* that is cited here.
ATL 1/1-018551-F

time between 1853 and 1856. Robinson evidently fired in the air and then Captain Muter aimed but missed. The seconds then intervened and the affair ended.

Charles Robinson lingered on in Akaroa, gradually selling his landholdings before returning to England in 1861. He returned briefly in 1864 to sell his remaining New Zealand assets and saw out his days in England.

What are we to make of this perplexing man, fastidious in his personal habits, clever (an adjective used by nearly all commentators) and who executed a brilliant mix of diplomacy and legal wisdom in a situation in Akaroa, which in the worst scenario, had it not been so sensitively handled, could have led to discord between two of the major powers. With all of that, however, there was some character flaw in his personal life which led him into shady land dealings and abuse of his wife. At the end of his magistrate's role in Akaroa he might have been destined for greater things. Instead, the path he chose was one that left his reputation in tatters in New Zealand and led him into obscurity in England.

Forty-five years on, presumably on hearing of Charles's death at the end of 1899, Helen asked her brother Francis in England to find out what he could about his later life. What little he found came largely from a lawyer and distant relative who had acted for Charles and also knew him socially. He evidently lived extremely modestly, having bought an annuity with what assets he had amassed during his time in New Zealand. His few belongings were left to his nephews, the sons of his brother George, who predeceased him. He had never told the distant relative that he was married.

After leaving her husband, Helen did not marry again, but retained her married name — which lives on today with her descendants, Keith and Bruce Robinson.

▲ Robinsons Bay in the Akaroa Harbor, on Banks Peninsula in the South Island, keeps the Robinson name alive in New Zealand. Charles Robinson purchased land in the area from local Māori, who knew the bay as Kākakaiau.
Google Earth

Pigeon Bay, the final years

With Helen and baby Aubrey's return to Pigeon Bay in 1855, the family at Craigforth consisted of Eliza (55), James (29), Helen (24), Aubrey (1), Frank (21) and Ann (16), while half a mile away in the bay lived Thomas Gay (46), Jane (26) and their two children, George (5) and Francis (3). Annie, a daughter born in 1851, died at the age of two and was buried at Pigeon Bay. Eliza's brother, John McHutcheson (39) (John Mack Hutcheson as he was known), had left Pigeon Bay long since, in 1848.

By this time James had taken over the day-to-day management of the farm, while Eliza continued to run the household, allowing Helen time to recover from the breakup of the marriage and to manage the baby.

In 1857 Thomas Gay, after spending the last few years at his home in Pigeon Bay, was approached by a group of Lyttelton businessmen, and this resulted in the following news item in the *Lyttelton Times*:

> The schooner Corsair has been purchased in Sydney on behalf of several gentlemen of this place, and is intended to be fitted as a whaler and to cruise off this coast. She is a staunch teak built vessel of 134 tons register, and is now in the experienced hands of Captain Gay, of Pigeon Bay. She sailed for Geelong with a general cargo on 3rd inst., and would return to Sydney to be fitted out.[90]

The fitting out didn't happen immediately as the *Corsair* made a trading run directly to Lyttelton, arriving on 21 December 1857, before presumably returning to Sydney to be fitted out. Jane and Helen were passengers on this latter voyage. During the refit the sail configuration was changed so that she emerged as a brigantine (square rigged on the foremast with fore-and-aft mainsail and a square topsail on the mainmast). The brigantine proceeded to Hobart and thence to Lyttelton, arriving on 13 March 1858. The two sisters were away from home for more than two months while their three little children must have been looked after by Eliza and Ann. There is no mention of James Gay, Thomas's son from his first marriage, being brought from Hobart with them.

A further trading trip across the Tasman was made before the brigantine *Corsair* sailed on a whaling voyage on 9 June 1858. Ten days later there was success, with a whale caught off Kaiapoi and tryed-out in Pigeon Bay, yielding nine tons of oil and eight hundredweight of bone.[91]

This early success was not to be repeated, however, and while a few more whales were caught, overall the season was a failure. From November 1858 to March 1859 the brigantine traded between Lyttelton, Timaru and Dunedin carrying passengers and general cargo and laying down some new moorings for the authorities at Timaru port. The 1859 whaling season was even worse, with only three whales caught and two crew lost and two boats smashed when a whale attacked. Again the brigantine traded south in the off-season and hopes were high for the 1860 season, but it was not to be. Again only a few whales were caught despite Thomas Gay refitting the vessel as a brig (fully square-rigged) to improve performance.

The owners decided to quit the enterprise and sold the *Corsair* at auction on 23 April 1861. Thus ended what had been a high-profile venture for Lyttelton, and high hopes had been held for it. Its failure cannot have enhanced Thomas Gay's reputation.

Pigeon Bay was becoming increasingly settled, with a consequential steady decline in Māori; in 1859 it was reported that there were only ten male and three female Māori remaining in the bay. Ship-building and repair was an expanding activity, and a steam-driven sawmill began operation in August 1859. Pigeon Bay was a prime source of premium lumber. A weekly steamer service to and from Lyttelton began in April 1858, with mail taken to Akaroa by packhorse.

Eliza's reputation for hospitality to travelers continued despite her increase in neighborly contacts. The Rev. James Stack, whose parish included all the outlying settlements on Banks Peninsula, visited in May 1859 and recounts this delightful story of his journey from Akaroa to Pigeon Bay in his *More Maoriland Adventures*:

> My companion [Ngaere Wiremu te Hau, or 'Little William,' a lay preacher] had talked incessantly all the way up the hill about a widow who was always kind to the Maoris, and lived with her family down near the beach. Her name, he said, was Tikara. I could not think of any name that might be its English equivalent, but whatever her name might be I refused to go near her house, and told William not to take me there.
>
> We were walking for some time under tall forest trees through which our path led when, without any warning I stepped through a natural arbour and found myself within a yard or two of a large house, and standing on the

▼ Pigeon Bay was a favorite place for whaling vessels to 'try out' their catch — the boiling out of the oil from the whale blubber. The bay was sheltered and had abundant wood available to fuel the fires.
ATL MNZ-0006-1/4-F

verandah, looking at me, were two young English ladies. I felt very angry with William for tricking me, but as there was no retreating I slipped off my knapsack and put on my coat, but, not having shaved before starting in the morning, I felt very dirty and travel-stained.

On turning the corner of the house I came face to face with the quaintest little lady I had ever seen. She was dressed in pale blue, with a little shawl over her shoulders, and a white starched sun bonnet on her head, beneath which her kindly grey eyes shone out a warm welcome. She seized my hand with both hers, and turned a deaf ear to my apologies for being in such an unfit state to meet ladies. "We are just going to dinner," [dinner was in the middle of the day in the household] she said, "and you must join us." After I had washed my hands the little lady escorted me into the dining-room where, at a long table, I saw a number of people seated. "Now I must introduce you to my family." And she took me up to each one, with whom I shook hands. "This is my daughter, Mrs. Robinson; and this is Captain Gay, my son-in-law; and this is Mrs. Gay; and this is Miss Aylmer,[92] the daughter of the clergyman at Akaroa; and this is my daughter Annie; and this is Jimmy Gay,[93] and Hamish[94] you have seen."

Master William had got such a good dinner that he was loth to move when the time came for us to continue our journey. His reason for disobeying my orders, and bringing me to Mrs. Sinclair's hospitable house was very evident. This visit, paid against my will, was the first of many.[95]

▲ Rev. James West Stack (1835–1919) was the Anglican parish priest for the Māori mission in the Christchurch diocese from 1859 to 1874. Born to Church Missionary Society parents in a Māori pā in the Waikato, James was educated in England and New Zealand. He followed in his father's footsteps and the Māori mission role was his first appointment. The mission covered the whole Canterbury Province, with the mission house, church and school located at Tuahiwi near Kaiapoi, well away from European influence. He traveled extensively, and stayed with the Sinclair family both before and after his marriage in 1861.
ATL PA2-2781

Two years later he visited again, this time with his new bride, and his journal gives insight into Ann's character:

We spent the best part of a week with Mrs. Sinclair, whom we found a most enchanting hostess. She was delighted to discover that my wife knew Edinburgh so well, and they enjoyed long talks about it and its notable people. I was glad to find my wife as charmed with Annie as I had been at first sight. Though brought up from childhood in the secluded little bay in which her home stood, shut out from all intercourse with companions of her own age and sex, and with nobody to speak to but the members of her own family, it was astonishing to find what an interest she took in everything going on in the world, and how wide and varied her interests were, and what a fund of information she had acquired on most topics that cropped up in the course of conversation.[96]

Ann was by this time 22, and she hadn't been as cloistered as it might have appeared to the reverend. While the Sinclair house was separated from the main activity in the bay, it was still a mecca for travelers and acquaintances. Ann had several admirers among the local community and lately had acquired a serious prospective suitor, James Montgomery. With a sunny temperament and broad interests she was sensitive and helpful to all. Consequently many and varied were the excuses for young men to call, particularly as "she was an active and gregarious person."[97]

Growing up she had been dominated by Helen, her attractive and intelligent older sister, on whom she had waited hand and foot, but who now had grown into a graceful and charming hostess. Both Ann and Helen had excellent singing voices.

Her nearest sibling in age was Francis (Frank), a romantic at heart, and they both shared a passionate love of literature. Ann encouraged him in his poetic writings.

James, the eldest of the children, thirteen years older than Ann, was the 'go to' person in the family. He had an encyclopedic memory and while a quiet personality, everyone sought his advice, which was always given sympathetically.

Jane was perhaps closest to James in having a sweet and soft personality, always helpful and unselfish, and while totally capable in every form of outdoor activity, was dainty and feminine.

Visitors of note during this period were William Fox and his wife Sarah. By 1859 Fox was a New Zealand parliamentarian who had already had a short spell as premier. He was also a gifted watercolorist of the New Zealand landscape. Ann must have showed interest in his work and on 17 January 1859, as a measure of their gratitude, he sent her some of his watercolors and some technical hints.

> I send by the steamer to Lyttelton a small packet addressed to you "to the care of Messrs. Cookson Bowler & Co." It contains a few water colors [unfortunately these could not be located] as intended as a Christmas present from Mrs. Fox and myself to Miss Sinclair. I have also added a few hints on water color drawing which she may find useful, the result of difficulties overcome in my own small experience in such matters.
>
> We had a very wet passage from Pigeon Bay to Lyttelton, but a fine run the following week to Wellington where we arrived all well.
>
> Mrs. Fox was very much delighted with her trip & with no part of it more than the visit to Pigeon Bay.

Despite the whaling failure and the sale of the *Corsair*, Thomas Gay had not been left idle:

> The port of Lyttelton has received a valuable accession to its list of vessels, in the shape of the screw steamer Maid of the Yarra, lately purchased by Captain Gay, on account of Messrs. Miles and Co. The Maid of the Yarra is a handsome iron boat of 142 tons register, and 14 horsepower. The limited power of her engines brings her under the class of auxiliary screws, but her excellent sailing powers more than compensate for this deficiency, as she is well known in the neighbouring colonies as a perfect clipper ... She is commanded by Capt. Gay, late of the Corsair, than whom no commander better known or more widely esteemed could have been chosen.[98]

I came face to face with the quaintest little lady I had ever seen

For the next nine months, until August 1862, the *Maid of the Yarra*, under Thomas Gay, was employed in the coastal trade, shuttling from Lyttelton down to Timaru via Akaroa and occasionally to Dunedin, and north as far as Kaiapoi and Amuri.

A rail tunnel under the Port Hills to connect the city of Christchurch with Lyttelton port had been mooted almost since the first settlers arrived. After much debate over the years, and one false start in 1859, a contract for the construction of a 1.6-mile tunnel and ancillaries was awarded to Holmes & Co. in April 1861. George Holmes needed lumber for construction and sleepers, and the most accessible source was Pigeon Bay, where the Sinclairs had several hundred acres of prime forest. Holmes would certainly have sounded Eliza out early in the tendering process, as would other tenderers.

It could well have been these discussions with George Holmes that prompted the family to review their situation. Although the farm was doing well, the family was getting larger, but their land was finite. Eliza was devoted to keeping the family together. The exciting pioneering days were over in Pigeon Bay; it was now becoming too settled. Although they had faced difficulties, particularly with the tragic loss of the patriarch, Eliza, Francis and Helen still had their adventurous spirit. Was it time for a major move?

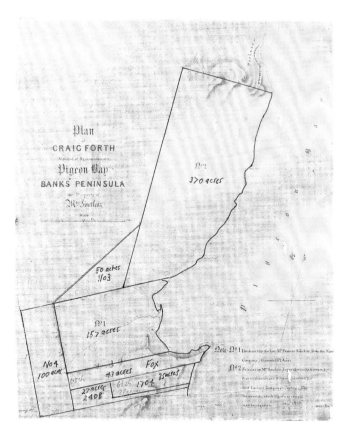

▲ The property in Pigeon Bay that was sold to George Holmes on 8 February 1863 consisted of 782 acres in seven titles, together with all improvements.

Robinson family

They had an experienced seafarer in the family, and British Columbia and California were spoken of as offering suitable opportunities.

Francis and Helen were both unhappy with their circumstances. Francis, romantic soul that he was, had just become estranged from the beautiful Blanche Campbell from Akaroa, whom all the family liked, and he was despondent. Helen was still recovering from the breakup of her marriage and the area held too many memories of that traumatic event. Pigeon Bay felt too circumscribed now and they should look for wider opportunities. Eliza was sympathetic. It had been 17 years since Francis Senior declared to his brother William in Scotland that Pigeon Bay 'was the sweetest spot you have ever seen,' but times and circumstances had now significantly changed.

Because of her blossoming relationship with James Montgomery, Ann was not at all keen on a move, and the easygoing James, happy with his present lot, was also reluctant to leave Craigforth.

The majority won the day and the family resolved to sell up and look first at possibilities in British Columbia. It was a huge decision after almost 20 years at Craigforth. Their friends were flabbergasted, but negotiations began with George Holmes over the sale of Craigforth. By this time Eliza had amassed 782 acres of land in seven titles. Both William Wakefield and William Fox had been true to their word, and Eliza had also bought further additions. The seven titles were made up of:

Section 1	157 acres bought by Francis from the Nanto-Bordelaise Co.
Section 2	370 acres, with 350 acres as compensation from NZ Company as per William Wakefield's agreement plus 20 acres allowance for roads
Section ?	43 acres as per agreement with William Fox
Section 3	50 acres later purchase
Section 4	100 acres later purchase
Section 1704	35 acres later purchase
Section 2408	27 acres later purchase
Total	782 acres[99]

* The pound sterling bought US$5.58 in 1862, and US$7.08 in 1863. The sale price for Craigforth was therefore around US$50,000.

In October 1862 Craigforth was sold to Holmes & Co. for £8707.*[100] The *Lyttelton Times*, in reporting the sale later in the month said:

> We shall miss the gentle and refined minds of the ladies and the hearty and genial welcome of Messrs. Frank and James Sinclair, and the honest grasp of Captain Gay, under

▲ The Craigforth property in Pigeon Bay in 1866, two years after Eliza Sinclair sold it to George Holmes. The homestead is behind the trees in the middle distance. This watercolor was painted by Nicholas Chevalier as part of a commission from the Canterbury Provincial Government to portray typical scenes from the province for publicity purposes. Russian-born Chevalier (1828–1902) came to the Southern Hemisphere in 1854, first to Australia and then on to New Zealand in 1865. He returned to Europe in 1871.
National Library of Australia, Rex Nan Kivell Collection

whose protection and command they are about soon to embark. It must be a regret that the country of our adoption should cease to have sufficient attractions for those who preceding us by many years have now determined to recross the equatorial line reseeking under the Polar star what they have failed to find under the Southern Cross — but such is life — they will carry with them our highest respect, and be always remembered in the catalogue of "absent friends".[101]

Thomas Gay did not have to look far for a suitable vessel. His brother William had been captaining a 264-ton bark, the *Bessie*, throughout 1861 and 1862 and had been on the Melbourne–Dunedin run at least three times. With Thomas on the southern coastal run they would have crossed paths, and thus Thomas would have known the *Bessie*. When the decision was made to purchase a vessel Thomas visited Melbourne and bought her, arriving back in Lyttelton with the bark on 3 January 1863. He then left shortly afterwards for Pigeon Bay.

Fitting out the vessel for its lengthy voyage and rearranging the accommodation to suit the family's needs took some time. The *Lyttelton Times* reported on the *Bessie*'s refit in Pigeon Bay that 'she stepped a new mainmast of sugar-loaf pine, and in a short time will be in good trim for her trip to British Columbia.'[102] With the refit completed, the task of loading the family's belongings began, and to quote from Ida von Holt's *Stories of Long Ago*:

> All sorts of supplies were put on board — a cow and hay and grain for her, chickens, fine merino sheep, jams and jellies made at home, quantities of apples from the orchard, also books, clothing and all the paraphernalia of a home, even to a piano.[103]

Once the decision to leave had been made and the vessel bought, Eliza took charge and was all hustle and bustle. Helen wrote in her diary: 'It all seems like a dream, mother being at her age the leader for such an undertaking. But she says *it will be done* and we trust her implicitly.'

And later, as departure neared:

> Mother was on the jetty from early morning until long after nightfall, forever dashing up and down the gangplank, checking cargo aboard, keeping the workers stepping lively, checking the working gear of the vessel, ordering the crew here and there to make everything shipshape.[104]

When all was ready and all farewells made, on a summer's morning in late February/early March 1863, the *Bessie* sailed northwards to Tahiti on the family's next adventure.[105]

CHAPTER SEVEN

THE PACIFIC JOURNEY AND PURCHASE OF NI'IHAU

The *Bessie*'s first port of call was Tahiti, 2500 miles away and perhaps four weeks sailing from Pigeon Bay. She arrived at Pape'ete on 3 April 1863 and left on 11 April, and is described in the *Bulletin Officiel des Établissements Français de l'Océanie* on her departure as 'trois-mâts barque anglais Bessie, 262 ton. cap. Gay, 12 passagers allant à Vancouver.'[1]

Tahiti does not seem to have been mentioned as a serious contender for their final destination; and it may have been a combination of a general search for land possibilities (and perhaps cargo) as well as the opportunity to supplement food and water supplies, that led to the decision to stop off there.

The best description available of the vessel in which the Sinclair family ventured out across the broad Pacific appeared in a Newcastle, Australia, newspaper two years after the *Bessie*'s extensive refit in Pigeon Bay:

> The Barque BESSIE
>   Register Tonnage, 264 tons
>   Length, 110 feet
>   Breadth, 24 feet 6
>   Depth, 15 feet 4
>
> The "Bessie" was built at Wallace, Nova Scotia in 1854, of the very best materials, and is in first rate order, and well found in sails, spars, rigging, ground tackle, boats &c. She has great stowage capacity, the cabins being on deck.[2]

The Pigeon Bay refit would have included constructing more extensive cabin and living space for the twelve passengers, and barnyard arrangements for the animals. The family's accouterments (piano and all) would have amounted to only a small fraction of the *Bessie*'s cargo capacity (354 tons), so she would have been ballasted for the journey as well.

▲ The *Bessie*'s arrival in Pape'ete on 3 April 1863 was duly reported; a similar notice appeared on her departure.
Messager de Taiti 11 April 1863

Although they took no servants with them, preferring to do for themselves,[3] there would have been perhaps ten or a dozen crew members aboard to work the ship, the latter directed by the first mate, Thomas Gay's brother William. William was the master of the *Bessie* when Thomas bought her on Eliza's behalf, and served as first mate under Thomas on subsequent voyages.

The twelve passengers included five children — Aubrey Robinson (9) and George (11), Francis (9), Eliza (6), and Charles Gay (2) — quite a handful on a small ship with limited deckspace. From all accounts grandmother Eliza took them all in hand from the start, bustling about purposefully throughout the voyage and setting the ground rules for family behavior. Eliza was in her element. According to Wilmon Menard,[4] at the start of the voyage Eliza told the family that despite Francis's tragic death 17 years earlier, he was with them in spirit. A place was set for him at the head of the table for every meal, and Helen wrote: 'It is as if Papa is actually sailing with us.'

The voyage was an adventure for the whole family, the weather was kind to them, and they settled in to the seagoing life under Eliza's kindly tutelage. The days went by and soon the harbingers of tropical seas arrived with sightings of flying fish and tropic birds.

In what must have seemed a relatively short time, under the captaincy of Thomas Gay, the stately peaks of Tahiti and Moʻorea hove into view. Approaching Matavai Bay for the first time, with its spectacular mountain backdrop, is an entrancing sight and as recounted by Wilmon Menard, Eliza wrote in her diary:

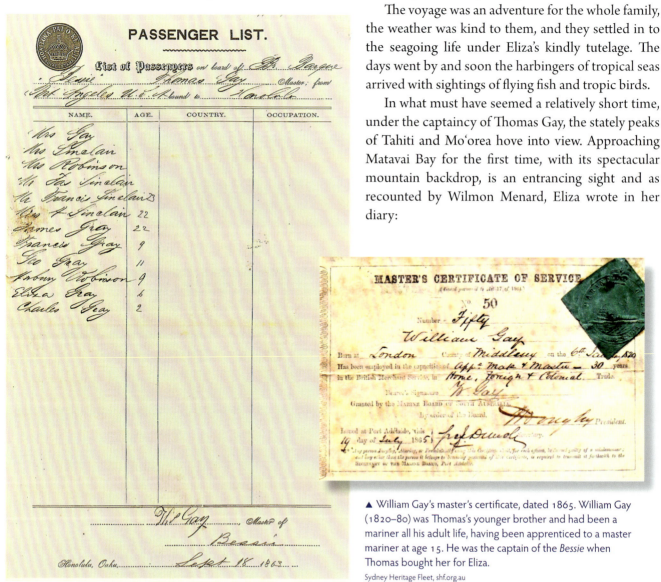

▼ The passenger manifest for the *Bessie* on her cruise across the Pacific.
Hawaiian State Archives

▲ William Gay's master's certificate, dated 1865. William Gay (1820–80) was Thomas's younger brother and had been a mariner all his adult life, having been apprenticed to a master mariner at age 15. He was the captain of the *Bessie* when Thomas bought her for Eliza.
Sydney Heritage Fleet, shf.org.au

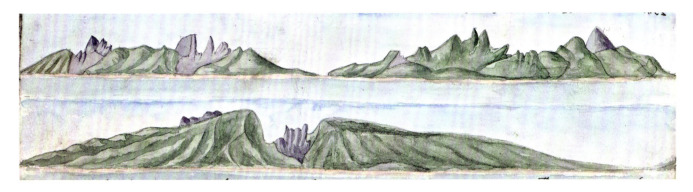

It was a lovely day, and in the sunlight the islands of Tahiti and Eimeo [Moʻorea] were very green and inviting after so many days at sea, with clouds festooned about their high pinnacles; waterfalls poured down some of the slopes, and there was the fragrance of tropical flowers in the breeze. We felt that this might be our home.[5]

Their impressions of the whaling town of Papeʻete (population 3000) were not, however, so favorable and Eliza notes: 'at all hours reeling men and their native bawds staggered along the waterfront, shouting, fighting and mouthing curses.' She found the town lawless, ugly and most unattractive.

Politics were also a consideration. In Tahiti the family would be under the protection of the French rather than the British Crown. The family had first-hand experience of the awkward situation that had emerged between the British and French at Akaroa, and would have been aware of the early British involvement in Tahiti, particularly that of the London Missionary Society, which was now considerably depleted. While Queen Pōmare IV was still on the Tahitian throne, she had accepted the protection of the French in 1847 in return for much reduced monarchical powers, and they were

▲ After weeks at sea the view of the lush, green, spectacular island of Tahiti must have been exciting for the Sinclair family. These two watercolors are by an unknown artist on the bark *Harpley* approaching Tahiti in June 1847, the upper one at six miles distance and the lower one four miles. The *Harpley* was on her maiden voyage and had sprung a leak which required major repairs. These took eleven weeks — to the crew's delight and the owner's despair, no doubt. She then proceeded to England to pick up migrants for the Australian colonies.
ATL E-113-f-48

◤ Looking out across Faʻaʻā, in urban Papeʻete, to the shipping roadstead beyond. The small island shown is now part of the international airport. The photo was taken in late 1863, only months after the *Bessie*'s visit, by Peruvian Eugenio Courret.
betweenthecovers.com

continuing to increase their influence in the kingdom, which in 1880 culminated in King Pōmare v's abdication in favor of French control.

Eliza's first call was on the long-serving British consul George Miller. According to Ida von Holt[6] the consul was immediately attracted to Ann, and during their short stay in Tahiti proposed to her. Consul Miller had been through a difficult time looking after British interests on the islands during the French Protectorate and, despite his romantic interest in Ann, was unlikely to have advised them to attempt to purchase land.

Miller introduced them to Scotsman John Brander, a prominent planter and trader and the founder of a wider commercial empire in the South Pacific — extending even to Rapa Nui (Easter Island). Brander was growing many kinds of crops — coconuts, coffee, sugar cane and oranges. He provided a carriage for the family to let them to explore the island. They found that only relatively small coastal margins existed suitable for plantations or ranching, and that Brander and other planters had most of it already planted in sugar cane and other crops. Eliza was also uneasy about Tahiti as a suitable place to bring up small children and felt the climate to be too warm for ranching. After only a little over a week in Tahiti the *Bessie* left Matavai Bay for the Pacific northwest — but not before 20,000 of John Brander's oranges were loaded aboard for sale there. Tahitian oranges were regarded at that time as the best in the Pacific, if not in the world.

News of the *Bessie*'s safe arrival in Tahiti reached New Zealand in a little over two months, and a notice informing all their New Zealand friends was published accordingly in the *Lyttelton Times* of 20 June.

That year an event occurred that directly concerned Pigeon Bay. On 17 January 1863, while the *Bessie* was refitted in the bay, but after George Holmes had taken over the Sinclairs' property, James Hay, Ebenezer's eldest son, lit a fire to drive some recalcitrant cattle out of the bush. The fire got away and over the next several weeks burned hundreds of acres of George Holmes' newly acquired Pigeon Bay land. Because of the valuable lumber lost, Holmes sued Ebenezer for damages of £5000. The case was heard in a jury trial in the Supreme Court in September 1863. Ebenezer was found guilty, and the jury awarded damages to Holmes of £3000[6] — an enormous sum in those days, bearing in mind Eliza sold Craigforth for £8707.

Two months later Ebenezer was found dead at the bottom of a cliff on the bridle path between Christchurch and Lyttelton. The inquest jury delivered a verdict of accidental death, but more than one witness spoke of the effect of the earlier trial on his health.[7] Eliza and her family most likely only heard of these sad events when they were settled on Niʻihau, but how different the story of Niʻihau could have been had Eliza not sold Craigforth when she did.

Victoria, Vancouver Island

With her precious passengers (and cargo of oranges) the *Bessie* set out on the longest leg of their long journey — 4800 miles from Papeʻete to Victoria, the main port of the Pacific northwest. With shipboard routines already established by Eliza, the family

▲ Queen Pōmare IV (1813–77) was only 13 when she succeeded her brother Pōmare III. She ruled Tahiti from 1827 to 1877. The early years of her reign were spent in combating French influence which culminated in a bloody war (1843–46). Her forces were defeated and she had to accept French Protectorate status. By the time of the *Bessie*'s arrival some 16 years later, that status was well established, with the queen having responsibility for all domestic affairs. The Sinclair family were well aware of the political situation as the French were still pushing for full annexation, with British diplomacy their only restraint. French annexation came only after Queen Pōmare IV's death.
Wikimedia Commons

◂ While the French had Tahiti in their grip politically, British entrepreneurs drove the economy. One in the ascendency at the time the *Bessie* visited was John Brander, who hosted the Sinclairs around the island when they inspected land. John was a Scotsman and had himself acquired large landholdings in Tahiti and throughout the South Pacific.
Wikimedia Commons

▲ The town of Victoria on Vancouver Island, the year before the *Bessie* arrived in June 1863. It was still a frontier town in the 1860s. The etching is from a photograph by Richard Roche titled 'Victoria from James Bay Looking up Government Street'.
Wikimedia Commons

settled into the long sea voyage through the tropics. Some weeks later, and halfway into the journey, they sighted the lofty snow-clad peaks of Mauna Kea and Mauna Loa on the island of Hawai'i. Some writers have insisted that the *Bessie* called at Honolulu, but there are no port records of that happening, and Ann in her journal noted that they merely sailed past the islands.[8]

From then on temperatures cooled and as they approached Puget Sound the skies became more sombre. Victoria, at the southeastern end of Vancouver Island, would have been known to Thomas Gay from his earlier sailing days.

The town began life in 1841 as a Hudson Bay Company trading post, becoming the capital of the British colony of Vancouver Island on its establishment in 1849. It remained a trading port of a few hundred people until the discovery of gold in the Fraser River in 1858. Victoria became the main port of entry to the mainland goldfields and the population mushroomed to over 5000 in a short time. Many Native Americans migrated to reserves on the town's outskirts to share in the vastly increased economic opportunities. In March 1862 disaster struck in the form of the first cases of smallpox brought to the island in vessels from the mainland. There was widespread panic — and the disease was particularly deadly to the native people. Although there was much criticism of the handling of the outbreak, with the use of the combined resources of government, media, churches and the medical fraternity, the epidemic was over by early 1863, but being so recent may have affected the Sinclair family's thinking.

On 9 June 1863, the following appeared in the local newspaper:

From New Zealand. — The bark Bessie, Capt. Gay, arrived from New Zealand last night, and came to anchor in the outer roads. She has been 108 days *en route* touching at Otaheite, comes in ballast, and brings no passengers, with the exception of the Captain's family.[9]

A passage of 108 days implies a Pigeon Bay departure date of 21 February, at variance with previous sources, but more reasonable given the time spent on the family's exploration of possibilities in Tahiti. While the newspaper indicates she arrived in ballast this was mostly true as the 20,000 oranges aboard only weighed only a few tons. These were advertised for sale.

They reached Victoria with high hopes. Vancouver Island was a British colony and many Scots had settled there. Victoria was probably in the same stage of development as the Christchurch they had observed arising during the latter days of their stay at Pigeon Bay — and well ahead of the Wellington they had left in 1843. Eliza wrote on arrival at Victoria: 'In some ways the scenery reminds me of Scotland in her more heavily wooded parts, the air is so crisp and clear, and how the sun shines down upon this blessed land. I am so hopeful of finding what we want here.'[10]

They met many people and traveled by carriage as far as was practicable throughout Vancouver Island. While many encouraged them to stay, the creation of ranching land from the heavily forested countryside appeared daunting, there were mosquitos everywhere, the locals did not seem to them as attractive as the Māori of New Zealand (Eliza found them 'alarming'), and, despite Eliza's first impressions, they found the climate cold and damp.

Eliza wrote towards the end of their stay: 'How sad I am that we cannot stay here in Canada! It has pleased us so many ways. The bay, the town, the English and Scotch people here are so attractive and interesting.'[11]

The family spent two months looking at possibilities on Vancouver Island but became disillusioned with the prospects. The family now had California in their sights, having hearing from many people of the vast lands available there. Then they met Henry Rhodes, a prominent Victoria businessman and consul for the kingdom of Hawai'i. An Englishman, Henry had spent thirteen years in Hawai'i before moving to Victoria in 1858. He advised against going to California as winter would be approaching by the time they got there, and suggested Hawai'i instead. He had an older brother, Godfrey, who had been in business there for many years and he volunteered to provide an introduction to him. Eliza wrote: 'Henry Rhodes … has now made what he seems to think is a very practical suggestion for us: go to the Sandwich Islands [Hawai'i], because there might be large lands at a very reasonable price. So I held a family meeting this evening, and it is agreed we will sail south to Honolulu.'[12]

The *Bessie* departed Victoria for Honolulu in early August, via Puget Sound.

Honolulu

On 17 August the *Bessie* sailed from Utsalady, a small town on the north end of Camano Island in Puget Sound 'with a cargo, principally composed of planed lumber …'[13] As the lumber was destined for Christchurch, Thomas Gay must have made arrangements for this during the time the *Bessie* was in Victoria.

Given the time that would have been required to sail to Utsalady across Puget Sound and to load the lumber, this implies a departure from Victoria in early August.

▲ Advertisement in the *Daily British Colonist* for 12 June 1863. The oranges came from John Brander's plantations.

▶ Henry Rhodes (1823–78) was the founder of a mercantile empire, Rhodes & Co., based in Victoria, British Columbia. How he met the Sinclairs is unknown, but Eliza had a knack of getting to know the important people around town quickly. In 1859, with the closure of the Hudson Bay Co.'s offices in Honolulu, King Kamehameha IV appointed Henry Rhodes honorary consul in Victoria for Hawai'i to look after Hawaiian citizens in the area, a task which had previously been undertaken informally by the Hudson Bay Co. Although born in England, Rhodes had lived for many years in Honolulu before moving to Victoria. The Sinclairs, disappointed with the prospects on Vancouver Island, became focused on California as their next target. It was Rhodes who convinced them they should look first at Hawai'i, and gave them an introduction to his older brother Godfrey in Honolulu.
Wikimedia Commons

Having cleared United States Customs in Port Angeles at the exit from Puget Sound on 20 August, the *Bessie* then set sail for Honolulu, 2700 miles away, on another long sea voyage (Some commentators have confused Port Angeles with Los Angeles. The *Bessie* did not go to California).

The seas were rough, particularly off the mouth of the Columbia River, and they didn't reach Honolulu until 17 September, after a passage of 28 days.[14] On the wharf to meet the *Bessie* was the legendary Reverend Samuel Damon, the Congregational missionary and port chaplain. After hearing the Sinclairs' story from him, Isabella Bird, in her book *Six Months in the Sandwich Islands* depicts the family's arrival:

> Mr. Damon, who was seaman's chaplain, on going down to the wharf one day, was surprised to find their trim barque, with this large family party on board, with a beautiful and brilliant old lady at [its] head, books, pictures, work, and all that could add refinement to a floating home, about them, and cattle and sheep of valuable breeds in pens on deck.[15]

Samuel Damon also assisted the family by finding a house for the winter in Sheridan Street,[16] which was then on the outskirts of town. There must have been sufficient adjacent land to accommodate their livestock. A house for the winter made sense, for if their search for suitable land in Hawai'i proved fruitless, it was still their intention to move on to California to look for prospects there in the spring.

When the Sinclairs arrived in 1863 Honolulu's population was around 13,000, made up largely of native Hawaiians — and three times the size of the town of Victoria they had left a few weeks earlier.

King Kamehameha IV (Alexander Liholiho) and his consort, Queen Emma, both Anglophiles, had been on the throne since 1855. During this time there had been a progressive loosening of the strict missionary social ethic which had pervaded the country. By 1863, with the tone set by royalty, both the theater and dancing were acceptable activities, for instance. For the first time 'style' was in evidence in Honolulu, which had been the capital of the kingdom since 1845. There had been talk of a reciprocity treaty with the United States and discussion of annexation, but both matters were in abeyance in September 1863.[17]

Physically the town was a muddle, having grown haphazardly around the port and later around the royal palace and government buildings. The era of thatch and adobe was at an end, with houses

▲ The Reverend Samuel Damon (1815–85) was on the wharf to greet the *Bessie* when she arrived. Born and bred in Massachusetts, he had just been ordained when a call came from the Port of Honolulu for a seaman's chaplain. He arrived in 1842 and remained in the role for more than 40 years. He was also editor of *The Friend* for the same period. His life was spent in good works. King Kalākaua attended his funeral in 1885 and said of him, 'He was one of nature's noblemen — of fine personal appearance, always pleasant and cheerful, happy and always laboring to make others happy here and hereafter — a truly model Christian man and it may justly be said that the world was made better by his having lived in it.'
Wikipedia Commons

◀ King Kamehameha IV (1834–63) and Queen Emma (1836–85). Kamehameha (Alexander Liholiho), the adopted nephew of Kamehameha III, reigned from 1855 until his death in 1863.
Wikimedia Commons

◀ Queen Street, Honolulu, in 1856, a few years before the Sinclairs arrived. It was still a casual country town. Hale pili (grass houses) are visible on the left. In the left foreground is the Hudson Bay Company's offices which closed in 1859, and in the middle ground on the right is what was generally known as the Old Court House. The legislature met in this building from 1857–74. The building was demolished in 1968 to make way for Hawaii Towers. In the background is the distinctive Kawaiahao Church while in the right foreground is the Honolulu Fort, which had been demolished before the Sinclairs reached the town. The lithograph is by George Henry Burgess.

now built of wood and more substantial buildings of stone. The streets were muddy or dusty depending on the season, water supply was a problem and most residences still used their own wells. Street lighting was yet to come. Movement around town was generally on horseback with carriages a relative rarity. Roads petered out into tracks only a few miles out — the first buggy was driven over the Pali road from Honolulu in 1861 and in the reverse direction in 1863.

Non-citizens had been able to buy land since 1850. The Sinclairs would have gleaned this information in Victoria from Henry Rhodes and this may have influenced the change in their plans.

The American Civil War was still in progress. Hawai'i had declared neutrality in 1861, but the war still had far reaching effects on the kingdom's economy. It accelerated the decline in the whaling industry, the servicing of which was the mainstay of the economy; but on the other hand commodity prices generally rose markedly, particularly sugar, rice, cotton and wool. Sugar production grew exponentially as a result. The Sinclairs may have been influenced by these prices, while realizing that with an end to the war the bubble might well burst, which of course it did.[18]

The Ni'ihau purchase

▲ Godfrey Rhodes (1815–97), seen here with his daughter, was the older brother of Henry. Having started out as a sea captain, he settled in Hawai'i early in his life and in partnership with Frenchman John Bernard in 1842 established the first coffee plantation on Kaua'i at Hanalei. He sold it to Robert Wyllie in 1853. He rose to become a privy councillor from 1867 to 1891 and a member of the House of Nobles from 1876–86.
Wikimedia Commons

The family's goods were unloaded from the *Bessie* in a matter of days. The *Bessie* did not wait. Thomas Gay and his crew sailed for Lyttelton, New Zealand, on 29 September, their cargo including lumber loaded at Utsalady.[19] The *Bessie*'s subsequent journeys under Thomas's captaincy are recounted in later sections.

The remainder of the family settled into the Sheridan Street property secured for them by Samuel Damon. Honolulu society they found welcoming, and their letter of introduction from Henry Rhodes to his brother, Godfrey, was most helpful. They met the British consul, William Synge, and his predecessor William Miller, and through him his great friend Robert Crichton Wyllie who had been Minister of Foreign Affairs for the kingdom since 1845 and was currently Minister of Finance as well, before giving up this latter role to Charles Manley Hopkins in early November. Miller and Wyllie had

▶ Robert Wyllie (1798–1865) was a key figure in the purchase of Niʻihau by the Sinclairs. He had been Minister of Foreign Affairs in the kingdom since 1845, deftly navigating the ruffled waters between the three external rival powers — the United States, Britain and France. When the *Bessie* arrived he was briefly also Minister of Finance. A Scotsman by birth and a doctor by profession, he arrived in the islands in 1844 and never left. As the photo indicates, he loved uniforms, and also arranged court etiquette. At one stage he suggested peerage titles be awarded — a idea promptly squashed. He was a deft and level-headed negotiator, serving in the foreign affairs role through three reigns, although it was said early in his career that no drama in the Pacific was complete without the 'fastidious, meticulous and verbose Scots busybody, Dr Robert Crichton Wyllie.' (From John Fox, 'Wyllie,' *Macnamara's Irish colony and the United States taking of California in 1846*, pp 83–86, McFarland.)
Wikipedia Commons

arrived in Honolulu together in 1844 after colorful careers elsewhere. The Gerrit Judds, Bishop Staley and his wife, the Thomas Browns and the Hermann von Holts also added to their circle of friends.

Gerrit Judd (1803–1873) arrived in Honolulu as a medical missionary in 1828. In 1842 he resigned from the mission to become an adviser to King Kamehameha III, assuming various roles within government — Minister of Foreign Affairs, Minister of the Interior and Minister of Finance — before turning to elected office as a Member of the House of Representatives 1858–9. He was in retirement in 1863. Thomas Staley (1823–98) was the first Church of England bishop of Hawaiʻi. He and his wife arrived in Honolulu in October 1862 amid a storm of protest from the Calvinist missionaries at his high church views and the hierarchical nature of the Anglican church. He was, however, supported by both Kamehameha IV and Kamehameha V. He retired in 1870. Thomas Brown's wife, Mary Ann, was the sister of Henry and Godfrey Rhodes and they would have met the Browns through Godfrey. Hermann von Holt had married Thomas Brown's daughter, Alice, in 1862, a year before the Sinclairs arrived.

The family was invited to a reception given by Minister Wyllie in honor of Kamehameha IV and Queen Emma at which none other than the king danced a hula which told the story of Kamehameha the Great — a far cry from earlier times when the hula was completely banned by the missionaries.[20]

All were well aware of the family's aspirations — that they had capital and had come to Honolulu to invest in suitable and sufficient land to keep the family together.

They were offered Ford Island in Pearl Harbor, but at 335 acres it was far too small for their purposes. More extensive lands at Kahuku, on the western side of the northernmost tip of Oʻahu, and lands at ʻEwa/Honouliuli to the north and west of Pearl Harbor were also available and examined. In both these areas the land was found to be interspersed with kuleana as a result of the 1848 Great Māhele.* They found this to be the general pattern throughout the islands, which was disconcerting, and after some time searching the family resolved to move on to California in the spring when the *Bessie* returned from New Zealand.

Minister Wyllie was keen to have the family remain in the islands, and in discussion with the king, the idea of offering the family the island of Niʻihau emerged. The Sinclairs were taken with the notion of an island of their own, and in company with the government land agent for Niʻihau, Mr J. Wahineaea, one of the two brothers (probably Francis — known as Frank) set off to inspect it. Wahineaea was familiar with the island, having had the unenviable task of attempting to collect government lease monies for

* The Great Māhele (land division) of 1848, instituted by Kamehameha III, abolished the traditional land use regime in the islands and divided the land between the king (Crown lands), the chiefs/konohiki (land administrators), and government. Kuleana could be awarded in all of the three divisions to commoners working the land if they could prove their claims. A Land Commission administered the division of the land to claimants. The Kuleana Act of 1850 established fee simple ownership. This Act enabled historical land tenants who had been awarded land to claim ownership of specific parcels of land (kuleana). Once fee simple title had been granted, a kuleana plot could be sold to any party, including foreigners.

*In 1863, government taxes included a poll tax (with a reduced amount for women and lesser again for children), an ad valorem assets tax, and an animal tax. In addition, able-bodied men were required to work six days a year for the government. These taxes were levied separately from the lease of the island from government. The government levied a land tax on privately owned land, but not on land leased from the government.

the island from the community — with little success, it must be said.* The difficult of tax collection from Niihauans had reached the stage that in April 1863 Wahineaea was moved to write to the clerk of the Ministry of the Interior suggesting that in view of their long-standing arrears, the islanders' assets should be seized in payment.[21] As far as is known no assets were in fact seized.

Some Niihauans had a five-year lease of the island from the government for $600 per annum, which expired in 1863. Although the lease itself has been lost, its existence is formally recorded in the State Archives.[22] On 22 September 1863 the eight lessees wrote to the Minister of the Interior requesting a meeting between the minister and their named representative to discuss a renewal of the lease, and also raising the possibility of the purchase of the island.

The letter then went on to advise the minister that there had been a considerable decline in the island's population over the previous two or three years and set down the current numbers living there.[23] These were somewhat lower than those shown on the government's taxation register.

The reason for the inclusion of the resident population reduction in the second half of the letter is unknown. Was it merely to 'correct the record,' subtly set the stage for the lease renewal discussions with the Minister, or some other reason?

Coincidentally or not, this letter was written only a week after the *Bessie*'s arrival. It was never replied to, as far as we know.

▶ The translation of Wahineaea's letter to the Minister of the Interior of 11 April 1863, suggesting that the king authorise asset seizures from tax delinquents on Niʻihau. This was not acted upon.

Hawaiian State Archives: Interior Dept. Lands: 1863 April 11

TRANSLATION:

Honorable S. SPENCER,
    Clerk of the Minister of the Interior.
Love to you.

    I wish to inform you that I went to Niihau to demand of the natives their rents for the fifth year, the natives said that there was no money to be had belonging to us now, I said, how about mats, if you have any on hand, let me have them, and I will take them to the King, who will buy (or sell) them, they replied, there are no mats made up now. That was the first time when I went in the month of Dec. In the month of March, I went again. This is the amount of money received ($21.50) from the hands of the land agent of Niihau. I am thinking about levying on their/own property, and to sell at auction right away, if it is agreeable to you and the King. Here are 280 goat skins, and twenty from the natives, making together 300 goat skins. It is coming by the hands of my servant which I am sending to you.
                        With thanks,
                            J. WAHINEAEA.
Hanapepe, 11th Ap., 1863.

◀ The Niihauans' letter to the Minister of Interior of 17 January 1864, requesting consultation. Translated, it reads:

The Honorable Robertson Lopikana,
Minister of the Interior

Greetings:

All of us are subjects of your kingdom currently living here on the island of Niihau.

We cordially request that you consult with us, the native citizens of your kingdom, because we have heard that Niihau is going to be purchased by a foreigner. So — according to what we have heard — Niihau is up for sale. Therefore, we desire that you sell the island to us; don't sell it to foreigners or else living here will no longer be beneficial to these native citizens, our lives will not be as they should if it becomes the property of foreigners. This is our suggestion to you. If you have any doubts concerning this letter of ours, we will forward to you a list of all the names.

S. Nawaalaau, scribe,
Niihau, January 17, 1864

Hawaiian State Archives: Series 526: Survey Grant #2944. Translation by Hōkūlani Cleeland.

There was disquiet among the Niihauans at the possible sale to a foreign owner. Other foreign visitors had already been approached. This concern culminated in a letter the Niihauans wrote to the Minister of Interior on 17 January 1864 asking the king to consult with them before any decision was reached.[24] In any event the letter was too late.

To inspect the island Frank probably traveled on the 400-ton government steamer *Kilauea* which made weekly trips to Kauaʻi, met there with Wahineaea, and journeyed from there to Niʻihau by whaleboat or canoe. Travel around the island would have been on horseback. The previous two years had seen abnormally heavy rainfall, and the island was looking exceptionally lush and green. Frank was enthusiastic about what he saw and felt that, at 47,000 acres, it would fulfil the family's needs admirably.

Early in the negotiations, on 30 November, the king, although still a young man, died. His successor and older brother, Kamehameha v (Lot Kapuāiwa) had, however, been a key figure in the discussions as Minister of the Interior, and now as sovereign, continued to be supportive. On 14 January 1864 the Sinclair brothers (James and Francis) made an offer of $6000 for the island. Their offer[25] and the government's reply to them of 19 January from the Ministry of the Interior is in the Hawaiʻi State Archives. Below is government's reply:

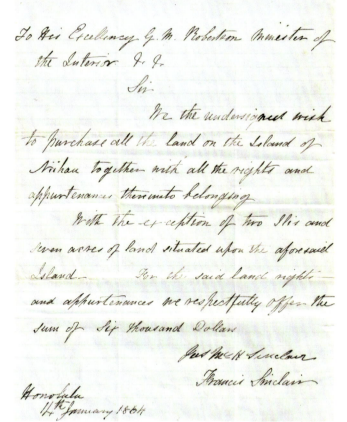

◀ The Sinclair brothers' 14 January 1864 offer to buy Ni'ihau Island.

Hawaiian State Archives: Series 526: Survey Grant #2944

▲ James McHutcheson Sinclair (1824–73), c.1870: the older of the Sinclair brothers who jointly purchased Ni'ihau.
Robinson family

▲ Francis (Frank) Sinclair (1834–1916), c.1865: the younger of the Sinclair brothers who jointly purchased Ni'ihau.
Canterbury Museum

Gentlemen:

In reply to your letter of 14th instant, making an offer of the sum of six thousand Dollars, for the Government lands on the island of Niihau, I have the honor to inform you that, having submitted your proposition to His Majesty the King in Cabinet Council, I am now authorized to offer you as follows, viz:

To sell you all the Government Lands on Niihau, in Fee Simple (reserving the rights of the Government in the two lands of Koakanu) for the sum of Ten Thousand Dollars; or to lease those lands to you, for a term of fifty years, at an annual rent of seven hundred and fifty Dollars.

The goats on the island are claimed by the Government, and reserved in this proposal.

I have the honor to be,
Gentlemen,
Your Obt Servant,
G. M. Robertson [26]

The king did not just pluck the figure of $10,000 out of the air, but in November 1863 had requested a valuation from Kaua'i businessman and founder of Grove Farm Plantation on Kaua'i, Hermann Widemann. He in turn recruited three 'helpers,' to use Widemann's term — rancher Valdemar Knudsen, missionary George Rowell and doctor James Smith — all of whom play some further part in Ni'ihau's story. Hermann Widemann and Valdemar Knudsen visited the island, the remaining two feeling that they already knew the island well enough to make an assessment. Widemann forwarded the valuations from his three 'helpers' separately, and in his own valuation, addressed to the new Minister of the Interior, George Robertson, cautioned: 'I formed this estimate of course only from what I saw during my recent visit which happened after an unusually propitious season of 3 or 4 months of rainy weather. Due deference should therefore be given to the estimates of helpers Rowell, Smith, and Knudsen who have seen the island in dry seasons.' Hermann Widemann's letter supports the widely held view that the island was looking particularly lush at the time of the Sinclair's visit. The four assessments of the value of Ni'ihau were:[27]

		Letter date
Valdemar Knudsen	$6000	31 December 1863
George Rowell	$7000	1 January 1864
James Smith	$7500	1 January 1864
Hermann Widemann	$10,000	5 January 1863 (should be 1864)

▲ Kamehameha V (1830–72) became king at age 33, on the death of his brother on 30 November 1863. As he had been serving as Minister of Interior since 1857, he was fully aware of Ni'ihau's prospective sale. As king, he commissioned an independent valuation of the island.
Wikipedia Commons

The king took no notice of Widemann's cautionary note and set the price at $10,000. This was accepted,[28] and the king signed off the sale on 23 January only four days after the Sinclair brothers' offer. Land Patent Grant #2944 is reproduced on the following page.[29] It shows that the whole island was not purchased initially, as even on Ni'ihau there were three kuleana.

No mention is made in the deed of Eliza's piano, which according to family tradition the king was keen to have included as part of the purchase price, nor of the goats on the island which the king wished to retain. The fate of the piano is unknown, but there is a letter in the archives of 25 January instructing Wahineaea to catch all the goats on Ni'ihau as any remaining after 1 May 1864 would become the property of the new owners.[30] The letter indicates how important the goat skins were for the coffers of the government.

This instruction regarding the goats shows that there were some side discussions that took place, and one persistent oral tradition is that the king particularly requested the Sinclairs to look after his subjects on Ni'ihau — a request the family took to heart and has always attempted to honor throughout the succeeding years. There were over 600 Niihauans resident on the island when the sale took place (see Appendix D for population figures). The government saw employment opportunities for them in the Sinclairs' proposed ranching operation.

In *Niihau: The Traditions of an Hawaiian Island* the authors state that after the sale King Kamehameha V issued the following statement to the new haole owners:

> The natives are yours and you are the new chief, and they will work and serve you according to the laws and customs of the King of Hawaii. They are subject to this rule only — if it [control of Ni'ihau] does not interfere with the people's rights of a grant of a little land to plant food, a place for a home, firewood and the right to fish their waters.[31]

▲ Hermann Widemann (1822–99), a German by birth, came to live on Kaua'i in 1846 after some time at sea. An entrepreneurial agriculturalist, he bought Grove Farm in 1854, and was elected to the House of Representatives in 1855. In 1863, despite no formal legal training, he was appointed Circuit Judge. In November 1863 the king asked him to appraise Ni'ihau for sale. He went on to have a distinguished career in the kingdom.
Wikimedia Commons

No reference is given in the book for the statement, and it is not held in the Hawai'i State Archives, but the sentiments expressed have been maintained by the family owners ever since.

▶ Royal Patent Grant No. 2944, dated 23 January 1864. The first two paragraphs (with amendments incorporated) read:

'Kamehameha v., By the grace of God, King of the Hawaiian islands, by this His Royal Patent, makes known unto all men, that he has, for himself and his successors in office, this day granted and given, absolutely, in Fee Simple unto James McHutcheson Sinclair and Francis Sinclair as Tenants in Common, for the consideration of Ten thousand dollars paid into the Royal Exchequer, The whole of the land now belonging to the Government on the island of Niihau, it being understood, that under this Patent the whole of the land on the said island of Niihau is conveyed to the said James McHutcheson Sinclair and James Sinclair; with the exception of the two lands known as Kahuku and Halawela, set off to Koakanu in the great Division of 1848, and that tract of land sold to Papapa, containing 50 acres, which is more particularly described in Royal Patent No. 1615 of Land Sales, which Patent, in the diagram, also describes the pieces of land set apart for Church and School lots, and also excepting and reserving to the Hawaiian Government, all Mineral and Metallic Mines of every description.'

Bureau of Conveyances, Honolulu

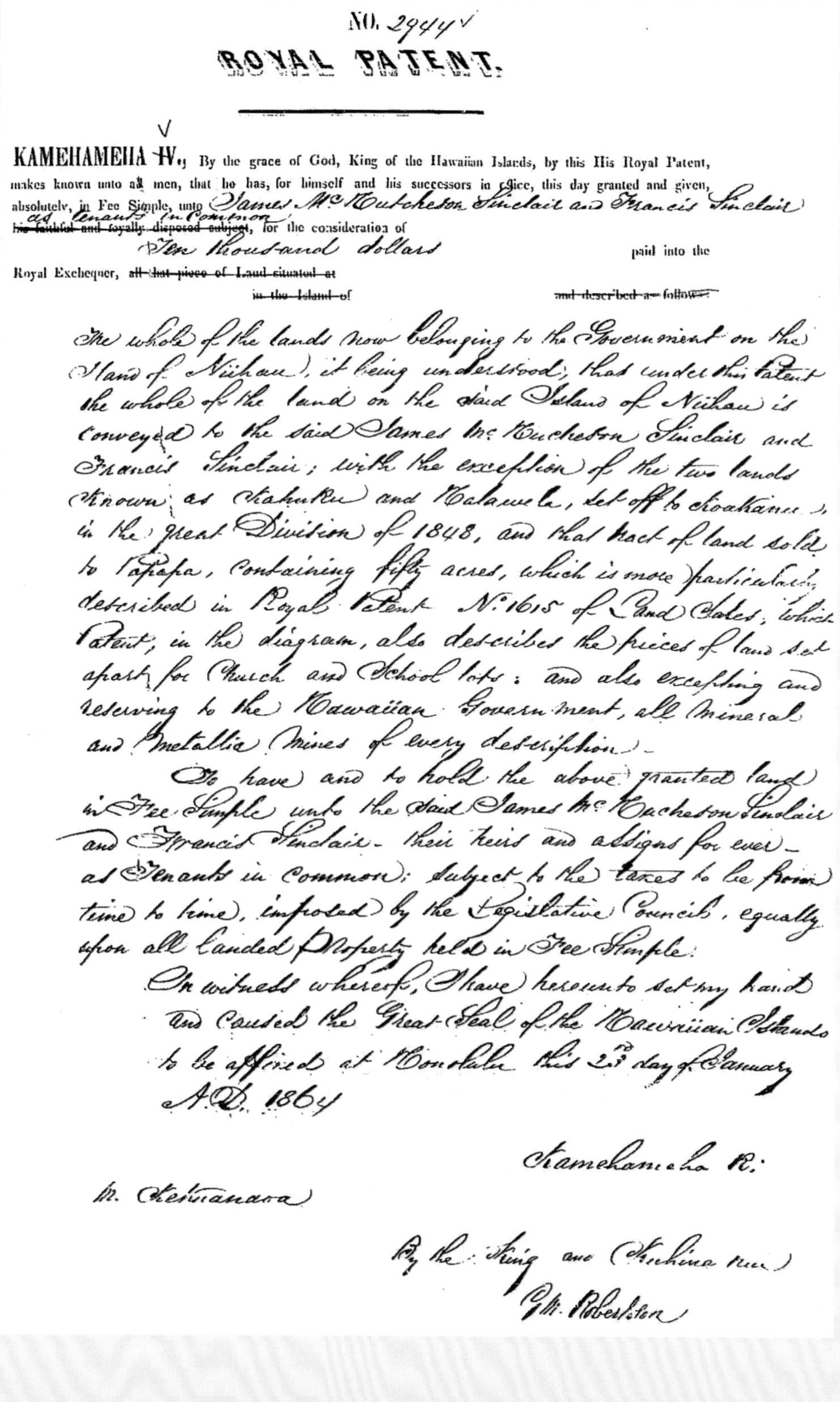
NO. 2944

ROYAL PATENT.

KAMEHAMEHA ~~IV.~~ V, By the grace of God, King of the Hawaiian Islands, by this His Royal Patent, makes known unto all men, that he has, for himself and his successors in office, this day granted and given, absolutely, in Fee Simple, unto James Mc Hutcheson Sinclair and Francis Sinclair as tenants in Common ~~his faithful and loyally disposed subject~~, for the consideration of Ten thousand dollars paid into the Royal Exchequer, ~~all that piece of Land situated at~~ ~~in the Island of~~ ~~and described as follows:~~

The whole of the lands now belonging to the Government on the Island of Niihau, it being understood, that under this Patent the whole of the land on the said Island of Niihau is conveyed to the said James Mc Hutcheson Sinclair and Francis Sinclair; with the exception of the two lands known as Kahuku and Halawela, set off to Koakanu, in the great Division of 1848, and that tract of land sold to Papapa, containing fifty acres, which is more particularly described in Royal Patent No. 1615 of Land Sales, which Patent, in the diagram, also describes the pieces of land set apart for Church and School lots: and also excepting and reserving to the Hawaiian Government, all Mineral and Metallic Mines of every description.

To have and to hold the above granted land in Fee Simple unto the said James Mc Hutcheson Sinclair and Francis Sinclair, their heirs and assigns for ever, as Tenants in Common; subject to the taxes to be from time to time, imposed by the Legislative Council, equally upon all Landed Property held in Fee Simple.

In witness whereof, I have hereunto set my hand and caused the Great Seal of the Hawaiian Islands to be affixed at Honolulu this 23 day of January A.D. 1864

Kamehameha R.

M. Kekuanaoa

By the King and Kuhina nui

C.M. Robertson

The sale of the island was made public a few days later in the *Pacific Commercial Advertiser*.[32]

The idea of selling Ni'ihau was not new. As far back as 1853, correspondence in the State Archives shows the idea being mooted.[33] Difficulties with lease money collection from the Niihauan residents (whether in cash or kind) had been going on for many years as indicated earlier, and there had been much grumbling by the Niihauans about how they had been treated by successive governments. The arrival of the Sinclairs must have been seen as a godsend by government and Minister Wyllie 'expressed his satisfaction at seeing people of such substance settle in Hawaii.'[34]

The new owners had much to do before they could take up residence. Whether they reconnoitered the island again before they moved there is unknown. Probably they did, and the sale arrangements may have included some assistance from government in arranging temporary accommodation. Although members of the family were fluent in Māori, which would have helped, none spoke Niihauan, and the resident Hawaiians no English. The closest source of bilingual speakers and labor was Waimea on Kaua'i and people here may have been recruited by the family to help erect temporary housing.

The *Bessie* arrived back from New Zealand via Newcastle, Australia with a load of coal on 30 March 1864 and the vessel was advertised for sale in Honolulu during April and the early part of May before departing for Ni'ihau, presumably with the family and their possessions, on 21 May.[35]

King Kamehameha V and his entourage visited Ni'ihau on 2 June, shortly after the Sinclairs arrived, and he spoke to his assembled subjects. The king's visit may also have been a part of the sale arrangements, in order to introduce the new owners to the residents. The visit was reported in the *Pacific Commercial Advertiser* by Minister Wyllie:

> On the 2d of June, His Majesty addressed His subjects on Niihau, inquired into their complaints, and advised them to congregate together in a village, on 2000 or 3000 acres of land fit for cultivation, where they could keep up their manufacture of mats, have their own church and school, expressing His confidence that the Messrs. Sinclair would treat them kindly and assist them so far as they could.
> The people dispersed after giving three hearty cheers for King Kamehameha V.
> I remain, my dear sirs, yours truly,
>   R. C. WYLLIE[36]

The visit to Ni'ihau by the king on the royal yacht *Nahienaena* was preceded by visits to Kaua'i and to Ka'ula, where the king planted the Hawaiian flag for the first time.

In accordance with the king's advice, over time, but rather slowly (see Appendix D) the pattern of settlement altered, consolidating gradually at Pu'uwai from the dozen or so hamlets scattered around the island.

The three kuleana landholdings on Ni'ihau

The kuleana lands owned by Koakanu and Papapa were specifically excluded from the sale of the island to the Sinclairs.

Papapa's kuleana was given to him by the king in 1854, probably for services rendered. For $12.50 payment from Papapa he received Land Grant 1615, which was recorded on 20 Jan 1855. The land was not part of the 1848 Great Māhele.

On 7 August 1880 Papapa's kuleana was recorded as having been sold to Mrs Elizabeth Sinclair for the sum of $150. The deed of sale was notarized by Frank Brandt, the government agent on Kaua'i.[37]

The diagram that located the land and formed an integral part of Land Grant 1615 has been lost, but the survey notes dated September 1854 are in the State Archives and describe the land as in Omaumalua and Kamalino and give bearings and chainages from points on the sea coast. The area is given as '50 acres more or less.' The survey notes show it as consisting of about 2000 yards of beach frontage extending back an average of 120 yards to a stone wall. It is centered on Kamalino about six miles south of Ki'e K'ie. Papapa must have been compliant and did not interfere with the ranching operation, so the Sinclairs found no necessity to purchase the land immediately after they bought the island.

The facts regarding Koakanu's land are very different. The land was awarded to Koakanu in the 1848 Great Māhele. It was recorded as receiving the Royal Patent, in Koakanu's and his wife's names, on 24 August 1864. The land is described as the ahupua'a (a traditional Hawaiian land division usually extending from the uplands to the sea) of Kahuku and the ahupua'a of Halawela, both on Ni'ihau. No locations or areas of the two ahupua'a are given in the Royal Patent. The name Kahuku cannot be found on any maps in the Hawai'i State Archives. Halawela as a name occurs only on a US Army map from 1954 and shows it at Ki'eki'e.[38] This location was important to the Sinclairs and is where they built 'The House.' Koakanu paid $200 for the Royal Patent, a large sum in those days.[39]

A deed dated 13 February 1864 records the sale of both of Koakanu's ahupua'a to the Sinclair brothers, James and Francis, for $800. The deed was notarized by Valdemar Knudsen and was recorded on 7 March 1864 by Thomas Brown, the Registrar of Conveyances.[40]

The timings of the deed and the Royal Patent are interesting in that the Royal Patent was actually issued to Koakanu five months after he had sold the land to the Sinclair brothers. The deed of sale of 13 February 1864 makes clear that the Ministry of the Interior had assured Koakanu by letter on 27 November 1861 that he was the rightful owner of the lands.

There is a persistent legend in the Sinclair/Robinson family that they paid $1000 for Koakanu's land. This could be accounted for by the Sinclairs paying $800 for the land and $200 for Koakanu to obtain the Royal Patent, the latter taking some months.

The deed of sale to Koakanu occurred before the sale of the island proper to the Sinclairs by King Kamehameha V. Both negotiations must have been going on in parallel. Koakanu had a reputation for being difficult among the Niihauans on the island — even stopping locals from landing on his shoreline. Frank must have discovered this on his initial reconnaissance, and they had begun talking to him early on. The family legend has it that they recruited Valdemar Knudsen, a fluent speaker of Hawaiian (and who subsequently married Ann Sinclair), to assist. These discussions must have occurred on Kaua'i or on Ni'ihau while other members of the family were negotiating with the government on O'ahu.

▲ Norwegian-born Valdemar Knudsen (1819–98) arrived at Kekaha on Kaua'i in 1856 at the age of 37. He initially managed Grove Farm Plantation, then owned by Hermann Widemann, became completely fluent in Hawaiian and in 1862 was entrusted by the Crown with taking an inventory of military equipment and supplies still at the Russian Fort in Waimea. He leased, on a 30-year term, 100,000 acres from the Crown at Mānā and built his home and ranch, Waiawa. He advised the king on the Sinclairs' Ni'ihau purchase, and later his life became interwoven with the family through his marriage to Ann Sinclair. He was subsequently appointed to the House of Nobles and later became a respected member of the House of Representatives.
Toulon/Knudsen family photos, colorised

Romanticized versions of Valdemar's role in discussions with Koakanu and his wife have appeared in Eric Knudsen's *Teller of Hawaiian Tales*[41] and Ruth Tabrah's *Ni'ihau: The Last Hawaiian Island*,[42] but Papapa's 50 acres is given as being the issue. From the evidence above it appears the problem was Koakanu's land, and it was solved with Valdemar's help — possibly using a bag of silver dollars as an added incentive as described in the two books.

Had negotiations with Koakanu not been successful, we can speculate as to whether the family would have bought Ni'ihau. They saw the kuleana landholdings as a problem wherever they looked to buy land in Hawai'i.

The *Bessie*'s subsequent travels

The *Bessie* under Thomas Gay had left Honolulu on 29 September 1863, only twelve days after dropping off the family, their belongings, and their menagerie in Honolulu. The ship was bound for Lyttelton, New Zealand, with the cargo of lumber from Puget Sound and also sugar, molasses, rice and other commodities which had been loaded in Honolulu — including '200 dozen oranges in prime condition.'[43] The vessel reached Lyttelton on 11 November without incident, after a swift passage.[44] The commodities appear to have been owned by the family while the lumber was on consignment. Both were auctioned, the lumber on behalf of the consignees, while the auctioneers for the commodities, having received instructions from Captain Gay, did likewise.[45] Having discharged and sold off all the cargo, the *Bessie* sailed on 24 December for Newcastle on the New South Wales coast, evidently in ballast.[46]

With many people interested in the doings of the Sinclairs, the *Lyttelton Times* reported, somewhat inaccurately:

> The barque Bessy [sic], Capt. Gay, arrived with a cargo of timber, sugar, and rice, from Fraser's River, Vancouver's Island, via the Sandwich Islands. He speaks very favourably of Port Victoria and the country generally, but the natives offer every resistance to the settlement of white people, and it is dangerous to venture far beyond the towns, unless in armed bodies.[47]

This was followed five days later by a minor correction and further information:

> In our notice of the arrival of the barque Bessie, the remark made about the settlers not venturing beyond the towns, except in armed bodies, has reference only to the North part of the island. Captain Gay describes the country as magnificent in scenery, and the climate as admirable. Although Mrs. Sinclair and family have for the present selected a residence at the Sandwich Islands, they are not yet determined on continuing there permanently, and it is possible on the return of the vessel that they will leave for Vancouver's Island, to carry out their first object on leaving Pigeon Bay.[48]

Thomas must have felt the earlier report had left the wrong impression and wished it amended. The comment that the family were staying in Hawai'i 'for the present' refers presumably to their intention to stay in Honolulu, at least for the winter.

After a slow passage across the Tasman, the *Bessie* reached Newcastle on 12 January 1864 to load coal for Honolulu.[49] The *Bessie* had been engaged in the Australasian coal trade before Captain Gay bought it on behalf of the family, and could load expeditiously. With 305 tons of coal aboard, she was cleared for departure for Honolulu on 23 January,[50] arriving there on 30 March. Thomas Gay was happily reunited with his family after an absence of six months. During his time away the decision had been made to settle in the Hawaiian islands, and Niʻihau had been bought. It was decided to sell the *Bessie*, as is where is, with the proviso that she first be used to take the family to Niʻihau. For six weeks she was advertised for sale in Honolulu, but no acceptable offers were made. The family decided that as she was suited to the coal trade, the *Bessie* should be offered for sale in Newcastle, Australia after transporting the family and their accouterments to Niʻihau.

While the vessel was in Honolulu, Thomas was asked to transport 70 mules to Auckland. As this dovetailed reasonably well with the plan to sell the *Bessie* in Newcastle, the task was accepted. First though the family was taken to Niʻihau, with the *Bessie*'s departure from Honolulu for the island taking place on 21 May as stated previously. Then with the family safely established on Niʻihau, the *Bessie* picked up the 70 mules — probably from either Hawaiʻi, Maui or Kauaʻi as there are no reports of the *Bessie* revisiting Honolulu.

Having just been carrying coal, some major rearrangements would have been necessary to transport live animals in pens below deck, and considerable feed supplies and water were vital. Ballast would also be needed, and arrangements for 'mucking out' — a considerable logistical exercise. Where all this took place is not known, but access to building materials and labor would have been essential. Maybe it took place in Hilo,

▼ Auckland waterfront, 1864. The *Bessie* was moored in Auckland from August 1864 until she left for Newcastle, Australia in January 1865. It is thus quite possible that one of the vessels at anchor here is the *Bessie*.
Auckland Libraries Heritage Collection 1-W718

but this is pure speculation as no shipping records from Hilo (or Lahaina on Maui or Kōloa on Kaua'i) have been found. Specialist personnel would also have to have been recruited to look after the mules on the lengthy voyage.

The *Bessie* arrived in Auckland via Apia, Sāmoa, on 15 August 1864,[51] after a most disturbing journey, as related in the next section.

Trial and anguish

The day after the *Bessie*'s arrival in Auckland the mules were advertised for sale:

MULES

EX BARQUE 'BESSIE', FROM THE SANDWICH ISLANDS

———

58 OF these VERY VALUABLE ANIMALS
FOR SALE, all young and broken in to
work. They may be seen on board, and as the
vessel is proceeding without delay to Lyttelton,
immediate application is necessary …[52]

Alas the voyage to Lyttelton was not to be. In the Police court the following day, 17 August, 'Charles Boyd was charged by Captain Thomas Gay, master of the barque 'Bessie' with having been guilty of wilful disobedience to lawful commands on board the said vessel, on 19th July last.'[53]

The prisoner pleaded not guilty, and in his deposition Thomas stated that on the day in question he asked the mate, his brother William, to get the flying jib set. He heard William pass on the instruction to Boyd, who did not obey. Boyd was then ordered aft and he refused to go. William in evidence confirmed this, and continued saying that on account of Boyd's wilful disobedience the Captain then ordered the mate to put him in irons (handcuffs). The Captain 'did not strike or ill use the prisoner.' William added that Boyd 'threatened to push me off the boom if I came out after [him].'[54]

Three seamen from the *Bessie* confirmed the Gay brothers' evidence. Boyd then made a rambling statement contending that both the Gays had ill used him in that they had 'kept him in irons for sixteen days down in the lazarette [space used for storage of ropes, sails, etc], upon biscuit and water, until he was nearly starved, and used to come down in the night time and gag him with an iron bolt.' Boyd produced the iron bolt and showed the court where three of his teeth had been broken.

The judge commented that there seemed to be some truth in Boyd's statement and adjourned the case to allow the police time to make enquiries.

Two days later it was reported from the Police court that 'Thomas and William Gay, master and mate of the barque "Bessie", were charged with an aggravated assault upon Charles Boyd, a seaman on board that vessel, whereby his life was endangered.'[55]

The tables had been completely turned.

After a day long hearing of evidence the judge decided that there was a case to answer and the two brothers were remanded to appear in the Supreme Court. Bail was set at two sureties of £500 each for each of the two accused — impossible for the Gays, and they were remanded in custody in Auckland pending the Supreme Court sitting.

There was great public interest in the trial, and it was widely reported in detail. The *New Zealand Herald* commented: 'The court was crowded during the hearing of this case, the particulars of which excited strong feelings of indignation against the prisoners, which broke out into open expressions of disgust as they were removed from the dock.'[56]

During this time the *Bessie* was anchored in Official Bay (now reclaimed land), just off what is now the Auckland central business district, presumably quietly gathering harbor dues.

The court sitting took place on 27 September, with the chief justice, Sir George Arney, presiding. A jury of twelve men were duly sworn in and were cautioned, in view of the public interest in the case, to base their decision solely on the evidence presented in court, and not be influenced by what they might have heard elsewhere.

Although some of the evidence was contradictory the main facts of the case were:

- On 19 July, on the high seas en route from Hawai'i to Auckland, seaman Boyle (his name seems to have morphed from Boyd to Boyle) was given an order 'to put a hank on the flying jib' which according to the Gays' evidence he refused to do.

▲ Chief Justice Sir George Arney (1810–83) was appointed to the role from England in 1857. The importance of the trial of Thomas and William Gay in the fledgling New Zealand colony was indicated by the fact that the chief justice presided.
ATL 1/1-014776-G

- The captain then ordered Boyle to go aft and be put in irons, an order with which he did not comply.
- It took the combined physical resources of the captain, the mate and the carpenter to put the irons on him.
- Boyle was extremely abusive to the captain.
- Boyle was then confined to the lazarette, where he continued shouting abuse and singing.
- The lazarette was next to the captain's cabin with only a thin bulkhead between, and was filled with ropes, sails and hay, so was effectively only four feet high. Boyle could not stand upright in it.
- The captain told Boyle several times to be quiet. When he wouldn't stop the captain called for a bolt which he and the mate secured across his mouth by tying a rope around his head, breaking three teeth in the process. Evidence was contradictory as to how long the bolt was in his mouth before the captain removed it. (The bolt itself was produced in court.)
- Evidence was also contradictory as to whether Boyle could still speak with the bolt in his mouth, which led to the following amusing exchange in the court:

His Honor [The Chief Justice]: It seems to be quite undecided whether the witness [Boyle] could speak when that bolt was in his mouth. It would not be amiss if some gentleman would try it on you Mr. Wynn [Counsel for the Gay brothers] — (laughter)

Mr Merriman [Counsel for Boyle]: That has been suggested your Honor as an admirable test (loud laughter.)[57]

Boyle was confined to the lazarette for 16 days, allowed out to wash etc. only periodically. Because of the treatment he received, Boyle refused to sign off from the *Bessie* and to receive his pay.

Thomas Gay produced four character witnesses: two in person — the Colonial Secretary, Hon. William Fox, and Christchurch businessman, William Montgomery,[8] who had made a special trip from Christchurch to speak in Thomas's favor. The Canterbury Superintendent, Samuel Bealey, and the Anglican Bishop of Christchurch, Henry Harper, wrote letters of support. Thomas was moved to tears by the testimony.

The judge would not allow evidence of any earlier altercations between Boyle and the Gays to be presented, but it is highly likely there had been earlier troubles with a feisty Boyle, and when these events occurred both brothers just 'lost their cool.'

In his summing up for the jury the chief justice explained: 'It was only a question of fact for the jury to satisfy themselves whether the assault had been committed or not, and then whether the two joined in doing it.'*

The jury retired briefly, and on their return pronounced 'both prisoners guilty of assault on the high seas.' The judge deferred sentencing.

There was an outpouring of sympathy in Canterbury at the account of the trial and its outcome, brought back by ship from Auckland — 'an account which will be read with a sorrowful interest by a great number of the settlers in Canterbury,' and assuring readers that the sentences were 'expected not to exceed imprisonment for a week, or at most a month.'[58]

After a peroration on the powers given captains at sea under English law and a recent similar case involving a mate who was sentenced to hard labor, in view of the splendid character testimony submitted: 'His Honor then sentenced Captain Thomas Gay to five calendar months' imprisonment in the common gaol of Auckland, and the mate, William Gay, to three calendar months' imprisonment in the same gaol.'[59]

The original charge against Boyd/Boyle for disobedience was never proceeded with, or if so, was not reported.

The last journey

The Gay brothers were completely devastated at the outcome of the trial. The loss of reputation was particularly hard for Thomas to bear after a career as a well-respected captain spanning over 25 years. William, nine years younger, had also acted as the master of vessels for many years. They had languished in prison for six weeks before the trial and, while they accepted the outcome, the thought of facing further detention was humiliating and debilitating.

As soon as the result of the trial was known, the *Bessie* was put up for sale — advertised as 'well suited for the Cattle Trade,' presumably on account of the mule pens.[60] It would appear that offers were not forthcoming — in December she was advertised as available 'for freight or charter.'[61]

Thomas was released from prison on 10 January 1865, almost five months since his arrest.[62] Presumably William had already completed the full term of his incarceration. William was fully capable of getting the *Bessie* ready for sea, which it appears he did. He

* *Was William Montgomery by any chance the father or another relative of James Montgomery, Ann Sinclair's New Zealand beau?*

then picked up Thomas on his release and the vessel sailed for Newcastle in ballast on 13 January 1865.[63]

The voyage to Newcastle was slow, if uneventful. The vessel is recorded as arriving on 1 February — a 17-day passage.[64]

The trial and the prison term took a huge toll on Thomas, psychologically and physically. On 11 February, ten days after the *Bessie*'s arrival, the Newcastle newspaper announced:

> DEATH
>
> At King Street, Newcastle, in his 57th year, Captain Thomas Gay, late of the barque Bessie.[65]

When the news got back to New Zealand, the following appeared in the newspapers throughout the country:

> By the arrival of the 'Kate Waters,' from Newcastle, last evening, we have intelligence of the sudden death of Captain Gay, of the barque 'Bessie,' who, it will be remembered, was sentenced in the Supreme Court here to a term of imprisonment for brutally ill-treating a seaman of the 'Bessie', on the passage to Auckland; but whose offence, it was said, had been exaggerated. Deceased was liberated before the expiration of his sentence, and proceeded to Newcastle, where he expired on the 9th inst. from exhaustion caused by loss of blood.[66]

No doubt the emotional stress of the trial coupled with the conditions in Auckland jail sapped his strength and reduced his ability to cope with any infection.

A touching letter on the circumstances of Thomas's final illness has been kept by his family. It was written by Rev. Charles Creed, who had officiated at the marriage of

▼ Newcastle, Australia, in the late 1860s or early 1870s. The port was a bustling affair when the *Bessie* arrived in 1865. The mainstay of the town was coal, which was exported around the Australian coast, to New Zealand and further afield in the Pacific, a trade in which the *Bessie* had been involved for some years.

Newcastle Herald, Archival Revival: Newcastle in the 1800s, photo 28 of 155

The Pacific journey and purchase of Ni'ihau

◀ Thomas Gay's headstone in Sandgate Cemetery, Newcastle, Australia. He was originally buried in the Honeysuckle Cemetery in Newcastle, which was closed in 1883 when the Sandgate Cemetery opened. In 1916 the Honeysuckle Cemetery land was required for railway extensions. All 63 bodies were exhumed, carefully documented and reburied in the Sandgate Cemetery. The headstones were shifted with them, so the misspelling of his surname occurred at the time of his original burial. Thomas was buried in the Presbyterian section.
Australian Cemeteries Index No. 8378289

Thomas and Jane in Dunedin on 18 August 1849, and was written to his widow Jane, expressing condolences and informing her of Thomas's last days.

Thomas had kept in touch with Charles Creed over the years and had last seen him in Newcastle a year earlier in March 1864, when loading coal for Honolulu on the *Bessie*. He had moved from New Zealand to Australia in the mid-1850s and Thomas had seen him on his visits to Australia.

Evidently Thomas was suffering from dysentery before they left Auckland and this continued throughout the journey to Newcastle. For the final two or three days of the trip he began bleeding from the nose and mouth, which they were unable to stop. On arrival he was brought ashore and taken to a quiet boarding house where doctors plugged his nose and managed to stanch the bleeding. There was some hope that he would be able to continue the journey home. This was not to be, however, and he died five days later, but not before he had made and signed his will and given instructions for the sale of the *Bessie* to his commission agent in Newcastle, George Dibbs, in whom he had complete trust.* Charles Creed and Thomas's brother William were with him at the end.

The pair of them arranged for his body to be sealed in a lead coffin in case Jane wished to bring him home. He was buried in a local Scots cemetery, as his family's wishes in this regard were unknown.

* Charles Creed is generous in his praise of Dibbs, who went on to become a long-time parliamentarian later in his career and was knighted.

▶ The Methodist missionary Reverend Charles Creed (1812–79) who married Thomas Gay and Jane Sinclair in Dunedin on 18 August 1849 and was present in Newcastle, Australia during Thomas's last days in February 1865. Over the years the two had kept in touch.
Wikimedia Commons

The Rev. Creed's letter to Jane is most poignant. Thomas was a devout Christian and took great succor from the presence of William and Charles.[67]

The *Bessie* was sold in Newcastle, and William continued captaining ships on the Australian coastal trade.

A pregnant Jane and the Gay children had been on Niʻihau for almost nine months when Thomas died, and by the time the tragic news reached them Alice Gay had been born. Thomas never saw his last child. The loss of Thomas in this fashion inevitably drew the Sinclair/Gay/Robinson family on Niʻihau even closer together.

▶ A shell from Niʻihau.
Colin Bassett

CHAPTER EIGHT

A FLEDGLING RANCH

When the Sinclair family purchased Niʻihau at the beginning of 1864, the clan consisted of 13 people:

- the matriarch, Eliza Sinclair (63)
- her unmarried son, James Sinclair (37)
- her married daughter, Jane Gay (35), who was pregnant with daughter Alice
- Jane's husband Thomas Gay (54), and their children George (13), Francis (11), Eliza (7), and Charles (2), together with Thomas's son from an earlier marriage, James Gay (23)
- Eliza's married daughter, Helen Robinson (33), estranged eight years from her husband, and their son, Aubrey Robinson (10)
- Eliza's unmarried son, Francis Sinclair, generally known as Frank (29)
- Eliza's unmarried daughter, Ann Sinclair (24).

All except Thomas Gay took up residence on Niʻihau in mid-1864. The few months between securing the island and moving there were extremely busy, with much of the work falling heavily on James and Frank. The family remained at the rented Sheridan Street house in Honolulu until the move was made following the *Bessie*'s return from New Zealand on 30 March. The schooner *Kalama* made three trips to Niʻihau during March and April, departing from Honolulu.[1] The *Kalama* was well known in the inter-island trade, but these were the only trips she ever made to Niʻihau, transporting goods there for the new owners.

Over many centuries there had been a symbiotic relationship between the Niihauans living on Niʻihau and those living in the western Kauaian villages — Waimea and Kekaha in particular. There was a trade in makaloa mats and shell lei in exchange for poi and taro, which would barely grow on Niʻihau. During droughts, many Niihauans migrated to Kauaʻi, returning home when times were better.

The Sinclairs soon learned that this symbiosis was as vital for their life on Niʻihau as it was for the locals. Early on they made the acquaintance of pioneer rancher Valdemar Knudsen and used him as negotiator and interpreter, both on Niʻihau and on Kauaʻi, where he lived. While the two brothers didn't speak the native language, both spoke Māori, and they adapted themselves to a language so similar in many ways.

There was much to think about in beginning a ranching operation where none had previously existed. James, at 37, must have remembered the similar situation the family faced 21 years earlier at Pigeon Bay. It was essential to gain the respect and trust of the local Niihauans, as they did with the Māori in Pigeon Bay. The visit of King Kamehameha V on 2 June, a few months after their arrival (see Chapter Seven) would have helped, but earning trust was largely up to the family members. In this they succeeded, although some inhabitants evidently left for Kauaʻi at this time rather than waiting to see how the relationship with the new owners developed. The sale of the island by the king had erased all hope of owning a kuleana, their own land, and this prompted some islanders to depart (see Appendix D).

▲ An extract from a 5 May 1945 letter from Alice Gay Robinson (1865–1960) to her daughter Eleanor. Alice was a prolific correspondent and many of her letters have been kept by her family. Her handwriting is distinctive, as this extract shows, but not easy to read today. This extract informs her daughter of inaccuracies about the Sinclair family in Eric Knudsen's book about his father, Valdemar, *Kanuka of Kauai*.
Robinson family

▼ An extract from an article in *Ka Kuokoa Nupepa* (4 June 1864) about the purchase of Niʻihau by the Sinclairs, written by P R Holiohana, a Hawaiian living on the island.

All accounts mention the speed and dedication with which the new owners and their family learned to speak Niihauan, but their most immediate task was to find somewhere to live. The Niihauans were in settlements scattered throughout the island. Tax records for 1863 show 165 taxpayers in twelve locations on Niʻihau (including 20 at Lehua village opposite Lehua Island).[2] The Sinclairs decided to settle initially at Kaununui on the west coast. The *Bessie* took them there, as a letter from Alice Robinson (née Gay) to her daughter Eleanor recounts: 'My father [Thomas Gay] took them in the Bessie and landed them at Kaununui & they put up temporary building on the hill on the makai [beach] side of the Kaununui gulch & lived there for quite a while …'[3]

They remained there for two years, according to the tax records. Two months after their arrival the Hawaiian language newspaper *Ka Kuokoa Nupepa* reported (in translation) under the headline *The Haole are Really Working Niihau*:

> [The Sinclairs] are pleasant and good, and speak nicely with the people, but they are not very proficient in the Hawaiian language. … There are ten Hawaiians, caretakers of the land, chosen from amongst the locals, but two are from elsewhere, they are newcomers, one from Hawaii and one from Maui, and including them there are ten caretakers. … Those caretakers are in charge of the three work days every month just like the konohiki of the chiefs, should there be work by haole owner to be done.
>
> … they live in Kaununui; they are religious, with one God, but their religion is very different; their houses were constructed in Britain and brought to Niihau: three houses, one currently stands, and two more to follow; we appreciate how nice and beautiful it is to see.[4]

The writer, P R Holiohana, an employee of the family, was writing from Niʻihau. How the Sinclairs managed to source three pre-cut houses in such a short time is unknown. A deal must have been struck over prefabricated houses that were already in the islands for some other purpose.

Once purchase of the island had been formally executed in Honolulu, both James and Frank returned to Kaua'i and then on to Ni'ihau in early March 1864 to arrange everything that needed attention for the family's move, and to commence farming activities. Their visit would have been timed to link with the arrivals of the schooner *Kalama*, which would have brought the houses, building materials, farm supplies and even some of the family's livestock. On two of the *Kalama*'s visits the vessel also called at Kōloa on Kaua'i, so they could have boarded her there to avoid a whaleboat or canoe crossing to Ni'ihau.

Meanwhile the *Bessie* had not been forgotten. In a letter of 2 April 1864 from the Department of the Interior to the family's livestock agents in Honolulu, permission was granted to transport 3000 sheep in the *Bessie* from Moloka'i to Ni'ihau.[5] As the inter-island trade was normally restricted to local vessels, it was highly unusual for a foreign-flagged vessel to be allowed this opportunity; authorisation may have been an outcome of negotiations at the time of the island's sale.

Whether the sheep transport ever took place on the *Bessie* has not been firmly established. Three thousand sheep would have required several voyages. The *Bessie* was for sale in the port of Honolulu from mid-April, and she left there for Ni'ihau on 21 May. The *Bessie*'s next known arrival is at the port of Auckland with a cargo of 70 mules on 17 August (see previous chapter). There would have been time during this interval to have sailed between Moloka'i and Ni'ihau before collecting the mules and leaving for New Zealand, but no records exist to determine if this indeed happened.

Goats still roamed the island freely despite the king's edict to remove as many as possible before the end of May, at which time those remaining would revert to the new owners. Goat skins were a valuable commodity. The letter to the Government Land Agent at Ni'ihau, Mr Wahineaea, urging the removal of the goats, dated 25 January 1864, had ended with the charming exhortation, 'Do not delay, work with all your might.'[6]

Wild pigs were also in evidence, descendants of those left by Captain Cook and other early European travelers. As ranching got under way, dogs were eliminated to avoid their worrying the sheep.

Although Gorham Gilman,[7] in reporting on his 1845 visit, states that there were no horses on Ni'ihau at that time, by the 1860s the Niihauans undoubtedly had them, and they were ubiquitous on the other islands by then. (An 1854 report complains of there being too many horses on the islands.[8]) Horses must have been used during the late-1863 reconnaissance visit. Many more would be required for ranching purposes, but while there is no early record of horses being brought from Kaua'i, the most likely source, it must have occurred.

Frank Sinclair was given the task of securing livestock for the island, which he would have relished. He had effectively managed Craigforth from the time James had been injured by a falling tree in New Zealand and had remained generally unwell ever since. Cattle were bought from Parker Ranch on Hawai'i and sheep from Moloka'i Ranch. Wool was planned to be the ranch's main source of income.

Even though the island had appeared lush, and the shallow lakes were full during the initial reconnaissance visit, the family would have been told about the periodic droughts and the general lack of rainfall. They knew there were no permanent streams on the

> 'Do not delay, work with all your might' [to remove goats]

▲ Gorham Gilman (1822–1909) arrived in Hawai'i from the East Coast as an 18-year-old in 1841. He visited Ni'ihau with the missionary Samuel Whitney in 1845. A record of his time there is held in the State Archives and is quoted from on page 195. Gilman returned to Boston in 1861, but retained a lifelong interest in the Hawaiian islands, for some time holding the position of honorary consul in New England for Hawai'i.
Pacific Commercial Advertiser

island and that the Niihauans relied mostly on rainwater for domestic needs. Wells and water sources were scarce, and they knew water would be necessary for a successful ranching operation. It would be very different from Craigforth, where there was always running water, even during summer droughts. Plans had to be made accordingly.

Another necessity that immediately became apparent was a safe and reliable form of transport across the 17-mile Kaulakahi Channel to Kauaʻi. Valdemar Knudsen recommended that the brothers employ Kapahe, a Kauaian who had been operating a whaleboat service taking poi and taro from the Kalalau valley across to Niʻihau for some time. He was immensely strong, a superb swimmer, and Valdemar saw him as having a great sense of responsibility for his passengers. Many tales were told of Kapahe's prodigious feats in trying circumstances. When asked by Frank, he readily agreed to be their captain. The whaleboat journey meant a row of five to six hours in good weather, but was reasonably reliable. Sailing across was not so dependable, and Ann recounts a three-day sailing trip because of contrary winds.[9]

Eliza took the lead in selecting the house site on their 72-square-mile island. She was an avid horsewoman and would have enjoyed her rides in search of a suitable location. Two miles south of Puʻuwai and two miles north of Nonopapa Landing rose a gentle bluff with a view to the southwest towards Kaʻula Island, 19 miles away. This she decided was where they should build, and the rest of the family agreed.

The Kiʻekiʻe mansion was built and called The House, a name which befitted it as the only European-style dwelling on the island. Craigforth as a name was not mentioned in this context; the family saw Niʻihau as a new beginning.

The House was a series of modules, connected by a wide lanai or verandah.[10] In 1867 the schooner *Nettie Merrill* arrived off Nonopapa with a load of building material for extensions. The vessel had left Honolulu on 24 June, stopped off at Kōloa, and arrived off Niʻihau in early July. A correspondent for the *Pacific Commercial Advertiser* described the unloading scene:

> The sun was slowly descending behind a curtain of crimson clouds, when we entered Cook's Harbor [Nonopapa] and cast anchor. The little hamlet on shore appeared to be alive with people. They crowded the white sandy beach as curious and anxious at the appearance of the *Nettie* as the natives were when the great discoverer anchored in the same place nearly a century ago…
>
> There are four halepilis [houses thatched with pili grass] and a halepili warehouse, which constitute this depot of the trade of Niihau…
>
> Next morning, daylight found all hands busy constructing a raft to land the lumber consigned to the Messrs. Sinclair, for the purpose of making additions to their hospitable mansion. And then the active, stalwart natives were busy on shore rolling down the bales of wool and cotton, the product of the Island, to be shipped on board the *Nettie*.[11]

▶ The House at Kiʻekiʻe, 1885.
Robinson family

Later that same day the correspondent walked to The House:

> We visited the residence of the Messrs. Sinclair, and although unknown and without those stereotyped passports of Society — letters of introduction — we were warmly welcomed and received and entertained in that genial, old-fashioned kind of Scotch hospitality that does one's heart good — that hospitality which springs spontaneously from a warm and generous nature, untrammelled by the cold conventional rules of society, or rather, mock society. That welcome, those exhilarating refreshments, aroused emotions that had long slept. Memory traveled back through the vista of the past, and recalled homely but cheering and hospitable scenes of home like this, 'o'er the glad waters of the dark blue sea.'
>
> The situation of the house is very beautiful and commands an extensive view. It is on a long cape-like ridge, on the northwest side of the Island, that terminates in the sand dunes referred to. Trees only are wanting to give it that rural air, which no country mansion can ever wear without trees to wanton in the breeze.[12]

This account reveals that the Sinclairs were growing cotton, presumably because of the high prices that could be obtained in the wake of the Civil War. The price crash came soon enough, but for now, wool and cotton were already being shipped — the ranch was up and running only a little more than two years after the family had arrived.

The correspondent also comments on attractive trade goods on offer:

> Native Island produce was on the shore [at Nonopapa] and the sharp Kanakas seemed ready for a trade. Sweet potatoes, onions and pineapples were in abundance and remarkably fine and cheap — the best we have seen in Hawaii. There were also those skillfully wrought and ornamented rush mats, the manufacture of which is peculiar to Niihau. They are pliable and elastic, and made of a material that grows nowhere else on the islands.[13]

The arrival of a vessel, unexpected as it would have been, gave the Niihauans and crew the opportunity to exchange goods while the unloading and loading operations were completed. Surprisingly, the distinctive shell lei are not mentioned in the account above. This vignette of life on Ni'ihau in 1867 shows that the Niihauans were entrepreneurial and keen to trade.

The wind was not always kind in those early years, as this translated article from an Hawaiian language newspaper from 1868 attests:

> Strong winds. — M. W. Keale of Niihau told us that on the 3rd of this month, toppled over were nine buildings on Niihau, for there were two in Kamalino; two in Kiekie; one in Puuwai; and three in Kaununui, one being a Protestant meeting house, one a Catholic meeting house, and one a private residence. And most of the others were tilted to the side by the dirt-stirring winds.[14]

▼ The House at Ki'eki'e on Ni'ihau. Built in stages from 1865, the family moved progressively to Makaweli on Kaua'i from the early 1870s. From then on The House remained mainly as a family vacation and entertainment venue, until it was largely destroyed in Hurricane Iwa in 1982. This photo probably dates from the 1890s.
Robinson family, colorised

191

The Makaweli purchase

Princess Victoria Kamamalu (also referred to as Kaʻahumanu IV), the younger (and only) sister of Kamehameha IV and Kamehameha V, was awarded vast lands on Hawaiʻi, Oʻahu, Maui and Kauaʻi in the Great Māhele of 1848. The siblings were grandchildren of Kamehameha the Great. Victoria Kamamalu had been kuhina nui of the monarchy since 1854 until her brother, Kamehameha V, abolished the position in 1864. This was not a reflection on his sister, but done in an aggregation of his monarchial powers. The office of kuhina nui was roughly equivalent to prime minister and regent in European 19th-century terms, so Princess Victoria had always had the ear of the king. She had thus been at the center of power for a decade when the Sinclairs arrived in Honolulu and began looking at land opportunities.

The ahupuaʻa of Makaweli on Kauaʻi, situated opposite Niʻihau, was one of the lands awarded to the princess.[15] The ahupuaʻa had been in the royal family's possession since 1824 when the lands were redistributed after the rebellion on Kauaʻi (see Chapter Five).[16]

At some point Eliza Sinclair realized that Niʻihau was not going to provide sufficient wherewithal as an inheritance for the family, and for her two elder daughters in particular. It may well have been that the Makaweli ahupuaʻa formed a part of the conversation when Niʻihau was purchased. Could it have been a quid pro quo for taking troublesome Niʻihau off the king's hands? We will probably never know.

Nor do we know why Princess Victoria Kamamalu might have wanted to sell the Makaweli ahupuaʻa. The kingdom was certainly strapped for cash and Niʻihau was nettlesome, but the princess herself was wealthy and made no further land sales in her short life. She died in May 1866, aged just 27. Her remaining immense landholdings eventually became part of the endowment of Kamehameha Schools.

Only a year after the Sinclair family took up residence on Niʻihau, on 29 June 1865, the sale of the 21,844-acre Makaweli ahupuaʻa to Eliza Sinclair was recorded at the Bureau of Conveyances.[17]

▲ Princess Victoria Kamamalu, the sister of Kamehameha IV and Kamehameha V, from whom Eliza Sinclair bought the ahupuaʻa of Makaweli in 1865.
Wikimedia Commons

◂ The ahupuaʻa of Makaweli (red) in relation to Niʻihau. It lies between the ahupuaʻa of Waimea on the west and that of Hanapēpē to the east.
Kauaʻi Nui Kuapapa

The Princess's trustee for her estate, who figures largely in the Deed of Sale, was Charles Harris, the Hawaiʻi Attorney General. He had this role from December 1863 until September 1866 so would have been involved in both the Niʻihau and Makaweli sales.

Discussions on the prospective Makaweli purchase must have been going on for some time. Valdemar Knudsen, with lands immediately to the north, may well have been involved. Minister Wyllie, who dearly wished the Sinclairs to remain in the islands, may also have had an influence.

Makaweli land was sold for $15,000: $10,000 in cash, with $5000 due in 60 days. The $5000 was discounted to $4900 as Eliza paid it all in cash on the day.

Why Eliza negotiated the phased payment arrangement may have been due to the uncertainty of timing of the sale of the *Bessie*. The vessel was a substantial family asset.

The Makaweli land purchase was made by Eliza, whereas the Niʻihau and Koakanu acquisitions were in James and Francis's names. For the next few years all the family's further land was bought in Eliza's name.

After the substantial Makaweli purchase, in the remaining 1860s, Eliza bought three blocks of land at Makaweli and two at Hanapēpē, presumably all kuleana-owned. Purchases continued into the 1870s with six additional Makaweli parcels, and on into the 1880s and beyond with many more parcels bought at both Makaweli and Hanapēpē.[18] Edward Gibbon Wakefield's 1830s dictum of 'Possess yourselves of the Soil and you are secure,' which had first led Eliza and the family to New Zealand, was truly fulfilled in the Hawaiian Isles.

The original Makaweli acquisition from Princess Victoria Kamamalu gradually became the focal point of the family's life from then on, but Ni'ihau remained a vital element in their commercial activities and kept its place in their hearts.

The early church on Ni'ihau

To give some context to the religious situation when the Sinclair family arrived it is necessary to go back in time to the founding of the mission stations on Kaua'i.

> Niihau — This small Isl. lies 20 miles west of Kauai. The want of good water, occasional famines when the people are obliged to leave & the sparce population, seem to exclude the hope that a foreign Miss[ry] [missionary] will be comfortably & usefully settled among them. There are on that Isl. 1,079 inhabitants, scattered over a sea coast of 40 miles of dry & barren country. Waimea is rather nearer than any of the other stations, though Hanalei is almost equally accessible, & the Isl. could be occasionally visited by a Miss[ry] from these stations.[19]

This is the first recognition of Ni'ihau in the formal missionary literature and comes from an 1833 report by Rev. Samuel Whitney for his superiors at the American Board of Christian Foreign Missions in Boston.

Samuel Whitney had arrived in the islands with the original company of missionaries in April 1820 and by July established the first mission station on Kaua'i, at Waimea. His bailiwick included Ni'ihau and the whole of Kaua'i. Samuel was 27 when he went to Waimea to found the mission. The board recruited him as a mission schoolteacher, and he was not ordained until 1825. Nevertheless he had spent two years at Yale College and in 1813 was judged to have become 'hopefully pious.'

By 1833 the mission was well established at Waimea, and from there he could service about forty percent of the Kaua'i population of over ten thousand. The demands on the mission were large, but Ni'ihau had not been completely forgotten. In April 1829 his assistant Peter Gulick reported:

> The schools of Niihau, a small island adjacent to Kauai, were examined. They are 4 in number, embrace 33 males and 43 females: 44 who read and 32 that spell.
>
> … In July last I assisted in teaching a number of the school teachers, the art of writing. Mrs. Gulick did the same for their wives. After filling 2 sheets most of the females wrote intelligibly and several of them a pretty hand. The best male writer received, as a premium, a shirt and pantaloons. The female that excelled was presented with a bonnet, which was made in school, under the directions and by the assistance of Mrs. Gulick. It was made of the cocoanut leaf. … Their seats and writing tables are chiefly made of those boards on which the natives used to spend much of their time, sporting in the surf.[20]

▲ Charles Coffin Harris (1822–81), Hawai'i's Attorney General and trustee for Princess Victoria Kamamalu's estate.
Wikimedia Commons, colorised

▲ Rev. Peter Gulick (1796–1877) and his wife Frances (Fanny) arrived in the islands with the third company of missionaries in March 1828 and he became Samuel Whitney's assistant in Waimea in April 1829. He was the first missionary to visit Ni'ihau, where native teachers had already set up schools. Gulick remained six years in Waimea before moving to other mission stations around the islands. This photo was taken in his later years.
Wikimedia Commons, colorised

It appears that Samuel Whitney visited Niʻihau much earlier in his mission, in 1822, and likely several times in the 1820s after that. William Beals, a young lad of mixed race who had been tasked with teaching English to Queen Kaʻahumanu, commented in a letter dated 16 August 1822 to Hiram Bingham's wife, Sybil, 'I am going to Niihau in the Tartar, and my scholars are going with me, so I teach them there. Mr. Whitney is going with us to Niihau.'[21]

▲ Rev. Samuel Whitney (1793–1845) arrived in Hawaiʻi in April 1820 and by July had made arrangements with King Kaumualiʻi of Kauaʻi to set up his mission at Waimea on Kauaʻi. Before sailing from Boston he had married Mercy Partridge and their first child was born at Kailua. The remainder of his life was spent in the islands, mostly on Kauaʻi. This painting by Samuel Morse was done immediately before his departure from Boston, when he was 27.

◥ Mercy Whitney (1795–1872) was drawn to missionary work from an early age. She met Samuel Whitney, who was imbued with similar fervor, and they married shortly before departing on the *Thaddeus* in 1819. After Samuel's death in 1845 she took over the missionary work there until a new person could be appointed, and she lived out her days in Waimea. Her extensive letters and diaries are preserved in the Mission Children's Society in Honolulu. Her portrait is also by Samuel Morse.
Find a Grave

The 1833 report quoted was the first major review by the board of the mission situation on Kauaʻi/Niʻihau. Whitney recommended further mission stations be established at Kōloa, Kapaʻa and Hanalei, and that Niʻihau be serviced by visits from Waimea or Hanalei. As a result, two further mission stations were established on Kauaʻi — those at Hanalei (Waiʻoli) and at Kōloa.

Now relieved of some of his responsibilities, Samuel Whitney should have had a little more time to consider his obligations to the Niihauans, but he doesn't appear to have done so. While in 1834 he reported there were ten schools on Niʻihau (and 84 on Kauaʻi), it wasn't until October 1842 that he himself visited Niʻihau. What apparently goaded him into action was the arrival of an evangelistic Catholic convert there, as he plaintively noted in 1840:

> It is with feelings of deep regret and concern that I often think of a part of our field [the island of Niʻihau] as almost entirely excluded from my personal labours, and never more so than just now. Owing to the fact that one of the Catholic converts, a woman of extensive family relations, and influence, has been at that Island scattering Catholic books, and setting up a school among her relatives.[22]

Again in 1841, in speaking of Niʻihau, he reports to his superiors:

> This Island, though included in the Station, is but seldom visited, and has not received that attention and labour which the wants of the people demand. It is separated from us by a somewhat dangerous channel of Sixteen miles in width, which is seldom passed except by natives in canoes. It has a population of one thousand and upwards, among them are nine schools in which are 214 children. … Within the past year, the Catholics have gained a footing there. They have a native teacher, who is said to be very zealous, and gaining quite a number of converts to the Catholic faith. It is with weeping eyes that we often look towards the rugged Clifts of that Island and ask what can be done for its wretched inhabitants. With the exception of these on Niihau there are no Catholics in the district.[23]

Catholic priest Father Robert Walsh visited Niʻihau for nearly three weeks in July/August 1842 and celebrated the first Catholic mass on the island on 31 July. Walsh had been preceded by a Hawaiian neophyte who prepared a small chapel for the occasion. At the conclusion of his visit he baptized more than one hundred souls into the Catholic faith.[24]

The sojourn was not without its difficulties, however. The first three Catholic missionaries had arrived in the islands from France in 1827, seven years after the New England Protestant missionaries, and were not made welcome. The Protestants saw the Catholics as rivals and had by this time established the written Hawaiian language, printed the Bible and set up schools. The Catholics, because of their statues and crucifixes, were accused of idol worship, anathema to the kingdom which had forbidden their own religious idols in 1819 only six months before the Protestants arrived.

The persecution of the Catholic missionaries began in earnest in 1830, led by the powerful Queen Ka'ahumanu, and resulted in the expulsion of the three Catholic missionaries. Until the arrival of Father Walsh in 1836 there was no Catholic priest in the islands but, being British, he was allowed to stay, so long as he did not attempt to convert native Hawaiians. His presence prompted the return of the original French priests, but they were met with renewed opposition and were again expelled in 1837.

Then followed a moment of gunboat diplomacy. In 1839, a French frigate entered Honolulu harbor, and its captain demanded religious freedom for Catholics, under threat of firing the ship's guns at the city. Kamehameha III capitulated and proclaimed 'that Catholic worship be declared free … the members of this religious faith shall enjoy in them the privileges granted to Protestants.'

It was against this backdrop that Father Walsh visited Ni'ihau. Many Niihauans had been exposed to the Protestant mission in Waimea, and they were aware of the political situation that the Catholics had found themselves in with respect to the Hawaiian government. Although new laws gave Hawaiian citizens the right to worship as they wished, there was friction on Ni'ihau during and after Father Walsh's trip, to the extent that Catholic church property there was desecrated and destroyed.

Despite his concerns for the lack of Christian education available to Niihauans in his earlier mission reports, Samuel Whitney records his visit in October 1842, only a few months after Father Walsh's stay. He stayed a week and held what he called:

> … a protracted meeting which was well attended; but the prospects of the people on that Island are exceedingly dark. They are ignorant in the extreme and almost entirely destitute of the means of instruction. The catholicks are rushing in upon them, and leading them by scores into the delusions of the Man of Sin.[25]

He visited Ni'ihau again in 1843 and this time was delighted 'with the evidence I saw of the Spirit of God among the people,' but:

> There may be about one in ten of the inhabitants of Niihau who profess to be followers of the Pope; but they know little or nothing of the Romish faith. They are in bad savor with the bulk of the people on account of their immoralities, and unless they have a Priest to guide them, there is not much danger that they will increase.[26]

In 1844 he again spent a short time on Ni'ihau and afterwards railed against the Catholic situation there, and talked of the need for a Protestant teacher.

Samuel Whitney, accompanied by Gorham Gilman and a Mr Tobey, traveled to Ni'ihau at the end of August 1845, and Gilman left a fascinating account of the visit. Whitney conducted student examinations in two villages, one of which must have been Pu'uwai. Gilman describes it thus:

> This village is the largest one on the island, having fourteen or sixteen houses, a Protestant and a Catholic Church, and is the principal place for the Catholics, their little chapel stands on a very conspicuous hill surmounted with its cross.[27]

When the churches may have been built is a matter for conjecture, but the Catholic church, at least, must have been quite new.

Unfortunately there is no mission report for 1845, as Samuel Whitney fell ill later in the year and died on Maui on 4 December. His widow, Mercy, filled in, and in reporting for 1846 remarked on the necessity for an urgent replacement as: 'unless there is some one to watch over and guide them, many will doubtless wander and go astray, from the paths of rectitude and uprightness.'

George Rowell was duly appointed, but he makes no mention of Niʻihau in his first report, which was for the two years 1848 and 1849.

George and his wife, Malvina, arrived in Hawaiʻi on the *Sarah Abigail* in 1842 and were assigned to the Waiʻoli (Hanalei) Mission Station. On Samuel Whitney's death they moved to Waimea in late 1846, where George was 'preaching to a diminished congregation' as Mercy Whitney had predicted. The Waimea church had physically collapsed due to heavy rains, and the congregation spiritually likewise. His efforts over the next few years were largely directed towards building a grand new church, a huge enterprise, and it is a testament to his determination and skills that it still stands today — now known as the Foreign Church. The first service was held in the church in 1854, although the building was far from complete. Rufus Anderson, secretary of the Missions Board, described the church after his islands-wide visit in 1863: 'The church is built of a whitish sandstone, obtained near the sea-shore, and is one of the best looking on the islands.'[28]

George Rowell visited Niʻihau in October 1850, ever alert to incursions on his patch:

The progress of popery in this field the past year has not been perceptible. On Niihau, which has been its strong hold, it has rather waned than otherwise. In my visit to that island in Oct. last, a larger congregation assembled on the Sabbath to hear the word than had ever before been known. This was owing to large numbers of catholics who rushed in & filled the house to overflowing. No part of my audience appeared more interested & attentive than they. In travelling, too, about the island, no part of the population more

▲ The Gulick-Rowell House in Waimea, Kauaʻi. The house, of coral blocks, was begun by Peter Gulick when he arrived in Waimea in 1829 and he and his family lived there until he moved to Waiʻoli six years later. It then remained empty until the Rowell family arrived. George Rowell was a carpenter and he renovated and extended it as his family of seven children grew. The family lived there until 1869, when it was sold into private hands. It is on the Historic Register and is currently being restored by Hale Puna as a museum and educational center.
Wikimedia Commons

◀ Rev. George Berkeley Rowell (1815–84), his wife Malvina, and probably their eldest child, also Malvina. They arrived in the islands with the tenth company of missionaries in 1842. George became one of the more controversial missionaries, and started his own church in Waimea in 1865. He was a regular visitor to Niʻihau, which was a part of his ministry.
Hawaiian Historical Society

cordially welcomed me to their houses & their hospitalities, than the catholics.²⁹

Both Catholic schools on Ni'ihau had closed, he wrote, while it appears the Protestant schools were reduced to five. The adult population by this time had learned to read and write, and with the population decreasing on Ni'ihau, school reductions were inevitable.

For various reasons, including church building and his own health, Rowell didn't report visiting Ni'ihau again until 1855, when he went twice, although a 'helper,' as he called him, Edward Johnson, a missionary from Wai'oli, made the journey on his behalf in 1853.

Mormonism appeared on the scene in 1854, but after an initial flicker of interest its influence waned and Rowell pronounced it 'defunct' in his district in 1854. In that same year he reports that the people of Ni'ihau raised the money for a bell for his new church in Waimea.

George Rowell's visits were complemented by those of medical missionary Dr James Smith from Kōloa. He visited Ni'ihau several times, from 1854. His mission was to vaccinate the whole Ni'ihau population against smallpox, a task he did well. In 1856 he was on the island with George Rowell and he describes the ten-day journey in his journal. He also undertook pastoral activities and for 28 August 1856 he writes:

> The next day I vaccinated all the children they brought to me, about 15 in all and Bro. R. preached three times. The following day was the Sabbath and we administered the Communion of the Lord's Supper. Our Communion furniture was certainly of the plainest kind — a couple of common blue plates for the bread — two pewter tumblers and a common earthen pitcher served for the wine — and water in a tin basin for baptismal purposes.³⁰

Rowell's reporting after 1858 was erratic (or records are missing). An amusing paragraph lamenting the Kaua'i locals' abiding interest in horse racing occurs in his 1862 report:

> One of the causes which has diminished the Sabbath congregations is the practice by the lovers of pleasure, of devoting Saturday to horse racing & other amusements. They gather by hundreds from the districts of Koloa & Waimea, men women & children, & spend the whole day in racing, betting, trading & all sorts of frolicking, & return home, many of them late at night, & wake Sabbath morning weary in body & dissipated in mind, & wholly indisposed to direct their feet or thoughts towards a place of worship.³¹

Rowell opens his 1863 report on a rather melancholy note: 'The past year at Waimea has been one of apparent spiritual dearth,' and this tone of despondency follows throughout. Mormonism had enjoyed a resurgence, he reports, which added to his woes. No mention is made of Ni'ihau.

When the Sinclairs stepped onto Ni'ihau in May/June 1864 the islanders had been exposed to the teaching of the Christian religion for over 40 years — almost two generations — and all were literate. The Sinclairs also arrived at the time of a major church scandal.

◀ Rufus Anderson (1796–1880), long-time secretary of the American Board of Commissioners for Foreign Missions, who visited all the missions in the islands in 1863 and reported that the board's task was done and the missions should now transition to independent churches. The engraving was by John Chester Buttre.
Wikimedia Commons

George Rowell's 1863 mission station report was to be his last. Rumors had been circulating for some time that over the past few years he had been in several inappropriate relationships with local women, and in particular with the married melodeon player at the church. The chatter peaked in early 1865, and the Kauai Evangelical Association, which comprised all the missionaries on Kaua'i, appointed missionary and doctor, James Smith, to investigate.

Smith was a good friend of George Rowell, both families having sailed from Boston together in the *Sarah Abigail*. While he was an appropriate choice, it was a painful assignment for the doctor. He confronted the Waimea pastor with the gossip, and while initially denying everything, Rowell finally conceded the truth of his relationship with the church melodeon player. As a result, the Evangelical Association called upon him to desist from preaching, which he was extremely reluctant to do, but after consulting his wife he finally consented.

This was not the end of it, however, as later in March 1865 Rowell confessed from the pulpit and suggested to the congregation that it was up to them, rather than his peers, as to whether he should preach or not. In the light of all this the Kauai Evangelical Association met on 29 March and withdrew their support for him.

Rowell had a lot of support among the Waimea congregation, however, and as Evelyn Cook writes in *100 Years of Healing: The Legacy of a Kauai Missionary Doctor*, 'the situation was beginning to spin wildly out of control.'[32]

Dr James Smith, as acting pastor, reported later on a bell-ringing protest:

> In the first place we were disturbed in our meetings [services]. Certain persons, not having the fear of God before their eyes, would enter the Church and ring the bell while we were engaged in worship. We endured the annoyance for a while, but at last the lunas [church elders] complained of this bell ringer to the magistrate [Valdemar Knudsen] & he imposed a fine on the offender. He appealed to the Circuit Judge, but did not escape & had to pay a fine and cost of court. Since this we have not been disturbed in our public worship.[33]

Later in 1865, while the Kauai Evangelical Association was holding its annual meeting at Wai'oli, individuals close to Rowell attempted to bar the church to outsiders:

> The Trustees then appealed to the Circuit Judge complaining that they had been deprived of their rights in being shut out of the Church — On hearing the case the Judge decided, that no just cause had been shown for closing the building; and ordered it to be opened.[34]

▶ Dr James William Smith (1810–87) and his wife Melicent arrived in Hawai'i on the same ship as the Rowells in 1842, and were stationed at Kōloa on the south coast of Kaua'i. As both a medical doctor and spiritual leader he made many trips to Ni'ihau. He was for many years the only doctor on Kaua'i and remained in Kōloa until his death.
Mission Children's Society

After a further court action over trespass by the Rowell faction, which they lost, the case about who were the rightful church trustees was appealed to the Hawaiian Supreme Court, which heard it over three days in April 1866. The court ruled on 7 August 1867 (after an unconscionable and inexplicable delay) in favor of the original trustees, i.e. those elected before the 'Rowell affair.'[35] Through all these trials George Rowell's wife, Malvina, stood by him.

The revelations do not seem to have featured in the Honolulu press, but the story was picked up on the mainland in an editorial in the *Daily Alta California* for 29 August 1866, much to the missionaries' chagrin, no doubt. After explaining the court case, the article concludes:

> There is considerable selfishness behind this foolish affair, which is a disgrace to all concerned who call themselves *missionaries*, and no credit to the American Board of Missions at home, who are unfortunately kept in darkness as to the sins of their *servants* at the Islands …[36]

In the interim, until the court ruled, both factions used the church, but at different times. By the end of December 1867 the governing arrangements had been resolved and Rowell's supporters ceased using the church but continued to worship, eventually building another church — what is now the Ohana Niihau O Waimea Church.

Aside from the court action, the American Board of Commissioners for Foreign Missions' 1865 annual report notes:

> Two Hawaiian preachers — one of them ordained — have been silenced the past year, on account of immorality; and the Committee feel it their duty to state, though they do it with the most painful emotions, that Mr. Rowell, long a missionary of the Board, has also been excluded from the ministry, and for the same cause; and in the church with which he has been connected, there has been great trouble in consequence of his proceedings.[37]

▲ Waimea Foreign Church today (Waimea United Church of Christ). The large coral block church has had a checkered career. The massive structure was begun by George Rowell in 1848 and the first service was held in 1854. After Rowell's break with the Hawaiian Board of Missions it fell gradually into disuse and a major storm in 1885 blew the shingles off the roof, exposing the interior to the elements. In 1894 a group of haole residents raised funds to reinstate the church building and hire a minister, a large but successful undertaking. Then in 1992 Hurricane Iniki inflicted major damage and reconstruction began all over again, faithful to the original design.

Hōkūlani Cleeland

No missionary pastor was appointed to succeed Rowell, despite some early attempts to do so. The times coincided with the withdrawal of the Missions Board from overall control of the mission stations. A succession of local pastors followed Rowell's demise.

The Sinclairs arrived on Niʻihau in mid-1864 in the midst of the affair, just when emotions were running at their highest. Of the part they may have played in it Ida von Holt, quoting from her mother Ann Knudsen's notes, says only:

> The Rev. Mr. Rowell who had charge of the Niihau Mission, lived at Waimea on Kauai, and made monthly visits to us [on Niihau]. We became very good friends and helped him all we could.[38]

Either they were not aware of the rumors swirling, or they chose to ignore them. George Rowell must have been pleased that the island had been bought by a devout Presbyterian family.

Dr Smith, as acting Waimea pastor following Rowell's departure, was able to report in 1866:

> D. S. Kupahu, another young man from the Wailua [Wailuku, on Maui] Seminary has been laborious at Niihau. The people there wish to have him ordained, and our Ecclesiastical Association appointed a Committee some time ago to visit Niihau for that purpose.[39]

The appointment of David Kupahu, 33, as pastor was a first for Niʻihau, and the hand of the Sinclairs can perhaps be seen at work. Kupahu reported to the Kauai Evangelical Association in 1867 that on 15 July 1866, in accordance with the wishes of the

Niihauans, the island now had an independent church called 'The Church of Niihau' with himself as pastor.

He reviewed his work during the year — a service every Sunday in the schoolhouse at Puʻuwai in the morning and one at Nonopapa in the evening — with often in the morning service some of Rowell's faction, the Catholics and the Sinclairs also attending.[40] He complains about the effect on church members of a whaling ship visit on a Sunday, which 'then becomes a day for gadding about and Sunday was not peaceful.'

He compliments the Sinclair family:

> The "haole" [white] people of Niihau live truly spiritual lives and their religious nature is made clear by their coming together with us in the work that promotes the Kingdom of God.[41]

When David Kupahu wrote this 1867 report, the Supreme Court had not made its ruling, and he remarks on the 'tenacity' of Rowell's flock, to which the majority of the Hawaiians belonged, at least pro tem. Relations with the Catholics had been strained over Sunday School attendances, but with the Sinclairs' help this was now resolved. Overall his report is positive, given the fact that it was his first year as Niʻihau pastor, and it is clear that the island's owners were extremely helpful, giving both financial and moral support.

In the February issue of *The Friend* an article appeared under the headline 'A Cheering Word from Niihau' which could only have been authored by one of the Sinclair family. It read in part:

> We had a very pleasant time here on New Year's Day with our natives. We had a grand feast, and some very good addresses. Mr. Kupahu (our Pastor) wrote a hymn for the occasion, which was set to music and sung beautifully. After which there was a Total Abstinence Society formed, and all our young people joined it to set a good example, and then a great many natives came forward and joined also, and more will in time. They seemed to enter fully into the spirit of it.[42]

The following year's report is not nearly so happy. After an account of church activities, Kupahu says:

> Concerning my being discharged.
>
> I am through with my service as pastor of the church of Niihau. I do not intend to return there in the future because of being discharged by the owner of the land … Because of this oral discharge the members wrote a document releasing me and I received the document from the members, so your fellow-worker is like a ship sailing here and there without casting anchor in any harbor …[43]

In any event he remained in the church and went to Kōloa as a schoolteacher.

It was Frank Sinclair who asked him to leave, and it would certainly have been discussed fully and agreed within the Sinclair family beforehand. Frank would also have talked to the church elders and received their support for his proposed course of action — but they may well have been in awe of the island's new owners; they were Frank's employees as well as elders. According to Kupahu's record of the event, Frank refused to give him the reason for his discharge, merely telling him that he did not wish to discuss it and that was his last word on the matter.

Are there echoes here of the Rowell affair, or was it merely a clash of personalities? As far as we know, Kupahu remained true to the mission church. Unless further records come to light, what happened will remain a mystery. The elders of the church, according to Dr Smith's record, wanted Kupahu ordained — did they change their mind about him when they saw his work? Smith described Kupahu's work on Niʻihau as 'laborious,' in the sense of industrious.

Niʻihau was again without a pastor. This was remedied after some time by the appointment of Deacon Andrew Kaukau from Maui, where he had been assisting Rev. Alexander. As Kaukau says in his report for 1871: 'F Sinclair commanded that I go and conduct services on Niihau. I cheerfully assented to his urging.'

He then lays down (in rather quaint English, as translated) the Niʻihau ground rules as set by Francis Sinclair as follows:

> The Hawaiians are very grateful for their haole chief in several ways
>
> [1.] April is the regular month for sheep-shearing. That is the time when 3,000 or more sheep are slaughtered; to eat the mutton and throw [the entrails] into the sea for the sharks.
>
> 2. To collect the tallow. The remaining tallow from the slaughtered sheep. The people take that tallow for them[selves] and everyone has from one to two barrels. They are well supplied with tallow every year.
>
> 3. F. Sinclair gave graciously an eighth of the whole island of Niihau as an open country where the horses of the people may run. He gave the posts and boards for the horse pasture from the uplands down to the sea. That is at Keawanui.
>
> 4. He gave freely lands for planting sweet potatoes — two planting places — at Pukeheke and below Kamalino, perhaps 100 or more acres.
>
> 5. To eat, people are to gather fish surrounding Niihau; there is no disputing about fish, like the days of the 'konohiki' [the chief's agent].
>
> 6. He will punish the persons indulging in sexual gratification and drinking liquor. The Government will punish persons outside of their house lots. He will punish the persons who drink liquor inside of all the houses, if discovered.
>
> 7. He and his family go regularly to the church service and urges the Hawaiians to come to church. He marks the children that do not go to Sunday School and punishes them if they always stay home. Therefore his Sunday School is full throughout the year. The Sunday School work is progressing finely on Niihau under the excellent leadership of F. Sinclair. There are very few haole here in Hawaii who do like this, for the two goods — physical and spiritual.[44]

The owners' generosity can be seen, but came with certain behavioral conditions applicable, of course, to all inhabitants, not just those of a particular faith. Punishment could possibly be suspension or loss of employment.

Kaukau numbers his congregation at 30 out of a population of 300 on the island, the Rowell faction being in the majority, with a sizeable number of Catholics and a few Mormons.

▲ The sad last paragraph of David Kupahu's 1868 report to his masters after his sacking by Frank Sinclair for reasons that are still obscure. The letter was translated from the Hawaiian by Rev. Henry Judd.
Mission Children's Society

In his 1872 report, the last on record, Kaukau covers much of the same territory with respect to the owners' wishes, and enthuses: '[Frank Sinclair] is like a father and acts rightly and helps the sincere people and is provoked at those who act mischievously. The Hawaiians produce true love for him.'[27]

How long Kaukau was on the island and what became of him is not known. From 1864 onwards, as a result of Rufus Anderson's 1863 reconnaissance visit to all the missions, the American Board of Commissioners for Foreign Missions, feeling that their work had been largely accomplished, began stepping back and encouraging the true independence of each church. The role of the Hawaiian Evangelical Association, while still important, changed and reporting was no longer required by the individual missions. The historical record then becomes that much more obscure.

The Niʻihau native population had decreased from about one thousand in 1834 to 233 in 1872 — not far out of line with what had happened to the native Hawaiian population as a whole, although the Niihauans always had the option of a temporary or permanent move to Kauaʻi. They had experienced massive changes to their culture over this time with the coming of the missionaries. Even at a distance the missionaries' ideas were persuasive, given the vacuum caused by the forced abandonment of their own religion and religious rites in 1819. Then, in 1848, came the Great Māhele, and instead of occasional tributes to their konohiki (headman of an ahupuaʻa under the chief), Niʻihau belonged to the Crown and land leases had to be paid for. As we have seen, these lease monies proved almost impossible to collect. In

▶ Niihauans in the 1870s, in photographs donated to the Auckland Museum by Frank Sinclair in 1875. From top: In their fishing canoes (both men in the water have caught fish on their spears); At Puʻuwai, with houses built by the Sinclairs in the background; In their Sunday best.
Auckland War Memorial Museum, PH-NEG-4724, PH-NEG-4716, PH-NEG-4729

1864 the Sinclair family arrived and brought with them yet another regime — and this within a conservative Christian framework. The people had to adapt yet again, and they did. It was after seven years of farming, in 1871, that Kaukau wrote down the Sinclair family's guiding principles. By this time the ranch was well established and fully stocked, and the Niihauans were dealing with all the consequences of the changes in their lives.

Protestations

For Niʻihau, 1874 was 'the year of the protests.' There was discontent in the relationship between the government and the Hawaiian populace regarding taxation, and also between the Niihauan residents and the island's owners.

Regarding the first of these, the *Hawaiian Gazette* on 29 April 1874, under the headline 'A Valuable Gift,' reported:

> His Majesty [King Kalākaua] received on Monday last a choice Niihau mat, presented to him by Mr. George Gay of Niihau. In this mat is wrought in red letters, a petition, praying that the taxes may be removed on all animals, and for other changes in the laws. The petition, which is in Hawaiian, is quite lengthy …⁴⁵

The decorated makaloa mat had been eleven months in the making by renowned Niihauan weaver Kalaʻi-o-Kamalino and her husband, for presentation to King Lunalilo. Unfortunately both Kalaʻi's husband and Lunalilo died before the mat was completed. It appears that the mat was an individual expression of protest and hope by Kalaʻi, and George Gay was merely the courier.

Little is known of Kalaʻi. She was from Kamalino on Niʻihau and according to the newspapers of the time was approaching 80 years old. The *Hawaiian Gazette* noted 'She is a very old woman, one of the few remaining links that connect the present generation with the time of Kamehameha I. She was twelve or fifteen years old when she saw the old warrior king …'⁴⁶

The makaloa mat, roughly six feet square and with the warp and weft both eleven to the inch, has essentially three messages:

- A heartfelt request for a return to 'The Golden Age' of peace in the early 1800s which occurred after the consolidation of the islands by Kamehameha and his promulgation in 1797 of Kānāwai Māmalahoe or 'The Law of the Splintered Paddle' — protection from wanton harm under the law.

- A plea to the king to do all in his power to reverse the decline in the numbers of the Hawaiian race.

- An appeal for the removal of all taxes on animals. At the time of the petition, horses, mules, asses, and dogs were taxed on a per head basis, while cattle and sheep were included in personal assets and taxed on their assessed value.

The text concludes with an exhortation to the king to release his people from the laws which make them slaves to the government.⁴⁷

▲ Frank Sinclair (1834–1916) in a formal portrait, towards the end of his time managing Niʻihau.
Robinson family

> **Kānāwai Māmalahoe, 'The Law of the Splintered Paddle':**
>
> In 1797 Kamehameha, in the heat of battle, was chasing an escaping fisherman carrying a child to safety when the king caught his foot in a coral crevice. The fisherman turned around and hit Kamehameha a tremendous blow on the head with his canoe paddle, shattering the paddle. Seeing the king's predicament the fisherman then turned away and, showing great compassion spared Kamehameha's life.
>
> Years later the fisherman was brought before the king for an offence punishable by death. Kamehameha, remembering the earlier incident, and realising that human life was precious and that the fisherman had only been protecting his family, with great empathy, chose a lesser punishment. As expounded by Kamehameha, in English translation, 'The Law of the Splintered Paddle' reads:
>
> Oh people,
> Honor thy God;
> respect alike [the rights of] people both great and humble;
> May everyone, from the old men and women to the children
> Be free to go forth and lie in the road (i.e. by the roadside or pathway)
> Without fear of harm
> Break this law, and die.
>
> The Law is enshrined in the Hawai'i State Constitution, Article 9, Section 10 as:
>
> The law of the splintered paddle, mamala-hoe kanawai decreed by Kamehameha I — Let every elderly person, woman and child lie by the roadside in safety — shall be a unique and living symbol of the State's concern for public safety.

▲ George Sinclair Gay (1850–1933), eldest son of Thomas and Jane Gay, who presented the Protest Mat to King Kalākaua. George married Marion Rowell, a daughter of George Rowell, and they lived in The House at Ki'eki'e on Ni'ihau for many years, taking over day-to-day management of the ranch from George's uncle, Frank Sinclair.
Robinson family

The key question is whether the protest mat had any effect; it is difficult to find written evidence to indicate that it did. The mat does not appear to have been presented to the king with any supporting documentation. Evidently it stood on its own, and George Gay would undoubtedly have made some verbal explanatory remarks.

Kalākaua was always a strong proponent of increasing the Hawaiian race. In his inaugural speech to the legislature, only a few days after the mat's presentation, he remarked: 'The subject, however, that awakens my greatest solicitude is to increase my people, and to this point I desire to direct your earnest attention.'[48] Maybe the mat's sentiments had some effect in reinforcing his views in this respect.

But on the question of animal taxes his views were diametrically opposed to those of Kala'i. The kingdom was desperate for money and the direct taxes on horses, dogs and other farm animals represented a sizeable proportion of the taxes levied (around 25%). In one form or another the animal taxes had been in place since 1840, so they were not new, but they had always been seen as disproportionately affecting the less well off — by this time almost all those who were capable of riding owned a horse, and probably a dog.

In 1874 the animal taxes were 75 cents for a horse, 50 cents for a mule and $1 for a dog. A bill was introduced on 14 May by Representative Joseph Martin to reduce the horse tax, which as it progressed through the legislature was reduced to 50 cents. The bill was passed and then forwarded to the king for his signature. Kalākaua refused to

A fledgling ranch

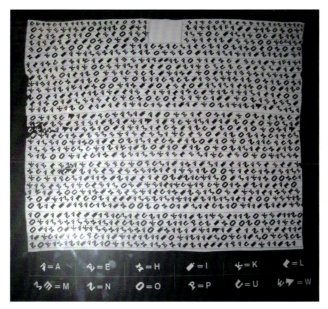

◀ A representation of the makaloa Protest Mat as it may have looked when presented to the king by George Gay in 1874. The original mat was woven by Kalaʻi-o-Kamalino, one of Niʻihau's most skilful weavers.
Steven Gentry photo from the Bishop Museum display in the Hawaiian Hall.

sign, and the bill died. As one commentator put it, the king admired the mat, but not the petition — or at least this part of it.[49]

The mat was initially hung in the palace, but with the formation of the Hawaii National Museum a few months later, the king donated the mat as one of its inaugural exhibits. It was transferred to the new Bishop Museum in 1889 when the Hawaii

> The full text of the Protest Mat, in English translation, reads:
>
> Kamehameha provided for all the chiefs of the land thus establishing the *ahupuaʻa, kalana, okana* land sections and islands. That was what Kamehameha did when he stood at the head of his government. He placed the chiefs over the lands; all kinds of chiefs settled on the land. Chiefs and commoners shared the peace under the one law, "Let the aged sleep on the highway unharmed; let the sugar canes grow till they fall over; let the bananas grow till they fall over." The king questioned his messengers to find out what they thought, "What are the old women and the old men like? Are they like the sugar cane and the banana stalks?" They told him what they were like. That was Kamehameha's constitution — his peace. Peace was the symbol of his kingdom; the old women and old men, his constitution. There was no ruthless seizing. It brought peace to the Hawaiian islands when it was issued. It was issued because of his love of the people. Therefore he laid down his Mamalahoa law that there be no more destruction of his foes.
>
> Therefore the people became free under the one law called the Mamalahoa, the giver of the greatest peace in his kingdom, an honor that has come to us from an old kingdom, that of Kamehameha I. Let us rise to study the great cause for the decrease of the Hawaiian people, a large population in the olden days under Kamehameha, and to ask the king to change the taxes on animals, cattle, horses, asses, mules, and sheep and let none of them remain.
>
> O Heavenly One — release [us] from the burden of the law that keeps us slaves under masters from the sky.
>
> By me, Kalaʻi.

▶ The third page (of four) showing the final paragraph of the Niihauans' 1874 petition to the Legislature, and 45 of the 101 signatures.
Hawaiian State Archives

▶▶ The back cover of the Niihauans' petition, indicating that it was 'laid on the table,' i.e. no action was taken on it.
Hawaiian State Archives

National Museum ended its days. It is presently on display in the Hawaiian Hall of the Bishop Museum.

Another protest emerged from the Niihauan community in 1874 and was directly concerned with their own island situation. The protest, addressed to the legislature, not the king, consisted of a list of itemized complaints (in Hawaiian) about the treatment by Frank Sinclair of those Niihauans living on the island. The document was signed by 101 residents — which must have represented the majority of the adult males on Niʻihau, given the population of 300 recorded by Andrew Kaukau in 1872.

The complaints would have arisen over a lengthy period, and some stem from Frank's sacking of Rev. David Kupahu without explanation in 1867, and the 'rules' described by Andrew Kaukau in 1871 (see pages 201 200–201).

Several of the complaints relate to the efforts of the Sinclair family to develop the island into an economic sheep and cattle ranch, all of which meant changes for a people who were used to roaming the island at will, limited only by their customary konohiki arrangements. Fencing may have required diversions of traditional tracks, for instance, and areas may have been designated as off-limits during lambing.

Some other complaints do, however, call into question the apparent arbitrary nature of Frank's decision-making and lack of communication. There appears to have been an underlying fear among the islanders that they could be capriciously sent off the island, never to return to their traditional home.

The petition of the Niihauan complainants
(English translation by Hōkūlani Cleeland)

To the Legislature of the Government with appreciation: We are the citizens of the island of Niihau. We are bringing our petition before your Distinguished House concerning our problems with which we are being burdened by Francis Sinclair, the Owner of Niihau.

Here are the complaints
1. We get kicked out for unfair reasons.
2. We are judged because of his personal desires, not by the law.
3. Oppressive laws are enacted because of his own personal desires.
4. We are used like slaves, not like the usual "konohiki" jobs from the old days.
5. Women and children are also put to work on "konohiki" days.
6. Our children are pulled out of the Government school and used to do his work.
7. Our children are not allowed to be married to outsiders, only to those from Niihau.
8. Our children are not given for adoption by those of other places, as was done in the old days, only on Niihau.
9. Guests are not allowed to come and stay as long as they like on Niihau.
10. Some of the people's blessings are limited in order to be sold [probably meaning that free mutton was being limited in order to be sold by the ranch].
11. It is forbidden to go to certain places on the island.
12. Parts of the Government pathways that were straightened in the old days have been closed. [This probably means that because of pathway closures by Frank Sinclair the residents have to take the old (and longer) ways around.]
13. It is not allowed to live in other places of the island, only where he wants.
14. Guests are not allowed to stay except for "konohiki" work.
15. Lawyers are not allowed to stand before the court.
16. No one may travel away from Niihau (or to Niihau from somewhere else), without his prior knowledge.
17. "Konohiki" days are assessed for the boat transport.
18. Independence of Churches is forbidden.
19. Certain harbors are forbidden for boats to be kept for an appropriate time.
20. All the people living on a piece of land are punished without knowing what was their offense.
21. Some of our things are taken without proper consultation.
22. Complaints by the citizens are forbidden to be made to the Legislature.
23. Animal skins that have not been tanned are not allowed to be taken and used to make whatever is needed.
24. Dogs cannot be kept, only by him.
25. No cooked meat can be taken away from Niihau.
26. People cannot choose the horses they want on the Government corral.

And even more is his oppression and the hardships placed upon us.

And for the person or persons who oppose these laws of his, there are three punishments:

1. To pay cash,
2. To be used however he wants,
3. To be permanently kicked out of Niihau. "Saying the people have no authority, nor the Government, I am the entire island, my words that I speak to you, and the laws, that is what you must follow. And if you don't follow them properly, whatever, just leave, go to Kauai."

As to verify the truth of the complaints and everything stated above in this document, we are placing our names below.

[*Then follows a list of 101 names*]

The complaint document was introduced to the House on 11 May 1874 by David Kaukaha, the Representative for Hanalei District, only days after the king was presented with the Protest Mat by George Gay. Its time in the House was short. It was agreed that it should 'lie upon the table', i.e. that it not be referred to a legislative committee for further discussion, and that no action should be taken on it.[50] In fact the petition itself did not request any action, but merely laid out the complaints.

Undoubtedly Frank Sinclair would have been aware of its existence. As far as we know he was not asked for a comment or a rebuttal and there is nothing further on file in the State Archives about it. Nevertheless, he may have improved his communication with the Niihauans as a result, as no further formal complaints eventuated.

Why these two very different protests should have emerged almost simultaneously is unknown. Kalākaua had been only elected as king in February 1874 after the untimely death of Lunalilo. The Protest Mat is evidence of wide dissatisfaction of native Hawaiians with their lot. They were concerned about their decreasing numbers and the excesses of previous reigns, and hoped that their monarch might be able to turn the situation around.

The Niihauans' petition to the Legislature was obviously born out of frustration with the situation the Niihauans found themselves in on their home island. It may have been the petition bringing their concerns into the open that precipitated Frank's stepping back from the detailed management of the ranch and effectively leaving his nephew George Gay in charge, except for major decisions.

▼ Frank and Isabella Sinclair, shortly after their wedding in New Zealand in 1866.
Canterbury Museum, New Zealand

Frank and Isabella

The family had been on Niʻihau for a little more than a year when Frank announced he was returning to New Zealand to marry his first cousin Isabella McHutcheson, the daughter of Eliza's brother, William McHutcheson. Elder brother James was available to keep an eye on things, and Frank felt that with the farm now reasonably stocked and with the Niihauans rapidly becoming excellent paniolo (cowboys) he could return to New Zealand to fulfil the promise he had made to Isabella before he left on the *Bessie*.

At first his sister Ann was predictably upset at the news, since she felt she had been unduly pressured to forsake her New Zealand beau, James Montgomery, in the interests of family unity. Frank assured her, however, that he intended to bring his bride back to Niʻihau and to remain part of the family. Just before he left, the Hawaiian government appointed him as district justice for Niʻihau.[51]

Isabella and her family had arrived in New Zealand on the second voyage of the *Silistria*, which entered Otago Harbor on 11 January 1862 after a 99-day passage from Scotland.[52] The William McHutchesons moved to Christchurch to be closer to the Sinclairs in Pigeon Bay. Eliza had been encouraging her

A fledgling ranch

brother William to come to New Zealand for years, but when he finally decided to emigrate, the Sinclair family must have been already thinking of their next move.

William McHutcheson opened a shop (the Cashel Store) in Cashel Street, Christchurch — quite an entrepreneurial venture for one who, like Eliza's husband (his late brother-in-law, Francis), had been a tax collector in Scotland. Born in 1810, he was ten years younger than Eliza. Some of his daughters, including Isabella, opened a school for young ladies in Christchurch run on Wesleyan principles. William himself became a staunch supporter and chairman of the Total Abstinence Society.

The McHutchesons' time in Christchurch was to be brief. With the Sinclairs' departure on the *Bessie*, they moved to be closer to the other member of the family who was in New Zealand, John McHutcheson, who had taken up residence in Blenheim in 1859.

John, by this time preferring to be known as John Mack Hutcheson, was born in 1817, the youngest of Eliza's brothers. He had come with Eliza's family to New Zealand in 1840, posing as one of her children. John remained with Eliza and her family until 1848 when he returned briefly to Scotland, where he became involved in sending the first emigrant vessels to Otago. He returned to Canterbury and married, moving later to Nelson and producing a large family. John then took up land briefly in the Mackenzie Country (Canterbury) before going into the insurance business in Blenheim. He became a pillar of Blenheim's St Andrew's Presbyterian church and by 1873 was mayor of the town. He is described as having a happy, humorous manner, tactful, and with unfailing amiability.

John sounds just the kind of person to welcome his brother William and family to Blenheim in 1864 and to settle the family comfortably there. William became the master of the Provincial Government's school in Blenheim, while two of his daughters also taught there.

Two years on from William's move to Blenheim the following notice appeared in the *Marlborough Press* on 15 August 1866:

> On the 6th instant, at Blenheim, by the Rev. A. Russell, Francis Sinclair, Esq. of Niihau, Sandwich Islands, to Isabella, third daughter of Mr William McHutcheson.[53]

Isabella was 26 and Francis 32. The wedding would have been conducted at St Andrew's Church, where Archibald Russell conducted the marriage of Isabella's eldest sister Jane a year later.

While Isabella appears to have been a schoolteacher, her artistic ability was evident from an early age. She had an abiding interest in the natural world, particularly the unique New Zealand flora. Her rambles with Frank in Pigeon Bay, with its still unspoiled bushclad hills, allowed the growing friendship between the pair to blossom. The time they were able to spend together between the McHutchesons' arrival in Christchurch and the departure of the Sinclair family a year later was relatively fleeting, given the difficult journey necessary between the burgeoning town of Christchurch and Pigeon Bay. It was evidently time enough for them to have come to an understanding that Frank would return to wed her as soon as he could. The surprising thing is that it seems Frank's family never got wind of the arrangement until he announced it to them on Ni'ihau.

▲ An example of Isabella Sinclair's artistic ability — her Christmas card to the family from 1890. Her botanical artistry is covered in Chapter One. The card must have been reproduced using chromolithography, the same process used for the production of her botanical book, and presumably executed by her publisher as the process is complex and exacting.
Robinson family

While in New Zealand Frank selected further stock for the ranch and arranged for them to be shipped. He had many friends in the Canterbury area who would have been delighted to see him and Isabella and to learn of their marriage plans. Shipping services between Hawai'i and New Zealand were most irregular. There were no steamships regularly traveling to the South Pacific at this time and Frank, and later the couple, may have had to take a circuitous route via Australia or San Francisco. The whole trip would have taken many months.

On the couple's return to Ni'ihau they lived in one of the cottages of The House close to the rest of Eliza's large family, and Frank resumed ranching duties. Water, and the dryness of the island in the ferocious heat, was the overriding problem, as it had been almost from the start, but wool, sheepskins, cattle hides and tallow were now being produced and provided an income of sorts. The viability of the ranch was, however, questionable.

Valdemar and Ann

Meanwhile the family on Ni'ihau had cause for further celebration. Shortly after Frank and Isabella returned from New Zealand, Ann and Valdemar Knudsen announced their engagement.

Knudsen had arrived in Hawai'i in 1853 and had been a great help to the Sinclairs in their purchase of Ni'ihau. It seems though that his interest in the Sinclairs went deeper than just land transactions. Ann soon became the object of his affections and he asked her for her hand in marriage.[54] Valdemar was 46 and ready to settle down, having led an adventurous and varied life.

Born in Norway in 1819 to well-off parents, Valdemar read science and botany at the University of Oslo (called Royal Frederick University in his day). From an early age he exhibited a gift for languages, and having toyed with medicine and the law, felt a need to spread his wings. With the blessing of his family he departed for New York and worked in a publisher's office for some years before the lure of the goldfields proved too much, and in 1849 he sailed around Cape Horn to San Francisco. Mining itself was not his great interest and he set up a successful trading establishment to service the miners at the junction of the Feather and Yuba rivers. Traveling via Panama on his return from visiting his elderly parents in Norway, Valdemar contracted Panama Fever — a term used then in Central America for both yellow fever and malaria. To recuperate he was advised to seek out a warmer and drier climate than northern California and, after several misadventures, landed at Kōloa on Kaua'i. Hilo, Hawai'i was his destination, but the schooner's master was a little short on navigational skills. After managing Grove Farm at Līhu'e for a time, Valdemar bought several leases at Kekaha, Poki and Mānā in the drier western part of Kaua'i, and by the early 1860s was a prosperous cattle rancher and sugar planter, with a substantial ranch house at Kekaha, known as Waiawa.[55]

The family were initially not altogether happy with Ann's engagement and her intention to move to Waiawa. According to her daughter, Ida:

▲ Valdemar Knudsen (1819–98) and Ann Sinclair (1839–1922) were married at Ki'eki'e on Ni'ihau on 12 February 1867. Ann was the youngest of Eliza Sinclair's children, and 20 years Valdemar's junior. The photo of Ann was taken eight years later, when she was well settled at Valdemar's ranch at Waiawa on Kaua'i.

Toulon/Knudsen family; Robinson family

A fledgling ranch

When late in 1866 she told the family of her engagement to Valdemar Knudsen, Frank asked 'Is it because I have married that you are leaving us?' To this question she laughingly replied, 'Nonsense, Frank, you must realise I want a life companion and home of my own as much as you do.' … All felt Anne* was cruel to leave them and want her own home, though, as they thought highly of Valdemar Knudsen they had no real reason for objecting to her marriage, and were glad of Anne's choice.[56]

* Ann was sometimes known as Anne (or Annie).

The Sinclairs' belief in the family as an indivisible unit had led to their move to the Hawaiian islands, so the news was a shock, until they realized that Waiawa was close to their Makaweli property and in reality Ann would not be far away.

The couple were married on Niʻihau on 12 February 1867, only six months after Frank and Isabella, as *The Friend* records:

> MARRIED
>
> KNUDSEN–SINCLAIR – On the 12th of February, at the residence of the bride's mother, Niihau, by the Rev. D. S. Kupahu, pastor of Niihau, Valdemar Knudsen, Esq. of Waiawa, Kekaha to Annie, youngest daughter of the late Francis Sinclair, Canterbury, New Zealand. No cards.[57]

Ida comments:

> Her simple white dress and the fresh orange blossoms picked early in the morning by her devoted brother Frank only enhanced her charm and loveliness.[58]

Despite her early misgivings, Eliza was generous and gave Ann her share of her projected inheritance as a wedding present — a substantial amount, in cash.[59] The day after the wedding the couple left in the family whaleboat to begin their life together at Waiawa on Kauaʻi. Valdemar was a sentimental soul. In a letter to his brother-in-law Frank only two

▲ Valdemar Knudsen and his family, in a photograph reputedly taken at The House on Niʻihau by a member of the 1874 Transit of Venus Expedition to Kauaʻi. From left: Augustus, Ida, Ann (holding Eric), Valdemar, Maud. Their fifth child, Arthur, was born in 1875.

Toulon/Knudsen family photos

▲ 'Mama's Favorite Walk 1898' — a painting of the Niʻihau landscape by Maud Knudsen Garstin, Ann Sinclair Knudsen's daughter.

With permission; painting loaned to Kauaʻi Museum by Mrs Cynthia Blackwell

days after his wedding, Valdemar wrote 'She is now my darling bride and she will always be that to me.'[60]

A month later the couple left for their honeymoon in Europe, via San Francisco, Panama and New York. They were accompanied on the journey by James Sinclair and Helen Robinson from Niʻihau and were away more than seven months.[61]

With James and Helen's return from overseas the family in The House consisted of Eliza Sinclair; James Sinclair; Jane Gay with her children George (16), Francis (14), Eliza (10), Charles (5), Alice (2) and stepson James Gay (26); together with Helen and son Aubrey Robinson (13), and Frank and Isabella Sinclair. Thirteen in all, and a large household by today's standards.

The children's education on Niʻihau was a problem, and tutors came and went with considerable rapidity. Recruiting teachers to Niʻihau was a continuing difficulty.

Eliza's move to Makaweli

Visitors to The House abounded and the family's hospitality seemed endless. The journalist on the *Nettie Merrill* quoted earlier (page 191), who arrived shortly after Valdemar and Ann's February 1867 wedding, wrote an article generously praising the hospitality received at The House when he arrived totally unannounced.[62]

That same year, 1867, two shipwrecks occurred on islands to the west and the survivors made their way to Niʻihau. The clipper *Kathay* was wrecked on Howland Island and the crew of 25 were rescued by the schooner *San Diego*, which took them first to Niʻihau and later Honolulu. Captain Popham of the *Kathay* enjoyed their Niʻihau stop:

> On Sunday last we touched at Cook's anchorage at Niihau, where Capt. Tengstrom [of the *San Diego*] received great kindness from Mr. Sinclair and his two nephews. They supplied us with three sheep and several bags of potatoes and brought them off after dark to the schooner, which kindness I shall never forget, as there was a heavy surf on at the time. Capt. Tengstrom has been very kind to us in this long tedious passage.[63]

A few months later the whaling bark *Daniel Wood* went aground and broke up on the dangerous French Frigate Shoals. After salvaging supplies from the wreckage, eight of the crew set off for Niʻihau in the most seaworthy of the ship's boats, the *Ann E Wilson*.

> For the first four days after leaving the ship the *Ann E. Wilson* encountered strong winds from the north and north-northeast, but made very good headway in the desired direction, sometimes pulling and sometimes sailing when the wind gave a slant. For prudential reasons all hands in the boat were put on an allowance of one pint of water and one biscuit a day. Thus they struggled on, until Sunday morning, April 23d, when they made the Island of Niihau. Landing there, they were most hospitably and kindly

received by the proprietors of the Island, Captain Sinclair and family, of whom Captain Richmond [of the *Daniel Wood*] speaks in the highest terms.⁶⁴

The *Ann E. Wilson* continued to Honolulu and Captain Richmond arranged for the remaining 27 members of the crew to be rescued from the Shoals.

Apart from these incidents and the aridity (and excepting for the inevitable ups and downs of sheep and cattle ranching) their life on Niʻihau seemed, at least to one observer, idyllic. In 1870 he describes the Sinclairs' Niʻihau establishment in glowing terms reminiscent of Pigeon Bay and Craigforth: 'On the island of Niihau the Sinclairs have, I think, their full heart's desire.'⁶⁵

But was it so? Earlier writers have always made much of the family's hospitality — but were the visitors as frequent as portrayed? Niʻihau was difficult to reach.⁶⁶ While Eliza still had most of her family around her, opportunities to socialise may not have been as easy or as frequent as she would have liked. There was also the grandchildren's education to think of. The youngest, Alice Gay, was only five in 1870 and her eldest sibling, George, was 19. Aubrey Robinson was 17. Eliza (by then affectionately called Mama by family and Hawaiians alike) turned 70 in 1870, and while showing no signs of slowing down, she was uncomfortable on Niʻihau in the summer heat. Her thoughts turned to building a residence on the uplands of the nearly 22,000-acre block she had bought at Makaweli on Kauaʻi. But she would have to move: the rich lands of Makaweli would be difficult to develop from a base on Niʻihau.

The large and picturesque Makaweli House was built on an elevated site at an altitude of 1800 feet with a view stretching across the rolling Kauaʻi countryside, and beyond to Niʻihau. This was to be Eliza's home for the rest of her long life. As Isabella Bird described it, as part-quoted in Chapter One:

Behind rise the forest covered mountains and in front a beautiful wooded ravine very precipitous widens to the rolling grassy hills and the blue sea 5 miles off on which at a

▲ 'Mama' — Eliza Sinclair (1800–92), the matriarch, in 1869, about the time the family began building Makaweli House and progressively moving there from Niʻihau.
Robinson family

◤ Makaweli House, nestled into its surroundings. Land clearance for the house began in 1868 and the house was completed in the early 1870s.
Photo by James Williams, Honolulu, Robinson family

▲ The family at Makaweli House in late 1888. From left to right:
Eliza Gay (Aunt Lila)
Francis Gay (seated)
Frank Sinclair
Jane Gay (seated)
Eliza Sinclair (the matriarch)
Isabella Sinclair (Frank Sinclair's wife, standing)
Helen Robinson (Aubrey's mother)
Alice Robinson (Aubrey's wife) with baby Aylmer
Aubrey Robinson
Sinclair Robinson (child)
James Wodehouse (family friend).
Robinson Family

distance of about 18 miles floats the island of Niihau which the sun turns every night to a living amethyst. There is no house native or foreign within 6 miles. It is the most beautiful scenery I have seen on the island in fact the place is perfection.[67]

As soon as the house was completed in 1872 the majority of the family departed, leaving behind as full-time occupants at Ki'eki'e only Frank and Isabella Sinclair and Frank's nephew, George Gay. Eliza divided her time between Ni'ihau and Makaweli until 1875 when she moved permanently to Makaweli House. With the family gone, the island's resident pastor, Andrew Kaukau, also departed, leaving the Ni'ihauans' spiritual needs to be looked after by their own people.

With the exception of Ann and Valdemar, the whole family had been living together on Ni'ihau for eight years. It must have been a hard decision to leave, not unlike that which they had made on leaving New Zealand.

Despite her aversion to the heat, the pull of having the family around her drew Eliza back to Ni'ihau in the summer holidays. Ida Knudsen von Holt, Ann's eldest daughter, vividly remembers the excitement of the summer of 1874 on Ni'ihau when she was six — the drama of the channel crossing, the two-hour buggy trip with cousin George to The House, the welcome 'with open arms' from Mama: 'There she stood, a little slim woman of 74, beautiful and fascinating in her dainty dress and with her lace cap showing under her shirred silk bonnet.'[68]

Then there were the greetings from the rest of the family, and all sorts of activities — shell collecting, swimming, storytelling, and in later years, surfing, fishing and horseback riding. Niʻihau had a captivation of its own for all the family, and many happy summer holidays were spent there.

With the permanent haole population of Niʻihau now reduced to three, even more emphasis could be placed on making the island profitable. The 1871 wool clip was expected to be 80,000 pounds (200–300 bales) and tallow, 10,000 pounds.[69] But more was required to make Niʻihau stand on its own financially.

Travels and a death

While Frank Sinclair and George Gay, with the vital support of the Niihauan families, devoted themselves to the ranch, Isabella pursued her botanical and artistic interests. Frank and Isabella never had children. Frank's nephew, George Gay, was twelve years his uncle's junior and was being trained in ranching duties.

George was at Makaweli when Isabella Bird visited in March 1873. Her letter to her sister in Scotland gives a perceptive description of the family at that time, not long after they had moved to Makaweli House (punctuation was not one of her strong points):

> The family living here consists of Mrs Sinclair a bright beautiful lady of 72 with a refined Scotch accent and charming manners. They all admire and adore her and say she is the youngest of them all. She usually wears a bonnet and is in and out all day and up at 5. She is very talented and sparkling like Dean Ramsays ladies* … Then there is a bachelor son [James] very quiet and an immense reader. Mrs Robinson [Helen] a widowed daughter highly cultivated and very intellectual and a most splendid rider.†

She praises Aubrey (as quoted in the following chapter) and then turns her attention to Jane Gay and her children:

> She has 2 sons [Frank and George] 19 and 21 over 6 feet very dark and handsome with great beards and mustachios a most attractive girl of 15 [Eliza] as graceful as she can be and very intellectual and a boy [Charles] and a girl [Alice] of 10 and 8 like the very nicest English children …
>
> I think I never was in a family which to an equal extent combined religion love and culture. They all speak Hawaiian as easily as English. They all dress nicely but not fashionably but when the young men go out on horseback they look so picturesque in scarlet shirts grey trousers leather belts and great boots and spurs riding brass bossed Mexican saddles with lassoes coiled up behind.[70]

Of Eliza's move to Makaweli she writes:

> Mrs Sinclair's great object has been to keep her family all together and she disliked leaving Niihau but as her grandsons grew up they could not have enough to do on so small an island.[71]

The only family members not present at Makaweli House were Frank and Isabella on Niʻihau, and of them she wrote: 'Mr Sinclair is said to reign there like a prince. He and his wife devote themselves to the natives who are said to be the most religious, moral and prosperous on the islands.'[72]

A few months later George was back on Niʻihau with Frank and Isabella, and Helen was preparing to take James to Boston to seek medical help he needed as a result of the injury he sustained in New Zealand. She also intended taking Francis, Aubrey, Eliza

▲ Isabella Bird (1831–1904), the fiercely independent 19th-century traveler and writer. She visited Hawaiʻi in March 1873, armed with an introduction to medical missionary Dr James Smith, whose wife rode with her the 23 miles to Makaweli. They stayed several days with the Sinclairs before riding back to Kōloa.
Wikimedia Commons

* Dean Ramsay was Dean of Edinburgh and is best known for his 'Reminiscences of Scottish Life and Character' which went through 22 editions. He died in 1872. The reference to 'Dean Ramsay's ladies' is to the genteel manners he attributes to the ladies of his generation and his lament at the passing of these ways.

† Helen was not in fact widowed, but may well have been introduced to Isabella Bird in this fashion.

and Charles to further their education. On the eve of their departure James suddenly collapsed and died. The briefest of death notices appeared in *The Friend*:

> SINCLAIR — At Makaweli, Kauai, September 22d, JAMES MCH. SINCLAIR, of Niihau, late of Craigforth, Canterbury, New Zealand.[73]

The planned trip was hastily rescheduled and, accompanied by Valdemar and Ann as far as Salt Lake City, the group left for the East Coast. Aubrey took law classes at Boston University and was eventually admitted to the bar in the Eastern Law Courts.[74] Having toured the East Coast, the remainder of the family returned to Makaweli and were reunited with Mama Sinclair, Jane and Alice.

George remained on Niʻihau with Frank and Isabella, apart from a visit to Honolulu in April 1874 when he presented the makaloa protest mat to King Kalākaua.

A little over a year later, in August 1875, it was noted in the press that both Francis and George Gay were students at Massachusetts Institute of Technology.[75] MIT records show that they attended for the 1874/75 academic year, both entered as 'Students Not Candidates for a Degree.' George took the third-year civil engineering course and Francis the fourth-year science and literature course: the latter included business law as well as political and industrial geography. They lived together at 25 Pemberton Square, Boston.

Soon after completing his studies at MIT, George became engaged to Marion Rowell, George Rowell's daughter. The marriage took place at Waimea on 16 January 1879, the officiating clergyman the bride's father George Rowell.[76] The wedding presumably took place at what is now the Ohana Niihau O Waimea Church — the congregation founded by George Rowell on his dismissal from the Kauai Evangelical Association. Marion had earlier taught George's younger siblings on Niʻihau and it seems that the 'Rowell affair' had not soured relationships between the families over the years.

The newly married couple took up residence at Kiʻekiʻe and remained there for well over ten years. Four of their six children were born at Kiʻekiʻe and the last two in California in the 1890s. According to a lifelong friend of Marion's:

> [Marion] remained on Niihau, cheerful and contented in that secluded spot, occupied with her household, the care and teaching of her children, and with her music, until the family moved to California. Her sisters lived near her there.[77]

George and Marion's marriage and their contentment with life on Niʻihau gave Frank and Isabella the opportunity to come and go from the island as they wished. Even though Frank remained in charge overall, George took over more managerial responsibilities. By 1884 *McKenney's Hawaiian Directory* had the following to say about Niʻihau (in part):

> A Mr. [George] Gay lives on the island, in charge for Mr. [Frank] Sinclair, and besides his family and servants, there are about two hundred natives.[78]

Frank and Isabella left Niʻihau for Makaweli some time in the early 1880s. Frank continued to visit Niʻihau, and Isabella continued her botanical work and flower studies on Kauaʻi. Frank had for some time been eager to retire from ranching to pursue his interest in writing. Aubrey Robinson's 1883 return from his extended European and Asian visit gave Frank the opportunity to pass the baton to the next generation.

▲ Aubrey Robinson (1853–1936), around the time he was called to the bar in the Eastern law courts.

Canterbury Museum 1951_35_59_A Robinson

▲ Marion Rowell Gay (1848–1912), daughter of missionary George Rowell, who tutored Aubrey and Alice's two youngest children on Niʻihau and later married their eldest son, George, and lived on Niʻihau for some years.

Robinson family, photographer James Williams, Honolulu

Ownership and management changes

James and Francis Sinclair bought the Crown-owned portion of Niʻihau as tenants in common. When James died in 1873 he left his interest in this land to his brother Francis (Frank), who thus became the single holder of what had been the remaining Crown land. The same applied to the kuleana of Koakanu, also bought by James and Francis as tenants in common. The kuleana of Papapa, on the other hand, was bought by Eliza, but not until 1880, well after James's death.

Apart from Eliza's small landholding, Frank was the sole owner of Niʻihau for 18 years until 31 January 1891, when he sold his interests in the island to his sisters, Jane and Helen, and his nephew Aubrey. The two sisters collectively paid Frank $35,000 and Aubrey $1 (essentially for the right to inherit his mother's half-share in the island after Helen's death).[79] By a separate deed dated 2 February 1891 the four partners of Gay and Robinson (Jane Gay, Helen Robinson, Francis Gay and Aubrey Robinson) agreed to pay Frank the sum of $3500 a year in gold coin for life, or for 28 years; this payment to commence on 31 December 1891.[80]

▲ Helen Sinclair Robinson (1831–1913), left, and Jane Sinclair Gay (1829–1916).
Robinson family

On 3 March 1891 Eliza Sinclair gave her daughters Jane and Helen 'all of my lands and all of my real estate situated on the islands of Niihau and Kauai.'[81] On Niʻihau all she owned was the kuleana of Papapa, but on Kauaʻi her landholdings were vast. The original Makaweli purchase was in her name, as were all subsequent purchases.

George Gay remained on Niʻihau after Aubrey's return from overseas in 1883, the latter event allowing Frank to retire from the family business to pursue his literary interests. Frank left for England in 1884 to assist in the publication of Isabella's outstanding book *Indigenous Flowers of the Hawaiian Islands* (see Chapter One). The first of Frank's own literary works was published in England in 1889, and in all he produced five major literary works, all of which are still available.[82]

While basing themselves principally in England, Frank and Isabella traveled widely, giving Frank the opportunity to collect material for his books. After Isabella died in 1901, Frank married her sister Willamina ('Ina') Sherriffs. Frank himself died on Jersey in 1916, aged 82.[83]

Although all the adult members of the family were involved, and especially his mother, Eliza, Frank had successfully established the ranch on Niʻihau and run it for almost 20 years. Elder brother James also played a part in the early years, but as a semi-invalid he could only do so much.

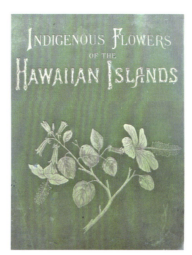

▶ Isabella Sinclair's *Indigenous Flowers of the Hawaiian Islands*, published in London in 1885.
Courtesy Lisa Schugart

▶▶ Hau (*Hibiscus tiliaceus*), one of the 42 much admired botanical plates in Isabella Sinclair's book, all painted on Niʻihau and Kauaʻi.

Water was the enduring problem on Niʻihau and right up to the end of his tenure Frank was attempting to secure more. An 1883 letter from the Minister of Interior in response to his plea for funding assistance to drill for water reads:

> Mr. Francis Sinclair
> Sir;
> After consulting my colleagues in reference to your proposition for boring a well on the island of Niihau. I am enabled to state to you the views of His Majesty's Government on the matter briefly, as follows. The Hawaiian Government agrees to pay one-half the expense for boring the proposed well, and further that the Government will not accede to any risk greater than five thousand dollars entire cost.
>
> I have the honor to remain
> Your Obedient Servant
> Jno E Bush
> Minister of Interior[84]

That the government was prepared to invest showed the importance it placed on improving the productivity of Niʻihau. The well, however, proved unsuccessful, much to the disappointment of Frank and the family.

Frank had served his time for Niihau Ranch well, and at 50 he was ready to begin his literary life.

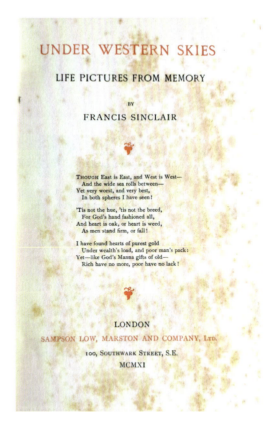

▶ Frank Sinclair's *Under Western Skies* was the fifth book he wrote after leaving the islands.
Steven Gentry

CHAPTER NINE

AUBREY ROBINSON TAKES THE REINS

Aubrey Robinson's 1883 return from his years abroad heralded great changes for the family's land arrangements. After his year at Boston University Law School in 1875, Aubrey must have spent time in Boston working for a law firm to obtain his law practicing certificate. He then departed on a major world journey which took him to Europe, the Middle East, India and Asia. Little is recorded of this period of his life; nor do we know how much of his time away was spent on investigations which might benefit the family ranching activities and how much was purely horizon-expanding. Given his enquiring mind, there would have been much interweaving of the two aspects.

As Aubrey plays such a large part in the story of Niʻihau, it is useful to step back in time for a moment to reflect on him as a person, as seen by Isabella Bird just before he departed for his Boston education and travels overseas. In 1873 Isabella wrote from Makaweli House to her sister, Henrietta in Scotland:

> [Mrs Robinson] has one son 6 feet high only 19 but with a mature mind and much culture. He has the most singular grace of manner and though not at all handsome he has a face you like to look upon. He is a delightful creature.[1]

This shows him as a most personable young man, just as he was about to embark on a journey which would fit him for a life in the family's adopted country.

▲ Aubrey Robinson (1853–1936), aged around 30, on his return from eight years at large in the world.
Robinson family, photographer James Williams, Honolulu

Gay & Robinson

In 1884 the two cousins, Aubrey Robinson and Francis Gay, together with their respective mothers, Helen Robinson and Jane Gay, and grandmother Eliza Sinclair, formed Gay & Robinson, a partnership, to foster their business interests and consolidate their owned and leased land.[2] Gay and Robinson, Inc. was incorporated in 1971. In 1991 Robinson Family Partners was formed as the land-holding entity, from which Gay and Robinson, Inc. leases land to operate its diverse enterprises.

On 11 July 1891 Eliza sold all her leased lands at Hanapēpē to Gay & Robinson by deed for a consideration of $1.[3] As the previous chapter indicated, on 3 March 1891 she gifted all her fee simple lands equally to her two daughters, Jane and Helen. Jane was free to do as she wished with her gift, but Helen's portion was essentially left in trust for Aubrey.

A third strand in this slightly tangled skein was that, for whatever reason, Francis Gay, one of the Gay & Robinson partners, on 2 February 1891, withdrew by deed from the Gay & Robinson partnership as far as Niʻihau was concerned.[4] Francis Gay remained in the partnership at this stage in all other respects. This deed implies that Francis had acquired an interest in Niʻihau via some arrangement made with the Gay & Robinson partnership which did not have to be recorded at the Bureau of Conveyances. The owners of Niʻihau after the deed was executed were Aubrey Robinson, Helen Robinson, Jane Gay and the Gay & Robinson partnership itself, which apparently took over Francis Gay's interests in the island.

All these ownership changes in 1891 were undoubtedly promoted by Eliza as she approached the end of her natural life. Her ambition had alway been to provide well for all her children and this she achieved. She had four surviving children in 1891:

- Francis (Frank) Sinclair, who received an income for life and a capital sum for his interest in Niʻihau
- Ann Knudsen, married to Valdemar Knudsen, who had been gifted land by her mother when she married
- Helen Robinson, separated from her husband for many years, with one child, Aubrey, married to Jane Gay's youngest child, Alice
- Jane Gay, widowed for a long time, with five children (George, Francis, Eliza, Charles and Alice)

▲ Francis Gay (1852–1928), around the time he and his cousin Aubrey Robinson founded Gay & Robinson in 1884.

ATL PA Coll-7027

Over time Aubrey Robinson became the sole owner of the island. In January 1902 he bought one fourth of his aunt Jane Gay's interests in Niʻihau for $25,000[5] and in January 1904 he bought her remaining interests for $50,000.[6] For both transactions Jane was to receive her share of the income from Niʻihau during her lifetime.

Thus the *Hawaiian Star* for 2 February 1904 pronounced:

> By the terms of this [second] deed [Aubrey] Robinson becomes the absolute owner of all of the island of Niihau and except for a life interest in the income, retained by Mrs. Gay, the owner of all her interests in the business of the firm of Gay and Robinson.[7]

Aubrey's mother Helen also had an interest in Niʻihau that was presumably passed on to Aubrey at her death in 1913, unless this had been transferred to him earlier without the need for it to be recorded at the Bureau of Conveyances.

In his personal life Aubrey had been moving forward too. On 8 June 1885 the following notice appeared in the *Pacific Commercial Advertiser*:

> ROBINSON/GAY — At Makaweli, Kauai, on the 3d instant, by the Rev. J. W. Smith, Aubrey Robinson Esq., of Makaweli, to Alice, youngest daughter of the late Captain Thomas Gay, of Fifeshire, Scotland.[8]

Alice was, of course, Aubrey's first cousin and they had been brought up in the same household together since Alice's birth on Niʻihau in 1865. Romance blossomed on Aubrey's return from overseas. Alice was only eight when he left, but an engaging young woman of 18 when he was reunited with the family after his years abroad. They had corresponded intermittently while he was away and one charming letter still exists, written to Alice on Niʻihau as a nine-year-old by Aubrey, at the ripe old age of 21, from his lodgings in Boston. It is dated 23 January 1875 and reads in part:

> King Kalakaua was over here in Boston not long ago but he soon left again, it was too cold for him but he said he was "lealea loa" [very pleased] to see the boys skating on the ice. But we both agreed that it was not such nice fun as "heenalu" [surfing].

Alice's thirteen-year-old brother Charles Gay was at school in Boston at the time, and Aubrey includes him in his story:

> Charlie has been trying it some [i.e. skating] but does not like it very much as he says the ice is not very elastic but very slippery so that his feet run away so quickly that his poor head comes down on the ice, which is not very comfortable.[9]

Aubrey used some Hawaiian words in the letter, which he knew Alice would understand. Alice's governess at the time was probably Marion Rowell Gay, George Gay's future wife (see previous chapter) who, like Aubrey, was bilingual.

Niihau Ranch

Aubrey arrived home from his world travels to a fully functioning ranch on Niʻihau overseen by his uncle Frank Sinclair, with his cousin George Gay and the latter's family living and working there. All able-bodied Niihauans were employed on ranching duties. Although numbers varied widely depending on the availability of water, when Aubrey returned there were at least 20,000 Merino sheep and upwards of 1000 head of Shorthorn cattle on the ranch.

One of the initiatives that Aubrey organized while overseas was to import Arabian horses to Niʻihau and Makaweli from Arabia and India. These were reputed to be the first of the breed brought to Hawaiʻi, and Aubrey felt they would be particularly suited to the Niʻihau ranching operation. This proved to be the case.[10]

Aubrey was determined to diversify the ecology of Niʻihau, to improve ranching opportunities and make the island more liveable. Thus as well as new varieties of grasses he imported exotic game birds, trees and honey bees.

Perhaps the most important of his imports was the kiawe tree or algaroba. The kiawe was a native of South America and reputedly was first brought to Hawaiʻi in 1828 by Father Alexis Bachelet, leader of the original Catholic mission. Since then it has been widely cultivated in the arid areas of the islands. Generally it is shallow-rooted but in drier areas it develops a long taproot. It can be invasive as it can reproduce by both suckering and seed dispersal. Although a coastal species it is not particularly salt-tolerant and can be defoliated by salt-laden winter

▲ Alice Gay Robinson (1865–1960) in her wedding gown, for her marriage to Aubrey Robinson on 8 June 1885.
Robinson family, photographer James Williams, Honolulu

▼ Cattle driven down for export from the island at the end of the 19th century.
Robinson family

▲ Descendants of Aubrey's Arabian horse imports, although mixed with other breeds, still roam the island today.

Honolulu Star Bulletin Archives; photographed at Puʻuwai in 1999 by Ken Sakamoto

◤ A typical kiawe forest.

Wikimedia Commons; photo by Forest and Kim Starr

▼ 1915 Niʻihau Beef advertisement.

The Garden Island Archives

storms. Surprisingly, perhaps, this has not been a problem on Niʻihau, where in many areas the trees now shade out other plant species as well as depriving them of moisture. The flowers produce valuable nectar for honey production and the dense heartwood makes a superior charcoal. Both the seedpods and the leaves make excellent stock fodder.

Charles Judd, director of forestry for the islands, visited Niʻihau in 1897 and again in 1929, after which visit he enthused about the kiawe:

> … I was deeply impressed with the thrift of the tree growth not only on the rolling coastal plain but also on the cliffs where the kiawe trees have been fostered and are growing up abundantly in the rank and verdant pili grass. This natural regeneration has been augmented with good results by the artificial establishment of trees on the barren, eroded sections of the high portions of Niihau … A tree nursery is maintained at the Kiekie homestead where about 60,000 trees are raised annually. These are grown in bamboo joints and during the rainy season are carried to the highlands where they are set out at the rate of 60 plants per man per day.[11]

Judd's second visit would have been after Aubrey's retirement from active ranching on Niʻihau, but the tree planting was undoubtedly his initiative to provide shade, fodder, and to attempt to increase moisture condensation on the higher ground, as George Munro had done on Lānaʻi.[12] Charles Forbes in his 1913 paper 'An Enumeration of Niihau Plants' noted that kiawe's cousin species, long-thorned kiawe (*Prosopis juliflora*) was present, but this may have been a misidentification, as it is clear that Aubrey began plantings much earlier than this 1912 visit.[13]

Aubrey corresponded with a wide variety of people and experimented with many different species of tropical fruit trees including avocado, mangosteen, sapote, star apple and mango.

In 1885 the first major contingent of Japanese contract laborers arrived in Honolulu on the *City of Tokio*. Francis Gay contracted a young man, Asahina Umekichi, for a three-year term and for his first three months he worked as a farmhand at Makaweli. As soon as he was sufficiently fluent in Hawaiian he was transferred to Niʻihau, as a handyman and houseboy for George Gay at The House. Aubrey took advantage of his background and arranged for him to source and experimentally plant green tea both at Makaweli and on Niʻihau. Unfortunately the plants on Niʻihau did not survive due to lack of water and insufficient nutrients. Asahina though, hard worker that he was, began a tradition of Japanese employees living and working for the family on the island.[14]

Pests were a problem, and none more so than the goats that roamed freely, competing with the sheep for feed and denuding the landscape. The King had not been successful in totally reaping his bounty before the new owners took possession (see the previous chapter). Charles Judd, on his visit in 1897, took part in a goat hunt:

> The task of exterminating them was not easy and I saw the work in 1897 when it was at its height. During the one week of daily drives in which I participated about 700 goats were captured. We had taken our rifles with us to shoot stragglers and at the first report of our guns the timid Hawaiian goat drivers, evidently unused to firearms, would hide behind rocks so that we could not know where they were and for the sake of safety had to desist from further shooting.[15]

The goats were particularly fecund and goats were still being culled out in 1910 as Aubrey's son, Sinclair writes from Harvard in March:

> I think that contract you made with Kualu ma to kill off the goats on Niihau was advisable, as the goats do a lot of damage, but I doubt if they will kill them all off. If we had been home we would have let the cash go and taken the contract for cartridges, horses and food supplied! But possibly it would be dangerous to guarantee us cartridges — I do not mean dangerous for the goats. However I have improved somewhat this winter in target practice …[16]

Sinclair obviously didn't have much faith in his own marksmanship. The goats were apparently exterminated not too long after this.

Flies and fly strike were also on occasions major problems. Francis Sinclair wrote to his sister Jane in 1898 while on holiday in Sweden: 'I was exceedingly sorry to learn by your last letter that another plague has come to Niihau in the shape of another fly, worse if possible than the old green fly in that it attacks the cattle as well as the sheep.'[17]

Not only animal pests had to be dealt with, but plant pests as well. Aubrey's son Selwyn writes from Niʻihau to Aubrey at Makaweli in 1918:

> Monday I took half of the men & went for kikania … Found conditions about usual except for Kapoka having quite a lot of kikania. Rennie [Niʻihau superintendent] went with the other half of the gang & the luna [foreman] to Awaawalua & reports few kikania … However the trip was just in time as the seed had not yet fallen although it was ripe in most places.[18]

Kīkānia is the Hawaiian name for *Datura stramonium*, an accidentally introduced shrub of the Solanum (nightshade) family which is highly poisonous to humans and stock. Hence the sweep across the island. Its seeds also have burrs that adhere to sheep's wool. Botanist Harold St John did not find it in his 1949 stay and it appears that even by the time of Judd's visit in 1929 it, along with many other weeds, had been successfully eliminated. Judd writes:

▲ Sinclair Robinson (1886–1964), the eldest of Aubrey and Alice's children, at Harvard. After graduating, he and his brother Aylmer worked for the Oahu Sugar Company. He then became assistant manager, and six months later, manager of the Gay & Robinson sugar plantation at Makaweli, where he remained throughout his career and came to be regarded as the doyen of the Hawaiian sugar industry. Sinclair married Ethel Glade in 1917 and they had four children.
Robinson family

▲ Kīkānia, known as jimson weed or thorn apple, is a poisonous annual of the nightshade family. All parts of the young plant shown here are dangerous — leaves, flowers and the thorny seed pods.
TeunSpaans / Wikimedia Commons

◂ The location of the island's reservoir and the pipeline to Kiʻekiʻe, shown in an extract from the USGS 1929 1:25000 map of Niʻihau, reproduced on the rear endpapers of this book. Contours are at 50-foot intervals. The reservoir is at 400-feet altitude and the pipeline four miles long. The reservoir had a major upgrade in 1909–10.
Wikimedia Commons

Not one undesirable weed was to be seen anywhere and it was always my understanding that the Robinson family used to lease the adjacent government island of Lehua for the sole purpose of eradicating the lantana upon it to prevent its seed from being carried by birds to Niihau.[19]

St John, in his flora, reported finding *Lantana camara* on the island, but commented that it was rare and removed whenever found.[20]

Overarching all these pest problems was the need for water, and water from a reliable source. Francis Sinclair's 1883 attempts to find an artesian supply had drawn a blank (see Chapter Eight). A second attempt at finding groundwater was undertaken by Aubrey in 1897–99, according to letters written to Aubrey by George Gay[21] and Frank Sinclair.[22] The results must have again been negative as no more has been heard of the bore results. Stearns in his 1947 survey of water resources on Niʻihau lists two bores 'drilled about 1905.'[23] These are probably the bores mentioned above. Aside from bores, many seeps and springs have been developed into waterholes for stock over the years by the family. Salinity has always been a problem due to salt spray and seepage, but most wells have been suitable for stock.

Rainwater storage has been the other avenue pursued and major efforts were made by Aubrey, particularly in relation to the pond constructed in Reservoir Cone, which was probably originally built during Francis Sinclair's time. The reservoir is in the ʻĀpana Valley, almost due west of Puʻuwai at an altitude of four hundred feet. The reservoir always suffered severely from leakage. In 1909 Aubrey hired Japanese contractors and a geological expert, a Mr Ewart, to plug the leaks (see page 235). This was apparently successful.

The major output of the ranch was unscoured merino wool, but getting it to the market was fraught with difficulties. It was transported in bales from Nonopapa by whaleboat to a steamer standing offshore — a weather-dependent operation. The wool eventually reached the European or American market where it fetched the prevailing price, good or bad. Aside from the transport challenges, an 1886 letter from the Hawaiian Legation in London gives a tactful picture of some of the trials of wool growing on Niʻihau:

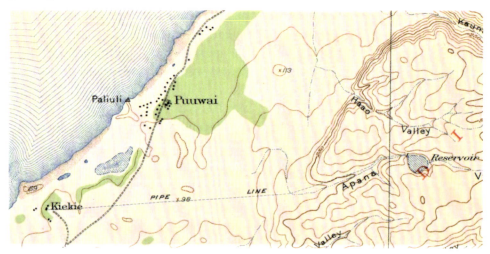

◀ Loading wool at Nonopapa.
Bishop Museum

▼ The wool bale stencil which Aubrey, and presumably Aylmer, used to identify wool from the island.
Steven Gentry

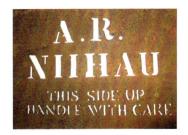

Apart from the course of the market — which nobody can control — the mistake which I made was to estimate your wool as being in all respects on a level with the Spencer wool on Hawaii or even with a large share of Gibsons wool on Lanai with which wools I had dealt the previous years and which formed the basis of my calculations.

I hope you will not think I am writing in a spirit of reproach or fault finding when I say that your wool is not in all respects on a level with those abovenamed — it is no doubt equal in staple and quality but it contains much more dirt and burr than either of the others and under normal conditions of the market it will bring within a penny to three halfpence per lb as much — which under the unfortunate conditions which have prevailed during the past half year it brought still less — in comparison, because you will readily understand that when a staple is cheap buyers give clear preference to the better and more easily workable qualities and this makes it relatively much worse for inferior sorts — I was quite aghast on two occasions to find that there was absolutely no bidding at all for it when it was put up and but for the fortunate spurt which took place later on — the result would have been very disastrous ...[24]

Then there were the physical risks involved, occasionally resulting in the loss of valuable cargo. Eric Knudsen in his delightful book, *Teller of Hawaiian Tales*, relates the story of one such loss, summarized as follows.[25]

The captain of the *Thunderer*, having loaded wool at Niʻihau, sailed the schooner across the channel to Waimea where he unwisely gave his crew permission to go ashore. Sailors being what they are, it was some days before he could induce them all to return aboard. By this time the weather had changed, with gusty winds blowing directly on shore preventing departure. Swells pushed the vessel inexorably towards the rocks that guard Waimea anchorage. As the schooner crashed on the reef the crew leaped overboard and swam to shore, leaving the captain to fend for himself. He stayed with the *Thunderer*, tying himself to the mast as the vessel slowly disintegrated.

All this was seen from the shore and a crowd gathered. One of the watchers, an eighteen-year-old girl named Mele asked one of the crew why the captain had stayed and was told that he could not swim. As none of the crew made any attempt to help the elderly captain, Mele stripped off her clothes, dived into the surf and swam strongly towards the wreck. Needless to say when she reached the vessel she found the captain terrified, but with sure hands she untied him and convinced him to trust her to get him safely to shore. After coaxing him into the water she pulled him steadily through the crashing surf towards the beach with her one free arm. With tearful gratitude, when they reached the beach the captain put his hand in his pocket where he found a small coin which he handed her. This Mele refused, feeling his need was greater than hers, and replied that what she did was only fun! Putting on her clothes she quietly disappeared into the crowd.

The source for Knudsen's story took some time to find. There are no press reports in the English language regarding a vessel named *Thunderer* trading in the islands and getting into trouble. Knudsen had obviously changed the vessel's name for reasons of anonymity. Research finally concluded that it must have been the schooner *Nettie Merrill*, a long-time visitor to Niʻihau. The *Hawaiian Gazette* report on the incident is included as an illustration at left. Press reports at the time differed somewhat in their telling of the story and Eric Knudsen has taken some liberties with it too.

Aside from wool, the ranch also traded cattle and sheep for the meat market in Honolulu and Līhuʻe, and in times of drought in particular, resorted to rendering stock down for tallow, and the sale of salted hides and skins.

▲ The *Hawaiian Gazette* report for 14 February 1888 on the wrecking of the schooner *Nettie Merrill* on Waimea beach. The rescue of Captain Crane was courageously effected by a young Niihauan woman.

▶ Cattle transport off the island to the waiting steamer and thence to market was not easy. Each whaleboat hauled out two cattle, one on each side, tied to the gunwale with their heads out of the water. The whaleboat was then rowed out to the ship where each cattle beast was craned aboard.
Robinson family

▶ Getting sheep to market was only slightly simpler than cattle …
Kauaʻi Historical Society

The Hawaiian Sugar Company

In an interview with the *Daily Bulletin* on 9 November 1889 Colonel George Macfarlane (part of King Kalākaua's military) announced the formation of the Hawaiian Sugar Company, with plans to grow sugar cane on almost 8000 acres of land at Makaweli, the bulk of which was to be leased from the Gay & Robinson partnership for 50 years.[26] A mill was to be built at Makaweli and water for irrigation was to be drawn from the Hanapēpē, Makaweli and Kōʻula rivers, all within the Makaweli ahupuaʻa. The venture was to be financed by a $2 million dollar share issue with investors drawn from both England and Hawaiʻi.

▲ Makaweli Mill, c.1920.
Robinson family

The driving force behind this venture was (William) Renny Watson of the sugar equipment manufacturing firm Mirrlees Watson Co. He was described as 'a multi-faceted mechanical engineer and public-spirited citizen, whose striking and energetic personality were of a type not uncommon in Victorian Glasgow's civic life.'[27]

Sugar cane was already widely grown on Kauaʻi and the possibility was on Aubrey's mind while he was overseas. Given his Scottish roots, he probably sought out Renny Watson in Glasgow. While there was little possibility of cane growing on Niʻihau, the Makaweli ahupuaʻa, with its gently undulating, fertile lower slopes offered considerable scope for sugar.

William Renny Watson was immediately struck by the prospect when he visited the islands, as was Henry P Baldwin, a founder of the entrepreneurial company Alexander & Baldwin. After quite some time spent in negotiations, an arrangement was struck with the Gay & Robinson partnership for the lease of nearly 7000 acres of land, while the partnership itself was to grow cane on a further 1000 acres to be processed at the mill. Gay & Robinson also invested in the new company, as did Renny Watson, Henry Baldwin and several other British and Hawaiian investors. Gay & Robinson were not represented on the eight-man board. Mirrlees Watson would build the mill and had a representative on the board, while Henry Baldwin became president and George Macfarlane vice president.

The plantation and mill were major undertakings and getting them off the ground absorbed an enormous amount of both Aubrey's and Francis Gay's energy and time. Once agreed, it all happened relatively quickly. Water was vital, and the Hanapēpē Ditch was completed in April 1891, allowing plantings to begin. The main thirteen-mile long ʻOlokele Ditch was finished in 1904. These ditches were major engineering achievements.[28] By 1914, over 30,000 tons of sugar were being produced annually.

By the mid-1890s there were thus three major components to the family's operations: ranching on Niʻihau, ranching on the Makaweli uplands and sugar production on the Makaweli lowlands.

Diversification trials: sisal and cotton

Headlines such as that in the *Pacific Commercial Advertiser* for 25 January 1903, 'Sisal One of Coming Island Industries,' showed the interest in sisal at this time. Sisal fiber was in growing demand worldwide and was already being produced on 600 acres at 'Ewa on O'ahu. A plantation was also about to be started on Kaua'i.

A large portion of the island of Lāna'i had recently been bought by the Robinson family and conditions there seemed similar to those on Ni'ihau. There appeared an opportunity to diversify from stock raising on both islands.

Sisal is one of the strongest natural fibers, and the Hawaii Agricultural Experiment Station had issued a monograph in 1903 on growing it in the islands.[29] The plant prefers poorer soils than sugar cane, needs less water, and produces a crop of fibrous leaves continuously for about ten years after a three-year juvenile period. Processing is relatively simple, requiring machinery to strip the fiber from the leaves (decortication), followed by air drying, baling and shipping to market for further processing into cordage and twine.

▲ A sisal plant (*Agave sisalana*) growing in a plantation. The leaf fiber is used principally for cordage because of its strength and durability, and competes well with other natural and synthetic fibers in many industries. It does not require much water and hence the interest in trialing it on Ni'ihau and Lāna'i.
Planting Man

Aubrey, Francis Gay, and Charles Gay on Lāna'i began investigating growing sisal on Ni'ihau and Lāna'i, and discussions were held with the O'ahu Sisal Company as early as 1907 to see if some arrangement could be entered into regarding planting sisal on Lāna'i in particular.[30] Negotiations ultimately proved unsuccessful, despite company officials visiting Lāna'i and agreeing the prospects looked good. The family continued investigations on their own. At the time Aubrey's sons Sinclair and Aylmer were at Harvard and volunteered to go south over Easter 1910 to investigate sisal plantations and processing in Florida. This never happened due to time constraints, but they did separately offer to visit manufacturers of decortication machinery in New York.[31] Test plantings of sisal took place on both Ni'ihau and Lāna'i in 1909, but the project did not proceed any further after Charles Gay, under financial pressure, had to sell the bulk of his landholdings on Lāna'i that same year.[32]

Aylmer and Sinclair had also begun making arrangements to visit Sea Island cotton plantations in the south, along with their sisal endeavors, before their trip was aborted. Sea island cotton was judged to be the most suitable species for the coastal situations found in the islands. Plantings were trialed on Ni'ihau over this period but the results were not encouraging and the venture was abandoned.

The passing of the matriarch

Eliza and her husband Francis Sinclair senior emigrated from Scotland to New Zealand as a God-fearing couple inspired by Edward Gibbon Wakefield's colonizing rhetoric 'Possess yourselves of the Soil & you are secure.' When, much later, land in New Zealand became too constrained for her large and growing family, Eliza took it on herself to seek new pastures, and again the family had ventured forth, this time finding resolution on Ni'ihau and Kaua'i.

▲ Sea Island cotton (*Gossypium barbadense*) has long and silky fibers.
Forest & Kim Starr, Wikimedia Commons

But the years were moving on and despite her robust health Makaweli House became ever more her refuge among her children and grandchildren, interrupted only by the family's legendary annual summer excursions to The House on Niʻihau. She was still riding horseback well into her eighties, and her mind had not dimmed with the years.

Finally, aged 93, she died on 16 October 1892 in her own fashion, after a short illness, as described in the *Pacific Commercial Advertiser*:

> A few weeks since she had an attack of grip [influenza] from which she recovered, but it left her so weak and helpless that she felt it was of no use to make any effort to recover and prolong life in such a helpless condition. Then calling her grand-children and friends to her bedside, she bade an affectionate farewell to each, closed her eyes and expired …[33]

Eliza is described in the same obituary as 'a most remarkable woman of Scotch birth, and possessed of an active business mind, which enabled her to be the ruling spirit and manager of her large property.'

Her great-grandson, Lawrence Kainoahou Gay, wrote much later of her relations with the local people:

> She was very kind and helpful to the Hawaiians. She spent many hours nursing the sick and providing them with food and other necessities. The Hawaiians loved and respected her. She had always told her family that she wanted Niʻihau to be kept in the true Hawaiian way of life.[34]

Edward Stepien, in his 1988 master's thesis on the history of Niʻihau, praised her for similar reasons:

> Eliza did all in her power to maintain the 'Hawaiian flavor' of Niʻihau, even in the face of the modernization occurring on other islands. … It was her desire to protect those who chose Niʻihau as their home from the horrors the haole brought to the other islands … While she did not see the Niʻihau Ranch become a financial success, she did lay the foundation for the attitude of her descendants: love Niʻihau and its people: protect them![35]

▲ Eliza McHutcheson Sinclair (1800–92); a portrait from the time she was making arrangements to divest herself of her assets, c.1890. Robinson family

In her will Eliza states that she had already provided all her children with "freehold estates" and gives now "all the property of whatsoever nature I may die possessed in equal shares to my two daughters Jane R. Gay and Helen McH. Robinson, their heirs and assigns, with the exception of the one third of my yearly income from Niihau which I have given to my son Francis Sinclair to be enjoyed by him during his life, and $5000 to my daughter Annie McH. Knudsen."[36]

Eliza must have felt she had achieved all that she and her husband set out to do on that damp and drizzly day in August 1840 when the *Blenheim* was towed down the Clyde to the Irish Sea on its way to New Zealand. She had certainly 'secured the soil' and had lived to see the land she had acquired developed into productive units by her growing family. She always seemed to have a deep mystical affection for Niʻihau, as did (and still do) the other members of the family. Niʻihau was the first piece of land she bought in the islands, and it was so separate and striking, particularly as viewed from Makaweli House which she loved so much.

Leprosy

The consensus is that leprosy probably arrived in the islands in the early 1830s. Known originally as maʻi-Pākē (Chinese sickness) by the Hawaiians, the disease spread throughout all the monarchy, and by the early 1860s it became serious enough for its control to be debated in the legislature. There was no cure at the time, and it was considered the disease could only be controlled by isolation of affected individuals from the healthy population. Niʻihau was destined to play a small part in one of the more dramatic incidents that occurred as a result of this policy.

In 1865 legislation was passed to establish a facility for the isolation of leprous persons capable of spreading the disease. Every person who knew someone with leprosy symptoms was to report them to the health authorities. After some false starts the isolation settlement decided upon was Kalaupapa on Molokaʻi, and the first patients arrived in 1866.

The pain and distress caused to families torn asunder by this decision was immense. For many it was seen as a death sentence, which in a sense it was, as there was no going back to communal Hawaiian society. The debate over forced incarceration did not diminish over the years.

On Niʻihau those suffering from leprosy had for some years chosen voluntarily to live separately at the southwestern corner of the island.[37] The remains of this leper colony were still visible when David Larsen visited Niʻihau in 1942: 'One place, called Pahau, contained the remnants of an old Hawaiian village — a broken down temple or church and lots of small stone platforms indicating houses. I was later told that this was once a leper settlement.'[38]

As large employers on Niʻihau and Kauaʻi, Gay and Robinson inevitably had employees whose families had the disease. Emotions ran high for decades, as exemplified in a letter from Francis Gay to his mother Jane in 1887 — more than 20 years after the legislation was passed. The letter reads in part: 'Tell Charles [Frank's younger brother] to be sure and not give the lepers any encouragement in running away as it will be all told against us.'[39] Instead, they should go to Molokai, 'the only alternative for them,' he wrote.

Francis Gay had just been elected to the House of Representatives and was writing from Honolulu. He would have had some foreknowledge of a governmental tightening of restrictions on recalcitrants.

Although not a Niihauan, Koʻolau, the central character in the most regrettable incident that took place during this emotional period had strong links with the island, having worked for Gay and Robinson both on Niʻihau and at Makaweli. The 'Battle of Kalalau' (see panel) and its aftermath resulted in six deaths in all.

No such tragic tale is told regarding the leprosy sufferers on Niʻihau, who apparently responded to Charles Gay's gentle urging, but whose self-segregation at Kawaihoa evidently inspired Koʻolau and his family, along with others, to seek isolation in the remote Kalalau valley.

▲ Charles Gay (1862–1937), the youngest son of Thomas and Jane Gay, was a toddler when the family embarked on the *Bessie*. He grew up on Niʻihau and at Makaweli. In 1874 he traveled to the east coast as a teenager with his Aunt Helen and his brothers to install Aubrey at Boston University, and on his return attended Punahou School for two years (1875–76). He later worked for Gay & Robinson both on Niʻihau and at Makaweli before he and the family bought the island of Lānaʻi in 1902. Charles and his family remained on Lānaʻi until 1926 when he retired and they went to live in Honolulu.

Robinson family

▲ Koʻolau (right) with his wife, Piʻilani and son, Kaleimanu, together with Koʻolau's mother, before they left for the Kalalau valley.
Hawaiian Historical Society

◄ Soldiers of Company A of the National Guard of Hawaiʻi camped in the Kalalau Valley during their deployment to search out Koʻolau and his family.
Hawaiian State Archives

Koʻolau and the 'Battle of Kalalau'
Kaluaikoʻolau, known as Koʻolau (1862–97), was born in Kekaha, attended George Rowell's school in Waimea and became a paniolo (cowboy), and later a luna (foreman) for both Francis Sinclair and Valdemar Knudsen. He was a man of great principle and, when he developed leprosy in 1892, refused to be separated from his family and exiled to Molokaʻi. They vanished to the remote Kalalau Valley on Kauaʻi and thus began the 'Battle of Kalalau.' A police posse led by Sheriff Louis Stolz pursued the family and Koʻolau shot Stolz dead, whereupon a platoon of the National Guard (complete with a howitzer) was mobilised to chase them down. This expedition was embarrassingly unsuccessful, with three National Guardsmen being killed and a further two injured in falls. The army was withdrawn and no further attempts were made to capture Koʻolau. Kaleimanu subsequently died of leprosy in his mother's arms, followed by Koʻolau himself some time later.

Aubrey's cousins, the Gay family

From the formation of Gay & Robinson until World War 1 and beyond, Francis Gay and Aubrey Robinson jointly managed the family business, with Aubrey having a more hands-on role on Niʻihau and Kauaʻi, and Francis more involved in Honolulu with the family's agents, Henry Waterhouse Trust Co., and attending to political matters.

All of Aubrey's five Gay cousins, Jane's children (George, Francis, Eliza, Charles and Alice), were involved one way or another with Niʻihau and developed great affection for the island.

On 18 April 1896 the *Hawaiian Star* reported an unusually restrained event:

> Francis Gay of Kauai and Miss Lillie Hart, daughter of Judge C. F. Hart were quietly married at the Waikiki residence of the bride's father Friday afternoon. Rev. Alex. Mackintosh officiated. Only about a dozen immediate friends were present. After the ceremony the bridal party drove to the steamer Ke Au Hou, upon which the happy couple departed for their future home on the Garden Island.[40]

At the time of their marriage Francis was 44 and Lillie 25. In 1897 the couple's only child, Francis Ernest (known as Ernest) was born. Throughout their married life their time was divided between Makaweli and Honolulu. When on Kauaʻi they lived at Makaweli in Kekepua, the family house, and in Honolulu at Young's Hotel or, earlier, with Lillie's parents. Their Honolulu living arrangements were not entirely satisfactory and early in the new century they bought a large property of 400 acres in the Kalihi valley, which they named Wailele (Waterfall). This home generally became the Honolulu base for visiting family members.

The interests of their son Ernest lay elsewhere and he took no direct role in the family business, although he did spend some holidays on Niʻihau.[41]

▲ Francis Gay (1852–1928) and Lillie Hart Gay Torrey (1871–1956). Lillie was a renowned beauty and a charismatic hostess. The daughter of Englishman Judge Charles Hart and Hawaiian Rebecca Kahoowakalani Kahalaiʻa, of the Kahekili family from Maui, she was privately tutored in Oakland and spoke with a decidedly British accent. Her marriage to Francis produced her only son, Ernest, who at age 13 was sent to prep school in New York. He was so homesick that Lillie followed him there, and, being a painter herself, met George Burroughs Torrey, well known as the 'painter of presidents'. The couple eventually moved back to Lillie's roots in Hawaiʻi, where Torrey died in 1942. Lillie had married him in 1924, well after her separation from Francis. Lillie's image is a detail from a rare photo of a full-length portrait by Torrey, which it is said, because of its risqué nature, was the final straw in the breakdown of her marriage to Francis Gay. The painting itself was destroyed in a fire.
Robinson family; Sanna Deutsch, colorised

Aubrey's eldest Gay cousin, George, lived on Niʻihau and managed the island day-to-day for many years. In the late 1890s he and his family moved to southern California and took up orange farming, while retaining close links with the family and relying on his mother Jane and uncle Aubrey for advice (and monetary assistance on occasions).

Nine years younger than Aubrey, and three years older than Aubrey's wife Alice, cousin Charles Gay also worked on the family estates at Makaweli and on Niʻihau. For some time he managed the boat runs between the two islands, and always had a love of the sea. He had bigger ideas, however, and in 1902, with his mother Jane's help, he bought at auction most of the land on the island of Lānaʻi. Negotiations for the remainder of the island, with Crown land, government land and several kuleana involved, proved intractable and expensive, while ranching income from the dry, denuded island was miserable. He built a large house there, but in the end financing discussions collapsed and in 1910 he had to sell much of the land he had bought.[42] The purchase and subsequent sale proved a great trial for the whole family, as their correspondence shows. Charles retained 600 acres and lived on Lānaʻi until 1926 when he moved back to Waimea on Kauaʻi.

While cousin Eliza (Aunt Lila) played no direct part in the ranching activities on Niʻihau, she remained a huge support for the family as a whole in many ways. In 1901 she married Mendell Welcker, a West Coast man, and went to live in Berkeley. Mendell died suddenly in June 1904 less than three years into their marriage, but the family rallied around and Lila stayed on in the large establishment (The Cedars) she owned in Berkeley. It became a West Coast home away from home for the family throughout the succeeding generation.

All of Aubrey and Alice's four sons (Sinclair, Aylmer, Selwyn and Lester) had a direct part to play in the story of Niʻihau and more will be told of their involvement in the following chapters. None of the children of Aubrey's Gay cousins (George had six and Charles twelve) became involved in the family business.

A family Christmas on Niʻihau

Robinson family holidays on Niʻihau were always regarded as something special, and Christmas 1909 was no exception. This particular Christmas was recorded in detail in a series of letters from Alice Robinson on Niʻihau to her mother, Jane Gay, who was in Boston with Helen Robinson (Aunt Helen) and Eliza Welcker (Aunt Lila), together with Alice's three older children, who were being educated there. Only Eleanor (11) and Lester (8) were on Niʻihau with Alice and Aubrey (see the family tree, rear endpapers).

Any visit to Niʻihau was a time for both work and play. Alice's letters were written or added to almost daily, beginning with the voyage over and particularly the landing — always a nervous time for all. Alice writes from Kiʻi on 20 December 1909:

> My Dear Mamma
>
> Here we are at the old shed again [it must have been more than just a shed; it was evidently very liveable] … Since arriving on Niihau we have just been resting here at Kii, and I really have been quite glad of the rest. … So Saturday and Sunday we had a fine rest & today I have been busy all day putting up Christmas cards & calendars for Kauai and Honolulu friends & writing a lot of letters as well. Aubrey went out for a ride this afternoon with the children after doing a lot of writing too. Eleanor & Lester enjoyed immensely being on horseback again & came back in great glee. Aubrey says that the stock is in poor condition up here, but there is some grass now … We expect to remain here till Thursday or Friday to get the mail as the boat returns again on Thursday and we are hoping to get letters from you all … How I wish dear Mamma you were all here with us. We miss each one of you awfully much. I think we have missed you all even more this time than ever before & that was quite enough …[43]

Aubrey asked the boat captain, on the latter's return to Kauaʻi, to ensure a cablegram was sent to the family in Boston informing them of their safe arrival on Niʻihau. This was standard practice when anyone visited the island.

The feelings of the rest of the family in Boston are encapsulated in a letter from Aylmer at Harvard to his mother, Alice, on Niʻihau written on 23 December:

> … I have been awfully homesick and would so like to be on Niihau with you. We got your cable-wireless to Grandma and thought that it would be perfect if we could spend Christmas together on Niihau.[44]

On 27 December, Alice reports on a cheerful Christmas:

> My Dear Mamma
>
> Since writing to you last we have had the pleasure of receiving dear letters from you all and also of getting Aunt Helen's cablegram in answer to ours saying we had arrived safely on Niihau, & it was good to hear you were all well, & everything going nicely with you. The boat came back from Kauai last Thursday with a large foreign mail, & lots of nice letters from you and the others, & then there were heaps of Christmas packages, which we put aside until Christmas morning, when the children had the pleasure of handing them around to us & then we all opened them up & there were many exclamations of delight as the parcels were opened. … The children got a lot of pretty things & had a happy Christmas tho' we missed you all dreadfully & wished we could all have been together here …

She adds more about Christmas, both for the family and the Niihauans:

> Well to return to our Christmas day — at one o'clock we had our Christmas dinner & the children got me to help them decorate the table with Bon Bon Crackers and little wild flowers etc. & with a nice cake Ichinose [their Japanese servant] had made for us, the table put on quite a festive air & their papa [Aubrey] was duly surprised when we went in to dinner which of course pleased the children very much. Most of our natives went down to Puuwai that day to a feast Aubrey gave the natives for Christmas. We got over a lot of poi by last boat & gave them a pipi [cattle beast], & Maria Hookano's wife said they had a fine time & had service at night in the church. It rained hard that day a regular kona

▲ Elizabeth Gay Welcker (Aunt Lila) (1859–1947) opened her home in Berkeley for the Hawaiʻi family. Sinclair and Aylmer lived there for the summer after completing Harvard and before they went to work for Oʻahu Sugar Company. While there they attended a trade school in San Francisco. Aylmer's project was to survey Aunt Lila's property, The Cedars.
ATL PA Coll-7027

storm but the natives made a lanai [verandah] near the church and covered it with tenting & so did not get wet. This has been quite a good kona storm and will do a lot of good they say there is water now in both of the lakes, tho' I hardly think there was heavy enough rain that lasted long enough to make much difference in filling up the reservoir, but we will likely have more for the weather is far from settled yet. All today it has blown quite a hurricane and the breakers rolling in to Kii and also breaking away out at sea are grand to watch. Now the wind is veering round to the south, so we may have rain again. …

The kona storm continued, bringing much needed water, but only indoor activities for the children:

> 28th Tuesday
>
> I wrote so far yesterday and will now add another word tho' there is no sign yet of the boat being able to get off for the kona is still on in full force. All today it has been pouring, and when it lifts a little we can see dozens of waterfalls pouring over the cliffs and the sea is all red from the mud washed out by the freshets. The natives say the reservoir is full, & it surely must be with all this heavy rain. All the lakes are full now and the pastures will be all right for months now — & it is likely with such a good commencement to the winter that we will have more rain later on …
>
> Thursday 30th
>
> The storm seems to be over at last & so I must finish up all my letters today for if it is good weather tomorrow the boat will go to Kauai & of course they like to get away in the early morning. This has been a fine rain & now the sun is out again & altho' the wind has not yet changed to the north still it looks as if the rain were over for the present & if so we will go down to Kiekie tomorrow. We have been much longer up here than we intended but of course this storm kept us here & as we all enjoy Kii we did not mind it & Aubrey has been busy with men planting sisal & cotton seed, whenever the rain kept off long enough for them to go and plant.
>
> How the boys [Sinclair, Aylmer, & Selwyn] would have enjoyed being here in this storm, but not more than we would have enjoyed having you all with us …

To The House at Kiʻekiʻe at last:

> January 1st 1910
>
> A Happy New Year dear Mamma. The boat [to Kauai] could not go yesterday on account of head wind, so I have a chance to add a few more words and to send you my best wishes … We came down to the House yesterday & found everything all right here the trees have grown up around the place and make it look quite pretty. The storm is now over & the wind seems calming down so I hope the boat will go on Monday …⁴⁵

▲ Aubrey, Alice, Eleanor and Lester — the family group that spent the Christmas and New Year holiday on Niʻihau in 1909–10. Eleanor was nearly eleven and Lester eight. This photo was taken at Kapalawai around this time.
Robinson family

▲ The 'old shed', at Kiʻi where the Robinson family, weatherbound, spent Christmas in 1909.
Kauaʻi Museum, colorised

Two and a half weeks later, on 18 January, Alice wrote again:

> My dear Mamma
>
> Today the boat arrived back from Kauai & brought a large mail with heaps of fine letters from you all ... We are having a nice time on Niihau — the children and I go quite often sea bathing at Nonopapa & sometimes out riding with Aubrey. He of course has been very busy, since coming over, trying to get things into proper shape. They are all so slow over here that everything falls behind. There is a gang of Japanese over working at the large reservoir & Mr Ewart is coming over in the boat on Saturday to lay out the work ... We plan to go up this week to Kii for a few days and be there to meet Mr Ewart when he arrives. We went down to Kawaihoa on Thursday of last week & spent a night there. It was blowing so hard though & too much surf so we did not get any good fishing. The boat was to have gone to Kauai last Friday but it was too stormy, and they did not get off till Saturday so that was why we only got back today, or rather last night late to Kii & they are going again on Thursday to bring Mr Ewart. We suggested for him to get the Japanese launch to bring him over. It is quite a good sized gasoline launch and goes about as fast as the steamer, but he says he would just as soon come by the boat & evidently does not mind a sea trip. Well we used not to think much of it ourselves & now this is a larger boat than we had before, the Captain said it just took them four hours crossing over this time as it was blowing a stiff breeze. We have gone to church every Sunday since coming down from Kii, & Kaomea has always preached till last Sunday when Kanahele took his place as Kaomea is quite sick, he has caught a cold. I hope he will recover soon for he is a good man. ... All the natives have enquired affectionately after you all & send aloha. We expect the steamer over next week to take us back to Kauai on Friday — so our stay over here will soon be pau [finished] ...

▼ Enjoying the ocean on Niʻihau, early 20th century.

▲ Fishing from the rocks: this photo from c.1909 shows Aubrey and Alice, probably John Rennie their Scottish overseer, and a Niihauan woman.
Robinson family

▼ The House at Kiʻekiʻe c.1910, then over 30 years old, showing mature trees and the front façade.
Robinson family, colorised

In 1909/10 when these letters were written Aubrey had owned and managed Niʻihau for over 25 years, and holidays there had become a family tradition. Letters were a vital means of communication when family members were

◀ A family picnic on Niʻihau in the early 1900s. Standing far left is Helen Robinson, while Aubrey can be seen seated on the ground on the right. Seated to the right of center is John Rennie, ranch manager (with mustache).
Robinson family

away from their Makaweli hub and much time and energy was devoted to writing and sharing them. There is a sense of excitement in Alice's letters when mail arrived from Boston. While telephones were used between the houses on Kauaʻi from about this time, the resident superintendent on Niʻihau, John Rennie, could only receive instructions from Aubrey either in person or by mail on the infrequent boat visits. Francis's wife Lillie owned an auto in Honolulu from 1907 and according to Francis was driving herself all over Oʻahu from then on. The family were on the island for over a month in all.

Emalia Licayan's account of a Niihauan community Christmas

In the last month of the year there is a big feast at the chapel on Niʻihau for the Christmas Feast. At night there are scripture readings with the children and the place is lit with kerosene lanterns. We all contribute money. You give ten percent of your earnings. It's in the Book of Malachi in the Bible.

Close to December, the pastor announces "Attention family!" When Niʻihau people hear that they know that it means it's the Sunday for reporting the contributions made to the church. That money is used for our food.

Some people are appointed to order the food and others are assigned to prepare it. There are two groups that are called 'hue kuene' or server groups. There is one server group for the men and one for the women. Two men take care of the cooking. The women join in the worship services. The men stay outside and cook. After the services, we have our feast and you hear "OK! Let's eat!" and everybody goes outside. We eat and then rest for a while — maybe one or two hours and then go back to church services. After that we go home.

At New Year it's the same. That Christmas Feast goes all the way to New Year's. It takes a lot of money. We actually eat our money.

The island's owner provides a cow for the Christmas Feast and one for the New Year's Feast. The poi would come from Kauaʻi. The owner knows to get the poi ready for the Christmas Feast. When the poi is ready it is sent over. The poi is usually enough, but if we run short on poi, we make flour poi. When flour poi gets sour it is delicious. We like that. We were raised on that kind of food.

▲ As a parallel story to Alice's letters, Mama Emalia Licayan (above), who was born on Niʻihau in 1929, wrote about Christmas and New Year festivities among the residents of Puʻuwai village. Her words here are based on her writings in *Aloha Niihau*, published in 2007, and are essentially timeless reflections of her life on Niʻihau.
Aloha Niihau, courtesy Kimo Armitage

A governess vacations on Niʻihau

Two and a half years later, in June 1912, the family was vacationing on Niʻihau and took with them Hettie Belle Matthew, their governess for Eleanor and Lester. Hettie Belle, aged 22, had been teaching music in the San Francisco Bay area. She was the daughter of a Methodist minister and Aubrey had interviewed her in Berkeley in 1911. With her family's blessing she was recruited for a year's tutoring of Aubrey and Alice's two youngest children, which was subsequently extended for a second year. Towards the end of her first year she accompanied the family to Niʻihau; by this time she had become a valued member of the extended family.

Her letters to her parents are fresh and frank about everything she saw and did during the four weeks on Niʻihau. These extracts are taken from the book *Robinson Family Governess* by kind permission of the author, Judith Burtner, Hettie Belle's granddaughter.

Hettie enthuses on 2 June 1912:

> As you see — we are on Niihau — and more than my fondest expectations are realized, it is a beautiful, *beautiful* island, and I am charmed by all that I see and by the novelty of everything.
>
> We had a *glorious* trip over — got up at one o'clock — coffee was ready for those who wished it, then to the wharf we went in autos, reaching the steamer by means of row boats at about two o'clock. It was the most *glorious* night — full moon and as bright as day — the ocean was as smooth as glass. Most of the way over we sat on the Captain's bridge — listening to his funny experiences, Irish stories (and swearing), and watching the moonlight on the water, and the glorious sunrise when it came — the flying fish and the bright red & white sea birds. We reached Niihau about seven o'clock. It is the *prettiest* island to look at as you approach it — so green & lovely and undulating. You know, they have no wharf — so we were carried from the steamer in row boats, and when they go in as far as possible,

▲ Hettie Belle Matthew (1888–1975), governess to Aubrey and Alice's two youngest children Eleanor and Lester from 1911 to 1913. Eleanor was thirteen and Lester ten when she arrived in September 1911.
Judith Burtner

◄ Kiʻi Landing on Niʻihau, where Hettie Belle disembarked.
Bishop Museum

you gracefully (not gracefully the *first* time, I fear) climb into the arms of two waiting natives, and are carried ashore. It was a *thrilling* experience for me — I was so excited that I wanted to put an arm around each neck — but as I had to hold my hand bag — and didn't want to be partial to *one* native by giving him my free arm — I discreetly held my hands in my lap, and was carried safely ashore. ...

We are to live in our bathing suits and riding skirts here. This is the *ideal* life. Yesterday we started in by having a swim & going canoeing & surf boarding — and eating two kinds of shellfish, which we pulled from the rocks. Now the excitement begins — about which I will write later. You can only have *one* letter a week now — for the steamer only comes once a week to this desert island. And isn't it quite extraordinary to hear from a marooned maiden *that* often?

June 6 ... This is surely the place for shells — millions and millions of them — the beaches are *covered* by them — and such *beauties*! It is certainly fascinating to gather them. How *you* would enjoy it! One of my earliest recollections is following you along a beach as you gathered mosses & shells. We all went to the beach yesterday afternoon — on the way home we stopped in an old garden & feasted on mangoes and cocoanuts — *delicious*!

Stacks of love to you *all*!

June 10 ... Since lunch — we have all been playing croquet — Selwyn was victorious, but we all enjoyed it immensely. This morning, immediately after breakfast, we went on a horse drive — and I have already told you how tremendously I enjoy them — this one, however, was especially enjoyable — for we had such a vast stretch to drive in — and *so many* horses — it was very exciting with none of the horrid part (branding, etc.) for we just drove all the horses into a certain pen — and then separated them — sending some to the mountains, some to this pen, and some to that. There were some *dear wee* colts today — and we each chose 'ours.'

Yesterday was Sunday, and one of the most enjoyable Sundays that I can remember. We all went to the native church — and tho' I couldn't understand a word, I was deeply impressed. The minister seemed *so* in earnest — and the people listened so attentively, nodding their heads at times — and saying to each other "Ai, ai" (yes, yes). The singing was beautiful — they have no organ — but their voices are *so* rich and powerful & melodious — and you feel that they *mean* what

▲ The beach house at the southern end of the island at Keāla (Kaunakahi) Bay, with the ramparts of Kawaihoa in the background.

▶ Hale pili at Kaunakahi Bay.

◀ Guests departing Nonopapa by whaleboat for the steamer. The seated women are Jane and Isabella Sinclair (right).
Robinson family

they are singing. I joined in the singing — for I knew the tunes and could read the words from their hymnal — tho' I couldn't understand them. After the service the people all, great and small — shook hands with each of the "white people" in turn — and after Mrs. R. told them that my Father was a minister, they looked at me with a kind of awe. The church is lovely — large, clean & airy — and practically *every* native on the island goes to church every Sunday in the year, both morning and evening. Here you see the results of Christian influence.

You should have seen me swimming, and better still, out in the canoe on Saturday. Oh! It was great fun — I enjoyed it immensely. I can paddle, some.

June 21

Last week was a *glorious* week! We spent it at Kii at the other end of the island. It was one round of fishing, swimming, horse-driving etc. You cannot imagine what a good time we had. The first day that I went fishing, I caught *eleven* fish — *beauties*! Am I not a worthy daughter of a splendid fisherman Father? The fish here are such *gorgeously* brilliant colored fish — and have such strange & beautiful markings — that it is especially fascinating to catch them.

One night we went Kupei hunting — the Kupei [kupeʻe, *Nerita polita*] is a small delicious shell fish that comes out of the sand and on to the rocks at night — the meat is good and the shells are *beautiful* — especially if you were as fortunate as I was to find a beautiful bright *red* one. When we went after these kupeis we were a strange looking procession, each armed with a lantern in one hand, and a cup in t'other — trotting along the beach in our bathing suits — stubbing our toes on every other rock — but enjoying it all *immensely* — and coming home tired but happy.

... One night we all went crawfishing — that was *the* exciting time! All the natives (at least about 12) went with us carrying flaming torches. We waded along in the water up to our waists — by the light of the torches we would see the crawfish [Hawaiian lobsters] on the bottom and *pounce* on them. I caught five and let three go — no, not on purpose — but they wriggled so horribly that I was terrified. You probably heard my shrieks even in Boise — didn't you? We got two sacks *full* of crawfish. My, but they are delicious when broiled. Wish you could have tasted them.[46]

In a 1973 memoir, Hettie Belle recalled how Aubrey settled disputes among the Niihauans in true baronial fashion:

If the people of Niihau had any disputes they could not resolve — they brought them to Mr. Robinson, when he was with them. There had been an 'episode' — and the Niihau parents did not know how to handle it. It seems that several of the teenage boys had disappeared, and been gone several days. They had taken with them a very lovely young Niihau girl. So — Mr. Robinson called them all together.

'Is it true,' he said, 'that you all disappeared, and were gone for many days — without permission?' They admitted it.

To the young girl he said, 'Were they unkind to you? Were you mistreated?'

'No,' she said, 'they were all kind to me — it was very nice.' And so — the verdict. Mr. Robinson said that she must choose one of the group — and be married immediately. And so it was.[47]

Hettie Belle returned to California and married Henry Marcus in 1916. They lived in San Francisco where they brought up their three daughters, but she never forgot the time she spent with the Robinson family and often returned to the islands.

▲ Hettie Belle's charges, Lester and Eleanor Robinson.
Robinson family

▼ Hettie Belle fishing during her stay on Niʻihau in June 1912.
Judith Burtner

▶ Set among kiawe trees, the local church which Hettie Belle and all the Niihauans attended.
Kaua'i Historical Society, colorised

As a postscript, Alice Robinson's daily diaries for the years covered by Hettie Belle's time as governess have recently been found by the family. Alice generally writes one page each day, heading it with her location, e.g. Ni'ihau, Kapalawai etc. Unlike her letters, her diaries follow a set pattern day by day simply chronicling the family routine without comment or reflection.

Each day she starts with the weather, followed by breakfast with the entire family and then a description of each family member's 'doings' during the morning. Often prayers after breakfast are mentioned. Generally the whole family gathers again for lunch, and the afternoon's activities are recorded person by person — often in order of descending age. Dinner, prayers and sometimes music or hymns follow, e.g. 'we all met at dinner and have had a pleasant evening with prayers as usual' (entry for 22 June 1912 while on Ni'ihau).

Hettie Belle is always referred to in the diaries as Miss Matthew, and Alice herself is almost always described in the third person. The daily routine is paramount, there is no mention of Alice's own household duties with servants to manage, but Hettie Belle herself is obviously regarded as a member of the family.[48]

Visitors

At the time of the sale of the island, King Kamehameha V enjoined the new owners to look after his subjects, which the family has made a mantra. In Aubrey's time this was interpreted, as it had been in the past, as allowing the Niihauans to live as they wished, while providing employment on the ranch to those who wanted it, and providing housing rent-free. Alcohol, dogs and tobacco were forbidden on the island, and movement of inhabitants was controlled to a degree.

With the transition from sail to steam, access to Niʻihau became easier. There was little publicity, but the following extracts from an article appeared in the monthly magazine *The Paradise of the Pacific* in 1893:

> LANAI AND NIIHAU: TWO INTERESTING ISLANDS RARELY VISITED BY TOURISTS
>
> [Niʻihau] lies to the southwest of Kauai, whence it is reached after an at-times agreeable passage by steamer, or the traveler whose time is valuable can cross the narrow passage which separates it from that island by the ever-convenient whale-boat … It was once more thickly populated, but is now little more than a large sheep ranch … being the property of Gay & Robinson … and the population consisting chiefly of shepherds and employees of that firm … Shells of great beauty and of many varieties are found upon the shores, and those with a reddish, coral-colored seed are gathered by the not-over-industrious natives, and being strung into necklaces and similar ornaments are disposed of to their fellow-countrymen and to foreigners. Considerable taste and ingenuity are displayed in the manufacture of these pretty articles; and as tourists are, as a rule, ready to pay liberally for curiosities, the natives derive a considerable income from their sale.[49]

▲ Typical of the interisland ferries of the period, the Interisland Steam Navigation Co's *Mikahala* at anchor off Niʻihau. A wooden vessel of 444 tons, she was built at Port Blakeley, Washington, in 1887 and remained in service until 1926.
Robinson family

By this time the interisland steamers were making regular calls and the curious must have been intrigued. According to many contemporary secondary sources, Aubrey closed the island to visitors in 1915, but no record of such an edict appears in the press of the time. What closure might have meant in this context is unknown, as visits had always been by invitation of the family, apart from those on official government business. It seems that it was from this era that Niʻihau received the appellation 'The Forbidden Island.'

That Aubrey was very much in control of movements to and from Niʻihau is seen in a letter from Sinclair to Aubrey while the latter was in Boston in 1913:

> The Niihau boat came over yesterday and returned last night. They had had splendid rains for five days. Aylmer & I let a George Kiu & his wife go over to stay pending hearing from you. He is a Honolulu native who recently married a daughter of Keale's and they want to live over there. He is a young fellow somewhat like Mokuwi[?] or Kakani mo[?]. Aylmer and I understood you always want natives to go to stay on Niihau so thought better not to refuse them.[50]

This letter shows there were clearly defined rules and that Aubrey was still managing Niʻihau in all respects, including visitors, at this time.

World War I

Although the United States did not enter World War I until 6 April 1917, because much of its populace was of European extraction, interest in the war was intense from its outset in August 1914. Conscription was introduced within days of the United States becoming involved, with passing the Selective Service Act on 18 May 1917. Under the Act all men aged between 21 and 30 had to register. Of Aubrey's four sons, Sinclair at 31 was too old, Lester at 17 was too young, but Aylmer (29) and Selwyn (25) both had to sign up for military service.

The Act divided registrants into five categories:

- Class 1: Eligible and liable for military service
- Class 2: Temporarily deferred, but available for service
- Class 3: Temporarily exempt, but available for service
- Class 4: Exempt due to hardship
- Class 5: Ineligible for induction into service (by reason of specific occupation)

Aubrey mounted arguments for the draft board that Aylmer and Selwyn's managerial responsibilities in food production were vital to the nation, and they should therefore be classified as Class 2. Much of the evidence depended on their respective managerial responsibilities for the ranch on Ni'ihau. A draft contract between Aubrey as ranch owner and Aylmer as manager exists in the Robinson family papers.[51]

Aylmer's case was heard first and the board found that the arguments put forward for deferral could not be sustained and he was declared as Class 1. The Act, however, included appeal provisions, with a final appeal direct to the United States president. Aubrey duly appealed the decision up to presidential level and was ultimately successful, with Aylmer reclassified as Class 2.[52]

Selwyn was similarly classified as eligible to serve. In his case the district appeal board unanimously upheld his eligibility and recommended that Aylmer's classification, despite presidential approval, should be revisited.[53] This latter recommendation was not taken up, and Aubrey made no further appeal. Selwyn was called up for military service, but before he could be sent overseas the war ended, on 11 November 1918.

▲ The young Aylmer Robinson (1888–1967). Two years younger than Sinclair, the eldest of Alice and Aubrey's children, he and Sinclair were educated together at high school in California, at the University of California, Berkeley, and finally Harvard, graduating in 1910. They both went to work for Oahu Sugar Company before returning to the family enterprises, Sinclair in sugar, Aylmer in ranching. The photo was taken around 1917.
Robinson family

Aubrey devolves control

In 1918 Aubrey was totally in charge of the island, but on Selwyn's return from military service in 1919 he was given managerial responsibility for Ni'ihau. When Selwyn married in 1922, Aubrey handed it on to Aylmer. The next definitive account is from 1924, when it appears Aubrey was still closely involved.[54] Unlike his mother and grandmother, who bequeathed their assets before they died, Aubrey remained the owner of Ni'ihau until his death in 1936, so always had proprietorial rights, while slowly devolving direct management of the ranch to his sons, and particularly to Aylmer. It was a slow transition, the more so with Aubrey's emotional ties to Ni'ihau and its people.[55]

As Edward Stepien writes of Aubrey's hopes for the island:

> He, like his grandmother, was extremely protective of Ni'ihau and wanted nothing more than to permit the residents to live in peace and contentment in whatever manner *they* desired. Always in the back of his mind, however was the goal to make the Ni'ihau Ranch Company a profitable business.[56]

Aubrey's extensive obituary in the *Honolulu Star Bulletin* was in the same vein: 'Mr Robinson, known throughout the islands for his aloha for the Hawaiian people, attempted to preserve as much as feasible of the old native life on Niihau …'[57] He was seen as having been 'prominent in island affairs since the days of the monarchy' and 'a man who paid his debts and taxes' — the latter driven by his strong Christian beliefs. He has also been described as somewhat reclusive, and certainly was not one for frivolity, as his regime on Niʻihau indicates. He was privately a most generous man, contributing to a wide variety of causes — educational, religious and humanitarian — to which family letters attest.

At the time of Aubrey's death in 1936, Sinclair (50) was manager of Gay & Robinson's sugar interests; Aylmer (48) had responsibility for Niihau Ranch, and was also business manager of Gay & Robinson; Selwyn (43) managed the family's Kauaʻi cattle ranching activities; and Aubrey's youngest son, Lester (34) was assisting Aylmer with the management of Niʻihau.

When Jane Gay's children moved away from the islands over the years they had received their inheritance from her property holdings in the form of land or other investments. (Jane died in 1916 and Helen in 1913.) By the time of Aubrey's death only he and his wife Alice remained to share ownership of the family lands. As a result, Aubrey's estate was reported as worth $3.4 million — a huge sum at the time.[58] Niʻihau contributed only $225,000 to that total.[59]

In his will Aubrey left Niʻihau three-quarters to Aylmer and one-quarter to Lester, but this was to take effect only after the death of Alice, which didn't occur until 1960.[60]

After Aubrey's death his five children entered into an agreement with their mother to give effect to Aubrey's will regarding land transfers.[61] It perhaps typifies the family's feelings for the importance of the continuance of their landholdings through time, binding Aubrey's heirs and successors, and *their* successors, to particular land transfer arrangements until such time as the agreement should be abrogated by the unanimous agreement of the current parties to it. If any rights to particular land assets are held by the Gay & Robinson Copartnership then they are to take precedence over the agreement. The document quotes liberally from Aubrey's will. All land is to continue to be held as tenants in common rather than severally. If, following the process set down, land is sold outside the family, the purchaser is obliged to be bound by the agreement. Should disagreements occur, arbitration arrangements are specified. Some minor portions of land have been sold outside the family over the years, but the family ethos to retain their lands has largely been maintained throughout the generations.

As regards Niʻihau, the will and the agreement required that should either Aylmer or Lester wish to sell their interest in the island they had to first offer it to the other, and to their mother, Alice. If neither were interested it was to be offered to Aubrey's other children.

Aubrey's will referred to his appointment of Aylmer as manager of Niʻihau and made provision for Alice to appoint a manager should Aylmer predecease her, perhaps an indication of the feelings Aubrey had for Niʻihau — and his wish that the island and its people remain in safe hands. A copy of the 1922 management agreement between Aubrey and Aylmer is appended to the document[62] and the overall agreement makes it clear that the Niʻihau management agreement was to remain in force during Aylmer's and Alice's lifetimes.

▲ Selwyn Robinson (1892–1984), around the time the United States entered World War I. Selwyn graduated from Harvard in 1916 and began his career as bookkeeper for Gay & Robinson before becoming assistant manager at Makaweli, and manager of Niʻihau.

Robinson family

In 1963, after he had managed Niʻihau for over 40 years, Aylmer wrote to his old schoolteacher and paid tribute to his father:

> My father passed away in 1936. He had given us all a splendid groundwork both in business and in Christian responsibility and since his death the reins of responsibility have rested on our generation although Mother remained the head of the family until her death in December of 1960 at the age of 95.[63]

▶ Father and son — Aubrey and Aylmer on Niʻihau in 1924.
Bishop Museum

▶▶ Aubrey Robinson as he would wish to be remembered, riding a trail on his favorite horse, one which still has unmistakable Arabian characteristics from his imports in the 1880s.
Judith Burtner

Niʻihau life in 1942 — extracts from David Larsen's letters

The village

The village of Puuwai is the principal settlement on Niihau and except for the Robinson homestead at Kie Kie, some two miles away, is the only habitated part of the Island. The homes are widely scattered through the village among Keawe [kiawe] trees and cactus thickets and rocks. The main street is about three-quarters of a mile in length and the homes sometimes a thousand or more feet apart. All of them are surrounded by individual stone walls forming little private yards, which are cleared of cactus and rocks. The area between these yards is used for tethering horses at night or when not let out into the adjoining pastures. Many of the stone walls are covered with Night Blooming Cereus. In the middle of the village is the church settled picturesquely among old Keawe trees in a spacious yard surrounded by a Cereus-covered stone wall.

David Larsen visited Niʻihau for a week in June 1942 and left an account of his time there in letters to his wife Katharine which are now in the Hawaiian State Archives. The letters give a rare snapshot of the life of the community on the island at the time. In 2009 they were included in a book called *Voices from our Past: Katharine and David Larsen*, edited and compiled by Donivee Laird, their granddaughter.

Hawaiian State Archives, Niʻihau, L D Larsen, Stacks 919.6942, L3n, pp 12–14, 24–25 & 28, 29

Food

The native population uses very little green vegetables and seem to care little for them. It is usually too dry to grow anything and when the weather is right, most of what they plant is sweet potatoes. They also raise some papayas and bananas and sometimes melons. The staple food for the native people is poi — which is all brought from Kauai. No taro is grown on the island, there being no suitable wet locations for it. Considerable flour is also brought over, which they mix with the poi and also use for hotcakes; pilot crackers, taro and miscellaneous canned goods are also staple articles of import. There is no store, but they send in a combined order to Aylmer by the weekly sampan, which is shipped over the following week … Just how they keep track of it I don't know, but somehow the individuals are charged with what they obtain. It is purchased for them by the Robinsons and billed through the payroll at invoice price. Transportation to the island is not charged for. Of local food products the principal ones are fish, pork, beef and mutton — also sweet potatoes. Beef and mutton are only given out occasionally on holidays or special occasions or when an animal gets hurt. Wild pig is plentiful and fish, opihi [limpets], limu [seaweed] and other sea products abound. The pork is usually dried in the sun like jerked beef.

A number of cows with calves are kept in a separate pasture near the Robinsons' home and anyone wanting milk can have all he wants by milking the cows for it. They make little use of this, however, as they prefer canned milk even for the babies — and it sure seems a lot easier than going two miles after work, milking a cow and going home again. Tobacco and liquor are taboo. Coffee

▶ Puʻuwai in 1928. When the Sinclair family bought the island from the king in 1864 there were a dozen scattered villages, Puʻuwai being one of them. Over time, as recommended by the king, the settlements coalesced at Puʻuwai as the Sinclairs built frame houses in European style for the Niihauan families. It took many years for the 30-plus houses in the village to be completed. The village has not altered in size to any extent over many decades.
Robinson family

is never brought over for the Hawaiians, but Aylmer says they manage to get it through other channels. He says he disapproves of it on account of their feeding it to the babies if they have it available. They are allowed to order tea, however.

Church

Last Sunday at Makaweli when I declined a church invitation from Mrs. Robinson [Aylmer's mother Alice], I was told that 'On Niihau we always go to church.'

About ten-thirty this morning we started off in the two-horse carriage, with two cowboys following on horseback to open gates. Sunday school was underway when we arrived. We sat in the rear pew. There was some sort of general discussion, interspersed with singing. Sunday school blended into church without interruption.

The women all sat on one side and the men on the other. There were about sixty or seventy women, many with their babies, and thirty or forty men and boys. People kept arriving, however, up to ten or fifteen minutes before the end. Sometimes they return in the afternoon for more singing … The young men wore fancy silk shirts and khaki or colored trousers. The older men wore dark suits. The women wore every conceivable thing. Some had long silk dresses — from light pink to black. Many of the younger ones wore loose white dresses, with no attempt at style or fit.

After the informal discussion and singing were over, one of the cowboys, my friend Kekuhina, stepped into the pulpit and talked and prayed and gave what seemed to be the main sermon.

The church singing, you can imagine, was just about perfect. I found a number of the young Hawaiian cowboys, with whom I have been associating during the week, singing at the top of their voices. Their lives apparently are very religious. Aylmer tells me that every single home has a prayer meeting both morning and evening. Even when the father has to get out at four o'clock in the morning, the family gets up in time for a prayer meeting and singing before he leaves.

After the service we went out on the church porch and as the congregation came out they all came up and shook hands with us.

Keeping Niʻihau a special place

The whole setup here is so precious and so naive it sounds like a fairy tale. They have kept it Hawaiian and Christian — perhaps more Christian than Hawaiian, and I am sure there is nothing like it anywhere else in the world.

Aylmer says people think it is peculiar that they do not allow casual visitors who are constantly besieging them with requests to go over for one reason or another. He said: 'You can see how they would spoil all this very fast.' I fully agree with him.

If the Hawaiians want relatives or others to visit, they ask permission, which is granted unless the persons wanted are found undesirable. They are brought over and back on the Robinsons' boat without charge. When the Niihau people want to go away to visit their friends or relatives on the other Islands, they also ask permission — which is granted if the occasion seems warranted.

Most of the men I talked with had visited Kauai occasionally.

> *You can see how they would spoil all this very fast.*

CHAPTER TEN

AYLMER'S STEWARDSHIP

As we galloped further southward the character of the coastal plain suddenly changed for the better. Extensive and closely cropped meadows of manienie grass were interspersed with larger groves of algaroba trees. These grassy fields, level as a billiard table, resembled huge polo fields and we were tempted to race our Arabian steeds for miles. Occasional clumps of coconut trees bent their graceful tops under the burden of closely packed clusters of nuts. A lonely loulu palm tree in a swale marked the site where once stood a native grass hut.

Mile after mile of this delightful coastal plain was passed over with the highlands on our left and sand dunes and ocean on our right until 12 miles from Kii we came finally to a heavier forest of kiawe trees under which were interspersed the houses of the ranch hands which constituted the scattered village of Puuwai.[1]

Charles Judd, the territorial forester and brother of territorial governor Lawrence Judd, was describing the party's ride from Kiʻi to Puʻuwai on the occasion of the first gubernatorial visit to Niʻihau in October 1929 (the island had to wait 32 years for the second visit of a governor). Judd's party of ten was hosted by Aylmer Robinson, assisted by his long-standing Niʻihau superintendent John Rennie. The passage gives a vivid picture of the island after rain:

Turkeys, an occasional peacock, cattle and sheep wandered contentedly over the level stretches of grassy plain which was dotted with flocks of plover which seldom hear the sound of a gun. There had been frequent rains during the summer and in consequence the foliage of the trees and the hue of the meadows were a brilliant green and these with the presence of the contented domestic animals gave this section every appearance of a well-groomed English park.[2]

Idyllic indeed. The governor's party was fortunate to see the island in such prime condition and the rains had helped, but due credit must also be given to Aylmer, who at this time had been in charge of Niʻihau for over ten years.

The governor's visit appears not to have been in any way investigative, but more of a goodwill tour and 'showing the flag.' Later in the year he also visited Kahoʻolawe, and became the only governor to have visited all eight major islands.

▲ Charles Judd (1881–1939), superintendent of forestry in the islands from 1915 to 1930. He wrote a lyrical account of his horseback ride from Kiʻi to Puʻuwai in 1929 when he accompanied the governor to Niʻihau. A keen hiker, he co-founded the Piko Club in 1931.
Hawaiian Journal of History, Vol. 37

Charles Judd describes meeting Niihauans at Puʻuwai:

> Dressed in their Sunday clothes, including shoes, these native men, women and children stood respectfully on one side and greeted with many subdued 'Alohas' the Governor and his party as they entered the school house …
>
> The school exhibit over, the party moved out into the yard where the noon sun filtered through the thin foliage of the kiawe trees upon the patiently waiting throng. Here followed introductions and speeches were made to a most attentive and respectful audience. As the speeches grew lengthy, fancy slippers were discarded to relieve pinched feet. The final wind up was the individual shaking of hands with the 98 inhabitants present who then placed upon our shoulders many coils of the pu-pu or shell leis for which Niihau is famed. Governor Judd, burdened with about ten pounds of leis, led the farewell singing of 'Aloha Oe', but the Niihau people promptly responded with 'The Star Spangled Banner' most excellently rendered.[3]

After the mandatory three cheers, the governor's party repaired to The House for lunch, after which a two-hour gallop back to Kiʻi brought the visitors to their embarkation point for Honolulu on the steamer *Kukui*. Judd again:

> The glorious day on the island had opened up to us a vision of beauty and a mode of living which was very unusual. And this is what we found: A well kept ranch which supported 750 shorthorn cattle, about 10,000 sheep, numerous turkeys and peacocks, and many aviaries, run by a manager, foreman and 30 cowboys … An industrious and contented people speaking nothing but the Hawaiian language, the entire population of 130 being members of the local church.[4]

He enumerates the unusual features of the island's lifestyle, such as the prohibition of alcohol and the complete lack of the trappings of civilization, and describes Niʻihau, perhaps with rose-tinted glasses, as an island 'flowing with milk and honey' — the rains and Aylmer's ranch management had enchanted him.

▲ Lawrence Judd (1887–1968), territorial governor from 1929 to 1934.
Wikimedia Commons, colorised

▲ John Rennie (1861–1941), a Scotsman, worked for Gay & Robinson for 34 years. For 17 of those years he lived and worked on Niʻihau as ranch manager.
Bishop Museum

◀ Looking north towards Puʻuwai with The House in the foreground, and the area the governor's party traversed on their way to a sumptuous lunch hosted by the Robinsons. The photo was taken in October 1928, just a year before the governor's visit in October 1929.
Robinson family

The ranch

Forester Charles Judd referred to Niʻihau as a well kept ranch, as indeed it must have been by 1929 after 66 years of operation, and with every effort made over the years to sustainably achieve profitability. It seems that Aubrey stepped back from the day-to-day management of the island in 1918, and when Selwyn was demobilized in 1919 he managed the island until his marriage in 1922, when Aylmer assumed day-to-day control.

An early initiative of Aylmer's was commercial-scale honey production. Aubrey had introduced bees early in his tenure, but the key to any possibility of honey production lay in the growth of the kiawe trees he had planted. This had been so successful that Judd noted in 1929, 'We rode through a field where young kiawe trees had recently been cut down and entirely eliminated so that they would not spoil the excellent grass crop in that section.' Like everything else in farming, it all required management expertise and balance. Honey production from the kiawe, with its abundant nectar, had been under way for many years when Judd visited.

Kiawe blossom yields a soft, white, creamy honey, and with kiawe growing extensively on all the islands it became the staple of the Hawaiian honey industry, with exports to the mainland commencing in the late 1890s and peaking in the 1930s. The First World War caused a dramatic price increase and this may have been the impetus for Aylmer to transfer bee colonies from Makaweli to Niʻihau at this time and begin commercial honey production.

The bee disease, American Foulbrood, was accidentally introduced to the Hawaiian islands around 1930, but never reached Niʻihau due to Aylmer's banning of further imports of bee colonies from Kauaʻi and his strict personnel travel restrictions.[5]

In its heyday, annual production of kiawe honey from Niʻihau totalled 80 tons, amounting to over 15,000 gallons, all packed in five-gallon tins, two to a box. Honey is heavy, with a specific gravity of 1.3 to 1.4, so cases could weigh up to 130 pounds. According to David Larsen, Aylmer's good friend who visited the island in 1942:

> Yesterday I was watching an old grey-haired Hawaiian loading honey cases down at the warehouse. He seemed pretty old to be working, but it looked like rather light work — until I tried to lift one of the cases. I couldn't budge it, whereas the old man picked them up quite casually and without apparent effort.[6]

This 'old man' was in fact Bene Kanahele, who in 1941 killed the Japanese pilot by picking him up and dashing his head against a rock — see Appendix C.

In the 1950s a second scourge hit the Hawaiian honey industry with another accidental introduction, this time a moth, *Ithome concolorella*, a kiawe pest, the larvae of which destroy the blossoms.[7] On this occasion the scourge did reach Niʻihau and by the early 1960s production had dropped to only 500 gallons a year, a dramatic decrease.

The harvesting of kiawe honey is particularly labor-intensive, as the timing is critical. Too early and the moisture content of the honey will be too high and it will ferment; too late and the honey will crystallise in the frame and can't be extracted without melting, in which case it cannot be considered raw. For the honey to be optimal, bees need water close to the beehive, and lack of water was always a problem.

▲ Loading honey on the Robinson sampan, *Lehua*, in the late 1940s.
Photo by Eugene Moroz, from *Before and Beyond the Niihau Zero* by Syd Jones

▼ Kiawe blossom, source of the pure white honey produced for many years.
Wikimedia Commons

Despite these constraints, and the discovery of a second parasite, the leaf-eating Monkeypod-Kiawe caterpillar, *Melipotis indomita,* in the early 1970s, honey production continued on Niʻihau into the 1990s.[8]

The loss of kiawe blossom to caterpillars also spelled doom for another project, the production and export of ground kiawe beans as a supplementary cattle feed. Cattle numbers fell as a result of all these problems, and also the cactus blight discussed below. Cattle numbered 1600–1700 at the time of Governor Quinn's visit in 1961. Sheep numbers had also dropped by then to only 7000.

Another attribute of the kiawe tree is that the wood makes a premium charcoal, and with a growing market in the islands and on the mainland for barbecue charcoal, Aylmer set out to exploit it, marketing the product as 'Sunset' charcoal from Niʻihau.

Charcoal is made by cooking wood in a low-oxygen environment, and is labor-intensive — most appropriate for the Niʻihau situation. The process takes days and, done properly, burns off all volatile compounds — water, tars, hydrogen and methane — leaving black lumps of charcoal and some ash. The lumps are about 25% of the original weight of wood.

▲ A kiln on Niʻihau producing Sunset brand premium charcoal from kiawe logs.
Greg Vaughn

Traditionally short logs were piled up (or a pit was dug for them) leaving an air chimney in the center free of wood. The pile or pit was covered with earth apart from the edges, to allow some air to enter. The chimney was then lit from some existing charcoal, with the average preparation time five days.

Brick kilns were erected on Niʻihau to fulfil the same function and were much more controllable, ensuring a consistent product for sale. A quality product needs to have the maximum number of charcoal lumps, a minimum of charcoal dust, and no ash. Sunset charcoal was regarded by the market as a quality product.

From the 1950s, if not earlier, production of charcoal was a part of everyday life for the paniolo. The *Star Bulletin* reported in 1957 that each week half of the 50 paniolo did the herding and ranch work, including the charcoal manufacture and honey production, while the other half went fishing, with the groups alternating week by week.[9]

Unfortunately freight costs from Niʻihau were such that the charcoal product ultimately proved uneconomic, with cheaper charcoal from Japan undercutting the Sunset brand from the island.

At some stage Aylmer decided to switch from wool growing to sheep rearing, producing lambs and hoggets for export to the other islands. During the Korean War in the early 1950s wool prices peaked, but when the war ended prices slumped. Given the difficult conditions on Niʻihau with consequent dirty and burr-ridden wool, it is likely that wool from the island became almost impossible to sell, and the switch was made at this time. The island had been stocked with a fine breed of sheep by Francis and Aubrey and this made good business sense.¹⁰

In a further attempt to supplement its income, in the 1950s the ranch entered the commercial fishing industry, fishing the near-shore area around the island over which they had konohiki (landlord) rights. The owners met with the representatives of the Niʻihau community in a continuing dialog over the commercial fishing, and because of concerns over depletion of the fish stocks, it was mutually agreed after some years that the activity should stop.¹¹ A project to resurrect the ponds in the island's lakes to grow and harvest mullet also proved unsuccessful.

The other seasonal output from the island was turkeys. These had multiplied to the extent they formed a useful addition to the ranch's income, and were supplied for the Thanksgiving and Christmas markets.

As mentioned in Chapter One, Aylmer had a serious plant disease to deal with in the 1940s — the loss of the prickly pear cactus (pāpipi) population. This cactus had been deftly cultivated in suitable areas as a vital source of food and water for the cattle, particularly in times of drought.

The extent of the cactus when the Sinclairs bought the island in 1864 is illustrated by comments made by Elia Helekunihi in the Hawaiian language paper *Ke Au Okoa* in 1871 after he had been the guest of Francis Sinclair in 1871. He wrote, in translation:

> Cactus is the commonest plant here, covering about one third of the island. The green coloring is a restful sight. When the light of the sun shines upon the silvery green of the plant, the image comes back to the eye as a pleasant scene, just like a forest.¹²

▲ A healthy prickly pear. Contrast this with the photo on page 23 of a sickly specimen on Niʻihau taken by Harold St John in 1947 before the species died out on the island. The cactus is thought to have been introduced in the early 1800s by Don Francisco de Paulo Marin.
JM Garg / Wikimedia Commons

On the Big Island and on Maui the cactus was regarded as an invasive species and efforts were made in the 1940s by the Department of Agriculture to control or eliminate it. Not so on arid Niʻihau, where it was regarded as a major asset to ranching. Unfortunately for the ranch a fungal disease (a species of *fusarium*) spread from Kauaʻi in 1943, causing major dieback and finally local extinction.

The botanist Harold St John, after his 1947 and 1949 visits, painted an ugly picture:

> [The *fusarium*] attacked the cactus like a wild-fire blight, whole plants turning yellow, then gray with black pustules, then the whole sturdy plant collapsing in a pile of soft, rotting tissue. Some joints may sprout new shoots and live for a while, but they soon are stricken and die.¹³

Although some cactus plants were alive at the time of St John's visits, he wrote that the ranch's carrying capacity had been reduced by 600 head of cattle as a result of the loss of the pāpipi. Aylmer had to rethink the ranching operation yet again, but was determined to continue to employ the local Niihauans. Their life changed but little — as described on pages 245–246 in David Larsen's 1942 letters.

The struggle against nature — in the form of drought, and plant and animal diseases (including fly strikes) — was continual for Aylmer and Lester. Attempts at diversification, including castor beans, sisal and Sea Island cotton proved disappointing for one reason or another. Regardless, the ranch continued to employ all the able-bodied men, albeit with some difficulty.

A treasure-seeking tale

The following event purportedly took place in 1934, but was not described in print until 1979, when it was published in Julius Scammon Rodman's book *The Kahuna Sorcerers of Hawaii, Past and Present*.[14] The Rodman story is referred to briefly in Tava and Keale's 1984 book *Niihau: The Traditions of an Hawaiian Island*.[15]

Julius Rodman was a member of the seafaring Rodman family of Massachusetts, and went to sea at 17. He arrived in Honolulu in 1930 at the age of 18 and spent his career in the islands adventurously researching old Hawaiian religious and burial rites until his retirement to Olympia, in Washington State, in 1979. He died in 2001.

In the fall of 1934 Rodman learned of the existence of a burial cave on the thousand-foot cliffs of Pueo Point from 'the Niʻihau man,' an elderly Honolulu news vendor named Maui Kaupo. This excited his curiosity and he decided to pay a clandestine visit to the island, recruiting a willing accomplice (named only as H Deuchare in the published account) and buying an old Japanese fishing sampan they named the *Saucy Maru*. Supplies were secured, including canned food, hiking packs, half-inch rope,* a block and tackle lifting mechanism and two surfboards. After a trial run from Honolulu to Molokaʻi and back, they left from Waiʻanae on the north side of Oʻahu early one Saturday morning, bound for Makaweli roadstead, where they arrived at midnight. The plan was to be at Niʻihau in the early hours of Sunday when few people would be around to notice them. At dawn the vessel was off Pueo Point and they were scanning the cliffs. According to Rodman's account they saw the blocked-off cave entrance about 200 feet below the top of the cliffs, just as old Kaupo had told him.

The *Saucy Maru* was anchored well outside the line of breakers pounding the shore, the equipment was lashed to the two surfboards and the pair slipped overboard to paddle for the island. Their landing was ignominious, both being separated from their surfboards at the first line of breakers and flung upon the rocky shore. No serious damage was done, however, to men or equipment. Having paused to collect themselves and repack their gear, they struck out for the summit of the steep cliffs above them.

The perilous ascent took them up a dry watercourse, with every step risking a fall to the boulder-strewn beach below. There was no vegetation, just crumbling lava rock. The grind upwards seemed endless, but at last they made the summit, secured the block and tackle to a large boulder and Rodman slowly lowered Deuchare down.

When Rodman had paid out about 200 feet of rope a cry from below told him to stop and throw down the remainder of the free end. After some moments' pause Deuchare asked Rodman to haul away, as he had spliced the two ends of the rope together. Rodman tied himself to one end of the loop and lowered himself down to where Deuchare was standing on a narrow ledge. In front of him was the cave entrance, covered by the lava rock they had espied from the *Saucy Maru*. The rock was rolled away, revealing a narrow gap through which they squeezed themselves.

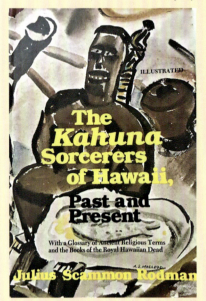

▲ Julius Rodman's book. The jacket design is from a watercolor by Alexander MacLeod, 1888–1976, entitled 'Polynesian God and Stone Fish.'

* *600 feet of half-inch manila rope weighs about 40 pounds.*

◀ Which ravine did they climb? A view of the east coast of Niʻihau, looking northeast towards Pānīʻau.

J Michael Anderson / Kauaʻi Historical Society

The pair were in the cave foyer with skeletons sprawled all over one another. As Rodman explained to Deuchare, often royal funerals were led by a kahu (guardian), specially trained to murder the rest of the burial party at the conclusion of proceedings, so that only a single person knew the secret burial place. Further in, their flashlights revealed whole mummies laid out in a row, adorned with whale-ivory pendants and featherwork, each lying beneath kapa sheets and covered with makaloa mats. Along the walls were calabashes, ornamented gourds, wooden weapons and stone artifacts. Deuchare tried to open a heavy chest he found, but the lock would not give. Rodman relates that three inches of fine dust lay on everything. (If this were so the pair must have caused massive disturbance to everything they described.)

At that moment Deuchare wriggled out to see how the *Saucy Maru* was faring. With a shout of alarm he saw that she had dragged her anchor and was moving closer inshore with each passing roller. With no further thought for the treasure they had just found, they clambered rapidly up the rope to the clifftop, then scrambled down the thousand feet to the beach and paddled furiously back to their vessel on their surfboards. By this time the *Saucy Maru* was only a hundred yards from the first of the breakers.

Then there was a nervous pause, until with a sigh of relief from both of them, the motor finally started and they were able to maneuver out of danger.

Here the 'treasure-seeking tale' ends. The narrative occupies only five pages in Rodman's 400-page book. Tava & Keale report that an elder, Tutu Kaui verified the existence of the cave.[16] Tutu Kaui also says, when speaking of the Niihauan people's stories, 'Call it what you wish … but many of these [stories] I have seen to be true.'

War preparations

Although World War I ended in November 1918, Selwyn Robinson was not demobilized until late 1919. Initially he helped Aylmer and Lester in the multifarious activities required to make the most of Niʻihau. In 1922, when Selwyn married, Aubrey gave him responsibility for Makaweli Ranch, a position he held for the rest of his working life.

Despite being billed as 'the war to end all wars', the seeds of another war were already sown, both in Europe and Asia. While the United States had deployed gunboats to protect American interests on the Yangtze River since 1854, with the deteriorating political situation in China the Yangtze River Patrol Force was formally created in 1921 — the same year the Chinese Communist Party was founded. China was in an increasing state of unrest, with warlords competing for control from the Yangtze to Manchuria in the northeast. In 1926 the Nationalist army of Chiang Kai-shek probed the Yangtze river valley and the Yangtze River Patrol became involved in several incidents over succeeding years. 1926 also saw the first Communist Party uprising which finally led to the civil war between the Nationalists and Communists.[17]

Meanwhile Japan was becoming ever more militaristic. There was antipathy towards the western colonial powers, who had taken advantage of Japan's inward-looking stance prior to the Meiji restoration of 1868. Since that time, the Japanese had been determined to compete and to vie for raw materials wherever they could be found. With a divided China on their doorstep, Japan invaded Manchuria near Mukden in 1931. US marines were protecting the foreign settlement there, and although they weren't directly attacked by the Japanese, they were subjected to fire from both sides in the first incident involving Japan and the United States. Over the ensuing five years Japan consolidated its gains in Manchuria, with a view to conquering all of China.

Shanghai fell to the Japanese in November 1937, and on 12 December a sustained Japanese bombing raid took place against the USS *Panay* on the Yangtze. After an attack lasting half an hour during which the gunboat received several direct hits the *Panay* sank

▶ The US Navy's river gunboat *Panay* during acceptance trials in 1928.
Wikimedia Commons, colorised

◀ Brigadier General Billy Mitchell (1879–1936) in 1920, posing beside a Vought VE-7 *Bluebird* designed as a two-seat trainer for the US Army and adopted by the US Navy as its first fighter aircraft.
Wikimedia Commons

in mid-river. "It is a type of aggression for which statements of deep regrets by smooth-tongued Japanese diplomats are totally inadequate," editorialized the *Washington Post*. US public sentiment was horrified at the attack.

The above dates and developments are important in this story of Niʻihau, but we now need to return to World War I and one of the American flying heroes of that conflict, Billy Mitchell, often dubbed 'the father of the US Air Force.' His ideas were crucial to war preparations carried out by the Robinson family on Niʻihau. In World War I he had been the first American officer to fly over enemy lines, and later led the largest number of aircraft to fly on a single bombing mission during the war, with over 1500 planes from four countries under his command.

At the age of 39, the outspoken (and within the confines of an army career, almost unmanageable), William (Billy) Mitchell ended the Great War as a brigadier general, despite having alienated most of his superiors with his campaign to improve American air capabilities.

Mitchell continued to speak out after the war, and in return received mid-level and generally administrative postings. In 1923 the services could see another stoush coming over his enthusiasm for the use of heavy bombers, and, perhaps unwisely, gave him leave for an extended honeymoon with his second wife, Elizabeth Trumbull Miller.

This did not turn out quite as the powers-that-be anticipated, as he spent his honeymoon touring American bases in Hawaiʻi and the Philippines and produced a highly critical 100-page report on their fitness for purpose. In it he predicted Japan would attack Pearl Harbor and Honolulu at 7.30 on a Sunday morning, using the island of Niʻihau as a forward base. His unsolicited report, and particularly this prediction, did not endear him to his superiors and needless to say was not acted upon.

By every means at his disposal Mitchell continued advocating for a greater role for air power, culminating in a press conference in September 1925 in which he made his views absolutely plain in an unprecedented outburst. The reaction in Washington was that this constituted an offense and a sensational court-martial resulted. Mitchell was found guilty and resigned from the army.

▲ Billy Mitchell and his second wife Elizabeth married in 1924.
Wikimedia Commons, colorised

▶ Colonel Gerald Brant (1880–1958) visited Hawai'i in 1925 and became convinced that Billy Mitchell was right — the islands were totally unprepared for war. In 1930 he was posted to Hawai'i for four years and during his time there the idea of furrowing Ni'ihau to prevent aircraft landing was developed with the Robinsons. Brant retired as a major general in 1944.
National Archives

One of the senior officers who gave evidence in Billy's defense was Colonel Gerald Brant, a 1904 West Point graduate and contemporary of Billy's. While he did not serve overseas in World War I, Brant showed an early interest in military aviation and in 1918 became chief of operations of the Office of the Director of Military Aeronautics, Washington. Other military aviation roles followed, including two months in Hawai'i in April/May 1925 as commander of the Hawaiian Air Depot.

Brant was one of the first to see Billy's unsolicited 1924 report on the deficiencies in the air defenses of the islands, and read with interest Billy's scenario of Ni'ihau as a possible staging post for a Japanese invasion force. He clearly agreed with Billy's conclusions. His own time in the islands reinforced his views and made him a logical choice to give evidence in Billy's defense later in 1925.

Whether he met any of the Robinsons and particularly Aubrey or Aylmer during his 1925 posting to the islands is unknown, but in 1930 Brant was assigned back to O'ahu in command of 18th Composite Wing, a position held until 1934. As a firm disciple of Billy's vision, he determined to do what he could to improve the islands' air defenses. According to Robinson family legend, Gerald Brant showed Aylmer Billy's report, which must have given Aylmer food for thought. Under Billy's scenario an improvement in the Hawaiian islands' defenses had to include the denial of the use of the unprotected island of Ni'ihau as a base, and between Aylmer, Aubrey and Gerald Brant they concocted the idea of furrowing all the flat land on Ni'ihau to prevent its use by aircraft.

By the early 1930s the world political scene was looking considerably more dismal. Militarism in Japan was rising, and Billy Mitchell's vision seemed to the Robinsons' eyes to be more and more credible.

The family was convinced and furrowing of the land commenced, using draft horses or mules and a single-share plow. The scheme was to plow all the flat or gently sloping land at 100-foot intervals, two ways at right angles, to create a chequerboard effect. The furrows were 20 inches deep and at least 30 inches wide, and thus large enough to prevent an aircraft landing without ripping off its undercarriage or turning turtle. The area to be furrowed was enormous, covering wherever an aircraft could land, approximately 50 square miles in all — of the order of 5–6000 miles of furrows, all of which took more than a single pass of the plow.

Furrowing was painfully slow and the global situation was continuing to deteriorate. It may have been the attack on 12 December 1937 on the USS *Panay* on the Yangtze, mentioned earlier, that convinced Aylmer that the furrowing needed to be greatly accelerated. The operation had to be mechanized to have any hope of success and accordingly he ordered a crawler tractor, at his own expense, from the Cleveland Tractor Co.

The tractor required fuel, lubricants and skilled maintenance, but unlike animal power did not need feed, water or rest. On arrival it was put to work immediately.

According to Keith Robinson, as quoted in *Before and Beyond the Niihau Zero* by Syd Jones, the driver was Joseph Keoua Kele. Oliva Kamala, Kauileilehua Keamoai and Kamakaukiuli Kawahalau formed a rough track for the machine by clearing away boulders and scrub.[18]

It was a massive job, and when it was finished in the summer of 1941 two-thirds of the island had been crosshatched with furrows. Faint traces can still be seen today on the beds of the shallow lakes. By the time it was completed it seemed inevitable that the United States would enter the war raging on the other side of the world, and closer to home the Japanese had become even more belligerent.

As it turned out, the furrowing was completed just in time. When the Japanese attacked Pearl Harbor on 7 December 1941, the island could not have been easily used as the launch pad for the attack envisaged by Billy Mitchell in 1924. Whether the Japanese were aware of the furrowing before formulating their aircraft carrier-led attack has never been explored, but the work was certainly never divulged to the American public. It seems that the Japanese did not know, as Niʻihau was nominated as an emergency landing place for Japanese planes that were damaged in the attack. Although the attack did not follow Billy's predictions exactly, it was entirely accurate as to timing — half-past seven on a Sunday morning. The base used as a springboard was, however, a carrier flotilla rather than the island of Niʻihau itself.

Aylmer could justifiably be proud of the massive work done in defense of his country, entirely at his own expense. This major event in the life of the island, and one which began with Billy Mitchell's one-man vision, then from him to his disciple Gerry Brant, and finally to Aylmer Robinson, the majority owner and manager of Niʻihau, is commemorated in a display at the Pacific Aviation Museum on Ford Island at Pearl Harbor. The Cletrac and the two plows used may now be seen there thanks to the generosity of Bruce and Keith Robinson and much hard work on the part of Syd Jones and many other volunteers. The moving of the various items in 2006 is fully described in *Before and Beyond the Niihau Zero*.[19]

The Niʻihau Incident

An extraordinary event in the life of Niʻihau took place in the immediate aftermath of the Japanese attack on Pearl Harbor on 7 December 1941 when a Japanese Mitsubishi Zero fighter aircraft crash-landed near the village of Puʻuwai. What followed has been

▶ Bruce (left) and Keith Robinson, the owners of Niʻihau, with the Cletrac Model AD tractor where it was parked after its retirement from work on the island. The photograph was taken in 2006 by Kathryn Budde-Jones just before the tractor was moved to the Pearl Harbor Aviation Museum as part of the exhibit on 'The Niʻihau Incident.'
Kathryn Budde-Jones

▲ The tractor, which sits alongside the plows and a replica of Nishikaichi's Zero in the museum.
Photograph by Anne Orndahl, Pearl Harbor Aviation Museum

▼ Traces of Aylmer Robinson's furrowing can still be seen today on the bed of Halulu Lake. To give an idea of scale, the furrows are roughly 100 feet apart. It would have taken several passes of the plow to create a ditch large enough to stop aircraft landing.
Google Maps

▲ The moment of impact, in a remarkably accurate depiction of Nishikaichi's plane as it clipped the barbed wire fence and crashed to the ground. This sketch by Paul Burlingham appeared in the *Honolulu Star Bulletin* on 7 December 1986, 45 years after the event, as part of a series of four articles on successive days which he researched and wrote.
Hawai'i State Library

▶ Shigenori Nishikaichi (1920–41), pilot of the ill-fated Zero. From the age of 13 he wanted to train as a naval flyer, and was selected for the competitive Yokotsuka Naval Training School in 1937. Later he transferred to the Naval Aviation School at Ōita, and in 1941 to Omura Air Field. After final training back at Ōita he joined the aircraft carrier *Hiryū* for the attack on O'ahu.
Wikipedia

described in news reports at the time, the inevitable official reports, a plethora of magazine articles and book chapters, and at least three books.[20] A film, *Enemy Within*, loosely based on the incident was released in 2019.[21]

The incident itself, often styled 'The Battle of Ni'ihau,' took place over a week and resulted in two deaths. What happened during that fateful week on Ni'ihau is set down in Appendix C, in the words of David Larsen (Aylmer Robinson's guest on the island in June 1942) when memories were still fresh. As Larsen concludes, it was 'an epic event crowded with heroic deeds, quick thinking and sound judgement.'

The Japanese pilot, Naval Airman 1st Class Shigenori Nishikaichi had two thoughts in mind when he crash-landed on the island, uninjured, and with his Zero more or less intact: to ensure his aircraft did not fall into the hands of the enemy, and to destroy his papers. The Mitsubishi AM62 model 21 Zero was a state-of-the-art fighter which the US military were keen to learn more about, and Nishikaichi had been drilled that he must not let that happen. His papers, including his orders and the location of the carrier fleet, were also of prime importance to him, as his subsequent actions showed.

The Japanese attack on Pearl Harbor and other military installations on O'ahu was carried out from a naval flotilla cruising about 230 miles north of the island. The flotilla consisted of over 50 vessels, including six aircraft carriers, which launched a total of 353 aircraft (fighters, bombers, dive bombers and torpedo bombers) against targets on O'ahu.

Nishikaichi's primary mission was to strafe Bellows Field on the northeast coast to stop American aircraft taking to the air. He and his seven companion Zeros strafed the airfield for about 15 minutes and put all twelve P-40 Tomahawk fighters on the ground out of action. Only three of the Tomahawk pilots were on the base, the others being on weekend leave. Two were killed and the third was wounded in the attack.

During the strafing Nishikaichi's Zero was hit several times by ground fire and he began losing fuel. At some point he realized that he was unlikely to have enough to get back to his carrier, so he turned his attention to Ni'ihau where he understood a submarine was waiting offshore to rescue any stranded pilots. It would appear he deliberately exhausted his fuel to prevent a fire and opted for a 'dead stick' landing with wheels down, presumably because he was unable to jettison his external fuel tank.

A week after his crash landing, Shigenori Nishikaichi lost his life at the hands of Bene Kanahele, as outlined in Appendix C.

Knowing nothing of the Pearl Harbor attack, during that fateful week the Niihauans tried hard to contact Kauaʻi and wondered why Aylmer Robinson had not arrived with their weekly supplies. In fact Aylmer had been forbidden by the military from making his normal sailing, due to the apparently imminent threat of a Japanese invasion of Niʻihau. The upshot was that, when all else failed, the Niihauans rowed a whaleboat to Waimea — a perilous journey.

As soon as the whaleboat arrived in the early hours of the Thursday (four days after Pearl Harbor) and Aylmer heard what had happened on Niʻihau, he alerted the military authorities. The lighthouse tender *Kukui* happened to be in the area extinguishing the lighthouses as a wartime measure. She was recalled to Waimea and a party of heavily armed soldiers under Lieutenant Jack Mizuha was assembled.

By the time the *Kukui* arrived at Niʻihau a week after the crash on Sunday 14 December, the action on the island was all over, however, with Nishikaichi and his local accomplice Yoshio Harada dead and buried. Having inspected the burned-out plane, the party returned to Waimea, carrying Bene Kanahele for medical treatment, together with his wife, and three prisoners — Yoshio Harada's widow and their daughter Irene, and Shintani. The latter three were headed for an uncertain future. Their fates are described in Syd Jones's *Before and Beyond the Niihau Zero*.[22]

Both the army and navy were still interested in what they could learn from the wreck of the Zero. A second visit by the military was mounted, traveling on the Robinson sampan, the *Lehua*. Not much more was learned, and the army decided it was not worth transporting the plane to Oʻahu as other crashed Zeros were available closer to hand. The navy did, however, remove the engine for further inspection. The remainder of the wreckage was hauled 200 yards from the crash site under some kukui trees, where it would be hidden from aerial observation.

▲ A restored Mitsubishi Zero in Pearl Harbor Aviation Museum painted in Nishikaichi's colors. The remains of his plane may be seen adjacent to this exhibit. The restored plane saw war service in the Solomon Islands in 1943. When the Zero was introduced into the Japanese navy in 1940 it was the best carrier-based fighter in the world. Over ten thousand were built.
Pearl Harbor Aviation Museum

▲ The Coast Guard lighthouse tender *Kukui* was in the area at the time extinguishing lighthouses because of the Japanese threat. When the whaleboat from Niʻihau arrived on 10 December 1941 she was immediately ordered to Waimea to pick up an armed party and proceed to Niʻihau.
US Coast Guard Service

Camp Niʻihau

As war started, the sudden intrusion of the outside world marked the beginning of rapid changes on Niʻihau. Aylmer did not find these changes comfortable, but patriot that he was, he accepted them while attempting to limit their impact on the Niihauans. With the United States at war with Japan, Niʻihau suddenly found itself on the front line with an invasion of Hawaiʻi by the Japanese armed forces a real possibility.

Early in 1942 members of the 299th Infantry Regiment of the National Guard visited the island and, with Aylmer's assistance, selected sites for a camp (north of Puʻuwai), and observation posts. Two posts were selected, one at Kāwaʻewaʻe, a volcanic cone, three hundred feet high in the south-center of the island, and one at Poʻooneone on the southeastern coast. The latter was subsequently moved to Pueo Point to provide better coverage of the western approaches to Kauaʻi.

The observers' mission was to provide early warning to the military on Kauaʻi by scanning the sea and sky for enemy vessels and aircraft. The necessary facilities were constructed and the first permanent observers, consisting of 26 Kauaians and five haole, arrived in June 1942. They landed with three jeeps and a three-quarter-ton truck — apart from the Cletrac, the first motorized vehicles seen on the island.

Aylmer had secured an agreement with the army about how the detachment was to behave on Niʻihau. Although happy to assist in the war effort, he was quite firm on the standards required of the soldiers. This included a ban on alcohol and as little social interaction as possible with the local population, within the limits of cordiality. Smoking was strongly discouraged because of the fire danger, but not prohibited. Sharing a meal with a local family was allowed, but overnight stays in Puʻuwai village were prohibited. Needless to say, fraternization with young women was off limits. The soldiers were freely permitted to hunt pigs and game birds.

As background for his 1988 master's thesis Edward Stepien spoke to several of those who served on Niʻihau during this time, and much of this account came from these interviews.[23]

The army had just begun occupying the newly constructed base camp the week before David Larsen spent his week on Niʻihau and wrote so graphically of 'The Battle of Niʻihau' (Appendix C). He was astonished at the extent of the Robinsons' assistance to the military. Aside from the huge scale of the furrowing, 'they transport troops and supplies back and forth from Kauai, furnish camp sites for the soldiers and some buildings for headquarters: they lend them horses to ride … and sometimes send men out to hunt wild pig to supply fresh pork for the troops.'[24]

There were occasional breaches of Aylmer's agreement with the army. Alcohol was smuggled in with the troops' supplies and tobacco was sneaked in for the locals, but the fraternization rules were generally obeyed. After the construction period, when engineers from 165 Regiment were on the island (and mostly haole) they left, which eased the situation.

The outside world was not aware of the deployment until a year after the troops arrived. On 19 June 1943 the *Honolulu Advertiser* headlined a story on page one, 'Once Isolated Niihau Greets Army: Joins Nation's War Effort,' by staff writer Laselle Gilman. While Gilman had never been to Niʻihau, his information was largely correct; his major theme

▲ The insignia of the US 299th Infantry Regiment, which had a detachment on Niʻihau from June 1942 to August 1944. The motto means 'Let us be alert.'

> The modern world of jeeps, radios, movies, electric lights, and bold-eyed strangers in uniform has invaded that legendary baronial estate which is the Territory's farthest-west inhabited island … Life on Niihau has been radically altered.

◀ US Coast Guard Landing Craft Mechanized (LCM) arriving at Nonopapa with supplies. Note the pierced steel plate laid to spread the load of the heavy machinery when it was brought in over the beach.
US Coast Guard Service

▼ A Caterpillar D7 bulldozer being unloaded at Nonopapa.
US Coast Guard Service

▼▼ The LORAN installation and camp north of Lē'ahi Point, June 1949.
US Coast Guard Service

was the changes that had been wrought to life on the island by the advent of the military: 'The modern world of jeeps, radios, movies, electric lights, and bold-eyed strangers in uniform has invaded that legendary baronial estate which is the Territory's farthest-west inhabited island … Life on Niihau has been radically altered.'[25]

Although the Battle of Midway, which took place from 4–7 June 1942, brought to an end the threat of invasion of Hawai'i, the army retained its observation posts on Ni'ihau until the summer of 1944.

LORAN

Army coastwatchers were not the only military personnel destined to call Ni'ihau their home. The island was to be used for another wartime purpose altogether.

A system of long-range navigation for ships and aircraft (LORAN) had been developed at Massachusetts Institute of Technology in 1941, and the Department of Defense considered it now ready for implementation. The task was given to the Coast Guard.

The system depended on bouncing the radio waves off the ionosphere (30–600 miles above the earth) and had a range of 800 miles in daytime and 1400 miles at night, with an accuracy of tens of miles. (Later developments increased the accuracy by orders of magnitude.)

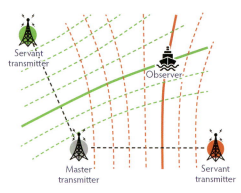

▲ The LORAN system involved transmitting short pulses of radio waves simultaneously from a pair of fixed transmitters hundreds of miles apart. These could be received on any vessel with the necessary equipment, and the microsecond time difference between the reception of the two signals could be translated into a distance difference. This time differential could only lie on a hyperbola between the two transmitting stations, creating a 'line of difference' along which the vessel lay. Using the same logic, the receipt of signals from a separate second pair of stations resulted in a second line. Where the two lines intersected was the location of the ship or aircraft.

To implement the scores of stations involved in the western Pacific where the major wartime usefulness was envisaged, the Coast Guard formed specialist construction units.

Siting surveys for the Hawaiian stations took place in late 1943 and it was decided that two master stations should be established on Niʻihau, with servant stations on French Frigate Shoals (400 miles from the first master station on Niʻihau), and the second servant station on the northwest tip of the Big Island (300 miles from the second master station on Niʻihau). A monitoring station was to be set up on Kauaʻi, with a base establishment on Sand Island in Pearl Harbor.[26]

The first of the Hawaiian stations built by the 40 men of Construction Detachment C was perhaps the most challenging — the two master stations on Niʻihau, where lack of landing facilities hindered access for the heavy equipment. The site selected was on the west coast, between Keʻelināwili Point and Lēʻahi Point, and about 200 yards inland. One rusty red Quonset Hut still stands today, while the foundations of the remaining six may still be seen beneath the kiawe trees. The materials and equipment were offloaded from US Navy landing craft at Nonopapa, eight miles away. Construction began in late April 1944.

When completed in July 1944 it was staffed by an officer and 14 enlisted men. Given the nature of the equipment the base was relatively sophisticated, with extensive electricity generating facilities, and a Cleaver-Brook boiler with water distillation plant.

The normal tour of duty for personnel was 18 months, and a movie theater, baseball diamond and soccer field were provided for leisure activities. Swimming and fishing were always popular. Aylmer came to a similar agreement with the Coast Guard as he had with the army regarding the behavior of personnel. The first such agreement had an end date of six months after hostilities ended, and was renewed several times as the station did not close until October 1952. By and large the required standards of conduct by Coast Guard personnel were complied with.

For the first six months of the LORAN station, both the army and the Coast Guard were on the island and great sporting rivalry existed between them, much to the amusement of the locals. Nevertheless life could be monotonous. Some likened their tours of duty on 'the rock' to an incarceration on Alcatraz.[27] After the war the station became quite popular with the Niihauans themselves, who rode from Puʻuwai for the movies or to suck ice cubes.[28]

When the stations finally closed in 1952 it marked the end of more than ten years of occupation of portions of the island by the military, with consequent changes in the lifestyles of the local Niihauans — changes which have continued, albeit more slowly, to this day.

The territorial senate investigates

The euphoria occasioned by the end of the war in 1945 engendered strong feelings among people across the world that governments should do more to ensure that all their citizens received a fair deal. These feelings echoed the sentiments in the 'Four

Freedoms' speech given by President Franklin Roosevelt as the State of the Nation address on 6 January 1941.

In his speech the president articulated four fundamental freedoms that people everywhere on the planet should be able to enjoy: freedom of speech, freedom of worship, freedom from want, and freedom from fear. These struck a chord, and the immediate postwar years saw the four freedoms become incorporated in the United Nations Universal Declaration of Human Rights in December 1948.

After the war some legislators in the islands became concerned that a proportion of their constituents were not fully able to experience the four freedoms. They felt that, particularly on the smaller islands, some citizens were not able to live the 'American Dream.'

The opportunity to explore the situation on Niʻihau arose in June 1946 when a belief surfaced that Kauaʻi County could not legally continue to subsidize the Niʻihau school, as its facilities were private and it stood on private land. The Senate pounced when they heard this, and a six-person Senate Investigating Committee was formed with a broad remit to inquire into the situation on both Niʻihau and Lānaʻi, with terms of reference:

> … to visit Lanai and Niihau to investigate what lands, roads, schools, parks, landing facilities and other public properties or improvements are owned by the territory or the county on such islands, and the welfare of the people of such islands, and their enjoyment or deprivation of the Four Freedoms, and to report their findings and recommendations to the senate at the next session of the Legislature.[29]

The wording indicates how prevalent knowledge of the Four Freedoms was at that time.

The appointed chair of the committee was Republican (R) Francis Hyde Īʻi Brown from Oʻahu, a senator of almost 20 years' experience. A wealthy man, often called 'the last aliʻi,' he was a grandson of John Papa ʻĪʻī, a superb athlete and renowned golfer. The other five members were Democrat (D) Clarence Crozier, an experienced senator from Maui with a reputation as a reformer; the fiery John Fernandes (D) from Kauaʻi, something of a maverick; William H Hill (R), a flamboyant senator from Hawaiʻi; Charles Silva (R), a ten-year veteran senator from Hawaiʻi; and Francis Sylva (R) from Oʻahu. The committee was accompanied by Senator Eugene Capellas, *Honolulu Advertiser* reporter Ernest May and photographer Danny Morse.

The party flew to Kauaʻi on 30 July 1946, crossed over to Niʻihau in a chartered boat, and were met at Nonopapa by Aylmer and Lester Robinson. The Coast Guard's command vehicle provided transport around the island. The committee left early afternoon the same day to return to Waimea, where they spent the night before flying from Barking Sands at six in the morning to return to Honolulu. Their time on the island was brief, but that didn't prevent senators from giving the press forthright and immediate impressions of their visit. Their minds may have been largely made up before the visit even took place.

On the evening of their return (31 July) the *Honolulu Star Bulletin* carried an article headlined 'Isolation of Niihau is Blasted,' in which Senator Clarence Crozier declaimed:

> Niihau, which has been preserved for three generations by the Robinson family as a last refuge of primitive Hawaii, is '80 years behind the times.'

▲ Francis Hyde Īʻi Brown (1892–1976), a member of the Territorial Senate almost continuously from 1927 to 1947 and chair of the Niʻihau Investigating Committee. He was also a champion golfer. Two golf courses on Hawaiʻi and many trophies have been named in his honor.
Find a Grave, colorised

'We are going to do something to bring the people over there up to date with the rest of the territory.'[30]

He delineated the deficiencies, as he saw them, in terms of communications, education, religion and medical care, and vowed to initiate improvements. Senator Francis Sylva, who was present during the interview, discreetly deferred all questions asked of him to Senator Brown as chair. In the same newspaper issue Senator John Fernandes stated the visit had confirmed that the Niʻihau school stood on private land and had been built with private funds.

The following morning the *Honolulu Advertiser* carried the first of four articles by Ernest May, the reporter on the visit. In the article Senator Brown announced that his committee would be recommending:

- Appointment of a full time medical representative on Niʻihau under the Territorial Board of Health
- Installation of modern communications with the other islands
- Maintenance by the territory of an adequate school program on Niʻihau.

He foresaw other recommendations once the committee had met after their visit.

In the same piece Senator Charles Silva echoed Senator Brown's sentiments, while Senator Crozier was concerned at the lack of religious freedom, with only a single church on the island, and with any disciplining required being done by the church rather than a government agency. He suggested building a wharf, making a road from the landing to the school, and constructing a health center and government-owned schools.[31]

The tone of all four of Ernest May's articles was essentially negative as regards the Niihauans' way of life. The Robinson family's progressive ranching methods, however, received praise.

Aylmer and Lester must have been horrified at the press reports, and it appears in retrospect that too little attention was given by either party to the planning of the quick visit the senators made. The school teachers were away (it was vacation time)

▲ Aylmer Robinson at the time of the Senate Investigation Committee's visit in 1946.

Saturday Evening Post / Kauaʻi Historical Society

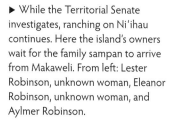

▶ While the Territorial Senate investigates, ranching on Niʻihau continues. Here the island's owners wait for the family sampan to arrive from Makaweli. From left: Lester Robinson, unknown woman, Eleanor Robinson, unknown woman, and Aylmer Robinson.

Private collection

and no opportunity was arranged for the committee to meet with a significant group of Niihauans. The visit was in sharp contrast to Governor Judd's 17 years earlier.

Ni'ihau was in the limelight, much to the distress of the Robinsons and the Niihauans. Publicity, most of it negative, appeared in magazines and on the radio. While it was conceded Niihauans appeared contented and healthy, an editorial in the *Honolulu Advertiser* opined that the island's isolation had deprived Niihauans of choice. The paper believed they had a right to know about the outside world, and this had been denied them.

Many letters to the editor supported the Robinsons' ethos and respected the Niihauans' desire to be left alone. Others had a different view. And all this before the committee's Ni'ihau recommendations were known. It was not until 24 March 1947 (nine months later) that Senator Brown and his committee reported to the Senate. Their report was, however, immediately withdrawn and resubmitted on 8 April on the suspicion there could be some government-owned land on Ni'ihau. The committee then reaffirmed that there was no public land on Ni'ihau; the whole island was owned by the Robinsons.

The central thesis of the report was that modern facilities should be brought to Ni'ihau, and to do this it was recommended that the government:

- Acquire sufficient land for a school
- Buy land to construct a landing pier
- Secure land and make a road from the pier to a government center at Pu'uwai, to include a grade school, teacher cottages, playground, health, policing and courthouse facilities
- Procure land for a small airfield, with roading to it
- Build a hospital and dispensary on land acquired for the purpose
- Appoint a Hawaiian-speaking district health nurse

◀ At the same time, paniolo also wait for the sampan from Makaweli.
Private collection

- Build a courthouse and police station on land obtained for the purpose, and appoint a magistrate and police officer
- Establish radio or telephone communications with Kaua'i and the other islands
- Acquire land for the building of a small church or churches to accommodate members of different faiths
- Draft a law to penalise landlords who prevent spiritual advisors from visiting tenants and administering the rites of the churches to which they belong.[32]

The committee wanted the superintendent of public instruction to explain why adequate provision had not been made to educate Niihauan children. It recommended that the school be extended from the fifth to the eighth grade as soon as possible, and when this was achieved, provision be made for scholarships for children to receive a high school education on Kaua'i or elsewhere.

The report's conclusion was sweeping:

> In short, your committee finds that either directly or by implication, three of the four freedoms, to-wit, freedom of speech, freedom of religion, and freedom from fear, either by name or in essence, are unknown upon the Island of Niihau.[33]

The committee had little to say regarding Lāna'i. Recommendations were made for improvements its roads and port, but there was no mention of the Four Freedoms there.

After two unsuccessful attempts at deferring discussion, the far-reaching conclusions and recommendations on Ni'ihau were adopted by the Senate on 11 April 1947. Senator Francis Brown immediately introduced two bills to give effect to the recommendations, the first to provide for the acquisition of the necessary land, the second to signal the Senate's concern regarding religious freedom by making it a misdemeanor for a landlord to interfere with the religious practices of his tenants. Both bills were passed by the Senate, the first by only one vote (8:7), the second comfortably (13:2), as it was of a more general nature.

Passage of these bills through the maze of Senate committees allowed many interested parties to take exception to the proposed legislation. Aylmer Robinson was among them and his lengthy letter was read before the Senate on 21 April 1947, countering the investigating committee's arguments and recommendations point by point. His central argument was that the changes contemplated 'would be very detrimental as well as distasteful to the Niihau people' and he gives detailed reasons for this belief. He emphasized that the current situation of those on the island is not driven by him alone, but that all issues are dealt with cooperatively in conjunction with the residents. He concluded: 'I have just returned from Niihau. The people there are greatly disturbed over the prospect of legislation to break up the type of community life [they lead] …'[34]

Also read before the Senate was a translation of a petition from 62 Ni'ihau residents to 'leave us alone,' and requesting the governor to veto any measure affecting the island.[35]

These and many other pleas were to no avail, and the Senate narrowly passed the bill as indicated above. The only member of the investigating committee to vote against the bill was Senator Francis Sylva.

The bill moved to the House, where it was seen quite differently. With the evident disquiet in the community, two members of the House, Rep. Flora Hayes and Rep.

I do not believe the initial group of senators who visited Niihau included a person who could speak Hawaiian.

Walter McGuire, decided to investigate for themselves. Both Hawaiian-speaking, they visited Niʻihau in conjunction with a visit by Department of Public Instruction officials and came back saying 'everybody seemed perfectly happy and contented.'[36]

Flora Hayes went so far as to say: 'I do not believe the initial group of senators who visited Niihau included a person who could speak Hawaiian. For this reason I believe that the residents did not express their views freely to the legislature.'[37]

The bill failed to garner support in the House. Perhaps because of the public outcry the proposed measure was roundly rejected. The governor never saw it and on Niʻihau the status quo remained. The Niihauans and the Robinsons had won the day, but the waves created by the investigation were felt for decades.

The debate and outcome also generated positive responses. George Mellen, scholar of Hawaiiana of the times, was moved to write tongue-in-cheek to the *Honolulu Advertiser*:

> Ably reporting the Legislative Committee's investigation of Niihau, the Advertiser has rendered valuable service to the Territory because on the face of the Committee's findings, the next Legislature can do nothing less than appropriate enough to hire the Robinson boys to run the rest of the Islands.[38]

He is, of course, referring to Sinclair, Aylmer, Selwyn and Lester.

Inquisitive strangers

Despite the conclusion of the Senate Investigating Committee that the government did not own the land upon which the school stood, the question of public lands on Niʻihau would not go away. In December 1955 the Attorney General reported that several documents had been found indicating that the government *may* own 14.76 acres of land on Niʻihau, including seven school sites, a church lot and landings at Ōmalumalua and Kamalino.[39] He accordingly wrote to the Robinson brothers, Aylmer and Lester, and their mother Alice, as co-owners, advising them that surveyors would be arriving to locate the supposed public lands and requesting assistance to access the island.

Lester, when questioned by a reporter before he had seen the letter, said that he didn't expect it would lead to any trouble with government. He was quoted as saying 'We have always had pleasant dealings with government.' And indeed it was so — as the survey party never arrived.

This was not the end of it, however, and the question dragged on through successive Attorneys General. It was raised again in 1959, 1960 and 1961 without any resolution.[40] Apart from the validity of the deed, the location of the pieces of land could not all be determined, defined as they were by landmarks that had long since disappeared. Governor Quinn stated that he favored negotiation, but it was not clear what there was to negotiate.[41] The governor had discussed the state's claims with Aylmer and Lester when he visited at the end of September 1961, and the matter then sank without trace, either because of their discussion, or after the governor had also read the Attorney General's latest report. While this battle was apparently averted, worse was to come in the 1970s.

Over the years Aylmer and Lester had always offered cordial access to the island to the relevant authorities, be they educational, public health, army, navy, Coast Guard, police, scientific or survey parties. They drew the line, however, at the accompaniment of these delegations by members of the press. Reporters had only been part of the official parties during the two gubernatorial visits (1929 and 1961) and the Senate Investigating Committee's visit (1946) during Aylmer's long tenure. Many members of the press had requested permission to be included in visits and had been refused so deftly that one, John Ramsey, was moved to publish extracts from Aylmer's refusal letter in the *Star Bulletin* as follows:

> We have made it a practice not to add others to the party. We have felt that when they have been kind enough to limit their own numbers for our convenience, it would be discourteous on our part to add others of our own selection.
>
> If we were to make an exception in your case, I think you can readily see that we might well be overwhelmed with applications in another year.
>
> It is unpleasant to be in a position of refusing requests such as yours, but under the circumstances I feel that such is the correct course to take, and I trust you will be willing to recognize the reasonableness of this decision.[42]

Sometimes members of delegations had themselves gone to the newspapers. There always seemed to be public interest in this mysterious island. Some people felt that with the paucity of information, perhaps the Robinsons had something to hide.

To satisfy this interest, Honolulu newspapers vied with one another to publish stories about Niʻihau. In November 1957 the *Star Bulletin* took matters into its own hands. The newspaper's chief photographer Warren Roll rented a Piper Cub, ostensibly to take aerial photos of Niʻihau. When some apparent engine trouble ensued over Niʻihau, the aircraft landed and in so doing damaged its landing gear and propeller. Pilot Joe Prigge stayed with the plane while Roll walked for a considerable time to reach Puʻuwai village early in the afternoon, a Saturday.

Meanwhile the authorities had been alerted that the plane was missing and a helicopter search was mounted. It was soon found disabled on Niʻihau and Prigge told the helicopter pilot who found him that repairs could be done on site if he could arrange the necessary spare parts. Later in the day a second Piper Cub successfully landed with the spares.

▼ Warren Roll (1922–2008). Regarded as assertive and audacious by his fellow photographers, his escapade on Niʻihau certainly shows this. As both the pilot, Joseph Prigge, and Warren Roll have now died the full story of the crash may never be known. At the time of the event Warren Roll was chief photographer for the *Star Bulletin*.
Honolulu Star Bulletin

Back in Puʻuwai, the first house Roll stumbled into, thirsty and exhausted, was that of school teacher Hannah Niau, where the family were stretched out on the lawn. 'Then an elderly woman with a friendly smile came toward me. I told her that our plane had crashed and I needed help. "I know," she said, "we heard it on the radio this morning".'[43]

The Niau family immediately invited him in and gave him a meal of poi, pork and bread — not forgetting water, which he gulped down. A curious crowd soon gathered at the sudden appearance of this haole stranger.

Dispelling rumors about life on the island, Roll noted that the men were in brightly colored aloha shirts and were wearing shoes and wristwatches. Feeling a little like the Pied Piper of Hamelin with the crowd trailing behind him, he went 'walkabout' in the village, observing and taking photographs as he went. 'The children were neat and clean,' he reported later. 'It seemed that the people — especially the children — were watching all my movements.'[44]

He noted the sturdy, well-built and tidy houses with their gardens and lawns, each surrounded by a perimeter stone wall to keep stock out, albeit with some homes in need of paint, but quite unlike the shacks he had expected. Bicycles were in evidence outside most houses. Cooking was done on kerosene stoves and all houses had kerosene refrigerators. Nearly all had battery-powered radios.

On inquiring, he found that shopping was done via mainland mail-order catalogs. The friendliness and openness of the people impressed him, and they certainly didn't appear to be oppressed. Aylmer Robinson was almost revered. Roll was told that Aubrey, Aylmer's father, had included in his will a stipulation that no Hawaiian was to be removed from Niʻihau unless the individual wished to leave. The promise had been kept.

Other myths dispelled were that the Robinsons' prohibition on smoking appeared under siege as he saw both men and women smoking.* Sunday was now not just for church-going, as a baby lūʻau was in progress at the time of his visit. All the village was invited, as was Roll himself. The paniolo told him that there were 50 of them and each week half fished while the other half worked on the ranch itself, with a few of the latter working on charcoal production. Fish-drying facilities and evidence of charcoal production were visible outside the houses.

Speculating on what the Niihauans would decide to do about him, the photographer inquired of the ranch foreman if the ranch hands could help in righting the Piper Cub. His reply was that he would have to ask Aylmer (by carrier pigeon) what to do, and that Roll should wait.

Shortly after this conversation finished, a Piper Cub flew low over Puʻuwai dropping candy, cigarettes and a message to the effect that Roll's plane had been repaired and would take off at five that afternoon. With that, more than two dozen residents, including two women with babies, piled into a war surplus truck to go to the take-off point:

'They told me to board the truck,' Roll said.

'It was the funniest thing to see how they packed the fenders, the hood and the front seat, all jabbering, laughing, eager to go.'

'I took a place in the stake body with a dozen others,' Roll said. 'We rode off standing up.'

'The ride, too, was one of the most hilarious things I have ever been on.'

▲ A house in Puʻuwai from the air, in a photograph taken by Warren Roll in 1957. The detail below shows residents coming out to see the plane overhead.
Honolulu Star Bulletin

* By the time of the state governor's visit two years later the restriction on smoking had been reduced to a ban on smoking outdoors because of the risk of fire.

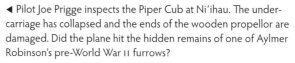

◀ Pilot Joe Prigge inspects the Piper Cub at Niʻihau. The undercarriage has collapsed and the ends of the wooden propellor are damaged. Did the plane hit the hidden remains of one of Aylmer Robinson's pre-World War II furrows?

◣ The view of the damaged Piper Cub which appeared in the *Star Bulletin* after the accident.

◣◣ The repaired plane and the ex-World War II truck that ferried Warren Roll back to the plane after his visit to Puʻuwai.

◣◣◣ A farewell low pass over the helpful Niihauans.

Warren Roll photographs, courtesy of Jonah Roll

'It had all the aspects of a picnic outing. Everybody got in the act in hooting stray cattle off the road.'[45]

With the passengers covered in the all-pervasive red dust, the truck arrived at the crash scene 45 minutes later, but the plane was nowhere to be seen. Joe Prigge had moved it to another cleared area after the repairs were done.

Then we said goodbye to the cheering Niihauans as we prepared to take off.

There were a few tense moments as Joe gunned the engine.

With the ground as bumpy as it was, we wondered whether the landing gear would give way again.[46]

The plane landed at Burns Field near Port Allen on Kauaʻi some little time later. Roll's story (written by reporter George West, and accompanied by Roll's revealing photos), covered three pages of the *Star Bulletin* on Saturday 16 November 1957. How much of the escapade was staged is still a matter for debate. Roll was familiar with light aircraft, as he was a pilot himself. The unvarnished description of life in Puʻuwai in the late 1950s is useful in that there was no involvement by the island's owners, and residents were at liberty to speak completely openly. Roll's impressions are worth contrasting with David Larsen's description of life on Niʻihau in 1942, 15 years earlier (see Chapter Ten). Change had occurred, but not too much.

Two years after Roll, a visitor who called at Niʻihau on official business and then chose to go public with his findings was Deal -, the assistant superintendent of public instruction (now the Department of Education). He visited as one of a delegation of three carrying out the department's annual school inspection. His enthusiastic observations were published in the *Sunday Advertiser* on 11 October 1959 under the headline 'Curtain Parts on Amazing Niihau.'

After detailing the journey to Kiʻi in the Robinson's ex-World War II landing craft and the subsequent panel truck ride to Puʻuwai, he turns to local scenes:

> It is difficult to describe as a village, however, as the houses are set so far apart. One hundred, 200 or 300 yards separate them. They are set in open pasture. The houses are protected from the cattle by stone fences …
>
> Of course, the usual signs of fishing activity surround the house — poles, throw-nets and covered screened racks for drying fish.
>
> The school is set in a large enclosure approximately 50 feet wide and 100 yards long. Dominating the center of this enclosure is the church. It is something out of 18th Century New England. It is a typical Congregational Church, beautiful in its design and stark simplicity, but devoid of ornamentation. It is painted dull buff.
>
> On either side and set back from the church are the two school rooms. Mrs. Hannah K. Niau teaches grades 1 to 4 and Gilbert Pahulehua [grades] 5 to 8. The school grounds were immaculate, covered with a light coating of sand to reduce dust. Night blooming cereus was on the stone wall …[47]

Apart from noting that all tuition was in English and that the children 'were very well ordered, in fact too well ordered,' doubtless due to their being subject to their annual inspection, he lavishes praise on Aylmer Robinson:

> Imagine if you can a Harvard man who speaks Hawaiian which sounds like flowing music. Imagine a man whose scientific understanding of conservation principles has saved an island from waste and erosion and made it productive — yet an island that still uses carrier pigeons to get messages back and forth.
>
> Imagine if you can a man 71 years old, in the peak of physical condition, spry enough to jump from an LCM [landing craft] into a small lighter in a surging sea. His dedication and love of his island, Niihau, and its wonderful people shines through his every word.[48]

After a picnic lunch on a secluded beach, the return journey from the Lehua landing to Makaweli ended a climactic day for Deal Crooker. The well set-out two-page spread in the *Sunday Advertiser* was too much for the *Star Bulletin*, which determined to fight back and 'regain the Niʻihau news initiative.'

A week or two later a *Star Bulletin* reporter, Shideler Harpe, secretly landed on the northwest coast of Niʻihau in the early hours of a Thursday morning, only to be found asleep on the beach by some paniolo on their way to work in a ranch truck. Eyeing the bearded haole stranger with a backpack full of canned food, and aware of the Cold War and remembering the events of December 1941, the ranch hands concluded he might be a spy who had landed from a Soviet submarine. While Aylmer was being contacted by carrier pigeon,* they took the visitor to Kiʻi Landing, where he remained for over 24 hours until Aylmer and Lester arrived with Kauaʻi police captain Anton Vidinha in the Robinson landing craft. On being questioned, Harpe admitted his assignment was to write a story on Niʻihau for

▼ An article in the rival newspaper on the Tuesday morning after the weekend crash. The headline implies a chilly reception was received from the Niihauans, but the body of the article makes it clear that the adjective was being used in relation to the overnight temperature. In fact the reception given Warren Roll in Puʻuwai was anything but chilly, as his extensive article the following week shows.
Honolulu Advertiser

'Saw Nobody, Took No Photos'
Cold Niihau Reception For Pair in Downed Plane

KAPAA, Kauai—Joe Prigge, pilot of a small plane that crash-landed on the "forbidden isle" of Niihau Saturday, said last night "we never saw nobody from Niihau all through the night."

Mr. Prigge, 45, of Kapaa told The Advertiser he and his passenger, Star-Bulletin Photographer Warren Roll,* slept alongside their Piper Cub Saturday night on the beach at Niihau. "It was really cold," he said.

HE SAID it was not true that he purposely tried to land on Niihau in order to give Mr. Roll a chance to get some otherwise unobtainable pictures.

"We didn't see nobody. He didn't take any pictures. We stayed right by the plane."

Mr. Prigge said "water in the gas" forced the plane down on Niihau.

WHEN THE CUB did not return to Kauai Saturday afternoon, according to its flight plan, Coast Guard Search-Rescue headquarters in Honolulu was alerted.

Already busy with rescue efforts in connection with the missing Pan American Airways plane, the Coast Guard managed to dispatch an 83-foot cutter from Nawiliwili, and ordered a helicopter to help in the search.

No trace of the Piper was found Saturday night, but Sunday morning at daybreak a helicopter pilot sighted the downed plane on the Niihau beach. Minutes later, both men were picked up and flown back to Kauai.

SPARE PARTS were obtained, and they were returned with the owner of the plane, Antone Texejra Jr. of Kauai. The plane was repaired in "about an hour," according to Mr. Prigge, and flown back to Kauai Sunday night.

* A three-way radio was installed in 1960 connecting Makaweli, Niʻihau, and the Robinson Landing Craft. Carrier pigeons were maintained for some time as a backup.

the *Star Bulletin*, but would not say how he got to the island. He was told he was under arrest for 'investigation' — a charge which allowed him to be held for 48 hours. He did not speak to Aylmer and Lester at Ki'i and they remained on the island.

Unfortunately for the *Star Bulletin*, the *Honolulu Advertiser* had the story almost immediately and on the Sunday morning couldn't resist running a page one account of the escapade under the headline 'Spy on Niihau? No, Just Sound of Harpe,' complete with a caricature of Harpe.[49]

The *Star Bulletin* had been well and truly upstaged, but despite that ran Harpe's own description of events and his observations on Ni'ihau on the following Sunday.[50]

▶ The caricature of Shideler Harpe which appeared in the *Sunday Advertiser* on 25 October 1959 under the headline: 'Spy on Niihau? No, Just Sound of Harpe.'
Sunday Advertiser

After traveling back to Makaweli in the Robinson landing craft, Harpe was questioned again at length by Captain Vidinha, and finally released. He caught the first plane to Honolulu. The Robinsons agreed not to file charges.

So what had his adventure achieved? A description of Ki'i and the paniolo in words and pictures. Extracts from Harpe's article follow:

> Kii Landing is a beautiful little bay where the Hawaiians once had a village. Nothing is left but half a dozen small, rotting houses.
>
> A crumbling stone pier pushes out into the bay. [Foreman Joseph Kelley] said part of it had been built in the 1800s. Empty corrals line the beach, and a dilapidated shed houses a battered whale boat.
>
> The cowboys stayed with me all day Thursday, waiting for the boat that never came. During the long, hot hours we talked, dozed, ate and swam.
>
> They all wore heavy work shoes, combat or Western boots.
>
> The men were dressed in army fatigues — although none had ever been in service — sports shirts, blue jeans, denim work shirts. On their heads were crumpled, sweat-stained, Stetsons and army fatigue hats.
>
> The cowboys were eager to display their knowledge of what's going on 'Outside,' and showed great pride in their radios — for some the only communication between Niihau and the rest of the world.
>
> The men said they work a 48-hour week 'just like everyone else' but it was apparent that many of their working days stretched far beyond eight hours.
>
> The Niihauans eat few vegetables, and very little food is grown on the island. Their basic menu is rice and poi.[51]

He remarks on the Robinsons' regulations regarding liquor and tobacco, but noted that many smoked roll-your-own cigarettes. 'Apparently the entire community pays the price if any person or group violates a Robinson taboo' and 'contrary to popular belief there's considerable traveling between Ni'ihau and "Outside," but the cowboys said they travel only on Robinson boats — free of charge, of course.' When asked if Aylmer was a hard man to deal with 'some agreed that he was,' but 'Basically they like their island and the kind of life they lead.'

While there was nothing startlingly new in the *Star Bulletin* article and Harpe failed to get to Pu'uwai, it gives a clear picture of the paniolo and the life they led at that time. These unusual and entrepreneurial incidents give the flavor of what Aylmer and Lester had to deal with in the 1950s and '60s.

Statehood — Governor Quinn visits

A cloud of red dust stirred up by the three Marine Corps helicopters announced the arrival of State Governor William Quinn to Lehua Landing on the northern tip of Niʻihau at 8.20 a.m. on 29 September 1961. The governor was completing a pledge to visit all of the inhabited Hawaiian islands during his term of office.

He had been elected the new state's first governor, assuming office on 21 August 1959 (having previously been territorial governor, appointed by President Eisenhower). In the plebiscite on statehood held on 27 June 1959 over 93% voted 'yes' in a turnout of over 90% of eligible voters. By contrast Niʻihau was the only precinct among the 240 in the islands to oppose statehood — by 70 votes to 18.[52] Niʻihau had 107 registered voters, and with three informal votes, the turnout was 85%. When Sinclair Robinson, Aylmer's elder brother, was asked why the voting pattern was so different on Niʻihau, his reply was that the Niihauans had told him, 'We are happy the way we are now. Why change it?'[53]

It had been 29 years since the previous visit of a governor and technology had changed, as well as much else — except perhaps the way of life on the island. (Governor Judd had toured on horseback — see Chapter 10.) Waiting to greet the governor at a respectful distance from the helicopters were Aylmer and Lester, accompanied by about 20 residents and two vehicles. 'When the dust settled, the party was greeted cordially by Aylmer and Lester Robinson — lean, elderly and looking much as they were described by one of the pilots: World War I soldiers.'[54]

This description of the Robinson brothers was apt given they were both wearing 'faded khaki shirts and breeches, well-worn leather puttees and work shoes' topped with broad-brimmed Stetsons.

The party moved to a two-vehicle convoy, with the governor and the Robinson brothers in a battered, windscreen-down jeep and the remainder, including three reporters, following in a red truck. (These were the first reporters invited to the island since 1946.) Then began a stomach-churning tour of the island while the Robinson brothers regaled the governor on the difficulties of ranching on Niʻihau — scarcity of water, intermittent droughts, death of the cactus, the major drop in honey production and wool quality problems all leading to a reducing ranch income despite major efforts at diversification.

The party finally drove into Puʻuwai, where the residents had turned out in force to see the governor. He inspected the school, which was in session, and met the two schoolteachers. On his return to Honolulu he said he 'wants to make certain that Niihau children get the best education they possibly can.'[55] Education of children on Niʻihau had long been a bone of contention between the legislators, the executive and the Department of Public Instruction.[56] The governor was introduced to Bene Kanahele, the hero of 'the Battle of Niʻihau' (see Appendix C). All visitors were presented with commemorative shell lei.

The party then moved to The House at Kiʻekiʻe, as reported in the *Star Bulletin*:

> Lunch was served in an austere, high-ceilinged dining room.
> Old lamps hung above the long table, which was covered with a white cloth and set with heavy crockery.

▲ Governor William Quinn (1919–2006) was raised in Missouri, before attending Harvard Law School. His studies were broken by naval service during World War II and when one of his postings was to Hawaiʻi he determined to return after the war when he completed his studies. He returned in 1947 and practiced law, but also involved himself in politics, running unsuccessfully for the Territorial Senate in 1956. He worked closely with the Hawaii Statehood Commission, and was subsequently appointed territorial governor by President Eisenhower in 1957. On the achievement of statehood in 1959 he defeated John Burns in the election and served until 1962.
Genealogy, colorised

A Robinson sat at each end and the table was served by a handsome, elderly Hawaiian cowboy who probably would have been happier working with cattle.

Aylmer offered a brief prayer before the lunch of cold beef, canned peas, fried taro, poi, roll slices, Niihau honey and canned peaches.

Aylmer dominated the conversation during and after lunch. He talked authoritatively about the Hawaiian language, culture, handicraft, history and geography.

Lester told stories and dispelled myths.

Calling Niihau the "Forbidden Island" is far-fetched, he indicated.

… About 600 passengers made the 20-mile journey last year in the Robinsons' boat.[57]

There was an extensive question and answer session as well as time for tale-telling and myth-dispelling. One of the reporters, Jack Teehan, wrote regarding the two brothers:

> Aylmer Robinson, elder of the two, is in his mid-70s. Robinson is thin, almost gaunt. The years and the elements have turned his skin as brown as the Hawaiian people he loves … Robinson has a restrained smile when he tells an amusing story — and he talks softly. [He] is obviously a true gentleman with gracious manners. He is accustomed to giving orders and having them obeyed. They sound more like friendly suggestions, but the undertone of command is there.
>
> Robinson, for all practical purposes, makes all the decisions about Niihau. His brother, Lester, some 12 years younger, is the assistant manager of the Niihau ranch operations. Lester possesses many of his brother's traits, but his humor is more unrestrained …
>
> Without appearing to do so they soon make it obvious that guests who behave like gentlemen will be treated as such — that there are certain unwritten rules beyond which a guest is guilty of impropriety.[58]

At 3 p.m. the helicopters met the party at Kamalino, south of Nonopapa, where they inspected the sheep shearing shed on their journey down from their lunch at The House. They then flew back to Barking Sands on Kaua'i.

Jack Teehan summed up his feelings after the visit: 'There is a simple dignity on Niihau that seems lost to the outside world. Niihau is not just an island — it is a way of life.'[59]

The governor's visit was one the Robinson brothers must have judged a great success.

Passing the baton

In response to a letter from Florence Boyer, one of his boyhood tutors on Ni'ihau, Aylmer wrote a long letter in 1963 to bring her up to date with the family's situation since those days at the turn of the 19th century. After describing the lives of his brothers and sister, Aylmer sums up his own career:

> My own work has been divided between two spheres. On Kauai I have been the business manager of our partnership dealing particularly with contracts and leases, legal problems, taxation and similar questions as they arise from time to time. These duties are exacting and take a great deal of time and close attention. My particular pleasure however has been the management of Niihau, with its cattle, sheep, horses and other

▲ The Ni'ihau Ranch landing craft *Hoio* in her berth at Makaweli Landing. (Ho'i'o is a Hawaiian fern with edible shoots.) At that time the vessel was an LCM 6 leased from the US Navy.

Robinson family

ranching activities. It still remains much as you saw it — a Hawaiian community, which is something distinctive now since other races — Japanese, Filipinos and others have become the larger elements in the population of the State.

He reveals what makes Niʻihau distinctive for him:

> Niihau is the last place where Hawaiian is spoken almost exclusively in the daily life of the place and where the jobs of importance are still filled by Hawaiians. The island life still centers around its church, and so far we have been able to keep out liquor, and the island has maintained its crime-free record. Outside pressure is heavy, wanting to break in on this last Hawaiian community, but so far that has been withstood.[60]

A second letter from Aylmer, written in 1948 in the aftermath of the war, answers some questions posed by a University of Hawaiʻi researcher. It gives a sensitive and sympathetic picture of the Niihauan community, which changed little during his stewardship of the island:

> [Niihauans] have friends and relatives all over the Islands and are continually travelling, either visiting on the other islands or having their friends or relatives visit them on Niihau. …
>
> The type of life on Niihau is by choice, not by reason of ignorance about the outside world, and has been little changed by the impact of the war. The strength of the community is due in considerable measure to the fact that liquor has been prohibited over a long period of years, and the community opinion solidly backs that prohibition. That was not changed by the war, the Army authorities realising the importance of that feature and cooperating fully, not allowing it at their post on the island. Tobacco has never been prohibited, the only regulations being by way of minimising the fire hazard on a very dry island. Radios, electric lights, and refrigerators were not new to Niihau, although with the higher wages of the war period there are more on the island now than there were before. Guns and ammunition had been used for many years in eradicating the wild goats. They had had little use since the goats were exterminated, but were in no sense unfamiliar. Neither were cats or dogs new, wild cats as well as tame being on the island in considerable numbers. Dogs are native to the islands, that is they were here when the islands were first discovered [by Europeans], but they are not kept now on Niihau on account of the sheep industry, and for that reason the Army also kept dogs away.[61]

There had been much speculation in the press that because of the war Niʻihau had somehow radically changed, and Aylmer wished to set the record straight. In fact, little about the community had changed as a result of the part the island played in the war.

The 'outside pressure' Aylmer speaks of in the first letter came in many forms. In October 1965 the US Navy inadvertently bombed the island in what was described at the time as 'The Second Battle of Niʻihau.' Two aircraft from the USS *Ticonderoga* on a close support exercise to bomb Kaʻula Rock bombed Niʻihau south of Kiʻi Landing by mistake (fortunately on the beach and under the cliffs). They were 34 miles off target, and many were the red faces in the navy. No injury or damage was sustained and the navy later checked for any unexploded ordnance. Aylmer wasn't overly concerned and understood that 'these things happen,' and Russell Robinson, his nephew (Sinclair's son) was led to remark, 'It's a good thing the bombs didn't hit Puuwai. Benny Kanahele wouldn't have been around to help them.' (Bene Kanahele had died in 1962.)[62]

▲ Aylmer and Lester Robinson greeted the governor in their trademark 'khaki shirts and breeches and brown leather puttees and broad-brim hats', as one reporter put it. Looking like soldiers from World War I, another wrote.
Private collection

The populace at large was highly indignant as the navy had insisted on keeping Kaʻula Rock for target practice, and a stinging editorial appeared in *The Garden Island* newspaper on 6 October.[63] In Washington Senator Inouye called for a moratorium on all live bombing exercises until an investigation was completed.

In November 1966, in response to increasing Cold War concerns, Maurice Myers, the state civil defense controller and his health department team paid a short visit to Niʻihau to assess the island's preparedness in case of nuclear attack — which was nil. Aylmer promised to build a fall-out shelter near Puʻuwai, but it never happened, probably due to his failing health.[64] He had been diagnosed with cancer and underwent an operation, but died on 2 April 1967. Ka Haku Makua, the Big Boss, was no more.

Aylmer's tenure as manager of Niihau Ranch covered almost half a century. The Niihauans had seen him as a gentle, wise friend, unlike some in the outside world who regarded him as the feudal lord attempting to preserve his baronial estate at all costs.

His death sparked concerns among the Niihauan community. For years the gap between costs and revenue for the ranch had been bridged by Aylmer from his own funds. The gap was widening. What would happen now? It was said Aylmer made provisions in his will for this support to continue, but there was no certainty.[65] Although Lester was well known to them and had gained their respect, what sort of person would he prove to be when in charge? There were bound to be changes — would Niʻihau be sold?

Aylmer never married and in his will left his three-quarter share in Niʻihau inherited from Aubrey to brother Lester, so the latter then owned the whole island. Lester willingly accepted his new responsibilities as Ka Haku on Niʻihau. Rumors surfaced that Niihauan families were forcibly moved to Kauaʻi to work on Robinson properties there, but this was publicly denied by Lester.[66] Gradually the islanders gained confidence in his management.

Then in one of those sudden quirks of fate, only 18 months after Aylmer's passing, Lester fell ill and died on 24 October 1969. For the Niihauans, uncertainty over their fate began all over again.

▶ Aylmer and Lester on horseback, their natural element.
Private collection

◀ Aylmer Robinson in 1961, at the time of Governor Quinn's visit to the island.
Honolulu Advertiser

> *Aylmer and Lester led by example. Several observers have said that orders were always given gently, e.g. 'Would you mind …,' 'Perhaps you would like to …' etc, and recipients responded in kind.*

As mentioned earlier, Aubrey, in his will, left a 75% share in Niʻihau to Aylmer and 25% to Lester. Three months before he died Lester handed on his one-quarter share in the island inherited directly from his grandfather, Aubrey, to his two sons, Keith and Bruce.67

Aylmer, in his turn, left his 75% share in Niʻihau to Lester and his wife Helen, with the stipulation that it was to go to Bruce and Keith after both Lester and Helen had died.68

In his will Lester left his remaining 75% share in the island half to his widow, Helen, with the other half to be shared equally between sons, Bruce and Keith.9 The upshot of all these changes was that upon their mother Helen's death in 2002, Keith and Bruce acquired complete ownership of Niʻihau. From Lester's passing until she died, Helen had a controlling interest in the island.

Keith was 27 at the time of his father's death, while Bruce was 25. Lester's will also stipulated that Helen was to make the decision as to which of the two boys was to become the manager of the ranch. Helen decided that Bruce should fulfil the role.

So what was Aylmer's legacy? He had succeeded in maintaining the language, culture and lifestyle of the community on Niʻihau according to the mores set by his father Aubrey, great-uncle Frank Sinclair, and great-grandmother Eliza Sinclair. The island and its people were his passion, and he was able to ensure that all able-bodied men had meaningful work from the time they left school, albeit by dipping into his own funds increasingly as the years progressed. Despite his several attempts at diversifying ranch income, Mother Nature can be cruel, and he felt these effects on many occasions — but persevered.

Over the years of his stewardship, schooling for the keiki improved and he set in motion, at his expense, scholarships to Kamehameha schools for the most able children. As technology became available, modern appliances such as kerosene-powered refrigerators and transistor radios began to be seen in Puʻuwai. Contact with the military during and after World War II accelerated the process of gradual change, despite the restrictions Aylmer placed on the military's behavior in relation to the local population.

▶ The grand mansion of Kapalawai standing on 157 acres of grounds, just after it was built by Aubrey outside Waimea, on Kauaʻi, in the 1890s. It became Aylmer's home for the rest of his life.
Robinson family

◂ Aylmer's distinctive hat still hangs on the wall at Kapalawai.
Steven Gentry

While churchgoing and learning from the Bible were still essential elements of the island way of life, it could not be said that the island was entirely stuck in the 'missionary culture of the 19th century' as some commentators claimed.

Aylmer and Lester led by example. Several observers have observed that orders were always given gently, e.g. 'Would you mind …,' 'Perhaps you would like to …' etc, and recipients responded in kind.

David Larsen, after spending time on Niʻihau in 1942, describes Aylmer's approach:

> Even when Aylmer was about there seemed to be no orders given — but a general discussion would take place in which one or several of the men would take part and then they would disperse to various tasks. Aylmer tells me that he never gives direct orders but asks if they can do this or that — and asks them how it should be done. He says it is the best way to get work and a sense of responsibility out of Hawaiians.[69]

It was an approach that won great respect towards the two brothers from the Niihauan community, but with both brothers now gone a new nervousness crept into their conversation.

Elama Kanahele: life on Niʻihau in the 1960s

As a counterpoint to David Larsen's description of life on Niʻihau in the 1940s (see pages 245–246) Elama Kanahele has written reminiscences of her time growing up there until the age of 13 in the 1960s. These memories, along with those of her mother, Virginia Nizo, and Emalia Licayan were published in both the Niihauan dialect and English in 2007 as *Aloha Niihau: Oral Histories*. They were translated into English by Elama Kanahele, Kimo Armitage and Kaeo NeSmith.

Time moves slowly on Niʻihau, as can be seen when contrasting these two accounts, one by a haole visitor and one by a Niihauan resident. This second description of life on the island, from which the following is drawn, comes towards the end of Aylmer Robinson's time on the island.

~

Life on Niʻihau isn't like it is on any other of the Hawaiian Islands. There are no cares or worries or bills or things like that. Our houses are just like the houses anywhere else in the islands except we have to deal with not having water. On Niʻihau there is no plumbing. Every house has a water catchment tank that holds the rainwater that is kept for cooking and drinking. You can't wash clothes or dishes with that water.

Life on Niʻihau is peaceful. There are no worries about being mugged or robbed or anything like that. Everyone who lives on Niʻihau is family.

On Niʻihau there is no hospital. We live every day according to the grace of God. We live by prayer and by our knowledge of traditional Hawaiian medicine.

Also the way we live is very family oriented. We watch out and care for each other's children. For instance if you go to the beach to pick Niʻihau shells there is nothing to worry about. The family watches out for the children until you get back.

There were no expenses for the house we had on Niʻihau; no rent or mortgage to pay. But there isn't any electricity either on Niʻihau — only kerosene lamps.

There was a wood-burning stove. We would go out and gather firewood and bring it home.

There are no cars on Niʻihau. Our means of transportation was the bicycle, or else we walked or rode horses. Every family has a horse or horses. There are different kinds of horses for different kinds of uses, like for work or to sell. Horses that were for sale could be used for whatever one wanted. But the 'work' horses were only used for working the land like when we drove cattle. The older boys would have their own horses to go fishing or to go gathering Niʻihau shells or to hunt pigs.

On Sundays everyone would be home. No one sleeps on the beach then. Sunday is a special day on Niʻihau. Everyone goes to church — when church is over everyone goes home. You have lunch and then you rest. At night you go and visit family.

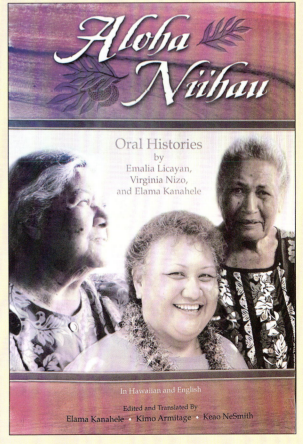

One day is set aside for the Lord God and we observe that day. That is a sacred day. No one works. Our houses are wood frame houses and there are separate houses for different functions. There is the main house that has sleeping rooms and a family room, and there is the cooking house that is made open so that the smoke doesn't fill up the house. Some families have propane stoves and other families have wood burning stoves. The cooking house has only a roof and a table. The cooking house is where we kept the food that was shipped in. The most important thing is that we have rice and flour. We bake bread and mix flour poi.

We have great love for God for watching over and caring for us. He provides all our needs. Sometimes when the ocean is rough there is no barge for a long time. Then we live by the grace of God. There are no problems living on Ni'ihau. You can go fishing at the beach or go pig or sheep hunting. Sheep are given to the families on Ni'ihau. Sometimes we slaughter a cow and make jerk meat. There were two families that had refrigerators but not like the electric refrigerators you plug in. It was the kind of refrigerator that runs by kerosene. That's what we used to keep the food cold.

The toilet is outside. A pit is dug and a small shack put over it and that's the outhouse. When the pit becomes full, you dig another pit and move the shack over it. The bathhouse is separate from the main house. We bathe using a bucket. Each person gets one bucket. We wash ourselves with soap and then we take the water and pour it over ourselves.

All families have devotional. Every morning we have family devotional before going to work or school or to the beach or anything like that. We have morning and evening devotional. Before going to sleep, we have devotional to give thanks to God. Then on Sunday we go to church.

There are three days in the week where we have services. We have them on Mondays, Wednesdays and Saturdays. When we were little we go to school and then we go to weekday services. The school and the church are in the same yard.

We observed and listened when we came together and prayed on Sundays, at weekday services, at home with our families, in the mornings and evenings, family devotional are very important to us. That's how we come to know these things so well and that's the tradition we continue.

There are two churches on Kaua'i that Ni'ihau families go to. We observe these things just like how they are observed on Ni'ihau. Those families who are capable of going go to the services. No one is compelled to go. Whenever it is possible for you to go, you remember God.

You should never forget God. These are important observances, but they are wise and important teachings for us, the younger generation. We need to continue these things. These are the things our parents established, and we, the younger generation must keep them up.

ELEVEN

AN ENDURING CULTURE

After the deaths of Aylmer and Lester, speculation about Niʻihau's future was rife. Would the island be put up for sale by the family? Possible overseas buyers were circling. The family denied that selling was on their minds, and stated it was 'business as usual.' Despite these denials there was much comment in the press, and Governor John Burns sensed an opportunity. Under pressure from ardent preservationists he felt strongly that a case could be made for the state to purchase what he regarded as the last remnant of the Hawaiʻi of old.

Governor Burns moved quickly. Three and a half months after Lester's death, on 10 February 1970, he wrote to the state legislature (reproduced in full overleaf).[1] The letter was prefaced by a lyrical quotation from 'Rocky Acres,' a poem by Robert Graves, possibly intended to evoke the spirit of Hawaiʻi as it had once been. Whether it did so is questionable; it is a poem of Scottish crags and windswept heather, not of waving palms and tropical splendor.

The message acknowledges that the original primeval environment no longer exists in Hawaiʻi due to human influence, but that the one island still relatively undisturbed is Niʻihau. (This was questionable even at the time, after a century of ranching and the even earlier introduction of goats.)

The purchase of Niʻihau was seen by the governor as an 'unparalleled opportunity to establish a controlled natural preserve while, at the same time, giving the residents of Niihau a choice of moving into the mainstream of contemporary Island life, and I mean a *real* choice.'

The governor was harking back to the results of the 1946 Senate Investigative Committee Report. He noted that the present assessed tax value was well within the means of the state and proposed 'that we take steps to acquire the entire island of Niihau,' and further, that the residents who preferred to continue their present mode of life could do so under a leaseback system.

A day after sending the letter the governor followed up with the introduction of bills to both the Senate and the House of Representatives[2] calling for an Act to make an

▲ Governor John Burns (1909–75) was born in Montana, but spent most of his formative years in Hawaiʻi. After gaining a BA from the University of Hawaiʻi he joined the Honolulu Police Department and it was here that his political interests began. He was elected chair of the Democratic Party in 1952 and a territorial delegate in 1956. As a delegate he played a key role in lobbying for Hawaiian statehood. Burns became state governor in 1962, and was re-elected in 1966 and 1970. He fell ill in 1973 and relinquished his duties that year. He is remembered for his role in stimulating the state economy by attracting investment and foreign tourism. He never visited Niʻihau.
Wikimedia Commons, colorised

281

▶ Governor Burns' letter to the Legislature.
Hawaiian Legislature Archives

EXECUTIVE CHAMBERS
HONOLULU
February 10, 1970

JOHN A. BURNS
GOVERNOR

GOVERNOR'S MESSAGE TO THE STATE LEGISLATURE
NIIHAU: A PROPOSED NATURAL PRESERVE

> This is a wild land, country of my choice,
>   With harsh craggy mountain, moor ample and bare,
> Seldom in these acres is heard any voice
>   But voice of cold water that runs here and there
>   Through rocks and lank heather growing without care...
>
>   Rocky Acres, by Robert Graves

From the time the Hawaiian Islands were discovered, Hawaii has been regarded and envied as the prime example of natural beauty. In the mountain forests exotic birds flew among trees found only in Hawaii. The offshore sea life presented a marine biologist's dream.

This primeval environment no longer exists. Man's intrusion has wrought irrevocable changes throughout the Islands.

There are, however, a few areas in the State where our biological and botanical riches are relatively undisturbed. These areas should be preserved and protected from further encroachment.

One such area, still relatively unspoiled by the physical trappings of progress is Niihau. This island is sometimes referred to today as "the Forbidden Island;" its people as the "the Forgotten People."

This Administration submits Niihau presents an unparalleled opportunity to establish a controlled natural preserve while, at the same time, giving the residents of Niihau a choice of moving into the mainstream of contemporary Island life, and I mean a real choice.

I propose we immediately take steps to acquire the entire Island of Niihau. This should be done before any private offers for the purchase of Niihau are entertained by its present owners. The possible sale of Niihau for commercial development would result in a tragic loss of a priceless treasure--a complete Island which could be restored to its primeval condition and maintained as a natural preserve for the enjoyment of all who cherish the old image of Hawaii.

Early acquisition would be well within our present means. The Island's present assessed tax value, at 100 per cent, is roughly $300,000.

Niihau lies about 17.5 miles west of Kauai. It has an area of 72 square miles and an altitude of 1,281 feet. Rainfall ranges from 18 to 26 inches per year.

Niihau once had extensive forests. Much of this growth has been ravaged by the goats, first introduced in 1794 by Captain Vancouver, and by the sheep and cattle introduced later. Through proper management and conservation practices, these forests can be regenerated, providing the environment necessary to support indigenous and rare birds such as the Elepaio, the Kauai Thrush, and Amakihi, the Creeper (Paroreomyza bairdii) and the Akepa (Loxops caeruleirostris).

Controlled regrowth would also create condition favorable to the further seeding of the Brighamia insignis, one of the most beautiful plants found in the Hawaiian chain. This plant is endemic to Niihau, growing only on the cliffs around the spring on Kaali Cliff on the northern part of the island.

Additionally, there are only a few areas in the State where lowland, shorezone and shallow water marine life still exist in a natural state. The waters around Niihau are among the best examples of such marine life, undisturbed by pollution and man.

Public acquisition of Niihau will also give the State an opportunity to offer additional services to the people who presently live there as employees of the island's owners. They should not remain "forgotten." It is our view that they should at least be given the choice of moving into the mainstream of Island life today. The State will give all who so desire special assistance to ease their transition.

The residents who prefer to continue their present mode of life can continue to do so under a leaseback system with the owners of the Island. It should be emphasized that the intent in this respect is to give the residents a free choice in their way of life.

I view the proposed acquisition of Niihau as part of a total effort to preserve, protect and enhance our total quality of life.

Too much of what is really native Hawaiian has already been irretrievably lost.

Accordingly, I herewith submit for your early and favorable consideration this proposal for the public purchase of Niihau.

John A. Burns

appropriation to purchase Niʻihau. The wording of the bills follows that of his message, and uses an identical rationale.²

For the next two months the political machine kicked into action. Everybody had an opinion, not least the governor:

> We don't want to upset the Hawaiians there, but it would be better for them than the present conditions … We would restore the island to what it was before; reforest it and replant it, and use the people there in the undertaking. We would let them be there with some injection of modern society without harming them.³

The injection of modern society included controlled access for visitors — was it to be a living museum? It appeared so, as in conversation with author Ruth Tabrah, Governor Burns told her:

> I'd like to see Niihau a state park, see the whole island one big conservation area and quiet retreat. We can use the people of Niihau as park keepers, and we can give them a good English education and commensurate state services.⁴

After the first reading in the House the bill was referred to its Committee on Lands. In the Senate the bill was referred to its Committee on Land and Natural Resources.

The House committee held a packed public meeting on Kauaʻi where residents, many of them Niihauan, were vocal in their opposition to the governor's proposal. The meeting became quite heated, with the Niihauans determined that the politicians should hear their views directly. The majority wanted the status quo to remain.⁵

▼ The owners of Niʻihau Island, Bruce (left) and Keith Robinson. Both attended the University of California, Davis, and graduated with agricultural degrees. Bruce became a rancher, managing the activities of the Robinson family, including Niihau Ranch, while Keith served in the US Army before returning to Kauaʻi. There he worked for Koʻolau Ranch, then ran a commercial fishing vessel for seven years around Kauaʻi. For many years now Keith has indulged his passion for saving rare plants from extinction at his Kauaʻi Wildlife Refuge on Robinson family land on the uplands of Kauaʻi.
Kathryn Budde-Jones

At the end of February, three weeks later, the Robinsons themselves wrote a strongly worded letter to the chairman of the Senate Committee on Land and Natural Resources. It was the Senate where they felt the future of the debate lay. The Robinsons strenuously opposed the plan to 'seize and nullify the results of more than a hundred years of hard work':

> The island of Niihau has not been, is not, and is not expected to be up for sale to anybody, anywhere, at any time. … If our continuous efforts at conservation are rewarded by the summary seizure of our land, who then will be encouraged to preserve and improve his own property?⁶

Their letter also challenged the governor's reafforestation rationale, regarding it as 'inaccurate and, unfortunately, [tending] to create a false impression about Niihau's ecological and social situation.'⁷

The committee's report and the debate in the House offered a glimmer of hope to the Robinsons. Rather than outright purchase, the amended House bill suggested that any island owned, or substantially owned, that is offered for sale should be first offered to the state, thus giving the state a right of first refusal. It was a compromise that many people, including the Robinsons, saw as a way to assuage the situation. Much of the rationale for this approach was taken from the Kaua'i public meeting, but as the debate in the Senate proved more critical, the bill in the House never came to a vote.

Seeing his initiative slipping away, Governor Burns drew attention to two recent developments that, in his view, reinforced the case for immediate state purchase of the island. Both implied a mistrust of the Robinsons' motives.

The first concerned the old Russian Fort Elizabeth at the mouth of the Waimea River (see Chapter Five), which the Sinclair/Robinson family acquired when purchasing land on Kaua'i. According to the governor, the Robinsons offered the fort area to the state if it would guarantee that it would not make future attempts to take over Robinson property.[8] Governor Burns rejected the suggestion out of hand. The state later acquired the land by condemnation.*

The second involved Selwyn Robinson. The state had an interest in some of Selwyn's land in Kalalau Valley. Governor Burns contended that Selwyn had sold the land to private interests while the state was carrying out its appraisal. Selwyn disagreed, saying that the state had been notified a year before and this was sufficient time to make up its mind before he offered it to the market. In response, the governor dismissed the allegation that the state procrastinated, and intimated the Robinsons had reneged on their agreement.[9]

Despite the governor's allegations, the House seemed to be becoming more sympathetic to the Robinsons. In the closing days of March the legislature received a petition opposing the governor's plan, signed by 102 Ni'ihau residents as well as several ex-residents.[10] The petition regarded the governor as being grossly misinformed about the ecological and social conditions on the island and prevailed upon him to recognize the travesty that would occur if the Senate approved the bill.

Burns then attempted to counter the rising feelings against his proposal by hosting an aerial tour of the island for the legislators, using a National Guard DC-6 aircraft. For many this was their first view of Ni'ihau.[11]

The Senate committee reported back on 7 April approving Burns' plan in an amended fashion, basing their conclusions on scientific evidence from experts who had knowledge of the island.[12]

The Senate's final version of the bill suggested there should be a more studied approach to acquisition and its consequences, and to that end recommended a sum of $100,000 for this purpose be appropriated. The bill passed its third reading on April 14, with the vote to be held the following day. Meanwhile the House bill was still meandering through its process.

Thirteen votes were needed in the Senate to pass the bill. After final debate the senators voted twelve ayes and twelve noes, with one senator having leave. In such a tie the status quo stands, and thus the bill narrowly failed.[13] It was a close thing for the Robinsons, with the new generation owners doubtless feeling they had been through a true baptism of fire.

The result left many unhappy. State Director of Administration Myron Thompson vented his feelings: 'What has been done is tantamount to the social injustices we thought our people would be spared after Statehood and forever.'[14]

* Condemnation: the legal process by which a government body exercises its right of 'eminent domain' to acquire private property for public uses. Owners must be paid fair compensation. This process is usually used for roading, national security reasons and the like.

* The 1920 Hawaiian Homes Commission Act provides for the rehabilitation of native Hawaiian people through a program of 99-year homestead leases at a nominal rental.

▲ Governor George Ariyoshi (born 1926) was raised in Honolulu, the son of Japanese immigrants. He attended McKinley High School, graduating in 1944, and served as an interpreter with the US Army in Japan. After his tour of duty he studied at the University of Hawai'i at Mānoa before transferring to Michigan State University and gaining a law degree in 1952. He soon entered politics back home in Hawai'i and was elected to the House of Representatives in 1954. This was followed by election to the Territorial Senate in 1958 and the Hawai'i State Senate upon statehood being achieved. Ariyoshi served on the Senate until 1970 when he was elected lieutenant governor. When John Burns fell ill, he assumed the acting governorship, and in 1974 was elected governor. He served until 1986, the longest-serving governor and the first Asian American in the role.
Wikimedia Commons

▶ Governor Ariyoshi speaking to Niihauans in front of the church at Pu'uwai on 21 December 1985.
Greg Vaughn

The governor was down but not out, still persisting in his crusade, and claiming later in the year that a sale of the island to private interests was imminent. He was supported in his acquisition quest in early 1972 by the Hawaiian Homes Commission,* a body that had been almost silent during the earlier debate. The commission wanted a state purchase of the island and wished funds 'to assure land tenure for the Hawaiians living there' with 99-year leases, and an ecological and social restoration program once ownership had been achieved.[15] Was the Hawaiian Renaissance just starting to emerge? Buoyed by this development, the governor tried again in early 1973 with a new House bill. This was referred to two House committees but sank without trace.[16]

Governor Burns died on 5 April 1975. Lieutenant Governor Ariyoshi had taken the helm as acting governor in October 1973 and had voted with the ayes in the Senate, but did not have the crusading zeal for purchase that Governor Burns expressed. It was reported in October 1975 that Ariyoshi was resurrecting the purchase proposal, but higher priorities were occupying his time and energy.[17] It wasn't until December 1985, over eleven years after he became governor, that he visited the island with his wife and daughter at the invitation of the Robinsons. They spent five hours there, talking to the residents and traveling round in a jeep. He was the first governor to visit since William Quinn in 1961. The visit changed his views and as he said on his return:

> I found the residents of the island very warm, contented, happy and at peace with themselves and their special place. It is not for us to impose change on them. Rather, it is important that we strive to protect their right to their own choice of lifestyle.[18]

He also said that he was 'touched by the close relationship between the Robinsons and the people of Niihau. Most of the communication between them was in Hawaiian, and its flavor and spirit, as with the people themselves, was also warm and gentle.'

With Governor Ariyoshi won over, the fight for state acquisition of Ni'ihau was at an end.

Who owns Niʻihau's beaches?

The Robinson family have always maintained that in purchasing the island from King Kamehameha v they purchased the konohiki rights,* and that they have managed the island in conjunction with the residents accordingly. In their view these konohiki rights allowed them to control shoreline access to the island. Over recent years ʻopihi (limpet) pickers and fishermen have increasingly reached the island's shores. In earlier times they were treated leniently, provided they did not move inland; now, since the resources have become depleted, sterner action has been taken over shoreline access.

The state has not regarded the shoreline access question in the same way. The first challenge to the Robinson's konohiki rights came in 1961 when state representative David McClung, chair of the House Committee on Lands, sought to add an investigation of the state's claim to Niʻihau's beaches to the ongoing state investigation of school and church sites. The legislature agreed and asked the Attorney General 'to look into the state's possible ownership of Niihau beach lands up to the high-water mark.'[19]

The Attorney General reported in May 1961 that in his opinion 'the beaches of Niihau below the high-water mark are public.' According to his opinion 'the study of the deed [of sale of the island] and history of the Hawaiian islands show that there could not have been any intent to convey the lands below the high-water mark.'

This conclusion followed a considerable discussion in the Attorney General's opinion as to what constitutes the high-water mark. The state had been using the 'debris line,' but the opinion suggests this may have to be tested in court. Other possibilities were seen as 'the seaward edge of the vegetation' or 'the highest wash of the waves.' It took until October 2006 for this matter to be finally resolved in the Hawaiʻi Supreme Court, when it unanimously agreed that the shoreline should be established 'at the highest reach of the highest wash of the waves.'[20]

A further attempt was made to alter the situation of the seaward areas of Niʻihau when, in 1969, officers of the State Land Use Commission proposed that the steep cliffs, beaches and valleys of the island be zoned as conservation districts.[21] This would place them under the control of the Department of Land and Natural Resources, although ownership of the land would not be changed. The proposal was vehemently opposed by the Robinsons who regarded it as a further diminution of their rights. A public meeting on the issue was held by the Land Commission on Kauaʻi and the matter was subsequently dropped.

Wherever the shoreline was decided upon made no difference to the Robinson brothers' view, one that Bruce Robinson reaffirmed in 1988: 'Our deed very clearly leads to the water. It is a separate deed quite unique in Hawaii. It stems directly from the monarchy, and with it comes the aboriginal rights of the old days.'[22] This view was reinforced by Keith Robinson in 1997 in a Special Report in the *Star Bulletin* when he asserted 'such private-property [konohiki] rights, granted during the monarchy, extend to submerged lands below the beach.'[23]

The coastline around Niʻihau was designated a Monk Seal Critical Habitat Area by the Federal Government in September

* 'Konohiki' means 'headman of an ahupuaʻa land division.' The konohiki traditionally controlled the land and fishing rights under his jurisdiction, known as the 'konohiki rights.'

▼ An east coast beach, taken from Poʻooneone Point looking north towards the east coast cliffs and Pueo Point.
Michael Anderson, Kauaʻi Historical Society

2015. In a nod to the ownership question the area designated extends from the 200-meter depth landward to only the 10-meter water depth. The designated areas on all the other islands extend from the 200-meter depth landward to five meters beyond the highest wash of the waves.[24] Critical habitat designation does not restrict access or fishing activities, but assists in Federal funding for research and other purposes.

And that is where the Ni'ihau shoreline access matter rests to this day — but see the next section regarding the 'opihi pickers.

Fishing rights and wrongs

Niihauans rely heavily on the ocean for food and have long been concerned at both recreational and commercial fishermen from Kaua'i (and even O'ahu) fishing near the island — and with increasing frequency. Not only was it taking longer for the islanders to catch fish, but the 'opihi* gatherers on the rocks in the intertidal zone were having a significant effect on these stocks too. By the end of the twentieth century residents of the island feared that their food resources were becoming depleted, and believed that action was necessary.

* Three species of 'opihi are found on Ni'ihau: the blackfoot or 'opihi makaiauli (Cellana exarata) in the upper wave wash, the yellowtail or 'opihi 'ālinalina (Cellana sandwicensis) in the lower portion of the wave wash, and the kneecap or 'opihi koele (Cellana talcosa) in the shallow intertidal zone.

State governor Linda Lingle was invited to visit the island to see for herself. This she did on 7 May 2003, five months after being elected, flying in the Robinsons' helicopter. She saw the problem of outsiders coming in and overfishing nearby waters, and of visitors taking large quantities of 'opihi. She also noted that with the encouragement of the Robinsons the island was becoming home to increasing numbers of the protected monk seals (numbering then about 100), which also competed for the fish resource. Keith Robinson assured her there were plenty of fish for both residents and seals; commercial and sport fishers from outside were the problem. The governor said her administration would see what regulations could be put in place to help the Niihauans. 'Perhaps a natural reserve is one approach.'[25]

Despite this commitment from the governor, no visible action was taken by her administration, and overfishing continued.

▼ A monk seal sleeping on a typical northern beach — but whose property is it on?
Michael Anderson, Kaua'i Historical Society

It was ten years before the issue appeared in the press again, this time in relation to a possible extension of the Hawaiian Islands Humpback Whale National Marine Sanctuary set up around the islands under the National Oceanic and Atmospheric Administration (NOAA) in 1992. The idea was floated of including Ni'ihau within an extended sanctuary. A Memorandum of Agreement between NOAA, the State Department of Land and Natural Resources (DLNR) and Niihau Ranch was suggested as a way forward. This proposal was greeted with grave concern by the Kaua'i fishermen, who called for wider community discussion.[26] The proposal was subsequently 'paused' and then abandoned when NOAA decided that the whale sanctuary extension should not be pursued.[27]

It must have been a frustrating decade for the Niihauan residents and the Robinsons. In spite of their best lobbying efforts for some fishing protection, all had been in vain. Therefore in late November 2013, in conjunction with state senator Clayton Hee, they took the extraordinary step of calling a press conference on the matter at the state capitol. Bruce

Robinson together with his Niihauan wife, Leiana, and eight Niʻihau residents traveled to Honolulu to make representations for fishing protection — an unprecedented step. They were supported by the Hawaiian caucus in the Senate (the six senators with native Hawaiian forebears), led by Senator Hee.

Bruce Robinson, in an impassioned speech in the state capitol, reminded the audience of politicians, state officials and community groups of King Kamehameha v's request to the new owners of Niʻihau in 1864 to 'take care of my people' and emphasized that 'We are here today for the fulfillment of that promise.'

Bruce explained how persistent activities by offshore interests had severely limited the islanders' capacity to source their food supply from the sea. More and more people were arriving to fish, pick ʻopihi from the rocks, and dive in the island's waters.

In addition 'pressure from the outside has strained [the islanders'] ability to maintain precious traditions and dying cultural practices ... without outside help we are going to lose that culture.'[28]

'... Our people are dependent on the sea shore, not only for food, but also for maluhia [peace, safety, tranquility],' said Robinson. 'It is a place where our people go for healing and spiritual well-being. Without that, our culture will not survive.'[29]

Leiana, who was raised on Niʻihau, backed up her husband: 'If we don't do something about it then we won't exist.'

The Robinsons and Niʻihau residents shared photographs and videos with the audience showing strangers fishing and gathering ʻopihi along the shoreline.

Senator Clayton Hee remarked on how unusual and difficult it was for the Niihauans to be present, which emphasized the seriousness of the issue to them. He said that

he, along with his fellow Hawaiian Caucus senators, intended introducing legislation in the 2014 legislative session that would prevent the waters around Niʻihau from being fished by anyone other than residents of the island.

William Aila, speaking as chairman of the Department of Land and Natural Resources said that, in addition to legislation, the department had a plan involving new rules and regulations to increase protection of Niʻihau's fish resources while allowing some offshore fishing.

Bruce Robinson concluded strongly: 'A promise to a king — that's important. It's the life of the people and you can't take that lightly.'

▲ ʻOpihi in the intertidal zone on the platform rocks on the northern side of Niʻihau.
Nancy Shaw

◀ Governor Linda Lingle was born in Missouri in 1953 and moved to California when she was twelve. Here she received her high school and college education, graduating in journalism from California State University in 1975. Soon after graduating she went to Hawaiʻi, working for the Teamsters and Hotel Workers Union before moving to Molokaʻi and starting a community newspaper, the *Molokaʻi Free Press*. Her political activities began here in 1980 when she was elected to the Maui County Council, where she served five two-year terms before being elected mayor in 1990. As a Republican, this was a major upset. She ran for state governor in 1998, but lost to Ben Cayetano. In 2002 she was successful, and served until 2010. She is remembered as governor for her generally conservative views on social issues and for revitalizing the Republican Party in Hawaiʻi.

◀ A fisherman on a lonely Niʻihau beach — but where are all the fish?
Michael Anderson, Kauaʻi Historical Society

▲ Bruce and Leiana Robinson in November 2013, at the press conference on the fishing situation around Niʻihau and the need for state action.
Honolulu Star Advertiser

▼ Senator Clayton Hee, who supported the Niihauan community and the Robinsons in their quest to have fishing around the island by non-residents banned or regulated. Hee was a state representative from 1982–84 and a state senator from 1984–88 and 2004–14. Of Hawaiian and Chinese ancestry, he speaks fluent Hawaiian and was in an admirable position to reinforce the control of traditional fisheries around Niʻihau.
Clayton Hee

While it sounded hopeful that some meaningful fishing restrictions might result, the next few weeks showed that the fishing interests on Kauaʻi had been readying themselves in opposition.

Clayton Hee was true to his word and a raft of bills was introduced in the Senate in early January 2014, with matching bills in the House introduced by Faye Hanohano. The House bills were all deferred at the committee stage on 29 January 'to allow more input by Niihauans and Kauaʻi fishermen and ocean users.' There was a preference in the committee (the House Committee on Ocean, Marine Resources and Hawaiian Affairs) for handling the complex issue by means of the DLNR rules process rather than legislation.[30] Bruce and Leiana Robinson submitted testimony, signed by dozens of the island's residents, in support of the bills.

Fishing interests were universally opposed to the bills, with the two main themes being that the two islands (Niʻihau and Kauaʻi) were one entity, and where was the evidence for the reduction in fish stocks around Niʻihau? This latter theme was echoed by some of the legislators. The fishermen indicated that they were open to some form of middle ground, but totally opposed to a blanket ban on outsiders fishing around Niʻihau.

The four Senate bills were:

- Marine Conservation District (SB180): The taking of aquatic life by non-residents would be prohibited within two miles of the shore of any island with a population of between 100 and 500 persons
  i.e. Niʻihau only.

- Konohiki (SB 2125): To manage the Marine Conservation District, a konohiki with traditional rights would be appointed from among the residents by the State Land Board chairman in conjunction with the owner.

- ʻOpihi (SB 2923): The giving of exclusive rights to gather ʻopihi to residents, or to visitors accompanied by a resident.

- Niʻihau County (SB 3003): The establishment of Niʻihau as a separate county for limited purposes, overseen by DLNR.[31]

The last of these bills came out of left field and particularly upset the incumbent Kauaʻi/Niʻihau mayor Bernard Carvalho who, along with other Kauaian politicians and officials, had not been consulted.[32] The bills underwent serious amendment during the committee process. Public hearings were held on them in late February.

The first House bill, for the Marine Conservation District, was considerably altered before it was sent back to the House, but it was recommended it be abandoned in favor of a DLNR rules process. The Robinsons gave testimony asking for the fishing ban to be extended to a ban on tour boats, surf skis, kayaks, surfboards and the like not owned by residents. This may have been a step too far, but was in line with the residents' use of the ocean for maluhia that Bruce had expressed at the press conference. The bill, as reported back to the House, included these further restrictions.[33]

The second bill, the Konohiki Management Bill, it was felt needed more discussion, and fish depletion around Niʻihau needed documentation. Again the Robinsons gave testimony, asking that the island's owners be responsible, in consultation with the residents, for appointing the konohiki. This was not acceptable to the Committee.

The third bill, the restrictions on ʻopihi gathering, was passed from the Committee to the House largely 'as is.' The Niʻihau County proposition it was felt required much more discussion with the community. It seemed to have been motivated by taxation rather than fishing considerations.

At a public meeting at Wilcox Elementary School in Līhuʻe on 7 February 2014, over a hundred people came to discuss the bills. The refrain was: 'What's the rush. Have the Robinsons an ulterior motive? Are the Robinsons just attempting to further privatise their island?' 'Why aren't the Robinsons here?' Others said: 'It's not the Robinsons that should be here, but the people of Niʻihau.'

At the meeting it was argued strongly that the two islands (Niʻihau and Kauaʻi) were 'brother and sister,' a relationship they felt the state didn't seem to understand. They should not be separated, neither as counties or as fishing areas. As one attendee said: 'We share the same ocean, we share the resources, we share ohana.' There was, however, support for a bill to appropriate money for a study of the whole issue.[34]

The politicians in the Senate, as in the House, ducked for cover and deferred all the bills, pending further study by DLNR and an appointed task force. At the time of writing, nothing further has been heard publicly on fisheries protection around Niʻihau. The fishing interests seem to have been successful in deferring the issue by convincing the authorities it is in the 'too-hard basket.' It is probable though that the wider community (fishermen, boaties, tour boats) that uses the waters around the island have taken note of the islanders' concerns and have taken a more responsible attitude since 2014. The issue may have been defused a little, but it has certainly not gone away.

Involvement with the US Navy

Keith Robinson proudly asserts that the Robinson family and Niʻihau have been involved with the US military since 1924, when Billy Mitchell came to the Hawaiian islands researching for his famous report described in the previous chapter. This ultimately led to the furrowing of Niʻihau by Aylmer in the late 1930s, and there has been almost continuous involvement by one or other of the armed services ever since. Immediately after the Japanese pilot crash-landed, the army and navy got involved. The army had observation posts there during World War II, the Coast Guard has set up the LORAN station, and since then there have been teams from the various services under the auspices of what is now the Pacific Missile Range Facility.

As a personal aside, Keith Robinson is the only person I have spoken to who, like me, witnessed the thermonuclear explosion from Johnston Island just before midnight on 31 July 1958. The test, known as Teak, was almost 50 miles up in the atmosphere and had a yield of 3.8 megatons (250

▲ Bernard Carvalho. An outstanding football player, he was employed by Kauaʻi Public Works and Recreation in 1985 after graduating from the University of Hawaiʻi with a degree in communications and public relations. He rose through the ranks to become director of the department in 2007, won the mayoralty of Kauaʻi County in 2008, and remained mayor until 2018.
Wikipedia Commons

▼ Leiana and Bruce Robinson, with their elder daughter Briana, listen as Senator Clayton Hee introduces the four bills about regulating the fishing around Niʻihau in January 2014.
Honolulu Star Advertiser

times as powerful as the Hiroshima bomb). I happened to be on Waikīkī Beach at the time and it was an awe-inspiring, frightening experience, even though Johnston Island was over 800 miles away. Immediately there was no doubt in my mind that it was a nuclear explosion, and with Cold War tensions extreme at the time, those of us on the beach wondered what was happening. The vision-shattering event lasted a full 20 minutes.

Keith Robinson said that the family was forewarned of the test by the navy. The Robinsons were advised, he told me, that the test had been delayed two hours by technical problems, so the family was very much 'in the loop.'[35] Niʻihau was being used by the US Navy for monitoring the test. A second atmospheric test was detonated from Johnston Island on 12 August. The Johnston Island test facility was used again in 1962 for another series of tests.

Monitoring these nuclear tests may have marked the beginning of Nʻiihau Ranch's long-standing relationship with the US Navy.

The Pacific Missile Range Facility based at Barking Sands on west Kauaʻi, which dates back to 1940 and World War II, has been managed by the navy since 1957. It describes itself as:

> … the world's largest instrumented multi-environment range capable of supporting surface, subsurface, air, and space operations simultaneously. There are more than 1,100 square miles of instrumented underwater range and more than 42,000 square miles of controlled airspace. This makes PMRF a premier facility for supporting operations which vary from small, single-unit exercises up to largescale, multiple-unit battle group scenarios.[36]

The facility provides an integrated range service, training personnel and testing missile systems of all types. Apart from its main base at Barking Sands, it also has outlying support facilities on Kauaʻi at Kōkeʻe, Mākaha Ridge, Port Allen and on Niʻihau. On Niʻihau the navy has:

- A remotely operated surveillance radar facility (Type APS-134) with generator and helipad, on the clifftop on Pānīʻau Ridge. Equipped with an electro-magnetic environmental simulator (EMES), and a moving target simulator for electronic warfare exercises.
- An electronic warfare and optical tracking installation known as Perch Site on Pānīʻau Ridge north of the radar facility, with generator and helipad, also equipped with EMES.
- Multiple sites for mobile EMES facilities on the north shore of Niʻihau.
- An 1100-acre test vehicle recovery site leased by the navy
- A helicopter terrain flight training course running diagonally across the island.
- Two emergency drone landing sites.

▲ Operation Hardtack — the Teak test, a 3.8-megaton thermonuclear bomb sent up on a Redstone missile and detonated 50 miles above Johnston Island at midnight Honolulu time on 31 July 1958. This is the view of the explosion from the south side of Oʻahu. It was widely reported in the press at the time, but the public were not forewarned. Niʻihau was used as part of the navy's monitoring arrangements.
Wikimedia Commons

An enduring culture

◀ The Pacific Missile Range Facility at Barking Sands on the west side of Kaua'i in 2004.
Wikimedia Commons

Ranch staff participate in exercises with service personnel in Special Warfare Operations, including amphibious landings and downed pilot training where they provide the 'enemy' component in tactical evasion training for all branches of the services — army special forces, air force pilots, marine snipers and navy seals.

The surveillance radar facility was installed in 1984 after four years of negotiation with the island's owners. The two-acre site selected was leased to the navy for a nominal rental. In return, for a like amount, the navy leases to the Robinsons a landing craft much superior to the one they had been operating. During installation the construction workers flew to the site by helicopter each morning and flew back to Kaua'i each evening.[37]

A downbeat description of downed pilot training is given in an official document from 1998:

▼ The US Navy's radar facility on the summit of Mount Pānī'au, on Ni'ihau. In the background distance (top right) is Ki'i Landing.
Steven Gentry

> Exercise provides training for downed aircrew in escape and evasion and coordination of recovery helicopter assets. Niihau Ranch personnel are hired to locate downed aircrew, who are trying to remain hidden, and the Niihau Helicopter is contracted to provide exercise support and medevac standby… Included in the pre exercise briefing, typically, is the [Niihau Ranch Government Point of Contact] Mr. Robinson, the aircrew personnel who will be on the ground, and the recovery force team. Personnel are briefed on general rules, boundaries, hazards, and safety procedures.

293

Personnel are also given tips by Mr. Robinson on evasion and detection avoidance. The exercise starts when the aircrew personnel are inserted at approximately 0730 by Niihau Helicopter … Aircrew execute escape and evasion plans and coordinate their rescue by helicopter at about 1600. Following the exercise, a debriefing session is held, bringing out strong and weak points of the mission.[38]

These exercises are a joint effort between the military service involved and ranch personnel. So far, no aircrew have managed to avoid detection. Each exercise must be a welcome diversion for the Niihauans involved.

Ranch staff are also employed for routine maintenance of the naval facilities on the island.

To protect the Niihauan way of life, all military personnel operate under a strict protocol agreed between Niihau Ranch and PMRF which includes:

- Coordination of all personnel entries to the island with Niihau Ranch
- No services are to be requested for a Sunday
- All non-technical labor required is to be furnished by Niihau Ranch
- A Niihau Ranch escort is required to be present for all services provided, and close coordination between the parties is required
- Niihau Ranch transportation is to be used for all PMRF transfers to and from Ni'ihau — helicopter for personnel, landing craft for equipment
- No smoking, consumption of alcohol, or firearms are permitted
- No foreign pests or weeds to be introduced (in particular the mongoose, brown tree snake and exotic seeds)
- No objects are to be removed from the island, other than those brought there for the particular program. All waste is to be removed.[39]

In the late 1990s PMRF announced it wanted to enhance the capabilities of the range to allow for the testing of anti-missile missiles. This would involve constructing two new launch pads for interceptor and target missiles, together with sundry tracking and other support facilities. Launch pads on Ni'ihau were suggested as an option, in which

▶ The US Navy's Perch Site electronic facility, with the island of Lehua to the north.
Steven Gentry

case a 6000-foot runway would need to be built at the southern end of the island. All suggested installations were to be well away from Puʻuwai village.

Public reaction was mixed but the Robinsons and the Niihauan community were in favor, eyeing the employment opportunities, and knowing the safeguards to the Niihauan culture that would be put in place based on their experience with the navy.[40] Public reaction ranged from 'the military shouldn't be on Niʻihau' to 'all in favor.'

For the first time ever, the Robinson brothers aired the possibility of selling the island if it became impossible for them to continue to subsidize the community — which expansion of the base would assist them to do. Keith Robinson was quoted in the *Honolulu Advertiser*: 'As long as the Niihau people, or a substantial element of the Niihau people, want us to keep on, we will do our utmost. But it may become impossible for us to keep on.'[41]

Governor Ben Cayetano was not enthusiastic, viewing the navy involvement in the island with suspicion, and concerned at the harm it may do to the way of life the islanders wished to lead. He determined to see for himself, and arranged to visit Niʻihau in May 1999, at the height of the controversy. On being briefed on the ranch's parlous finances, and seeing how the islanders' culture was being protected by the arrangements made with the navy (which was providing vital employment), he was won over, stating after his visit 'I feel in my heart that I must do everything I can to help the people of Niihau.'[42] He completely withdrew state objections to the use of Niʻihau as part of the proposed new missile testing program.

That battle was won, but the Department of Land and Natural Resources was insisting on a complete archeological survey of the island before approving the Environmental Impact Statement. This the Robinsons would not countenance. All proposed sites, which were minor areas in the context of the whole island, had already been investigated for cultural artifacts. A stalemate occurred, only broken when the Pacific Missile Range Facility decided to place the launch pads at Barking Sands rather than on Niʻihau. Instrumentation for test monitoring would still be located on the island.

Niʻihau remains as an integral part of the PMRF, with Niihau Ranch responding to program requests along the lines indicated, and with an increased intensity since the Missile Defense Agency's program began in earnest in 2007. It is common knowledge that the navy, one way or another, is now providing 80% of the island's income.[43]

▼ Governor Ben Cayetano and his wife Vicky visited Niʻihau in 1999 to see for themselves the situation of the Niihauans in view of the proposed expansion of the Pacific Range Missile Facility. In the end the expansion did not take place. Cayetano was state governor from 1994–2002.
Honolulu Advertiser

Tourism

To supplement the ranch's poor economic performance, low-impact tourism was an idea that exercised the minds of the island's owners for some time. The problem was how to achieve it without disrupting the islanders' way of life. It may have been the successful completion of the radar station in 1984, with workers flown in daily, or hints from the navy about the possibility of training on the island, with its concomitant employment opportunities, that led to some serious thinking about the purchase of a helicopter. There was also the nagging pressure from the authorities and the Robinsons' concern for better medevac arrangements for the island's residents.

The protocol established with the navy for building the radar station, four years in the negotiating, showed what could be done. Impacts on the residents were negligible, and this protocol became the basis for further work with the navy, as well as the rationale for low-impact helicopter tourist flights. Ni'ihau Helicopters LLC was thus born, and a new twin-engined, seven-seat Agusta 109A helicopter was purchased in 1986. It was a huge investment for the ranch.

The Agusta model 109 helicopter first flew in 1971 and versions are still in production. The company is based in Italy and the 109 model was the first mass-produced Italian helicopter. It has been used all around the world in both military and civilian roles. The helicopter is powered by two Allison turboshaft engines and the 109A version, with a widened six-seat cabin, was offered for the first time in 1981. It is one of the most popular helicopters in its class worldwide — fast, reliable and easy to control.

As the helicopter tours were to be a commercial venture, approvals from authorities (in particular the Kaua'i Planning Commission) were required — including flight path and landing pads on Ni'ihau. The Office of Hawaiian Affairs was initially concerned at the effect the proposal might have on the residents' way of life, but were finally convinced that the idea had merit.[44] This all took time and it wasn't until 1987 that the venture was able to begin.

Half-day tours from Kaua'i are offered, and as the company's website says:

> Now YOU can escape to this private Hawaiian island! In our executive class, Agusta 109A, twin engine helicopter, you can go back in time and visit this pristine island,

▶ The Robinsons' Agusta 109A helicopter taking off from Port Allen for Ni'ihau.

Michael Anderson, Kaua'i Historical Society

untouched by development and crowds, where monk seals laze on the beach and glass balls still wash up on the shore.[45]

As an adjunct to the half-day tours, two years later in 1989 Niihau Safaris Ltd was registered and began offering full-day hunting safaris. In addition to the pigs and sheep originally introduced for ranching, the island has eland and oryx (antelopes) and aoudad (aka Barbary sheep, but not a true sheep).

Some of these animals were imported from Moloka'i Ranch Wildlife Safari Park when the park downsized, and additions were made when the park closed in 1997. The eland, in particular, has done extremely well on Ni'ihau. With 1800 animals, it is the largest privately owned herd in the world.

When ranching was scaled down in 1999, feral pigs and sheep increased to the extent that culling was necessary to prevent further degradation of the fragile environment. Thus the idea of Niihau Safaris was born and hunting participants can take satisfaction that they are taking part in a controlled kill. Hunters have a trained local guide and the activity is monitored so as not to impact on the lives of residents:

> At Niihau Safaris, we are dedicated to the principles of good game management, fair chase hunting, and support good game management around the world. We, the game managers on private land, and you, the hunter, work as a team to harvest the right number and type of game in as efficient and humane a manner as possible.
>
> We work hard to achieve results, and expect the same from our clients. Hunting on Niihau is done according to the principles of free chase. Game is plentiful and hunters are certain to get an opportunity to shoot, but it is not an easy hunt. Shooting and stalking skill is required and tested to the utmost. The clients should come expecting a challenge.[46]

These two exclusive operations are the only tourism ventures that enable the public to access the island. Both rely on the helicopter which, with careful management, has provided an entrée to the island without harmful effects on the inhabitants or their culture.

The changing nature of ranching on Ni'ihau

On Lester's death in 1969, elder son Keith took over immediate responsibility for the ranch, but Lester's will required that his widow, Helen, name Lester's successor as manager. Helen decided, doubtless after much family consultation, to give the role to Bruce, a role he has now had for more than 50 years.

Bruce Robinson, at 25, and at that time not long out of the University of California with a degree in agricultural science, can have had little involvement in the management of the ranch before his father's death. The island, with all its financial problems and a nervous cohort of residents, was suddenly thrust upon him. His mother, Helen, was strong and knowledgeable, and must have been a great support, along with elder brother Keith. Soon after Lester's death the family was faced with Governor Burns' bid for state purchase of the island, which required immense energy to combat, and increased the tension being felt by the residents.

The ranch was rearing cattle and sheep and producing honey and charcoal when Lester died, but it was not financially viable and had not been for a long while. During

his short time as manager Lester had attempted to improve the ranch's financial performance, primarily by investing in further charcoal production. It must have been tempting to offer the island for sale, but the Robinsons determined not to, and the commitment given to King Kamehameha V to care for his people played a major role in that decision. All male island residents were still given employment on the ranch upon leaving school.

Like all farming operations, the ranch had its ups and downs. Major intermittent droughts and the occasional hurricane, as well as the usual highly variable 'farm gate' prices, make planning difficult. Transport costs to market are also an inevitable drawback for any offshore island operation such as Ni'ihau.

Beginning in the early 1970s, the two brothers began constructing further water storage facilities with the goal, as Bruce said, 'not to let a single drop of fresh water from Niihau run into the ocean.'[47] The increased water allowed sheep numbers to rise and the problem then became the need to provide sufficient feed during dry summers. When winter rains were insufficient in 1982, reducing sheep numbers became imperative as severe drought prevailed.[48] Fortunately Gil-Trans International of Bakersfield contracted to take 10,000 sheep to California at reasonable rates. A destocking regime in early summer became the norm, and the idea of growing winter hay to use during the summer dry season was floated. Drought was always lurking in the background, as it had since the ranch was founded.

Despite a recent drought, Bruce was upbeat in December 1985 when he and Keith hosted Governor George Ariyoshi for the day. The demand for charcoal had increased and production from their five brick kilns had now reached 900 tons per year (2000 45-pound bags) with half of it being exported to the mainland. Kiawe availability was not a constraint for a further increase. A new apiarist had been recruited and was currently under training.[49] Sheep production looked positive.

In 1946 Ariyoshi had voted in the Senate for the island to be compulsorily acquired, so when he visited in 1985 the owners put their best foot forward. The governor could not, however, be accorded the elaborate lunch at The House given Governor Quinn in 1961, as the Ki'eki'e mansion had been partially destroyed by Hurricane Iwa in 1982. The governor ate a sandwich lunch at the schoolhouse and said some heartening words to the large number of residents gathered there. 'I have a sense and a feeling that in many ways you want to be left alone,' was the crux of his message.[50]

Hurricane Iwa had blown through the islands in November 1982, three years before Governor Ariyoshi's visit, and hit Kaua'i, with its developed infrastructure, particularly hard. By contrast Ni'ihau, with practically no infrastructure, only suffered building damage, with four houses (out of over 30) totally destroyed and many others damaged, as well as The House. In the Robinsons' view, outside help was not needed. Nobody had been hurt, all could still be housed, repairs could be effected and insurance was in place. The authorities nevertheless wished to assess the damage, but as assistance wasn't needed, the owners resisted the assessment. This caused a furore in the press.[51] Eventually a flyover only was done.

When Hurricane Iniki hit in September 1992, again Kaua'i suffered extensively while Ni'ihau escaped lightly, but the press of the time was silent. In both cases the damage assessment and compensation was settled directly between the insurers and owners.

Despite Bruce Robinson's hopes in 1985, the projected turnaround in the island's financial fortunes did not eventuate. Japanese charcoal undercut the local product. Honey never became viable and intermittent droughts massively affected ranch production. The Robinsons could no longer sustain the continuing losses. By the time *Star Bulletin* writer Catherine Enomoto flew to the island in July 1997, Keith Robinson was saying: 'We will try to maintain the place as long as we reasonably can, but can obviously make no permanent guarantees. Hard times exist everywhere. At the moment, we have very little extra money to subsidize Niihau.'[52]

Two years later, in May 1999 when Governor Cayetano visited, Bruce Robinson said: 'Cattle ranching is dead. Sheep ranching is dead. Honey is dead. Even charcoal is dead …'[53] The ranching era was over. After 135 years the Robinsons had given up the unequal struggle to maintain full employment on Niʻihau.

What finally contributed to the decision to re-evaluate the ranching operation was the continuing attacks by pests on the Niʻihau pasture. Haole koa (*Leucaena leucocephala*), while a pest plant on the other islands, was a significant source of cattle feed on Niʻihau. Here it was under siege from an insect pest, and was being replaced by inedible weeds, while the sugar cane aphid was attacking one of the staple grazing grasses on the island.

▲ A Niʻihau lamb on the crags of the east side pali.
makawelimeatcompany.com

But some major ranching elements continue. While the charcoal and honey industries have gone, harvestable animals remain, and a new venture, Makaweli Meat Company, was formed to provide local meat for the Hawaiian market. Today the island still boasts 8000 to 10,000 sheep, 1800 eland and several hundred cattle. The offtake is processed and marketed through Makaweli Meat Co, which is organized into four divisions according to source and product type:[54]

- Makaweli Ranch: beef and beef products, sourced largely from Kauaʻi
- Niihau Ranch: lamb and eland (with Niʻihau-sourced beef sold through Makaweli Ranch)
- Maui Nui Venison: venison, with deer sourced from Maui
- Makaweli Reserve: speciality meat products imported from the mainland.

A new Department of Agriculture-certified processing plant, designed with the assistance of renowned animal behavior expert Dr Temple Grandin, has been built at Kaumakani on western Kauaʻi and opened at the end of 2013.

Sheep are selected for slaughter and transported by the Robinson landing craft from Niʻihau to Kauaʻi in mob sizes of 100–200 depending on the market. They are held on pasture at Makaweli Ranch for a period to ensure they are in prime condition before they are processed at the Kaumakani abattoir.

Eland, the largest of the antelope family, are handled differently. The eland on Niʻihau are a mixture of Lord Derby or giant eland (*Taurotragus derbianus*) and common eland (*Taurotragus oryx*) that the Robinsons bought from Molokaʻi Ranch for trophy hunting in 1998. Old males can weigh up to a ton and are larger than a horse. Eland for meat consumption are selected and shot on the island. The carcass is then lifted into a dump

▶ Makaweli Landing, on the west side of Kaua'i, just north of Pakala and the slaughterhouse. It is here that lambs from Ni'ihau are offloaded from the Robinsons' landing craft, and Niihauans are transported to and from the island.
Steven Gentry

▼ Eland, the largest of the antelope family, on Ni'ihau.
Michael Anderson, Kaua'i Historical Society

◂ The Department of Agriculture-approved eland dressing facility in the middle of Ni'ihau.
Marcia Braden

truck by a large tractor and driven to a purpose-built dressing facility completed in 2016. There the carcass is winched up, skinned and gutted, and the carcass is quartered. The quarters are then helicoptered to the Kaumakani slaughterhouse. There they are held in a temperature-controlled environment before wholesale or retail cuts are prepared (and frozen if required).

The emphasis in marketing for all of Makaweli Meat Company's products is grass-fed quality, sustainability of production without the use of antibiotics and steroids, with minimally stressed animals right through the production, transport and humane slaughter process. The target market is high-end restaurants and hotels throughout the islands.

Niihau Ranch is a vital component in the mix, and employment opportunities for Niihauans are embedded in the thinking for the whole operation. Thus ranching on the island is not dead, but has become less intensive in character, made possible by a growing interest in 'buying local' and a curiosity to try new products and recipes. Feral pork from the island is a possibility, but Department of Agriculture regulations are such that a separate slaughter facility would be needed.

An enduring culture

Conservation

While in an ecological sense the island has been severely modified by two distinct human migrations, the indigenous culture, while changed, has been retained in a large measure despite massive pressure from the modern world. Since Niʻihau's purchase by Eliza Sinclair in 1864, successive generations of the family have been mindful of King Kamehameha v's exhortation to preserve the Niihauan culture according to the residents' wishes.

Niihauans have always been conservation-minded, whether in the use of water or their pattern of fishing to sustain fish stocks; when enough fish have been caught for food, then the fishing stops.

The greatest visual change to the landscape in European times was Aubrey Robinson's introduction of the ubiquitous kiawe tree, motivated by ranching needs, as were his imports of exotic grasses and other plants to feed increasing herds of grazing animals. Exotic game birds and fruit trees followed as recreational elements, in what is now a diverse ecology.

The Robinson brothers are both environmentally conscious, and Keith in particular has developed a well deserved reputation as a sometimes controversial advocate for species conservation. He believes firmly in the ability of the private sector to achieve significant conservation results.

The largest biological conservation initiative currently being undertaken on the island is the protection of the monk seal population in a cooperative arrangement between the Robinsons and the National Oceanic and Atmospheric Administration, NOAA (see also Chapter One). The growing population of monk seals on Niʻihau is all now tagged and an annual census is undertaken by the two parties jointly, by land and from the air.

The island owners' relationship with the US Fish and Wildlife Service over Critical Habitats, and the State Department of Land and Natural Resources (DLNR) over ownership of the beaches has not been an easy one, however.

Niihau Ranch's contracts with the navy have environmental and cultural safeguards. For instance the beaches where the tiny shells for lei are collected are strictly off limits for any naval purposes.

Care for the environment is exemplified by the Robinsons forbidding any movement by vehicle (including motorbikes) across the northern sand dunes on the island, to protect this fragile ecosystem.

Lehua Island, the 276-acre volcanic tuff cone a mile north-west of Niʻihau, is a Hawaiʻi State Wildlife Sanctuary and is home to 17 varieties of seabirds. Rabbits were eliminated from the island in 2006 and an attempt to exterminate the Polynesian rat (*Rattus exulans*) population in 2009 failed, apparently for operational reasons. When a second attempt to destroy the rats was mooted, the Robinsons/Niihauans became willingly involved, allowing Niʻihau to be used as a bait and fuel depot for the helicopter used. Residents of the island were trained in loading and refueling. The operation was carried out in three

▼ A monk seal on Niʻihau wakes up on the approach of the photographer.
Honolulu Star Bulletin

bait drops in August and September 2017. Monitoring is continuing. While the project has been a success and seabird visitations have increased already, a few remnant rats were sighted in August 2018. These are being dealt with.⁵⁵

The above example illustrates how the resident Niihauans are becoming involved in selective activities since the ranch's long-standing full-employment policy was abandoned in 1999. Others are the collaboration with the navy and the eland dressing operation.

In a cultural preservation sense the main lever has been the restrictions on visitor access to the island (and to Puʻuwai village itself) to allow islanders to lead their lives as they wish. Residents have generally always had freedom of access, with free passage to and from the island on the Robinsons' landing craft — a point that has often been misunderstood. Only in cases where it is felt that the return of an islander will be detrimental to the community as a whole has passage been withheld, and this has not been done lightly.

Visitor access has been strictly controlled and hence the epithet 'The Forbidden Island.' As on any private property, visitors must have a genuine need to visit. The state authorities (education, health, etc) have always been allowed access, but approval for the media has not been so easy, to protect the islanders' way of life. Scientific expeditions have fared better, but there is still much that can be learned about the island's natural history.

The contemporary Niihauan community

In 1998 Hoomana Ia Jesu Church Inc. (the Niihauan church organization) published a landmark study by economist Philip Meyer on the present and future situation of the people of Niʻihau.⁵⁶ The study had its genesis in 1986 when the National Marine Fisheries Laboratory engaged Meyer to study the fishing patterns of islanders throughout Hawaiʻi.

A chance encounter with Keith Robinson led to an invitation for Meyer to visit Niʻihau as part of this work. Contact with the Niihauans continued over the years and when the US Navy was planning for the major extension of its facilities on Niʻihau in 1997, Meyer was engaged by the navy as part of their environmental assessment. This study, translated into Hawaiian by a group of seven Niihauan women, is the result. Although now dated in parts, much of what Meyer says still resonates today. He concludes:

▶ Looking across to Lehua from the base on Niʻihau, during the successful Lehua deratting operation in 2017.
Department of Land and Natural Resources

> ... Niihau has been able to sustain itself as a traditional Hawaiian community because it still has the material and cultural capability to offer a broad range of Hawaiian choices for its people. As noted Niihauans are private people — who seldom articulate their preferences to outsiders. When they do speak, however, their preference for traditional life on Niihau is clear.⁵⁷

Meyer quotes Henry Judd, writing as an outside observer after a week on the island in 1943:

> On Niihau one gets down to the elemental things of life. Family life looms up large over there. Religion is the compelling force in individual life. One gets close to nature, to the cliffs and the slopes, the sea beaches and the reefs, the pastures and lonely stretches, the valleys and coves. One can commune with nature in her variable moods.⁵⁸

The 'simple life,' to a greater or lesser degree, has its attractions for many of us. Of those fortunate enough to have been raised on Niʻihau during ranching times, Meyer concluded in 1998:

> To the present, Niihauans who choose to remain Hawaiian have done so at little cost — for they have been assured of a home and enough food for themselves and their families. Each Niihauan can aspire to a highly satisfactory personal role that is fully integrated into the fundamental productive structure of the island and is recognized as 'worthwhile' by island society. These 'Hawaiian choices' have remained viable because of two underlying factors — **sufficient island control**, so that the island inhabitants have been able to protect themselves from cultural inundation, and **sufficient basic resource and economic capability** to support an appropriate level of jobs and other meaningful human activity on the island.⁵⁹ (Meyer's emphasis)

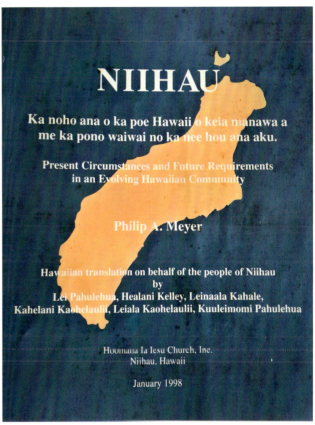

▲ The front cover of Philip Meyer's sociological study.

Since Philip Meyer wrote this, the 'sufficient island control' remains but with the demise of ranching the appropriate level of jobs has not been able to be maintained, and fishing stocks have fallen precipitously. The symbiotic relationship with Niihauan ʻohana on Kauaʻi has been crucial to the survival of the culture. Henry Judd's word picture of life on Niʻihau has become just a dream for many, and can only be exercised for a part of the year, or not at all.

Niihauans resident on the island, as given by the ten-year census figures, dropped somewhat when employment for all able-bodied men ceased with the changes to ranching in 1999, but not as much as might have been expected (230 residents in 1990 and 160 in 2000). As Appendix D shows, the island population then remained essentially constant between 2000 and 2010 (160 residents in 2000 and 170 in 2010) before dropping to 80 in the 2020 census.

In the last ten years since the 2010 census, however, all evidence points to a dramatic fall in numbers of residents who could be considered as 'living' on Niʻihau today. An informal head count in September 2019 indicated that around 60 adults and children could be viewed as resident on the island, but this number varies dramatically, up and down, depending on family, community or religious events taking place either on Niʻihau or on West Kauaʻi. Numbers swell particularly during the Christmas/New Year festivities, when most of the 34 houses at Puʻuwai are inhabited.

For Niihauans the symbiotic relationship with their ʻohana on West Kauaʻi has become even more important, and interchanges are frequent. Some have shifted more or less permanently to West Kauaʻi to be with their ʻohana there, because of health issues or for employment — many working in Gay & Robinson enterprises, but still from time to time they will spend a period at their house on Niʻihau.

The Niihauan community has shown considerable adaptability in the face of this situation. Fundamental to the survival of any culture is retention of the language. As more Niihauans moved away from the island those on West Kauaʻi realized that outside influences would destroy their culture unless strenuous efforts were made to keep the language alive, and to do that the Niihauan children on Kauaʻi needed special schooling. As a result, in the late 1990s two charter schools[60] were formed aiming to promulgate and perpetuate the Niihauan language and culture among those Niihauan children living on Kauaʻi. Each school now has an enrolment of around 50 and teaches through grade 12, while the school on the island itself now has fewer than a dozen pupils. The two charter schools in Kekaha have different language teaching philosophies, which are outlined in Appendix B. The language is seen as the main tool for cultural survival.

All Hawaiians share a profound sense of place, and none more so than Niihauans who, wherever they are, closely identify with their home island. This is exemplified in Tava and Keale's 1984 book *Niihau: The Traditions of an Hawaiian Island*.[61] While keeping alive the island's legends and sayings, the book also includes a large collection of island place names, a sure sign of the importance of place to the islanders.

As families have migrated and the public charter school rolls have risen, the proportion of pupils speaking the Niihauan language at home has severely dropped over time, making it even harder for the schools to maintain the Niihauan culture.

On Niʻihau itself, the school has suffered a corresponding reduction in numbers. It was the first in the state to benefit from solar cells, with a system for the school up and running from 2007 — a huge boost for technology education in particular.

The challenge for the island's owners and residents is to create sufficient gainful opportunities for employment. One singular success has been the production and marketing of Niʻihau shell lei, which has been assisted by two state initiatives.

Firstly, as a result of his own online retail business, in late 2003 Jon Riki Karamatsu, a member of the State House of Representatives, became aware of some products being labelled of Hawaiian origin when in fact they were not, and in this context set out to protect authentic Niʻihau shell lei by means of legislation. He found support among the Niihauan community and the legislators, and in a remarkably short time bills were introduced, debated and passed in both the House and Senate.

In May 2004 the Act was signed into legislation by Governor Linda Lingle. It requires that a shell lei cannot be described as a Niʻihau shell lei unless a minimum of 80% of

◀ An aerial view of the three classrooms of Niʻihau School, and below, the solar panel array which powers the school.
Honolulu Star Bulletin

the shells are from Niʻihau and the lei was made entirely in the state of Hawaiʻi. If the proportion of Niʻihau shells is less than 100% the actual percentage must be stated on the Certificate of Authenticity. One of the drivers of the legislation was the unique luster of the Niʻihau shells compared with the same species found elsewhere in the islands, which are being made into competing shell lei. The legislation is under the aegis of the Department of Agriculture and has been welcomed by all parties, including the Office of Hawaiian Affairs. Broadly the Act mirrors the protection given in 1998 to the labeling of Kona coffee.

The second initiative has been the formation in 2005 of the Niʻihau Cultural Heritage Foundation to help lei makers with marketing and to provide an avenue for the sale of their products to benefit the artists more directly. The website (niihauheritage.org) provides advice for those wishing to purchase lei, including what to look for in the shells themselves, in the workmanship, and how to ensure authenticity.[62]

The foundation's beginnings were inauspicious. In 2005, La France Kapaka-Arboleda, the Kauaʻi representative for the Office of Hawaiian Affairs, had a dream to establish a foundation to enable Niʻihau shell lei-makers to sell directly to the public and also provide health insurance for them and their families.

On 26 May, she called a meeting of the lei-makers at the Waimea plantation cottages. Only five Niʻihau women attended and they represented only three different families of lei-makers. Kapaka-Arboleda was concerned that as she did not speak Hawaiian there might be a communication problem, as the first language of the lei-makers was Niʻihau Hawaiian. She prevailed upon Hōkūlani Cleeland, a Hawaiian language teacher who had been involved with the Niʻihau community for many years, to assist with interpretation, and called a second meeting for 15 June 2005. Only the same lei-makers appeared, but Kapaka-Arboleda persisted and it was decided to call a community meeting at the Kekaha Neighborhood Center four weeks later on 13 July, with Cleeland facilitating. All Niihauan families were informed about the meeting, and 43 people attended. At this meeting, 20 family groups were identified as having members involved in lei-making to some extent, and it was decided to have each family identify a representative who would attend meetings to establish a foundation and communicate progress back to their

▲ Representative Jon Riki Karamatsu, promoter of the Niʻihau shell lei legislation passed in 2004.
Jon Riki Karamatsu

▶ Rhonetta Tate of Nā Mea Hawaiʻi/Native Books models two sets of Niʻihau shell lei on the occasion of the signing into law of Act 91 protecting the identity of Niʻihau shell lei.
Honolulu Star Bulletin

family groups. Of the 20 family groups, 16 families chose to participate and designated their representatives.*

Kapaka-Arboleda obtained a $30,000 grant from the Office of Hawaiian Affairs to help this culturally appropriate industry maintain its place in the art, history and future of the island residents.

With the grant money, legal and accounting advice was sought. At the first meeting with attorney Brian Ezuka and accountant Alan Arakaki held on 5 August, the nonprofit organization — to be called the Niʻihau Cultural Heritage Foundation — was established 'to perpetuate and preserve the culture and language of Native Hawaiians through, among other activities, education and development of self-sufficiency.'

Ezuka and Arakaki continued to meet with the group and facilitated the writing of the Articles of Incorporation. Approval for the Foundation as a 501(c)(3) tax-exempt organization was given by the Internal Revenue Service on 26 January 2006. La France Kapaka-Arboleda, the prime mover in the formation of the foundation, died shortly afterwards, but not before her dream had been realized.

The current Niʻihau Cultural Heritage Foundation board members are:

- President: Diane Hiipoi Kanahele (member of a Niihauan lei-making ʻohana)
- Vice president: Byron Hōkūlani Cleeland (educator and Hawaiian speaker)
- Secretary/treasurer: Lorna Contrades (active in Hawaiian issues on Kauaʻi)
- Director: Charles Baker (involved for many years in marketing Niʻihau shell jewellery)
- Director: Edward Lilikalani Punua (accountant)

* The chosen family representatives were: Noelani Kaaumoana, Sana Pahulehua, Kaehulani Kanahele, Naui Kanahele, Ulu Kanahele, Mapuana Beniamina, Minoaka Kanahele, Uilani Kelley, Kaleo Kaohelaulii, Luana Kaohelaulii, Kaimi Keamoai-Strickland, Kauilei Kelley, Loke Niau, Lu Niheu Koerte, Awapuhi Kahale and Haunani Kahokuloa.

An enduring culture

◀ The successful lei-makers meeting at the West Kaua'i Technology and Visitor Center in October 2005. From left: Rep. Mina Morita, Loke Mawae, Haunani Kahokuloa, Ella Kanahele, Kanani Beniamina, Awapuhi Kahale (holding baby Ola Vainuku), Rep. Jon Riki Karamatsu, Hōkūlani Cleeland, Ehulani Kanahele, Kaleo Kaohelaulii, Ululani Kanahele, Mokihana Kanahele, Mapuana Beniamina, Susana Pahulehua, Noelani Kanahele and Ileialoa Beniamina.

Jon Riki Karamatsu

A second grant of $15,000 from the Office of Hawaiian Affairs was awarded to the foundation on 20 June 2008, to 'provide marketing and brand development services to the Ni'ihau shell lei-making families' including development of a website to highlight 'the importance of Ni'ihau shell leis in preserving the culture, language and history of Ni'ihau and provide information on the lei-making process and materials.'

Hōkūlani Cleeland developed the website in 2009 and it can be reached at niihauheritage.org. The website averages between 2000 and 3000 visits every month and receives questions of all kinds about Ni'ihau shell lei — particularly requests about appraisals. These latter are answered by referring the questioner to appropriate lei appraisers whose reputations are well known to the Foundation.

Aside from these initiatives, in late 2018 the County of Kaua'i (which includes Ni'ihau) signed a memorandum of understanding with the Mālie Foundation, a local charitable organization 'that works to educate, promote, preserve and perpetuate Hawaiian culture.' The particular focus of the memorandum is the preservation of the 'ōlelo Ni'ihau (Ni'ihau language), with both the foundation and the county contributing.[63] A further collaborative program to promote the language is the partnership between Hamline University of Minnesota* and the charter school Ke Kula Niihau O Kekaha. The initiative has received funding from the Department of Education's Title 1: Comprehensive Support and Development Program. Hamline University has provided language and cultural learning resources for students and professional development for teachers. As of September 2019, more than 60 reading books written in the Ni'ihau dialect by the students at the school, and edited by their teachers, have been published for use in the school.

▲ Gladys Awapuhi Kahale wearing a lei she crafted consisting of three cascading strands of color-matched kahelelani shells.

Charles Baker/Gladys Kahale

* *Hamline University, in St Paul, Minnesota, is a small private liberal arts college with 2000 undergraduates and 1500 postgraduate students. The university, the first in Minnesota, was founded in 1854 by Methodist visionaries and the ethos of John Wesley still resonates. It is known for its emphasis on experiential learning, service and social justice.*

So how have things changed over the last half century for those living on the island? Undoubtedly the decision to curtail ranching operations in 1999, with the loss of guaranteed employment, has had a profound effect. Since then the availability of

▶ Puʻuwai Village Center with the church on the left, and school buildings.
Nancy Shaw

work has been sporadic, forcing many to leave the island and others to seek the unemployment benefit.

There has been little change to the rules and arrangements applying to those living on the island since Frank Sinclair's time there over 160 years ago. As of now:

- Alcohol is still forbidden
- Dogs are not allowed, but cats are
- Smoking is discouraged (and strict rules apply because of the fire danger)
- Tattoos and body piercings are forbidden
- Beards are not allowed and the men must have short hair
- Firearms are not completely forbidden, and may be used for supervised hunting
- Housing is free
- Wild pigs and sheep may be hunted
- Access is controlled by the Robinsons, with the only means of access being by their landing craft, the so-called 'barge,' or by the Robinson's helicopter.

While island access is organized by Leiana Robinson, Bruce's wife, residents and their families and friends are generally able to travel to and from the island. Access to the island, it is reasonable to say, does cause some angst from time to time, and has probably always done so ever since the Sinclairs took ownership. Brandi, younger daughter of Bruce and Leiana, has now taken over the operation of the barge from Bruce.

With the curtailment of ranching activities in 1999 and the population decrease, barge trips have become less frequent — generally only when stock are sent to the Makaweli Meats slaughterhouse. This has made life more constrained for those living on the island.

This apart, life on Niʻihau has changed little from that described in *Aloha Niihau* (see pages 279–80). The book's authors set out to record the lifestyle as it was for them on the island and to create a textbook that children who speak the Niʻihau dialect of the

An enduring culture

Hawaiian language could use, 'thereby empowering them to seek literature as a creative outlet.'

David Larsen's letters from 1942 describing the lives the Niihauans were leading then give a different perspective at a slightly earlier time (see pages 245–246).

Both accounts depict the islanders' strong spirituality and Protestant faith and the way that this faith is woven into their daily and weekly life.

Since these accounts were written, modern domestic appliances are becoming more prevalent and solar power is now ubiquitous. The fishing resource is greatly diminished. Water still has to be carefully husbanded, but generally daily life just flows on within the spiritual and cultural framework outlined in these narratives.

When the island was bought from Kamehameha v by the Sinclair family with their strict Protestant convictions, the islanders had been exposed for 30 years to similar beliefs by the missionaries. There was no clash, only a melding of ideologies. These same beliefs have been the bedrock of the relationship between the island's owners and the islanders to this day.

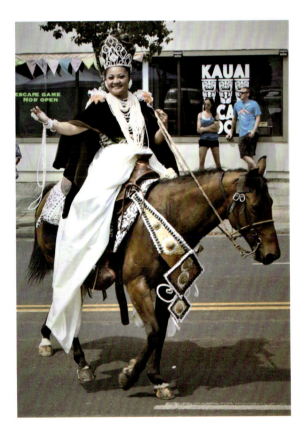

◀ Ashlee Aviguetero, Niʻihau Pāʻū Princess, King Kamehameha Day Parade, Kauaʻi, June 2018. King Kamehameha Day goes back to 1871 when the king decided to honor his great-grandfather by announcing an annual day of festivities throughout the islands. Today it is celebrated by parades, the ceremonial draping of lei on the statues of Kamehameha the Great, and many other events. Each of the islands has its own color and flower, with the exception of Niʻihau which has the white momi shell as its color and emblem. The riders in the parade wear long skirts called pāʻū, and from among the princesses a pāʻū queen is crowned.
Courtesy Ashlee Aviguetero

▲ The church at Puʻuwai.
Greg Vaughn

THE LEI IMAGES ON CHAPTER HEADING PAGES

The Niʻihau shell lei images shown on the chapter heading pages are drawn from various sources. The lei is described, the shell types are named, and where possible, the lei maker's name, and where the lei is currently held. The lei length refers to the length from clasp to clasp around the curve.

Contents page 19¾-inch crown-flower lei with multi-colored momi and kahelelani shells, and finished with a matching double cowrie shell clasp — by Kahea Niau.

Introduction 40-inch, seven-strand shell lei with strands of different colored kahelelani shells, completed in 1970 by Ane Kanahele and now held in the Hawaiʻi State Art Museum.

Chapter One Three-strand kipona lei of rarest colors of momi and kahelelani shells. Courtesy of Niʻihau Cultural Heritage Foundation.

Chapter Two 23½-inch, three-strand kipona lei with momi shells pīkake-style and kahelelani shells mauna loa-style — by Kaleohoomana Kaohelaulii.

Chapter Three 1¼-inch diameter kipona (mixed shell) flower style earrings of yellow/white laiki shells, brown striped paʻalima shells and maroon kahelelani shells — crafted by a Niihauan family. Courtesy of Charles Baker.

Chapter Four Ten-strand, 22½-inch kahelelani shell lei with double cowrie shell clasp — by Gladys Awapuhi Kahale.

Chapter Five Four-strand 28-inch pohelo lei strung in pīkake style. The pohelo shells are rare golden brown and black. Pīkake refers to a particular style of stringing which is reflective of the much prized flower of the pīkake plant — crafted by a top Niʻihau artist. Courtesy of Charles Baker.

Chapter Six Mauna Loa style 7¾-inch kahelelani shell bracelet strung in green, medium pink, rare hot pink, dark brown and yellow kahelelani shells, finished with a secure magnetic clasp — strung by a Niʻihau artist. Courtesy of Charles Baker.

▼ The size of the smallest kahelelani and kāmoa shells, in relation to a historic Hawaiʻi Statehood quarter from 1959.
Courtesy Niʻihau Cultural Heritage Foundation

Chapter Seven 20½-inch multi-colored kahelelani shell lei, four-tie poepoe block-style, with double cowrie shell clasp.

Chapter Eight A five-strand 20¾-inch kahelelani shell lei strung in mauna loa block style in colors of rare hot pink, pink blush, dark brown, kamoa (yellow and orange), maroon, green and medium flower pink. The lei is finished with a traditional double bumpy cowrie shell clasp — strung by a Niʻihau artist, courtesy of Charles Baker.

Chapter Nine 20¾-inch crown-flower and poepoe kahelelani kipona lei. Multicolored momi and kahelelani shells in poepoe and crown-flower styles. Matching double cowrie clasp — by Kaleohoomana Kaohelaulii.

Chapter Ten Ten-strand, 23⅓-inch white laiki or rice shell lei, with a white double cowrie shell clasp — by Gladys Awapuhi Kahale.

Chapter Eleven Five-strand, 24½-inch paʻalima necklace with ʻopihi pendant encrusted with kahelelani and laiki shells. — by Kaleohoomana Kaohelaulii, from the collection of Baryn Futa of Denver, Colorado.

Acknowledgements 48-inch, 20-strand lei with strands of different colored kahelelani shells, completed in 1993 by Ane Kanahele and now held in the Hawaiʻi State Art Museum.

Appendices (page 315) Choker-length lei wili of kahelelani shells by Ane Kanahele, crafted by winding the strung shells tightly around a cloth foundation, a rare skill. Courtesy of Niʻihau Cultural Heritage Foundation.

A note on shell types

There are three major shell types. The smallest shells are from the turban family, the kahelelani and kāmoa shells. The other shells commonly used are the momi from the dove shell family and lāiki (rice shells). All of these are mentioned in the lei descriptions above.

For further information see Linda Moriarty's book *Niʻihau Shell Leis*, published in 1986 by Kolowalu Press, or visit the Niʻihau Cultural Heritage Foundation website: www.niihauheritage.org.

ACKNOWLEDGEMENTS

Any project such as this book begins with a series of events — coincidences, perhaps. In 2013 I published my book on the Kermadec Islands, shortly after Doff, my wife of 50 years, passed away. Around the same time my Honolulu friend from graduate school days in Berkeley, Mary Ann McCrea, also lost her spouse. In due course I visited Honolulu and our longtime friendship blossomed.

In a sense I was unconsciously looking for another project, and while I was visiting her, Mary Ann acquired a new tenant, Jamie Emberson, a member of the Robinson family. Jamie kindly lent us Ida Knudsen von Holt's *Stories of Long Ago*, which describes her ancestors' time in New Zealand and their purchase of the island of Ni'ihau. We were both intrigued, and the idea of the book was born.

Mary Ann has been with me all of the way, and I thank her for her deep knowledge of the islands, for her sage advice on all aspects of the book, and for opening so many doors which I would otherwise have found hard to open. Without her willing and generous support, the book could never have been realized. Sadly Mary Ann did not live to see the culmination of our efforts, as she passed away in 2022.

The Robinson family are owed huge thanks for their participation in the project. Nancy Shaw in particular, as our go-to person on questions about the family's relationship with Ni'ihau, was always willing to go the extra mile. I feel privileged to have had complete access to the Sinclair/Robinson family letters and photographs, some of which date back to 1840 in New Zealand and came with the family to Hawai'i on the *Bessie*. I also acknowledge Nancy's mother, Lois Somers, keeper of the family archives, for letting us use the information she collected over the years concerning the family's involvement with Ni'ihau. This mantle has now been passed to Nancy, after her mother's death in 2022.

On my first meeting with him, Keith Robinson, co-owner of the island with his brother Bruce, supported the book concept and has remained involved. Bruce has freely given information, and his wife Leiana has also been generous. I thank them all.

Hōkūlani Cleeland, kumu (teacher) at Ke Kula Niihau O Kekaha, has been my entry into the Niihauan community: those living on Kaua'i, and more at a distance, those on the island itself. I am deeply grateful for his unfailing efforts to answer every question I put to him. His bilingual skills, and particularly his intimate knowledge of the Niihauan dialect, have been invaluable.

Special mention must also be made of the invaluable exchange of emails I had with Hōkūlani and with Pila Wilson, which turned my first attempts at the book's appendix on the Niihauan dialect into an accurate and readable addition. My sincere thanks to both of them.

Ane Kanahele (Mama Ane) introduced Mary Ann and me to Niihauan shell lei-making and later, with her daughter Ehulani and Thomas Kanahele, to wider aspects of Niihauan culture. We treasure our time with them.

Charles Baker, a longtime friend to the Niihauan community and ardent promoter of their shell lei, has been most helpful throughout the production of the book, and I thank him sincerely.

Mary Ann and I were fortunate to spend time with Betsy Knudsen Toulon and her son Eric before she died in 2018 at the age of 98. I thank her and Eric for their memories and images of the Knudsen family.

In New Zealand Hugh Laracy, who wrote about Eliza Sinclair and the family's time voyaging, kindly gave me all his working notes.

Individuals from many institutions have been especially helpful: Clyde Imada from the Bishop Museum; Jason Achiu from the Hawai'i State Archives; George Lee from the *Honolulu Star Advertiser*; David Lorence from the National Tropical Botanical Garden; Christine Fayre from the Kōke'e Museum; Donna Stewart and Delia Akaji from the Kaua'i Historical Society; and John Barker from the Hawaiian Mission Houses, to name but a few.

My thanks also to Sam and Mary Cooke, Susie Somers, Mary Sue Matter, Ian Birnie, Rosemary Steele, my sister Sally Mathieson, and the many others who have helped with information, advice and checking parts of the text.

Institutions that have been invaluable sources of information include the Akaroa Museum; National Library of New Zealand; Auckland Libraries; Auckland War Memorial Museum; Bishop Museum; Bureau of Conveyances, state of Hawai'i; Canterbury Museum; Christchurch City Libraries; Hamilton Library at the University of Hawai'i, Mānoa; Hawai'i State Library; Hawaiian Historical Society; Hawaiian Mission Children's Society; Hawai'i State Archives; *Honolulu Star Advertiser*; Kaua'i Historical Society; and Kaua'i Museum.

I am indebted to the following for permission to quote from publications: Kimo Armitage for extracts from *Aloha Niihau*. Mutual Publishing LLC for extracts from *Niihau: The Traditions of an Hawaiian Island*. Judith Burtner for extracts from *Robinson Family Governess*. Also to the very many other authors quoted who have written about Ni'ihau, all of whom are acknowledged in the bibliography. I thank you all.

Finally my thanks are due to Roger Steele, Christine Roberts and Matthew Bartlett of Steele Roberts Aotearoa Publishers, and to the University of Hawai'i Press, Mānoa for distribution of the book. It has been a real pleasure to have been so involved in the publication process, and one which I gratefully acknowledge.

APPENDICES

A	Timeline	316
B	The Niihauan dialect: Past and present	320
C	The Battle of Niʻihau	327
D	Niʻihau population numbers	333
E	Botanical explorations on Niʻihau	335

APPENDIX A

TIMELINE

mya ~ millions of years ago   ya ~ years ago   Page

6 mya	Niʻihau begins to emerge from the ocean, and volcanism continues for a million years, then ceases.	14
2.5 mya	Volcanism on Niʻihau renews, and cones are formed from tuff (light porous rock formed by consolidation of volcanic ash).	16
0.5 mya	Volcanism ceases for the second time.	
c. 50,000 ya	Humankind, having emerged from Africa, reaches Southeast Asia.	32
c. 5000 ya	The Austronesian diaspora begins with the movement of humans from Taiwan through the north coast of Papua to the western islands of the Pacific.	
800–900 ya	Tonga and Sāmoa are settled.	
1025–1125 ya	The Marquesas and Society Islands are settled.	
1200–1290 ya	The Hawaiian islands are discovered and inhabited by Polynesians from Tahiti and the Marquesas.	33
17th century	Aliʻi nui Kahelelani reigns over Niʻihau and Kauaʻi.	41
1730–70	Peleʻioholani reigns and divides Niʻihau/Kauaʻi into six districts, with Niʻihau being one of them.	
20 January 1778	The Hawaiian islands are sighted for the first time by Cook's third expedition.	57
29 January 1778	Captain Cook anchors off the west side of Niʻihau, and barters for supplies, going ashore himself on 1 February.	59
9 March 1779	Captain Clerke, after Cook's death, returns to Niʻihau for supplies.	58
c 1780	Kaumualiʻi born to Kamakahelei and Kaʻeokūlani (Kaʻeo).	106
8 June 1786	Captains Portlock and Dixon arrive at Yam Bay, Niʻihau, for supplies, and in particular, yams. Kaʻeo is ruler of Niʻihau and Kauaʻi.	106
14 March 1792	Captain George Vancouver anchors at Niʻihau for yams for the first time.	87
29 March 1793	At Waimea, Kauaʻi, Vancouver drops off the two Niihauan girls he picked up from James Baker of the *Jenny* on the northwest coast; he did not visit Niʻihau.	92
13 March 1794	A year later Vancouver arrives at Waimea again, takes the two Niihauan girls aboard again, and returns them to Niʻihau.	
14 December 1794	Kaumualiʻi becomes king of Niʻihau and Kauaʻi after his father is killed in battle at ʻAiea. Civil war erupts between Kaumualiʻi and his half brother Keawe.	106

May 1796	Kamehameha's Kaua'i invasion force encounters a great storm en route and the invasion is abandoned.	107
28 July 1796	HMS *Providence*, commanded by William Robert Broughton drops anchor in Yam Bay, Ni'ihau and on the following day two of his marines are murdered in what seemed like a premeditated plot, perhaps as retaliation for Broughton's refusal to trade yams for muskets.	98
1796	Keawe is victorious in the civil war and Kaumuali'i is placed under house arrest. Keawe dies months later and Kaumuali'i reassumes power.	107
1804	Kamehameha attempts a second invasion of Kaua'i, but is thwarted by a devastating illness among his troops.	108
1810	Kaumuali'i accepts Kamehameha's invitation to visit him in Honolulu and as a result of discussions agreement is reached that Kaumuali'i's domain should become a vassal state of Kamehameha's 'empire' and that tributes be paid accordingly.	110
28 May 1816	Despite their agreement Kaumuali'i does not trust Kamehameha not to invade, and spends considerable effort looking for foreign support. When Dr Schäffer and the Russians appeared to secure cargo from a wrecked Russian vessel Kaumuali'i grasps the opportunity to best his rival and signs treaties on 2 June putting Kaua'i and Ni'ihau under Russian protection in return for trading opportunities throughout the islands. Fort Elizabeth at Waimea is constructed. The tsar, however, does not agree with the treaties signed and Dr Schäffer passes out of the picture.	113
May 1819	Kamehameha dies and his 21-year-old son Liholiho (Kamehameha II) succeeds him.	117
1820	Kaumuali'i's son Humehume arrives back in Kaua'i after 15 years in America.	120
February 1821	Liholiho, apparently on a whim, sails to Kaua'i and tours it with Kaumuali'i. Subsequently Liholiho kidnaps Kaumuali'i and sails to Honolulu where the latter has to marry Ka'ahumanu, the most powerful woman in the land. Kaumuali'i remains in exile in Honolulu until his death.	119
May 1824	Kaumuali'i dies and a period of great uncertainty ensues on Kaua'i. Prime Minister Kalanimoku visits Kaua'i to calm the situation and confirms the overlordship agreement of 1810 which leaves many unhappy.	121
August 1824	Humehume rebels and attempts to take Fort Elizabeth at Waimea. Later the rebels are routed in the battle at Hanapēpē, 'The Pig Eating'. Humehume is exiled to Oahu.	122
1825	Ka'ahumanu appoints Kaikio'ewa governor of Kaua'i/Ni'ihau and political stability is finally achieved. He remains governor for 14 years.	124
3 May 1826	Humehume dies of influenza.	123
July 1828	The first visit to Ni'ihau by a Protestant missionary takes place when Rev. Peter Gulick and his wife visit and he reports that there are already four schools on the island.	193
25 August 1840	The Sinclair family sails from Scotland to New Zealand in the *Blenheim*, disembarking in Wellington on 26 December.	131
July/August 1842	Catholic priest Father Robert Walsh spends three weeks on Ni'ihau and celebrates the first Catholic mass held there.	194
May 1843	The Sinclair family sails from Wellington to Pigeon Bay in the *Richmond*, the boat built by Francis Sinclair Snr.	140
May 1846	Francis Sinclair senior and eldest son George are lost at sea while sailing from Pigeon Bay to Wellington.	147

October 1850	Rev. George Rowell visits Niʻihau and rails against the foothold the Catholic faith has achieved on the island. The rivalry continues.	196
February 1863	The Sinclair family sail from Pigeon Bay on their bark *Bessie*, bound for Victoria on Vancouver Island.	162
17 September 1863	The *Bessie*, with the Sinclair family aboard, arrives in Honolulu via Tahiti, Victoria (on Vancouver Island), Utsalady and Port Angeles in Washington Territory.	163
23 January 1864	King Kamehameha V sells Niʻihau Island to the Sinclair brothers, James and Francis, for $10,000.	175
2 June 1864	King Kamehameha V visits Niʻihau, introduces the new owners and addresses the islanders after the Sinclairs had established themselves temporarily at Kaununui on the northwest coast of the island.	177
1864	Ranching begins on Niʻihau with a gradual build-up of livestock from the other Hawaiian islands and New Zealand over the next few years.	188
1865	The first pastor for the island, David Kupahu, is appointed.	199
1865	The House at Kiʻekiʻe is started.	190
1874	'Protest mat' presented to King Kalākaua by George Gay on behalf of the mat maker on Niʻihau, objecting to the imposition of the animal taxes. It is also a wistful harkening back to the 'good old times' of Kamehameha the Great. The mat is on display in the Bishop Museum.	205
1884	The formation of Gay & Robinson by cousins Francis Gay and Aubrey Robinson and other family members, with a mandate to manage all the family's landholdings, including Niʻihau.	219
16 October 1893	Eliza Sinclair, the family matriarch, dies at the age of 92, but not before she had divested herself of her landholdings to her sons and daughters.	228
January 1902	Aubrey Robinson becomes sole owner of Niʻihau by purchasing the interests of the other members of the family over time.	220
1922	Aylmer Robinson takes over managerial responsibility for Niihau Ranch from his father and owner, Aubrey.	242
October 1929	The first gubernatorial visit to the island when the Territorial Governor Lawrence Judd visits for the day with his brother Charles Judd, the Director of Forestry.	247
1933	The furrowing of all flat and undulating land commences to foil a possible Japanese invasion by aircraft. The task is completed in the summer of 1941 when two thirds of the island has been plowed.	256
6 July 1936	Aubrey Robinson dies at Makaweli aged 82 and in his will leaves Niʻihau Island 75% to his son Aylmer, 25% to his son Lester upon the death of his wife Alice.	242
7 December 1941	In the aftermath of the Pearl Harbor attack a Japanese Zero aircraft crash lands close to Puʻuwai village with dire consequences for the pilot.	257
June 1942	Coastwatchers from the US Army's 299th Regiment arrive and remain on the island until October 1944. They are closely followed by a Coast Guard team to set up and operate LORAN facilities until 1952.	260
1946	A Territorial Senate Investigation Committee visits Niʻihau for a few hours and after a nine-month hiatus recommends major infrastructure investments, which the Senate approves, but the House rejects the bill.	262
29 September 1961	With statehood achieved in 1959, the first state governor, William Quinn, visits.	273

29 April 1967	Aylmer Robinson dies.		276
24 October 1969	Lester Robinson dies.		276
10 February 1970	Governor John Burns announces plans for the state to acquire Niʻihau. The attempt fails.		281
1984	A US Navy surveillance radar facility is constructed on Mount Pānīʻau. Other arrangements for selective use of parts of the island by the navy are also agreed with the owners.		292
1987	Half-day commercial helicopter tours to the island commence using the Robinsons' helicopter, followed by hunting safaris in 1989. Puʻuwai is avoided to limit the impact on the islanders.		296
1998	Two charter schools in Kekaha are formed, dedicated to the preservation of the language and culture of the Niihauans living on western Kauaʻi.		304
1999	Ranching effectively ceases on Niʻihau. The population subsequently declines over time.		299
May 2004	The governor signs legislation into law to protect the use of the term *Niʻihau shell lei* to those made largely of shells from the island.		304
2005	The Niʻihau Cultural Heritage Foundation is formed to market Niʻihau shell lei.		305
2013	After many years of concern at dwindling fish stocks around the island due to Kauaian fishermen, the island's owners call a press conference at the Capitol to request legislative action to protect fish stocks. Further discussions follow but no action is taken.		288

APPENDIX B

THE NIIHAUAN DIALECT: PAST AND PRESENT

> On being shown the live pigs which we had on board, and which we had brought with us from Tahiti they immediately cried *Booa*, and from this and from the rest of their speech it was evident that the language in use here was not unlike that of the Tahitians.
> H. Zimmermann, 1781, *First contact with Hawaiians — The Third Voyage of Captain Cook* [1]

Niihauans are justifiably proud of their distinct form of the Hawaiian language. Language is central to any culture and the Niihauan language is a prime example. The island community remains the only group still speaking Hawaiian (in their own dialect) as a first language, in an unbroken line from pre-European times.

The spoken word

When Captain James Cook first made contact with the Hawaiian people at Kauaʻi he noted in his journal, with some astonishment given the distance he had sailed from Tahiti, 'We were agreeably surprised to find that they spoke a dialect of the Otaheitean language.'* A week later at Niʻihau, having been driven from his anchorage at Waimea by the weather, he noted, 'The people [Niihauans] who were in them [canoes] resembled in their persons the inhabitants of Atooi [Kauaʻi].' There is no mention in any of the journals of there being any dialectical difference between Kauaʻi and Niʻihau at this time.

David Samwell, surgeon on the *Discovery*, was the first to notice and record a dialectical difference between the windward (eastern) and leeward islands of the Hawaiian archipelago. Fourteen months after their first Niʻihau visit, in March 1779, after the death of Cook, and as they were leaving Niʻihau for a second visit to the Bering Strait, he wrote in his journal:

> The Inhabitants of this Island [Niʻihau] and of Atowai [Kauaʻi] differ in nothing material, either in dress, Language or appearance, from those of Ouwaihee [Hawaiʻi] & the other Islands to the Eastward. These people constantly make use of the T, where the others use the K, such as in the Name of the Island Atowai which is called Akowai at Ou-waihee. [2]

Cook had no Tahitians or other Polynesians with him to assist, but given the length of time his vessels had just spent in the Society Islands, it is not so surprising that Samwell, and presumably others, could pick up and remark upon such a dialectical difference.

---

* *Cook was familiar with the Tahitian language, having just spent some months there, and had visited previously on his earlier voyages. He often spelled Tahitian and Hawaiian place names with an initial 'O' or 'A', which combines the actual place name with the short vowel 'o' meaning 'it is,' thus: Otaheiti, O Tahiti, it is Tahiti; Atooi, O Kauaʻi, it is Kauaʻi; and Oneeheeou, O Niʻihau, it is Niʻihau.*

That said, Samwell was aware how superficial their knowledge of the language and culture was. A few days earlier at Waimea, before his second visit to Niʻihau, he wrote in regard to their dialog: 'There is not much dependence to be placed on these Constructions that we put upon Signs and Words which we understand but very little of, & at best can only give a probable Guess at their Meaning.'[3]

Despite this, Samwell produced a commendable word list from his windward and leeward island visits, using his own phonetic spelling, which included K, but not T.

This geographical difference in pronunciation lingered after the islands were unified, as the 1880s Judge Abraham Fornander noted:

> ... as late as fifty years ago it was easy to distinguish a native from the leeward islands from one of the windward by his manner of pronouncing the letters *k* and *l*, which Kauai and Oahu natives, adopting the Tahitian style, pronounced *t* and *r*. Since the conquest of Oahu by Kamehameha I in 1796, and the cession of Kauai in 1809, the fusion of the people of the leeward and windward isles of the group has been so great as to nearly obliterate the ancient difference of speech between them.[4]

Judge Fornander was evidently not aware that because of its relative isolation the old style of speech had been retained of Niʻihau — and this continues today. In the early 1980s Tava and Keale explained:

> Today, the Niihauans have preserved the purity of the Hawaiian language of their forefathers and on Niihau it is spoken in its purest form. As with the older language of the Hawaiians, the use of the "T" and the "K" are interchanged. The "L" and "R" change, as do the "L" and "N". Although the language is written with the "K", Niihauans remain true to the ancestral tongue in speech with the use of the "T". As Captain James Cook noted during his visit to the islands in 1778, this style of language has almost the same sound as in Tahiti, though it is much softer and less brash and guttural in sound. ...
>
> The isolation of Niihau has preserved it from language changes that occurred on other islands.[5]

The written word

Hawaiian is one of the most melodious languages in the world. As *The Friend* enthused in 1878, when the language was in danger of extinction, 'Long live the grand old, sonorous, poetical Hawaiian language.' This poetic beauty of the language created an additional problem for the early Congregational missionaries who took on the task of rendering these sounds into written form, something none of them had been trained to do. Work on the written language, critical to their evangelical mission, began almost as soon as the missionaries arrived. One early report gave reason for optimism:

> During the following year [1821], some progress was made in settling the orthography of the language, a task, which the great prevalence of liquid sounds rendered extremely difficult. The alphabet adopted, was that proposed by Hon. John Pickering, of Salem,

▲ The first page of the first item printed by the missionary press in Honolulu, in 1822 — a three by five inch 16-page Hawaiian spelling booklet, *The Alphabet*.
Palapala, University of Hawaiʻi, Mānoa, Vol. 1, 2017

Mass. in his 'Essay on a Uniform Orthography for the Indian Languages of North America,' published in the Memoirs of the American Academy of Arts and Sciences; excepting that the Hawaiian language requires a less number of letters than that alphabet contains. Every sound has its appropriate sign; every word is spelled exactly as it is pronounced; and thus the art of reading and writing the language, is rendered to the natives simple and easy.[6]

The Tahitian orthography had been settled some years before and there was a feeling that the Hawaiian alphabet should follow that as closely as possible, while recognizing some sounds were different. Māori offered a further model.

The alphabet the missionaries finally settled on in 1826 consisted of only seven consonants (h, k, l, m, n, p, w) and five vowels (a, e, i, o, u). This alphabet was finally agreed after some books had already been printed. The first was a Hawaiian spelling book, in January 1822, which included b and d, and a mix of other consonants. In general the missionaries were not happy with the result and b and d were subsequently excluded, except in borrowed foreign words.

A lot of discussion also took place on the necessity in the written word to choose between 't' or 'k,' 'l' or 'r' and 'w' or 'v.' It was recognized that the spoken dialect varied between islands and it was these sounds that created the major differences. Most Hawaiians found it difficult to distinguish the sound difference between the pairs, a difference that was quite apparent to the English-speaking missionaries. A majority decision was arrived at with the choices made after all the missionaries, including those on every island, had been consulted — and polled. The winners were 'k', 'l' and 'w.'

This agreed alphabet was used for printing the catechism and Gospels, and a revised hymnal.[7]

In the missionary schools this alphabet was used to teach Hawaiians to read and write. Literacy was a huge and extremely successful venture — a lasting legacy of the missionaries. This orthography was used in all the monarchy's official records and in the Hawaiian-language newspapers that grew in number over the next 40 years.

The use of the 'glottal stop' ('okina, literally 'cutting off/separation') as an additional letter in written Hawaiian to clarify meaning was recognized quite early, with its sparing inclusion by the missionaries in the first complete Hawaiian Bible published in 1839. It was not used in the Bible as extensively as it is used in the language now. It was shown in the Bible as an apostrophe.* It is typeset today as an inverted comma.

The missionaries also recognized the desirability of a diacritical mark to signify a vowel lengthening or emphasis. Several early attempts at introductions were made, and there was confusion between the use of the second mark to indicate vowel lengthening or to signify an accented syllable. Although outsiders who wanted to learn the language would benefit from the use of 'okina (') and kahakō (macrons), to native speakers of Hawaiian their use was not important when learning the written language. These native Hawaiians were the missionaries' target market.

The missionaries were severely hampered by the lack of the special typefaces required, despite constant requests to their superiors in Boston. The macron or kahakō was not used at all in the first Bible, and this lack of the special typeface required persisted throughout the 19th century.

---

* The use of the apostrophe in the Hawaiian Bible to mark an 'okina is basically restricted to first person pronoun forms to distinguish them from second pronoun forms, e.g. kaʻu/koʻu (my), noʻu/naʻu (for me), oʻu/aʻu (of me). The apostrophe is also used in the Bible to mark a dropped 'a' as in i hanaʻi = i hana ai.

It wasn't until 1922 that any serious attempt was made to use diacritical marks to indicate pronunciation.[8] The formal addition of the kahakō gave the alphabet a further five vowels: ā, ē, ī, ō and ū. This set of letters (eight consonants and ten vowels) are those generally in use today, although it has been a long and slow process of recognition as far as the kahakō and ʻokina are concerned. As Albert Schutz relates in *The Voices of Eden*: 'If linguists have been slow to recognize that long vowels and the glottal stop are essential features of Hawaiians' sound system, non-linguists have been even slower to accept the symbols as part of the alphabet.'[9]

Among the Niʻihau community the ʻokina and kahakō have never been accepted. The old family and church ledgers were written without them and there is a reluctance to use them today. Teaching of the written word to the children of the Niʻihau community does not include their use on the grounds that their inclusion tends to alienate the students from their elders who are fluent speakers of the dialect. Likewise for teaching purposes, to reinforce the difference, T is being written in preference to K.

The Niihauan dialect today[10]

Today the Niʻihau community is the only Hawaiian society remaining where the native language is spoken as a first language in an unbroken line from ancient times.* The dialect is sufficiently different for Niihauan speakers to comment that when speaking Hawaiian with 'outsiders' they tend to speak 'standard Hawaiian' to make themselves more easily understood.

There is also the matter of vocabulary. Like any isolated community the Niihauans have developed their own vocabulary. This is particularly true of the names of plants and animals. Harold St John, after his 1947 visit to Niʻihau, listed 153 species of plants of which almost a third (49) had unique names on Niʻihau, and a further 25 had a name which applied to a different plant on the other islands. Except for the names of species introduced after European contact, these plant names would undoubtedly be ancient in origin. Overall St John comments, 'The evidence here presented on the Niʻihau vernacular plant names suggests that Niʻihau was also notably distinct in its vocabulary.'[11]

Allied to vocabulary is phraseology, and there are many phrases and sayings that distinguish the dialect — as will be found in any community that is relatively isolated from a broader society.

Because of the possible extinction of the Hawaiian language and consequent disappearance of the common interisland speech that existed through to the end of the monarchy in 1893, the vocabulary for Western-introduced concepts has developed on an island-by-island basis. This is true for Niihauan speakers as new ideas have given rise to new words and phrases, and will continue while the dialect lives.

Dr William H Wilson, Hawaiian linguist at the University of Hawaiʻi, Hilo, has monitored the language:

> While the 't'-pronunciation of Hawaiian in the Niʻihau community appears to have been quite stable from the earliest time of contact, the vocabulary and grammar of the language has clearly gone through some change, especially in recent years, compared to the earliest written and taped records of Hawaiian from Niʻihau.[12]

* The Hawaiian language is undergoing a revitalization throughout Hawaiʻi with schools teaching entirely in Hawaiian now to be found in many areas of the islands. There are some families who learned Hawaiian as a second language, where the families decided to raise their children speaking only Hawaiian at home. Children from some of these families have gone on to raise their own children as first-language speakers of Hawaiian. While grandparents may have spoken Hawaiian, there is a gap in transmission of the language that does not exist for the Niʻihau community.

◄ The first page of the Bible in Hawaiian (*Baibale Hemolele*). Translation began in 1826; the New Testament was published in its entirety in 1835 and the complete Bible in 1838. The work was done jointly by missionaries and Hawaiian scholars of the language.

Hōkūlani Cleeland

Over the generations, grammatical and vocabulary changes have occurred in both Niihauan and in the Hawaiian language generally. Until younger generations of Hawaiians abandoned Hawaiian for Creole English in the early 20th century, these changes occurred in parallel. Since then the changes to the Niʻihau dialect have occurred independently.

Unfortunately for the dialect, what Gavan Daws and Timothy Head wrote over 50 years ago is not so applicable today:

The Niihauans themselves recognize that they are different, not only from the rest of the world but also from other Hawaiians. In their non-English-speaking microcosm, they have kept the speech patterns that were peculiar to their end of the island chain in pre-white days, though the allegorical richness of classical Hawaiian thought and expression has long since withered away. In their church they celebrate God in Hawaiian-language hymns of their own composition; their secular festivals are not the holidays observed by most Americans, but birthdays and other occasions of a simple, basic sort. In numerous other ways their universe is bounded by their coast line.[13]

With a dwindling population on Niʻihau itself and a growing community of Niihauans in Kekaha on Kauaʻi, Niʻihau Hawaiian is no longer the first language of many of the keiki (children) in the Niʻihau community, even though this is still true of the kūpuna (elders) and many in their thirties. Change is in the air, and efforts to ensure the distinctive dialect lives on in the Niihauan keiki began in the 1990s with the founding of two charter schools at Kekaha on Kauaʻi, both devoted to the preservation of the Niihauan language and culture.

The future of any language is ultimately in the hands of the young people speaking it, and thus it is important to take a brief look now, in the 2020s, at the status of the Niʻihau dialect among today's younger generation.

Although the Niʻihau dialect is still the primary means of communication in many Niihauan homes on both Niʻihau and Kauaʻi, particularly where the extended family includes kūpuna, the degree of use varies from family to family. When a Niihauan living on Kauaʻi marries an 'outsider,' who does not speak the language, English often becomes the predominant — or only — means of daily communication within the family unit.

For families who attend a Niʻihau church either on Niʻihau or Kauaʻi, services are conducted entirely in Hawaiian, and there are families who continue to hold daily devotions in the Niʻihau dialect at home. The language is also commonly heard at family parties or special events and holiday gatherings.

Nevertheless, with the large number of Niʻihau families moving away from their home island, schooling opportunities vary significantly for Niʻihau youth.

On Niʻihau, in the Department of Education's school at Puʻuwai, the traditional philosophy has been that because children speak the Niʻihau dialect at home, school needs to be a place to learn English, so all classes are taught in English from Grade One through Twelve. If a student does not understand a particular concept or lesson, however, it may be explained in the Niʻihau dialect. All teachers and other employees at Niʻihau School live on the island and are native speakers of the Niʻihau dialect.

On Kauaʻi, the two Niʻihau Public Charter Schools — both in Kekaha — have different ways of addressing use of the language. At Kula Aupuni Niihau A Kahelelani Aloha (KANAKA school) the philosophy is similar to Niʻihau School's. Since Niʻihau students in the school speak the Niʻihau dialect at home, the role of the school is to have all core subjects taught in English by native speakers of English. This curriculum is supplemented with elective courses, such as music and Biblical literature, taught by native speakers of the Niʻihau dialect.

At the other Niʻihau charter school, Ke Kula Niihau O Kekaha, the mission is to strengthen and perpetuate the Niʻihau dialect. Therefore, all subjects in the early grades are taught in that medium except for a limited amount of time devoted to teaching English each day beginning in elementary school and gradually increasing as students move into higher grades. All of the teachers for preschool through middle school (except the English teacher) are native speakers of the Niʻihau dialect.

For Niʻihau students attending any of the other public schools on the western side of Kauaʻi, all classes are taught in English, and there is no language-specific support for students who speak the Niʻihau dialect. Teachers or aides who are hired to assist students learning English as a second language are mostly Filipino.

All three schools offer educational opportunities designed to foster success in the modern world, but they also provide a valuable setting for perpetuation of the Niʻihau dialect among students from grades 1 through 12, or even from preschool through grade 12 as in one of the charter schools. Although their approaches vary, these schools support use of the dialect in the home and at church, and they also serve as a key resource for students from families in which the dialect is not the primary language of the home. So as established elements of the community, each school plays a significant role in helping to ensure that the Niʻihau dialect will continue to live and thrive in the next generation.

A further note on the Niʻihau *t*

The following brief, simplified description of how *t* is used in the Niʻihau dialect was prepared by Hōkūlani Cleeland, a longtime teacher at Ke Kula Niihau O Kekaha Learning Center on Kauaʻi, and its accuracy has been verified by fluent native speakers of the Niʻihau dialect teaching at the same school.

The *t* used in Niʻihau speech is an unaspirated* sound that is commonly used in a variety of locations to replace *k*. However, its use may vary between different individuals or family groups, and even in the speech of a single individual, due to context issues.

* Unaspirated consonants are not pronounced with the sound of a breath. To tell the difference between aspirated and unaspirated sounds, put a hand or a lit candle in front of your mouth, and say 'spin' and then 'pin'. You should feel a puff of air or see a flicker of the candle flame with an aspirated sound (spin) that you do not get with an unaspirated sound (pin).

The *t* in some words is immutable, such as the *t* in the second syllable of all plural pronouns except lākou (they), and some words, like lākou or kino (body), never take a *t*. There are no invariable patterns, although a number of words with two *k*s retain use of the *k* for the first one and then use *t* to replace the second one such as in kātou (we) and kōtua (help). For some words, both variations may be heard as the more common kātau (write) is sometimes pronounced tākau.

When the definite article ke (the) comes before a word beginning with a *k*, it frequently changes to *ta* or possibly *ka*, and the phrase may go either way as in ta kai or ka tai (the sea). Although less common, some speakers may say te tai or even ta tai. Finally, some words with two *k*s use *t* for both such as tāto'o (support) or mōatāta (clear), and for the word tūtātūtā (discuss), all of the *k*s change to *t*, although this is admittedly a duplication of the more common tūtā, which has only two *k*s.

Even though use of the *t* is not entirely predictable in Ni'ihau speech, incorrect use or pronunciation quickly identifies someone as a non-native speaker.

For a more detailed description of the use of *t* and other variations in the Ni'ihau dialect, see the 2010 doctoral dissertation written in Hawaiian by Annette Kuuipolani Kanahele Wong, 'Pukaiki Kula Maniania: No Niihau, Na ka Niihau.' This dissertation has now been adapted by its author and published in Hawaiian by University of Hawai'i Press in 2019 as *Mai Pukaiki Kula Maniania a Puuwai Aloha o ka Ohana*.

For a basic Hawaiian language textbook that also identifies Ni'ihau perspectives in the language — particularly in regard to vocabulary — see the revised edition of *'Ōlelo 'Ōiwi: Hawaiian Language Fundamentals* by Hōkūlani Cleeland, Kamehameha Publishing, 2022.

APPENDIX C

THE BATTLE OF NIʻIHAU
by David Larsen

This account was written by David Larsen while on Niʻihau as a guest of Aylmer Robinson. It was included in a letter written to his wife, Katherine, on 18 June 1942, a little over six months after the events described took place. As he says in his introduction to the account, the story was told to him 'by eye witnesses and participants, chiefly by Willie Kaohelaulii, a Niihau boy with whom I rode and also by his brother, Kekuhina Kaohelaulii … and by Benehakaka Kanahele who was the man who finally killed the aviator.'

David Larsen and Aylmer Robinson were contemporaries and old friends. They had arrived on Niʻihau some days earlier than the letter was written. Their objective was to work together on some lease difficulties Gay & Robinson were having concerning the use of ʻOlokele Ditch water by the Hawaiian Sugar Company. As it turned out the lease work had to await their return to Makaweli, partly due to life on the island being restricted to daylight hours as it was still wartime and there were no black-out curtains. During the day Aylmer was busy with ranching affairs. As a result, David was left much to his own devices while on Niʻihau.

Larsen graduated from the University of Massachusetts in 1908 before taking up a role as plant pathologist at Hawaii Sugar Planters Association. In 1918 he became manager of the Kilauea Sugar Plantation on Kauaʻi, a job he held till 1930 when he was appointed vice-president of C Brewer & Co. In 1932 he became Brewer's vice-president with special responsibility for the operations of their plantations and ranches, and it would have been with this background and experience in mind that Aylmer must have asked for some help, and offered David some time on Niʻihau as his guest. His account has a freshness about it which many other accounts lack.

▲ Lametsius David Larsen (1886–1944) in his student days at the University of Massachusetts, Amherst. He went on to a career in the sugar industry in the islands, and became a firm friend of Aylmer Robinson.

Charles Hearn, Boston; University of Massachusetts, Amherst, Department of Special Collections and University Archives, WEB Du Bois Library

---

On Sunday, December 7th [1941], while the villagers were arriving at church, two planes were seen passing overhead. One of them was noted to be sputtering and smoking badly. They circled once around the village and then passed out to sea towards Kaula. The Hawaiians, who by nature are astonishingly observant, had noted the rising sun emblem on the planes and speculated as to the meaning of this, some even suggesting the possibility of their having come from an attack on Pearl Harbor and Honolulu.

About two o'clock in the afternoon one of the planes returned and kept hovering back and forth over the village and over the adjoining pastures — frequently coming low down as if trying to locate a place to land. This continued for a considerable time causing speculation and concern among the inhabitants. Finally it came to the ground on a slope just a few hundred feet below the village, coasted up the hill, crashed into some boulders which had been hidden under tall grass and weeds, went some distance beyond these boulders through a wire fence and came to a stop about seventy-five feet from a house occupied by one of the cowboys, Hawila Kaleohano. Hawila, who had been watching the contortions of the plane, ran out immediately, pulled open the door and grabbed the pilot who was in the act of drawing a revolver. Hawila grabbed the revolver arm with one hand and pulled the pilot out of the plane with the other, breaking the harness by which he was fastened into the plane. When the pilot was out and away from the plane he began feeling in his shirt for some papers which apparently were still intact. Seeing this Hawila tore open the shirt and took the papers away — the pilot protesting and trying to resist this action. When Hawila and the others who had gathered around tried to question the pilot in English he only shook his head, indicating that he did not understand, although it turned out later that he understood and talked English fluently. So they sent to Kie Kie for Harada, one of two Japanese on the island, to act as interpreter. Harada was a Kauai-born American citizen of Japanese ancestry, about 30 years of age. He lived with his wife, also an Island-born Japanese, in a cottage near the Robinson home where he acted as caretaker during the absence of the Robinsons. Harada was also an assistant bee man. The head bee man was another Japanese by the name of Sintani [more generally spelled Shintani] who had lived on Niihau for many years, had married a Niihau woman and had grown up half-Japanese half-Hawaiian children. Harada on the other hand, was more of a newcomer, having been on the island only a year. He had come from Waimea, Kauai, and had been engaged, with his wife, as housekeepers for Reni [John Rennie], an old Scotsman who for many years had been in charge of Niihau during the absence of the Robinsons and who had died a few months previously. While waiting for Harada to arrive the villagers noted several bullet holes in the plane and speculated some more about the possibilities of the plane having been in a raid on Pearl Harbor. When Harada arrived they questioned the pilot about this and about the reason for his trip — and the bullet holes. The pilot claimed to have come from Honolulu but denied everything about a raid. Some days later, however, he told them about the raid on Pearl Harbor and said all the planes had been shot down except the two. When they came over Niihau Sunday morning (December 7th) they had been returning to their carrier, which was supposed to be located somewhere north of Kauai. While hunting for the carrier the other plane which had been smoking, caught fire and crashed into the ocean. After seeing his friend go down and failing to locate the carrier, he decided to return and try a landing on Niihau. He later got to talking to them through the interpreter about the place and the owners and expressed a desire to settle there and work after the war was over.

There being no radios on the island, the Islanders had not yet heard about the Pearl Harbor attack but had decided nevertheless to hold the pilot prisoner until Aylmer's arrival, which was to have been on the following day, Monday the 8th. On Monday morning they took the prisoner to Kii landing, some fifteen miles to the North, where the sampan was to land with Aylmer and their weekly supplies. As no sampan arrived on Monday, they took the prisoner back to the village where they kept him under guard. On Tuesday they again went to Kii with their prisoner and spent the night there. When no sampan arrived on Wednesday and Thursday they feared something must be wrong and decided to signal Kauai. So on Friday a group of the men went to a high point on the mountains facing Kauai and built a signal fire, which by prearrangement, would indicate trouble on the island.

On Thursday afternoon, Harada, who had been one of the guards, as well as interpreter, suggested they move the prisoner down to his place at Kie Kie since keeping him in the village only kept the place in a turmoil. This sounded like a good idea, so the prisoner was moved to Harada's place adjoining the Robinson home at Kie Kie — still under guard by Harada and some of the Hawaiians.

On Friday afternoon while being guarded by one of the overseers (Hanakiki by name), the prisoner expressed a desire to go over to the honey house across the yard where Harada was working, saying he wanted to talk with Harada. By this time he had made it known that he could read and write English but could not speak it. So he had been communicating with them in writing whenever Harada was absent. After talking with Harada in Japanese for awhile, the three of them went to the adjoining warehouse where bee equipment was stored.

As soon as they got into this house the aviator grabbed a shotgun which had been hidden behind the door and Harada grabbed a revolver. They threatened to shoot Hanakiki if he made any noise and took him to the rear of the warehouse where they warned him to remain. The two of them then went out through the front door which they closed and locked from the outside. Hanakiki, on seeing what had happened, climbed to the loft where there was a window about twenty feet from the ground and jumped out. By this time Harada and the aviator had disappeared so Hanakiki ran to one of the other sheds in the yard where some others were gathered and informed them what had happened. The shot gun with some shells and the revolver with no ammunition had been taken from the Robinsons' house for which Harada, as caretaker, had the keys.

Harada and the aviator in the meantime had started down from the yard through some underbrush to a road that led to the village. Here they spotted a Hawaiian woman with seven children riding in a sulky drawn by one horse — one girl, a cousin, about seventeen years of age was riding the horse. Harada called to them but as they did not stop the two Japanese ran and soon caught up with them.

The family was made to get out of the sulky and line up on the ground in a row, one in back of the other. Harada then put the shot gun against the back of the last one and threatened to kill them all with one bullet if they moved or made any noise. While they

▲ Nishikaichi's Zero soon after it crash-landed on the island. A Niihauan is inspecting the engine, and the cockpit canopy has been shut after the pilot was dragged out. The external drop tank was torn off by the force of the crash.
Photographer unknown

were standing thus with their backs toward the two Japanese, the Japs hopped into the buggy and threatening the girl on horseback with the gun, made her drive as fast as possible toward the village.

Upon reaching the village they let the girl and the buggy go and started for Hawila's house (Hawila was the man who had taken the papers and the revolver from the aviator). Hawila saw them coming and disappeared behind some outhouses in back of his home. He had sensed that something was wrong and was on the lookout because a short while before Sintani, the other Japanese, had been to see him and had offered him on behalf of the aviator a roll of bills containing about $200 if he would give up the papers and let them be burned. This he refused to do and said he would surrender them only to Mr. Robinson. Harada and the aviator called for Hawila and, getting no response, searched his house thoroughly. Then they went to Sintani's house, but he ran away from them. After giving him chase for awhile they started through the other houses calling for Hawila and threatening to shoot everybody unless Hawila gave up the papers.

The villagers hearing the commotion and the threats and seeing the two men with the guns, took to the cactus thickets behind the village. The two Japs finally found an old lady, Mrs Huluoulani, who had refused to run out with the others because she was too old. She sat reading her Bible when the Japanese came in and asked her if she knew where Hawila had gone. She said she knew but would not tell and when they threatened to kill her she said that only God had power over life and death and anyone else who interfered with it would be punished — then turned around and continued reading her Bible. The two Japs stood and talked for a spell and then walked off and left her.

Hawila in the meantime had headed for the mountains to tell Kekuhina and the others who had gone to make the signal fire, what had happened.

Most of the other villagers in the meantime had gathered in the cactus grove behind the village to discuss what to do. It was decided to go back to the hills, leave the women and children in some caves and then return under cover of darkness and try to capture the two Japanese. It was just about dusk when this took place and, just before starting, one of the men said he thought it would be better to ask for Divine guidance before starting. So they all returned to the church where they prayed for guidance, after which they all felt much better and started for the mountains. The cactus thicket, incidentally, leads from behind the village clear to the mountains. It is covered with large cactus and koa [trees], but is full of cow trails and roads as it is used for pasturing cattle, it being considered one of the best fattening paddocks.

When Hawila found Kekuhina and the others on the mountain top signalling Kauai, they held a brief consultation and decided to go at once to Kii landing and take the whale boat for Kauai to notify Aylmer. The six of them — Hawila, Kekuhina with three of his brothers and one other, started off in the whale boat shortly before midnight and reached Waimea, Kauai about three the next afternoon, which was Saturday.

▼ A Ni'ihau whaleboat at Ki'i, similar to the one the Niihauans rowed to Waimea for help after the Zero crash. The journey took them 17 hours.
Kaua'i Museum

They said it was rough and they were pretty tired after sixteen hours of rowing, but they got in touch with Aylmer at once and told him their story. He immediately got in touch with the military authorities who dispatched the lighthouse tender, *Kukui*, with some soldiers and Aylmer and the six Hawaiian boys.

In the meantime things had been happening fast on Niihau. Harada and the pilot, failing to find Hawila, returned to the plane and took off the two machine guns together with all the ammunition and carried them up to the village where they threatened to shoot the place up and kill everybody unless they found Hawila. They captured one of the men (Kaahakila by name) who had been watching their operations from ambush. They tied his hands securely behind his back and sent him to Kie Kie with a message for Mrs. Harada. He started off obediently on his mission but as soon as he was out of sight, turned back through the underbrush — found Bene Kanahele, told him about the machine guns and ammunition and under cover of darkness stole up while the Japs were ransacking a home and stole all the ammunition from the machine guns.

▲ The Zero a few days after Nishikaichi and Harada burnt it to reduce its usefulness to the United States.
Wikipedia Commons

The two Japs were now very angry and ransacked all the houses thoroughly. In Hawila's house they found the pistol that had been taken from the aviator and also the map, but could not find the papers — which seemed to be the aim of their search. These papers Hawila had hidden in a special place where he knew the Hawaiians would look if he should disappear. It seems that such hiding places are customary in Hawaiian communities and are never disclosed to other races even when they are inter-married with them.

The activities of the two Japs were being watched by several of the men and all their movements were followed until about three o'clock in the morning when they disappeared somehow. They kept quiet and out of sight until just about daylight. At daylight they went to Hawila's home to ransack it once more and when they were through they set fire to the house and burned it to the ground. Then they set fire to the airplane, after sprinkling gasoline over it.

The story of the slaying of the Japanese aviator I had from Benehakaka Kanahele, the man who did the deed. He looks like an old man, but is strong as an ox — works at all sorts of hard labor on the ranch and is fifty-one years old.

After going with Kaahakila to steal the machine gun ammunition and hiding it, Bene, as he is called, took his wife and family to the beach to spend the night in comparative safety.

About seven o'clock in the morning (Saturday) Bene and his wife were returning from the beach to see what was happening in the village — when they were surprised and captured by the two Japanese. Bene told Harada that they should take the revolver away from the aviator before he would kill somebody. Harada said he could not do this or he might be killed himself. So Bene grabbed the aviator himself and tried to take the revolver away from him. The aviator got his arm with the revolver in it loose and Bene's wife grabbed at his arm and tried to take the revolver away. Harada then piled in and pulled Bene's wife away, threatening to kill her. Bene told Harada to leave his wife alone; that if he hurt her he would kill him (Harada) as soon as he was through with the aviator. When Harada pulled Bene's wife away the aviator got his arm loose and fired three close-up shots at Bene, one hitting him in the stomach, one in the groin and one in the upper part of the leg. When Bene saw the blood he got angry and thought he might die so he decided to kill the aviator first to prevent his killing the other people. So he picked up the aviator by his leg and neck (the way he was accustomed to picking up sheep) and dashed his head against a nearby stone wall.

The story that appeared in the papers that Bene's wife hit the aviator with a big stone, they say, is not true as she was struggling with Harada at the time.

After Bene was shot Harada loaded his shot gun, which, according to Bene's wife, had not been loaded up to that time. After getting it loaded he pointed it at his own stomach and Bene's wife now struggled with him to prevent him shooting himself. He finally managed to empty both barrels into his stomach. Since he was not dead Bene and his wife tried to patch him up a bit and then went to get assistance from the villagers. The aviator apparently died immediately with a badly crushed skull — Harada died a few hours later.

Thus ended the Battle of Ni'ihau — an epic event crowded with heroic deeds, quick thinking and sound judgement. In this battle a naive group of Hawaiians, without modern weapons of any kind, out-maneuvered and destroyed a modern and fully equipped enemy who had gotten the upper hand by treachery.

By the time Aylmer and the soldiers arrived on Sunday morning, the battle was over.

Benehakaka (Bene) Kanahele was subsequently awarded the Medal for Merit, the highest United States civilian decoration at the time, for the courageous part he played in the 'Niihau Incident.'[1]

▲ Benehakaka Kanahele with the citation for his Medal for Merit, presented to him by Lieutenant General Robert Richardson, Commander of the Armed Forces of the Central Pacific on 13 August 1945.

Hawai'i State Archives

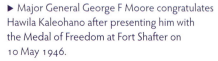

▶ Major General George F Moore congratulates Hawila Kaleohano after presenting him with the Medal of Freedom at Fort Shafter on 10 May 1946.

Hawai'i Official War Records, Hamilton Library, University of Hawai'i, Mānoa

APPENDIX D
NIʻIHAU POPULATION NUMBERS

Samuel Whitney, missionary at Waimea, says that there were 1079 people on Niʻihau in 1831, and 993 in 1835.[1]

The population of Niʻihau, from the United States census figures, is:[2]

Year	Pop.	Year	Pop.	Year	Pop.
1850	714	1900	172	1970	237
1853	790	1910	208	1980	226
1860	647	1920	191	1990	230
1866	325	1930	136	2000	160
1872	233	1940	182	2010	170
1878	177	1950	222	2020	84
1896	164	1960	254		

Note that the population halved between 1860 and 1866. The island was sold quite abruptly by the king to the Sinclair family at the beginning of 1864. To attempt to establish whether the drop in population occurred before or after the sale, I examined the Annual Tax Assessment ledgers for the years 1855 to 1872. The ledgers record the adult males on Niʻihau and are given below. From 1864, when the island was purchased by the Sinclairs, the haole taxpayers have been omitted so only the indigenous taxpayers are shown:

Year	Males	Year	Males	Year	Males
1855	190	1862	186	1868	89
1856	192	1863	165	1869	79
1857	181	1864	176	1870	77
1858	205	1865	137	1871	74
1860	190	1866	111	1872	73
1861	214	1867	100		

Although records before 1858 are incomplete it appears that individuals were leasing portions of the island from 1853, and in 1858 eight individuals banded together and leased the whole island for five years at an annual rent of $600. The lease was due for renewal at about the time the island was sold. The tax assessment shows the lease in 1860 as a $3000 sum.

Further corroboration of the population numbers in 1864 comes in the Hawaiian newspaper *O Kuakoa* on 11 June 1864.[3] In an article by PR Holiohana, written from Kaununui on Niʻihau on 19 May 1864, the population is broken down into categories with the total given as 626 (cf. 1860 census 647). It appears, however, that there has been some double counting in respect of the church members and if these are excluded the population is 559, a drop of 14% since the 1860 census figure of 647, but nothing like the drop of 42% from 559 in 1864 to 325 in 1866. The numbers of taxpayers over time generally corroborates these percentage drops.

Martha Noyes contends that the population decline began earlier than the Sinclair purchase as a result of lease increases, but this is only partially supported by the facts.[4] In their letter of 22 September 1863 the Niihauans told the Minister of Interior that a marked population decline took place over the previous two or three years, but again this is only partly correct.

By using the tax assessments as a proxy for the total island population, the numbers show a halving of the population between 1864 (the year of the Sinclair purchase) and 1869. It would appear that the population decline was largely due to the purchase of the island by the Sinclair family.

When the king visited the island shortly after the Sinclair's purchase he exhorted his subjects to consolidate their living arrangements. The taxpayer records show that there were eleven settlements scattered over the island at the time. In the years following there were many more leaving the island than moving house to consolidate around Puʻuwai. By 1872 there were only 73 indigenous taxpayers at five locations on the island, with only 15 at Puʻuwai and 20 still at Kamalino. This may have been due to the rate of housebuilding at Puʻuwai by the Sinclairs, who were providing rent-free housing.

Note that the population dropped by 50% between 2010 and 2020, presumably due to the lack of employment opportunities. This reduction is corroborated by the numbers of Niihauan children attending the schools on Niʻihau and Kekaha.

APPENDIX E

BOTANICAL EXPLORATION ON NIʻIHAU

While most of the early European exploratory expeditions had one or more naturalists aboard (See Chapter Four), little systematic botanical work was done on Niʻihau; the priority was to procure food. David Nelson, the naturalist on the *Discovery* with Cook in 1778 did not go ashore on Niʻihau and his botanical collecting was confined to the island of Hawaiʻi.

David Samwell, surgeon on the *Resolution* at the same time, wrote the first description of the plants under cultivation then on Niʻihau:

> Neehaw for the most part consists of low land entirely bare of Trees, the Soil is rich & capable of producing all kinds of fruit was it properly cultivated, but as the Island is thin of Inhabitants, the small Patches which are here & there planted with yams, Taroo and sweet potatoes afford a sufficient supply for them while large plains of fine Land is suffered to lie waste … Saw a few small Plantations of Sugar Canes & Plantains and two or three Palm Trees …[1]

In his paper on the plants found on Niʻihau on Cook's voyage, Harold St John records that in addition to the above, kava (*Piper methysticum*), paper mulberry (*Broussonetia papyrifera*), gourds (*Lagenaria siceraria*) and sida (*Sida fallax*) were also seen growing by members of Cook's expedition.[2]

Twelve years later, on his way to Alaska in 1792 George Vancouver anchored where Cook had off the southwest point of Niʻihau (Kawaihoa Point), in sight of Kaʻula. His botanist on the *Discovery* was Archibald Menzies, the ship's surgeon who left a fascinating account of his time ashore on Niʻihau:[3]

> In the forenoon of the 15th, I went on shore to examine the adjacent extremity of the island … The coast opposite to the ship being very rocky, and at this time quite inaccessible by a high sea breaking incessantly against it, we[4] were carried by some of the natives in a canoe to a small sandy cove near the bluff, and there artfully landed by placing the canoe upon the top of the highest swell, which carried us safe over some sunken piled rocks, by an accelerated motion, to the beach. Here we found a few small huts, seemingly the temporary residence of a party of fishermen, with some little stages to dry their fish on, and about one hundred of the natives who, impelled by a curiosity of being near the vessel, had taken shelter in the caverns of the rocks round the cove …
>
> After examining this romantic bluff, which we found composed of dark porous rocks, intermixed with hardened volcanic sand and gravel, we crossed a low narrow

▲ *Sida fallax* (yellow ʻilima) growing in sand on the north end of Niʻihau. It was identified during Cook's visit in 1788.
Steven Gentry

335

neck of land and pursued our journey along the eastern shore for nearly two leagues [six miles] without seeing anything deserving of notice excepting the desolate and barren appearance of the country we traveled through, covered with loose stones of a black and porous texture and a few stinted vegetables in a shrivelled state — no trees or bushes — no houses or any trace of cultivation were to be seen in the whole tract. The shore was bound by rocky indented caverns, rugged and bleak in the extreme. We therefore struck across the island to within a short distance of the western shore, and its whole width did not appear to us to be above 6 or 7 miles at any part. We then directed our way back to the vessels through the interior parts of the island, making in all a circuit of four or five leagues [12 to 15 miles]. On the western shore we saw a few villages and some appearance of cultivation, but in the interior part of the country the same effete[5] appearance prevailed. We passed indeed some small fields of sweet potatoes, which the natives were obliged to cover over with a layer of grass to preserve the little moisture of the soil from being exhaled by the sun's powerful heat. In the middle of the island we saw a large patch of low land encrusted over with salt, which the natives told us was overflowed with water in the rainy season, and shows that the soil must be strongly impregnated with that mineral. Though we here and there met with little natural tanks in the rocks which were carefully shaded over with stones to preserve the water that fell in them in rainy weather, yet these were at this time either drained up or their contents not drinkable, so that for quenching our thirst, we were chiefly indebted to some water melons we obtained from the natives.[6]

▶ Archibald Menzies, in a sketch probably drawn from the portrait shown in Chapter Three.
Hawaii Nei 128 Years Ago

Clearly Archibald Menzies was not impressed with the island. No mention is made of any botanizing on this lengthy walk, which took in the southern third of the island. Maybe he felt the plant life too meagre to bother collecting, but this seems unlikely. His journal indicates he collected on both Maui and Hawai'i. If he did collect on Ni'ihau, and as a botanist he would have felt compelled to, according to St John his collection records have been lost due to a dispute between Vancouver and Menzies. All his specimens are merely labelled 'Sandwich Islands.'[7]

This seemed to have been the pattern among the early botanists. Little account was taken of the specific island on which the specimen was collected, the thinking possibly being that all the islands in the archipelago would harbor identical species. This is far from the case, but does make it difficult to identify those collected on Ni'ihau.

Vancouver called at Ni'ihau two years later in March of 1794, again in search of yams, this time anchoring in Yam Bay (Nonopapa). There were none to be had and Menzies did not go ashore.

Many scientific expeditions to Hawai'i came and went around this time. HMS *Providence*, under Captain Broughton, in the course of surveying the Asian coast, visited Ni'ihau twice, in February and July 1796. Broughton had a naturalist, Alexander Bishop, aboard, but it seems unlikely that he went ashore on Ni'ihau; on the first visit because of the weather, and on the second on account of the tragedy described in Chapter Four. In any event no record of Bishop's time in Hawai'i survives. Botanists were part of an expedition under Russian auspices, captained by Otto Kotzebue, and one under the sponsorship of the French king captained by Louis de Freycinet, but neither investigated Ni'ihau.

It was to be 34 years before another naturalist stepped ashore. Frederick Beechey and his crew on board HMS *Blossom* left Honolulu for Ni'ihau on 31 May 1826. Beechey's task was to explore the Bering Strait, but he needed a supply of yams for the purpose. He had on the voyage as naturalist George Tradescant Lay, but unfortunately Lay was incapacitated with dysentery while the vessel was in Honolulu and was left behind to recover in the care of a British settler. He later rejoined the voyage, but in the interval, Alexander Collie, Beechey's surgeon on the *Blossom,* had shown interest and an aptitude for plant collecting, so Beechey appointed him interim botanist in Lay's stead.

HMS *Blossom* anchored in Yam Bay on 1 June 1826 eager to trade for yams. Beechey commented that like Vancouver, he was disappointed in the supplies, 'not from their scarcity, but in consequence of the indolence of the natives.'[8] By this time the islanders preferred muskets and powder to nails and trinkets, but Beechey as a Royal Navy captain refused to trade these, which may have accounted for their apparent indolence. The vessel's stay there was thus brief, but must have afforded Collie the only chance he had to gather plants from Ni'ihau for his collection, as this was Captain Beechey's only visit to the island.

The botanical account subsequently produced (in 1841) named both Lay and Collie as collectors.[9] Of the 207 Hawaiian species described, only 16 are identified as coming from Ni'ihau, ten are labelled O'ahu, and the remainder only Sandwich Islands.

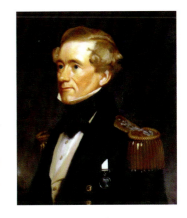

◥ Captain Frederick Beechey (1796–1856) entered service in the Royal Navy at the age of ten as a ship's boy, and retired as a rear admiral. He is best known as a geographer. In 1825 he was appointed to command HMS *Blossom* with the task of exploring the Bering Strait. In this context the *Blossom* visited Ni'ihau and some plants were collected, as was done in all the places the ship visited. He ultimately became president of the Royal Geographic Society.
National Portrait Gallery

◂ The title page of the botanical findings from Beechey's expedition in HMS *Blossom*, with Sir Joseph Hooker as the lead author. It was not published until 1841, many years after the expedition.
Wikimedia Commons

Although the record describes only Lay and Collie's collection, reference is made in the account to Archibald Menzies' work and to that of both Kotzebue's botanist on the *Rurik*, Adelbert von Chamisso, and de Freycinet's botanist on the *l'Uranie*, Charles Gaudichaud-Beaupré, for plant species comparison purposes.

The next significant botanical visitor to Niʻihau was Frenchman and gentleman explorer, Jules Rémy, who spent time on all the islands between 1851 and 1855 collecting botanical, historical and ethnographic material. For most of his stay he teamed up with Englishman Julius Brenchley, ten years his senior. They climbed Mauna Loa together and Rémy subsequently published his journal of the trek.[10]

▶ Jules Rémy (1826–93) visited Niʻihau in the 1850s and collected plant specimens in the course of his world travels as an amateur naturalist. These were deposited in Paris, but Rémy never wrote about them. A century later, in the 1960s, they were examined and evaluated by Harold St John.
Wikimedia Commons

Rémy was assisted on Kauaʻi by Valdemar Knudsen, who had only recently arrived there (see Chapter Eight). He befriended the young Rémy and probably facilitated his visit to Niʻihau. As Knudsen had an abiding interest in the natural world they collected botanical specimens together on Kauaʻi, and most likely also on Niʻihau.

While Rémy wrote about Hawaiian history and social customs, he published nothing on his large plant collection, but it was not lost to the world. Harold St John said that his plant specimens …

> were deposited in the Museum d'Histoire de Naturelle, Paris, where they were determined, arranged taxonomically, and then numbered. A list of his 726 plants was compiled … For each the only locality data given was the name of the island. The first set was kept in Paris, and one set of duplicates was sent to Asa Gray at Harvard University.[11]

▲ William Brigham (1841–1926) in old age, a far cry from the enthusiastic 23-year-old who competed with Valdemar Knudsen for Annie Sinclair's hand. After his visit to the Hawaiian islands with Horace Mann he attended law school in Boston and practiced law on the East Coast. He later made a disastrous investment in a Guatemalan plantation and lost all his assets. He became the founding director of the Bernice P Bishop Museum in 1892, a position he held for 20 years.

◀ William Hillebrand (1821–86), the German doctor and botanist who spent 1850 to 1871 in Hawaiʻi. As well as being physician to the royal family, he collected plants wherever he traveled. His home was in what is now Foster Gardens, and several of the trees there go back to his day. After his return to Germany he continued working on the botany of the Hawaiian islands and his major work, the first flora of the islands, was published two years after his death.
Wikimedia Commons

St John was able to write this having had the good fortune, in the 1960s, to examine the Rémy collection in Paris, but he found the labelling regarding Kauaʻi/Niʻihau was not quite as he described it above. Only five of the 726 species were recorded as having been collected on Niʻihau, and a further 35 were labelled 'Kauai ou [or] Nihau.' Of these latter 35 St John found four that are endemic to Niʻihau and three that occur on both islands. Fifteen are unknown on Niʻihau and are unlikely to have ever been present, but are well known on Kauaʻi. He makes no comment on the remaining 13 specimens.

The next botanical visitors to Niʻihau were William Brigham and Horace Mann in May 1864, shortly after the Sinclairs bought the island from King Kamehameha V. Brigham had recently graduated from Harvard and was studying botany when he was approached by Horace Mann to accompany him on an expedition to Hawaiʻi to collect plants for Mann's Harvard thesis.[12]

On Kauaʻi they were assisted by the well-established rancher, Valdemar Knudsen, who was now seeking a bride and had eyes for no one but Ann Sinclair on Niʻihau. It was inevitable therefore that Valdemar should accompany the two botanists to the island. Ann ('Annie') also had a great interest in the world of nature and all four may well have collected together. Unbeknown to Valdemar, William Brigham was also smitten with Annie, and on their return to Kauaʻi told Valdemar so and asked him to arrange a further visit to Niʻihau. Needless to say Valdemar tactfully refused — and subsequently married Annie himself (see Chapter Eight).

William (Wilhelm) Hillebrand, the German trained medical practitioner and founder of the Hawaiʻi Medical Association also had a keen interest in botany and in his spare moments during his 20 years on the islands, became an avid plant collector. In 1888 he published the first flora of the islands, his *Flora of the Hawaiian Islands: A Description of their Phanerogams and Cryptogams*. Sad to say he did this without ever visiting Niʻihau, and for Niʻihau he had to rely completely on those who had gone before him.

Three years before the publication of Hillebrand's *Flora*, in 1885, Isabella Sinclair, Ann Sinclair's sister-in-law, published in London her magnificent *Indigenous Flowers of the Hawaiian Islands*, a series of 44 exquisite color plates illustrating 45 species, with accompanying text for each. These were painted over a considerable period on both Niʻihau and Kauaʻi. Harold St John, as a botanist, reviewed the book in 1954 saying in part:

▲ A color plate from Isabella McHutcheson Sinclair's *Indigenous Flowers of the Hawaiian Islands*. This is the wiliwili (*Erythrina monosperma*). In Isabella's words: 'The Wiliwili is found in the driest districts, not only sustaining life, but growing luxuriantly where few other trees could exist. … The wood, when dry, is almost as light as cork, and is much used by the natives as out-riggers for their canoes. This is one of the few Hawaiian trees which shed their leaves in autumn. It blooms in early spring, and the tree may often be found covered in flowers while the leaf-buds are only forming.'

> Eliminating the one introduced ornamental and the seven species of aboriginal introduction and cultivation, there remain 37 indigenous Hawaiian plants described and illustrated in color in Mrs. Sinclair's book. Of these 37 there are 23 [20] species unknown to Niihau but certainly natives of Kauai. The remaining 15 [17] species occur as natives in both Kauai and Niihau. These 15 [17] are all abundant in the lowlands and occur near the old Sinclair homestead at Kiekie on Niihau. Though they could have been obtained on Kauai, it seems probable that all or most of these 15 [17] were gathered, painted, and studied by Mrs. Sinclair during her long residence [eight years] at the remote family home on Niihau.[13]

Note: While not all of the plants included in Isabella's book were indigenous, Harold did not have the numbers quite right in the quotation above. The numbers shown in square brackets are the author's inclusion taken from the individual species included in his paper, as categorized in the body of his review.

Isabella's book has been the subject of lavish praise over the years. It was the first to be published with color plates of Hawaiian flowering plants, and is still regarded as the 'gold standard' in this regard.

While she was not a professional botanist, Isabella was a skilled observer,

◄ The milo (*Thespesia populnea*). Another of Isabella Sinclair's splendid plates: 'The Milo … cannot be called a forest tree, as it is seldom found far from the abodes of men, or places which have been inhabited in former times … It attains a height of from thirty to forty feet, and is a handsome shade-tree. The leaves are beautifully glossy and the wind moves them in a most graceful way, not unlike the quivering of the aspen. The milo blooms freely and flowers may be found almost all the year round.'

and to further ensure the correctness of her text, took the audacious step of sending her specimens and notes to Sir Joseph Hooker, director of Kew Gardens and the pre-eminent Pacific botanist of the day. Hooker supplied her with the botanical names of the plants and encouraged her to have the work published.

Isabella's early life and marriage to her first cousin, Francis Sinclair, are described in Chapter Eight. Her time in New Zealand allowed her to contrast the New Zealand flora with that of Kaua'i and Ni'ihau. She well recognized the fragile nature of Hawaiian ecosystems, and warned:

> The Hawaiian flora seems … to grow in an easy careless way, which, though pleasingly artistic, and well adapted to what may be termed the natural state of the islands, will not long survive the invasion of foreign plants, and changed conditions. Forest fires, animals, and agriculture, have so changed the islands, within the last fifty or sixty years, that one can now travel for miles, in some districts, without finding a single indigenous plant; the ground being wholly taken possession of by weeds, shrubs, and grasses, imported from various countries.[14]

How right she was, even when writing in the 1880s.

When Frank Sinclair passed the management of the family estates to his nephews Aubrey Robinson and Francis Gay in 1883, Isabella and Frank moved to London to pursue their respective literary careers (see Chapter Eight). Isabella died in California in 1900.

The next visit to Ni'ihau of botanical interest took place in 1912 when John Stokes, curator of Polynesian ethnology at the Bishop Museum, spent time there at the invitation of Aubrey Robinson — perhaps due to the influence of William Brigham, the Bishop Museum director, who would have met Aubrey as a boy during his 1864 visit. John Stokes' field notes indicate he was investigating heiau (see Chapter Two), but he did not publish anything of cultural interest from his visit. What he did do was undertake a comprehensive plant collection with the aid of a local guide, Kalua Keale.

His collection was given to Charles Forbes, his brother-in-law and botanist colleague at the Bishop Museum, and must have been undertaken at his request. The outcome was a paper by Forbes, *An Enumeration of Niihau Plants*.[15] Forbes considered the collection of 115 species to be reasonably comprehensive, divided between:

- 25 species endemic to the Hawaiian islands
- 39 species indigenous to the islands
- 10 species of native Hawaiian introduction
- 41 species introduced since the arrival of Europeans

Any species not found that was identified by earlier botanists he felt reasonably certain would be extinct on Ni'ihau. He notes the changes wrought by the impact of grazing and European introductions and delights in the elimination of goats. He makes no mention of any plants endemic to Ni'ihau alone, but notes that *Schiedea amplexicaulis* and *Euphorbia stokesii* 'are probably peculiar to Niihau.' The latter he considered a species new to science and named it after John Stokes.[16]

Botanical exploration on Ni'ihau remained dormant for a further 35 years until Harold St John visited, in 1947 and 1949. His interest in Ni'ihau had been aroused not long after he arrived at the University of Hawai'i in 1929 when examining unidentified plant material at the Bishop Museum. In rummaging he found two bundles of Ni'ihau plants which had been collected by Stokes and which hadn't been included in Forbes' 1913 *Enumeration*. St John subsequently produced a paper on the find — *Additions to the Flora of Niihau*, listing nine species new to the island.[17]

While a prolific publisher, St John's visits did not produce an immediate written record. He published *Botanical Novelties on the island of Niihau*[18] in 1959 when almost at his retirement from the University of Hawai'i, but the world had to wait over 40 years after his sojourns there to see his and Juliet Rice Wichman's *A Chronicle and Flora of Niihau*[19] — published when he was in his ninety-eighth year. In compiling this he could include the work of later collectors such as John Fay in 1976, Charles Christensen in 1977, and others. As far as is known there have been no further collectors of vascular plants on Ni'ihau since the book was published in 1990. It is now over 30 years since then, and an 'on the ground' review is long overdue.

The Bishop Museum has the largest collection of Ni'ihau vascular plant specimens — nearly 500 in all. Harold St John's contribution totals 242 of these, while John Stokes' collection numbers 141. Other collectors who figure in this history are Ann Sinclair, her brother James, her grand-nephew Aylmer Robinson, and George Munro of Lāna'i fame, all of whom have a number of plant specimens included in the herbarium collection.

BIBLIOGRAPHY

Books and booklets (including online)

Alexander, W. D., 1891, *A Brief History of the Hawaiian People*, originally published by American Book Company, reprint by Pranava Books, India

Anderson, R., 1864, *The Hawaiian Islands: Their Progress and Condition under Missionary Labors*, Gould & Lincoln, Boston

Arago, J., 1823, *Narrative of a Voyage Round the World in the 'Uranie' and 'Physicienne,' Corvettes Commanded by Captain Freycinet, during the Years 1817, 1818, 1819 and 1820 etc.*, Treuttel & Wurz, London

Beaglehole, J. C., 1967, *Captain James Cook's Voyage of Discovery in the Resolution and Discovery 1776-1780*, Volume III, University of Cambridge Press

Beckwith, M. (editor), 1951, *The Kumulipo: A Hawaiian Creation Chant*, University of Hawaiʻi Press, Honolulu, reprinted 1972

Beckwith, M. W., 1940, *Hawaiian Mythology*, University of Hawaiʻi Press, Honolulu, reprinted 1970, 1985

Beechey, F. W., 1831 (1968), *Narrative of a Voyage to the Pacific and Beering's Strait*, Da Capo Press, New York reprint

Beekman, A., 1982, *The Niihau Incident*, Heritage Press of the Pacific, Honolulu

Bingham, H., 1848, *A Residence of 21 Years in the Sandwich Islands*, Sherman Converse, New York

Bird, I. L., 1881, *Six Months in the Sandwich Islands* (2007 edition by Mutual Publishing LLC, Honolulu)

——— (edited by Chubbuck, K.), 2002, *Letters to Henrietta*, Northeastern University Press, Boston

Broughton, W. R., 1804, *A Voyage of Discovery to the North Pacific Ocean Performed in His Majesty's Sloop Providence and her Tender in the Years 1795–98*, London

Buck, P. H. (Te Rangi Hiroa), 1938, *Vikings of the Sunrise*, 1958 edition, Whitcombe & Tombs, New Zealand

———1945, *An Introduction to Polynesian Anthropology*, Kraus Reprint Co, New York

———1953, *Explorers of the Pacific: European and American Discoveries in Polynesia*, Bishop Museum Special Publication 43, Honolulu

Buck, P. H. (Te Rangi Hiroa), 1957, *Arts and Craft of Hawaii*, Bishop Museum Press, Honolulu

Buick, T. L., 1928, *The French at Akaroa: An Adventure in Colonisation*, New Zealand Book Depot, Wellington

Burns, P., 1989, *Fatal Success: A History of the New Zealand Company*, Heinemann Reid

Burtner, J. M., 2019, *Robinson Family Governess: Letters from Kauaʻi and Niʻihau 1911–1913*, Publication Consultants, Anchorage, Alaska

Campbell, A., 1822, *A Voyage Round the World from 1806 to 1812*, Duke & Browne, Charleston, South Carolina

Clark, J. R., 1990, *Beaches of Kauaʻi and Niʻihau*, University of Hawaiʻi Press, Honolulu

Colnett, J., 1798, *A Voyage to the South Atlantic, and around Cape Horn into the Pacific Ocean for the Object of Investigating Spermaceti Whale Fisheries and other Objects of Commerce*, London

Cook, E. E., 2003, *100 Years of Healing: The Legacy of a Kauai Missionary Doctor*, Halewai Publishing, Kōloa, Kauai

Cook, J. & King, J., 1784, *Voyage to the Pacific Ocean etc* — John Stockdale etc, London

Corney, P., 1896, *Narrative of Several Trading Voyages from 1813 to 1818 between the Northwest Coast of America, the Hawaiian Islands and China etc*, T. G. Thrum, Honolulu

Croft, L. B., 2017, *Kaumualii and the Last of the God Kings*, Sphynx Publications, Arizona

Damon, E. M., 1931, *Koamalu: The Story of the Pioneers on Kauai, and of what they Built in that Island Garden*, privately printed, Honolulu (2 vols)

David, A. (editor), 2010, *William Robert Broughton's Voyage of Discovery to the North Pacific 1795–1798*, Ashgate, Vermont

Daws, G., 1968, *The Shoal of Time: A History of the Hawaiian Islands*, University of Hawaiʻi Press, Honolulu

———2006, *Honolulu: The First Century: The Story of the Town to 1876*, Mutual Publishing, Honolulu

Dibble, S., 1843, *A History of the Sandwich Islands*, 1909 edition, T. G. Thrum, Honolulu

Dixon, G., 1789, *A Voyage around the World but more particularly to the North-West coast of America performed* in 1785, 1786, 1787 and 1788 in the King George and Queen Charlotte: Captains Portlock and Dixon, Geo. Goulding, London

Donohugh, D., 2001, *The Story of Koloa, A Kaua'i Plantation Town*, Mutual Publishing, Honolulu

Ellis, W., 1782, *An Authentic Narrative of a Voyage performed by Captain Cook and Captain Clerke in His Majesty's ships Resolution and Discovery in Search of a North-West Passage*, Robison, Sewell & Debrett, London

——— 1825, *A Journal of a Tour around Hawaii, the Largest of the Sandwich Islands*, Crocker & Brewster, New York

Forbes, C. N., 1913, 'An Enumeration of Niihau Plants,' *Occasional Papers*, Vol. 5, No. 3–2. Bishop Museum, Honolulu

Fornander, A., 1996, *Fornander's Ancient History of the Hawaiian People to the Times of Kamehameha I*, Vol. 2 with foreword (reprint), Mutual Publishing, Honolulu

——— 1917, *Fornander Collection of Hawaiian Antiquities and Folk-Lore*, Vol. 4, 'The Story of the Formation of these Islands and Origin of this Race,' edited by T. G. Thrum, Bishop Museum Press, Honolulu

——— 1918, *Fornander Collection of Hawaiian Antiquities and Folk-Lore*, Vol. 5, edited by T. G. Thrum, Bishop Museum Press, Honolulu

——— 1920, *Fornander Collection of Hawaiian Antiquities and Folk-Lore*, Vol. 6, edited by T. G. Thrum, Bishop Museum Press, Honolulu

Galois, R., 2004, *A Voyage to the North West Side of America: The Journals of James Colnett 1786-89*, UBC Press, Vancouver

Gast, R. S. & Conrad, A. C., 1973, *Don Francisco de Paula Marin: Biography & Letters*, University of Hawai'i Press, Honolulu

Gay, L. K., 1981, *Tales of the Forbidden Island of Ni'ihau*, TopGallant Publishing, Honolulu

Gibson, J. R., 1992, *Otter Skins, Boston Ships, and China Goods: The Maritime Fur Trade of the Northwest Coast*, McGill-Queens University Press, Montreal

Hay, Hannah L.G., 1901, *Annandale Past and Present 1839–1900*, Whitcombe & Tombs, Christchurch

Hay, J., 1915, *Reminiscences of Earliest Canterbury (principally Banks Peninsula) and its Settlers*, Christchurch Press, Christchurch

Hayes, E., 1981, *Log of the Union: John Boit's Remarkable Voyage*, Massachusetts & Oregon Historical Societies

Henke, L. A., 1929, *A Survey of Livestock in Hawaii*, University of Hawai'i, Honolulu

Howarth, F. G. & Mull, W. P., 1992, *Origin of the Hawaiian Insect Fauna*, University of Hawai'i Press, Honolulu

Howay, F. W. (editor), 1940, *The Journal of Captain James Colnett aboard the Argonaut from April 26 1789 to nov. 3 1791*, the Champlain Society, Toronto

Howay, F. W. (editor), 1941, *Voyages of the Columbia to the North West Coast*, Massachusetts Historical Society, Da Capo Press, New York

'Ī'ī, J. P., 1959, *Fragments of Hawaiian History*, Bishop Museum Press, Honolulu

Iselin, I., *Journal of a Trading Voyage Around the World 1805–1808*, McIlroy & Emmet, New York

Jarves, J. J., 1872 (first published 1843), *History of the Sandwich Islands* (fourth edition), Henry M Whitney, Honolulu

Joesting, E., 1984, *Kauai: The Separate Kingdom*, University of Hawai'i Press, Honolulu

Jones, Syd, 2014, *Before and Beyond the Niihau Zero*, Signum Ops, Florida

Judd, B., 1974, *Voyages to Hawaii before 1860*, Hawaiian Mission Children's Society & Hawaiian Historical Society

Kaeppler, A. L., 1978, *Artificial Curiosities: An Exposition of Native Manufactures Collected on the Three Pacific Voyages of Captain James Cook R. N.*, Bishop Museum Press, Honolulu

——— 1978, *Cook Voyage Artifacts in Leningrad, Berne, and Florence Museums*, Bishop Museum Press, Honolulu

Kalakaua, D., 1888, *Ancient Hawaiian Creation Story: Hawaiian Legends Introduction*, available online

Kamakau, S. M., 1961 (revised 1992), *Ruling Chiefs of Hawaii*, Kamehameha Schools Press, Honolulu

Kay, E. A., 1994, *A Natural History of the Hawaiian Islands, Selected Readings II*, University of Hawai'i Press, Honolulu

Knudsen, E. A., 1946, *Teller of Hawaiian Tales*, Mutual Publishing, Honolulu

——— 1999, *Kanuka of Kauai*, Mutual Publishing, Honolulu

Kuykendall, R. S., 1938, *The Hawaiian Kingdom, Vol. 1, 1778–1893*, University of Hawai'i Press, Honolulu

——— 1953, *The Hawaiian Kingdom Vol. 2, Twenty Critical Years 1854–1873*, University of Hawai'i Press

Laird, D. M., 2009, *Voices From Our Past: David and Katharine Larsen*, blurb.com

Lamb, W. K. (editor), 1984, *A Voyage of Discovery to the North Pacific Ocean and Around the World 1791-1795 by George Vancouver*, Hakluyt Society, London

Langdon, R., 1984, *Where the Whalers Went: An Index to the Pacific Ports and Islands Visited by American Whalers (and some others) in the Nineteenth Century*, Pacific Manuscripts Bureau, Australian National University, Canberra

Laracy, H., 2013, *Watriama and Co*, Australian National University E Press, Canberra

Ledyard, J., 1783, *A Journal of Captain Cook's Last Voyage to the Pacific Ocean and in Quest of a North-West Passage between Asia and America performed in the Years 1776, 1777, 1778, and 1779*, Nathaniel Patten, Hartford

Licayan, E., Nizo, V. & Kanahele, E., 2007, *Aloha Ni'ihau: Oral Histories*, Island Heritage Publishing, Honolulu

Liliuokalani, Queen, 1897 *The Kumulipo: An Account of the Creation of the World According to the Hawaiian Tradition*. Originally published by Lee & Shepard, Boston, USA (reprinted 2020)

Loebel-Fried, C., 2002, *Hawaiian Legends of the Guardian Spirits*, University of Hawai'i Press, Honolulu

London, J. 1985 (editor A. Grove Day), *Stories of Hawaii*, Mutual Publishing Paperback Series, Tales of the Pacific, Honolulu

Lydgate, J. M., 1915, *Kaumuali'i the Last King of Kauai*, Hawaiian Historical Society, 24th Annual Report

Macrae, J., 1922, *With Lord Byron in the Sandwich Islands in 1825*, BiblioBazaar Reproduction

Malo, D., 1903 (republished 1987), *Hawaiian Antiquities*, Bishop Museum Press

Manby, T., 1798, edited by Dale Torlesse 1992?, *Journal of the Voyages of HMS Discovery and Chatham*, Ye Galleon Press, Fairfield, Washington

McKenney's Hawaiian Directory, 1884, L.M. McKenney & Co

McPhail, H., 2015, *The Blenheim People*, blenheim175.wordpress.com

Meares, J., 1790, *Voyages Made in the Years 1788 and 1789 from China to the West Coast of America in which are included an Introductory Narrative of a Voyage performed in 1786, from Bengal, in the ship Nootka*, London

——— c.1916, *Extracts from Voyages Made in the Years 1788 & 1789 etc*, Hawaiian Historical Society reprint, Honolulu

Menzies, A., 1920, *Hawaii Nei 128 Years Ago*, Nabu Public Domain Reprints

Meyer, P. A., 1998, *Present Circumstances and Future Requirements in an Evolving Hawaiian Community*, Hoomana Ia Iesu Church, Niihau

Mills, P. R., 2002, *Hawai'i's Russian Adventure*, University of Hawai'i Press, Honolulu

Moriarty, L. P., 1986, *Ni'ihau Shell Leis*, University of Hawai'i Press, Honolulu

——— 2001, *Pupu o Niihau*, Honolulu Academy of Arts, Honolulu

Mouritz, A. A. St M., 1916, *The Path of the Destroyer*, Star Bulletin, Honolulu

Munro, G. C., 2007, *The Story of Lana'i*, privately printed, Honolulu

Nellist, G. F., 1925, *The Story of Hawaii and its Builders*, Honolulu Star Bulletin

Nokes, J. R., 1998, *Almost a Hero: The Voyages of John Meares, R. N. to China, Hawaii and the Northwest Coast*, Washington State University Press, Pullman

Ogilvie, G., 2007 (3rd edition), *Banks Peninsula: Cradle of Canterbury*, Phillips & King Publishers, Christchurch

Portlock, N., 1789, *A Voyage around the World; but more particularly to the North-West Coast of America: performed in 1785, 1786, 1787 and 1788, in the King George and Queen Charlotte, Captains Portlock and Dixon*, John Stockdale and George Goulding, London

Pratt, H. G., 1963, *The Hawaiians: An Island People*, Charles C Tuttle & Co., Vermont

Rickman, J., 1781, *Journal of Captain Cook's voyage to the Pacific Ocean, on Discovery performed in the Years 1776, 1777, 1778, 1779*, 2nd edition, Newberry, London

Rodman, J. S., 1979, *The Kahuna Sorcerers of Hawaii: Past and Present*, Exposition Press, New York

Roe, M., (editor) 1967, *The Journal and Letters of Captain Charles Bishop on the North-West Coast of North America, in the Pacific and in New South Wales 1794–1799*, published for the Hakluyt Society by Cambridge University Press

Samwell, D., 1957, *Captain Cook and Hawaii: A Narrative by David Samwell*, David Magee, San Francisco & Francis Edwards, London

Schutz, A. J., 1994, *The Voices of Eden: A History of Hawaiian Language Studies*, University of Hawai'i Press, Honolulu

Sinclair, F., 1911, *Under Western Skies*, Sampson Low, Marston & Co., London

Sinclair, Mrs. Francis Jr., 1885, *Indigenous Flowers of the Hawaiian Islands: Forty Four Plates Printed in Watercolour*, Sampson Low, Marston, Searle and Rivington, London

St John, H. & Jendrusch, K., 1980, *Plants introduced to Hawaii by the Ancestors of the Hawaiian People*, Polynesian Seafaring Heritage and Kamekameha Schools

Stepien, E. R., 1988, *Ni'ihau: A Brief History*, University of Hawai'i Working Paper Series, Honolulu

Straubel, C. R., 1948, *The Schooner Richmond and Canterbury's First Farmers*, The Rigamont Press, Wellington

Tabrah, R. M., 1987, *Ni'ihau: The Last Hawaiian Island*, Press Pacifica, Kailua

Tava, R. & Keale, M. K. (Sr.), 1984, *Niihau: The Traditions of an Hawaiian Island*, Mutual Publishing, Honolulu

Thomas, M., 1983, *Schooner from Windward: Two Centuries of Hawaiian Interisland Shipping*, University of Hawai'i Press, Honolulu

Townsend, E., 1888, *The Diary of Ebenezer Townsend Jnr (Vessel Neptune)*, Hawaiian Historical Society Reprints no 4, Honolulu

Turnbull, J., 1813, *A Voyage Round the World in the Years 1800, 1801, 1802, 1803, and 1804*, second edition, A Maxwell, London

Vancouver, G., 1798, *A Voyage of Discovery to the North Pacific Ocean and Round the World 1791–95*, London

Varez, D., 2011, *Pele and Hi'iaka: A Tale of Two Sisters*, Petroglyph Press, Hilo

von Holt, I. K., 1985 (revised edition), *Tales of Long Ago*, Daughters of Hawaii, Honolulu von Kotzebue, O., 1821, *Voyage of Discovery to the South Sea and to Behring's Strait*, Sir Richard Phillips & Co., London

Westervelt, W. D., 1916, *Hawaiian Legends of Volcanoes: How Pele Came to Hawaii*, G. H. Ellis Press, Boston

White, L. D., 1996, *The Canoe Plants of Ancient Hawaii*, www.canoeplants.com

Wichman, F. B., 1985, *More Kauaʻi Tales* (illustrated by Chris Faye), Bamboo Ridge Press, Honolulu

———2003, *Na Pua Aliʻi o Kauaʻi: Ruling Chiefs of Kauaʻi*, University of Hawaiʻi Press, Honolulu

Wichman, J. R. & St John, H., 1990, *A Chronicle and Flora of Niihau*, National Tropical Botanical Garden, Kauaʻi

Wilcox, C., 1996, *Sugar Water: Hawaii's Plantation Ditches*, University of Hawaiʻi Press, Honolulu

Yzendoorn, R., 1927, *History of the Catholic Mission in the Hawaiian Islands*, Honolulu Star Bulletin

Zimmerman, E. C., 1948, *Insects of Hawaii*, Vol. 1, Introduction, University of Hawaiʻi Press

Zimmermann, H., 1781, *Dernier voyage du capitaine Cook autour du monde, où se trouvent les circonstances de sa mort*, Berne (translation by U. Tewsley & J. C. Andersen, 1926, published by the Alexander Turnbull Library, Wellington, New Zealand)

Key papers and articles

'A Geologic Tour of the Hawaiian Islands: Kauai and Niihau,' *Volcano Watch*, 10 January 2016

Aloha Magazine, May/June 1986, 'Niihau: Special Feature & photos by Greg Vaughn,' Aloha Airlines

Andersen, J. C., 1908, 'Old Identities Book 1,' Alexander Turnbull Library, Wellington MS-0063

Beardsley, J. W. & Tuthill, L. D., 1959, 'Additions to the known Insect Fauna of Niihau,' *Proceedings, Hawaiian Entomological Society*, Vol. 17, August

Bolkhovitinov, N. N., 1973, 'The Adventures of Dr Schäffer in Hawaii 1815–1819,' translated from the Russian by Igor Vorobyoff, *Hawaiian Journal of History*, Vol. 7

Campbell, J., 1840, 'Journal Kept on Board the Ship *Blenheim*,' Alexander Turnbull Library, Wellington qMS-0370

'Coastal Geology of Niʻihau, The,' undated, University of Hawaiʻi, Coastal Geology Group

Conover, A., 1996, 'A Onetime Rancher Wages Lonely War to Save Rare Plants,' *Smithsonian Magazine*, 1 November 1996

Conter, F. E., 1903, 'The Cultivation of Sisal in Hawaii,' Hawaii Agricultural Experiment Station, Honolulu

Cooke, C. M., 1931, 'The Land Snail Genus Carelia,' *Bishop Museum Bulletin* 85

Coral Reef Assessment & Monitoring Program, 2008, 'CRAMP Study Sites: Island of Niihau'

Daws, G. & Head, T., 1963, 'Niihau: A Shoal of Time' *American Heritage Magazine*, Vol. 14, Issue 6

Enomoto, C. K., 1997, 'Niihau: Island at the Crossroad: Special Report,' *Honolulu Star Bulletin*

Fisher, H. I., 1951, 'The Avifauna of Niihau Island, Hawaiian Archipelago,' *The Condor*, January 1951

Flinders, A. F., Ito, G. & Garcia, M. O., 2010, 'Gravity Anomalies of the Northern Hawaiian Islands: Implications on the Shield Evolutions of Kauai and Niihau,' American Geophysical Union, *Journal of Geophysical Research: Solid Earth* (1978–2012)

Fullaway, D. T., 1947, 'Niihau Insects,' *Proceedings of the Hawaiian Entomological Society*, Vol. 13, No. 1, May 1947

Gilman, G., 1845, 'Rusticating on Kauai and Niihau in the Summer of 1845 by Makaikai,' Hawaiian Mission Children's Society unpublished manuscript

Hinds, Norman E. A., 1930, 'The Geology of Kauai and Niihau,' *Bishop Museum Bulletin* 71

Hitt, C., 2010, 'Keepers of the Flame: How Cultural Practitioners are Preserving Niihau's Unique Traditions,' *Hawaiʻi Magazine*, May, hawaiimagazine.com

Howay, F. W., 1930, 'Early Relations between the Hawaiian Islands and the Northwest Coast,' Capt. Cook Sesquicentennial

Kawaharada, D., 1999, 'Notes on the Discovery and Settlement of Polynesia: Hawaiian Voyaging Traditions (updated to include Hunt's findings),' Polynesian Voyaging Society

Kirch, P. V., 1982, 'The Impact of the Prehistoric Polynesians on the Hawaiian Ecosystem,' *Pacific Science*, Vol. 36/1

Larsen, L. D., 1942, 'Letters to his Wife, Katharine,' Niihau Stacks 919.6942 L3n, Copy 1, Hawaiʻi State Archives

Lepage, D., 2014, 'Avibase: Bird Checklists of the World: Niihau'

'Livestock in Hawaii,' *Hawaiian Gazette*, 21 May 1901

Maly, K. & Wilcox, B., 2000, 'A Short History of Cattle and Range Management in Hawaiʻi,' University of Hawaiʻi

Mann, H., 1866, 'An Enumeration of Hawaiian Plants,' *Proc. of American Academy of Arts and Sciences*, Vol. 7

Matisoo-Smith, E. et al, 1998, 'Patterns of Prehistoric Human Mobility in Polynesia indicated by mtDNA from the Pacific Rat,' *Proceedings of the National Academy of Science*, Vol. 95

Menard, W., 1969, 'Willie Maughan and the Wonderful Widow Sinclair,' *Foreign Service Review*, October

———1981, 'The Widow Sinclair and her Sea Search for Paradise,' *The Beaver*, Summer

———1982, 'The Cloistered Island: The Lively Widow and Lonely Island,' *Aloha Magazine*, April Issue

Menzies, A., 1923, 'Menzie's Journal of Vancouver's Voyage April to October 1792,' Archives of British Columbia, Victoria, BC

Hawaii's Comprehensive Wildlife Conservation Strategy, Niʻihau 2005, US Fish & Wildlife Service

La Paz (*nom de plume*), 1867, Review of Kauai and Niihau, *Pacific Commercial Advertiser* 17 Aug., 31 Aug., 5 Oct.,12 Oct., 19 Oct., 21 Dec., 28 Dec. 1867

Niʻihau Cultural Heritage Foundation, www.niihauheritage.org

Pritchardia aylmer-robinsonii, Wikipedia, en.wikipedia.org/wiki/Pritchardia_aylmer-robinsonii

Ramones, I., 2014, 'Niʻihau Family makes Rare Public Address,' *Indigenous Issues*

'Reports of Waimea, Kauai 1822–1866,' unpublished manuscripts, Hawaiian Mission Children's Society, Honolulu

Richardson, R. C., 1984, 'The Barque "Blenheim": Its Place in the Early Colonisation of New Zealand,' Alexander Turnbull Library, Wellington, MS-Papers-2137

Robinson, K., 1997, 'Niihau: Other Views,' *Star Bulletin*, July 26

Rose, R. G., 1990, 'Patterns of Protest: A Hawaiian Mat-Weaver's Response to 19th-Century Taxation and Change,' *Bishop Museum Occasional Papers*, Vol. 30

Soehren, L. J., 2002, 'A Catalog of Kauaʻi Place Names: Including Niʻihau, Lehua and Kaʻula,' unpublished

St John, H., 1982, 'Vernacular Plant Names used on Niʻihau Island,' *Bishop Museum Occasional Papers*, Vol. 25/3

——— 1959, 'Botanical Novelties on the island of Niihau, Hawaiian Islands,' Hawaiian Plant Studies 25, *Pacific Science*, Vol.13, April

——— 1979, 'The Botany of Niihau Island, Hawaii, as seen on Captain Cook's Voyage, 1778-1779,' *Pacific Science* (1979) vol. 33, No. 4

——— 1931, 'Additions to the Flora of Niihau,' *Bishop Museum Occasional Papers*, Vol. 9, No. 14

Stearns, H. T., 1947, *Geology and Ground-water Resources of the Island of Niihau, Hawaii*, Bulletin 12, Hawaii Division of Hydrography

US Department of Commerce, 2013, 'Endangered and Threatened Species: Final Rulemaking to Revise Critical Habitat for Hawaiian Monk Seals,' NOAA National Marine Fisheries Service

US Department of Commerce, Pacific Islands Region, 2016, 'Main Hawaiian Islands Monk Seal Management Plan,' NOAA National Marine Fisheries Service

US Fish and Wildlife Service, 2001?, 'Critical Habitat for 83 Plant Species from Kauai and Niihau,' Proposed Rule

——— 2003, 'Final Critical Habitat for Plant Species from the Island of Niʻihau'

Valauskas, E. J., 2014, 'Isabella in Hawaii: The Adventures of an Amateur Botanist in the 1860s,' Chicago Botanic Garden

Williams, R., 2014, 'The 'Olelo Odyssey,' in *Hana Hou! The Magazine of Hawaiian Airlines*, April/May

Wilson, J., 2010, 'Niihau and Kauai Mokopuni,' *Ea O Ka Aina*, islandbreath.org

——— 2005, 'The Potential of the Robinson Legacy,' *Ea O Ka Aina*, islandbreath.org

Yim, L. & Downes, P., undated, 'Capsule History of the Catholic Church in Hawaii,' www.ssccpicpus.com

ENDNOTES

Chapter One: A volcanic ark

1. Bird, I. L., 2002, *Letters to Henrietta*, edited by Kay Chubbuck, Northeastern University Press, p 93.
2. Forbes, C. N., 1913, An Enumeration of Niihau Plants, Bishop Museum, *Occasional Papers* Vol. 5(3), pp 17–18
3. Dana, J. D., 1849, *United States Exploring Expedition 1838–1842, Geology*, Geo. P. Putnam, New York, p 155
4. Dana, J. D., 1890, *Characteristics of Volcanoes with Contributions of Facts and Principles from the Hawaiian Islands*, Dodd Mead & Co., New York p 312
5. Powers, S., 1920, 'Notes on Hawaiian Petrology,' *American Journal of Science*, Vol. 50, pp 257–258
6. Hinds, N. E. A., 1930, 'The Geology of Kauai and Niihau,' *Bishop Museum Bulletin* 71, Honolulu, p 53
7. Stearns, H. T., 1947, *Geology and Ground-water Resources of the Island of Niihau, Hawaii*, Bulletin 12, Hawaii Division of Hydrography, pp 29–31
8. Clague, D. A. & Dalrymple, G. B., 1989, 'Tectonics, Geochronology and Origin of the Hawaiian-Emperor Volcanic Chain,' as reprinted in *A Natural History of the Hawaiian Islands* edited by Alison Kay, University of Hawai'i, 1994, p 20, figure 6
9. Palmer, H. S., 1936, *Geology of Lehua and Kaula Islands*, Bishop Museum Occasional Papers XII, p 13
10. *Volcano Watch*, 7 Jan 2016, 'A Geologic Tour of the Hawaiian Islands: Kaua'i and Ni'ihau'
11. Stearns, 1947, p 37
12. Wichman, J. R. & St John, H., 1990, *A Chronicle and Flora of Niihau*, National Tropical Botanical Garden, Kaua'i, Hawai'i, p 43
13. St John, H., 1978, The First Collection of Hawaiian Plants by David Nelson in 1779, *Pacific Science*, Vol. 32(2), pp 315–324. The four weeds Nelson found that are growing on Ni'ihau are *Oxalis corniculata, Digitaria setigera, Waltheria indica* and *Merremia aegyptia*.
14. St John, H., 1959, 'Botanical Novelties on the island of Niihau, Hawaiian Islands': Hawaiian Plant Studies 25, *Pacific Science* Vol. XIII. The species is now felt to be a variety of the Nihoa island Pritchardia, *Pritchardia remota* (var. *aylmer-robinsonii*). See Hodel, D. R., 2007, 'A Review of the Genus Pritchardia,' *Palms* 51, Supplement to Vol. 4, pp 1–53
15. 'Federal Register: Endangered and Threatened Wildlife and Plants; Final Designation or Non-designation of Critical Habitat for 95 Plant Species from the Islands of Kauai and Niihau,' HI; Final Rule 27 February 2003, US Fish and Wildlife Service, Department of the Interior.
16. Keith Robinson, personal communication, 20 August 2014
17. 'Federal Register: Endangered and Threatened Wildlife and Plants; Final Designations, 27 February 2003, US Fish and Wildlife Service, Plant Species from the Islands from the Islands of Kauai and Niihau'
18. 'Critical Habitat for 83 Plant Species from Kauai and Niihau (date unknown),' US Fish and Wildlife Service, p 3
19. 'Federal Register: Endangered and Threatened Wildlife and Plants; Final Designations, 27 Feb 2003, US Fish and Wildlife Service, Plant Species from the Islands from the Islands of Kauai and Niihau,' p 9118
20. Kirch, P. V., 1982, The Impact of Prehistoric Polynesians on the Hawaiian Ecosystem, *Pacific Science*, Vol. 36, pp 434–435
21. NOAA Fisheries, 2019, Hawaiian Monk Seal, Hawaiian Monk Seal Research Program, Pacific Islands Fisheries Science Center
22. NOAA Fisheries, 2018, 'What's the Latest on Hawaiian Monk Seals?'
23. NOAA Fisheries, Pacific Islands Regional Office, 2014, Hawaiian Monk Seal Historical Timeline
24. Nordtvedt Reeve, L. L., Reeve, R. B. & Cleghorn, P. L., 2013, The Hawaiian Monk Seal in Traditional Hawaiian Culture, prepared for NOAA National Marine Fisheries Service, Pacific Islands Regional Office
25. Department of Commerce: National Oceanic and Atmospheric Administration 2015, 'Endangered and Threatened Species: Final Rulemaking to Revise Critical Habitat for Hawaiian Monk Seals,' National Marine Fisheries Service, pp 143, 154 & 200
26. NOAA, National Marine Fisheries Service, 2007, *Recovery Plan for the Hawaiian Monk Seal*

27 *The Garden Island*, 1 June 2003
28 US Department of Commerce, NOAA, National Marine Fisheries Service, Pacific Islands Region, 2016, Main Hawaiian Islands Monk Seal Management Plan.
29 I was privileged to be invited by Keith Robinson to attend the annual planning meeting, hosted by NOAA, and attended by the Robinsons and the navy, at which the logistics for the annual seal count was arranged, and suitable flipper tags were agreed that it was felt would not attract sharks.
30 Kirch, P. V., 1982, 'The Impact of Prehistoric Polynesians on the Hawaiian Ecosystem,' *Pacific Science*, Vol. 36, p 432
31 Fisher, H. I., 1951, 'The Avifauna of Niihau Island, Hawaiian Archipelago,' *The Condor*, Vol. 53, p 34
32 avibase.bsc-eoc.org
33 U.S. Fish & Wildlife Service, 2010, 'Hawaiian Islands Animals — Listed Species,' as designated under the US Endangered Species Act
34 Fullaway, D. T., 1947, 'Niihau Insects,' *Proceedings, Hawaiian Entomological Society*, Vol. XIII, No. 1, pp 51–53
35 Beardsley, J. W. & Tuthill, L. D., 1959. 'Additions to the Known Insect Fauna of Niihau,' *Proceedings, Hawaiian Entomological Society*, Vol. XVII, No. 1, pp 56–61
36 Nishida, G. M., 2002, 'Hawaiian Terrestrial Arthropod Checklist,' Bishop Museum Technical Report, No. 22, pp 29–230
37 Nishida, G. M., 2002. 'Hawaiian Terrestrial Arthropod Checklist,' Bishop Museum Technical Report No. 22, pp 21–28, 235–239
38 *Sarasota Herald Tribune*, 21 September 1978, p 78
39 For example Bonato, L., Foddai, D., Minelli, A. & Shelley, R. M., 2004, 'The Centipede Order Geophilomorpha in the Hawaiian Islands (Chilopeda),' Bishop Museum, *Occasional Papers* 78, or Howarth, F. G., 1990, Hawaiian Terrestrial Arthropods: An Overview, Bishop Museum, *Occasional Papers*, Vol. 30, or Beardsley, J. W., 1966, 'Insects and other Terrestrial Arthropods from the Leeward Hawaiian Islands,' *Proceedings*, Hawaiian Entomological Society, Vol. XIX, p 157 *et seq*
40 Zimmerman, E. C., 1948, *Insects of Hawaii*, Vol. 1, Introduction, University of Hawai'i Press, p 104.
41 Cowie, R. H., 1995, 'Variation in Species Diversity and Shell Shape in Hawaiian Land Snails: In situ Speciation and Ecological Relationships,' *Evolution* 49(6), pp 1191–1202
42 In his field notebooks for 1908 Cooke states that he collected *Endodonta, Lyropupa, Tornatellina, Tornatellinaides perkinsi*, and *Helicina* shells at Halehaa on Ni'ihau, Regina Kawamoto, personal communication, 2016
43 Cooke, C. M. Jr., 1931, 'The Land Snail Genus Carelia,' *Bishop Museum Bulletin* 85, p 23
44 Neal, M. C., 1934, *Hawaiian Helicinidae*, Bishop Museum, *Bulletin* 125
45 Zimmerman, E.C., 1948, pp 98–101. The two families are the Achatinellidae (2 species) and the Pupillidae (1 species). In Cowie, Evenhuis & Christensen, 1995, *Catalogue of the Native Land and Freshwater Molluscs of the Hawaiian Islands*, Backhuys Publishers, Leiden, the three species are not identifiable, presumably because they were described from shells found on another island, and from the catalog can't be identified as also existing on Ni'ihau.
46 *Ibid*, p 48
47 Fornander, A., 1985, *Fornander Collection of Hawaiian Antiquities and Folk-Lore*, History of Kuali, as edited by Thomas Thrum, Bishop Museum, Honolulu, Vol. 4, p 372–

Chapter Two: The Polynesian footfall

1 Chambers, G. K. & Edinur, H. A., 2015, 'The Austronesian Diaspora: A Synthetic Total Evidence Model,' *Global Journal of Anthropology Research*, Vol. 2, pp 53–65
2 Wilmshurst, J. M., Hunt, T. L., Lipo, C. P. & Anderson, A. J., 2011, 'High-precision Radiocarbon Dating Shows Recent and Rapid Initial Colonization of East Polynesia,' *Proceedings of the National Academy of Sciences*, Vol. 108(5), pp 1815–1820. Also: Rieth, T. M., Hunt, T. L., Lipo, C. & Wilmshurst, J. M., 2011, 'The 13th Century Polynesian Colonization of Hawai'i Island,' *Journal of Archaeological Science*, Vol. 38, pp 2740–2749
3 Matisoo-Smith, E., Roberts, R. M., Irwin, G. J., Allen, J. S., Penny, D. & Lambert, D. M., 1998, Patterns of Prehistoric Human Mobility in Polynesia Indicated by mtDNA from the Pacific Rat, *Proceedings of the National Academy of Science*, Vol. 95, p 15149
4 Chang, C., Liu, H., Moncada, X., Seelenfreund, A., Seelenfreund, D. & Chung, K., 2015, A Holistic Picture of Austronesian Migrations Revealed by Phylogeography of Pacific Paper Mulberry, *Proceedings of the National Academy of Science*, Vol. 112, p 13537
5 Hinkle, A. E., 2007, 'Population Structure of Pacific Cordyline fruticosa (Laxmanniaceae) with Implications for Human Settlement Patterns of Polynesia,' *Journal of American Botany*, Vol. 94, pp 828–839
6 Beckwith, M. W., 1940, *Hawaiian Mythology*, Yale University Press (reprinted University of Hawai'i Press, 1970, p 5)
7 Liliuokalani, Queen, 1897 *The Kumulipo: An Account of the Creation of the World According to the Hawaiian Tradition*
8 Beckwith, M. W., 1951, *The Kumulipo: A Hawaiian Creation Chant*, University of Hawai'i Press, Honolulu
9 Luomala, K., 1971, in the foreword to the second edition of *The Kumulipo* by Martha Beckwith, p xviii
10 Beckwith, 1940, pp 42–46

11. Elliott, D., 1995, *Hawaiian Creation Myths.* witchswell.wordpress.com/2019/12/02/hawaiian-creation-myths/
12. Buck, P. H. (Te Rangi Hiroa), 1938, *Vikings of the Sunrise*, J. B. Lippincott & Co, Philadelphia, pp 255–256
13. Westerfelt, W. D., 1916, *Hawaiian Legends of Volcanoes*, Ellis Press, Boston, pp 4–6
14. Nimmo, Harry Arlo, 1987, 'Pele's Journey to Hawaii: An Analysis of the Myths,' *Pacific Studies*, Vol. 11/1, p 31
15. Tava, K. & Keale, M. K. Sr., 1984, *Niihau: The Traditions of an Hawaiian Island*, Mutual Publishing, Honolulu, p 11
16. *Ibid*, p 29
17. Buyers, C., 2008, Kauai Genealogy, www.royalark.net/Hawaii/Kauai.htm
18. Tava, R. & Keale, M. K. Sr., 1984, *Niihau: The Traditions of an Hawaiian Island*, Mutual Publishing, Honolulu, p 14
19. *Ibid*
20. Tava, K. & Keale, M. K. Sr., 1984, *Niihau: The Traditions of an Hawaiian Island*, Mutual Publishing, Honolulu, p 26
21. *Ibid*, p 27
22. Meyer, P. A., 1998, *Niihau: Present Circumstances and Future Requirements in an Evolving Hawaiian Community*, Hoomana Ia Iesu Church Inc., Niihau, p 33. (Drawn from Titcomb, M., 1952, 'Native Use of Fish in Hawaii,' *Journal of Polynesian Society*, Mem. No. 29, New Plymouth, pp 1–2)
23. Fornander, A., 1920, *The Fornander Collection of Hawaiian Antiquities and Folk-Lore*, edited by Thomas G. Thrum, Bishop Museum Press, Honolulu, p 168
24. St John, H., 1959, 'Botanical Novelties on the island of Niihau, Hawaiian Islands,' *Pacific Science*, Vol. 13, p 162
25. Tava & Keale, 1984, p 34
26. Krauss, B. H., 1993, *Plants in Hawaiian Culture*, University of Hawai'i Press, Honolulu, p 32
27. Rose, R. G., 1990, 'Patterns of Protest: A Hawaiian Mat-Weaver's Response to 19th-Century Taxation and Change,' Occasional Papers, Vol. 30, Bishop Museum, Honolulu, pp 88–117
28. Soehren, L. J., c 1976, Archaeology at Nualolo-kai, Bishop Museum, Manuscript SC Soehren, Box 1.5, p 85
29. Kaeppler, A. L., 1978, *Artificial Curiosities: An Exposition of Manufactures Collected on the Three Pacific Voyages of Captain James Cook, R.N.*, Bishop Museum Press, Honolulu, pp 75 & p 94
30. Wichman, F. B., 2003, *Nā Pua Ali'i O Kaua'i: Ruling Chiefs of Kaua'i*, University of Hawai'i Press, p 7
31. Fornander, A., 1880, *An Account of the Polynesian Race: Its Origins and Migrations*, Vol. II, Trubner & Co, London, pp 45–46
32. Brigham, W. T., 1912, Grant 234 in Carnegie Institution of Washington Yearbook, No. 11, p 239
33. Stokes, J. F. G., 1912, Field Notes, Typescript Stokes Grp 1 Box 9.48, Bishop Museum Archives
34. Brigham, W. T., 1913, Director's Annual Report for 1912, Bishop Museum *Occasional Paper*, Vol. 5, No. 4, p 9
35. Knudsen, E. A., 1946, *Teller of Hawaiian Tales*, Mutual Publishing, Honolulu, pp 193–195
36. *Ibid*, & Tava & Keale, 1984
37. Kinney, W. M., 1907, in A Collection of Historical Accounts and Oral History Interviews with Kama'aina Residents and Fisher-people of Lands in the Halele'a-Napali Region on the island of Kauai, ulukau.org
38. Fornander, A., Vol. 5, pp 164–168
39. Adapted from Barrere, D. B. & Pukui, M. K., 1980, 'Hula: Historical Perspectives,' *Pacific Anthropological Records*, No. 30, Bishop Museum, Honolulu, pp 7–8
40. Pukui, M. K., 1983, *'Olelo No'eau: Hawaiian Proverbs and Poetical Sayings*, Bishop Museum Press, Honolulu, p vii
41. Tava & Keale, 1984, pp 16–17

Chapter Three:
A fateful European encounter

1. Kamakau, S. M., 1961 (revised edition 1992), *Ruling Chiefs of Hawaii*, Kamehameha Schools Press, Honolulu, p 92
2. Beaglehole, J. C., 1967, *The Journals of Captain James Cook on his Voyages*, Cambridge University Press for the Hakluyt Society, Vol. III, part 2, p 263
3. *The Three Voyages of Captain Cook Round the World With a Map of the World, a Portrait, and a Memoir of His Life*, 1824, publisher: J. Limbird, pp 308-9
4. Beaglehole, 1967, p 275 footnote 1
5. Rickman, J., 1781 *Journal of Captain Cook's Last Voyage to the Pacific Ocean etc*, Da Capo Press, New York, reprint, p 225
6. Cook, J. & King, J., 1784, *A Voyage to the Pacific Ocean etc*, John Stockdale etc, London, Vol. II, p 152
7. *Ibid*, pp 152–153
8. Beaglehole, 1967, p 275, footnote 2
9. Cook & King, 1784, Vol. II, p 153
10. Beaglehole, 1967, p 276, footnote 2
11. Rickman, 1781, p 228
12. Beaglehole, 1967, pp 1349–1350 (Williamson's Journal)
13. Cook & King, 1784, Vol. II, p 153
14. *Ibid*, p 216
15. Beaglehole, 1967, p 276
16. *Ibid*, pp 276–277
17. *Ibid*, p 277
18. *Ibid*
19. *Ibid*
20. Rickman, 1781, p 226
21. Cook & King, 1784, Vol. II, pp 167–168

22 Cook, J. & King, J., 1784, *A Voyage to the Pacific Ocean etc*, John Stockdale etc, London Vol. III, p 86
23 Beaglehole, J. C., 1967, *The Journals of Captain James Cook on his Voyages*, Cambridge University Press for the Hakluyt Society, Vol. III, Part 1, p 572
24 *Ibid*, p 573
25 *Ibid*, p 575
26 *Ibid*, p 579
27 *Ibid*, p 580
28 *Ibid*, p 581
29 *Ibid*, pp 581–582
30 Beaglehole, J. C., 1967, *The Journals of Captain James Cook on his Voyages*, Cambridge University Press for the Hakluyt Society, Vol. III, Part 2, p 1084
31 *Ibid*, p 1085
32 *Ibid*
33 *Ibid*, pp 1222–3
34 Rickman, J., 1781, *Journal of Captain Cook's Last Voyage to the Pacific Ocean on Discovery performed in the years 1776, 1777, 17778, and 1779*, second edition, E. Newbery, London, p 330
35 Beaglehole 1967, Textual Introduction, p ccv
36 Ellis, W., 1782, first edition *An Authentic Narrative of a Voyage performed by Captain Cook and Captain Clerke, in His Majesty's ships Resolution and Discovery etc.*, London, Vol. II, pp 130–131
37 Beaglehole 1967, Textual Introduction, p ccvii
38 Ledyard, J., 1783. *A Journal of Captain Cook's Last Voyage to the Pacific Ocean and in Quest of a North-West Passage etc.*, Hartford, Connecticut, p 156
39 Ellis, 1782, Vol. 1, pp 177–179

Chapter Four: Early Western voyagers

1 Portlock, N., 1789. *A Voyage Around the World, but more particularly to the North-West Coast of America in the Years 1785–1788*, John Stockdale, London, p 75
2 *Ibid*, p 83
3 *Ibid*, p 84
4 *Ibid*, pp 84–85, Harold St John, in *A Chronicle and Flora of Niihau* notes on p 109 that Portlock's description of 'the tree with spreading branches' etc. was most likely hau (*Hibiscus tiliaceus*) and on p 103 St John notes that Portlock's tree with the nuts used as a substitute for candles would have been kukui (*Aleurites moluccana*) St John does not comment on Portlock's nine-foot high tree with 'blossoms of a beautiful pink colour' but this, according to Clyde Imada of the Bishop Museum, could possibly have been naio (*Myoporum sandwicense*).
5 *Ibid*, p 90. Yam Bay is now known as Nonopapa
6 *Ibid*, p 173
7 *Ibid*, p 184
8 *Ibid*, p 198
9 *Ibid*, p 303
10 *Ibid*
11 *Ibid*, p 306. Captain Dixon's account of the Ni'ihau incident is somewhat at variance (*A Voyage Round the World* etc by George Dixon second edition 1789, George Goulding, pp 257–258):

> Soon after this Tyheira ['Ōpūnui/Abbenooe's son] came on board, and (on our asking after Abbenoe) began to tell us a very lamentable story, the purport of which was, that since we had left Atoui [Kaua'i] a ship had been there; that the Captain used the inhabitants very ill, and even killed several of them … From what [he] had told us respecting the strange vessel, we were inclined to think that it was Captain Meares who had quarrelled with the natives, especially as our Captain had recommended him to touch at Atoui in preference to any of the islands. On our asking Abbenooe about this circumstance, he informed us that the Nootka had left Atoui 20 days, and that the Captain was *enou*, or a bad man, and had not given any present whatever, though he had been plentifully supplied with every refreshment the island afforded.

12 *Ibid*, p 307, The ship mentioned as 'lying under Imperial colours commanded by captain Barclay' was in fact the Imperial Eagle captained by Charles Barkley. The vessel never called at Ni'ihau, see *The Remarkable World of Frances Barkley 1769–1845* by Beth Hill and Cathy Converse, 2008, Touchwood Editions, Victoria, BC
13 *Ibid*
14 Meares, J., 1790. *Voyages Made in the Years 1788 and 1789 from China to the North West Coast of America, with an Introductory Narrative of a Voyage Performed in 1786 from Bengal in the Ship Nootka*, J. Walter, London p xxxix. Also of interest is *Almost a Hero: The Voyages of John Meares, R.N., to China, Hawaii and the Northwest Coast* by J. Richard Nokes, Washington State University Press, 2008.
15 *Ibid*, 1790, pp 280–281
16 *Ibid*, Appendix V, 'Extract from Mr. Meares Instructions to Capt. Douglas on leaving the American Coast.' Hawaiian Historical Society reprint of Meares Voyages, c.1916, p 47
17 *Ibid*, 1790, pp 357–358
18 Colnett, J. & Galois, R. M. 2003. *Voyage to the North West Side of America: The Journals of James Colnett 1786–1789*, University of British Columbia Press, Vancouver, p 193
19 *Ibid*, p 193
20 *Ibid*, p 193
21 *Ibid*, p 200
22 Taylor, A. B., 1788 *Journal of the Prince of Wales 1786–1789*, in the Taylor Papers, 1781–99, Mss. A2106, Mitchell Library, State Library of New South Wales
23 Meares, 1790, p 361

24. Colnett, J. & Howay, F. J., 1968, *Journal of Captain James Colnett Aboard the Argonaut from April 26 1789 – November 3 1791*, The Champlain Society, Toronto, p 221
25. Howay, F. J., 1925, Captain Simon Metcalfe and the Brig Eleanora, *Washington Historical Quarterly*, Vol. 16(2), pp 114–121
26. Ingraham, J., 1792. 'The Papers of Joseph Ingraham: Journal of the Voyage of the Brigantine Hope from Boston to the North West Coast of America 1790–1792,' Library of Congress ms, Vol. 2 Chart, p 32 and Vol. 3 Chart, p 43
27. Howay, F. J., 1941, *Voyages of the Columbia to the North West Coast 1789–1790 and 1790–1793*, Boston Massachusetts Historical Society, Israel Amsterdam, New York, pp 418–419
28. Judd, B., 1974 (second edition). *Voyages to Hawaii before 1860*, University of Hawai'i Press, pp 5–7.
29. Roe, M., 1967. *The Journal and Letters of Captain Charles Bishop on the North-West Coast of America, in the Pacific and in New South Wales 1794–1799*, Published for the Hakluyt Society by Cambridge University Press, p 139
30. Cook, J. & King, J., 1785, *A Voyage to the Pacific Ocean etc*, John Stockdale etc, London, Vol. II, p 296
31. Gibson, J. R., 1992, *Otter Skins, Boston Ships, and China Goods: The Maritime Fur Trade of the Northwest Coast, 1785–1841*, McGill-Queen's University Press, Montreal.
32. Vancouver, G., 1798
33. Manby, T., 1798 (1992), edited by Dale Torlesse, *Journal of the Voyages of HMS Discovery and Chatham*, Ye Galleon Press, Fairfield, Washington, pp 142–43
34. Vancouver, G., 1798, *A Voyage of Discovery to the North Pacific Ocean and Round the World*, London, Vol. 1, p 186
35. *Ibid*, Vol. 3, p 79
36. Roe, M., 1967. *The Journal and Letters of Captain Charles Bishop on the North-West Coast of America, in the Pacific and in New South Wales 1794–1799*, published for the Hakluyt Society by Cambridge University Press, pp 139–40
37. *Ibid*, p 141
38. Kamakau, S. M., revised edition, 1992, *Ruling Chiefs of Hawaii*, Kamehameha Schools Press, Honolulu, p 190
39. Turnbull, J., 1815 (second edition), *A Voyage Round the World in the Years 1800–1804*, A. Maxwell, London, p 221
40. *Ibid*, p 221
41. *Ibid*, p 222
42. Campbell, A., 1822 (third american edition), *A Voyage Round the World from 1806 to 1812*, Duke & Browne, Charleston, South Carolina, pp 91, 103, 118
43. These were: The Russian ship *Neva* (Captain Hargomeister) (on which Campbell arrived), the British ships *Duke of Portland* (Captain Spence) (on which Campbell departed) and the *Otter* (Captain Jobelin), the American ships *Catherine* (Captain Blanchard), *O'Cain* (Captain Winship), *Otter* (Captain Hill), *Vancouver* (Captain Swift), *Liddy* (Captain Brown), *Dromo* (Captain Woodward) and four or five others. How many of these called at Ni'ihau is unknown, but this gives some idea of the volume of traffic at that time.
44. Corney, P., 1896, *Narrative of Several Trading Voyages from 1813 to 1818 Between the Northwest Coast of America, the Hawaiian Islands and China etc*, T. G. Thrum, Honolulu, p 96
45. Langdon, R., 1984, 'Where the Whalers Went: An Index to the Pacific Ports and Islands Visited by American whalers (and some others) in the Nineteenth Century,' Pacific Manuscripts Bureau, Australian National University, Canberra, pp 72–123. Whaling ship visits to Ni'ihau were by the *Phoenix* 1823, *Atkins Adams* 1848, *Mechanic* 1854 (twice), *Oliver Crocker* 1858, *Cambria* 1860, *John Howland* 1861 and *Navy* 1862
46. Menzies, A., unpublished journal 1792–1794, Hawaiian entries published 1920 as *Hawaii Nei 128 Years Ago*, edited and published by W. F. Wilson, Honolulu, p 132
47. *Westminster Review* March–June 1846, Vol. 45, No. 2, George Luxford, London, Footnote, pp 432–433
48. Vancouver, G., 1798 *A Voyage of Discovery to the North Pacific Ocean and Round the World 1790–1795*, Vol. II, London, p 227
49. Menzies, 1920, p 132
50. Vancouver, 1798, Vol. II, p 229
51. *Ibid*, p 229
52. *Ibid*, p 228
53. Menzies, A., Journal for 2 December 1792, as published in *California Historical Society Quarterly*, Jan 1924, Vol. 2, No. 4
54. *Ibid*, p 114
55. *Ibid*, p 129
56. Vancouver, 1798, Vol. II, p 231
57. Menzies, 1920, p 130
58. *Ibid*, p 131
59. Vancouver, 1798, Vol. III, p 74
60. Menzies, A., 1794. Journal, Alexander Turnbull Library, Wellington, MS-Papers-0890-3 (entry for 14 March, unnumbered pages)
61. Manby, T., 1798, edited by Dale La Torlesse 1992? *Journal of the Voyages of HMS Discovery and Chatham*, Ye Galleon Press. Fairfield, Washington, p 11
62. Vancouver died in 1798 at the age of 41, just as his journals were being prepared for publication. The editing was completed by his brother John and others. Archibald Menzies' journal has never been published in its entirety. The sections dealing with his three Hawaiian visits on the *Discovery* were published in 1920 as *Hawaii Nei 128 Years Ago* under the editorship of W F Wilson. The

sections concerning his visits to the Californian coast were published in the *Hawaiian Historical Review* in 1924. Menzies died in 1842 at the age of 88.

63 For an account of Broughton's journey see Jim Mockford's 2004 article in Terrae Incognitae, Vol. 36, pp 42–58, titled *The Journal of a Tour across the Continent of New Spain from St Blas in the North Pacific Ocean to La Vera Cruz in the Gulph of Mexico* by Lieut. W. R. Broughton in the Year 1793.

64 David, A., editor, 2010 *William Robert Broughton's Voyage of Discovery to the North Pacific*, Farnham, Burlington, Vermont

65 Broughton, W. R., 1804. *A Voyage of Discovery to the North Pacific Ocean; in which the Coast of Asia … Japan … as well as the coast of Corea have been Examined and Surveyed, Performed in His Majesty's Sloop Providence and her Tender in the Years 1795–1798*, Cadell & Davies, London, pp 46–47. Note that the extracts from Broughton's journal in this section have been taken from the above reference rather than the original manuscript version, published in 2010 as William Thomas Broughton's *Voyage of Discovery to the North Pacific 1795–1798*. There are wording differences, but the sense remains generally the same.

66 *Ibid*, p 48
67 *Ibid*, pp 64–65
68 *Ibid*, p 74
69 *Ibid*, pp 74–75
70 *Ibid*, pp 75–76
71 *Ibid*, pp 77–78
72 *Ibid*, p 76
73 *Ibid*, pp 76–77
74 *Ibid*, p 77
75 *Ibid*, p 79–80
76 Cartwright, B., 1888. *Extracts from the Diary of Ebenezer Townsend Jr. Supercargo of the Sealing Ship "Neptune" etc*, Hawaiian Historical Society Reprints (No. 4), Honolulu, pp 21–22

Chapter Five: Rebellion on Kauaʻi

1 Wichman, F. B., 2003, *Nā Pua Aliʻi o Kauaʻi: Ruling Chiefs of Kauaʻi*, University of Hawaiʻi Press, Honolulu, p 92
2 *Ibid*, p 93
3 Kuykendall, R. S., 1938, *The Hawaiian Kingdom*, Vol. 1, 1778–1854, Foundation and Transformation, University of Hawaiʻi Press, Honolulu, p 30
4 Joesting, E., 1984, *Kauai: The Separate Kingdom*, University of Hawaiʻi Press and Kauaʻi Museum Association, p 59
5 Wichman, 2003, p 93
6 Daws, G., 1974, *Shoal of Time: A History of the Hawaiian Islands*, University of Hawaiʻi Press, Honolulu, p 31
7 Portlock, N., 1784, *A Voyage Round the World, but more particularly to the North-West Coast of America etc*, John Stockdale, London, p 176
8 Wichman, 2003, p 97
9 Joesting, 1984, p 56
10 Kuykendall, 1938, p 46
11 Bishop, C., 1794–1799, *The Journal and Letters of Captain Charles Bishop to the North West Coast of America, in the Pacific and in New South Wales*, edited by Michael Roe, published for the Hakluyt Society by Cambridge University Press, p 145–6
12 *Ibid*, p 146
13 Broughton, W. R., 1804, *A Voyage of Discovery to the North Pacific Ocean etc Undertaken in the Years 1796–1798*, Cadell & Davies, London, p 73
14 Cleveland, R. J., 1842, *A Narrative of Voyages and Commercial Enterprises, in Two Volumes*, John Owen, Cambridge, Vol. I, p 232
15 Turnbull, J., 1813, *Voyage Round the World in 1800–1804 etc*, A. Maxwell, London, second edition, p 210
16 Vancouver, G., 1798, *A Voyage of Discovery to the North Pacific Ocean and Round the World 1790–1795*, Vol. I, London, p 181 & p 184 (p 394 & p 400 Hakluyt)
17 Shaler, W., 1808, 'Journal of a Voyage Between China and the North-Western Coast of America made in 1804,' as extracted from *American Register* for 1808, Vol. 3, p 172
18 Iselin, I., 1897?, *Journal of a Trading Voyage Around the World 1805–1808*, McIlroy & Emmet, New York, p 75
19 *Ibid*, p 80
20 *Ibid*, p 67, Iselin states: '[Kamehameha] is said to possess about two thousand muskets, twenty carriage or ship, guns, a ship formerly the *Lelia Bird* (an American), several large three masted schooners, besides small vessels of twenty to fifty tons.'
21 Kamakau, S. M., 1961, *Ruling Chiefs of Hawaii* (revised edition), Kamehameha Schools Press, Honolulu, p 194
22 *Ibid*, p 196
23 ʻĪʻī, J. P., 1959, *Fragments of Hawaiian History*, Bishop Museum Press, Honolulu, p 82
24 Kuykendall, 1938, p 50
25 ʻĪʻī, 1959, p 83
26 Franchere, G., 1820 (Trans. 1854) *Narrative of a Voyage to the Northwest Coast of America in the Years 1811, 1812, 1813 and 1814*, Redfield, New York, pp 67–68
27 Gast, R. H. & Conrad, A. C., 1973, *Don Francisco de Paula Marin: Biography, Letters and Journal*, University of Hawaiʻi Press, Honolulu, p 210
28 Mills, P. R., 2002, *Hawaiʻi's Russian Adventure: A New Look at Old History*, University of Hawaiʻi Press, Honolulu, p 101
29 McClellan, E. N., 1928, John M. Gamble, Hawaiian Historical Society, 1927 Annual Report, p 48

30. Lydgate, J. M., 1915, 'Ka-mu-alii: The Last King of Kauai, Hawaiian Historical Society,' Annual Report, 1915, p 36
31. The 'Log of the Atahualpa' is by an unknown writer, and is held in MS form in the Massachusetts Historical Society Library. The quotation is from Ref 29 above, p 105
32. Croft, L. B., 2017, *Kaumuali'i and the Last of the God Kings*, Sphynx Publications, Phoenix, Arizona, p 82
33. Bolkhovitinov, N. N., 1972, *Avantyura Doktora Sheffers na Gavayakh v 1815–1819 Godakh (The Adventures of Doctor Shäffer in Hawaii 1815–1819)*, Novaya i Noveyshaya Istoriya, Russian, No. 1, translation by Igor V. Vorobyoff, December 1972, as published in *Hawaiian Journal of History*, Vol. 7, 1973, p 60
34. *Ibid*, p 60
35. *Ibid*, p 62
36. *Ibid*, pp 65–66
37. *Ibid*, p 72
38. Corney, P., 1896. *Voyages in the Northern Pacific … from 1813 to 1818*, T. G. Thrum, Honolulu, p 85
39. *Ibid*, p 89
40. Croft, 2017, p 106
41. Arago, J., 1823, *Narrative of a Voyage Round the World in the "Uranie" and "Physicienne", Corvettes Commanded by Captain Freycinet, during the Years 1817, 1818, 1819 and 1820 etc.*, Treuttel and Wurz, London, Vol. II, p 106
42. Kuykendall, 1938, p 68. The quotes are from an account given by Kaahumanu to Rev. Bishop in 1826.
43. Bingham, H., 1847 *A Residence of Twenty-One Years in the Sandwich Islands* (second edition), Sherman Converse, New York, p 140
44. *Ibid*, p 146
45. Jarves, J.J., 1872 (first published 1843), *History of the Hawaiian Islands* (fourth edition), Henry M. Whitney, Honolulu, p 110.
46. *Ibid*, p 110
47. Bingham, 1847, p 173
48. As quoted in Croft, 2017, pp 129–130
49. *Ibid*, pp 130–131
50. Bingham, 1847, p 232
51. *Ibid*, pp 233–234
52. Joesting, 1984, p 106
53. Bingham, 1847, p 236
54. Jarves, 1872, p 116 gives the numbers killed as 130 insurgents and one loyalist. Both he and Bingham may be correct, with Bingham's numbers being the battlefield casualties, and Jarves's including non-combatants. These latter were significant as the Dibble extract shows.
55. Bingham, 1847, p 239
56. Dibble, S., 1843, *A History of the Sandwich Islands*, 1909 edition, T. G. Thrum, Honolulu, pp 172–173.
57. Jarves, 1872, p 116
58. Bingham, 1847, p 242
59. *Ibid*, p 243

Chapter Six: Sinclairs, Gays and Robinsons in New Zealand

1. Scotland, Marriages 1561–1910, FHL microfilm 102945, 1042982, 1042984.
2. The Old Parish Register for Renfrew records her birth on 23 April 1800 and baptism on 27 April 1800, her parents being James Hutchison and Jean Robertson, as reported at blenheim175.wordpress.com
3. von Holt, I. E. K., 1940, *Stories of Long Ago: Niihau, Kauai, Oahu*, revised edition, Daughters of Hawaii, Honolulu, 1985, p 158
4. *Ibid*, pp 5–6
5. Called Jean in *Stories of Long Ago*, but Jane elsewhere. Jane has been used herein.
6. von Holt, 1940, p 6 and the children's birth records.
7. Novitz, R., 2014, 'Sinclair, Elizabeth,' from the *Dictionary of New Zealand Biography. Te Ara: The Encyclopedia of New Zealand*. Jane Sinclair's second name was Robertson.
8. Burns, P., 1989, *Fatal Success: A History of the New Zealand Company*, Heinemann Reed, Auckland, p 14 and elsewhere.
9. *Ibid*, p 89
10. *Ibid*, pp 85–86
11. As quoted in Richardson, R. C. H., 1984, 'The Barque "Blenheim": Its Place in the Early Colonisation of New Zealand,' ATL MS papers 2137, p 1
12. Burns, P., p 106
13. *Ibid*, pp 115–116
14. *Ibid*, p 131
15. *John McHutcheson*. The Old Parish Register for Glasgow records that James McHutcheson, manufacturer, and Jean Robertson had a son, John, born on 6 October 1816. (Traveled to New Zealand as John Sinclair.)
    George Sinclair. The Old Parish Register for Glasgow records that Francis Sinclair, Excise Officer and Elizabeth McHutcheson, had a lawful son George, born on 5 November 1824.
    James McHutcheson Sinclair. The Old Parish Register for Kinloss in Morayshire records that Francis Sinclair, Excise Officer, and Elizabeth McHutcheson had a son, James McHutcheson, in Findhorn, born on 23 June 1826 and baptized on 25 July.
    Jane Robertson Sinclair. The Old Parish Register for Glasgow records that Francis Sinclair, Officer of Excise, and Elizabeth McHutcheson had a daughter Jane Robertson, born on 22 March 1829.
    Helen McHutcheson Sinclair. The Old Parish Register for Stirling records that Francis Sinclair, Officer of Excise,

and Elizabeth McHutcheson had a daughter, Helen McHutcheson, born on 29 May 1831 and baptized on 26 June. One of the witnesses was William McHutcheson, Eliza's brother.

Francis Sinclair. The Old Parish Register for Stirling records that Francis Sinclair, Officer of Excise, and Elizabeth McHutcheson had a son, Francis, born on 12 January 1834.

Ann McHutchison Sinclair. The Old Parish Register for Stirling records that Francis Sinclair, Officer of Excise, and Elizabeth McHutchison had a daughter, Ann McHutchison, born on 7 March 1839 and baptized on 22 March.

All the above as reported at blenheim175.wordpress.com. Published as a pdf, *The Blenheim People* in 2015. Note the different spellings of McHutchison.

16 Francis Sinclair's land order may be seen in National Archives of New Zealand, Christchurch, Canterbury Association papers L and S 40/2, no.35. Reproduced here as Image 6.13

17 *Stirling Observer*, 1840, September 3. As reported in Ancestry.com, rootsweb

18 Richardson, R. C. H., 1984, 'The Barque "Blenheim": Its place in the Early Colonisation of New Zealand,' ATL MS-papers-2137, pp 1–2

19 Campbell, J., 1840, Journal on Board Blenheim, p 1, ATL qMS-papers-0370.

20 *Ibid*, p 12

21 *Ibid*, p 56

22 *Ibid*, p 68

23 *Ibid*, p 70

24 *Ibid*

25 Campbell, J., 1840, Journal on Board Blenheim, ATL qMS-papers-0370, p 71

26 Francis Sinclair letter to William McHutcheson, 3 January 1841, ATL fMS-Papers-0460, p 1, typed version (fragile original also in file). Unfortunately no later letters exist in these papers.

27 Lower Hutt Past and Present, Roads, 1941, Hutt City Libraries Online Heritage Collection, p 25

28 For more fanciful tales of this journey see I. E. K. von Holt, 1985, *Stories of Long Ago: Niihau, Kauai, Oahu,* Daughters of Hawaii, p 9. Ida von Holt sourced her information largely from her mother, Ann Sinclair, who was only a toddler at the time of this voyage.

29 *The Press*, 30 January 1899, 'Death of a Settler: Some Memories of Old Times,' p 5

30 *New Zealand Gazette and Wellington Spectator*, 3 April 1841, p 2

31 Hay, H.L.G., 1901, p 64. Also, the promissory letter from William Wakefield dated April 1845 reproduced on page 139, from the Robinson family papers.

32 *Ibid*, p 60

33 As quoted in Geoff Park, 1995. *Ngā Ururoa: Ecology and History in a New Zealand Landscape*, Victoria University Press, Wellington, pp 92–93

34 *New Zealand Gazette and Wellington Spectator*, 17 August 1842, p 2, Launch of the *Richmond* Schooner. The shipyard was nearly a mile up the river from the present mouth.

35 Some refinements must have been required as, after advertising for cargo for Nelson, she didn't leave Port Nicholson again until 29 September 1842, arriving back from Nelson and Kāpiti with whale oil, pigs and potatoes on 8 October. Her next voyage was again to Nelson on 16 October. She returned to Port Nicholson on 8 November, before sailing for the Manawatū on 14 November, returning to Wellington on 11 December with a load of lumber and potatoes. The schooner left Port Nicholson again on 29 December, this time for Poverty Bay, and arrived back in Wellington on 18 January 1843 with a cargo of pigs, fowls, hams and bacon. She next sailed for 'the coast' on 29 January (presumably the east coast of the North Island), returning with general cargo on 6 February 1843.

36 Straubel, C. R., 1948. *The Schooner Richmond and Canterbury's First Farmers,* The Rigamont Press, Wellington, p 5 (ex. Alexander Turnbull Library ATL Pam 6422)

37 *New Zealand Gazette and Wellington Spectator*, 26 April 1843, p 2

38 Charles Barrington Robinson figures later in this story.

39 *New Zealand Gazette and Wellington Spectator*, 13 May 1843, p 3

40 *Ibid*, 27 May 1843, p 2

41 Best, S., 2013 *Frontiers: A Colonial Dynasty,* Steele Roberts Aotearoa, Wellington, p 54

42 *New Zealand Spectator and Cook's Strait Guardian*, 26 July 1845, p 2

43 Hay, H.L.G., pp 70–71

44 *Ibid*, pp 88–89

45 *Ibid*, pp 89–90

46 *Ibid*, p 113

47 Shortland, E., 1851, *The Southern Districts of New Zealand: A Journal, with Passing Notices of the Customs of the Aborigines*, Longman, Brown, Green and Longmans, London, pp 269–270.

48 Selwyn, G. A., 1844, Journal of the Bishop's Visitation Tour as quoted in Paul, R. B. 1857, *Letters from Canterbury, New Zealand*, Rivingtons, Waterloo Place, London, footnote on p 65

49 Sinclair, F., 14 April 1845, letter to William Sinclair, published in the *New Zealand Journal*, London, 25 October 1845, pp 272–273
50 *Ibid*, p 273
51 Renaud, R., 6 May 1845 letter to Sinclair Squire, Pigeon Bay, Robinson family collection:

   Akaroa le 6 Mai 1845

   My dear Sir,

   In answer to your request, I inform you that I shall be very much pleased to make your commission; you may be assured of my attention and care to do it well.

   I hope when I come back, I shall be able to pay my visit to you; I wish I could have done it in these last days, but I have had no opportunity.

   Pray, present my respectful[?] compliments to Mrs. Sinclair and all your family, and believe me

   my dear Sir
   Your Sincere friend
   Reymond[?]

52 *New Zealand Spectator* and *Cook's Strait Guardian* 11 July 1846
53 Hay, H.L.G., 1901, pp 110–111
54 Sinclair, H., 1846, as quoted in Ruth Tabrah's *Niʻihau: The Last Hawaiian Island*, Press Pacifica, Kailua, 1987, p 95
55 *Akaroa Mail and Banks Peninsula Advertiser*, 13 June 1913.
56 Letter from Charles Robinson in Wellington to Eliza Sinclair, 6 June 1850, Robinson family letters, pp 2–3
57 Hay, H.L.G., p 135
58 Torlesse, C.O., 1958, *The Torlesse Papers: The Journals and Letters of Charles Obins Torlesse concerning the Foundation of the Canterbury Settlement 1848–51*, edited by Maling, P.B., Pegasus Press, Christchurch, pp 78, 148 & 158
59 *Wellington Independent*, 24 Oct 1849
60 *The Britannia and Trades Advocate*, Hobart, 3 January and 7 February 1850, Shipping Intelligence
61 *Colonial Times*, Hobart, 23 February 1849, Shipping Intelligence, Departures
62 genforum.genealogy.com.mytrees.com
63 Godley, C.W., 1951, *Letters from Early New Zealand 1850–1853*, Whitcombe & Tombs, Christchurch, letter of 18 November 1851, p 257–258
64 *Colonial Times*, Hobart, 13 February 1852, Shipping Intelligence. The schooner Mumford is reported as having sailed for New Zealand on 12 January with 'Mrs Gay, child and servant' as passengers.
65 Annie 1851, Francis 1852, Elizabeth 1858, Charles 1862, Alice 1865. All were born at Pigeon Bay except Alice, the first non-native Hawaiian-born on Niʻihau. Annie died at age two at Pigeon Bay.
66 genforum.genealogy.com, mytrees.com
67 Hay, H.L.G., p 60
68 Evans, F.J., 29 April 1849 letter to Eliza Sinclair, Robinson family papers
69 Godley, C.W., 1951, *Letters from Early New Zealand 1850–1853*, Whitcombe & Tombs, Christchurch, letter of 18 November 1851, pp 250–251
70 *Ibid*, p 257 and p 250
71 Hay, H.L.G., 1901, p 199
72 Godley, J.R. 13 August 1852 letter to Eliza Sinclair, Robinson family papers
73 Hay, H.L.G., 1901, p 160
74 *Ibid*, p 158
75 *Lyttelton Times*, untitled, 31 January 1852, p 10
76 Godley, C.W., 1951, p 258
77 *New Zealand Advertiser* and *Bay of Islands Gazette*, July 2 1840, p 4 (ex ancestry.com)
78 Buick, T.L., 1928. *The French at Akaroa*, New Zealand Book Depot, Wellington, p 249 footnote
79 Wakefield, W., 1844, letter to Secretary, Otago Association, Dunedin 31 August 1844 in Hocken, T.M. 1898 Contributions to the Early History of New Zealand, Appendix D, p 273
80 Letters from C.B. Robinson to Captain Sinclair dated 13 December 1845, 4 January 1846 and 23 April 1846. The quote is from the second of these letters, pp 3–4, Robinson family papers
81 *Star*, 15 December 1900, 'Old Akaroa: Reminiscences of Mr. S.C. Farr
82 Andersen, J.C. Notes, *Old Identities and Old Occurrences*, Vol. 1, p 5, entry for 25 August 1908, unpublished manuscript ATL MS-0063
83 *Lyttelton Times*, 29 January 1853, p 6
84 von Holt, I.E.K., 1985, *Stories of Long Ago: Niihau, Kauai, Oahu*, revised edition, Daughters of Hawaii, Honolulu, p 23
85 *Press*, 15 June 1984, article by Gordon Ogilvie on Charles Robinson, p 14
86 Sewell, H., edited by David McIntyre, 1980. *The Journal of Henry Sewell 1853–57*, Whitcoulls, Christchurch, Vol. 1, p 331
87 Andersen, 1908, pp 5–6
88 Hay, J., 1915, *Reminiscences of Earliest Canterbury (Principally Banks Peninsula) and Its Settlers*, Christchurch Press Co., Christchurch, p 133
89 *Lyttelton Times*, 28 January 1854, Untitled, p 10
90 *Ibid*, 21 November 1857, 'Shipping News,' p 4
91 *Ibid*, 19 June 1858, 'Local Intelligence,' p 5
92 Rev. William Aylmer was the vicar of Akaroa from 1851–73
93 The 18-year-old son of Thomas Gay by his former marriage.
94 Unknown

95 Stack, J. W., 1936. *More Maoriland Adventures of J W Stack* (edited by A. H. Reed), A. H. & A. W. Reed, Dunedin, pp 236–238
96 Stack, J. W., 1994, *Further Maoriland Adventures of J W and E Stack* (edited by A. H. Reed), Southern Reprints, Auckland, p 62
97 Joesting, E., 1984, *Kauai: The Separate Kingdom*, University of Hawai'i Press, Honolulu, p 192
98 *Lyttelton Times*, 7 December 1861, p 413.
99 Robinson family papers
100 Laracy, H., 2013, *Watriama and Co.: Further Pacific Island Portraits*, ANU EPress, p 45. This sale price of £8707 is borne out by a letter of guarantee from the Bank of New Zealand dated 4 November 1862 in the sum of £8477-10-00 payable on 3 February 1863. The slight difference (2.6%) may well be a bank margin or alternatively a transaction tax. This letter is in the Robinson family papers.
101 *Lyttelton Times*, 29 October 1862, Town and Country News, p 5
102 *Ibid*, 7 February 1863, *Shipping Intelligence*, p 4
103 von Holt, I. E. K., 1940, *Stories of Long Ago: Niihau, Kauai, Oahu*, revised edition, Daughters of Hawaii, Honolulu, 1985, p 26
104 Robinson, H., 1863, as quoted in Ruth Tabrah's *Ni'ihau: The Last Hawaiian Island*, Press Pacifica, Kailua, 1987, p 96
105 The *Bessie* arrived at Lyttelton from Melbourne on 3 Jan 1863 (*Lyttelton Times*, 7 January) and left immediately for her refit in Pigeon Bay. It was reported on 7 February that a new mainmast had been stepped (*Lyttelton Times*) and that she was nearly ready to leave. Both *Stories of Long Ago* and *Ni'ihau: The Last Hawaiian Island* are incorrect in stating the *Bessie* left in April. In fact it was late February/early March.

Chapter Seven: The Pacific journey and purchase of Ni'ihau

1 *Messager de Tahiti*, 11 April 1863, p 4 and 18 April 1863, p 4
2 The *Newcastle Chronicle and Hunter River District News*, 24 June 1865, p 4. (To put these measurements in a familiar context, the Bessie was the same length as Captain Cook's Resolution, but much narrower and thus of smaller cargo capacity.)
3 Ida von Holt in *Stories of Long Ago* mentions their taking servants, but if so they would have been shown on the passenger manifest for the Bessie.
4 Menard, W., 1982, April. *Aloha Magazine,* The Cloistered Island: The Lively Widow and Lonely Niihau, p 50
5 *Ibid*, p 51
6 *Lyttelton Times*, 26 September 1863, p 4
7 *Ibid*, 1 December 1863, p 4
8 von Holt, I. E. K., 1985, *Stories of Long Ago: Niihau, Kauai, Oahu*, Daughters of Hawaii, p 29. Also the published Honolulu Port records in the *Pacific Commercial Advertiser* and *The Friend* for April and May of 1863 make no reference to the *Bessie* having arrived or departed from Honolulu
9 *The British Colonist*, Victoria, Vancouver Island, 9 June 1863, p 3
10 As quoted in Menard, W., 1981, The Widow Sinclair and her Sea Search for Paradise, *The Beaver*, Summer Issue, p 50
11 *Ibid*, p 50
12 As quoted in Menard, 1981, p 50
13 *The British Colonist*, Victoria, Vancouver Island, 11 September 1863, p 3 Despatch from Utsalady
14 *The Friend*, 2 Oct 1863, Vol. 20, No. 1, p 80
15 Bird, I. L., 1881, *Six Months in the Sandwich Islands*, G. P. Putnam's Sons, New York (second edition), p 202
16 Daws, G., 2006 *Honolulu the First Century: The Story of the Town to 1876*, Mutual Publishing, Honolulu, pp 220–265
17 *Joesting in Kauai: The Separate Kingdom* (1984), p 190 states the house was on King Street and was rented from George Luce, onetime Honolulu harbor pilot. It may well therefore have been on the corner of King and Sheridan Streets.
18 Vance, J. W. & Manning, 'A The Effects of the American Civil War on Hawai'i and the Pacific World,' *World History Connected*, Vol. 9, No. 3, worldhistoryconnected.press.illinois.edu
19 *The Friend*, 2 Oct 1863, Vol. 20, No. 1, p 80.
20 von Holt, I. E. K., 1985, *Stories of Long Ago: Niihau, Kauai, Oahu*, Daughters of Hawai'i, p 31
21 Letter from J. Wahineaea to the Clerk of the Ministry of Interior, 11 April 1863, Hawai'i State Archives: Interior Department Lands, see Image 7.16
22 Registration of lease from government to Niihauans, Hawai'i State Archives, Register of Government Leases 1845–1882, Series DLNR2, Vol. 19 Item 49
23 Letter from Niihauans to Minister of the Interior 22 September 1863, Hawai'i State Archives: Series 526: Survey, Grant #2944
24 Letter from Niihauans to Minister of the Interior 17 January 1864, Hawai'i State Archives: Series 526: Survey, Grant #2944. See Image 7.17 & Translation
25 Letter from James and Francis Sinclair to Minister of the Interior 14 January 1864, Hawai'i State Archives: Series 526, Survey, Grant #2944. See Image 7.19

26   Letter from Ministry of Interior to J. H. & F. Sinclair 19 January 1864, Hawai'i State Archives, Int. Dept. Bk.7, pp 504–505
27   Four letters in Hawai'i State Archives, Series 526 Grant #2944
28   Letter from James Sinclair to Minister of the Interior 20 January 1864, Hawai'i State Archives, Series 526, Grant #2944.
29   Land Patent Grant #2944, Sinclair, James McHutcheson and Francis, District of Niihau, Island of Niihau, Vol. 14, pp 514–515, Bureau of Conveyances
30   Letter from Ministry of Interior to J. Wahineaea, 25 January 1864, Hawai'i State Archives, Int. Dept. Bk.7, p 508
31   Tava, R. & Keale, M. K., 1987, *Niihau: The Traditions of an Hawaiian Island*, Mutual Publishing, Honolulu, p 47
32   *Pacific Commercial Advertiser*, 4 February 1864, p 2
33   Letter from Ministry of Interior to Rev. G. B. Rowell, 1 June 1853, Hawai'i State Archives, Int. Dept. Bk.6, p 100. Ditto, letter to D. B. Marsh, 19 August 1854, Int. Dept. Bk.6, p 223
34   Daws, G. & Head, T., 1963, Niihau Shoal of Time, *American Heritage*, Vol. 14, Issue 6, p 51
35   *Pacific Commercial Advertiser*, 2 April, 16 April, 23 April, 30 April, 7 May, 14 May, 28 May, p 2, 1864
36   *Ibid*, 11 June 1864, p 3
37   Bureau of Conveyances Deed dated 7 August 1880, Kaua'i/Ni'ihau Grantors Book 64, p 271
38   G4382.N5 1954.A7, US Army
39   Bureau of Conveyances, Royal Patent RP5573 dated 24 August 1864
40   *Ibid*. Deed dated 13 February 1864, Kaua'i/Ni'ihau Grantors Book 18, p 16
41   Knudsen, E. A., 1946, *Teller of Hawaiian Tales,* Mutual Publishing, Honolulu, pp 232–237
42   Tabrah, R. M., 1987, *Ni'ihau: The Last Hawaiian Island*, Press Pacifica, Kailua, Hawai'i, p 113
43   *Lyttelton Times*, 14 November 1863, p 5. Oranges were grown extensively around Kona on the Big Island at this time. See Mark Twain's 1866 visit titled *Roughing it in the Sandwich Islands* (republished 1990 by Mutual Publishing, Honolulu). When journeying through the area he writes 'We rode through one orange grove that had ten thousand trees in it. They were all laden with fruit.' (p 47)
44   *Ibid*, 12 November 1863, p 4
45   *Ibid*, 14 November 1863, p 5
46   *Ibid*, 26 December 1863, p 4
47   *Ibid*, 12 November 1863, p 4
48   *Ibid*, 17 November 1864, p 4
49   *Newcastle Chronicle and Hunter River District News*, 12 January 1864, p 2
50   *Ibid*, 23 January 1864, p 2
51   *New Zealand Herald*, 15 August 1864, p 3
52   *Ibid*, 16 August 1864, p 1
53   *Ibid*, 18 August 1864, p 5
54   *Ibid*
55   *New Zealand Herald*, 20 August 1864, p 5
56   *Ibid*
57   *New Zealand Herald*, 28 September 1864, p 5
58   *Ibid*
59   *Daily Southern Cross*, 1 October 1864, p 5
60   *New Zealand Herald*, 3 October 1864, p 1
61   *Ibid*, 16 December 1864, p 1
62   *Daily Southern Cross*, 13 January 1865, p 4
63   *New Zealand Herald*, 18 January 1865, p 4
64   *Newcastle Chronicle and Hunter River District News*, 4 February 1865, p 8
65   *Ibid*, 11 February 1865, p 2
66   *Daily Southern Cross*, 24 February 1865, p 4
67   Letter from Rev. Charles Creed in Newcastle to Jane Gay on Ni'ihau 27 January 1865, Robinson family papers

Chapter Eight: A fledgling ranch

1   *Pacific Commercial Advertiser*, 26 March, 9 April, 30 April 1864 re movements of the schooner *Kalama*. (Not to be confused with the steam-powered sidewheeler *Kalama* wrecked at Kōloa in 1856).
2   Hawai'i State Archives, Tax Records for Ni'ihau 1855–1872 (Extracted on 28 May 2019). Lehua village opposite Lehua Island is mentioned by name in Gorham Gilman's 1845 'Rustications on Kauai and Niihau' referred to below.
3   Letter from Alice Robinson at Makaweli to Eleanor Robinson in Honolulu, 6 May 1945, Robinson family papers
4   nupepa-hawaii.com, Kuokoa Blog for 29 May 2012
5   Hawai'i State Archives, Department of the Interior, Letterbook No.7B, Jan 2 1861 to June 16 1866, pp 538–539. (The sheep population of Moloka'i Ranch was likely of the order of 15,000–20,000 at this time.)
6   Hawai'i State Archives, Department of the Interior, letter 25 January 1864, p 508
7   Gilman, G. 1845, 'Rustications on Kauai and Niihau in the Summer of 1845,' Mission Houses Museum, Honolulu, unpublished MS, p 64
8   Report of Committee on Horses, 1854, Transactions Royal Hawaiian Agricultural Society, Vol. 2, No. 1, pp 105–107
9   Tabrah, R., 1987, *Ni'ihau: The Last Hawaiian Island*, Press Pacifica, Kailua, Hawai'i, pp 103–104
10 Joesting in *Kauai: The Separate Kingdom* (1984), p 192 says 'three precut houses were carried ashore and assembled …,' but gives no reference for this statement.

Isabella Bird, writing after staying with the Sinclairs at Makaweli in March 1874, mentions their having taken three wooden houses with them to establish themselves on Niʻihau (Isabella Bird *Letters to Henrietta*, edited by Kay Chubbuck 2002 and published by Northeastern University Press, p 94). There seems to be confusion here between the precut houses erected at Kaununui and the construction of The House at Kiʻekiʻe. It is likely that in the fullness of time the precut houses were disassembled at Kaununui and reerected to form part of The House. Certainly in 1867 the material on the Nettie Merrill arrived as lumber. Labor, admittedly unskilled, was readily available for house building, and could be supplemented by skilled locals from Kauaʻi.

11 *Pacific Commercial Advertiser*, 3 August 1867, p 1
12 *Ibid*, p 1
13 *Ibid*
14 nupepa-hawaii.com, Kuokoa Blog for 30 October 2014
15 Bureau of Conveyances Book 9, p 262, Royal Patent 4476
16 Edward Joesting, in *Kauai: The Separate Kingdom* (p 113) relates the history of the Makaweli ahupuaʻa from the point of view of a claimant called Ahukai who gave evidence to the Land Commission:

> One of the longer and more carefully documented claims for land on Kauai was sent to the Land Commission by a man named Ahukai. Ahukai stated that when Kaʻeo was king of Kauai he gave the land division of Makaweli to his sister or to a female cousin. When Kaumualii reigned, he likewise granted the use of Makaweli to either his sister or a female cousin. After Kaumualii died [in 1826] and the revolt had been put down, Kalanimoku gave the land to Kahalaia, the short time governor of Kauai, who then gave Makaweli to Ahukai. But at the death of Kahalaia, Kalanimoku and Kaahumanu jointly gave Makaweli to Kinau, a daughter of Kamehameha I. Kinau became regent of the kingdom after the death of Kaahumanu [in 1832]. Before Kinau died she told Kekauluohi [the Kuhina Nui] or Kamehameha III that Makaweli belonged to Ahukai. The king sent Ahukai back to Kauai and the claimant stayed on the land unopposed until 1846 when Kekuanaoa, the husband of Kinau and father of Victoria Kamamalu, claimed the land. Ahukai closed his claim by stating, "When the day comes to work on it and you direct me to come, I will go, with the proper witnesses."

Ahukai's claim is unusual because it extends back to the days of Kaʻeo. Ahukai was obviously a resourceful, patient man. It appears he had been deported to another island (presumably after the rebellion), but had been allowed to return to Kauaʻi by no less authority than Kamehameha III. In the end Ahukai's claim was not granted. His documentation was good, but the competition he faced (from Victoria Kamamalu) was much too great.

17 *Ibid*. Book 19, p 416 Sale of RP 4476 to Elizabeth Sinclair. Date of Record 29 June 1865
18 *Ibid*, Kauaʻi Grantors Books 1845–1869 and 1870–1884
19 Whitney, S., 1833, 'Kauai Answers to Questions 1, 3 & 4' in circular dated Boston, Mass, 16 March 1833, sent by B. P Wisner, R. Anderson and David Greene, Secretaries to the missionaries of the American Board of Commissioners for Foreign Missions, Mission Houses Museum, Honolulu, unpubl. MS
20 As quoted in *Koamalu: The Story of the Pioneers on Kauai and What They Built on That Island Garden*, Damon, E. M., 1931, published privately, pp 274–275
21 Bingham, H. 1848 *A Residence of Twenty-One Years in the Sandwich Islands*, second edition, Sherman Converse, New York, pp 172–173. The ship *Tartar*, under the command of John Turner was notable in that it brought the frame for the Mission House in Honolulu, which still stands today. The vessel arrived in Kona where the mission was then headquartered on Christmas Day 1820. Freight on the frame was given free by the ship's owners and agents Messrs Bryant and Sturgis of Boston. The *Tartar* then made several trips to Canton with sandalwood, finally leaving the islands in May 1823. Captain John Turner, by all accounts a very pious man, died suddenly on the *Tartar* in Honolulu harbor, on 4 August 1822.
22 Whitney, S., 1840, 'Mission Station Report for Waimea, Kauai,' Mission Houses Museum, Honolulu, p 1. Note: This reference and all those from the Mission Reports that follow are taken from typed versions of the originals and have been included as typed.
23 Whitney, S., 1841, 'Mission Station Report for Waimea, Kauai,' Mission Houses Museum, Honolulu, p 2
24 Yzendoorn, R., 1927, *History of the Catholic Mission in the Hawaiian Islands*, Honolulu Star-Bulletin, p 177
25 Whitney, S., 1842, 'Mission Station Report for Waimea, Kauai,' Mission Houses Museum, Honolulu, p 1
26 Whitney, S., 1843, 'Mission Station Report for Waimea, Kauai,' Mission Houses Museum, Honolulu, p 2
27 Gilman, G., 1845, 'Rustications on Kauai and Niihau in the Summer of 1845,' Mission Houses Museum, Honolulu, unpublished MS, p 63
28 Anderson, R., 1864 *The Hawaiian Islands: Their Progress and Condition under Missionary Labors*, Gould and Lincoln, Boston, p 223
29 Rowell, G. B., 1851, 'Mission Station Report for Waimea, Kauai,' Mission Houses Museum, Honolulu, p 2
30 As quoted in Cook, E. E., 2003, *100 Years of Healing: The Legacy of a Missionary Doctor,* Halewai Publishing, Kōloa, Hawaii, p 49

31 Rowell, G. B., 1862, 'Mission Station Report for Waimea, Kauai,' Mission Houses Museum, Honolulu, p 1
32 Cook, E. E., 2003, p 65. This book gives an excellent account of 'The Rowell affair.'
33 Smith, J. W., 1866, 'Mission Station Report for Waimea, Kauai,' Mission Houses Museum, Honolulu, p 1
34 Ibid, p 1
35 Reports of Decisions Rendered by the Supreme Court of the Hawaiian Islands in Law, Equity, Admiralty and Probate 1866–1877, Honolulu: H. L Sheldon, pp 50–63
36 Daily Alta, California, San Francisco, 29 August 1866, Missionary Squabbles at the Sandwich Islands, p 6
37 American Board of Christian Foreign Missions, 1865 Annual Report, p 132
38 von Holt, I. E K., 1985, Stories of Long Ago: Niihau, Kauai, Oahu, Daughters of Hawaii, Honolulu, p 33
39 Smith, J. W., 1866, p 3
40 Kupahu, D. S., 1867, Church of Niihau Report, Mission Houses Museum, Honolulu, p 1. Note: This Niʻihau Report and those that follow are handwritten translations in English from the Hawaiian which have been executed for the Mission Houses Museum by Rev. Henry Judd, a Hawaiian scholar and grandson of missionary Gerrit P. Judd. They are reproduced here verbatim.
41 The Friend, 1 February 1868, p 9
42 Kupahu, D. S., 1868, Church of Niihau Report, Mission Houses Museum, Honolulu, pp 3–4
43 Kaukau, A., 1871, Church of Niihau Report, Mission Houses Museum, Honolulu, pp 2–3
44 Kaukau, A., 1872, Church of Niihau Report, Mission Houses Museum, Honolulu, pp 1–2
45 Hawaiian Gazette, 29 April 1874, Honolulu, Notes of the Week, p 3
46 Ibid, 6 May 1874, Honolulu, Notes of the Week, p 3
47 Rose, R.G. 1990 'Patterns of Protest: A Hawaiian Mat-Weaver's Response to 19th-Century Taxation and Change,' Bishop Museum Occasional Papers Vol. 30, pp 96–97
48 Pacific Commercial Advertiser, 2 May 1874, Royal Speech
49 Jason Achiu, Hawaiʻi State Archives 14 February 2019, personal communication
50 Jason Achiu, Hawaiʻi State Archives, 12 February 2019, personal communication
51 Lyttelton Times, 16 May 1866, p 2
52 freepages.genealogy.rootsweb.ancestry.com
53 Marlborough Press, 15 August 1866, p 2
54 See also the delightful story of the May 1864 visit of Valdemar Knudsen and the young William Brigham to Niʻihau in Appendix E.
55 von Holt, I. E. K., 1985, Stories of Long Ago: Niihau, Kauai, Oahu, Daughters of Hawaii, Honolulu, pp 46–59 and Nellist, G. F., 1925, 'The Story of Hawaii and its Builders,' Honolulu Star Bulletin, Territory of Hawaii, pp 143–144
56 von Holt, 1985, p 38
57 The Friend, Honolulu, 1 March 1867, p 17. Note: Ida von Holt writes that they were married 'in the little Hawaiian church on Niihau,' which is at variance with the statement in The Friend. (which also appeared in the New Zealand in the Lyttelton Times of 27 May 1867) The reception would certainly have been at The House, but the marriage ceremony itself could have been there or at the Puʻuwai church. As the two venues are two miles apart, and guests would have required carriages, perhaps having The House as the sole venue is more likely. It probably depended on how much the Niihauan community themselves were involved. The House was very new with little room for visitors so it would have been a small wedding.
58 Tabrah, R. M., 1987, Niʻihau: The Last Hawaiian Island, Press Pacifica, Kailua, Hawaii, p 107. Note: Ann bought the 6500-acre ahupuaʻa of Kōloa in 1872, presumably using her inheritance. (Source: Eric A. Knudsen Trust website)
59 Knudsen, V., 14 February 1867 letter to Frank Sinclair, Robinson family papers
60 von Holt, 1985, p 40
61 Ibid, pp 42–43
62 The Pacific Commercial Advertiser, 3 August 1867, p 1
63 The Friend, 1 April 1867, p 32
64 Ibid, 1 May 1867, p 37
65 Ibid, 1 October 1870, p 94
66 In Stories of Long Ago Ida von Holt writes that Lord and Lady Brassey visited Niʻihau, and this has been repeated by later writers. Lady Brassey's published journal makes it clear that they only visited Hilo and Honolulu in the course of their world cruise on the Sunbeam, which occurred in 1876 — after the Sinclairs had moved to Makaweli. The Brasseys could possibly have met a visiting Sinclair in Honolulu.
67 Bird, I. L., Letters to Henrietta, edited by Kay Chubbuck, Northeastern University Press, p 93
68 von Holt, I. E. K., 1985, Stories of Long Ago: Niihau, Kauai, Oahu, Daughters of Hawaii, Honolulu, p 77
69 Pacific Commercial Advertiser, 13 May 1871, p 3
70 Bird, I. L., 2002 Letters to Henrietta, edited by Kay Chubbuck, Northeastern University Press, pp 94–96. After her return from her travels Isabella Bird's modus operandi was to severely edit the letters she had written to her sister, eliminating many personal details and produce the sequence of letters together in book form. Her Hawaiian journey, Six Months in the Sandwich Islands, was first published in 1881 by John Murray, London. Many subsequent editions have followed.

71. *Ibid*, p 94
72. *Ibid*
73. *The Friend*, 1 November 1873, p 93
74. *The National Cyclopaedia of American Biography*, Vol. XI, 1909, James T. White & Co, pp 283–284. His name appears in the Boston University Law yearbook for 1874 and is listed with the Junior Class. He does not appear thereafter. Personal communication, email 16 February 2016, Boston University
75. *The Friend*, 3 August 1875, p 65
76. *Ibid*, 1 February 1879, p 13
77. findagrave.com
78. *McKenney's Hawaiian Directory*, 1884, L. M McKenney & Co, p 374
79. Bureau of Conveyances Grantees Book 189, pp 9–10 Deed for Sale of Ni'ihau from Francis Sinclair to Jane Gay, Helen Robinson and Aubrey Robinson, Instrument dated 31 January 1891
80. Bureau of Conveyances Grantees Book 195, pp 37–38 Deed of Agreement for Annual Payment to Francis Sinclair, Instrument dated 2 February 1891
81. Bureau of Conveyances Grantees Book 136, p 461 Deed of Agreement for Gift of Lands etc from Eliza Sinclair to Jane Gay and Helen Robinson, Instrument dated 3 March 1891
82. *Ballads and Poems from the Pacific* (1899), *Where the Sun Sets: Memories from Other Years and Places* (1905), *Under North Star and Southern Cross* (1907), *From the Four Winds* (1909), *Under Western Skies: Life Pictures from Memory* (1911). All were published by Sampson Low, Marston & Co, London, who also published his wife Isabella's *Indigenous Flowers of the Hawaiian Islands*. Apart from his first book the others are all in short story format, four to seven to a book, recounting, somewhat fancifully, true stories of adventure that he had been told.
83. *Honolulu Star Bulletin*, 8 September 1916, p 4
84. Hawaiian State Archives, Bush Correspondence, 16 March 1883, Int. Dept. Bk 22, p 227

Chapter Nine:
Aubrey Robinson takes the reins

1. Bird, I., 2003, *Letters to Henrietta* (edited by Kay Chubbuck), Northeastern University Press, Boston, p 95
2. In 1902 Alice Robinson was admitted to the partnership. After the deaths of Helen Robinson and Jane Gay they were both formally excluded in 1916. In 1917 Sinclair Robinson and Aylmer Robinson were admitted, and so on. See *The Garden Island*, 17 October 1916 and 6 March 1917.
3. Bureau of Conveyances Grantees Book 134, pp 176–177 Deed of Lease Transfer from Eliza Sinclair to Gay and Robinson, recorded 3 August 1891
4. Bureau of Conveyances Grantees Book 250, pp 117–118 Deed, Francis Gay Withdrawal from Gay and Robinson with respect to Ni'ihau.
5. Bureau of Conveyances Grantees Book 234, p 108
6. Bureau of Conveyances Grantees Book 253, p 345
7. *The Hawaiian Star*, 2 February 1904, p 1
8. *The Pacific Commercial Advertiser*, Honolulu, 8 June 1885, p 3
9. Letter from Aubrey Robinson in Boston to Alice Gay on Ni'ihau, dated 23 January 1875, Robinson family letters. A month earlier, King Kalākaua had been the guest of honor at the White House at the first dinner given to a ruling Hawaiian monarch by a United States president (Ulysses S. Grant).
10. Henke, L. A., 1929, *A Survey of Livestock in Hawaii*, University of Hawai'i Research Publication No. 5, p 6
11. Judd, C. S., 1932, *The Hawaiian Forester and Agriculturist*, Vol. 29, Jan–Mar, p 8
12. Munro, G. C., 2007 *The Story of Lāna'i*, Privately printed, Honolulu, p 134–135
13. Forbes, C. N., 1913, 'An Enumeration of Niihau Plants,' Bishop Museum Occasional Papers, Vol. 5, No. 3, p 22
14. Tabrah, R. M., 1987, *Ni'ihau: The Last Hawaiian Island*, Press Pacifica, Kailua, pp 121–122
15. Judd, 1932, p 8
16. Extract from letter of 2 March 1910 from Sinclair Robinson at Harvard to Aubrey Robinson at Makaweli, Robinson family papers
17. Extract from letter of 8 August 1898 from Frank Sinclair in Stockholm to Jane Gay at Makaweli, Robinson family papers
18. Extract from letter of 12 June 1918 from Selwyn Robinson on Ni'ihau to Aubrey Robinson at Makaweli, Robinson family papers
19. Judd, 1932, p 6
20. Wichman, J. R & St John, H., 1990, *A Chronicle and Flora of Niihau*, National Tropical Botanical Garden, Kaua'i, p 129
21. letter of 7 July 1897 from George Gay at Coronado to Aubrey Robinson at Makaweli, Robinson family papers
22. Letter of 29 December 1899 from Frank Sinclair in Berkeley to Aubrey Robinson at Makaweli, Robinson family papers
23. Stearns, H. T., 1947, 'Geology and Ground-water Resources of the Island of Niihau, Hawaii,' *Bulletin* 12, Hawaii Division of Hydrography, pp 34–35
24. Extract from letter of 10 September 1886 from the Hawaiian Legation in London to Aubrey Robinson at Makaweli, Robinson family papers
25. Summarized from Knudsen, E., 1946, 'The Wreck of the Thunderer' in *Teller of Hawaiian Tales*, Mutual Publishing, Honolulu, p 157, and the *Hawaiian Gazette*, 14 February 1888, p 5

26 *The Daily Bulletin*, Honolulu, 9 November 1889, p 3
27 *Who Was Who*, 2007, Watson, Sir William Renny, Oxford University Press, online edition, www.ukwhoswho.com
28 Wilcox, C., 1996, *Sugar Water: Hawai'i's Plantation Ditches*, University of Hawai'i Press, p 89
29 Conter, F.E., 1903, 'The Cultivation of Sisal in Hawaii, Hawaii Agricultural Experiment,' *Station Bulletin*, No. 4, US Department of Agriculture, Honolulu
30 Letter from Francis Gay in Honolulu to Aubrey Robinson at Makaweli, 25 April 1907, Robinson family papers
31 Letters from Aylmer Robinson at Harvard to Aubrey Robinson at Makaweli January 26, 17 February, 16 March 1910, Robinson family papers
32 Munroe, G.C., 2007 *The Story of Lāna'i*, Privately Printed, Honolulu, p 24
33 *The Pacific Commercial Advertiser*, Honolulu, 21 October 1892, p 3
34 Gay, L.K., 1981, *Tales of the Forbidden Island of Ni'ihau*, Topgallant Publishing, Honolulu, p 17
35 Stepien, E., 1988, Ni'ihau: A Brief History, Working Paper Series, Center for Pacific Island Studies, University of Hawai'i at Mānoa, p 47
36 Wichman, J.R & St John, H., 1990, *A Chronicle and Flora of Niihau*, National Tropical Botanical Garden, Kaua'i, p 30
37 *The Garden Island*, Līhu'e, Kaua'i, 19 December 1916, The Story of Piilani, p 6
38 Larsen, L.D., 1942, letters to his wife Katherine, Hawaiian State Archives, Ni'ihau, Stacks 919.6942, L3n, p 31
39 Letter from Francis Gay in Honolulu to Jane Gay at Makaweli, 21 November 1887, Robinson family papers
40 *The Hawaiian Star*, 18 April 1896, 'Quietly Married,' p 3
41 Ernest (as he was known) had a distinguished career on the stage in New York. He retired to Maui and was buried there. See obituary in the *Honolulu Star Bulletin* for 4 January 1984
42 Munro, G.C., 2007, *The Story of Lāna'i*, Privately printed, Honolulu, p 24
43 Extracts from letter of 20 December 1909 from Alice Robinson to Jane Gay, Robinson family papers
44 Extract from letter of 23 December 1909 from Aylmer Robinson to Aubrey Robinson, Robinson family papers
45 Alice Robinson to Jane Gay, letter 27 December 1909 to 1 January 1910, Robinson family papers
46 Burtner, J.M., 2019, *Robinson Family Governess: Letters from Kaua'i and Ni'ihau 1911–1913*, Publication Consultants, Anchorage, Alaska, pp 141–148. Hettie Belle Matthew's letters authored during the time she spent as tutor to Aubrey and Alice Robinson's two youngest children have recently been published by Judy Burtner, Hettie Belle's granddaughter. I am deeply indebted to Judy for permission to include these extracts from her book.

47 *Ibid*, p 147
48 Alice Robinson's diaries for the years 1906–7 and 1911–15 are held by the Robinson family in their collection
49 *The Paradise of the Pacific*, Honolulu, Apr 1893, Vol. 6, No. 4, p 51, published monthly Frank Godfrey Managing Editor, founded Jan 1888 with the tagline 'Devoted to the Interests of the Hawaiian Islands.' In 1966 it became *Honolulu Magazine*.
50 Letter from Sinclair Robinson at Makaweli to Aubrey Robinson in Boston, 1 November 1913, Robinson family letters
51 'Employment Agreement between Aubrey Robinson as owner of Niihau Island and Aylmer Robinson as manager of Niihau Ranch.' Unsigned draft dated 1918, with some pencil additions, Robinson family papers
52 Letter of 23 March 1918 from Senator Shafroth, chairman of the United States Senate Committee on Pacific Islands and Puerto Rico, Washington to Aubrey Robinson at Makaweli, Robinson family papers
53 *Hawaiian Gazette*, 31 May 1918, 'Selwyn Robinson Must Remain in Fighting Class,' p 8
54 Letter of 7 September 1924, from Alice Robinson in London to Aubrey Robinson at Makaweli wherein Alice writes "in your last letter you said you had arranged for a steamer to go to Niihau at the end of August for the wool", Robinson family letters
55 As an aside, in 1924 Francis Gay withdrew from the Gay & Robinson partnership, the consideration being $150,000 paid by Aubrey Robinson; see Bureau of Conveyances Book 748, pp 154–155. This did not affect the ownership of Ni'ihau from which he had already withdrawn in 1902.
56 Stepien, E., 1988, 'Ni'ihau: A Brief History,' Working Paper Series, Center for Pacific Island Studies, University of Hawai'i at Mānoa, p 49
57 *Honolulu Star Bulletin*, 8 July 1936, 'Aubrey Robinson, of Niihau, Dies,' p 1
58 *Honolulu Advertiser*, 19 June 1943, 'Once Isolated Niihau Greets Army: Joins Nation's War Effort,' p 6
59 Daws, G. & Head, T., 1963, 'Niihau: A Shoal of Time,' *The American Heritage*, Vol. 14, Issue 6, October 1963, p 2
60 Wichman, J.R & St John, H., 1990, *A Chronicle and Flora of Niihau*, National Tropical Botanical Garden, Kaua'i, p 34
61 Bureau of Conveyances Grantees Book 1370, pp 229–242. Agreement dated 11 March 1937 between Alice Robinson and her Five Children regarding the execution of certain elements of the will of her husband Aubrey Robinson.
62 Bureau of Conveyances Grantees Book 1370, pp 240–241 Agreement of Management of the Island of Niihau between Aubrey Robinson and Aylmer Robinson. This is the successor document to the 1918 draft agreement mentioned earlier which is in the Robinson family papers.

63 Robinson, A. F., 26 May 1963, letter to Florence Boyer, Hawaii State Archives, Eleanor B. Waldo Collection, U-126, p 4 Florence Boyer was a tutor for Aubrey and Alice Robinson's children

Chapter Ten: Aylmer's stewardship

1 Judd, C. S., 1932, *The Hawaiian Forester and Agriculturalist*, Vol. 29, Jan–Mar, p 6
2 *Ibid*
3 *Ibid*, pp 6–7
4 *Ibid*, p 7
5 Roddy, K. M. & Arita-Tutsumi, L., 2008, *A History of Honey Bees in the Hawaiian Islands*, p 4
6 Larsen, L. D., 1942, 'Letters to his Wife Katharine,' unpublished manuscript, Hawaiian State Archives, Niʻihau Stacks, 919.6942 L3n, p 8
7 Roddy & Arita-Tutsumi, 2008, p 4
8 Oda, C. S & Mau, R. F. L., 1974, Description and Life Cycle of the Monkeypod-Kiawe Caterpillar Melipotis indomita Walker, Hawaii Agricultural Experiment Station Journal Series No. 1596, p 1
9 *Honolulu Star Bulletin*, 16 November 1957, 'They're Happy on Niihau,' p 14
10 Tabrah, R. M., 1987, *Niʻihau: The Last Hawaiian Island*, Press Pacifica, Kailua, p 213
11 Testimony of Bruce Robinson Before the Senate Committee on Water and Land, 14 February 2014, in Consideration of Senate Bill 180, SD1 Relating to Ocean Management, p 1
12 Ke Au Okoa, September 1871, reprinted in translation in *The Garden Island*, 26 January 2020
13 Wichman, J. R & St John, H., 1990, *A Chronicle and Flora of Niihau*, National Tropical Botanical Garden, p 114
14 Rodman, J. S., 1979, *The Kahuna Sorcerers of Hawaii, Past and Present*, Exposition Press, Smithtown, New York pp 249–255
15 Tava, R. & Keale, M. K., 1984, *Niihau: The Traditions of an Hawaiian Island*, Mutual Publishing, Honolulu, pp 14–15
16 Tutu Kaui, who died in 1988, was the main source for many of the stories told in Tava and Keale's book. See Preface, p xii
17 Kolb, R. K., 1991, 'Gunboat Diplomacy on the Yangtse', *VFW Magazine*, April
18 Jones, S., 2014, *Before and Beyond the Niihau Zero*, Signum Ops, Florida, p 16
19 *Ibid*, pp 83–119
20 Jones, S., 2014. *Before and Beyond the Niihau Zero*, Signum Ops, Florida 32952. Paul, C., 2006, *East Wind, Rain*, HarperCollins Publishers, New York. Beekman, A., 1982, *The Niihau Incident*, Heritage Press of Pacific, Honolulu.

21 *Honolulu Star Advertiser*, 12 May 2017, 'Casting of Non Hawaiian in Niʻihau Movie Upsets Some' (Note: This decision was subsequently reversed)
22 Jones, 2014, p 59 and pp 75–82
23 Stepien, E. R., 1988, 'Niʻihau: A Brief History,' Center for Pacific Island Studies University of Hawaiʻi at Mānoa, unpublished master's thesis, pp 58–61
24 Larsen, L. D., 1942, 'Letters to his Wife Katharine,' unpublished manuscript, Hawaiian State Archives, Niʻihau, Stacks 919.6942, L3n, pp 8–9
25 Gilman, L., *Honolulu Advertiser*, 19 June 1943, 'Once Isolated Niihau Greets Army,' p 1, p 6
26 'The Coast Guard at War 1946,' Vol. IV, in 'LORAN,' Vol. II, Historical Section, US Coast Guard Headquarters, pp 59–64
27 May, E. R., *Honolulu Advertiser*, 4 August 1946, 'Niihau Called Alcatraz by Military Garrison,' p 1
28 Stepien, E. R., 1988, *Niʻihau: A Brief History*, Center for Pacific Island Studies University of Hawaiʻi at Mānoa, unpublished master's thesis, pp 58–61
29 State of Hawaiʻi, 1947, *Senate Journal*, p 248.
30 *Honolulu Star Bulletin*, 31 July 1946, 'Isolation of Niihau is Blasted,' pp 1–2
31 May, E., 1 August 1946, *Honolulu Advertiser*, 'Niihau facing Inroads of Modern Living Trends,' p 1, p 7
32 Territory of Hawaiʻi, Senate Journal 1947, p pp 248–49
33 *Ibid*, p 249
34 The full text of Aylmer's letter ex *Senate Journal* 1948:631–634 is given in E. R. Stepien, 1988, *Niʻihau: A Brief History*, Center for Pacific Island Studies University of Hawaiʻi at Mānoa, unpublished master's thesis, Appendix C, pp 211–20
35 *Honolulu Advertiser*, 25 April 1947, 'Senate to Act on Niihau Land Seizure Bill,' p 3
36 Tabrah, R. M., 1987, *Niʻihau: The Last Hawaiian Island*, Press Pacifica, Kailua, p 169
37 *Honolulu Star Bulletin*, 3 June 1947, 'Rep. Hayes Says People of Niihau Seem Happy, Contented and Informed,' p 3
38 *Honolulu Advertiser*, 11 August 1946, A Suggestion from George Mellen, p 32
39 *Honolulu Advertiser*, 17 December 1955, 'Territory Stakes Claim to 15 Acres on Niihau,' p 1
40 *Star Bulletin*, 4 November 1959, 'State's Niihau Land Rights Vague,' p 1A; 28 January 1960, 'Ruling May Say State Owns Church, School Sites on Niihau,' p 19; 31 March 1961, 'Action Looms on Niihau School Sites,' p 15
41 *Ibid*, 2 October 1961, 'Quinn Favors Negotiating for Niihau School Sites,' p 1B
42 *Ibid*, 28 September 1957, 'Aloof Niihau is Private Bali H'ai,' p 1

43 *Ibid*, 16 November 1957, They're Happy on Niihau, p 15
44 *Ibid*, p 15
45 *Ibid*
46 *Ibid*
47 *Sunday Advertiser*, 11 October 1959, 'Curtain Parts on Amazing Niihau,' p A26
48 *Ibid*
49 *Sunday Advertiser* 25 October 1959, 'Spy on Niihau? No, Just Sound of Harpe,' pp 1, A2
50 *Sunday Star Bulletin*, 1 November 1959, 'Niihau: A *Star Bulletin* Reporter Visits the "Forbidden Isle",' p 6
51 *Ibid*, pp 6–7
52 *Honolulu Advertiser,* 30 June 1959, Niihau Rejects Statehood by 70 to 18 Vote, p 1
53 *Star Bulletin*, 26 June 1964, 'Sinclair Robinson Dies,' p 1A
54 *Ibid*, 30 September 1961, '20th Century Problems Hit 19th Century Niihau,' p 1
55 *Honolulu Advertiser*, 2 October 1961, 'Nature's Blows Bring Hardship to Niihau,' p. A4
56 For the detail see Edward Stepien's 1988 University of Hawai'i master's thesis, 'Ni'ihau: A Brief History,' Chapter X and Ruth Tabrah's 1987 book, *Ni'ihau: The Last Hawaiian Island*, Chapter XIX
57 *Star Bulletin*, 1 October 1961, '"New" Niihau Stories Eclipse "Old" Ones,' p 6
58 *Honolulu Advertiser*, 1 October 1961, 'Frontier Days Still Live among Niihau Dust,' p. A1A
59 *Honolulu Advertiser*, 30 September 1961, '250 Fight Relentless Nature for Friendly Niihau Dream,' p A 4
60 Robinson, A. F., 26 May 1963, letter to Florence Boyer, Hawaii State Archives, Eleanor B. Waldo Collection, U-126, pp 6–7
61 Robinson, A. F., 31 December 1948, letter to Gwenfread Allen, Kaua'i Historical Society, Ni'ihau files, p 1
62 *Honolulu Advertiser*, 8 October 1965, 'This "Attack" on Niihau is Different,' p. A6
63 Tabrah, R. M., 1987, *Ni'ihau: The Last Hawaiian Island*, Press Pacifica, Kailua, p 196
64 *Ibid*, p 196
65 There appears to be confusion here. Aylmer left a provision in his will for deficits to be covered during the time of probate (See *Star Bulletin*, 24 April 1968, Estate Appraisal Gives Unusual Peek at Niihau, p A7) while Ruth Tabrah, p 206, indicates the arrangement was permanent. The former is more likely to be correct. As of late 2018 Almer's will was still in probate.
66 *Honolulu Advertiser*, 11 January 1968, 'Niihau Exodus is Denied,' p 1. It was true though that volunteers were being recruited on Ni'ihau to work on Makaweli canefields during harvest time to reduce losses on Ni'ihau.
67 Bureau of Conveyances, 11 July 1969, Book 6592, pp 269–271
68 *Honolulu Advertiser*, 5 November 1969, 'Wife Inherits Niihau Control,' p 36
69 Larsen, L. D., 1942, 'Letters to his Wife Katharine,' Hawaiian State Archives, Niihau, Stacks 919.6942, L3n, p 11

Chapter Eleven: An enduring culture

1 Governor's Message No. 135 to the Legislature, *Journal of the Senate* 1971, p 128. The letter, originally over three pages, has been reproduced in full on two pages. A typo ('Graves,' not 'Graces') has been corrected.
2 House Bill 1678-70, *Journal of the House,* 1971, p 138. Senate Bill 1516-70, *Journal of the Senate,* 1971, p 129
3 *Honolulu Star Bulletin*, 24 March 1970, 'Burns Urges Quick State Action to Acquire Niihau,' pp 1 & 4
4 Tabrah, R. M., 1987, *Ni'ihau: The Last Hawaiian Island*, Press Pacifica, Kailua, p 209
5 *Honolulu Star Bulletin*, 28 February 1970, 'Niihauans Plead "No Change",' p 1. *Honolulu Advertiser*, 1 March 1970, 'Niihauans Plead for Status Quo,' p 5
6 *Honolulu Advertiser*, 4 March 1970, 'Plans to Sell Niihau Denied,' p 6
7 *Honolulu Star Bulletin*, 3 March 1970, 'Robinson Family Says Niihau Not for Sale to Anyone,' p 1
8 *Honolulu Advertiser*, 24 March 1970, 'Niihau Option not Purchase,' p 7
9 *The Garden Island,* 25 March 1970, 'Burns Pushes for Niihau Purchase,' p 1
10 *Honolulu Star Bulletin*, 26 March 1970, 'Niihauans Ask Burns to Halt Takeover,' p 2
11 *Honolulu Star Bulletin*, 1 April 1970, 'Lawmakers Want Niihau; How, When Questioned,' pp A2 & A14
12 Senate Standing Committee Report No. 513-70, 7 April 1970. The scientists cited were Dr Allison Kay (Malacologist), Dr Harold St John (Botanist), and Dr Charles Lamoureux (Botanist).
13 *Journal of the Hawai'i State Senate*, 1971, pp 456–7 (reproduced in Stepien's thesis)
14 *Honolulu Advertiser*, 17 April 1970, 'Official Assails Foes of Niihau Purchase,' p 10
15 *Honolulu Star Bulletin*, 23 November 1972, 'State is Asked to Purchase Niihau,' p. A22
16 Much of this section has been drawn from Edward Stepien's unpublished 1988 master's thesis, Stepien, E. R., 1988, 'Ni'ihau: A Brief History,' Center for Pacific Island Studies, University of Hawai'i at Mānoa, pp 120–132
17 *Honolulu Advertiser*, 31 July 1975, 'Niihau Not Top Concern of State,' p. A12

18 Kresnak, W., 21 December 1985, 'Governor Visits Forbidden Island,' United Press International
19 *Honolulu Star Bulletin*, 31 March 1961, 'Action Looms on Niihau School Sites,' p 15
20 Supreme Court of the State of Hawaii, No. 26997, Appeal from the Fifth Circuit Court, 24 October 2006, pp 29–30
21 *Honolulu Advertiser*, 27 June 1969, 'Fight Expected as State Moves to Zone Niihau,' p 1
22 *Honolulu Advertiser*, 29 October 1988, Trespassing?, pp 1 & 4
23 *Honolulu Star Bulletin*, 14 July 1997, Privileged Few View by Invitation only, p 5
24 National Oceanic and Atmospheric Administration 21 August 2015, 'Endangered and Threatened Species: Final Rulemaking to Revise Critical Habitat for Hawaiian Monk Seals.
25 *Honolulu Star Bulletin*, 8 May 2003, 'Outsiders are Overfishing in Niihau Waters,' p 4
26 *The Garden Island*, 10 October 2013, 'Niihau Protection Proposal on Pause,' pp 2–3
27 *Christian Science Monitor*, 28 January 2016, 'Why did Feds Scale Back the Whale Sanctuary in Hawaii,' pp 1–2
28 *Hawaii News Now*, 27 November 2013, 'Ni'ihau Residents Plead with Lawmakers for "No Fishing" Zone,' p 1
29 *The Hawaii Independent*, 27 November 2013, 'Hawai'i's Over-fishing Problems Reach Ni'ihau, Endanger its Community,' p 2
30 *The Garden Island*, 30 January 2014, 'Niihau Bills Go Belly Up,' pp 1–2
31 *Honolulu Star Advertiser* 30 March 2014, Protecting the 'Last Hawaiian Island,' pp E1, E4–E5
32 A second bill establishing Ni'ihau as a separate county, SB 172, was also introduced, but it appears both bills were discussed together in the committees. Likewise there was a second bill on 'opihi gathering (SB 2124) with submissions heard on 3 February 2014. The pairs of bills were quite similar.
33 *The Garden Island*, 18 February 2014, 'No Surfing Near Niihau?,' pp 2–3
34 *Ibid*, 9 February 2014, 'Keeping the Islands One,' pp 2–4
35 Keith Robinson, personal communication, 26 August 2014
36 www.themilitarystandard.com/navy_base/hi/barking_sands.php
37 Tabrah, R., 1987, *Ni'ihau: The Last Hawaiian Island*, Press Pacifica, Kailua, pp 212–213
38 Pacific Missile Range Facility: Enhanced Capability: Final Environmental Impact Statement December 1998, Attachment H, Niihau Island Ongoing Activities, p 1
39 *Ibid*, 1998, Appendix G, 'Terms and Conditions for Use of Niihau Island Facilities and Helicopter Services (Protocol),' pp 1–4
40 *Honolulu Star Bulletin*, 14 July 1997, 'Island at the Crossroads: On the Cusp,' pp 3–4
41 *Honolulu Advertiser*, 17 June 1997, 'Owners may Sell Niihau: Navy's Role Critical to Robinsons Plan,' pp 1 & 8
42 *Honolulu Star Bulletin* 14 May 1999 'Ni'ihau Opening Up,' p 4
43 Keith Robinson, personal communication, 21 December 2016
44 *Honolulu Advertiser,* 26 March 1987, 'OHA Joins in Support of Helicopter Tours to Niihau,' p 3 and 29 January 1987, 'Niihau Discovers the Forbidden in Isles,' p 1
45 niihau.us/heli.html
46 niihau.us/safaris.html
47 *Honolulu Advertiser,* 22 December 1985, 'Niihau: Charcoal, Sheep, Aid Economic Outlook,' pp 1 & 4
48 *Honolulu Advertiser*, 28 June 1984, 'Drought: Dry Lakes, Dusty Trails, Graying Grass on Parched Niihau,' p 48
49 Ishimatsu Shintani, the long-time beekeeper, had retired in Aylmer's time and died at Makaweli in 1970. See Appendix C for the part he played in 'The Battle of Ni'ihau'
50 *Honolulu Advertiser*, 20 December 1985, 'It's Aloha, Governor, on Niihau,' p 4
51 *Honolulu Star Bulletin*, 27 November 1982, 'Niihau Owners Won't Permit Damage Assessment,' p 1
52 *Honolulu Star Bulletin,* Features: Story 2, 14 July 1997, 'Niihau: Island at a Crossroad, On the Cusp,' p 4
53 *Honolulu Star Bulletin,* 14 May 1999, 'Niihau: Opening Up,' p 2
54 makawelimeatcompany.com
55 islandconservation.org/lehua-island-hawaii
56 Meyer, P. A., 1998, *Niihau: Present Circumstances and Future Requirements in an Evolving Hawaiian Community*, Hoomana Ia Iesu Church, Inc, Niihau, Hawaii
57 *Ibid*, p 137
58 Judd, H. P., 1943, *A Week on Niihau: Paradise of the Pacific*, December, p 10 (as quoted by Philip Meyer)
59 Meyer, P. A., 1998, p 141
60 Ke Kula Niihau O Kekaha and Kula Aupuni Niihau A Kahelelani Aloha
61 Tava, R. & Keale, M. K. Sr., 1984, *Niihau: The Traditions of an Hawaiian Island*, Mutual Publishing, Honolulu
62 For further information on Ni'ihau shell lei see Linda Paik Moriarty's two excellent books *Niihau Shell Leis* (1986), University of Hawai'i Press, and *Pūpū 'o Ni'ihau: Shell Leis of Ni'ihau* (2001), Honolulu Academy of Arts
63 *The Garden Island*, 28 November 2018, 'Memo Supporting Niihau Language Signed

APPENDICES

B: The Niihauan dialect: Past and present

1. Zimmermann, Heinrich, 1781, *Account of the Third Voyage of Captain Cook 1776–1780*. Translated by L. Tewsley of the Alexander Turnbull Library, Wellington, New Zealand and published as Bulletin No. 2 1926, p 27
2. Beaglehole, J. C., 1967, *The Journals of Captain Cook on the Resolution and Discovery Expedition 1776–1780*, Cambridge University Press, Vol. 3, Pt. 2, pp 1230–1
3. Ibid, p 1223
4. Fornander, A., 1880, *An Account of the Polynesian Race*, Trubner & Co, London, Vol. II, p 59
5. Tava, R. & Keale, M. K. Snr., 1984, *Niihau: The Traditions of an Hawaiian Island*, Mutual Publishing, Honolulu, p 15
6. Anonymous author, 1825, in Preface to *A Journal of a Tour Around Hawaii, the Largest of the Sandwich Islands* by William Ellis, Crocker & Brewster, New York, p IV
7. 'Minutes of General Meeting of the Mission May 16 – June 20 1825,' Mission Houses Museum Archives, Honolulu, pp 18–22
8. In Rev. Henry Hodges Parker's 1922 revision of Lorrin Andrew's 1865 *Dictionary of the Hawaiian Language*.
9. Schutz, A. J., 1994, *The Voices of Eden: A History of Hawaiian Language Studies*, University of Hawai'i Press, Honolulu, p 146
10. The invaluable assistance of Hōkūlani Cleeland is gratefully acknowledged in the preparation of the latter part of this section.
11. St John, H., 1982, 'Vernacular Plant Names Used on Ni'ihau Island,' Bishop Museum Occasional Papers Vol. 25/3, p 10
12. Dr William (Pila) Wilson, 12 October 2016 Pers. Comm.
13. Daws, G. & Head, T., 1963, 'Niihau: A Shoal of Time,' *American Heritage*, Vol. 14, Issue 6, p 7

C: The Battle of Ni'ihau

1. Hawaiian State Archives, Niihau, L D Larsen, Stacks 919.6942, L3n, pp 14–24. The original letters have been typed up by David Larsen's then secretary, Miss Flannigan, but are not in electronic form. They have been transcribed here, word for word, with the only changes being some additional paragraph breaks to make the account more readable. In 2009 the letters were included in a book called *Voices from the Past: Katharine and David Larsen*, edited and compiled by Donivee Laird, their granddaughter.

D: Ni'ihau population numbers

1. Kumu Hawaii, 23 December 1835, see nupepa-hawaii.com
2. US Census Bureau, via Hawai'i State Archives
3. KaNupepa Kuokoa, Buke III, Helu 24, Aoao 4, 11 June 1864. See nupepa-hawaii.com. It is noted in the article that there were three Protestant churches and one Catholic church on the island
4. Noyes, M. H., May, 1993, Oneehow, *Honolulu Magazine*

E: Botanical exploration on Ni'ihau

1. David Samuel's Journal, in Beaglehole, J. C., ed. *The Journals of Captain James Cook*, 1967, Vol. 3 Parts 1 and 2 'The Voyage of the Resolution and Discovery 1776–1778,' University of Cambridge Press, p 1231
2. St John, H., 1979, The Botany of Niihau Island as seen on Captain Cook's Voyage 1778–1779, *Pacific Science*, Vol. 13, no 4, p 327
3. Not Cook's vessel, but a new *Discovery* launched in 1789.
4. His companion was Thomas Manley, the master's mate
5. In this context, unable to produce, i.e. sterile
6. Menzies, A., 1792, as reproduced in *Hawaii Nei 128 Years Ago*, edited by W. F Wilson and published in 1920, pp 40–41
7. Wichman, J. R. & St John, H., 1990, *A Chronicle and Flora of Niihau*, National Tropical Botanical Garden, p 39
8. Beechey, F. W., 1831, *Narrative of a Voyage to the Pacific and Beering's Strait*, New York, Da Capo Press, 1968, p 320
9. Hooker, W. J., Arnott, G. A. W., Beechey, F. W., 1841, *The Botany of Captain Beechey's Voyage: comprising an account of the plants collected by Messrs Lay and Collie and other officials of the expedition, during the voyage to the Pacific and Bering's Strait performed in His Majesty's ship Blossom under the command of Captain F W Beechey in the years 1825, 26, 27, 28*, H. G Bohn, London, pp 78–111
10. Rémy, J., 1892, *Ascension de MM. Brenchley et Rémy au Maunaloa Polynesie. Extrait du Journal de M. Jules Rémy*, Chalons-sur-Marne: Martin Freres (translated by Molly Summers and published in English in the *Hawaiian Journal of History*, Vol. 22, 1988)
11. Wichman & St John, 1990, p 39. Asa Gray at Harvard was the pre-eminent American botanist of his day. Originally selected for the United States Exploring Expedition of 1838–42, he resigned before it left, but ended up coordinating the reporting on the thousands of plant specimens collected due to the inadequacy of his replacement, William Rich. The expedition did not visit Ni'ihau so is irrelevant to this account.
12. Mann's thesis was subsequently published in 1867 by Welch, Bigelow & Co, Cambridge as *Enumeration of Hawaiian Plants*. The study lists 667 vascular plants, but does not include the approximately 50 grasses. Unfortunately no account is given regarding the islands on which the individual species occur (or were collected). Horace Mann died in 1868 at the age of 24.

13 St John, H., April 1954, 'Review of Mrs. Sinclair's "Indigenous Flowers of the Hawaiian Islands",' *Hawaiian Plant Studies* 23, Pacific Science, Vol. VIII, p 145.

14 Sinclair, I. McH, 1885, *Indigenous Flowers of the Hawaiian Islands*, Sampson Low, Marston, Searle & Rivington, London, Introduction

15 Forbes, C. N., 1913, 'An Enumeration of Niihau Plants,' Bishop Museum, *Occasional Papers*, Vol. 5(3), pp 17–26

16 *Schiedea amplexicaulis* is now regarded as extinct by St John, while the Euphorbia is found on the other islands and is now known as *Euphorbia celastroides var.stokesii*.

17 St John, H, 1931, 'Additions to the Flora of Niihau,' Bishop Museum, *Occasional Papers* 9(14) pp 1–11

18 St John, H., 1959, 'Botanical Novelties on the island of Niihau, Hawaiian Islands,' *Hawaiian Plant Studies* 25, Pacific Science 13(2), pp 156–190

19 Wichman & St John, 1990, pp 37–157

HAWAIIAN WORDS IN THE TEXT

(*Note: terms that are defined in their context are not included in this glossary*)

ahupuaʻa	land district
aliʻi	high chief, monarch
aliʻi ʻai moku	chief who rules a district
aliʻi nui	high chief
ao	light, daylight
ʻaumakua	personal god, benevolent guardian spirit
hala	pandanus tree
hale	house
hale pili	house thatched with pili grass
hale nui	big house
haole	foreign(er)
heiau	shrine
hōʻiʻo	a Hawaiian fern
hula kiʻi	dance with marionettes
ʻiore	Polynesian rat
kahakō	a macron over a vowel to lengthen and strengthen it
kahuna	priest
kālaimoku	prime minister, high official
kapa	cloth made from the bark of the paper mulberry tree (= tapa)
kapu	taboo, prohibition
kauwā	slave, servant
keiki	child/children
kiawe	algaroba tree, *Prosopis pallida*
kona	westerly (leeward) side of island or wind from that direction
konohiki	headman of an ahupuaʻa or land district; (rights) land or fishing rights under his control
kualā	dorsal fin
kuhina nui	premier, regent, highest office next to monarch
kukui	candlenut tree
kuleana	small piece of property within an ahupuaʻa
kūpeʻe	sea snail
lūʻau	a party or feast, especially accompanied by entertainment
mahimahi	a fish, dorado
makaʻāinana	the people of the land, commoners
makaloa	the sedge *Cyperus laevigatus*
maluhia	tranquility, serenity
ʻohana	family, kin group
ʻokina	glottal stop
ʻōlulu	shrub, 'cabbage on a stick'
pali	cliff
paniolo	cowboy(s)
pāpipi	cactus
pāpio	fish, trevalli
pō	night, darkness
poi	a Polynesian staple food, made from taro
pueo	short-eared owl
puʻuhonua	place of refuge
uhi	yam
ʻuala/uwala	sweet potato
wā	epoch
wāhane	palm, *Pritchardia aylmer-robinsonii*
wili	twist(ed)

INDEX

(*passim* = to be found at various places between the pages indicated)

A

Abbenooe *see* 'Ōpūnui
ahupua'a 46, 52, 178, 192, 202, 205, 227, 287
Aila, William 289
albatross, Laysan 27
alcohol prohibition 245, 248, 260, 272, 275, 294, 308
algaroba *see* kiawe
ammunition *see* arms
Ancey, César 29-30
Andersen, Johannes 155
Anderson, J Michael 253, 287, 289, 296, 300
Anderson, Rufus 196-97, 202
Anderson, William 58, 66
antelopes 13, 299-300
aoudad 297
Arabian steeds *see* horses
Arago, Jacques 117
Arakaki, Alan 306
Ariyoshi, George 286, 298
Armitage, Kimo 279
arms trading 67, 71, 82-83, 85-86, 89, 98, 100-2, 105-6, 114, 130, 139, 317, 337 *see also* firearms
Arney, George 182
Aviguetero, Ashlee 309
Aylmer: Lucy 158; William 154

B

Bachelet, Alexis 221
Baker, Charles 306-7, 311-12, 314
Baker, James 92-93, 103, 316
Baldwin, Henry P 227
Baranov, Alexandr 114
barbary sheep *see* sheep
Barking Sands 263, 292-93, 295
Battle of Ni'ihau, the 257, 327-32
Beaglehole, John Cawte 60, 63, 71
Bealey, Samuel 183
Beals, William 194
Beckwith, Martha 35-37
Beechey, Frederick 337

beef 245, 299
Bell, Edward 92
Bengal Fur Company 80, 83
Beniamina: Ileialoa 307; Kanani 307; Mapuana 306-7
Bennett, James 113
Bernard, John 170
Bible, the 324-25, 330; Hawaiian 322
Bingham, Hiram 118-25, 194
Bird, Isabella 10-11, 169, 213, 215, 219
Bird, Jonathan 101
Bishop, Alexander 100
Bishop, Charles 87, 89, 103, 107
Bishop Museum 55, 338
Blackwell, Cynthia 12, 212
Bligh, William 58-60, 68, 75, 101
Boit, John 86-87
Boki (Poki, born Kamā'ule'ule) 124
Boyd, Charles 181
Boyer, Florence 274
Boyle (seaman) 182-83
Braden, Marcia 17, 300
Brander, John 166, 168
Brandt, Frank 178
Brant, Gerald 256-57
breadfruit 20, 34, 41-42, 55, 101
Brenchley, Julius 338
Brewer & Co 327
Brigham, William 22, 48, 338-40
Broughton, William Robert 87, 90, 98-103, 107, 317, 336
Brown, Francis Hyde I'i 263-66
Brown, Thomas 171, 178
Buck, Peter *see* Te Rangi Hiroa
Budde-Jones, Kathryn 257
Burlingham, Paul 258
Burney, James 58
Burns, Governor John 281-82, 284-86, 297, 319
Burns, Patricia 130
Burtner, Judith 237, 239, 244
Bush, Jno E 218
Byng, Frederick 124

C

cactus *see* prickly pear cactus
Campbell, Archibald 91
Campbell, Jessie 132-33, 135
candlenut tree *see* kukui
cannibalism 49, 61
Capellas, Eugene 263
Carrington, Frederic 149
Carvalho, Bernard 290-91
castor beans 251
Cawley, John 100
Cayetano, Ben: 289, 295, 299; Vicky 295
centipedes 28
Chamisso, Adelbert von 338
charcoal production 250, 299
Chevalier, Nicholas 161
Chiang Kai-shek 254
Chinese Communist Party 254
Choris, Louis 94
Christensen, Charles 19, 341
Christianity 246, 322
Christmas on Niʻihau 58, 134, 159, 209, 232-34, 236, 251, 304
church 246, 248, 264, 271, 278, 310, 323-24
cigarettes *see* tobacco
Clague, D. A. 15
Cleeland, Hōkūlani 305-7, 324-26
Clerke, Charles 58, 61-69, 74-75, 103, 316
Cleveland, Richard 108
Coast Guard, US 261-63
coffee 170, 237, 245, 305
Cold War, the 271, 276, 292
Collie, Alexander 337
Colnett, Captain 79, 81-85, 88, 93, 103
Constantine 34
Contrades, Lorna 306
Cooke, Charles Montague 29
Cook, Captain James 8, 44, 57-60, 63, 74-76, 87-88, 103, 105, 189, 316, 320-21, 335; death of 64, 66, 69, 316; postage stamp 58
Cook, Evelyn 198
Corney, Peter 92, 116
cotton 94, 170, 190-91, 228, 234, 251
cowboys *see* paniolo
Cowie, Robert 29
Craigforth 128, 143, 146, 148, 150-51, 154, 156, 160-61, 166, 189-90, 213, 216
Crane, Captain 226
Creed, Charles 149, 184-86
Creole English 324
Critical Habitat designations 22, 25-26, 287-88, 301
Crooker, Deal 270-71
Crozier, Clarence 263-64
Cullen, Tom 143, 145

D

Daggett, Herman 121
Dalrymple, G.B. 15
Damon, Samuel 169-70
Dana, James 13-14
Davidson, George 86
Davis, Captain 112
Davis, Isaac 121
Daws, Gavan 324
Deans, William 139-40, 152
deer 299
Defoe, Daniel 7
Dell, Daniel 101
Deuchare, H 252-53
Dibble, Sheldon 123
Dixon, George 75-77, 79, 81-82, 103, 106, 316
Douglas, William 80-81, 84, 103
Downed Pilot Training 293
Duncan, James 81, 103

E

Easter Island *see* Rapa Nui
Edgar, Thomas 58
Eisenhower, President 273
eland 297, 299-300, 302
Ellis, William 57-58, 60-61, 63, 66, 71-73, 105
Emma, Queen 169, 171
Emory, Kenneth 55
endemic species 19, 22
Enomoto, Catherine 299
Environmental Impact Statement 295
Ewart, Mr 224, 235
Ezuka, Brian 306

F

Fay, John 19, 341
Feher, Joseph 35
Fernandes, John 263-64
Finlay, Captain 141
firearms 8, 223, 294, 308 *see also* arms trading
Fisher, Harvey 26-27
fishing 88, 204, 239, 251, 269, 271, 287-91, 302, 319, 335
Fitzgerald, James Edward 146
folklore, Hawaiian 35, 39
Forbes, Charles 12-13, 222, 340-41
Fornander, Abraham 42-43, 46, 321
Fort Elizabeth 115, 285, 317
Fort Shafter 332

Foster Gardens 338
Four Freedoms 262-63, 266
Fox, William 148-49, 151, 153, 159-60, 183
Francis, Gavin 7
Freycinet, Louis de 336-38
frogs 30
Fullaway, David 27-28
Funter, Robert 103
furrowing (defensive) 13, 256-57, 260, 270, 291, 318
fur trading 75-77, 82-87, 92, 108, 113-14 *see also* sea otters
Futa, Baryn 312

G

Gamble, John 111
Garg, J M 251
Garstin, Maud Knudsen 12, 211-12
Gaudichaud-Beaupré, Charles 338
GAY
— Alice *see* Robinson: Alice
— Annie 156
— Charles 164, 187, 212, 215, 220-21, 228, 230-32
— Eliza (Elizabeth/'Aunt Lila') *see* Welcker: Eliza
— Francis 156, 164, 187, 214-15, 217, 219-20, 222, 227-28, 230-32, 318, 340; (Francis) Ernest 231-32
— George 149, 156, 164, 187, 203-5, 208, 212, 214-17, 220-21, 223-24, 231, 318
— James (Jimmy) 149-50, 157-58, 187, 212
— Jane (née Sinclair) 13, 128, 131, 143, 149, 154, 156-59, 185, 187, 204, 212, 214-15, 217, 219-20, 229-30, 232, 238, 243
— Lawrence Kainoahou 229
— Lillie *see* Torrey: Lillie Hart Gay
— Marion Rowell 216, 221
— Thomas (Captain) 149-61 *passim* 164, 167-68, 170, 179-88 *passim*, 220, 230
— William, 161, 164, 181-83, 185-86
Gay and Robinson (copartnership) 217, 219-20, 223, 227, 230-31, 241, 243, 248, 304, 318, 327
Gear, J W 124
Gebbie family 140
geckoes 23
George III 105
Gilman, Gorham 189, 195
Gilman, Laselle 260
Gil-Trans International, Bakersfield 298
Glade, Ethel 223
glottal stop *see* 'okina
goats 18, 23, 63, 65, 67, 92, 174-75, 189, 223, 275, 281, 340
Godley: Charlotte 150, 152; John 150-51
Golding, William 7
Gore, John 58, 62-64, 66, 68-69
gourds 19, 42-44, 67

Grandin, Temple 299
Graves, Robert 281
Gray, Robert 103
Great Māhele 124, 171, 177-78, 192, 202
Grey, George 148
Grey, John (Captain) 133
Gulick, Peter 193, 196, 317

H

Halāliʻi: chief 53-54; lake 17, 54
Hale pili/grass houses 61, 170, 238
Halulu, Lake 17, 41, 52-53, 257
Hamline University of Minnesota 307
Hanakiki 329
Hanner, Ruth Knudsen 128
Hanohano, Faye 290
Haole koa (plant) 299
Harada: Irene 259; Mrs 259, 328, 331; Yoshio 259, 328-32
Harpe, Shideler 271-72
Harper, Henry 183
Harris, Charles Coffin 192-93
Hart, Lillie *see* Torrey, Lillie
Harvard University 48, 242
Harvey, William 66
Haumea (goddess) 35, 53
Hawaiʻi, first European visitors 88
Hawaiʻi State Department of Social Services 55
Hawaiʻi State Wildlife Sanctuary 301
Hawaiʻi Statehood Commission 273
Hawaiʻi Sugar Planters Association 327
Hawaiʻi Supreme Court 287
Hawaiian Evangelical Association 202
Hawaiian Homes Commission 286
Hawaiian Islands Humpback Whale National Marine Sanctuary 288
Hawaiian language 55, 251, 275, 305, 320-326 *see also* Niihauan language
Hawaiian Music Foundation 55
Hawaiian religion 252
Hawaiian Renaissance 286
Hawaiian State Archives 245
Hawaiian State Land Use Commission 287
Hawaiian Sugar Company 227, 327
HAY
— Agnes 137, 143
— Ebenezer 102, 137-45, 147-48, 150-51, 155, 166
— family 147, 154
— Hannah Guthrie 138, 142, 150
— James 137, 143, 145, 151, 155, 166
— John 143
Hayes, Flora 266-67

Head, Timothy 324
Health Department, Hawai'i 276
Heaphy, Charles 134, 136
Hee, Clayton 288-91
heiau (sacred sites) 47-48, 57, 340
Helekunihi, E 251
Hi'iaka 38-39
Hill, William H 263
Hillebrand, William 338-39
Hinds, Norman 15
Hinkle, Anya 33
Hitchcock, Howard 13
Hobson, Governor 152
Holiohana, P R 188, 334
Holmes, George 159-61, 166
Holt: Hermann von 171; Ida 154, 161, 166, 199, 214
honey industry 221-22, 248-50, 273-74, 297, 299, 329
Honolulu Museum of Art 55
Hookano, Maria 233
Hooker, Joseph 337, 340
Ho'omana Ia Jesu Church 302
Hopkins, Charles Manley 170
horses 23, 92, 94, 150, 189, 201, 203-7, 221-23, 238, 244-45, 247, 256, 260, 274, 279
House Committee on Ocean, Marine Resources and Hawaiian Affairs 290
House Committee on Lands 287
House, The (at Ki'eki'e) see Ki'eki'e homestead
Hudson Bay Company 170
Huluolani, Mrs 330
Humehume 119-23, 125, 317
hunting 22, 260, 279-80, 297, 299, 308, 319
hurricanes: 27, 234, 298; Iniki 199, 298; Iwa 191, 298
Hutcheson, John Mack 156, 209 see also McHutcheson, John

I

'Ī'ī, John Papa 111, 263
Inamo'o 96, 106-7
Infantry Regiment (299th) 260
Inouye, Senator 276
ipu pāwehe 19, 42
Iselin, Isaac 109-10

J

Japan (World War II) 249, 254-60, 291, 318, 328-31; Japanese vessels 61; Japanese workers 222-24, 233, 235
Jarves, James 120, 123
Joesting, Edward 122
Johnson, Edward 197
Johnston Island 292
Jones, Syd 257, 259

Judd: Charles 222-23, 247-49, 318; Lawrence 247-48, 265, 273, 318
Judd: Gerrit 171; Henry 303

K

Kaahakila 331
Ka'ahumanu, Queen 113, 117-25, 192, 194-95, 317
Kaaumoana, Noelani 306
kahakō (macrons) 9, 47, 55, 322-23
Kahalai'a 121, 124, 232
Kahale, Gladys Awapuhi 306-7, 311-12
Kahekili, King 95, 105-6, 232
Kahelelani (ali'i) 41, 55, 316, 325
Kaho'olawe 38, 247
Kahokuloa, Haunani 306-7
Kahokuloa, Kuramatsu 50-51
Ka'eo 41, 67, 76, 81, 83, 95, 105-7, 316
Kaikipa'anānea, King 46
Kala'i-o-Kamalino 203-5
Kalākaua, King 35-36, 169, 203-4, 208, 216, 227, 318
Kalanikūpule 106-7
Kalanimoku 116, 119, 121-22, 124, 317
Kaleimanu (son of Ko'olau) 231
Kaleohano, Hawila 328, 330-32
kalo 19-20, 36, 41, 46, 77-78, 187, 190, 245, 274
Kamakahelei 67-68, 105-6, 316
Kamakau, Samuel 57, 110, 123
Kamala, Oliva 257
Kamāmalu, Queen 124-25, 192-93

KAMEHAMEHA
— I 43, 87, 90-91, 95, 98-99, 106-19, 122-24, 192, 203-5, 317-18, 321; death of 117
— II (King Liholiho) 111, 117-19, 121, 124-25, 169, 317
— III 125, 169, 171, 195
— IV 125, 168-69, 171, 192
— V 8, 43, 111, 171, 175-78, 188, 192, 205, 240, 287, 289, 298, 301, 309, 318, 333-34, 338
Kamehameha Schools 192, 277

KANAHELE
— Ane 311-12
— Benehakaka 249, 258-59, 273, 275, 327, 331-32
— Diane Hiipoi 306
— Ehulani 307
— Elama 279
— Ella 307
— Kaehulani 306
— Kealohaohana 332
— Minoaka 306
— Mokihana 307
— Naui 306
— Noelani 307
— Ulu 306-7

Kānāwai Māmalahoe 203-4
Kaneoneo 41, 63, 67, 105-6
Kaohelaulii, Kaleohoomana 306-7, 311-12; Kekuhina 327; Luana 306; Willie 327
kapa cloth 20, 33, 53, 253, 367
Kapahe (boatman) 190
Kapaka-Arboleda, La France 305-6
Kapalawai, house at 278
Kapoulakinau (daughter of Haumea) 53
kapu (taboo) 45-48, 79, 82-83, 97, 117-19
Karamatsu, Jon Riki 304-5, 307
Kauaʻi: Museum 55; Planning Commission 296; Public Works and Recreation 291; Wildlife Refuge 284; Evangelical Association 198, 216
Kaui, Tutu 253
Kaukaha, David 208
Kaukau, Andrew 201-3, 206, 214
Kaumualiʻi 90, 96, 106-23, 194, 316-17
Kaupo, Maui 252
Kāwaʻewaʻe 260
Kawahalau, Kamakaukiuli 257
Kawaihoa 12-13, 16, 41, 60, 70, 230, 235, 238, 335
Keale, Kalua 340
Keale, Moses 47, 55, 191, 252, 304, 321
Kealiʻiahonui 119-21
Keamoai, Kauileilehua 257
Keamoai-Strickland, Kaimi 306
Keawe 105-7, 245, 316-17
Kekuhina 246, 327, 330
Ke Kula Niihau O Kekaha 50, 307, 325
Kele, Joseph Keoua 257
Keliʻimalolo 52-53
Kelley, Joseph 272
Kelley, Kauilei & Uilani 306
Kendrick, John 103
Kewelani (daughter of Haumea) 53
kiawe trees 13, 18, 221-22, 240, 245, 247-50, 298, 301, 367
Kiʻekiʻe homestead 178, 190-91, 204, 210-12, 214, 223, 229, 234, 245, 248, 273-74, 298, 318, 329
Kiha (chief) 105-6
King George's Sound Company 75-77, 79-81, 83
King, James 58, 61-62, 66-68, 71-72, 105
Kirch, Patrick 23, 26
Kiu, George 241
KNUDSEN
— Ann ('Annie', née Sinclair) 22, 48, 128, 131, 143, 156-58, 178, 183, 187, 199, 208, 210-12, 229, 338-39, 341
— Arthur, Augustus & Ida 211
— Eric 48-49, 179, 188, 225-26
— Maud see Garstin, Maud Knudsen
— Valdemar 48, 174-75, 178, 188, 190, 192, 198, 210-12, 220, 231, 338

Koakanu 174, 176-79, 192, 217
Koerte, Lu Niheu 306
Koʻolau 46, 230-31, 284
Kona kings 46
kona winds 11-12, 233-34
konohiki rights 46, 171, 188, 201-2, 206-7, 251, 287, 290-91, 367; Konohiki Management Bill 291
Korean War 250
Kotzebue, Otto 115, 336, 338
Krauss, Beatrice 44
Kuhaimoana, shark-god 51, 55
Kūkaʻilimoku 105
Kūkona, King 46
kukui (candlenut) 20, 65, 76, 259, 367
Kumulipo 35-38
Kupahu, David 199-201, 206, 211, 318
Kuykendall, Ralph 111, 117

L

Laird, Donivee 245
land snails see snails
language, Niihauan 9, 304, 307, 320-26
Larsen, (Lametsius) David 230, 245-46, 249, 251, 258, 260, 270, 278-79, 309, 327-32; Katharine 245
La Tendresse, Dale 98
Lavaud, Captain 152
Law, John 58, 66
'Law of the Splintered Paddle' 204
Lay, George Tradescant 337
Ledyard, John 72-73
Lehua Island 97, 249, 259, 271, 294, 301-2
lei, shell 42, 44-45, 187, 191, 248, 273, 304-7, 311-12, 314, 319
leprosy 230-31
Licayan, Emalia 236, 279
Liholiho, King see Kamehameha II
Likelike, Princess 43
Liliha, Kuini 124
Liliʻuokalani, Queen 35-37
Lingle, Linda 26, 288-89, 304
lizards 23, 30, 36
Lono 37, 40, 57, 61, 63
LORAN (long range navigation) 261-62, 291
loulu palm tree 247
Lunalilo, King 203, 208
Luomala, Katharine 36
Lydgate, John 111

M

Macfarlane, George 227
MacLeod, Alexander Samuel 252
macrons see kahakō

Mahiole 110
Maihinenui 119, 121
makaloa: mats 33, 42-44, 53-54, 74, 187, 203, 253; sedge 22, 42
Makaweli: House 213-15, 219, 229; Landing (Kauaʻi) 274, 300 Meat Company 299-300, 308; purchase 192-93; Ranch 254, 299; Reserve 299
Mālie Foundation 307
maluhia 289-90
Manby, Thomas 88, 98
Manchuria 254
manienie grass 247
Mann, Horace 338
Manookian, Arman 37
Manson family 140
Mantell, Walter 144
Māori language 322
Marcus, Henry 239
Marin, Don Francisco de Paulo 251
Marine Conservation District 290
Marine Sanctuary 288
Martinez, Esteban José 84-85
Martin, Joseph 204
Massachusetts Institute of Technology 216, 261
Matisoo-Smith, Lisa 32-33
Matsu *see* Kahokuloa, Kuramatsu
Matthew, Hettie Belle 236-40
Maui Nui Venison 299
Mawae, Loke 307
May, Ernest 263-64
McClellan, Edwin 111
McClung, David 287
McGuire, Walter 267
MCHUTCHESON
— Isabella 208-9
— James 128
— John 131, 136, 143, 156, 209
— William 135, 137, 208-9
McIntosh, Alexander (Sandy) 148
Meares, John 79-81, 83, 86, 103
medevac arrangements 293, 296
Mellen, George 267
Menard, Wilmon 164
Menzies, Archibald 88, 92-98, 335-36, 338
Meyer, Philip 302-3
Midway, Battle of 261
Miller, Elizabeth Trumbull 255-56
Miller, George 166
Miller, William 170
Mills, Peter 115
Mirrlees Watson 227
Missile Defense Agency 295

missionaries 7-8, 36, 55, 119-25 *passim*, 149, 169, 171, 174, 185, 189, 194-94, 197-99, 215-16, 278, 317, 321-22, 333
Mitchell, William (Billy) 255-57, 291
Mizuha, Jack 259
Molodin, Alexander 115
Molokaʻi 252; Molokaʻi Ranch Wildlife Safari Park 297, 299
momi shells 309, 311-12
monk seals 13, 24-26, 287-88, 297, 301
Montgomery, James 158, 160, 183, 208
Montgomery, William 183
Moore, George F 332
Moriarty, Linda 312
Morita, Mina 307
Mormonism 197, 201
Morse, Danny 263
Morse, Samuel 119, 194
mtDNA 33
mullet 17
muskets *see* arms trading
Munro, George 222, 341
Muter, Douglas 155-56
Myers, Maurice 276

N

Nā Mea Hawaiʻi/Native Books 306
Nanto-Bordelaise Company 145, 148, 160
National Marine Fisheries Laboratory 302
National Oceanic and Atmospheric Administration 288, 301
National Tropical Botanic Gardens 97
Nawaalaau, S 173
Neal, Marie 29
Nelson, David 335
NeSmith, Kaeo 279
New Zealand Company, the 128-32, 135-36, 138-39, 144-45, 148, 151, 153
Niau, Hannah 268, 271
Niau, Kahea 311
Niau, Loke 306
Nicolson, Adam 7
Night blooming cereus 245
Nihoa Island 14, 30, 56, 102, 120
Niʻihau County establishment 290-91
NIʻIHAU
— Cultural Heritage Foundation 305-6, 311-12, 319
— 'Niʻihau Incident' *see* Battle of Niihau, the
— Public Charter Schools, Kauaʻi 325
— purchase by Sinclair family 334
— Ranch 248-49, 276-77, 284, 292, 294, 297, 299
— School 263-73 *passim*, 277, 304-5, 325
— Shell Lei Legislation 2004 305
— Helicopters 293-94, 296
— Safaris Ltd 297

Niihauan language 8, 40, 304, 320-326
Nimmo, Harry Arlo 39
Nishikaichi, Shigenori 249, 257-59, 291, 328-332
Nizo, Virginia 279
Nootka: Conventions 86, 88, 92, 95, 99; Crisis 85, 88
northwest passage 58, 64-66, 68
Noyes, Martha 334
nuclear attack preparations 276
nuclear weapon 291-92

O

Oʻahu, attack on 258-59
Oʻahu Sisal Company 228
Oahu Sugar Company 223, 242
Office of Hawaiian Affairs 55, 296, 305-7
ʻokina 9, 322-23
ʻOlokele Ditch 227
ʻōlulu 20-22
Operation Hardtack 292
ʻopihi (limpet) 288-91
ʻŌpūnui 76, 78-79, 81-83, 106
oryx 297, 299
otters *see* sea otter

P

Pacific Missile Range Facility 25, 291-95
Pahulehua: Gilbert 271; Sana 306; Susana 307
pandanus 20, 33, 41, 43
paniolo 208, 231, 246, 250, 265, 269, 271-72
Papapa 176-79, 217
paper mulberry 33, 41, 335
pāpipi *see* prickly pear cactus
Park, Robert 140
peacocks 247-48
Pearl Harbor 50, 91, 171, 255, 257-59, 262, 318, 327-28
Pele 31, 35, 38-40, 51, 53
Peleʻioholani 41, 105, 316
Peru 85
petition (1874) 206-7
Pickering, John 321
Pigeon Bay 138-63, 166, 168, 179, 188, 208-9, 213, 317-18
pigs 245, 308
Piʻilani (wife of Koʻolau) 231
Piko Club 247
Pitcairn Island 7
poi 41-42, 49-51, 187, 190, 233, 236, 245, 268, 272, 274, 280, 366
Pollard, R 80
Polynesian Triangle 32-34
Pōmare, Queen 166
Popham, Captain 212

population numbers 333
Portlock, Nathaniel 75-79, 81, 83, 103, 106, 316
Powers, Sidney 15
prickly pear cactus (pāpipi) 22-23, 245, 250-51, 273, 330
Prigge, Joseph 268, 270-71
Protest Mat 204-5, 208
pueo 27, 47, 65
Puʻuwai village 55, 177, 190, 195, 200, 245, 247-48, 257, 260, 262, 265, 269-73, 276-77, 302, 304, 308, 310, 319, 325, 334
Pukui, Mary Kawena 54
Punua, Edward Lilikalani 306

Q

Quimper, Manuel 84-85
Quinn, William 250, 267, 273, 277, 286, 298, 318

R

rabbits 301
RAC *see* Russian-American Company
Ramsay, Dean 215
Ramsey, John 268
Rapa Nui 11, 33, 166
rats 24, 97, 301-2
reafforestation 284
religious freedom 264, 266,
Rémy, Jules 22, 338
Rennie, John 223, 235-36, 247-48, 328
Rhodes, Godfrey & Henry 168, 170
Rhodes, William Barnard 141-42
Richardson, Mary Ellen Kaukalilani 150
Richardson, Robert 332
Richards, William 125
Richmond, Captain 213
Rickman, John 58, 60-62, 64, 71-72
Robertson, George 173-75
Robertson, Jean 128
ROBINSON
— Alice (née Gay) 186-88, 212-15, 220-21, 227, 230-35, 237, 240, 244, 246, 267
— Aubrey 8, 18, 48, 154, 156, 164, 187, 212-46 *passim*, 249, 256, 277-78, 301, 318, 340
— Aylmer 8, 19, 23, 154, 223, 225, 228, 232, 234, 241-81, 291, 318-19, 327-28, 330, 332, 341
— Brandi 308
— Briana 291
— Bruce 156, 257, 277, 284, 287-91, 295-99, 301
— Charles 148, 152-56
— Eleanor 188, 232, 234, 237, 239, 264
— family (general) 7, 9, 27, 42, 44, 127, 155-56, 178, 186, 219, 224, 228, 232, 237, 245-46, 248, 252, 255-56, 260, 263-69 *passim*, 284-304 *passim*, 308, 319, 328-29, 348, 353

— George 156
— Helen (née Sinclair) 128, 131, 143, 154-59, 162, 187, 212, 214, 217, 220, 229, 232, 236
— Helen (née Matthew, wife of Lester) 277, 297
— Keith 156, 257, 277, 284, 287-88, 291-92, 295-99, 301-2
— Leiana 289-91, 308
— Lester 232, 234, 237, 239, 242-43, 251, 254, 263-64, 267, 272-76, 281, 297-98, 319
— Russell 275
— Selwyn 232, 234, 238, 242-43, 249, 254, 267, 285
— Sinclair 214, 223, 232-34, 241-43, 267, 273, 275
Robinson, Joseph (not related) 138
Rockwood, Paul 38
Rodman, Julius 252-53
Roll, Warren 268-70
Roman Catholics 191, 194-97, 200-1
Roosevelt, Franklin 263
Ropes, George 119
Rowell: George 174-75, 196-99, 204, 216, 231, 318; Malvina 196; Marion 204, 216
Royal Geographic Society 337
Ruggles, Samuel 121
Russell, Archibald 209
Russia 113; Russian-American Company 113-16
Russian Fort 115, 178, 285

S

Samwell, David 58, 66, 69-72, 320-21, 335
sandalwood ('iliahe alo'e) 63, 91-92, 109, 112, 114, 116-19, 122
Sandwich, Earl of 64
Schäffer, Georg 113-16, 317
Schauinsland, Hugo 24
schooling 248, 304-5
Schutz, Albert 323
scorpions 28
sea otters 8, 75-77, 79, 86 *see also* fur trading
seals *see* monk seals
Selwyn, George 146
Senate Committee on Land and Natural Resources 284-85
Senate Investigating Committee (1946) 263, 267-68, 281
Sewell, Henry 155
Shaler, William 108-9
sheep 245, 250, 297-300, 308
shell lei *see* lei, shell
Sherriffs, Willamina 217
Shintani, Ishimatsu 50, 328, 330
Shortland, Edward 145, 152
Silva, Charles 263-64
Simpson, Roger 87, 103

SINCLAIR
— Ann *see* Knudsen: Ann
— Eliza (Elizabeth) 4, 29, 127-29, 131, 136-37, 139, 141, 143, 146-52, 154-168 *passim*, 175, 178, 187, 190, 192-93, 208-20 *passim*, 228-29, 242, 277, 301, 318
— family 8, 29, 126-38 *passim*, 141, 143, 147-55 *passim*, 158, 163, 165-67, 187-88, 192-93, 200, 203, 206, 209, 245, 285, 309, 317-18, 333-34; the Sinclair purchase of Ni'ihau 334
— Francis (Snr) 127-29, 131-34, 135-43, 145-48, 150-51, 153, 160, 164, 209, 211, 228, 317
— Francis Jnr ('Frank') 128, 131, 142, 145, 156, 158-60, 164, 171, 173-74, 176, 178, 187, 189, 192, 200-4, 206-9, 212-24 *passim*, 229, 231, 251, 308, 318, 340
— George 127-28, 131, 139, 142-43, 147, 215, 317
— Helen *see* Robinson: Helen (née Sinclair)
— Isabella 208-9, 212, 214-15, 217, 238, 339-40
— James 19, 22, 128, 131, 137, 139, 143, 145, 151, 156, 158-60, 173, 178, 187-89, 192, 208-, 212, 215-17. 318
— Jane *see* Gay: Jane
— John *see* McHutcheson, John
— William 145-46
Sintani, Ishimatsu *see* Shintani, Ishimatsu
sisal 228, 234, 251
skinks 23
Smith, Henry 154
Smith: James 174-75, 197-99, 201, 215, 220; Mrs 215
smoking prohibition *see* tobacco
snails 23, 29-30
snakes 30
solar power 304-5, 309
Spain 85
Special Warfare Operations 293
spiders 28
Splintered Paddle, Law of the 203-4
St John, Harold 18-23, 26, 43, 63, 223-24, 251, 323, 335-36, 338-41
Stack, James 157-58
Staley, Thomas 171
Stanley, Lord 140
Stearns, Harold 15-18, 224
Stepien, Edward 229, 242, 260
Stevens, Philip 69
Stewart, Charles 125
stilt, Hawaiian 26-27
Stokes, John (curator) 29, 47-48, 340-41; Captain 142, 152
Stolz, Louis 231
supercargo 102, 108, 110
surfing 72-74, 214, 221
sweet potatoes 41, 191
Sykes, John 89, 94, 96, 99
Sylva, Francis 263-64, 266
Synge, William 170

T

Tabrah, Ruth 179, 284
Tahiti 55, 320-21; Tahitian language 320, 322
Taiwan 32-34, 316
taro *see* kalo
Tate, Rhonetta 306
Tava, Rerioterai 47, 55, 252-53, 304, 321
taxation 333-34
Taylor, Andrew 83
Te Rangi Hiroa 38, 43, 45
Teamsters and Hotel Workers Union 289
Teehan, Jack 274
Tengstrom, Captain 212
Territorial Board of Health 264
Thompson, Myron 285
tobacco 130, 240, 245, 260, 269, 272, 275, 294, 308
Tobey, Mr 195
Torlesse, Charles 149
Torrey: George Burroughs 232; Lillie Hart Gay 231-32, 236
tourism 281, 296-97
Townsend, Ebenezer 102
Tsar Alexander 114
Tupararo 100-2
turkeys 85, 247-48, 251
Turnbull, John 90, 108
Tuthill, Leonard 26-28

U

Umekichi, Asahina 222-23
Under Western Skies 218
UNITED STATES:
— Air Force 255
— Army 178, 255, 259-62, 267, 275, 284, 291, 293, 318
— Coast Guard Landing Craft Mechanised 261
— Department of Agriculture 251, 299-300, 305
— Department of Defense 261
— Department of Education 270, 307, 325
— Department of Land and Natural Resources 287-291, 295, 301-2
— Department of Public Instruction 267, 270, 273
— Fish and Wildlife Service 22, 301
— Navy 255, 259, 262, 275, 292, 294-96, 301-2
Universal Declaration of Human Rights 263
University of California 242, 284, 297
University of Hawai'i 19, 275, 281, 291, 323

V

Vainuku, Ola 307
Vancouver, George 86-89, 92-99, 101-3, 108, 316, 335-36
Varez, Dietrich 39
Vaughn, Greg 286, 310
venereal disease 62, 67, 72, 76, 99
Vidinha, Anton 271-72
visitor access 302

W

Wahineaea, J. (government land agent) 171-73, 175, 189
Wairau Incident 144
Wakefield: Arthur 144; Edward Gibbon 129-31, 148, 193, 228; William 129-31, 138-39, 145, 148, 151, 153, 160
Wallace, Alfred 143, 145, 147
Walsh, Robert 194-95, 317
Watson, (William) Renny 227
Webber, John 58, 61-62, 68, 70-72, 75
Welcker: Eliza 13, 164, 187, 212, 214-15, 220, 231-33; Mendell 232
Westervelt, William 38-39
West, George 270
whales 4, 11, 157, 288
White, Tom 144
Whitney: Mercy 194, 196; Samuel 121, 189, 193-96, 333
Whittemore, Captain 111
Wichman, (Frederick) Bruce 46
Wichman, Juliet Rice 19, 341
Widemann, Hermann 174-75, 178
Wilkes, Charles 13
Williamson, John 58, 62
Wilson, William H 323
Winship, Jonathan & Nathan 110-11
Wodehouse, James 214
Wong, Annette Kuuipolani Kanahele 326
wool growing 224, 250
World War: I 242, 249, 254; II 48, 254, 270, 273, 292
Wyllie, Robert Crichton 170-71, 177

Y

yams 20, 41, 55, 64, 66-67, 75, 82, 85-87, 91-92
Yangtze River Patrol 254

Z

Zimmerman, Elwood 28-29
Zimmermann, Heinrich 320

THE SINCLAIR/GAY/ROBINSON FAMILY TREE, IN RELATION TO NI'IHAU

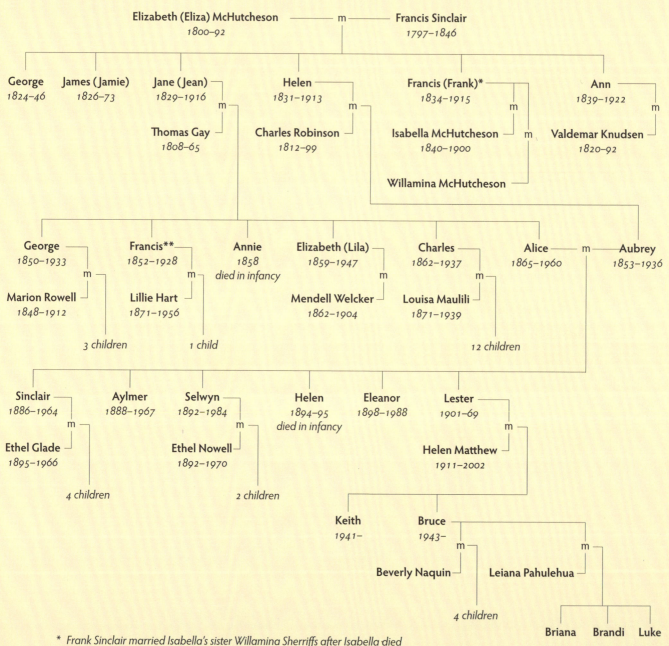

* Frank Sinclair married Isabella's sister Willamina Sherriffs after Isabella died
** Francis Gay married Marie Edmondson after his divorce from Lillie Hart